GOLF
CALIFORNIA SURVIVAL GUIDE

by Shaw Kobre and Bob Fagan

GOLF
CALIFORNIA SURVIVAL GUIDE

Shaw Kobre and Bob Fagan

Published by:

1206 4th Street
Santa Rosa, CA 95404

Text copyright Shaw Kobre and Bob Fagan 2001
All rights reserved
Maps and Illustration copyright In The Loop Golf 2001

ISBN: 0-9710918-0-3
1st edition - September 2001

 Front Cover Photo: JoAnn Dost Golf Edition, LLC
The Golf Club at Genoa Lakes, pg. 73
Cover image scanning provided by Nikon Imaging Equipment

Distributed to the book trade in the United States by Sunbelt Publications
Printed in the United States by Banta Books

Publisher:	Greg Redmond
Associate Publisher:	Chris Bronis
Layout design:	Sandy Loam
Director of Research:	Nancy Bernstein
Directory Researcher:	Dricilla Bronis
Editors:	Carolyn Perkins
	Nancy Bernstein
Cover Design:	Randi Morehead
	Studio M Graphic Design
Production:	Kelly Townsend

NOT ALL COURSES ARE CREATED EQUAL

You are holding the internet in your hand. The **GOLF CALIFORNIA SURVIVAL GUIDE** is designed to give quick, pertinent, and accurate information on golfing in the Golden State (plus Las Vegas and Reno).

At the same time, we realize that not all golf courses are created equal. So we have provided you with helpful lists, ratings and opinions on some of California's most popular facilities.

The **GOLF CALIFORNIA SURVIVAL GUIDE** also includes details on important golf services, such as organizing a tournament, golf travel agents, schools, associations, and more.

But that isn't enough, is it?

It wasn't enough for us either. You deserve more. So we created a web portal, **www.InTheLoopGolf.com,** to give you course updates, reviews, humorous articles and breaking news about golf in the Golden State.

Play golf and...

Stay In The Loop

REGIONAL MAP

Shasta Cascade
pg. 51

EUREKA

REDDING

North Coast
pg. 119

RENO

Gold Country
pg. 89

SACRAMENTO

SANTA ROSA

High Sierra
pg. 67

SAN FRANCISCO

San Francisco Bay Area
pg. 145

SAN JOSE

FRESNO

LAS VEGAS

MONTEREY

Central Valley
pg. 217

Central Coast
pg. 183

Desert
pg. 367

SANTA BARBARA

Los Angeles
pg. 249

LOS ANGELES

Inland Empire
pg. 289

PALM SPRINGS

Orange County
pg. 315

IRVINE

San Diego
pg. 337

SAN DIEGO

CONTENTS

SURVIVAL GUIDE
HOW TO USE YOUR

SEARCHING FOR COURSES

By name or by city: Simple, just use the indexes in the back of the book.

By Region: Even simpler, just flip back to the handy regional map. Each region has a page number next to it, i.e. North Coast Page 119. Go to that page and you will find a location map that contains all of the cities with courses.

BOB'S MINI-BOOK OF LISTS

Bob Fagan, one of the most extensively traveled golfers in America, has played nearly 1,450 courses, more than 400 in California alone. Bob ties the state together, giving readers rankings on public and private courses throughout the state. *See the complete "Bob's Mini Book of Lists" starting on page 45.*

REGION vs. HOT DESTINATION:
WHAT'S THE DIFFERENCE?

Regions:
Within the 12 regions of California and Nevada there are nearly 1,000 golf facilities. Some regions could take you all day to drive through; others are fairly small. The regions are based on both geographical boundaries and course density.

Destinations:
Within California and Nevada there are 11 golf destinations. We define a golf destination as a place where golfers can stay and play a variety of courses within a short drive. A region, in some cases, can also be a destination, i.e. San Diego. Each destination contains:
• Convenient airports
• Climate profile
• Overview of things to do in the area besides golf

To assist you in finding a place to play, each destination includes:
• Main Courses (courses every golfer should play if he or she gets the chance)
• Muni-Me (reasonably priced municipal or public courses for those on a budget)
• Rooms with a View (resort courses)
• XXX-Rated (courses that pose an eXtreme challenge for low handicappers)
• Off the Beaten Path (courses out of the way but worth the drive)

If you still can't find a course to suit your needs or have questions, concerns, or just want to report changes, corrections, improvements, or bad service, email us at intheloopgolf@aol.com or call us at 707-569-8481.

captured in the GOLF CALIFORNIA SURVIVAL GUIDE *besides golf courses*

We want to draw your attention to nine extremely helpful services that can save you money or broaden your horizons. Listed are some things just for fun:

1) Our Alpha Index / Scoring Log - Our index is also a convenient scoring log, so you can keep track of every course you played, your score, and the date you played. The **Golf California Survival Guide** now becomes a permanent record and keepsake of all your golf adventures.

2) Nike Parent-Child Golf School: We are not Nike freaks, and like so many people, we are tired of seeing the swoosh logo everywhere we turn. But you have to acknowledge a good idea when you find one, and this is a good idea. What better way to learn about the game and spend quality time with your children. *For more information see page 458.*

3) Discount Golf: You may be paying too much for your green fees unless you check out this section. There are several great books covering the entire state that feature discounts on green fees, travel, lodging, and even tickets to PGA Tour events. *For more information see page 439.*

4) The Junior Golf magazine website: This website run by the publishers of Junior Golf Magazine is well thought out, easy to get around, and contains information you can actually use. If you have a junior golfer, we recommend you log onto www.juniorgolf.com. *For more information see page 453.*

5) Golf Trade: If you want to break into the golf business, visit www.golftrade.com. It lists hundreds of golf careers.

6) Stand-by Golf or Next Day Golf: Both companies are located in the desert and are based on the same principle. They sell unused tee times at discount prices. This is not for someone who needs to plan golf in advance, but for someone who wants to play a nice course and isn't too picky about the time, it's a chance to save some money. There is also something intriguing about not knowing exactly where you are going to play. Who knows? You might find yourself playing a great course for less than you thought possible. *For more information see page 439.*

7) The Publications Section: This is an interesting section for a couple reasons. First, many of the local magazines are a great place to find coupons for discounted golf. Second, the golf entrepreneur looking to market his or her product, now has access to nearly every golf publication covering the entire state. *For more see page 452.*

8) Pin-up Golf: This is one of our favorite ideas; we wish we had thought of it. It's 50% fun and 50% practical. What better way to separate money from the wallets of golfers at your next charity event than having models sell your raffle tickets and mulligans. They will greet your guests and work your on-course contests. *For more information see page 460.*

9) www.InTheLoopGolf.com: Hey, if we don't promote ourselves, who will?

KEEPING SCORE

Here are the new facilities that opened in 2000 and 2001

Course	City	Type	Page
Bailey Creek Golf Course	Lake Almanor	Public	57
Bali Hai Golf Club	Las Vegas	Public	391
Barona Creek Golf Club	Lakeside	Public	350
Bear's Best	Las Vegas	Public	392
Black Gold Golf Course	Yorba Linda	Public	335
Cimarron Golf Resort	Cathedral City	Public	373
Coyote Moon Golf Course	Truckee	Public	84
Cross Creek Golf Club	Temecula	Semi-Private	311
D'Andrea Golf & Country Club	Sparks	Semi-Private	82
Darkhorse Golf Club	Auburn	Public	94
Landmark Golf Club at Oak Quarry	Riverside	Public	307
Legends Golf Club at Rancho Lucerne	Lucerne Valley	Public	300
Lost Canyons Golf Club	Simi Valley	Public	211
Marriott's Shadow Ridge Golf Club	Palm Desert	Resort	409
Mayacama Golf Club	Santa Rosa	Private	135
Mission Hills Golf Course	Hayward	Public	156
Pasadera Country Club	Monterey	Private	196
PGA of Southern California	Calimesa	Public	294
Rancho del Pueblo	San Jose	Public	171
Rio la Paz Golf Club	Nicolaus	Semi-Private	107
Shadow Lakes Golf Club	Brentwood	Public	224
Shady Canyon Golf Club	Irvine	Private	325
Siena Golf Club	Las Vegas	Public	398
Sierra Lakes Golf Club	Fontana	Public	297
SilverStone Golf Club	Las Vegas	Resort	398
Southern Highlands Golf Club	Las Vegas	Private	399
StoneTree Golf Club	Novato	Public	131
Talega Golf Club	San Clemente	Public	332
The Auld Course	Chula Vista	Public	342
The Bridges at Rancho Santa Fe	Rancho Santa Fe	Private	354
The Club at Roddy Ranch	Antioch	Public	149
The Crosby National Golf Club	Rancho Santa Fe	Private	354
The Golf Club at Boulder Ridge	San Jose	Private	170
The Preserve Golf Club	Carmel	Private	190
Tuscan Ridge Golf Club	Chico	Semi-Private	55
Twin Creeks Golf Course	Salinas	Public	205

THE GOOD NEWS: Due to the size of California, its topography, and diverse weather conditions, the state is blessed with the ability to provide golfers with a wide variety of courses. You can play desert courses, ocean courses, mountain courses, links style, and parkland layouts. And no matter what time of year it is in California, it is always peak season somewhere in the state.

THE BAD NEWS: Most golfers do not have three or four years to travel and play all these wonderful courses. So what do you do if you only have a few weeks, or even a few days, to play golf?

THE ANSWER IS SIMPLE: you pick a golf destination. California has 11 destinations where you can play a variety of courses within minutes of each other. You can also visit a remote, but outstanding, course within a short drive.

HOT DESTINATIONS

As you have noticed, we have included Reno and Las Vegas in this book. Why? Because both areas are supported by California golfers and those visiting the Golden State.

Destination	Region
Reno - Lake Tahoe	High Sierra
Sacramento	Gold Country
Wine Country	North Coast
San Francisco Bay Area	San Francisco Bay Area
Monterey	Central Coast
Santa Barbara/San Luis Obispo	Central Coast
Los Angeles	Los Angeles
Orange County	Orange County
San Diego	San Diego
Palm Springs	Desert
Las Vegas	Desert

HOT DESTINATIONS:
The Good, the Bad and the Ugly

Best Destination for Affordable Daily Fee Golf
Sacramento - You will find excellent service, availability, price and selection.
Reno - Lake Tahoe - This area is destined to be a golf destination powerhouse.

Most Days per Year of Economical Daily Fee Golf
San Diego - This destination does not win one category, yet add up year-round good weather, value, and selection, it is the clear choice for the traveler in search of good golf anytime of year.

Worst Destination for Public Access Golf and Pricing
San Francisco Bay Area - The courses aren't the problem - just too few, too far between, and too crowded.

Best Destination for Selection of Upscale Daily Fee Golf
Orange County - Excellent variety and conditioning are Orange County hallmarks.

Least Affordable Destination for Year Round Daily Fee Golf
Orange County - It will be interesting to see what happens in the near future, now that the economy isn't booming and golfers, not corporations have to pick up the tab for green fees. Our guess is that lower green fees, or incentives in the way of specials, will be popping up. Nevertheless, the golf ain't cheap.

One Last Wish and You Could Only Pick One Golf Destination
Monterey - Why? It has the world's best public access course and several other worthy layouts as well. The ambience, beauty, and history aren't too bad either. We just hope one of your previous wishes was for a lot of money.

Best Destinations for Things Other than Golf
Las Vegas: The adult version of Disneyland™ has become family friendly.
Los Angeles: The attractions are endless.
San Francisco: It lives up to its reputation as one of Americas favorite tourist destinations.

Most Romantic Destinations
Wine Country: Romance abounds, and the courses are fun too. There are just too few of them.
Monterey: Carmel, the Pacific, Pebble Beach, and an unbelievable coastline.

THE AREA: Originally known for skiing and gambling, the Reno-Lake Tahoe area has experienced an explosion of golf. For the time being, the supply exceeds the demand. Don't wait too long to take advantage of the abundance of beautiful layouts and reasonable green fees. With an increasing population and a well-organized marketing group, this area is becoming a leader in destination golf.

THE COURSES: Abundance and variety make this a great place to take your golf vacation. Course styles range from classic mountain golf with Sierra pines, to high country, desert, target golf. For a change of pace, you can even find several wetland, valley courses. Fueled by many additional courses opening in the past ten years, most of them offering public access, Reno-Lake Tahoe is one of the top three golf regions in the state.

CLIMATE: In some parts of Reno-Lake Tahoe golf, can be played year-round, but don't count on it on any of the higher elevations.

PEAK SEASON: Late spring through fall.

AIRPORTS

Reno/Tahoe International Airport
Reno
775-328-6400
renoairport.com
Most major airlines serve Reno.

Sacramento International Airport
916-929-5411
sacairports.org
Sacramento Airport is about two hours west of Reno.
Most major airlines serve Sacramento.

MAIN COURSES

Courses every golfer should play if he or she gets the chance

ArrowCreek Golf Club
Reno, NV
775-850-4653
page 78

Coyote Moon Golf Course
Truckee, CA
530-587-0886
page 84

Dayton Valley Golf Club
Dayton, NV
775-246-7888
page 72
Lots of bunkers and water make this one of the area's most challenging layouts, undoubtedly so in the afternoon wind.

Edgewood Tahoe Golf Course
Stateline, NV
775-588-3566
page 83
Long the most famous of the area's courses and the annual host to a televised celebrity tournament, the scenic lakeside layout is surprisingly playable.

Golf Club at Genoa Lakes
Genoa, NV
775-782-4653
page 73
This is an imaginatively designed layout that mostly plays along the valley floor. It is nicely maintained and well bunkered, with water coming into play at critical points. Much tougher in the wind.

Red Hawk Golf Club
Sparks, NV
775-626-6000
page 82

MUNI-ME

Reasonably priced municipal and public courses for those on a budget

Rosewood Lakes Golf Course
Reno, NV
775-857-2892
page 80

Wildcreek Golf Course
Sparks, NV
775-673-3100
page 83

Silver Oak Golf Club
Carson City, NV
775-841-7000
page 71

Eagle Valley Golf Course
Carson City, NV
775-887-2380
page 71

ROOMS WITH A VIEW

Resort Courses

Resort at Squaw Creek
Olympic Valley, CA
530-581-6637
page 77

The Dragon at Gold Mountain
Graeagle, CA
800-368-7786
page 74

XXX-RATED

Courses that pose an eXtreme challenge for the low handicapper

Northgate Golf Club
Reno, NV
775-747-7577
page 79

Resort at Squaw Creek
Olympic Valley, CA
530-581-6637
page 77

**The Dragon at
Gold Mountain**
Graeagle, CA
800-368-7786
page 74

OFF THE BEATEN PATH

Courses that are out of the way, but worth the drive

Graeagle Meadows Golf Course
Graeagle, CA
530-836-2323
page 74

**The Golf Club at
Whitehawk Ranch**
Clio, CA
800-332-4295
page 72

OUTSIDE THE ROUGH

Life outside of golf

The Reno - Lake Tahoe area is now a year-round destination. The winter is dominated by world-class skiing. If you are in Reno or South Lake Tahoe, gambling is available for the over-21 set. From about April to October, life around the Lake takes on a new face. Everything from biking to jet skiing to hot air ballooning, not to mention golf, goes on. The nightlife in Reno has its own merits. For car buffs, do not miss those Hot August Nights!

You can find more information about Lake Tahoe by receiving the State of California Official Visitor's Guide. To order a free copy log onto www.visitcalifornia.com or call 916-322-2881.

Tahoe-Douglas Chamber of Commerce & Visitors Center
775-588-4591
tahoechamber.org

Reno-Sparks Convention & Visitors Authority
888-HIT-RENO
renolaketahoe.com

Truckee-Donner Chamber of Commerce
530-587-2757
truckee.com

RENO-LAKE TAHOE

DESTINATION: SACRAMENTO

THE AREA: Picture the flat terrain around Sacramento and you might conclude that the courses here must be extremely horizontal and uninteresting. Your conclusion would be wrong. Yes, there are some flattish courses, but most of the courses use mature trees, distinctive bunkering, and water to create interest and keep it challenging. Venture out from the city and you will discover the foothills, which range from rolling to hilly. The scenery and golf in this area can be downright exhilarating.

THE COURSES: With the price of land being relatively cheap by California standards, the past decade has seen an explosion of new courses. Many of them are upscale daily fee layouts, easily comparable to the exclusive private clubs in the area. The good news for golfers is that this has encouraged the older public courses to upgrade their facilities to remain competitive. Even better news, there seem to be more courses than golfers who are willing to pay high-end daily fees. In the next few years the facilities in this region will be fighting for your business. The end result for you will be affordable, quality golf.

CLIMATE: Golf can be played year round. Summers can sizzle, while winters can be cool and damp.

PEAK SEASON: Spring and fall.

AIRPORTS

Sacramento International Airport
916-929-5411
sacairports.org
Most major airlines serve
Sacramento.

MAIN COURSES

Courses every golfer should play if he or she gets the chance

Pine Mountain Lake Country Club
Groveland
209-962-8620
page 103
Friendly folks, a beautiful mountain surrounding and an interesting, playable layout combine for a worthwhile jaunt.

Saddle Creek Golf Club
Copperopolis
209-785-3700
page 98
Eighteen solid holes together with wooded, mountain, and meadow vistas make the layout top notch. Regrettably, their policy of no carts off the path forces everyone to make long, arduous walks, which detracts from the experience.

The Ridge Golf Course
Auburn
530-888-7888
page 95
This is the kind of challenging, well-bunkered, and nicely maintained layout that you would expect to find at the best private clubs.

Twelve Bridges Golf Club
Lincoln
916-645-7200
page 104
Play where the LPGA plays on an interesting, challenging design that is devoid of housing.

Turkey Creek Golf Club
Lincoln
916-434-9100
page 104
There is a minimum of fairway bunkers, but this is still a very interesting and demanding tee shot course. There is attractive shaping and framing along with golf challenges to engage you.

MUNI-ME

Reasonably priced municipal and public courses for those on a budget

Ancil Hoffman Golf Course
Carmichael
916-482-3284
page 97

Castle Oaks Golf Club
Ione
209-274-0167
page 103

Dry Creek Ranch Golf Course
Galt
209-745-2330
Page 230

Haggin Oaks Golf Complex - Mackenzie Course
Sacramento
916-481-4653
page 114

La Contenta Golf Club
Valley Springs
209-772-1081
page 116

Plumas Lake Golf & Country Club
Marysville
530-742-3201
page 105

Teal Bend Golf Club
Sacramento
916-922-5209
page 114

XXX-RATED

Courses that pose an eXtreme challenge for the low handicapper

XXX

Greenhorn Creek
Angels Camp
209-736-8111
page 92

Whitney Oaks Golf Club
Rocklin
916-632-8333
page 110

The Ridge Golf Course
Auburn
530-888-7888
page 95

OFF THE BEATEN PATH

Courses that are out of the way, but worth the drive

Bailey Creek Golf Course
Lake Almanor
530-259-4653
page 57

**Pine Mountain Lake
Country Club**
Groveland
209-962-8620
page 103

**Fall River Valley
Golf & Country Club**
Fall River Mills
530-336-5555
page 56

Saddle Creek Golf Club
Copperopolis
209-785-3700
page 98

OUTSIDE THE ROUGH

Life outside of golf

There is more to do at the state's capital than meets the eye. The Capitol itself has an abundance of tours and museums. Old Town Sacramento can be fun, as well as educational. The Gold Rush started nearby. If the season is right, you can catch a Kings (NBA) or a Monarchs (WNBA) basketball game. There is even a new water park to help out with that scorching valley summer heat.

You can find more information about this destination by receiving the State of California Official Visitor's Guide. To order a free copy, log onto www.visitcalifornia.com or call 916-322-2881.

Sacramento Convention and Visitors Bureau
916-264-7777
sacramentocvb.org

DESTINATION: WINE COUNTRY

THE AREA: This may be one of the most beautiful places in the entire world — a rugged coastline, lush valleys, and stunning vistas. In a little more than an hour, you can travel from the Pacific Ocean to the Napa Valley. Both Sonoma and Napa counties have a well-deserved reputation for world-class wines. For all the beauty, the Wine Country does not boast an abundance of great golf courses. Wine, not golf, is king here. That said, the courses here are attractive, enjoyable, historical, and a few are extremely difficult. This is still active agricultural country, with few new courses on the drawing boards. The result is that the prices are a little higher than one might expect, but not nearly as expensive as the Bay Area.

THE COURSES: Along the coast, you will find very challenging ocean courses. Inland, you will find a few mountain courses and several traditional layouts.

CLIMATE: Golf is played here year-round; however, winter golf is inconsistent, sunny and cool one day, rainy and cold the next.

PEAK SEASON: Spring through fall.

AIRPORTS

SFO - San Francisco International Airport
650-821-7275
sfoairport.com
1.5 hour drive north from San Francisco

Oakland International Airport
510-577-4000
oaklandairport.com
1.25 hour drive north from Oakland

MAIN COURSES

Courses every golfer should play if he or she gets the chance

Chardonnay Golf Club - The Vineyards Course
Napa
707-257-1900
page 128
If you like playing among the vineyards and on quirky, unusual greens, you will love the flow of this layout.

The Fountaingrove Club
Santa Rosa
707-579-GOLF
page 135
Hilly vistas and some dramatic tee shots make this course a worthwhile bet.

Hiddenbrooke Golf Club
Vallejo
707-558-1140
page 141
An attractive and stout test of your skills and nerves.

Silverado Country Club & Resort - North Course (private resort)
Napa
707-257-5460
page 129
It is probably the tougher and better of the Silverado's two courses.

Sonoma Mission Inn Golf and Country Club (private resort)
Sonoma
707-996-0300
page 139
Except for the absurd twisting cart paths, this classic layout is both challenging and scenic. This is probably the area's best all-around course.

StoneTree Golf Club
Novato
415-209-6090
page 131
This new course features a combination of wetland holes with some very formidable and scenic hilly, wooded holes.

MUNI-ME

Reasonably priced municipal and public courses for those on a budget

Bennett Valley Golf Course
Santa Rosa
707-528-3673
page 134

Mare Island Golf Club
Vallejo
707-562-4653
page 142

Napa Golf Course
Napa
707-255-4333
page 129

Oakmont Golf Club
Santa Rosa
707-538-2454
page 136

Paradise Valley Golf Course
Fairfield
707-426-1600
page 124

Windsor Golf Club
Windsor
707-838-7888
page 143

ROOMS WITH A VIEW

Resort Courses

Sonoma Mission Inn Golf and Country Club
Sonoma
707-996-0300
page 139

Silverado Country Club & Resort - North and South Courses
Napa
707-257-5460
page 129

XXXXXX-RATED

Courses that pose an eXtreme challenge for the low handicapper

Bodega Harbour Golf Links
Bodega Bay
707-875-3538
page 122

Hiddenbrooke Golf Club
Vallejo
707-558-1140
page 141

The Sea Ranch Golf Links
Sea Ranch
707-785-2468
page 137

OFF THE BEATEN PATH

Courses that are out of the way, but worth the drive

The Sea Ranch Golf Links
Sea Ranch
707-785-2468
page 137

OUTSIDE THE ROUGH

Life outside of golf

A person is hard-pressed to find a more beautiful and romantic destination than the Wine Country. If you start your tee times early enough in the day, you'll have plenty of time to check out the rest of the area. You can head out to the rugged Sonoma Coast for seafood right off the boat. Mud baths and hot springs are great for relaxing. If you choose, hit some world-class wineries, located in both Sonoma and Napa counties. Be adventurous, try the wineries you have never heard of - you're in for a treat. Try a Russian River Valley Pinot Noir - trust me. Many world-renowned chefs have restaurants here, due to the proximity of fresh, local ingredients and the finest wines.

You can find more information about this destination by receiving the State of California Official Visitor's Guide. To order a free copy, log onto www.visitcalifornia.com or call 916-322-2881.

Sonoma County Tourism Program
800-576-6662
sonomacounty.com

Napa Valley Conference & Visitor Bureau
707-226-7459
napavalley.com

DESTINATION: SANFRANCISCO BAY AREA

THE AREA: The greater San Francisco Bay Area includes Oakland/East Bay, Marin County, and San Jose. It possesses some of the most interesting topography and open areas, yet is one of the most under-served golf areas in the United States. The result is that you can expect a lower value as dictated by higher fees and more crowded conditions.

THE COURSES: The cost to join private clubs may be the highest in America, and adequate practice facilities are at a premium. However, the area is rich in golf tradition and, together with the Monterey area, possesses some of the best courses west of the Mississippi. Affordable new golf has not been forthcoming, but as you head away from the urban areas, some excellent upscale daily fee courses are springing up.

CLIMATE: There are a couple of things to keep in mind with the Bay Area. First, there are several microclimates. The coast can be damp and cool, so the ball will not carry nearly as far. Away from the ocean, the air becomes arid and warmer during the more mild months. Conditions are more likely to be firm, especially in the rough, and the ball will fly. Golf is played year-round but winter months can be rainy and cold.

PEAK SEASON: Spring through fall.

AIRPORTS

SFO - San Francisco International Airport
650-821-7275
sfoairport.com
All major airlines serve SFO.

Oakland International Airport
510-577-4000
oaklandairport.com
Most major airlines serve Oakland. Oakland is right across the bay from San Francisco. It is often easier to get into SF from the Oakland Airport than SFO.

San Jose International Airport
408-501-7600
sjc.org
Most major airlines serve San Jose.

MAIN COURSES

Courses every golfer should play if he or she gets the chance

Cinnabar Hills Golf Club
San Jose
408-323-7815
page 170
This 27-hole complex features hilly terrain, dramatic bunkering, fast greens and some excellent views.

Coyote Creek Golf Club
San Jose
408-463-1400
page 161
This Jack Nicklaus design combines both flat wetlands and some hilly golf to make for a challenging course that has also hosted the PGA Senior Tour.

Monarch Bay Golf Club - Tony Lema Course
San Leandro
510-895-2162
page 172
John Harbottle's renovations, with dramatic bunkering, spice up this dramatic site that includes a spectacular view of the San Francisco skyline.

Pasatiempo Golf Course
Santa Cruz
831-459-9155
page 177
This Alister Mackenzie course features some of golf's best green sites and is included in America's 100 Best.

Presidio Golf Course
San Francisco
415-561-4661
page 168
This historic, former military course is quietly one of the area's best layouts, with the trees and terrain characteristic of the Peninsula.

The Club at Roddy Ranch
Antioch
925-978-4653
page 149
Carved from a working cattle ranch, this authentic links-style course is fun and scenic.

The Course at Wente Vineyards
Livermore
925-456-2475
page 158
Wonderful views, smartly framed greens, and superior ambience make this the best course in the East Bay.

MUNI-ME

Reasonably priced municipal and public courses for those on a budget

Boundary Oak Golf Course
Walnut Creek
925-934-4775
page 180

De Laveaga Golf Course
Santa Cruz
831-423-7212
page 176

Harding Park Golf Course
San Francisco
415-661-1865
page 168

Poppy Ridge Golf Course
(NCGA members)
Livermore
925-456-8202
page 157

Tilden Park Golf Course
Berkeley
510-848-7373
page 150

SAN FRANCISCO BAY AREA

ROOMS WITH A VIEW
Resort Courses

Half Moon Bay Golf Links
Half Moon Bay
650-726-4438
page 155

XXX-RATED
Courses that pose an eXtreme challenge for the low handicapper

The Bridges Golf Club
San Ramon
925-735-4253
page 175

Oakhurst Country Club
Clayton
925-672-9737
page 151

Coyote Creek Golf Club
San Jose
408-463-1400
page 161

The Course at Wente Vineyards
Livermore
925-456-2475
page 158

OFF THE BEATEN PATH
Courses that are out of the way, but worth the drive

Diablo Grande Golf Club
Patterson
209-892-4563
page 236

Stevinson Ranch
Stevinson
209-668-8200
page 239

OUTSIDE THE ROUGH
Life outside of golf

The Bay Area has an excess of activities outside of golf. A person can spend days experiencing the city of San Francisco alone. The NBA, NFL, MLB, and NHL (I could keep going, but all the acronyms start to run together) all have at least one team here. Some of the finest restaurants in country are in the Bay Area as well. Throw in theSilicon Valley, Stanford, some amusement parks, spectacular shopping and cultural sights, and you have your hands full. There is a good reason so many people want to live here.

You can find more information about this destination by receiving the State of California Official Visitor's Guide. To order a free copy log onto www.visitcalifornia.com or call 916-322-2881.

San Francisco Convention & Visitors Bureau
415-283-0177
sfvisitor.org

San Jose Convention & Visitors Bureau
888-847-4875
sanjose.org

DESTINATION: MONTEREY

THE AREA: Most serious golfers will at least be familiar with Monterey and the Pebble Beach Golf Links. Many will have heard the praises of the fiercely private Cypress Point Club. While Pebble Beach is the ultimate public access golf experience, and nearby Cypress Point is among the best private layouts anywhere, they are not the only attractions. South all the way to Santa Barbara and somewhat inland, you will find many wonderfully entertaining layouts well worth playing. Twenty years ago the area offered many golfing bargains—now there are few.

THE COURSES: As with the San Francisco Bay Area, don't expect the ball to go as far when playing near the coast. All along this area the land drops fairly steeply into the ocean. Therefore, you can more expect hilly terrain.

CLIMATE: The summer months can mean fog, which can be surprisingly cold. Late spring or fall may actually be better times if you are looking for warmer weather. If you want a better chance of playing the premier courses, wintertime is a good bet. Winter can mean rain, but often it means less fog and mild conditions.

PEAK SEASON: Spring through fall.

AIRPORTS

Monterey Peninsula Airport
831-648-7000
montereyairport.com
Major Airlines: American, America West, United

San Jose International Airport
408-501-7600
sjc.org
San Jose International Airport is a viable alternative, approximately 1.5 hours north.

MONTEREY

MAIN COURSES
Courses every golfer should play if he or she gets the chance

Bayonet Golf Course
Seaside
831-899-7271
page 210
Formerly a restricted military course, this gem is not very well known, but PGA Tour hopefuls know it is one of the toughest tests in California.

Blackhorse Golf Course
Seaside
831-899-7271
page 210
Long the "other" course at the former Ft. Ord, it has been enhanced and is the equal of its attractive neighbor, the Bayonet.

Eagle Ridge Golf Club
Gilroy
408-846-4531
page 191
If you like an abundance of bunkers and wildly curvaceous greens, this is the course for you.

The Links at Spanish Bay
Pebble Beach
831-647-7495
page 203
Love it or hate it, we say that this links course has lots of character and deserves its Top 100 in the U.S. ranking by most major golf publications.

Pebble Beach Golf Links
Pebble Beach
831-624-3811
page 202
Simply America's best public access course. Everybody should play it once in their life—and that's all many of us could afford.

Poppy Hills Golf Course
Pebble Beach
831-622-8239
page 202
Home to the Northern California Golf Association (NCGA) and the only present course in the forest without ocean frontage, this Robert Trent Jones Jr. design sits high on the hill and rewards patient, accurate shotmaking.

Spyglass Hill Golf Course
Pebble Beach
831-625-8563
page 203
With five holes reminiscent of Pine Valley and thirteen similar to Augusta National, this Robert Trent Jones masterpiece is one of the toughest and best public access courses in all of America.

MUNI-ME
Reasonably priced municipal and public courses for those on a budget

Bayonet & Blackhorse Golf Courses
Seaside
831-899-7271
page 210
This is a good value for weekday play.

Laguna Seca Golf Club
Monterey
831-373-3701
page 196

Pacific Grove Golf Course
Pacific Grove
831-648-5777
page 200

Pajaro Valley Golf Club
Royal Oaks
831-724-3851
page 204

Poppy Hills Golf Course (NCGA Members)
Pebble Beach
831-622-8239
page 202

Rancho Cañada Golf Club - East & West Courses
Carmel
800-536-9459
page 190
This is a good value on weekdays.

ROOMS WITH A VIEW
Resort Courses

Carmel Valley Ranch
Carmel
831-626-2510
page 189

The Lodge at Pebble Beach
Pebble Beach
831-624-3811
page 202

The Links at Spanish Bay
Pebble Beach
831-647-7495
page 203

Quail Lodge Resort
Carmel
831-620-8808
page 189

XXXXXX-RATED
Courses that pose an eXtreme challenge for the low handicapper

Spyglass Hill Golf Course
Pebble Beach
831-625-8563
page 203

Pebble Beach Golf Links
Pebble Beach
831-622-8239
page 202

Bayonet Golf Course
Seaside
831-899-7271
page 210

OFF THE BEATEN PATH
Courses that are out of the way, but worth the drive

San Juan Oaks Golf Club
San Juan Bautista
831-636-6115
page 206

Ridgemark Golf & Country Club
Hollister
831-634-2222
page 194

OUTSIDE THE ROUGH
Life outside of golf

The Monterey area is not just rich in golf. Besides enjoying its picturesque coastline and equally gorgeous courses, you can truly relax here. The spas are enough to tempt anyone off the course. The Monterey Bay Aquarium is unequaled. A stroll, some shopping, and dinner in the village of Carmel can take your mind off of anything. John Steinbeck's Cannery Row is here. All this, and great wineries, too.

You can find more information about this destination by receiving the State of California Official Visitor's Guide. To order a free copy, log onto www.visitcalifornia.com or call 916-322-2881.

Monterey County Convention and Visitors Bureau
888-221-1010
gomonterey.com

Carmel California Visitor & Information Center
800-550-4333
carmelcalifornia.org

DESTINATION: SANTA BARBARA/ SAN LUIS OBISPO

THE AREA: Known for its spectacular coastline and good weather, this is one of the favorite getaways for Southern Californians. As you move inland, the topography is varied and equally beautiful. Although Santa Barbara and San Luis Obispo are about two hours apart, they are close enough to make an easy day trip for golfers.

THE COURSES: Within the two regions you will find a variety of ocean, mountain and meadow courses. The greens fees are not the lowest in the state; however, you will find them more reasonable than those up the coast in the Bay Area or down the coast in Los Angeles.

CLIMATE: Golf can generally be played year-round. Watch out for the "June Gloom", which is morning coastal fog. Morning fog is more frequent during the summer; however it will burn off. Summer afternoons can be on the hot side, but nothing like the desert.

PEAK SEASON: Spring through fall.

AIRPORTS

Santa Barbara Airport
805-967-7111
flysba.com
Airlines: American Eagle,
America West Express, United

San Luis Obispo County Airport
805-781-5205
thegrid.net
Airlines: American Eagle,
America West, United Express

MAIN COURSES

Courses every golfer should play if he or she gets the chance

Hunter Ranch Golf Course
Paso Robles
805-237-7444
page 200
This is an attractive, challenging lay-out of an expansive scale, dotted with bunkers, and set in rolling terrain and a wealth of mature oaks. Good players will definitely want to play here.

Cypress Ridge Golf Course
Arroyo Grande
805-474-7979
page 186

La Purisima Golf Course
Lompoc
805-735-8395
page 195
A combination of distant ocean breezes, length, demanding landing areas, and difficult greens make the layout quietly one of the most difficult in California. It is a wonderfully attractive layout, too.

Rancho San Marcos Golf Course
Santa Barbara
805-683-6334
page 208
This valley setting back in the mountains in one of Robert Trent Jones, Jr.'s best, as well as one of the best in California.

Sandpiper Golf Course
Goleta
805-968-1541
page 193
This is the area's version of Pebble Beach with its dramatic cliff holes. All in all, it's one of the best munis in America.

MUNI-ME

Reasonably priced municipal and public courses for those on a budget

Morro Bay Golf Course
Morro Bay
805-782-8060
page 197

Marshallia Ranch Golf Course
Vandenburg AFB
805-734-1333
page 214

The Links Course at Paso Robles
Paso Robles
805-227-4567
page 200

ROOMS WITH A VIEW

Resort Courses

Ojai Valley Inn & Spa
Ojai
805-646-2420
page 199

XXX-RATED

Courses that pose an eXtreme challenge for the low handicapper

La Purisima Golf Course
Lompoc
805-735-8395
page 195

Cypress Ridge Golf Course
Arroyo Grande
805-474-7979
page 186

Hunter Ranch Golf Course
Paso Robles
805-237-7444
page 200

OFF THE BEATEN PATH

Courses that are out of the way, but worth the drive

Marshallia Ranch Golf Course
Vandenburg AFB
805-734-1333
page 214

Rancho San Marcos Golf Course
Santa Barbara
805-683-6334
page 208

OUTSIDE THE ROUGH

Life outside of golf

People come to this area for quiet relaxation. The beaches are phenomenal. Spas, as well as golf, are among the main attractions. The coastline is beautiful. The little town of Solvang has the Old World feel and is the "Danish Capital of America." Quality wineries also populate this area.

You can find more information about this destination by receiving the State of California Official Visitor's Guide. To order a free copy, log onto www.visitcalifornia.com or call 916-322-2881.

Santa Barbara Visitors & Convention Bureau
805-966-9222
santabarbaraca.com

San Luis Obispo Chamber of Commerce
805-781-2777
visitslo.com

Solvang Conference & Visitors Bureau
800-468-6765
solvangusa.com

THE AREA:
Fly over the LA area and you will find that golf courses offer one of the few oases from the structures and asphalt that dominate the landscape. Golf here is busy and expensive, but the quality of courses is impressive. Though not possessing as many of the marquee-name private clubs as Northern California, the bench strength of private clubs may outclass their neighbors to the North.

THE COURSES:
One can expect flattish, tree-lined parkland-style courses closer to the coast. Moving inland, the elevation changes tend to become more pronounced. A plethora of impressive, upscale public access courses have been added during the 1990s, that are comparable in challenge and conditioning to most of the private alternatives. The downside is many are expensive and built on difficult terrain, so you should expect to ride a cart. The older public courses tend to be less stylized with much less mounding and earth moved. The conditioning and challenge can vary widely.

CLIMATE:
The sun is usually shining in Los Angeles, even in the winter. Summers can get a little too warm to stay out on the course all afternoon, especially when you add in the hot, dry Santa Ana winds. Coastal morning fog burns off in time to make for a good day. Don't forget your sunglasses any time of the year in Los Angeles.

PEAK SEASON: *Year-round.*

AIRPORTS

LAX - Los Angeles International Airport
310-646-5252
airports.ci.la.ca.us
LAX is located on the west side of the Los Angeles area.
All major airlines serve LAX.

Burbank Airport
818-840-8840
BurbankAirport.com
Burbank is located 15 minutes north of downtown Los Angeles.
Major Airlines: Alaska, America West, American, Southwest, United

Long Beach Airport
562-570-2678
lgb.org
Long Beach is located halfway between LAX & John Wayne Airport in Orange County.
Major Airlines: American, America West, jetBlue

Ontario International Airport
909-937-2700
airports.ci.la.ca.us
Ontario Airport is located in between Los Angeles and Palm Springs. Ontario is served by most major airlines.

MAIN COURSES

Courses every golfer should play if he or she gets the chance

Industry Hills Golf Club - Eisenhower Course
City of Industry
626-810-4653
page 256
The rough has been softened some over the years, so at least you can find your balls, but this hilly, long layout remains one of the state's most challenging. Built on landfill, its attractive design is a testament to how golf can enhance the environment. The sister course, the Zaharias, is also recommended.

Ocean Trails Golf Club
Rancho Palos Verdes
877-799-GOLF
page 275
When the new holes are completed sometime in 2001, the layout will undoubtedly receive terrific acclaim if for no other reason than its ocean views. It is a very fair, though demanding, golf course with a plethora of bunkers and difficult putting surfaces.

Lost Canyons Golf Club
Simi Valley
805-522-4653
page 211
For the serious golfer, this is simply a course (actually two courses) that can't be missed. Watch out for the wind.

Rancho Park Golf Course
Los Angeles
310-839-4374
page 269

Griffith Park - Wilson Course
Los Angeles
323-664-2255
page 267

Robinson Ranch
Santa Clarita
661-252-7666
page 278
Designed, built, and owned by Ted Robinson, the architect who has more credits to his name than almost any other designer in the state, they have two attractive golf courses.

MUNI-ME

Reasonably priced municipal and public courses for those on a budget

Brookside Golf Club
Pasadena
626-796-8151
page 273

Los Verdes Golf Course
Rancho Palos Verdes
310-377-7888
page 275

Rancho Park Golf Course
Los Angeles
310-839-4374
page 269

Griffith Park - Wilson Course
Los Angeles
323-664-2255
page 267

Hansen Dam Golf Course
Pacoima
818-896-0050
page 272

XXX XXX-RATED
Courses that pose an eXtreme challenge for the low handicapper

Industry Hills Golf Club - Eisenhower Course
City of Industry
626-810-4653
page 256

Robinson Ranch - Valley Course
Santa Clarita
661-252-7666
page 278

Lost Canyons Golf Club
Simi Valley
805-522-4653
page 211

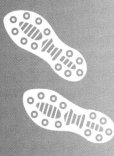

OFF THE BEATEN PATH

Courses that are out of the way, but worth the drive

Lost Canyons Golf Club
Simi Valley
805-522-4653
page 211

Robinson Ranch
Santa Clarita
661-252-7666
page 278

OUTSIDE THE ROUGH
Life outside of golf

If you want something besides peace and quiet, LA surely has it, complete with the laid-back attitude. Shopping, spas, beaches, restaurants, nightlife, sporting events, Hollywood, and amusement parks are just a small sampling of what the area has to offer. Contrary to popular belief, Los Angeles is not culturally deficient, either. If you are in LA and say you are bored, you obviously didn't walk outside your door.

You can find more information about this destination by receiving the State of California Official Visitor's Guide. To order a free copy, log onto www.visitcalifornia.com or call 916-322-2881.

Los Angeles Convention & Visitors Bureau
lacvb.com
213-624-7300

THE AREA:
If you're walking along Michigan Avenue in Chicago, Rodeo Drive in Beverly Hills or 5th Avenue in Manhattan, you understand that you'll be paying full retail if you walk into any of the shops. Consider Orange County golf along the same lines. If you live around here, fine. If you have a lot of money, even better. The bottom line is, unless you come here with clients and a corporate credit card, or enjoy playing twilight golf, most upscale daily fee courses are out of reach of most golfers' budgets. If you're in this area and you are priced out of the market and are looking for quality at a reasonable price, try the Inland Empire region.

THE COURSES:
Now that we are done complaining about the price of golf in Orange County, we should tell you that overall the destination courses here receive an A+ for diversity, conditioning, and quality.

CLIMATE:
Orange County is nice and golf-friendly year-round. It averages over 325 days of sun, with an average temperature of 73°. The farther inland you move, the more desert-like it becomes; humidity is not a problem. Summers tend to heat up, but temperatures rarely surge over 100°. Expect some morning coastal fog in June.

PEAK SEASON:
Year-round.

AIRPORTS

John Wayne Airport, Santa Ana
949-252-5200
ocair.com
Orange County is served by most major airlines.

LAX - Los Angeles International Airport, Los Angeles
310-646-5252
airports.ci.la.ca.us

MAIN COURSES

Courses every golfer should play if he or she gets the chance

Oak Creek Golf Club
Irvine
949-653-7300
page 324
This upscale layout features wide fairways framed by many bunkers. It is an attractive, well-conditioned layout that is very playable for all skill levels.

Pelican Hill Golf Club
Newport Coast
949-760-0707
page 330
Take your pick of two outstanding and similiar layouts, but expect to pay top dollar. Both courses overlook the Pacific. If you can only play one course, play the Ocean South.

Tijeras Creek Golf Club
Rancho Santa Margarita
949-589-9793
page 331
The front nine is solid, though hardly remarkable, as it plays among housing, but the back nine is terrific, maybe the best in the area. It plays along a ridgeline and roams into a valley for some beautiful and exciting golf.

Talega Golf Club
San Clemente
949-369-6226
page 332

MUNI-ME

Reasonably priced municipal and public courses for those on a budget

Anaheim Hills Golf Club
Anaheim
714-998-3041
page 318

Costa Mesa Country Club (Los Lagos Course)
Costa Mesa
714-340-7500
page 320

Mile Square Golf Club
Fountain Valley
714-968-4556
page 322

ROOMS WITH A VIEW
Resort Courses

Monarch Beach Golf Links - St. Regency
Dana Point
949-240-8247
page 321

XXX-RATED

Courses that pose an eXtreme challenge for the low handicapper

Coyote Hills Golf Course
Fullerton
714-672-6800
page 323

Strawberry Farms Golf Club
Irvine
949-551-1811
page 326

OFF THE BEATEN PATH

Courses that are out of the way, but worth the drive

PGA of Southern California Golf Club at Oak Valley
Calimesa
877-742-2500
page 294

Eagle Glen Golf Club
Corona
909-272-4653
page 296

Cross Creek Golf Club
Temecula
909-506-3402
page 311

SCGA Members' Club
Murrieta
800-752-9724
page 303

Goose Greek Golf Club
Mira Loma
909-735-3982
page 301

Hidden Valley Golf Club
Norco
909-737-1010
page 304

OUTSIDE THE ROUGH

Life outside of golf

Disneyland. Need we say more? Actually, we will. Orange County has a full array of amusement parks - enough to keep kids and adults busy for at least a week. Head west to the Pacific and you will find beaches most people only get to dream about. As we mentioned once or twice, Orange County is an upscale area. This translates into fabulous shopping and great spas — activities that can keep adults busy for at least a week. Depending on the time of year, you can catch the Angels or the Mighty Ducks. If you somehow manage to get bored, Los Angeles and San Diego are both about an hour away.

You can find more information about this destination by receiving the State of California Official Visitor's Guide. To order a free copy, log onto www.visitcalifornia.com or call 916-322-2881.

Anaheim/Orange County Convention Bureau
anaheimoc.org
714-765-8888

DESTINATION: SAN DIEGO

THE AREA: From the flatter coastline to the hilly country inland, golf is popular in San Diego. When you add the wonderful climate, you can appreciate why San Diego and golf go well together.

THE COURSES: By and large, there are relatively few private, exclusive courses; hence, most are open for public play. The rates compared to Orange County and LA are more modest. However, with the addition of new, upscale resort or daily fee courses, low green fees may be on the way out.

CLIMATE: San Diego has sun year-round, with an average temperature of 70°. It also has micro climates, ranging from the coastal to mountain to desert. Humidity is low.

PEAK SEASON: Year-round.

AIRPORTS

San Diego International Airport
619-686-6200
portofsandiego.org
Most major airlines serve San Diego.

MAIN COURSES

Courses every golfer should play if he or she gets the chance

La Costa Resort & Spa
Carlsbad
760-438-9111
page 342
Either well-bunkered course will
entertain you.

The Meadows Del Mar Golf Club
San Diego
877-530-0636
page 359
This is cart-golf, but it nonetheless
has some very scenic, engaging
holes.

Mt. Woodson Golf Club
Ramona
760-788-3555
page 353
Uniquely beautiful and challenging despite its short length, the
course puts the premium on accuracy, but don't be distracted by
the views.

Four Seasons Resort Aviara
Carlsbad
760-603-6900
page 341
This is one of the Arnold Palmer
Group's best designs, and the
waterscaping here is something to
behold.

Torrey Pines Golf Course -
South Course
La Jolla
858-452-3226
page 349
If you can get a tee time on this
busy muni, you will enjoy the cliff
side views and good solid simple
golf, and, of course, revel in playing where the pros play.

Barona Creek Golf Club
Lakeside
619-387-7018
page 350

Maderas Golf Club
Poway
858-726-4653
page 352

MUNI-ME

Reasonably priced municipal and public courses for those on a budget

Carlton Oaks Country Club
Santee
619-448-8500
page 362

Singing Hills Resort - 3 courses
El Cajon
619-442-3425
page 344

Torrey Pines Golf Course
La Jolla
858-452-3226
page 349

Encinitas Ranch Golf Course
Encinitas
760-944-1936
page 345

Balboa Park Golf Course
San Diego
619-387-7018
page 357

Coronado Municipal Course
Coronado
619-435-3121
page 343

ROOMS WITH A VIEW
Resort Courses

Four Seasons Resort Aviara
Carlsbad
760-603-6900
page 341

La Costa Resort & Spa
Carlsbad
760-438-9111
page 342

Barona Creek Golf Club
Lakeside
619-387-7018
page 350

Rancho Bernardo Inn
San Diego
858-675-8470
page 361

Temecula Creek Inn Golf Resort
Temecula
800-642-4653
page 312

XXX-RATED
Courses that pose an eXtreme challenge for the low handicapper

Steele Canyon Golf Club
Jamul
619-441-6900
page 348

OFF THE BEATEN PATH
Courses that are out of the way, but worth the drive

Barona Creek Golf Club
Lakeside
619-387-7018
page 350

OUTSIDE THE ROUGH
Life outside of golf

This is the land dominated by sun and fun. The sensational climate invites it. The beaches are great, evidenced by the array of water sports. Keeping with the theme, Sea World is a major draw. The zoo is not to be missed, either. Add downtown San Diego to your list of "to do's." Drive a bit out of San Diego and you'll hit the mountains for hiking and biking. Some of the country's best spas are in the San Diego area - don't miss them.

You can find more information about this destination by receiving the State of California Official Visitor's Guide. To order a free copy, log onto www.visitcalifornia.com or call 916-322-2881.

San Diego Convention & Visitors Bureau
sandiego.org
619-236-1212

DESTINATION:
PALM SPRINGS

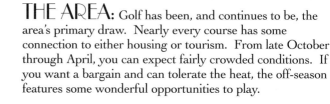

THE AREA: Golf has been, and continues to be, the area's primary draw. Nearly every course has some connection to either housing or tourism. From late October through April, you can expect fairly crowded conditions. If you want a bargain and can tolerate the heat, the off-season features some wonderful opportunities to play.

THE COURSES: While the best courses are private, over the last twenty years many solid resort and daily fee courses have come onto the area scene. Players can expect to see much earth moved to create interest from the formerly flat desert floor. That means digging lakes and building mounds, hence, many water hazards. Also, there is an abundance of parkland, or oasis courses, with more of the new ones incorporating the natural desert features and target golf. Typically, because of an older recreational clientele, most of the courses are relatively benign in their challenge.

CLIMATE: This is truly a desert climate-hot and dry. Come here for warmth and sunshine. Summer is usually too hot to play unless you get up early. The area has a lot of 100°+ days. Bring your shorts, even in the winter. Winter days are usually warm, but winter nights can be downright freezing. Many Californians love the desert for quick getaways fall through spring.

PEAK SEASON: October through April.

AIRPORTS

**Palm Springs
International Airport**
760-318-3800
ci.palm-springs.ca.us
Major Airlines: Alaska,
American, America West,
Continental, Delta,
Northwest, United

**Ontario International Airport,
Ontario**
909-937-2700
airports.ci.la.ca.us
Hardcore golfers know to fly
into Ontario and make the
drive to Palm Springs.

MAIN COURSES

Courses every golfer should play if he or she gets the chance

Desert Dunes Golf Club
Desert Hot Springs
760-251-5360
page 375
This Robert Trent Jones, Jr. course is laid out among large dunes and mature desert trees. It has a links feel in several spots. It easily compares to any of the private courses. Beware of the wind.

Desert Willow Golf Resort -
Firecliff Course
Palm Desert
760-346-7060
page 407
Huge sand bunkers dominate the landscape of this Hurdzan/Fry/Cook collaboration. Landscaped dunes and water give it an oasis look and feel.

Landmark Golf Club
Indio
760-347-2326
page 384
Two similar, but enticing, new courses with an abundance of bunkering enhance the Indio area. The site now hosts the annual Skins Game.

La Quinta Resort & Club -
Mountain Course
La Quinta
760-564-7686
page 386
Long considered one of the premier desert courses, the holes set against the mountains are particularly memorable.

PGA West - Jack Nicklaus
Tournament Course
La Quinta
760-544-7170
page 388
This is one of the tougher, meaner resort courses with fairly generous landing areas, but real trouble when you miss them. This is surprisingly similar to the neighboring Pete Dye work.

PGA West -
Greg Norman Course
La Quinta
760-544-7170
page 387
Thoughtful use of bunkering, land, and strategy make this one layout you will want to play.

PGA West -
TPC Stadium Course
La Quinta
760-564-7170
page 388
Famous for its difficulty, the course attracts golfers who pay the premium price to torture themselves here. Actually, the course is surprisingly fair with generous landing areas, especially if you play the tees that fit your ability. Actually, the Stadium Course may be underrated.

Tahquitz Creek, Golf Resort
Palm Springs
760-328-1005
page 415
A fun, challenging design and an engaging valley setting make this newer course definitely worth the visit, especially for the better player.

Westin Mission Hills Resort -
Pete Dye Course
Rancho Mirage
760-328-3198
page 421
Dye has a habit of repeating his hole designs, and here is a good place to sample his work. This is an entertaining and slightly more forgiving challenge than some of his other work.

Westin Mission Hills Resort -
Gary Player Course
Rancho Mirage
760-770-9496
page 421
Good aesthetics and playability here. The mounding and water is definitely present, but not overdone. A tough test from the tips nonetheless.

MUNI-ME
Reasonably priced municipal and public courses for those on a budget

Tahquitz Creek, Golf Resort
Palm Springs
760-328-1005
page 415

ROOMS WITH A VIEW
Resort Courses

The Westin Mission Hills Resort
Rancho Mirage
760-328-3198
page 421

La Quinta Resort & Club
La Quinta
707-564-7686
page 386

The Golf Resort at Indian Wells
Indian Wells
760-346-4653
page 382

XXX-RATED
Courses that pose an eXtreme challenge for the low handicapper

PGA West - TPC Stadium Course
La Quinta
760-564-7170
page 388

OUTSIDE THE ROUGH
Life outside of golf

Golf, golf, golf. That's all there is to Palm Springs, right? Wrong. The desert is the place to relax. A place to work on your tan during the winter — complete with someone delivering icy drinks by the pool. It is a place to let yourself be pampered at the spa. Another relaxing choice is haunting the flea markets and other open-air shopping. Check out some of the amazing restaurants. If it is not too hot, play some tennis or go horseback riding. Whatever you choose, golf included, don't forget your sunglasses and sunscreen.

You can find more information about this destination by receiving the State of California Official Visitor's Guide. To order a free copy, log onto www.visitcalifornia.com or call 916-322-2881.

Palm Springs Tourism
760-778-8415
palm-springs.org

DESTINATION: LAS VEGAS

THE AREA: Tourists are flocking to Las Vegas and surrounding areas for golf. Unfortunately, the golfers are coming quicker than the courses. The result is that there are no longer many great values, but the good news is that most of the courses, more than fifty now in the greater area, are open to the public. The new ones being built have spared few expenses, and the quality is consistently good.

THE COURSES: In the land of excess and imagination, why should the golf be any different? You will find plenty of desert, traditional, and natural courses in Las Vegas and surrounding areas. But where else in the world will you find courses where a limo picks you up for your tee time, castles replace clubhouses, and a tropical paradise is imported to create— well, a tropical paradise? If you are coming during peak season, don't forget your Mastercard, Visa, American Express, or your home-equity line of credit. Imagination and excess aren't cheap.

CLIMATE: Las Vegas is smack in the middle of the desert, so expect hot and dry conditions year round. This is great for fall, winter and spring. You can golf and relax by a pool. Summers sizzle with multiple 100°+ days. If you are there during the summer, play early and retreat to your hotel or casino of choice — they'll have air conditioning.

PEAK SEASON: October through May.

AIRPORTS

McCarran International Airport, Las Vegas
702-261-5211
mccarran.com
Most major airlines service Las Vegas.

Laughlin/Bullhead International Airport
520-754-2134
Air Laughlin services this airport.

MAIN COURSES

Courses every golfer should play if he or she gets the chance

Angel Park Golf Club
Las Vegas
888-446-5358
page 390

The Oasis Golf Club
Mesquite
702-346-7820
page 402
The Oasis Course is the center-piece of this 27-hole complex.

Las Vegas Paiute Golf Resort
Las Vegas
800-711-2833
page 396
Paiute offers a winning combina-tion of excellent service and fun golf courses.

Primm Valley Golf Club
Primm
702-679-5510
page 417
Two courses provide the Tom Fazio look and high-end experi-ence. They are comparable to each other, so don't worry about which one you play if you can only play one.

Reflection Bay Golf Club
Henderson
702-740-4653
page 379
There is nothing very easy about this Jack Nicklaus layout that enjoys an engagingly unique lakeside view.

The Revere at Anthem
Henderson
702-259-4653
page 378
This is a scenic course with great views of the Las Vegas Strip that will push your shot making ability to the limit.

Rio Secco Golf Club
Henderson
888-867-3226
page 380
While guests of a certain hotel have first priority, this course is open to the public. This Rees Jones course has any number of spectac-ular views and challenges.

Shadow Creek Golf Club
North Las Vegas
866-252-4653
page 404
Technically public (open to guests of any MGM Mirage property), the Steve Wynn/Tom Fazio creation remains the standard for the area. Completely fabricated from the flat desert, it has the spectacular look and feel of a traditional course in a mountain environment. The green fees here maybe the most expen-sive in the nation.

Wolf Creek at Paradise Canyon
Mesquite
866-252-GOLF
page 403
This course will take your breath away, and the views aren't bad either.

MUNI-ME

Reasonably priced municipal and public courses for those on a budget

Desert Rose Golf Course
Las Vegas
702-431-4653
page 393

Los Prados Golf Course
Las Vegas
702-645-5696
page 396

ROOMS WITH A VIEW
Resort Courses

Primm Valley Golf Club
Primm
702-679-5510
page 417

Reflection Bay Golf Club
Henderson
702-740-4653
page 379
There is nothing very easy about this Jack Nicklaus layout that enjoys an engagingly unique lakeside view.

XXX-RATED
Courses that pose an eXtreme challenge for the low handicapper

Wolf Creek at Paradise Canyon
Mesquite
866-252-4653
page 403
The course is about an hour drive from Las Vegas.

Badlands Golf Club
Las Vegas
702-382-4653
page 391

TPC at the Canyons
Las Vegas
702-256-2000
page 401

OFF THE BEATEN PATH
Courses that are out of the way, but worth the drive

The Oasis Golf Club
Mesquite
702-346-7820
page 402

Wolf Creek at Paradise Canyon
Mesquite
866-252-GOLF
page 403

OUTSIDE THE ROUGH
Life outside of golf

What is there to do in Vegas? A better question is, what can't you do? I'm still trying to figure that one out. You can golf, gamble, and experience some of the finest restaurants in the country (yes, you read that correctly). Feel like relaxing? Choose a spa or stay by the pool and get waited on. To satisfy the high rollers and the lucky that populate Vegas, you can find some of the best shopping money can buy. It is hard to find better nightlife or shows than what Las Vegas has to offer. If you can dream it, you can probably find it, or get it done, in Las Vegas.

Las Vegas Convention & Visitors' Authority
702-892-0711
lasvegas24hours.com

Laughlin Visitors Bureau
800-4-LAUGHLIN
visitlaughlin.com

Bob is one of the most extensively traveled golfers in America. During his 38 years of golf, he has played nearly 1,450 courses, more than 400 in California alone. A fine player, Fagan owns more than seventy-five course records.

PUBLIC COURSES

Ten Best Resort Courses

1a. Pebble Beach Golf Links
1b. Spyglass Hill Golf Course
2. The Links at Spanish Bay
3. Ojai Valley Inn & Spa
4. La Quinta Resort & Club - Mountain Course
5. Four Season Aviara
6. La Costa Resort & Spa - Combination Course
7. Sonoma Mission Inn & Spa
8. Marriott's Shadow Ridge
9. Westin Mission Hills Resort - Gary Player Course
10. The Golf Club at Quail Lodge

California's Most Demanding Courses - The Top 6

1. PGA West: TPC Stadium Course
2. Industry Hills Golf Club - Eisenhower Course
3. Spyglass Hill Golf Course
4. La Purisma Golf Course
5. Bayonet Golf Course
6. The Dragon at Gold Mountain

Toughest Shortest Courses

Bodega Harbour Golf Links - don't let the yardage fool you. It's a wolf in sheep's clothing.

Honorable Mention: Mt. Woodson Country Club, Palos Verdes Golf Club

Best Nine-Hole Courses

Glenbrook Golf Course - on the Nevada side of Lake Tahoe. It is so narrow that the fairways seem almost like tunnels.

Northwood Golf Club - just as narrow as Glenbrook, but with giant redwoods and the ninth hole is as demanding as any you will find.

7 Remote Public Access Golf Courses Worth the Trip *(alphabetical order)*

Bodega Harbour Golf Links
Fall River Valley Golf & Country Club
La Purisma Golf Course
Marshallia Ranch Golf Course
Saddle Creek Golf Club
The Golf Club at Whitehawk Ranch
The Sea Ranch Golf Links

Best Value Public Access Golf Courses *(alphabetical order)*

Bennett Valley Golf Course
Boundary Oak Golf Course
Fall River Valley Golf & Country Club
La Contenta Golf Club
Las Verdes Golf & Country Club
Morro Bay Golf Course
Pacific Grove Golf Course
Plumas Lake Golf & Country Club
Poppy Hills Golf Course (NCGA Members)
Poppy Ridge Golf Course (NCGA Members)
Rancho Park Golf Course
Ridgemark Golf & Country Club
SCGA Member's Club (SCGA Members)
Singing Hills Resort

The Best Public Courses designed before 1960

1. Pebble Beach Golf Links
2. Pasatiempo Golf Course
3. Ojai Valley Inn & Spa
4. Presidio Golf Course
5. Bayonet Golf Course (formerly Ft. Ord)
6. Torrey Pines Golf Course - South Course
7. Blackhorse Golf Course (formerly Ft. Ord)
8. Harding Park Golf Course

The Best Public Access Courses designed after 1960

1. Spyglass Hill Golf Course
2. The Links at Spanish Bay
3. PGA West: TPC Stadium Course
4. Pelican Hill Golf Club - Ocean South
5. Saddle Creek Golf Club
6. La Quinta Resort & Club - Mountain Course
7. The Course at Wente Vineyards
8. Desert Dunes Golf Club
9. Rancho San Marcos Golf Course
10. The Meadows Del Mar Golf Club
11. The Golf Club at Whitehawk Ranch
12. Four Seasons Resort Aviara
13. La Purisima Golf Course
14. Pelican Hill Golf Club - Ocean North
15. San Juan Oaks Golf Club
16. Redhawk Golf Club
17. La Costa Resort & Spa (Composite Course)
18. Desert Willow Golf Resort - Firecliff Course
19. Industry Hills Golf Club - Eisenhower Course
20. Stevinson Ranch
21. Twelve Bridges Golf Club
22. The Ridge Golf Course
23. Sandpiper Golf Course
24. Cinnabar Hills Golf Club
25. Too many fun Palm Springs desert courses to mention individually

Best 36-Hole Golf Complexes - Public

1. Pelican Hill Golf Club
2. Half Moon Bay Golf Links
3. Lost Canyons Golf Club
4. PGA of Southern California
5. Landmark Golf Club
6. Robinson Ranch
7. Diablo Grande Golf Club
8. Primm Valley Golf Club
9. Rancho Murieta Country Club
10. Industry Hills Golf Club
11. Torrey Pines Golf Course
12. Desert Willow Golf Resort
13. Silverado Country Club & Resort
14. Los Serranos Country Club

Best Complex Over 36 Holes

The Pebble Beach Company owns Pebble Beach Golf Links, The Links at Spanish Bay, Spyglass Hill Golf Course, and Del Monte Golf Course.

Best Complex Over 36 Holes At One Site

PGA West: Public and Private Combined

Best Bridges on a Course

Mt. Woodson Golf Club

Best Opening Stretch of Golf

Spyglass Hill Golf Course - The first six holes may be the best start in America.

Best Courses Finishing with a Par Three

Pasatiempo Golf Course
Mesa Verde Country Club

Sandpiper Golf Club

Toughest Eighteenth Holes - Public (all par-fours)

1. Four Seasons Resort Aviara
2. Bodega Harbour Golf Links
3. Carlton Oaks Country Club
4. Cypress Golf Club
5. Oakhurst Country Club
6. Pelican Hill Golf Club - Ocean South Course

Longest Eighteenth Hole

Lake Chabot Golf Course - 677 yards, par-six

Most Dramatic Finishing other than Pebble Beach

Half Moon Bay Golf Links - Links Course

Best Approach Shot - Public

Pebble Beach Golf Links - par four 8th hole

Scariest Par Three

The Meadow Del Mar Golf Club -17th hole from the tips

Best City Views

Lincoln Park Golf Course 17th - Golden Gate Bridge & San Francisco

Best Opening Tee Shot

The Course at Wente Vineyards

Best Back-To-Back Par Threes

Pelican Hill Golf Club - Ocean South, holes 12 &13 (S. Course)

Best Back-To-Back Par Fives

Hunter Ranch Golf Course, holes six and seven

Monarch Bay Golf Links - Several holes afford a panoramic view of San Franciso

Best Ocean Views Other than Monterey *(alphabetical order)*

Bodega Harbour Golf Links
Half Moon Bay Golf Links(both courses)
Los Verdes Golf Course
Ocean Trails Golf Club

Sandpiper Golf Course
Sea Ranch Golf Course
Torrey Pines Golf Course (both courses)

PRIVATE COURSES

Thirteen Best Private Classic Club Courses (Through 1960)

1. Cypress Point Club
T2. The Olympic Club - Lake Course
T2. San Francisco Golf Club
T2. Riviera Country Club
T2. The Los Angeles Country Club - North Course
6. The Valley Club of Montecito
7. Monterey Peninsula Country Club - Dunes Course
8. Lake Merced Golf & Country Club
9. Bel Air Country Club (renovated so often it might not be considered a classic)
10. Sherwood Country Club
11. Lakeside Golf Club
12. Pauma Valley Country Club
13. Rancho Santa Fe Golf Club

Dozen Best Modern Private Club Courses (since 1960)

1. Lahontan Golf Club
2. CordeValle Golf Club
3. Winchester Country Club
4. The Preserve Golf Club
5. Tradition Golf Club
6. The Plantation Golf Club
7. The Quarry at La Quinta
8. Granite Bay Golf Club
9. The Vintage Club - Mountain Course
10. Mission Hills Country Club - Dinah Shore Course
11. Sherwood Country Club
12. The Club at Morningside

Two Dozen Other Worthy Private Club Contenders - Golf Courses *(alphabetical order)*

Annandale Golf Course
Bakersfield Country Club
Bear Creek Golf Club
California Golf Club
Coto de Caza Golf & Racquet Club - North Course
Del Rio Country Club
Green Hills Country Club
Hacienda Golf Club
La Jolla Country Club
Meadow Club
Monterey Peninsula Country Club - Shore Courses

North Ridge Country Club
Oakmont Country Club
The Olympic Club - Ocean Course
PGA West: Nicklaus Private
San Diego Country Club
Saticoy Country Club
Serrano Country Club
Stanford University Golf Course
Sunnyside Country Club
Valencia Country Club
The Vintage Club - Desert Course

Five Best 36-Hole Golf Complex - Private

1. The Olympic Club
2. Monterey Peninsula Country Club
3. The Los Angeles Country Club
4. The Vintage Club
5. PGA West

Toughest Private Course You Never Heard Of
Canyon Oaks Country Club

Most Exclusive Private Clubs
1. Cypress Point Club
2. The Los Angeles Country Club
3. The Valley Club at Montecito
4. San Francisco Golf Club

Most Unusual Routing
Bel Air Country Club - Here you follow several tunnels, an elevator, clubhouse hallways, and a swinging bridge to get yourself around the golf course.

Most Ostentatious Clubhouse
Sherwood Country Club - Anyone who has ever visited it would have a difficult time believing that golf is not a rich man's game.

Least Ostentatious Clubhouse
Cypress Point Club - Perhaps that is the essence of its classiness.

Best Eighteenth Hole - Private
1. Granite Bay Golf Club
2. Mission Hills Country Club
3. The Wilshire Country Club
4. Riviera Country Club

Best Finishing Stretch
The Quarry at La Quinta

Best Course Starting With a Par Three
Napa Valley Country Club

Best Course Finishing With A Par Three
Mesa Verde Country Club

Longest Par Four
Pasadera Country Club, 560 yards

Scariest Tee Shot
Cypress Point Club - 16th hole - Private

Best Back-to-Back Par Threes
Cypress Point Club - holes 15 and 16   Lahontan Golf Club - holes 15 and 16

Best City Views
Bel Air Country Club - 1st hole - Views of the nearby Westwood section of Los Angeles

Best Opening Tee Shot
1. Bel Air Country Club
2. Castlewood Country Club - Hill Course
3. Riverview Golf & Country Club
4. Riviera Country Club

Best Par Three Course (private)
The Olympic Club - Cliffs Course 9-hole par three private course

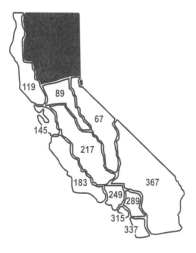

119
89
67
145
217
183
367
249
289
315
337

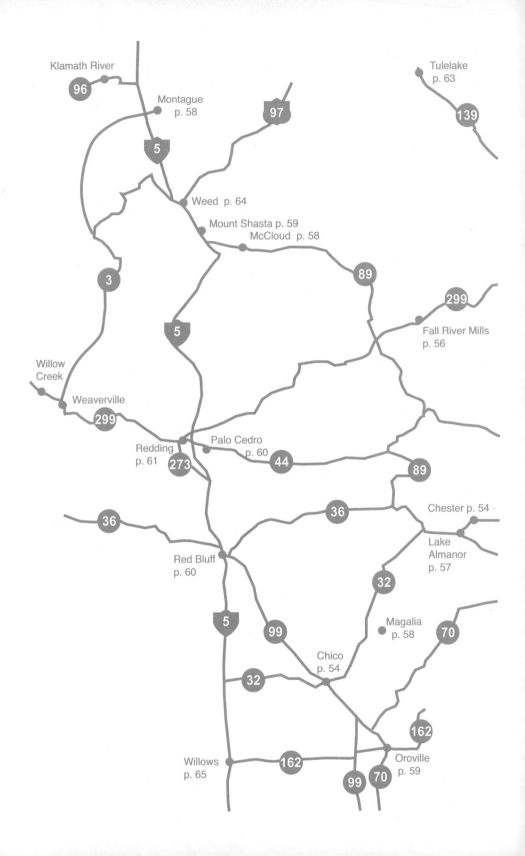

Map not to scale

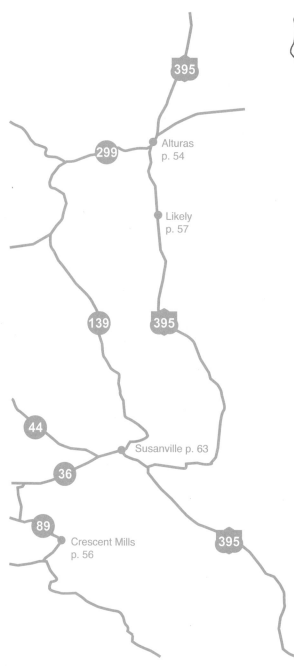

395

299   Alturas
        p. 54

        Likely
        p. 57

139   395

44

36

89   Crescent Mills
       p. 56

Susanville p. 63

395

ARROWHEAD GOLF COURSE (public, 9 holes, john briggs 1969) . . . .

1901 North Warner Street
Alturas, CA 96101
(530) 233-3404

	YARDAGE	PAR	RATING	SLOPE
FRONT	2743	36	70.6	120
MIDDLE	3118	37	74.2	128
BACK	3118	36	68.2	112

$10 - $18

WHAT TO EXPECT: Bring the big stick, because you are almost guaranteed to hit a fairway. Of course, it may not be the one you intended, but a fairway is a fairway. Arrowhead is not void of hazards, as irrigation ditches come into play on almost every hole. You will find the greens small and sloping.

DIRECTIONS: From within Alturas: Off Highway 299, head north on Warner Street, to the course.

LAKE ALMANOR WEST GOLF COURSE (public, 9 holes, homer flint 1977) . . . .

111 Slim Drive
Chester, CA 96020
(530) 259-4555

	YARDAGE	PAR	RATING	SLOPE
FRONT	2684	36	69.6	115
MIDDLE	-	-	-	-
BACK	3144	36	69.9	119

$19 - $27

WHAT TO EXPECT: The biggest obstacle to scoring well at Almanor West is the large sloping greens, which can be tricky to read. The fairways are surrounded by trees but are large enough to hit driver. Views of Mount Lassen can be found throughout the nine holes.

DIRECTIONS: From Chico (about 75 miles northeast to the course): Take Highway 32 east about 55 miles to Highway 36. Turn right on Highway 36 to Highway 89. At Highway 89, go south to Lake Almanor West. Turn left on Slim Drive.

BIDWELL PARK GOLF COURSE (public, 18 holes) . . . .

3199 Golf Course Road
Chico, CA 95973
(530) 891-8417
americangolf.com

	YARDAGE	PAR	RATING	SLOPE
FRONT	5440	73	70.2	120
MIDDLE	5991	70	68.5	117
BACK	6363	72	70.8	123

$13 - $25

WHAT TO EXPECT: This is a parkland-style golf course with lots of trees and some water. The fairways are wide enough to use your driver, but the course is not long, so it may not be your best option. Keep the ball in play and you will do fine.

OUR OPINION: The course is entertaining, cheap and will give up low scores. Isn't that what golf is all about? – Shaw

DIRECTIONS: From within Chico: Off Highway 99, take the East Avenue exit and drive east. Turn left on Wildwood. Drive about two miles to Golf Course Road. This leads directly to the course.

BUTTE CREEK COUNTRY CLUB (members only, 18 holes, bob baldock 1965) . . . .

175 Estates Drive
Chico, CA 95928
(530) 343-8292
buttecreek.com

	YARDAGE	PAR	RATING	SLOPE	
FRONT	5236	72	69.5	115	**$35 - $65**
MIDDLE	6581	72	71.1	122	
BACK	6978	72	73.0	126	

WHAT TO EXPECT: Butte Creek runs through the property and affects five holes. The layout is a flat, but scenic, course, with plenty of mature trees and undulating, yet puttable, greens. The course offers a fair test of your skills, but does not torture members with higher handicaps.

NOTES: Reciprocal play with other members only clubs is allowed.

DIRECTIONS: From Sacramento (about 85 miles north to the course): Take Highway 99 north. After the Welcome to Chico sign, take a left at Estates Drive. If you go over Butte Creek on Highway 99, you've gone too far.

CANYON OAKS COUNTRY CLUB (members only, 18 holes, jim summers 1985) . . . .

999 Yosemite Drive
Chico, CA 95928
(530) 343-1116
americangolf.com

	YARDAGE	PAR	RATING	SLOPE	
FRONT	5031	72	70.8	125	**$35 - $45**
MIDDLE	6401	72	71.7	132	
BACK	6804	72	73.9	142	

WHAT TO EXPECT: Canyon Oaks is one of the most difficult in the region. This is a hilly course that plays along a creek. Narrow fairways with trouble on both sides spell doom for wayward hitters.

NOTES: Reciprocal play with other members only clubs is allowed.

DIRECTIONS: From within Chico: Off Highway 99, take Highway 32 east. Turn left on Bruce Road. Make a right on California Park Drive and another right on Yosemite Drive.

TUSCAN RIDGE GOLF CLUB (semi-private, 18 holes, algie m. pulley, jr. 2001) . . . . . .

Skyway Avenue
Chico, CA
(530) 343-3862
tuscanridge.com

	YARDAGE	PAR	RATING	SLOPE	
FRONT	-	-	-	-	**$30 - $50**
MIDDLE	-	-	-	-	
BACK	-	-	-	-	

WHAT TO EXPECT: The nines are being opened on separate dates. The current nine that is open is a compilation of holes from the front and back nines.

NOTES: The additional nine are due to open in fall of 2001.

DIRECTIONS: From within Chico: Off Highway 99, exit at Skyway Avenue, and head east about five miles.

MOUNT HUFF GOLF COURSE (public, 9 holes, sy brand 1954) . . . .

15301 Highway 89
Crescent Mills, CA 95947
(530) 284-6204

	YARDAGE	PAR	RATING	SLOPE
FRONT	1887	33	61.1	93
MIDDLE	2138	33	60.2	92
BACK	2301	32	60.8	95

$15 - $18

WHAT TO EXPECT: This is an executive course with a river running through four holes and ponds coming into play on two more. The greens are small and sloping. As many as 60 trees have been planted over the last few years.

DIRECTIONS: From Truckee (about 85 miles northwest to the course): Off I-80, take Highway 89 north to Crescent Mills. The course is located at the Taylorsville Junction.

FALL RIVER VALLEY GOLF & COUNTRY CLUB (resort, 18 holes, clark glasson 1978) . . .

42889 Highway 299E
Fall River Mills, CA 96028
(530) 336-5555

	YARDAGE	PAR	RATING	SLOPE
FRONT	6001	72	73.2	128
MIDDLE	6991	72	72.8	128
BACK	7375	72	74.9	131

$15 - $29

WHAT TO EXPECT: Nature is the dominant feature on this long, beautiful course that has no hidden agenda. If you keep the ball in the wide, rolling fairways, you will be rewarded with an easy shot into the greens. If you miss them, the native grasses and hazards will punish your score. The greens are large, and the course is dotted with oaks. Three lakes come into play on five holes.

OUR OPINION: What can you say about a fantastic layout, at an excellent price, out in the middle of nowhere? We say if you get a chance, play it before word gets out. There maybe no better value in California. – Shaw

DIRECTIONS: From Redding (about 75 miles northeast to the course): Off I-5, take Highway 299 east to Fall River Mills. The course is on the right. It is right before the town of Fall River Mills.

EAGLE'S NEST GOLF COURSE (public, 9 holes, orville reiersgaard 1972) . . . .

22112 Walker Road
Klamath River, CA 96050
(530) 465-2424
eagles-nest-resort.com

	YARDAGE	PAR	RATING	SLOPE
FRONT	1642	32	61.2	106
MIDDLE	1794	32	61.2	106
BACK	1872	32	61.2	106

$9 - $20

WHAT TO EXPECT: This is a natural course that features plenty of trees and the Klamath River. The fairways are tight and the greens are smallish, so accuracy is far more important than distance.

OUR OPINION: Imagine a place where a round of golf takes less than four hours, costs less than $20, and is surrounded by magnificent beauty. Eagle's Nest may not be the best golf course in the state, but it may be one of the better golf experiences. – Shaw

DIRECTIONS: From Yreka (about 35 miles northwest to the course): Take Highway 263 north to Highway 96. Drive west on Highway 96 for about 25 miles. Turn left over the Walker Bridge, which is about four miles west of the town of Klamath River. Follow the signs to the course.

BAILEY CREEK GOLF COURSE (public, 18 holes, homer flint 2000) . . . .

433 Durkin Drive
Lake Almanor, CA 96137
(530) 259-4653
baileycreek.com

	YARDAGE	PAR	RATING	SLOPE	
FRONT	5329	72	-	-	**$25 - $40**
MIDDLE	-	-	-	-	
BACK	6508	72	-	-	

WHAT TO EXPECT: Forested, undulating terrain, complete with sweeping mounding, expansive bunkering, and large putting surfaces make for a very playable and attractive golf course.

OUR OPINION: This is a scenic course that is well worth playing if you are in the area. – Bob

DIRECTIONS: From Chico (about 80 miles northeast to the course): Take Highway 32 east about 55 miles to Highway 36. Make a right and follow to Chester. Turn right on County Road A13 (Walker Road) and then another right on Clifford Drive to the gate. Durkin Drive, and the course, is on the right.

LAKE ALMANOR COUNTRY CLUB (semi-private, 9 holes, ed clifford 1960) . . . .

951 Clifford Drive
Lake Almanor, CA 96137
(530) 259-2868

	YARDAGE	PAR	RATING	SLOPE	
FRONT	2919	35	68.3	-	**$18 - $36**
MIDDLE	-	-	-	-	
BACK	2954	35	67.5	115	

WHAT TO EXPECT: This is a well-maintained mountain course with narrow tree-lined fairways and large sloping greens.

NOTES: In July and August public play is not permitted until after 3:00 p.m.

DIRECTIONS: From Chico (about 80 miles northeast to the course): Take Highway 32 east about 55 miles to Highway 36. Make a right on Highway 36 and follow it to Chester. Turn right on County Road A13 (Walker Road) and then another right on Clifford Drive to the gate.

LIKELY PLACE R.V. & GOLF (public, 9 holes, rich hamel 1999) . . . .

Jess Valley Road
Likely, CA 96116
(530) 233-6676
likelyplace.com

	YARDAGE	PAR	RATING	SLOPE	
FRONT	2565	36	67.4	112	**$10 - $17**
MIDDLE	3178	36	68.8	119	
BACK	3351	36	70.2	122	

WHAT TO EXPECT: Located within 480 acres, covering more than four miles, this is one of the longer nine-hole courses in the state. Each hole is individually framed, so you will encounter no parallel holes. For the less-than-accurate driver, the fairways are super-sized. There are three lakes to keep you on your toes. With long stretches in between holes, walking is not recommended.

DIRECTIONS: From Alturas (about 25 miles south to the course): Take US 395 south and go east on Jess Valley Road/County Road 64. The club is on the right.

PARADISE PINES GOLF COURSE (public, 9 holes, bob baldock 1974) . . . .

13917 South Park Drive
Magalia, CA 95954
(530) 873-1111

	YARDAGE	PAR	RATING	SLOPE
FRONT	2402	34	63.8	118
MIDDLE	-	-	-	-
BACK	2494	34	67.4	101

$12 - $16

WHAT TO EXPECT: There is no need to bring your driver out on this course. Paradise Pines is about precision. Tiny greens and uneven lies are what golfers will encounter on this tricky nine-hole course.
DIRECTIONS: From Chico (about 33 miles northeast to the course): Off Highway 99, take the Skyway exit and head east, through Paradise. Turn left on South Park Drive.

MCCLOUD GOLF COURSE (public, 9 holes) . . . .

1001 Squaw Valley Road
McCloud, CA 96057
(530) 964-2535

	YARDAGE	PAR	RATING	SLOPE
FRONT	2623	36	-	-
MIDDLE	-	-	-	-
BACK	2983	37	-	-

$12 - $18

WHAT TO EXPECT: McCloud is a walkable, scenic course with tree-lined fairways, plenty of water and views of Mount Shasta from nearly every tee box.
NOTES: The course is open April through November.
DIRECTIONS: From Redding (about 75 miles north to the course): Drive north on I-5. Then take the Highway 89 exit and drive east to McCloud. Turn right on Squaw Valley Road. The course is on the right.

SHASTA VALLEY GOLF COURSE (public, 9 holes, clark glasson 1965) . . . .

500 Golf Course Road
Montague, CA 96064
(530) 842-2302

	YARDAGE	PAR	RATING	SLOPE
FRONT	2717	36	70.8	116
MIDDLE	-	-	-	-
BACK	3100	36	68.5	114

$11 - $17

WHAT TO EXPECT: This is a walkable course with trees, water and other hazards.
DIRECTIONS: From Yreka (about 15 miles east to the course): Off I-5, head east on Highway 3 to Montague. Take a right on Golf Course Road. There is a sign. If you go over the Shasta River Bridge, you have gone too far.

MOUNT SHASTA RESORT GOLF COURSE (resort, 18 holes, tatum & summer 1993) . . . .

1000 Siskiyou Lake Boulevard
Mount Shasta, CA 96067
(530) 926-3052
mountshastaresort.com

	YARDAGE	PAR	RATING	SLOPE	
FRONT	5092	71	65.4	116	**$45 - $59**
MIDDLE	5673	70	66.3	117	
BACK	6036	70	67.7	121	

WHAT TO EXPECT: This is a rolling, narrow, tree-lined course with dramatic greens and eye-pleasing views. The course, by today's standards, is short in length, but that doesn't mean it's a pushover. Mount Shasta is designed to make players think, giving them several options for each shot.

OUR OPINION: Bring a few extra balls. It's a drive, but for the price you pay for golf and a night at the chalet, you probably couldn't get on the putting green of some high-end Bay Area courses. – Frank

DIRECTIONS: From Redding (about 60 miles north to the course): Drive north on I-5. Take the Mount Shasta Central, exit and turn left over the freeway. The resort is visible from there.

KELLY RIDGE GOLF COURSE (semi-private, 9 holes, homer flint 1974) . . . .

5131 Royal Oaks Drive
Oroville, CA 95966
(530) 589-0777

	YARDAGE	PAR	RATING	SLOPE	
FRONT	1863	33	63.7	103	**$9 - $16**
MIDDLE	2080	33	62.5	106	
BACK	2207	33	61.2	110	

WHAT TO EXPECT: Whether you are in the fairway or on the green, remember the ball will run toward town. This is a narrow course with constant elevation changes. Kelly Ridge is surrounded by homes, with plenty of out-of-bounds and well-placed traps.

DIRECTIONS: From Marysville (about 40 miles north to the course): Drive north on Highway 70 to Oroville. Take the Oro Dam Boulevard exit and head east. Make a right on Olive Highway and a left on Kelly Ridge Road. Turn left on Royal Oaks Road to the course.

TABLE MOUNTAIN GOLF CLUB (public, 18 holes, bob baldock 1956) . . . .

2700 Oro Dam Boulevard
Oroville, CA 95965
(530) 533-3922

	YARDAGE	PAR	RATING	SLOPE	
FRONT	5000	72	67.1	106	**$10 - $21**
MIDDLE	6254	72	69.0	114	
BACK	6990	72	71.2	118	

WHAT TO EXPECT: This course has water on ten holes, wide-open fairways and hard fast greens in the summer months. The traps are all in front, left and right, so it is better to be long than short. Trees come into play if you miss the fairways by the slightest margin. To avoid being under a tree, make sure your errant shots are bad enough to reach the hard pan or another fairway.

DIRECTIONS: From Chico (about 25 miles southeast to the course): Drive south on Highway 99 and then east on Highway 162. Follow Highway 162 to Oroville and the course.

PALO CEDRO GOLF CLUB (semi-private, 9 holes, bert stamps 1992) . . . .

22499 Golftime Drive
Palo Cedro, CA 96073
(530) 547-3012

	YARDAGE	PAR	RATING	SLOPE
FRONT	2700	36	70.1	123
MIDDLE	3000	36	67.5	114
BACK	3100	36	68.9	117

$10 - $20

WHAT TO EXPECT: This is a flat course with water on every hole. The greens are sloping and undulating.
DIRECTIONS: From Redding, about ten miles east to the course, take I-5 north to Highway 44 and head east. Go about eight miles to Silver Bridge Road and make a left. The course is on the left.

OAK CREEK GOLF COURSE (public, 9 holes) . . . .

2620 Montgomery Road
Red Bluff, CA 96080
(530) 529-0674

	YARDAGE	PAR	RATING	SLOPE
FRONT	2503	35	68.0	114
MIDDLE	2622	35	64.6	108
BACK	2654	35	64.6	106

$6 - $17

WHAT TO EXPECT: Your driver is rarely your best option. This is a flat course with narrow fairways. There is water or out-of-bounds on seven of the nine holes. A good short game is a must because the greens are small and slightly crowned. If you miss them on the wrong side, trouble awaits.
DIRECTIONS: From within Red Bluff: Off I-5, take the Main Street exit and head north. Turn left on Montgomery Road and the course is on the right.

WILCOX OAKS GOLF CLUB (members only, 18 holes) . . . .

Two Wilcox Golf Road
Red Bluff, CA 96080
(530) 527-7087

	YARDAGE	PAR	RATING	SLOPE
FRONT	4468	72	69.7	120
MIDDLE	6144	72	68.9	118
BACK	6329	69	66.4	111

$25 - $45

WHAT TO EXPECT: This is a tricky course, where knowing the layout will help your score. The front nine is fairly wide open with lots of trees. On the back nine, there are only three holes that allow you to see the green from the tee. If you hit your ball into the trees lining the fairway, you might as well leave bread crumbs as you search for your ball – it may be the only chance you will have to find your way out.
NOTES: Reciprocal play with other members only clubs is allowed.
DIRECTIONS: From within Red Bluff: Off I-5, take the Wilcox Golf Road exit west to the course.

ALLEN'S GOLF COURSE (public, 9 holes, dick manning 1962) . . . .

2780 Sacramento Drive
Redding, CA 96001
(530) 241-5055

	YARDAGE	PAR	RATING	SLOPE	
FRONT	1662	31	58.8	92	**$7 - $13**
MIDDLE	-	-	-	-	
BACK	1706	31	57.6	90	

WHAT TO EXPECT: This is flat, walkable course with a creek running throughout and small greens. With plenty of trees, out-of-bounds and lateral water hazards, accuracy is a must.
DIRECTIONS: From within Redding: Off I-5, take the Bonnyview (Bechelli Lane) exit and head west. Turn left on Eastside Road. Take another left on Star Road. Follow this to the course.

CHURN CREEK GOLF COURSE (public, 9 holes) . . . .

7335 Churn Creek Road
Redding, CA 96002
(530) 222-6353

	YARDAGE	PAR	RATING	SLOPE	
FRONT	2686	36	-	-	**$9 - $18**
MIDDLE	2724	36	-	-	
BACK	2724	36	-	-	

WHAT TO EXPECT: This is a flat course with plenty of mature trees, small greens, and out-of-bounds on several holes.
DIRECTIONS: From within Redding: Off I-5, take the Knighton Road exit and head east. Knighton turns into Churn Creek Road. The course is on the left.

GOLD HILLS COUNTRY CLUB (semi-private, 18 holes, phil holcomb 1978) . . . .

1950 Gold Hills Drive
Redding, CA 96003
(530) 246-7867
goldhillsgolf.com

	YARDAGE	PAR	RATING	SLOPE	
FRONT	4836	72	68.8	120	**$25 - $40**
MIDDLE	6164	72	70.3	132	
BACK	6562	72	72.2	135	

WHAT TO EXPECT: This is a demanding golf course. The fairways are narrow and mostly uphill. Miss the short grass and you will find yourself hitting out of the trees, with little chance to reach the green. The greens are small and they slope slightly, back to front.
DIRECTIONS: From within Redding: Off I-5, exit on Oasis Road and drive east. Turn right on Gold Hills Drive to the course.

LAKE REDDING GOLF COURSE (public, 9 holes) . . . .

1795 Benton Drive
Redding, CA 96003
(530) 243-5531

	YARDAGE	PAR	RATING	SLOPE	
FRONT	1790	31	-	-	**$9 - $15**
MIDDLE	-	-	-	-	
BACK	1895	31	-	-	

WHAT TO EXPECT: This executive course has narrow, tree-lined fairways, small greens, and water that comes into play on four holes.
DIRECTIONS: From within Redding: Off I-5, take the Highway 299 east exit. Turn left and proceed to Market Street. Make a left on Market Street and a right on Benton Drive, to the course.

RIVER BEND GOLF & COUNTRY CLUB (members only, 9 holes, bill ralston 1989) . . . .

5369 Indianwood Drive
Redding, CA 96001
(530) 246-9077
riverbendgolfandcc.com

	YARDAGE	PAR	RATING	SLOPE	
FRONT	1828	32	60.5	95	**$10 - $20**
MIDDLE	-	-	-	-	
BACK	2075	32	59.0	93	

WHAT TO EXPECT: The smart player will never take the head cover off the driver. With trees, the Sacramento River slough, and water coming into play, there is little room for error off the tee. If you can navigate the fairways, the greens are medium sized with very subtle breaks and will reward a good putt.

NOTES: Reciprocal play with other members only clubs is allowed.

DIRECTIONS: From within Redding: Off I-5, take the South Bonnyview Road/Churn Creek exit and head west. Turn right on Indianwood Drive.

RIVERVIEW GOLF & COUNTRY CLUB (members only, 18 holes, henry rother 1947) . . .

4200 Bechelli Lane
Redding, CA 96002
(530) 224-2250

	YARDAGE	PAR	RATING	SLOPE	
FRONT	5769	72	72.6	120	**$36 - $60**
MIDDLE	-	-	-	-	
BACK	6482	72	70.5	123	

WHAT TO EXPECT: This is a traditional course with tree-lined fairways, small greens and demanding par 3s. To score low, keep it in the fairway and bring your best short game. That's so easy to write.

NOTES: Reciprocal play with other members only clubs is allowed.

DIRECTIONS: From within Redding: Off I-5, take the South Bonneyview Road/Churn Creek exit and head west to Bechelli Lane. Take Bechelli Lane north one-half mile to the course.

TIERRA OAKS, THE GOLF CLUB AT (members only, 18 holes, tatum & summer 1993) .

19700 La Crescenta Drive
Redding, CA 96003
(530) 275-0887
americangolf.com

	YARDAGE	PAR	RATING	SLOPE	
FRONT	6830	72	73.3	138	**$35 - $65**
MIDDLE	6375	72	71.4	135	
BACK	5111	72	71.2	125	

WHAT TO EXPECT: The main obstacles at Tierra Oaks are the rolling hills and fairways that are lined by trees. There are relatively few bunkers.

NOTES: Reciprocal play with other members only clubs is allowed.

DIRECTIONS: From within Redding: Off I-5, exit on Oasis Road and drive east for about three and one-half miles. The course is on the left.

TUCKER OAKS GOLF COURSE (public, 9 holes, jim roa 1964) . . . .

6241 Churn Creek Road
Redding, CA 96002
(530) 365-3350

	YARDAGE	PAR	RATING	SLOPE
FRONT	2977	37	71.6	111
MIDDLE	-	-	-	-
BACK	3173	36	69.0	106

$8 - $16

WHAT TO EXPECT: Mount Shasta sits right behind the first hole. OK, not exactly, but it looks like if you miss the green, your ball will be resting at the base of the mountain. The course is level and tree lined. Plenty of parallel fairways will benefit the golfer who can't hit it straight.

NOTES: Cart paths and new practice greens have been added.

DIRECTIONS: From within Redding: Head south on I-5 and take the Anderson exit through Anderson. Cross the Sacramento River. At the four-way stop, turn left on Churn Creek Road. The course is on the right.

EMERSON LAKE GOLF COURSE (public, 9 holes, dave tanner) . . . .

470-835 Wingfield Road
Susanville, CA 96130
(530) 257-6303

	YARDAGE	PAR	RATING	SLOPE
FRONT	2699	36	69.0	117
MIDDLE	3227	37	74.9	130
BACK	3227	36	69.2	114

$10 - $16

WHAT TO EXPECT: This is a tree-lined golf course with two creeks and a lake that come into play. The greens are slick and subtle. A new nine is under construction, and will be surrounded by Ponderosa Pines. The course will play to 6,700 yards.

NOTES: Construction to finish the 18-hole layout should be completed in early 2002. The original nine is still open.

DIRECTIONS: From Reno (about 90 miles northwest to the course): Drive north on US 395. Right before Susanville, turn left on Richmond Road. Go four to five miles and turn left on Wingfield Road, to the course.

INDIAN CAMP GOLF COURSE (public, 9 holes, malcolm crawford 1981) . . . .

17334 Stateline Road
Tulelake, CA 96134
(530) 667-2922

	YARDAGE	PAR	RATING	SLOPE
FRONT	1421	28	-	-
MIDDLE	-	-	-	-
BACK	1512	28	-	-

$7 - $18

WHAT TO EXPECT: This is an irons course well suited for beginners and juniors. There are plenty of trees, side-hill lies and tall grass to keep it interesting for the better player.

DIRECTIONS: From Klamath Falls, Oregon (about 40 miles southeast to the course): Go south on Highway 39. In Merrill, turn right on Malone Road. At Stateline Road, follow the signs.

TRINITY ALPS GOLF & COUNTRY CLUB (semi-private, 9 holes, fred eastwood 1973) ..

111 Fairway Drive
Weaverville, CA 96093
(530) 623-5411

	YARDAGE	PAR	RATING	SLOPE
FRONT	-	-	-	-
MIDDLE	-	-	-	-
BACK	1981	31	-	-

$10 - $15

WHAT TO EXPECT: This is a short course with plenty of trees, tight, rolling fairways and small greens. Water comes into play on four holes and out-of-bounds on another three. Views of the Trinity Alps abound.

DIRECTIONS: From Redding (about 45 miles west to the course): Off I-5, take Highway 299 west to Weaverville. Take Glen Road and drive south. Turn left on Fairway Drive to the course.

LAKE SHASTINA GOLF RESORT (resort, 27 holes, robert trent jones jr. 1973) ....

5925 Country Club Drive
Weed, CA 96094
(530) 938-3205
lakeshastinagolfresort.net

	YARDAGE	PAR	RATING	SLOPE
FRONT	5530	72	70.0	121
MIDDLE	6536	72	70.6	130
BACK	6969	72	72.6	132

$30 - $45

WHAT TO EXPECT: There are two courses, the Championship Course and the nine-hole Scottish Links Course. The Championship Course has many doglegs, blind shots, and trees to keep you focused. The course is fairly level, but does have some elevation changes on the back nine. The nine-hole Scottish Links Course is more wide open, with great views of Mount Shasta. Watch out – if you miss the fairways, you will find yourself in thick, native grasses or deep bunkers.

NOTES: The yardage listed is for the Championship Course.

DIRECTIONS: From Redding (about 70 miles northeast to the course): Take I-5 north to Highway 97 and drive east about seven miles. Turn left to Lake Shastina. Follow the signs for the golf resort.

WEED GOLF COURSE (public, 9 holes) ....

27730 Old Edgewood Road
Weed, CA 96094
(530) 938-9971

	YARDAGE	PAR	RATING	SLOPE
FRONT	2371	35	67.3	116
MIDDLE	2673	35	70.9	124
BACK	2796	35	65.5	112

$10 - $15

WHAT TO EXPECT: This little gem of a nine-holer is hidden only a stone's throw off I-5. Though there are no sand bunkers, this neatly manicured course with its tiny, plateaued greens is definitely a challenge for the better player, yet easy for the average golfer.

DIRECTIONS: From Yreka (about 30 miles south to the course): Take I-5 south, just past Edgewood. Take the Klamath Falls/Hwy. 97 exit. Follow the signs for "golf".

BIGFOOT GOLF & COUNTRY CLUB (semi-private, 9 holes) . . . .

333 Bigfoot Avenue
Willow Creek, CA 95573
(530) 629-2977

	YARDAGE	PAR	RATING	SLOPE
FRONT	2501	35	68.5	118
MIDDLE	-	-	-	-
BACK	2501	35	64.1	115

$15 - $20

WHAT TO EXPECT: Bigfoot is a tree-lined course with water on more than half the holes. Out-of-bounds comes into play on the perimeter of the course.
DIRECTIONS: From Eureka (about 45 miles east to the course): Go north on US 101 to Highway 299 and drive east. Turn left at Country Club Road. Cross the Trinity River, and make a left on Patterson. Turn right on Bigfoot Avenue.

GLENN GOLF & COUNTRY CLUB (public, 9 holes, ben harmon 1961) . . . .

6226 County Road 39
Willows, CA 95988
(530) 934-9918

	YARDAGE	PAR	RATING	SLOPE
FRONT	2959	36	73.2	118
MIDDLE	-	-	-	-
BACK	3255	36	70.1	113

$9 - $20

WHAT TO EXPECT: Homes line the course, so you can find out-of-bounds on nearly every hole. The good news is the fairways are fairly wide and water is nowhere to be found.
DIRECTIONS: From within Willows: Off I-5, just north of the town of Willows, take the Blue Gum Road/County Road 39 exit. Head west to the course.

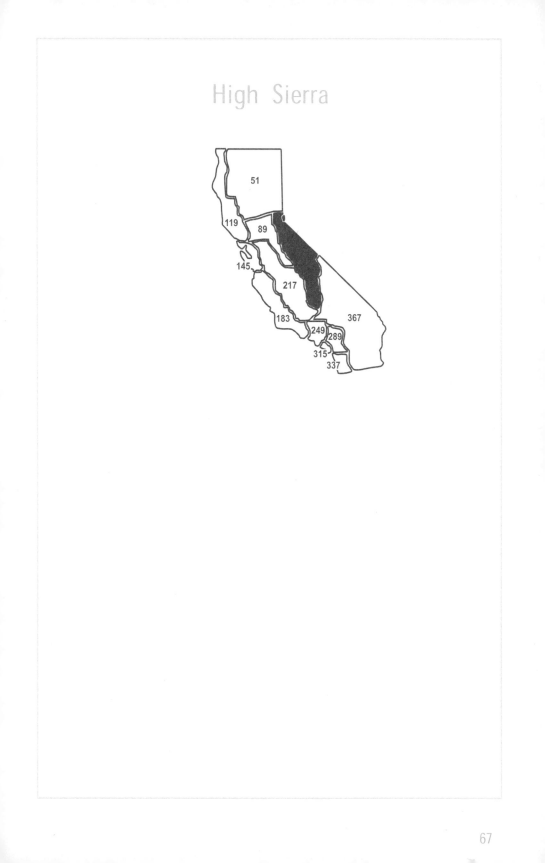

High Sierra

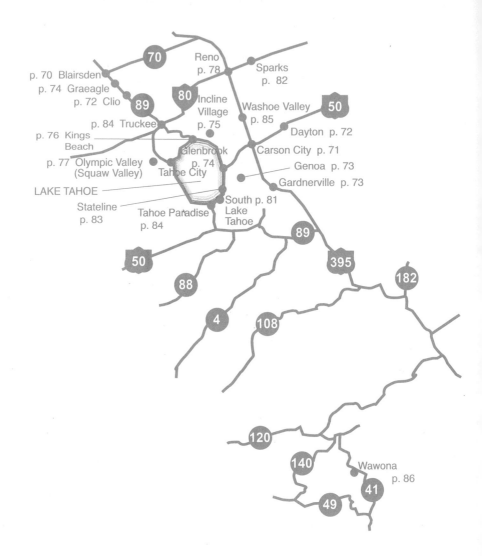

p. 70 Blairsden
p. 74 Graeagle
p. 72 Clio
p. 84 Truckee
p. 76 Kings Beach
p. 77 Olympic Valley (Squaw Valley)

Reno p. 78
Sparks p. 82
Incline Village p. 75
Washoe Valley p. 85
Dayton p. 72
Carson City p. 71
Genoa p. 73
Gardnerville p. 73

Glenbrook p. 74
Tahoe City

LAKE TAHOE
Stateline p. 83
Tahoe Paradise p. 84
South Lake Tahoe p. 81

Wawona p. 86

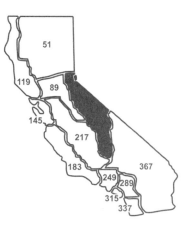

Map not to scale

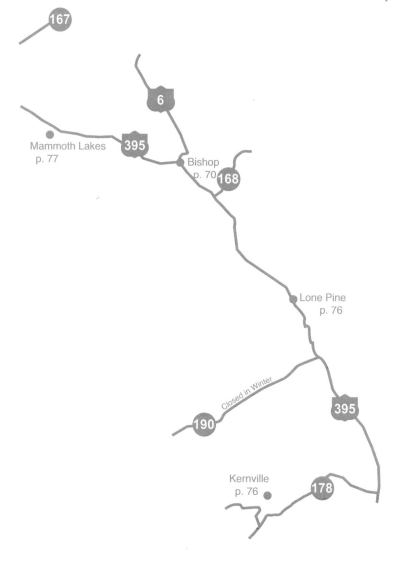

167

6

395

Mammoth Lakes
p. 77

Bishop
p. 70

168

Lone Pine
p. 76

Closed in Winter

395

190

Kernville
p. 76

178

BISHOP COUNTRY CLUB (semi-private, 18 holes) . . . .

South Highway 395
Bishop, CA 93514
(760) 873-5828

	YARDAGE	PAR	RATING	SLOPE
FRONT	5459	71	70.3	123
MIDDLE	6138	71	68.4	121
BACK	6661	71	70.8	125

$18 - $32

WHAT TO EXPECT: Bishop is a challenging course with an abundance of water (15 holes), trees and rough. The two nines were built about 30 years apart. The front nine is longer with small greens, while the back nine is shorter with large greens.
DIRECTIONS: From within Bishop: Go south on US 395. The club is on the right, about a mile and a half out of Bishop.

FEATHER RIVER INN GOLF COURSE (public, 9 holes, harold sampson 1919) . . . .

65899 Highway 70
Blairsden, CA 96103
(530) 836-2722

	YARDAGE	PAR	RATING	SLOPE
FRONT	-	-	-	-
MIDDLE	-	-	-	-
BACK	2818	35	-	-

$14 - $21

WHAT TO EXPECT: Set among the trees of the Plumas National Forest, you will find the fairways open and forgiving.
OUR OPINION: This is a course, at a reasonable price, that the entire family can enjoy. – Shaw
DIRECTIONS: From Reno (about 60 miles northwest to the course): Take US 395 north to Highway 70 west. The course is on the right, just past the intersection of Highway 70 and Highway 89. From Truckee: Drive north on Highway 89 and then west on Highway 70.

FEATHER RIVER PARK RESORT (public, 9 holes, bert stamps 1922) . . . .

8339 Highway 89
Blairsden, CA 96103
(530) 836-2328

	YARDAGE	PAR	RATING	SLOPE
FRONT	-	-	-	-
MIDDLE	-	-	-	-
BACK	2663	35	-	-

$16 - $18

WHAT TO EXPECT: Feather River is a good place to learn the game. The fairways are copious and level.
DIRECTIONS: From Truckee (about 55 miles northwest to the course): Drive north on Highway 89, just past Graeagle. From Reno (about 65 miles northwest to the course): Take US 395 north to Highway 70 and drive west to Highway 89. Go south on Highway 89 to the course.

EAGLE VALLEY GOLF COURSE (public, 36 holes) . . . .

3999 Centennial Park Drive
Carson City, NV 89706
(775) 887-2380
eaglevalleygolf.com

	YARDAGE	PAR	RATING	SLOPE	
FRONT	5293	72	68.9	121	
MIDDLE	6245	72	69.3	132	**$5 - $39**
BACK	6851	72	72.0	138	

WHAT TO EXPECT: The East Course is an open, high-desert golf, where low scores are a real possibility. The West Course is a much more difficult links-style course, with more punishing hazards such as natural vegetation, water, and plenty of strategic bunkering. The West Course also features more elevation changes throughout.
NOTES: The yardage listed is for the West Course.
DIRECTIONS: From South Lake Tahoe (about 30 miles northeast to the course): Take US 50 east. After passing through Carson City, turn left on Centennial Park Drive.

EMPIRE RANCH GOLF COURSE (public, 27 holes) . . . .

1875 Fair Way
Carson City, NV 89701
(775) 885-2100
empireranchgolf.com

	YARDAGE	PAR	RATING	SLOPE	
FRONT	4854	72	67.4	118	
MIDDLE	6392	72	69.6	125	**$25 - $40**
BACK	6840	72	70.5	127	

WHAT TO EXPECT: This 27-hole layout plays through a valley setting enhanced by many water hazards.
NOTES: The yardage listed is for the Sierra-Comstock combination.
DIRECTIONS: From South Lake Tahoe (about 29 miles northeast to the course): Take US 50 east. Turn right on Empire Ranch Road and then left on Clubhouse Way.

SILVER OAK GOLF CLUB (public, 18 holes, duncan & salomon 1999) . . . .

1251 Country Club Drive
Carson City, NV 89703
(775) 841-7000
silveroakhomes.com

	YARDAGE	PAR	RATING	SLOPE	
FRONT	5716	71	66.6	118	
MIDDLE	6110	71	68.7	126	**$30 - $45**
BACK	6564	71	70.8	130	

WHAT TO EXPECT: Silver Oak is situated alongside the Sierra Nevada. The course has subtle elevation changes and 1,600 trees. Luckily most of the them are young and not large enough to create any problems – yet. There are homes lining some of the fairways.
DIRECTIONS: From Reno (about 31 miles south to the course): Take US 395 south. Go west on College Parkway toward the mountains. Turn right on GS Richard Boulevard and then left on Country Club Drive.

SUNRIDGE GOLF CLUB (public, 18 holes, bill wellman 1997) . . . .

1000 Long Drive
Carson City, NV 89705
(775) 267-4448
sunridgegolfclub.com

	YARDAGE	PAR	RATING	SLOPE
FRONT	4922	72	62.9	119
MIDDLE	6583	72	70.5	133
BACK	7055	72	72.7	138

$30 - $75

WHAT TO EXPECT: Twenty-two acres of stonewalled lakes characterize the challenge. The valley views are excellent, but a cart is needed.

NOTES: They have a par 3 19th playoff hole to finish the round.

DIRECTIONS: From Reno (about 36 miles south to the course): Take US 395 south. Turn left on North Sunridge Drive. This eventually turns in to Long Drive. Follow this to the course.

WHITEHAWK RANCH, THE GOLF CLUB AT (resort, 18 holes, dick bailey 1996) . . . . . .

768 Whitehawk Drive
Clio, CA 96106
(800) 332-4295
golfwhitehawk.com

	YARDAGE	PAR	RATING	SLOPE
FRONT	4816	71	64.2	115
MIDDLE	6422	71	70.2	122
BACK	6928	71	72.4	130

$75 - $115

WHAT TO EXPECT: Arguably the area's finest public access course, the layout is set into natural wooded and valley meadow terrain. Streams flow through cedars, pines, and quaking aspens to create both a challenging and enjoyable experience.

OUR OPINION: This is a fantastic facility. On a scale of one to ten we rate this course a 9.95. Whithawk Ranch is well worth playing. – Shaw

DIRECTIONS: From Truckee (about 40 miles northwest to the course): Off I-80, drive north on Highway 89. The course is on the left.

DAYTON VALLEY GOLF CLUB (semi-private, 18 holes, palmer & seay 1991) . . . .

51 Palmer Drive
Dayton, NV 89403
(775) 246-7888
daytonvalley.com

	YARDAGE	PAR	RATING	SLOPE
FRONT	5161	72	67.4	118
MIDDLE	6637	72	72.1	134
BACK	7219	72	74.2	143

$30 - $85

WHAT TO EXPECT: Long considered among the area's best challenges, and home to many competitions, this flat course meanders over sculptured fairways. There is some fierce bunkering and lakes guard some huge, sloping greens. When the afternoon winds pick up, this course is an absolute beast.

NOTES: Dayton Valley has played host to Stage 1 of PGA Tour Qualifying since 1995.

DIRECTIONS: From South Lake Tahoe (about 37 miles northeast to the course): Take US 50 east. Exit Dayton Valley Road. Turn right on Palmer Drive. The course is on the right.

CARSON VALLEY GOLF COURSE (public, 18 holes) . . . .

1027 Riverview Drive
Gardnerville, NV 89410
(775) 265-3181
carsonvalleygolfcourse.com

	YARDAGE	PAR	RATING	SLOPE
FRONT	4684	72	69.6	119
MIDDLE	5489	71	65.0	108
BACK	6003	71	66.8	111

$16 - $40

WHAT TO EXPECT: This is a friendly, parkland-style course on the banks of the Carson River. You will find plenty of water and majestic cottonwoods. Carson Valley is suited for all abilities.

DIRECTIONS: From Reno (about 49 miles south to the course): Go south on US 395. Two miles south of Gardnerville, turn right on Riverview Drive. The club is on the left.

GENOA LAKES, THE GOLF CLUB AT (resort, 18 holes, peter jacobsen) . . . .

One Genoa Lakes Drive
Genoa, NV 89411
(775) 782-4653
genoalakes.com

	YARDAGE	PAR	RATING	SLOPE
FRONT	5008	72	67.6	117
MIDDLE	6738	72	71.2	127
BACK	7264	72	73.7	134

$23 - $105

WHAT TO EXPECT: The course occupies a flat valley area, with a gorgeous backdrop of the eastern slope of the Sierra Nevada. This excellent layout features water and well-placed bunkering. The course becomes much more difficult in the afternoon wind.

OUR OPINION: This maybe a better course than its more famous neighbor over the hill, Edgwood Tahoe. – Bob

DIRECTIONS: From Reno (about 48 miles south to the course): Go south on US 395. Past Carson City, turn right on Jacks Valley Road. Go about seven and one-half miles, and Genoa Lakes is on the left.

SIERRA NEVADA GOLF RANCH (public, 18 holes, miller & harbottle 1998) . . . .

2901 Jacks Valley Road
Genoa, NV 89411
(775) 782-7700
americangolf.com

	YARDAGE	PAR	RATING	SLOPE
FRONT	5129	72	68.5	124
MIDDLE	6820	72	72.9	132
BACK	7359	72	75.3	137

$25 - $125

WHAT TO EXPECT: The site of a former cattle ranch, the course carries a cowboy theme. There are dramatic elevation changes, an abundance of water, and 114 bunkers, all with lush valley and rugged mountain views.

OUR OPINION: A good, high-desert course. – Bob

DIRECTIONS: From Reno (about 48 miles south to the course): Head south on US 395 and turn right at Jacks Valley Road. The course is on the left.

GLENBROOK GOLF COURSE (members only, 9 holes) . . . .

2070 Pray Meadow Road
Glenbrook, NV 89413
(775) 749-5201

	YARDAGE	PAR	RATING	SLOPE
FRONT	2585	36	68.6	121
MIDDLE	-	-	-	-
BACK	2907	35	66.3	121

$45 - $70

WHAT TO EXPECT: Glenbrook has long been considered one of the West's best nine-hole golf courses. The fairways seem more like dark, narrow corridors, over which the trees touch. Tiny, tricky greens make this short layout much more challenging than you could imagine.

DIRECTIONS: From South Lake Tahoe (about 11 miles north to the course): Take US 50 east. About two and one-half miles, after traveling through the tunnel, there is a sign for Glenbrook. The gate is on the left.

DRAGON AT GOLD MOUNTAIN, THE (resort, 18 holes, robin nelson 1997) . . . .

3887 County Road A-15
Graeagle, CA 96103
(800) 368-7786
dragongolf.com

	YARDAGE	PAR	RATING	SLOPE
FRONT	4611	70	66.6	128
MIDDLE	6746	72	72.5	139
BACK	7080	72	74.2	147

$120 - $120

WHAT TO EXPECT: This is a target golf course with rolling fairways and excellent views. The fairways are narrow and surrounded by trees. The smart golfer will use their driver sparingly, because if you miss the short grass, you will find yourself in the trees or taking a drop from a lateral water hazard. The greens are on the small side and sloping, but are kept at a manageable speed. Keep the ball in play and enjoy the scenery.

OUR OPINION: Their motto is "Send me your heroes". Many of those heroes have ended up in body bags, or have retreated to the clubhouse; which may be even more spectacular than the course. The Dragon evokes strong emotion. We like that. You may love it, you may hate, but you won't forget it. – The Mole

NOTES: This course was admitted into the Audubon International signature program. The course is open May to November.

DIRECTIONS: From Truckee (about 50 miles northwest to the course): Take Highway 89 north to Sierraville (26 miles). At Sierraville, turn left at the stop sign. Five miles before Graeagle, there is a sign, Highway 89 splits (A-15); go right for five miles. The course is on the right.

GRAEAGLE MEADOWS GOLF COURSE (semi-private, 18 holes, ellis van gorder 1968) . .

107 Highway 89
Graeagle, CA 96103
(530) 836-2323
playgraeagle.com

	YARDAGE	PAR	RATING	SLOPE
FRONT	5589	72	71.0	127
MIDDLE	6345	72	70.1	128
BACK	6726	72	72.1	129

$40 - $60

WHAT TO EXPECT: Lofty pines, mountain views, and the Feather River embrace a course that is simple, good golf.

DIRECTIONS: From Truckee (about 50 miles northwest to the course): Off I-80, drive north on Highway 89. The course is right off the highway, just south of Highway 70.

PLUMAS PINES GOLF RESORT (resort, 18 holes, homer flint 1980) . . . .

402 Poplar Valley Road
Graeagle, CA 96103
(530) 836-1420
plumaspinesgolf.com

	YARDAGE	PAR	RATING	SLOPE
FRONT	5240	72	69.9	126
MIDDLE	5894	72	68.5	123
BACK	6505	72	71.3	132

$35 - $70

WHAT TO EXPECT: The greens are usually quick, but it is the rolling, narrow, tree-lined fairways that keep golfers honest. Hitting a driver off the tee is not always your best option.

OUR OPINION: On a few holes, we forgot about the golf and were entranced with the beauty of the surroundings. Hey, after two double bogeys in a row, you have to live for something. – Frank

DIRECTIONS: From Truckee (about 52 miles northwest to the course): Off I-80, take Highway 89 north to Graeagle. Turn left on A14, and follow it for two miles; then turn right on Poplar Valley Road. The golf course is at the end of the road, on the right.

INCLINE VILLAGE, THE GOLF COURSES AT (resort, 36 holes, r. trent jones, sr. 1964) .

690 Wilson Way
Incline Village, NV 89451
(775) 832-1146
golfincline.com

	YARDAGE	PAR	RATING	SLOPE
FRONT	5245	68	64.1	108
MIDDLE	6447	72	70.2	129
BACK	6932	72	72.2	133

$30 - $125

WHAT TO EXPECT: There are two courses, the Championship Course and the Mountain Course. The Championship Course is a long and humbling layout, with excellent views of Lake Tahoe. Fairly high rough, pine trees and fir trees create narrow fairways. Add water, a few blind shots, and demanding greens to the mix, and you can see why many golfers consider this one of the hardest courses in the Reno-Lake Tahoe area. The Mountain Course is a short, steep, executive target course with many of the same hazards as the longer Championship layout.

OUR OPINION: For every golfer on our staff, who loves the Championship Course, there is another who says it's overrated. Incline Village is well worth playing, to form your own opinion.

NOTES: Golf season runs May through October. The yardage listed is for the Championship Course.

DIRECTIONS: From Truckee (about 19 miles southeast to the course): Take Highway 267 to Lake Tahoe. Turn left onto Highway 28 and go six miles to Incline Village.

KERN VALLEY COUNTRY CLUB (public, 9 holes, jack wing 1957) . . . .

9472 Burlando Road
Kernville, CA 93238
(760) 376-2828

	YARDAGE	PAR	RATING	SLOPE
FRONT	2927	37	-	116
MIDDLE	-	-	-	-
BACK	3184	36	68.0	106

$10 - $24

WHAT TO EXPECT: Hit the ball left off the tee, and you will probably be out-of-bounds. Go right off the tee, and you will most likely be in the trees. Your best option is to hit it straight, which will give you a good chance at hitting the well-guarded greens in regulation.

DIRECTIONS: From Bakersfield (about 54 miles northeast to the course): Off Highway 99, go northeast on Highway 178 for about 50 miles. At Highway 155, keep going north. The course is located one-half mile south of Kernville on Highway 155.

OLD BROCKWAY GOLF COURSE (public, 9 holes, john duncan dunn 1926) . . . .

7900 North Lake Boulevard
Kings Beach, CA 96143
(530) 546-9909
oldbrockway.com

	YARDAGE	PAR	RATING	SLOPE
FRONT	2472	36	66.9	113
MIDDLE	3034	36	67.6	116
BACK	3315	36	69.8	125

$37 - $60

WHAT TO EXPECT: Old Brockway is long enough to satisfy the low handicapper and forgiving enough to accommodate the high handicapper.

DIRECTIONS: From Truckee (about 12 miles southeast to the course): Take US 80 to Highway 267 south. Brockway is on the corner of Highway 267 and Highway 28. Highway 28 circles along the north shore of Lake Tahoe. Descending toward the lake, the course is visible from Highway 267.

MOUNT WHITNEY GOLF CLUB (public, 9 holes, bob baldock 1958) . . . .

2559 South Main Street
Lone Pine, CA 93545
(760) 876-5795

	YARDAGE	PAR	RATING	SLOPE
FRONT	2846	35	71.0	112
MIDDLE	3080	36	69.6	119
BACK	3233	36	71.0	122

$15 - $22

WHAT TO EXPECT: Think twice before hitting your driver. Narrow fairways lined by trees make precision a must. The greens are small and tend to slope toward the highway. The views are awesome.

DIRECTIONS: From within Lone Pine: The club is about one mile south of Lone Pine, on the west side of US 395.

SIERRA STAR GOLF CLUB (resort, 18 holes, cal olson 1999) . . . .

2001 Sierra Star Parkway
Mammoth Lakes, CA 93546
(760) 924-4653
mammoth-golf.com

	YARDAGE	PAR	RATING	SLOPE
FRONT	4912	70	68.7	128
MIDDLE	6617	70	70.6	124
BACK	6709	70	71.0	133

$85 - $115

WHAT TO EXPECT: Located 8,000 feet above sea level, this is a level course with narrow tree-lined fairways and excellent alpine views. The greens putt true and will reward the good putter. However, reaching the greens is another story. The smart player will sacrifice distance for accuracy.

DIRECTIONS: From San Bernardino (about 290 miles north to the course): Take I-15 north to US 395 north to Highway 203 west to Mammoth Lakes. Make a left on Minaret and a right on Meridian. Turn right on Sierra Star Parkway. The course is on the right.

SNOWCREEK GOLF COURSE (resort, 9 holes, ted robinson 1991) . . . .

Old Mammoth Rd/Fairway Drive
Mammoth Lakes, CA 93546
(760) 934-6633
snowcreek.com

	YARDAGE	PAR	RATING	SLOPE
FRONT	2925	35	66.0	118
MIDDLE	3098	35	67.8	121
BACK	3255	35	69.2	124

$27 - $48

WHAT TO EXPECT: There is little room for error off the tee or around the green, as water comes into play on seven of the nine holes on this fairly level course. The greens are moderate in size and have been know to be hard and fast. If the game isn't going as planned, don't worry; there are plenty of mountain views to enjoy.

DIRECTIONS: From San Bernardino (about 290 miles north to the course): Take I-15 north to US 395, north to Highway 203, and then west to Mammoth Lakes. At the light at Old Mammoth Road, turn left and drive one mile to the course.

RESORT AT SQUAW CREEK (resort, 18 holes, robert trent jones jr. 1991) . . . .

400 Squaw Road
Olympic Valley, CA 96146
(530) 581-6637
squawcreek.com

	YARDAGE	PAR	RATING	SLOPE
FRONT	5097	71	69.1	127
MIDDLE	6453	71	70.8	132
BACK	6931	71	72.9	140

$55 - $115

WHAT TO EXPECT: Set in a beautiful mountain meadow, there is nothing gentle about the challenge. The fairways are like island targets amidst Environmentally Sensitive Areas. Precise play is required, so bring plenty of golf balls.

OUR OPINION: The trick to enjoying yourself at Squaw Creek is picking the correct tee boxes and playing when the green fees aren't a $115. – The Mole

NOTES: Squaw Creek is a four-star resort and spa. The course uses no chemicals in order to protect the environment.

DIRECTIONS: From Truckee (about 14 miles south to the course): Take I-80 east, to the Squaw Valley/Hwy. 89 south exit. Go about eight miles and turn right into Squaw Valley. Turn left on Squaw Creek Road.

ARROWCREEK GOLF CLUB (public, 36 holes, palmer, harbottle & zoeller 1999) . . . . .

2905 ArrowCreek Parkway
Reno, NV 89511
(775) 850-4653
arrowcreek.com

	YARDAGE	PAR	RATING	SLOPE	
FRONT	5007	72	68.6	126	**$28 - $90**
MIDDLE	6353	72	70.2	130	
BACK	7116	72	74.0	135	

WHAT TO EXPECT: Two high desert courses, located 20 minutes southwest of Reno in the foothills, are equally challenging. The Legend Course is open to the public and is more traditionally shaped with extensive bunkering. The private Challenge Course is more of a throwback to Scottish design, with pot bunkers, and it stretches more than 7,500 yards.
NOTES: The yardage is listed is for the Legends Course.
DIRECTIONS: From within Reno: Off I-80, take US 395 south, exit on Damonte Ranch Road and turn right. This turns into ArrowCreek Parkway. Stay to the left at the fork. The gates to the course are on the left.

BROOKSIDE GOLF COURSE (municipal, 9 holes) . . . .

700 South Rock Boulevard
Reno, NV 89502
(775) 856-6009

	YARDAGE	PAR	RATING	SLOPE	
FRONT	2450	35	62.3	95	**$7 - $12**
MIDDLE	2721	35	64.8	105	
BACK	3018	35	68.0	116	

WHAT TO EXPECT: This is a flat, open course and good place to learn the game.
DIRECTIONS: From within Reno: Off I-80, take Exit 17, onto Rock Boulevard, and head south. The course is on the right.

HIDDEN VALLEY COUNTRY CLUB (members only, 18 holes) . . . .

3575 East Hidden Valley Drive
Reno, NV 89502
(775) 857-4742

	YARDAGE	PAR	RATING	SLOPE	
FRONT	4776	72	65.8	113	**$50 - $80**
MIDDLE	6694	72	70.1	126	
BACK	7062	72	71.3	129	

WHAT TO EXPECT: The oldest and for many years the only private club in Reno, the layout is traditional and more park-setting than high desert in nature.
DIRECTIONS: From within Reno: Off I-80, exit on McCarran Boulevard and head south. Turn left on Pembroke and right on Piping Rock. Then turn left on Hidden Valley Drive. The club is on the right.

LAKE RIDGE GOLF COURSE (public, 18 holes, robert trent jones sr. & jr. 1969) . . . . .

1200 Razorback Road
Reno, NV 89509
(775) 825-2200
lakeridgegolf.com

	YARDAGE	PAR	RATING	SLOPE	
FRONT	5159	71	68.5	121	**$45 - $88**
MIDDLE	6141	71	69.1	132	
BACK	6716	71	72.3	137	

WHAT TO EXPECT: This is an open, shot-maker's course. Mature trees and homes line Lake Ridge. Don't let the yardage fool you; from the back tees, this is a stiff test of golf. As long as they choose the regular tees, the less-skilled player can have fun at Lake Ridge.
OUR OPINION: On the 15th hole, the view from the 120' elevated tee down to the large island green, with the City in the background, is worth the price of admission; easily the area's most photographed hole. – Bob
DIRECTIONS: From within Reno: Off I-80, take US 395 south. Take the South Virginia exit, and go left. Turn right on McCarran and left on Plumas. Turn right on Razorback Road and follow the signs.

MONTREUX GOLF & COUNTRY CLUB (members only, 18 holes, jack nicklaus 1997) . . .

18077 Bordeaux Drive
Reno, NV 89511
(775) 849-9496
montreauxgolf.com

	YARDAGE	PAR	RATING	SLOPE	
FRONT	5342	72	70.0	133	**$88 - $225**
MIDDLE	7053	72	73.6	138	
BACK	7558	72	75.3	142	

WHAT TO EXPECT: The longest of the area courses, most of the layout plays among the tall pines on this beautifully manicured property.
NOTES: Montreux is host to the PGA's Reno-Tahoe Open.
DIRECTIONS: From within Reno: Off I-80, take US 395 south. Take the Mount Rose Highway (Highway 431) west. Turn left on Bordeaux Drive.

NORTHGATE GOLF CLUB (public, 18 holes, robert benz) . . . .

1111 Clubhouse Drive
Reno, NV 89523
(775) 747-7577

	YARDAGE	PAR	RATING	SLOPE	
FRONT	5521	72	70.2	127	**$40 - $60**
MIDDLE	6411	72	69.8	126	
BACK	6967	72	72.3	131	

WHAT TO EXPECT: If you want a flat lie, you're going to have to bring your own. This is a hilly, links-style course that will force you to hit shots you didn't know even existed. Be careful judging your distances, they can be deceiving. The wind can make this course downright hard.
OUR OPINION: If you are looking for something out of the ordinary, Northgate will not disappoint. – Brad
DIRECTIONS: From within Reno: Off I-80 exit on McCarran Boulevard and head north. Turn left on Mae Anne, and then right on Avenida DeLanda. Turn left on Beaumont Parkway and Clubhouse Drive is on the left.

ROSEWOOD LAKES GOLF COURSE (municipal, 18 holes, brad benz 1991) . . . .

6800 Pembroke Drive
Reno, NV 89502
(775) 857-2892
rosewoodlakes.com

	YARDAGE	PAR	RATING	SLOPE	
FRONT	5073	72	67.8	118	**$18 - $55**
MIDDLE	6104	72	68.0	115	
BACK	6694	72	70..7	125	

WHAT TO EXPECT: Sixty acres of "wetlands" defines both the challenge and motif. The course is flat and plays tough when the wind picks up.

DIRECTIONS: From within Reno: Off I-80 east, take the East McCarran Boulevard, Exit 19, and head south. Turn left on to Pembroke Drive.

SIERRA SAGE GOLF COURSE (public, 18 holes) . . . .

6355 Silverlake Boulevard
Reno, NV 89506
(775) 972-1564

	YARDAGE	PAR	RATING	SLOPE	
FRONT	5573	72	69.6	113	**$25 - $30**
MIDDLE	6207	71	68.1	119	
BACK	6623	71	70.4	122	

WHAT TO EXPECT: This is a open, walkable course with large fairways. If for some reason you happen to miss the fairways, you will find yourself in sagebrush. The greens are open in the front, and they tend to break toward Peavine Mountain.

DIRECTIONS: From within Reno: Off I-80, take US 395 north and take Exit 76, Stead Boulevard, and head east. Turn left on Silverlake Boulevard.

WASHOE COUNTY GOLF COURSE (public, 18 holes, w.p.a. 1936) . . . .

2601 South Arlington Avenue
Reno, NV 89509
(775) 828-6640
washoegolf.com

	YARDAGE	PAR	RATING	SLOPE	
FRONT	5863	73	72.4	120	**$16 - $39**
MIDDLE	6468	72	70.0	116	
BACK	6695	72	71.0	119	

WHAT TO EXPECT: This is the oldest course in Reno. The course is level, with ample fairways, lots of trees and parallel fairways.

NOTES: The season runs April through October. Ben Hogan set the course record in 1948 when the Reno Open was played here.

DIRECTIONS: From within Reno: Off I-80, exit on McCarran, and take McCarran south to Plumb Lane. Turn left on Plumb Lane. Turn right on Arlington Avenue. Follow the signs to the course.

WOLF RUN GOLF CLUB (semi-private, 18 holes, fleming & eiguren 1998) . . . .

1400 Wolf Run Road
Reno, NV 89511
(775) 851-3301
wolfrungolfclub.com

	YARDAGE	PAR	RATING	SLOPE
FRONT	5294	71	69.7	128
MIDDLE	6489	71	70.1	126
BACK	6937	71	72.1	130

$20 - $75

WHAT TO EXPECT: Excellent views of Mount Rose can be seen throughout the course. This is a rolling course with liberal fairways, but few flat lies. Water comes into play on 15 of the 18 holes. The greens are undulating and quick.

NOTES: The course is home to the University of Nevada Reno golf team. New owners took over at the end of 2000.

DIRECTIONS: From within Reno: Off I-80, take US 395 south. Take Exit 59, Damonte Ranch Parkway, and turn right. At the Y, turn right on Zolezzi Lane. Turn left on Silver Wolf Drive. Follow the signs from there.

BIJOU MUNICIPAL GOLF COURSE (public, 9 holes) . . . .

3464 Fairway Avenue
South Lake Tahoe, CA 96150
(530) 542-6097

	YARDAGE	PAR	RATING	SLOPE
FRONT	1733	32	-	-
MIDDLE	-	-	-	-
BACK	2002	32	-	-

$15 - $25

WHAT TO EXPECT: Built in 1920, this is an open meadow course surrounded by trees. With no hidden obstacles and no holes longer than 300 yards, this is an excellent place for the whole family to golf.

NOTES: This is the oldest nine-hole course in South Tahoe.

DIRECTIONS: From Sacramento (about 100 miles east to the course): Take US 50 east into South Lake Tahoe. Turn right on Johnson Boulevard. Turn left on Fairway Avenue, which leads to the course.

LAKE TAHOE GOLF COURSE (resort, 18 holes, william bell, jr. 1959) . . . .

2500 Emerald Bay Road, Hwy. 50
South Lake Tahoe, CA 96150
(530) 577-0788

	YARDAGE	PAR	RATING	SLOPE
FRONT	5688	72	70.1	115
MIDDLE	6170	71	68.9	116
BACK	6708	71	70.9	120

$30 - $67

WHAT TO EXPECT: This busy mountain meadow course is scenic and fun. Though flat, it has enough trees and creeks in play to keep your attention. The greens provide small targets, so don't let the mountain views distract you.

DIRECTIONS: The course is located on US 50, south of South Lake Tahoe and north of Meyers. It is about 10 miles south of the casinos, on the right.

D'ANDREA GOLF & COUNTRY CLUB (semi-private, 18 holes, keith foster 2001) . . . . . .

2351 North D'Andrea Parkway
Sparks, NV 89434
(775) 331-6363
jenamar.com

	YARDAGE	PAR	RATING	SLOPE	
FRONT	6272	71	68.5	121	
MIDDLE	6501	71	70.4	126	**$70 - $80**
BACK	6850	71	71.8	129	

WHAT TO EXPECT: Accuracy is important because each hole is separated by desert, so the likelihood of hitting another fairway is slim to none. The course rises 450 feet above the valley floor and provides some excellent views. There are a few forced carries, so keep it in the fairway, and you will be ok.

NOTES: Reciprocal play with other members only clubs is allowed.

DIRECTIONS: From Reno: (about eight miles northeast to the course) Take I-80 east. Exit on Vista Boulevard. Go left over freeway and continue almost two miles. Turn right on North D'Andrea Parkway and follow the signs.

RED HAWK GOLF CLUB (semi-private, 36 holes, r.t. jones jr. 1997 & irwin 2000) . . .

6600 North Wingfield Parkway
Sparks, NV 89436
(775) 626-6000
wingfieldsprings.com

	YARDAGE	PAR	RATING	SLOPE	
FRONT	5115	72	69.2	125	
MIDDLE	6629	72	70.7	132	**$45 - $145**
BACK	7128	72	72.9	137	

WHAT TO EXPECT: The Lakes Course has generous fairways, gigantic bunkers (lots of them) and large, quick, undulating greens. Use the GPS system on the carts; it will help you choose the correct club to hit into the deep greens. The members only Hills Course is one of the few Hale Irwin designs around. You will find the fairways generous and the greens well protected and small. To be successful here, bring your best Hale Irwin iron game.

OUR OPINION: Red Hawk combines fun golf with great service, which makes it a favorite among visiting golfers. – Bob

NOTES: The Lakes Course is open to the public, while the Hills Course remains members only. The yardage is for the Lakes Course.

DIRECTIONS: From Reno (about 17 miles northeast to the course): From I-80 take Exit 21, Vista Road, and turn left and go north. Go about seven miles until it ends and turn left. This leads straight to the course.

WILDCREEK GOLF COURSE (resort, 27 holes, benz & poellot 1978) . . . .

3500 Sullivan Lane
Sparks, NV 89431
(775) 673-3100

	YARDAGE	PAR	RATING	SLOPE	
FRONT	5472	72	69.9	127	**$33 - $65**
MIDDLE	6656	72	71.2	131	
BACK	6933	72	72.5	133	

WHAT TO EXPECT: There are two courses, one 18-hole championship course and a nine-hole course. They are creatively named Course One and Course Two. On Course One, you will find the greens and the fairways generous in nature. On the second course, Course Two, you will find the fairways narrow and the greens small. Confused yet?
NOTES: Wildcreek hosted a Senior Tour stop from 1984 to 1986. It has also hosted several USGA qualifying events, as well as the Nevada State Ladies Championship.
DIRECTIONS: From Reno (about six miles north to the course): Take US 395 north. Take McCarran Boulevard and head east. Turn right on Sullivan Lane.

EDGEWOOD TAHOE GOLF COURSE (public, 18 holes, george fazio 1968) . . . .

180 Lake Parkway
Stateline, NV 89449
(775) 588-3566
edgewood-tahoe.com

	YARDAGE	PAR	RATING	SLOPE	
FRONT	6365	72	70.2	127	**$200 - $200**
MIDDLE	6846	72	72.3	132	
BACK	7380	72	75.7	139	

WHAT TO EXPECT: This gorgeous Lake Tahoe course does not give up low scores without a fight. The greens are fast and undulating. The fairways seem to get tighter with each passing hole. This course will challenge you both mentally and physically.
OUR OPINION: This is a beautiful course that will have you hitting a variety of golf shots. You can't go wrong if you choose to play Edgewood. – Val
DIRECTIONS: From South Lake Tahoe: Edgewood is located on the north side of US 50, behind Harvey's and the Horizon Hotel casinos.

TAHOE CITY GOLF COURSE (public, 9 holes, mae webb dunn 1917) . . . .

251 North Lake Boulevard
Tahoe City, CA 96145
(530) 583-1516
tcgc.com

	YARDAGE	PAR	RATING	SLOPE	
FRONT	2403	34	65.7	105	**$22 - $55**
MIDDLE	-	-	-	-	
BACK	2692	33	65.1	111	

WHAT TO EXPECT: Set in the mountains, this is a short course that derives its challenge from narrow fairways and hard-to-read greens. The course affords excellent views of Lake Tahoe from almost everywhere on the course.
DIRECTIONS: From Truckee (about 15 miles south to the course): Off I-80, take Highway 89 south. Just past the only light in Tahoe City, the course is on the left.

TAHOE PARADISE GOLF COURSE (public, 18 holes, bruce beeman 1959) . . . .

3021 US Highway 50
Tahoe Paradise, CA 96150
(530) 577-2121
tahoeparadisegolf.com

	YARDAGE	PAR	RATING	SLOPE	
FRONT	3768	69	61.7	96	**$21 - $32**
MIDDLE	-	-	--	-	
BACK	4034	64	60.9	103	

WHAT TO EXPECT: Set on a hillside, this is a short steep course with tight tree-lined fairways and small greens. The course affords terrific mountain views.

DIRECTIONS: From South Lake Tahoe: Head west on US 50. It is about three miles past the airport, on the left.

COYOTE MOON GOLF COURSE (public, 18 holes, brad bell 2000) . . . .

10685 Northwoods Boulevard
Truckee, CA 96161
(530) 587-0886
coyotemoongolfcourse.com

	YARDAGE	PAR	RATING	SLOPE	
FRONT	6211	72	69.1	130	**$85 - $135**
MIDDLE	6704	72	71.1	134	
BACK	7178	72	74.1	138	

WHAT TO EXPECT: Coyote Moon is an upscale daily-fee course with no homes surrounding the property. The fairways are generous, with granite outcroppings found throughout. The fairways have a funnel effect as you approach the medium-sized greens. The greens are well protected by sand, water, and trees. At 6,800 feet above sea level, expect to get up to ten percent more distance on each shot.

OUR OPINION: Must play, must play, must play. – Shaw

NOTES: Season typically runs May through October. For a short while, they tried out the name PineRidge, but fortunately they have returned to Coyote Moon.

DIRECTIONS: From Sacramento (about 100 miles northeast to the course): Take I-80 east to the Donner Pass Road exit. Turn left onto Donner Pass Road, and drive one-half mile to the first light. Take a left on Northwoods Boulevard. The golf course iis on the right.

GOLF CLUB AT TAHOE DONNER, THE (semi-private, 18 holes, bob williams 1976) . . .

11509 Northwoods Boulevard
Truckee, CA 96161
(530) 587-9440
tahoedonner.com

	YARDAGE	PAR	RATING	SLOPE	
FRONT	6032	74	73.1	138	**$25 - $100**
MIDDLE	6587	72	71.2	128	
BACK	6918	72	72.4	133	

WHAT TO EXPECT: If you can make it to the greens, you will find them very puttable. The rest of the course is not so amiable. Tahoe Donner is a very narrow, mountain layout that winds between the pines and will discipline golfer's who stray off the fairway.

OUR OPINION: This beautiful trek through the mountain woods is good for the soul and makes for fun golf as well. – Bob

DIRECTIONS: From Sacramento (about 100 miles northeast to the course): Take I-80 east to Truckee. Take the first Truckee exit (Donner Pass Road). Turn left on Donner Pass Road and then left on Northwoods Boulevard to the course.

LAHONTAN GOLF CLUB (members only, 18 holes, tom weiskopf 1998) . . . .

12700 Lodgetrail Road
Truckee, CA 96161
(530) 550-2424
lahontan.com

	YARDAGE	PAR	RATING	SLOPE
FRONT	5158	71	68.8	120
MIDDLE	6753	72	71.7	133
BACK	7214	72	73.7	138

$100 - $100

WHAT TO EXPECT: Mountain and meadow vistas, along with constant elevation changes, characterize Lahontan. The course has a superb flow of memorable holes taking advantage of the spectacular woods. All of the above make this course the best one in the Reno-Lake Tahoe area.
DIRECTIONS: From within Truckee: Off I-80, go south on Highway 267. Turn right on Schaffer Mill Road. The course is on the left.

NORTHSTAR AT TAHOE GOLF COURSE (resort, 18 holes, robert muir graves 1975) . . .

1680 Basque Drive
Truckee, CA 96161
(530) 562-2490
skinorthstar.com

	YARDAGE	PAR	RATING	SLOPE
FRONT	5470	72	70.8	136
MIDDLE	6260	72	69.5	129
BACK	6777	72	72.4	137

$60 - $95

WHAT TO EXPECT: Northstar is two courses in one. The front nine is the friendly meadow course, with free-flowing fairways and beautiful mountain views. The back nine is the evil twin, with narrow tree-lined fairways that devour golf balls and greens that seem to get smaller with each hole.
OUR OPINION: Northstar has a goofy, target-like layout on the back. – Frank
DIRECTIONS: From within Truckee: Off I-80, take Highway 267 south. Turn right on Northstar Drive, into Northstar. Follow the signs to the course.

PONDEROSA GOLF COURSE (public, 9 holes, bob baldock 1961) . . . .

10040 Reynold Way
Truckee, CA 96160
(530) 587-3501

	YARDAGE	PAR	RATING	SLOPE
FRONT	2557	35	68.2	108
MIDDLE	2900	35	66.6	111
BACK	3022	35	67.8	113

$30 - $48

WHAT TO EXPECT: This is a flat, straightforward, user-friendly golf course.
DIRECTIONS: From within Truckee: Off I-80, take Highway 267 south. The course is at the corner of Highway 267 and Reynold Way, just past the baseball fields. If you hit Northstar, you have gone too far.

THUNDER CANYON COUNTRY CLUB (members only, 18 holes, r. muir graves 1994) . .

19 Lightning W Ranch Road
Washoe Valley, NV 89704
(775) 884-4597

	YARDAGE	PAR	RATING	SLOPE
FRONT	4908	72	67.2	119
MIDDLE	6788	72	70.6	134
BACK	7204	72	72.6	137

$105 - $105

WHAT TO EXPECT: You will find plenty of water, excellent views, and many pine trees on this classic rolling layout.
NOTES: Reciprocal play with other members only clubs is allowed.
DIRECTIONS: From Reno (about 24 miles south to the course): Take US 395 south, exit at Bellevue, and turn right. Turn left at the end. Make a quick right into the entrance, which says "Lightning W Ranch." Follow the signs to the club.

WAWONA GOLF COURSE (public, 9 holes, walter g. favarque, alister mackenzie 1918)

Yosemite National Park
Wawona, CA 95389
(209) 375-6572
YosemitePark.com

	YARDAGE	PAR	RATING	SLOPE	
FRONT	-	-	-	-	
MIDDLE	-	-	-	-	**$13 - $22**
BACK	2998	35	69.1	117	

WHAT TO EXPECT: The course is part of Yosemite National Park. Set near the historic Wawona Hotel, this short golf course alternates between meadow golf and mountain golf, with narrow fairways lined with pine and cedar trees. Be aggressive with your putts – the greens are usually on the slower side. Mule deer regularly graze on the fairways.

NOTES: This was the first golf course to open in the Sierra Nevada.

DIRECTIONS: From Fresno (about 90 miles north to the course): Take Highway 41 north. The course is located at the south end of Yosemite Park.

Gold Country

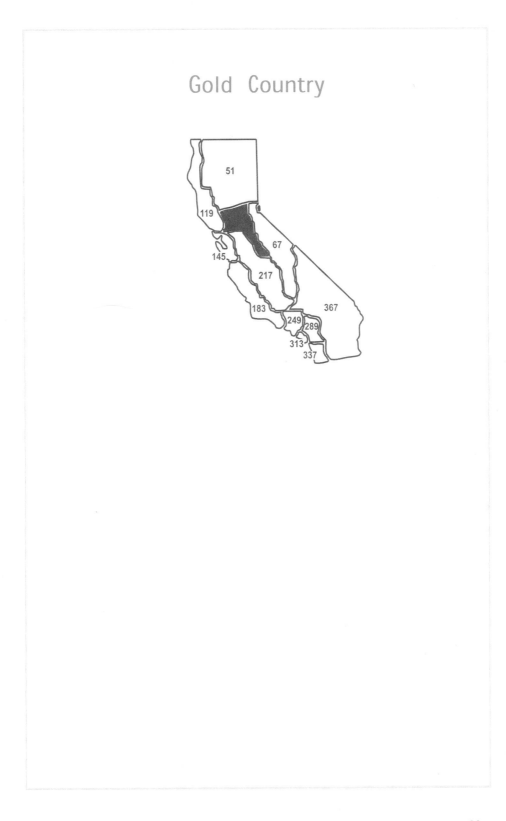

51

119

67

145

217

183

367

249

289

313

337

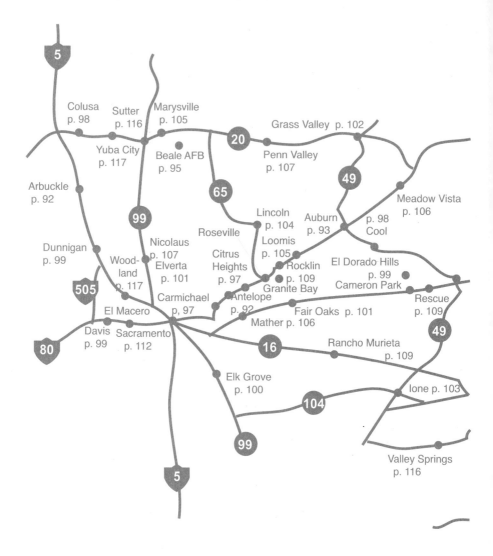

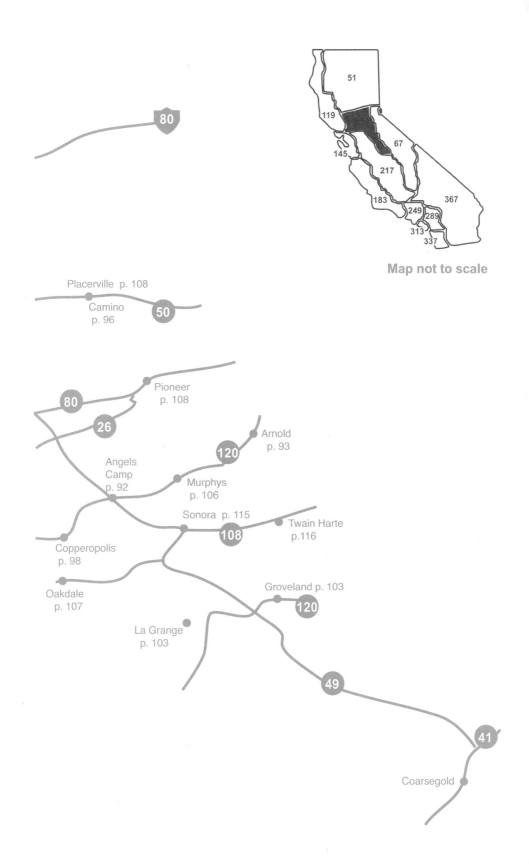

Map not to scale

GREENHORN CREEK (semi-private, 18 holes, don boos 1996) . . . .

711 McCauley Ranch Road
Angels Camp, CA 95222
(209) 736-8111
greenhorncreek.com

	YARDAGE	PAR	RATING	SLOPE	
FRONT	5200	72	71.3	126	**$55 - $80**
MIDDLE	6180	72	70.0	124	
BACK	6801	72	72.7	130	

WHAT TO EXPECT: Situated in a panoramic setting, this relatively new course has been fine-tuned to make it more playable. Lateral water hazards, rolling hills, and wooded fairways make a very challenging layout.

OUR OPINION: Greenhorn Creek is a fun layout but has seen the good, the bad and the ugly in course conditioning. Luckily, the course has been dramatically improved and is now a must-play if you are in the vicinity. – Frank

DIRECTIONS: From Stockton (about 50 minutes east to the course): Take Highway 4 east to Angels Camp. Turn right on Greenhorn Creek Drive, which is just before Highway 49.

ANTELOPE GREENS GOLF COURSE (public, 18 holes, don reiner 1994) . . . .

2721 Elverta Road
Antelope, CA 95843
(916) 334-5764

	YARDAGE	PAR	RATING	SLOPE	
FRONT	3007	58	56.1	81	**$14 - $17**
MIDDLE	3007	58	57.0	80	
BACK	3215	58	57.6	81	

WHAT TO EXPECT: This is an executive course with mostly par 3s. The longest hole on the course is a 350-yard par-4.

DIRECTIONS: From Sacramento (about 15 miles northeast to the course): Take I-80 east and exit on Watt Avenue. Go north about eight miles and turn left on Elverta Road. The course is on the right.

LAWRENCE LINKS GOLF COURSE (public, 9 holes, bert stamps 1970) . . . .

3825 Blackfoot Way
Antelope, CA 95843
(916) 332-7800
golf4cheap.com

	YARDAGE	PAR	RATING	SLOPE	
FRONT	2616	36	69.7	124	**$14 - $24**
MIDDLE	-	-	-	-	
BACK	3033	36	69.6	129	

WHAT TO EXPECT: Once a military course, Lawerence Links is now open to the public. Bring plenty of golf balls because this is a long nine-hole layout with water on every hole.

DIRECTIONS: From Sacramento (about 15 miles northeast to the course): Go east on I-80, exit onto Watt Avenue and head north. Turn right on Blackfoot Way.

ARBUCKLE GOLF CLUB (semi-private, 9 holes, local membership 1925) . . . .

5918 Hillgate Road
Arbuckle, CA 95912
(530) 476-2470

	YARDAGE	PAR	RATING	SLOPE	
FRONT	2956	36	72.7	120	**$15 - $25**
MIDDLE	-	-	-	-	
BACK	3230	36	70.2	120	

WHAT TO EXPECT: Rolling hills, tight tree-lined fairways, and elevated greens are the trademark of Arbuckle.

DIRECTIONS: From Sacramento (about 50 miles northwest to the course): Take I-5 north for about 45 minutes to Arbuckle. Take the Arbuckle exit. Turn left (west) on Hillgate Road, and drive about five and one-half miles. The course is on the left.

MEADOWMONT GOLF COURSE (public, 9 holes, dick fry 1963) . . . .

1684 Highway 4
Arnold, CA 95223
(209) 795-1313
meadowmontgolf.com

	YARDAGE	PAR	RATING	SLOPE	
FRONT	2713	36	70.4	124	**$9 - $26**
MIDDLE	-	-	-	-	
BACK	2845	36	66.8	121	

WHAT TO EXPECT: This simple, playable course is flat with small greens, and is, as its name suggests, set in a meadow up in the mountains, lined with pine trees.
DIRECTIONS: From Stockton (about 75 miles northeast to the course): Take Highway 4 east to Arnold. The course is on the left.

SEQUOIA WOODS COUNTRY CLUB (members only, 18 holes, bob baldock 1970) . . . . .

1000 Cypress Point Drive
Arnold, CA 95223
(209) 795-2141
sequoiawoods.com

	YARDAGE	PAR	RATING	SLOPE	
FRONT	4918	70	67.1	118	**$35 - $50**
MIDDLE	5261	70	64.9	116	
BACK	5600	70	66.1	120	

WHAT TO EXPECT: Sequoia Woods combines an open meadow with a tightly wooded, hilly section to make a scenic and deceptively challenging layout.
NOTES: Reciprocal play with other members only clubs is allowed.
DIRECTIONS: From Stockton (about 75 miles northeast to the course): Take Highway 99 south to Highway 4 east. Stay on Highway 4 past Angels Camp and through the town of Arnold. Turn right Moran and follow the signs.

AUBURN VALLEY COUNTRY CLUB (members only, 18 holes, bissett & curtola 1961) . .

8800 Auburn Valley Road
Auburn, CA 95602
(530) 269-1837
auburnvalley.com

	YARDAGE	PAR	RATING	SLOPE	
FRONT	5785	73	73.5	132	**$40 - $70**
MIDDLE	6486	72	71.0	125	
BACK	6822	72	72.7	129	

WHAT TO EXPECT: With narrow fairways, elevated tee boxes that provide excellent views, and rugged terrain, Auburn Valley plays much longer than the yardage indicates. If you survive tee to green, you will have to negotiate around notoriously quick greens.
OUR OPINION: This course is a hidden gem. – Bob
NOTES: Reciprocal play with other members only clubs is allowed.
DIRECTIONS: From Sacramento (about 40 miles east to the course): Take I-80 east to Auburn, then take Highway 49 north. Exit at Lone Star Road, and head west to Auburn Valley Road. This leads to the course.

BLACK OAK GOLF COURSE (public, 9 holes, john walker 1986) . . . .

2455 Black Oak Road
Auburn, CA 95602
(530) 878-1900

	YARDAGE	PAR	RATING	SLOPE	
FRONT	2640	36	70.0	119	
MIDDLE	3000	36	68.8	121	**$9 - $20**
BACK	3163	36	70.1	130	

WHAT TO EXPECT: Nothing is subtle about Black Oak. This is a hilly, challenging course where you will encounter uphill, downhill, and side-hill lies. Plenty of water, creeks, native oaks, and traps come into play. For the right-handed player who has a penchant for snap hooking off the tee, be prepared to re-tee most of the day.
DIRECTIONS: From Sacramento (about 40 miles east to the course): Drive east on I-80 to Auburn. Take the Dry Creek exit and head west. Turn on Black Oak Road, and follow to the course.

DARKHORSE GOLF CLUB (public, 18 holes, keith foster 2002) . . . .

13450 Combie Road
Auburn, CA 95602-8917
(530) 269-7900
darkhorsegolf.com

	YARDAGE	PAR	RATING	SLOPE	
FRONT	5180	72	-	-	
MIDDLE	-	-	-	-	**$40 - $60**
BACK	7031	72	-	-	

WHAT TO EXPECT: The course will use the 5,000 mature oak trees to line the fairways. Six ponds and eight streams will come into play. Elevation will change from 1,400 to 1,700 feet through out the round.
NOTES: The course is due to open in spring of 2002.
DIRECTIONS: Directions to the course were not available at time of press. Please check our website www.InTheLoopGolf.com for updates.

LAKE OF THE PINES COUNTRY CLUB (members only, 18 holes) . . . .

11665 Lakeshore North
Auburn, CA 95602
(530) 269-1544

	YARDAGE	PAR	RATING	SLOPE	
FRONT	4517	70	66.8	118	
MIDDLE	5897	71	69.2	118	**$27 - $32**
BACK	6140	71	70.3	122	

WHAT TO EXPECT: With the lake on one side, and houses on the other, this is a narrow course with lots of out-of-bounds. This hilly layout makes its way around the lake, with no parallel holes. Accuracy is crucial to scoring well. Ignore the distance on the scorecard — this course can put up a fight.
NOTES: Reciprocal play with other members only clubs is allowed.
DIRECTIONS: From Sacramento: Drive east on I-80 to Highway 49 north. Exit Combie Road, headed east. Turn right and drive to Lakeshore North. Take another right on Lakeshore North.

RASPBERRY HILL, GOLF COURSE AT (public, 9 holes, fred strong 1980) . . . .

14500 Musso Road
Auburn, CA 95603
(530) 878-7818

	YARDAGE	PAR	RATING	SLOPE
FRONT	1533	29	56.3	84
MIDDLE	-	-	-	-
BACK	1533	29	56.6	89

$9 - $20

WHAT TO EXPECT: This is a short course with small, quick greens and water on five holes. Holes two, three, and four are long, challenging par 3s.
DIRECTIONS: From Sacramento (about 40 miles east to the course): Take I-80 east to Auburn and exit at Bell Road. Make a right on Bell and a left onto Musso Road. The course is on the right.

RIDGE GOLF COURSE, THE (public, 18 holes, robert trent jones jr. 1999) . . . .

2020 Golf Course Road
Auburn, CA 95602
(530) 888-7888
RidgeGC.com

	YARDAGE	PAR	RATING	SLOPE
FRONT	4954	71	68.5	123
MIDDLE	6345	71	70.1	132
BACK	6735	71	72.2	137

$40 - $52

WHAT TO EXPECT: This is an interesting course, the equal of any of the area's private clubs. Large oaks, rock outcroppings and meandering creeks give the layout a mature feel.
OUR OPINION: The course receives high marks from our contributors for value, design, and service. Interestingly, these comments came from both our female and male writers.
NOTES: The Ridge is only 300 yards from the Auburn Airport, and the staff at the Ridge is happy to pick up golfers.
DIRECTIONS: From Sacramento (about 40 miles east to the course): Take I-80 east to the Bell Road exit in Auburn. Go north on Bell Road almost two miles. Make a right on New Airport Road, and another right on Golf Course Road.

REECE POINT GOLF COURSE (military, 18 holes, golf plan 1998) . . . .

17440 Warren Shingle Boulevard
Beale AFB, CA 95903
(530) 788-0192

	YARDAGE	PAR	RATING	SLOPE
FRONT	4624	69	66.8	112
MIDDLE	6347	72	70.3	124
BACK	6814	72	72.4	132

$22 - $24

WHAT TO EXPECT: Reece Point is an honest course with water on five holes. You will encounter mature trees on the front side and immature trees that pose little threat on the back. However, don't miss the fairways on the back nine, because you will be knee-deep in thistle.
NOTES: Public play is accepted.
DIRECTIONS: From Sacramento (about 50 miles north to the course): Take Highway 99 north to Highway 70 and drive north, almost to Marysville. Turn right, heading east off the freeway, following the Beale AFB signs. Follow the signs to Beale AFB signs to get to the course.

CAMERON PARK COUNTRY CLUB (members only, 18 holes, bert stamps 1962) . . . . . .

3201 Royal Drive
Cameron Park, CA 95682
(530) 672-7900

	YARDAGE	PAR	RATING	SLOPE	
FRONT	5894	73	74.0	134	**$45 - $65**
MIDDLE	6303	72	70.2	126	
BACK	6532	72	71.0	128	

WHAT TO EXPECT: Quick, sloping greens and narrow landing areas make this layout both interesting and rigorous. (Hey, aren't you glad we didn't say "challenging"?)
NOTES: Reciprocal play with other members only clubs is allowed.
DIRECTIONS: From Sacramento (about 35 miles east to the course): Take US 50 east. Take the Cameron Park Drive exit and turn left. Make another left onto Country Club Drive and a right onto Royal Drive.

APPLE MOUNTAIN GOLF RESORT (resort, 18 holes, algie pulley 1997) . . . .

3455 Carson Road
Camino, CA 95709
(530) 647-7400
apple-mountain.com

	YARDAGE	PAR	RATING	SLOPE	
FRONT	4652	71	67.4	117	**$45 - $60**
MIDDLE	5663	71	67.8	116	
BACK	6427	71	70.6	127	

WHAT TO EXPECT: Dogwood and pine trees line the fairways of this mountain course. Apple Mountain's varied terrain makes even lies the exception, rather than the rule. Beware of the grass hollows; they can ruin a perfectly good round.
DIRECTIONS: From Sacramento (about 50 miles east to the course): Take US 50 east past Placerville. Make a left to Carson Road and then an immediate right on Carson (like a frontage road). Turn left at the Apple Mountain sign, to the course.

CAMINO HEIGHTS GOLF CLUB (semi-private, 9 holes) . . . .

3020 Vista Tierra Drive
Camino, CA 95709
(530) 644-0190

	YARDAGE	PAR	RATING	SLOPE	
FRONT	1532	31	57.6	92	**$10 - $16**
MIDDLE	1819	31	60.4	100	
BACK	1896	31	60.8	102	

WHAT TO EXPECT: This is a hilly course with average-sized, sloping greens. There are houses along the fairways, but they only come into play for the mediocre, or worse, golfer.
NOTES: The public is welcome, but members get priority for tee times.
DIRECTIONS: From Sacramento (about 50 miles east to the course): Drive east on US 50, past Placerville, to Camino. Make a right on Camino Heights Drive and a left on Vista Tierra Drive to the course.

ANCIL HOFFMAN GOLF COURSE (public, 18 holes, william bell 1965) . . . .

6700 Tarshes Drive
Carmichael, CA 95608
(916) 482-3284

	YARDAGE	PAR	RATING	SLOPE	
FRONT	5954	73	74.2	126	
MIDDLE	6434	72	70.9	125	**$14 - $24**
BACK	6794	72	72.8	128	

WHAT TO EXPECT: A traditional, tightly treed course with oak and pine, Ancil Hoffman requires accurate tee and approach play. When in good condition, the layout compares favorably to some of the best in Northern California.

DIRECTIONS: From Sacramento (course is about 12 miles east): Head east on I-80, and exit on Madison. Go south to Sunrise Boulevard, and turn right. Turn right on Fair Oaks Boulevard and then left on California. Turn left on Tarshes Drive.

SUNRISE GOLF COURSE (members only, 9 holes) . . . .

6412 Sunrise Boulevard
Citrus Heights, CA 95610
(916) 723-0481

	YARDAGE	PAR	RATING	SLOPE	
FRONT	2041	31	62.3	105	
MIDDLE	-	-	-	-	**$7 - $15**
BACK	2041	31	60.4	98	

WHAT TO EXPECT: This is a nine-hole executive course with small greens. The fairways are rolling with trees. Some of the holes are outlined by an apartment complex, creating out-of-bounds opportunities.

NOTES: Reciprocal play with other members only clubs is allowed.

DIRECTIONS: From Sacramento (about 15 miles east to the course): Go east on I-80, exit at Greenback Lane and turn right. Turn left on Sunrise Boulevard. The entrance is on the right, just a block from Greenback Lane.

YOSEMITE LAKES PARK GOLF COURSE (members only, 9 holes, bob baldock 1970) . . .

30250 Yosemite Springs Parkway
Coarsegold, CA 93614
(559) 642-2562

	YARDAGE	PAR	RATING	SLOPE	
FRONT	1471	31	59.2	83	
MIDDLE	-		-	103	**$7 - $12**
BACK	1471	31	59.2		

WHAT TO EXPECT: This is a narrow course with plenty of hills and water that comes into play on more than half the holes.

NOTES: Reciprocal play with other members only clubs is allowed.

DIRECTIONS: From Fresno (about 33 miles north to the course): Drive north on Highway 41 toward Yosemite. Turn left on Yosemite Springs Parkway, and drive four miles to the course.

COLUSA GOLF & COUNTRY CLUB (semi-private, 9 holes) . . . .

2224 Highway 20
Colusa, CA 95932
(530) 458-5577

	YARDAGE	PAR	RATING	SLOPE	
FRONT	2898	37	72.2	120	**$10 - $20**
MIDDLE	3262	36	70.9	120	
BACK	3322	36	71.4	122	

WHAT TO EXPECT: This is a hilly course, with no trees lining the fairways. If you can't par anywhere, you can par here. Reverse that, the course plays just the opposite. We just thought you were tired of reading the same old thing.

DIRECTIONS: From Williams (about 15 miles east to the course): Off I-5, go east on Highway 20 to Colusa. The course is on the right.

AUBURN LAKE TRAILS GOLF COURSE (members only, 9 holes) . . . .

1400 American River Trail
Cool, CA 95614
(530) 885-6526
auburnlaketrails.org

	YARDAGE	PAR	RATING	SLOPE	
FRONT	1352	29	56.2	87	**$10 - $15**
MIDDLE	-	-	-	-	
BACK	1393	29	56.1	86	

WHAT TO EXPECT: This is a rustic nine-hole course with plenty of trees and rolling terrain.

DIRECTIONS: From Sacramento (about 45 miles northeast to the course): Take I-80 east to Highway 49 south. After about eight miles, turn left onto Highway 193. The course is on the left.

SADDLE CREEK GOLF CLUB (semi-private, 18 holes, carter morrish 1996) . . . .

1001 Saddle Creek Road
Copperopolis, CA 95228
(209) 785-3700
saddlecreek.com

	YARDAGE	PAR	RATING	SLOPE	
FRONT	4471	72	65.4	111	**$35 - $66**
MIDDLE	6356	72	71.2	127	
BACK	6773	72	73.1	137	

WHAT TO EXPECT: Saddle Creek features wonderful views and an excellent variety of holes. Bold, artistic bunkering and quick, smooth greens make this the "must play" in the Gold Country. Each hole is individually framed, so you often have the feeling that you have the course all to yourself.

OUR OPINION: There is no quick way to Saddle Creek, but it is definitely worth the drive. When this course first arrived on the scene, arrogance took precedence over service. Things have changed, so if you were put off before by the attitude, you might want to take a second look. – Shaw

DIRECTIONS: From Stockton (about 40 miles east to the course): Off Highway 99, take Highway 4 east for 35 miles toward Copperopolis. Turn right on O'Byrnes Ferry Road, and go about four miles. Turn right on Copper Cove Drive. At the end, turn left on Little John. The course is on the right.

DAVIS GOLF COURSE (municipal, 18 holes, bob baldock 1964) . . . .

24439 Fairway Drive
Davis, CA 95616
(530) 756-4010
davisgolfcourse.com

	YARDAGE	PAR	RATING	SLOPE	
FRONT	4428	67	63.9	95	**$8 - $16**
MIDDLE	4472	67	61.0	96	
BACK	4953	67	62.9	102	

WHAT TO EXPECT: This is a diminutive, and flat muni course with a bounty (OK, we were tired of writing "plenty") of water.
DIRECTIONS: From Sacramento (about 15 miles west to the course): Take I-80 west to Highway 113 north, toward Woodland. The course is five miles up the highway on the left. Take the Road 29 exit.

WILDHORSE GOLF COURSE (public, 18 holes, jeff brauer 1999) . . . .

2323 Rockwell Drive
Davis, CA 95616
(530) 753-4900
eaglgolf.com

	YARDAGE	PAR	RATING	SLOPE	
FRONT	4925	72	72.9	134	**$22 - $50**
MIDDLE	6212	72	70.4	128	
BACK	6736	72	69.0	126	

WHAT TO EXPECT: Environmentally Sensitive Areas, which require forced-carry approach shots, make the course quite intimidating for the weaker hitter. Otherwise, you can expect a well-bunkered, flat links-like landscape where the wind can be a strong factor.
DIRECTIONS: From Sacramento (about 13 miles west to the course): Drive west on I-80 toward Davis. Take the Mace Avenue exit and turn right. Proceed to Wright Boulevard and turn right. Make another right on Moore and then a left on Rockwell Drive to the course.

CAMPERS INN RV & GOLF COURSE (public, 9 holes) . . . .

2501 Road 88
Dunnigan, CA 95937
(530) 724-3350

	YARDAGE	PAR	RATING	SLOPE	
FRONT	-	-	-	-	**$6 - $20**
MIDDLE	-	-	-	-	
BACK	1134	27	-	-	

WHAT TO EXPECT: Wind often comes into play on this short par-3 layout, which is part of a recreational area.
DIRECTIONS: From Sacramento (about 35 miles northwest to the course): Take I-5 north to Dunnigan. Take the Dunnigan exit and turn left, which is Road Six. Turn right on Road 88.

EL DORADO HILLS GOLF CLUB (public, 18 holes, robert trent jones, sr. 1962) . . . . . .

3775 El Dorado Hills Boulevard
El Dorado Hills, CA 95762
(916) 933-6552
edhgc.com

	YARDAGE	PAR	RATING	SLOPE	
FRONT	3530	61	59.2	91	**$20 - $25**
MIDDLE	3860	61	61.1	102	
BACK	4012	61	61.8	103	

WHAT TO EXPECT: There are few straight holes on the course. El Dorado Hills will give golfers plenty of opportunity to hone their skills on working the ball left to right and right to left. If you don't keep it in the fairway, you will find yourself in one of the many trees that line the fairways.
DIRECTIONS: From Sacramento (about 25 miles east to the course): Travel east on US 50. Take the El Dorado Hills Boulevard exit north. The course is on the right.

SERRANO COUNTRY CLUB (members only, 18 holes, robert trent jones jr. 1996) . . . .

5005 Serrano Parkway
El Dorado Hills, CA 95762
(916) 933-5716
serranocountryclub.com

	YARDAGE	PAR	RATING	SLOPE
FRONT	5232	72	69.9	124
MIDDLE	6525	72	69.7	127
BACK	6976	72	74.2	134

$60 - $125

WHAT TO EXPECT: Located in the Sierra foothills, Serrano features rolling hills, and fairways which are outlined by large native oaks. The landing areas are fairly generous, but water comes into play on six holes. Wind can be an issue. The greens break toward Folsom Lake.

NOTES: Reciprocal play with other members only clubs is allowed.

DIRECTIONS: From Sacramento (about 25 miles east to the course): Take US 50 east. Exit at El Dorado Hills Boulevard and drive north to Serrano Parkway. Turn right and travel east to the course.

EL MACERO COUNTRY CLUB (members only, 18 holes, bob baldock 1961) . . . .

44571 Clubhouse Drive
El Macero, CA 95618
(530) 753-5621

	YARDAGE	PAR	RATING	SLOPE
FRONT	5816	72	73.5	124
MIDDLE	6489	72	70.6	119
BACK	6836	72	72.1	123

$40 - $60

WHAT TO EXPECT: This flat, long course is made interesting by its wooded fairway corridors, which demand a good driving game.

NOTES: Reciprocal play with other members only clubs is allowed.

DIRECTIONS: From Sacramento (about 12 miles west to the course): Take I-80 west to Mace Boulevard. Exit on Mace Boulevard and head south. Turn left at the blinking light, after crossing over the freeway. Go right at the Y in the road. Turn right on Clubhouse Drive.

EMERALD LAKES GOLF CENTER (public, 9 holes, rick yount 1991) . . . .

10651 East Stockton Boulevard
Elk Grove, CA 95624
(916) 685-4653

	YARDAGE	PAR	RATING	SLOPE
FRONT	1982	33	61.4	97
MIDDLE	-	-	-	-
BACK	2282	33	61.8	99

$9 - $19

WHAT TO EXPECT: This is a level, executive course with lakes coming into play on six holes. The greens are undulating and guarded by traps.

DIRECTIONS: From Sacramento (about 15 miles south to the course): Drive south on Highway 99 to the Grant Line Road exit west. Go east and cross over Highway 99 to East Stockton Boulevard. Drive south on East Stockton Boulevard. Travel one-quarter mile to the course.

VALLEY HI COUNTRY CLUB (members only, 18 holes, william bell 1959) . . . .

595 Franklin Boulevard
Elk Grove, CA 95758
(916) 423-2170

	YARDAGE	PAR	RATING	SLOPE	
FRONT	5426	73	70.5	115	**$35 - $55**
MIDDLE	6543	72	70.7	121	
BACK	?	72	71.7	123	

WHAT TO EXPECT: The growth of the trees, together with play around three lakes, has made this flat valley course more challenging over time. Though the greens are fairly flat, they can be deceptively hard to putt when the speed is increased.
NOTES: Reciprocal play with other members only clubs is allowed.
DIRECTIONS: From Sacramento (about 15 miles south to the course): Take I-5 south, exit on Elk Grove Boulevard and head east. Turn left on Franklin Boulevard. The course is on the right.

CHERRY ISLAND GOLF COURSE (municipal, 18 holes, robert muir graves 1990) . . . . .

2360 Elverta Road
Elverta, CA 95626
(916) 991-6875
empiregolf.com

	YARDAGE	PAR	RATING	SLOPE	
FRONT	5173	72	70.0	117	**$19 - $23**
MIDDLE	6201	72	70.1	118	
BACK	6562	72	71.6	122	

WHAT TO EXPECT: The low handicapper should pick spots to be aggressive. With water hazards or out-of-bounds on nearly every hole, the inpatient player will rack up plenty of penalty strokes. The front side has far more trees to contend with than the back. You will find several of the greens elevated throughout.
DIRECTIONS: From Sacramento (about 14 miles north to the course): From I-80 take the Watt Avenue exit and head north. Turn left on Elverta Road.

NORTH RIDGE COUNTRY CLUB (members only, 18 holes, billy bell, jr. 1954) . . . .

7600 Madison Avenue
Fair Oaks, CA 95628
(916) 967-5716

	YARDAGE	PAR	RATING	SLOPE	
FRONT	5839	72	74.6	136	**$50 - $70**
MIDDLE	6251	71	70.1	127	
BACK	6554	71	71.5	130	

WHAT TO EXPECT: Small, well-bunkered greens, tightly treed fairways and many uphill holes make this one of the region's better courses and an excellent test of your skills.
NOTES: Reciprocal play with other members only clubs is allowed.
DIRECTIONS: From Sacramento (about 20 miles east to the course): Drive east on I-80. Take the Madison exit and drive southeast about five miles to Mariposa. Make a right into the club.

GRANITE BAY GOLF CLUB (members only, 18 holes, robert trent jones jr. 1994) . . . .

9600 Golf Club Drive
Granite Bay, CA 95746
(916) 791-5379
granitebayclub.com

	YARDAGE	PAR	RATING	SLOPE
FRONT	4942	70	67.9	118
MIDDLE	6520	71	71.5	134
BACK	6910	71	73.3	137

$55 - $175

WHAT TO EXPECT: Granite Bay Golf Club is a rugged, but simple, course. It was designed to incorporate nature in both beauty and challenge. The course features rolling fairways and is surrounded by oaks, with creeks running throughout. The views on the course are even more spectacular than the design.

NOTES: This is a members only course, but outside play is accepted on Mondays.

DIRECTIONS: From Sacramento (about 20 miles northeast to the course): Take I-80 east, exit on Douglas Boulevard, turn right and head southeast. Turn right on Roseville Parkway. Turn right on Golf Club Drive, which is past Sierra College Boulevard.

ALTA SIERRA GOLF & COUNTRY CLUB (semi-private, 18 holes, bob baldock 1964) . . .

11897 Tammy Way
Grass Valley, CA 95949
(530) 273-2010
altasierragolf.com

	YARDAGE	PAR	RATING	SLOPE
FRONT	5984	73	75.6	136
MIDDLE	6340	72	70.1	125
BACK	6537	72	70.9	127

$22 - $50

WHAT TO EXPECT: There are no adjacent fairways on this course. Alta Sierra is a tree-lined, mountain course with abundant-sized greens. The course favors the player with local knowledge. Don't forget any of your clubs; you will have an opportunity to use them all.

NOTES: Limited public play is accepted.

DIRECTIONS: From Sacramento (course is about 50 miles northeast): Take I-80 east to Highway 49 north. Drive about 20 miles, heading toward Grass Valley. Turn right at Alta Sierra Drive. Follow Alta Sierra Drive to Tammy Way and the course.

NEVADA COUNTY COUNTRY CLUB (semi-private, 9 holes) . . . .

1040 East Main Street
Grass Valley, CA 95945
(530) 273-6436

	YARDAGE	PAR	RATING	SLOPE
FRONT	2550	35	68.5	119
MIDDLE	-	-	-	-
BACK	2690	35	65.4	116

$12 - $18

WHAT TO EXPECT: For the inaccurate driver, Nevada County Country Club is paradise. With plenty of parallel fairways, if you can't hit your own fairway, you still have a good chance of landing on the short grass. The course creates a challenge with small greens that feature subtle breaks, favoring the player with course knowledge.

NOTES: Non-members can play after 2:00 p.m. on weekdays and anytime on weekends.

DIRECTIONS: From within Grass Valley: Off Highway 49, exit at Idaho Maryland and go west. Turn right on East Main Street and head up the hill. The course is on the left.

PINE MOUNTAIN LAKE COUNTRY CLUB (semi-private, 18 holes, billy bell, jr. 1969) . .

19228 Pine Mountain Drive
Groveland, CA 95321
(209) 962-8620
pinemountainlake.com

	YARDAGE	PAR	RATING	SLOPE	
FRONT	5355	70	70.8	128	**$35 - $35**
MIDDLE	6146	70	69.0	123	
BACK	6358	70	70.1	125	

WHAT TO EXPECT: This is definitely a "local knowledge" course. Tight, slanted, tree-lined fairways that often turn, put a definite premium on accuracy off the tee. The other engaging factor is the wonderful views around the property; many of the holes are exquisitely framed. The course plays a little more difficult than the yardage would suggest.

OUR OPINION: Friendly, scenic, interesting and a good value, make for a winning combination. – Bob

DIRECTIONS: From Modesto (about 65 miles east to the course): Take Highway 99 north to Highway 120 east to Groveland. Be sure to take the Yosemite Junction to stay on Highway 120. Once in Groveland, turn left on Ferretti and then right on Mueller.

CASTLE OAKS GOLF CLUB (public, 18 holes, bradford benz 1994) . . . .

1000 Castle Oaks Drive
Ione, CA 95640
(209) 274-0167
castleoaksgolfclub.com

	YARDAGE	PAR	RATING	SLOPE	
FRONT	4953	71	67.3	114	**$18 - $48**
MIDDLE	6356	71	70.8	127	
BACK	6739	71	72.7	131	

WHAT TO EXPECT: This popular layout winds among oak-studded hills and features tight fairways. Water is the primary hazard. The course forces you to hit a variety of shots. Beware of the 18th hole – it has ruined many promising rounds.

OUR OPINION: Castle Oaks has a high enjoyment-to-price ratio. In other words, we like it.

DIRECTIONS: From Sacramento (about 45 miles southeast to the course): Take Highway 99 south. Take the exit for Highway 104 toward Jackson (east). About 30 minutes later, turn right on Castle Oaks Drive, right before the town of Ione.

HIDDEN HILLS GOLF CLUB & RESORT (resort, 18 holes) . . . .

7643 Fachada Way
La Grange, CA 95329
(209) 852-2242

	YARDAGE	PAR	RATING	SLOPE	
FRONT	5568	72	-	-	**$20 - $35**
MIDDLE	6145	72	-	-	
BACK	6387	72	-	-	

WHAT TO EXPECT: The course is currently undergoing renovations. Call for more information.

DIRECTIONS: From Modesto (about 40 miles east to the course): Head east on Highway 132 through La Grange. Turn right (south) on Hayward Road and then left on Ranchito Drive. Make a left on Hernandez Drive and another left on Fachada Way.

LINCOLN HILLS GOLF CLUB (public, 18 holes, casper & nash 1999) . . . .

1005 Sun City Lane
Lincoln, CA 95648
(916) 434-7450
delwebb.com

	YARDAGE	PAR	RATING	SLOPE	
FRONT	5411	72	70.5	117	**$33 - $50**
MIDDLE	6464	72	70.8	120	
BACK	6985	72	73.2	127	

WHAT TO EXPECT: Break out your oversized, graphite-shafted, titanium-headed driver and let it rip. This is an open, well-conditioned layout with liberal fairways and large undulating greens. There are homes on the course, but they only come into play on a couple of holes. Beware of trouble lurking out of sight, off the tee boxes, on several holes on the back nine.

OUR OPINION: This is a fun course at a reasonable price that doesn't punish golfers for every bad shot. – Bob

NOTES: A cart is recommended.

DIRECTIONS: From Sacramento (about 30 miles northeast to the course): Go east on I-80 to Highway 65 north. Go nine miles to Sterling Parkway and head east. Turn right into Sun City Lincoln Hills and follow the signs to the course.

TURKEY CREEK GOLF CLUB (public, 18 holes, brad bell 1999) . . . .

1525 Highway 193
Lincoln, CA 95648
(916) 434-9100

	YARDAGE	PAR	RATING	SLOPE	
FRONT	4796	71	67.3	121	**$20 - $65**
MIDDLE	6498	72	71.3	131	
BACK	6930	72	73.4	136	

WHAT TO EXPECT: Rolling, tree-lined fairways with minimal bunkering and more than a few blind shots highlight this beautiful layout.

OUR OPINION: This is an excellent new addition to the Sacramento golf scene. – Bob

DIRECTIONS: From Sacramento (about 30 miles northeast to the course): Take I-80 east to Highway 65 north. Go about ten miles and turn right on Highway 193 east. The course is about one and one-half miles out on the left.

TWELVE BRIDGES GOLF CLUB (public, 18 holes, dick phelps 1996) . . . .

3070 Twelve Bridges Drive
Lincoln, CA 95648
(916) 645-7200
twelvebridges.com

	YARDAGE	PAR	RATING	SLOPE	
FRONT	5310	72	71.0	123	**$30 - $60**
MIDDLE	6693	72	72.6	131	
BACK	7109	72	74.6	139	

WHAT TO EXPECT: An LPGA Tour stop, the course has a wonderful routing along streams and natural outcroppings. To score well here, you must hit your fairways.

OUR OPINION: Twelve Bridges is one of the best courses in the region. For the local golfer, the greens fees are considered on the high end, but for the Bay Area and the Southern California golfer, Twelve Bridges is a bargain. – Shaw

DIRECTIONS: From Sacramento (about 30 miles northeast to the course): Take Highway 65 north off I-80. Take Twelve Bridges Drive east to the course.

INDIAN CREEK COUNTRY CLUB (public, 9 holes, bill williams 1958) . . . .

4487 Barton Road
Loomis, CA 95650
(916) 652-5546

	YARDAGE	PAR	RATING	SLOPE	
FRONT	1996	32	61.2	103	**$8 - $17**
MIDDLE	2170	32	64.2	107	
BACK	2215	32	61.2	107	

WHAT TO EXPECT: This is an open, walkable course, drawing about 60 percent of the play from seniors. The course has plenty of out-of-bounds, trees, a lake and a creek. The greens are crowned.

DIRECTIONS: From Sacramento (about 25 miles northeast to the course): Drive east on I-80. Take the Rocklin Road exit and turn right. Follow Rocklin Road to Barton Road, and turn left and drive to the course.

PEACH TREE GOLF & COUNTRY CLUB (members only, 18 holes, bob baldock 1959) . . .

2043 Simpson-Dantoni Road
Marysville, CA 95901
(530) 743-2039

	YARDAGE	PAR	RATING	SLOPE	
FRONT	5045	70	68.8	117	**$40 - $75**
MIDDLE	6500	72	71.0	124	
BACK	6819	72	72.6	127	

WHAT TO EXPECT: This is a level, walkable course with trees guarding the perimeter of the fairways. The greens are generally slanted back to front.

DIRECTIONS: From Sacramento (about 40 miles north to the course): Take Highway 99 north to Highway 70 north to Marysville. Take Highway 20 east, and turn right on Ramirez Road. Stay on Ramirez Road to the course. Peach Tree is on the left, after the race track.

PLUMAS LAKE GOLF & COUNTRY CLUB (semi-private, 18 holes, bob baldock 1960) . . .

1551 Country Club Avenue
Marysville, CA 95901
(530) 742-3201

	YARDAGE	PAR	RATING	SLOPE	
FRONT	5759	72	73.4	127	**$21 - $26**
MIDDLE	6153	71	70.3	128	
BACK	6437	71	71.3	130	

WHAT TO EXPECT: This is a tight, scenic course where trees, homes, condos, and hazards can consume golf balls.

DIRECTIONS: From Sacramento (about 40 miles north to the course): Take Highway 99 north to Highway 70 north. Right before Marysville, exit at Feather River Boulevard and turn left under the freeway. After about six and one-half miles, turn left on Country Club Avenue.

MATHER GOLF COURSE (public, 18 holes, jack fleming 1959) . . . .

4103 Eagles Nest Road
Mather, CA 95655
(916) 364-4353
courseco.com

	YARDAGE	PAR	RATING	SLOPE	
FRONT	5876	74	72.4	119	**$22 - $27**
MIDDLE	6270	72	70.3	121	
BACK	6686	72	71.8	125	

WHAT TO EXPECT: This former military facility is a park-setting course with tree-lined, wide, rolling fairways and many elevated tees. Mather has no hidden tricks, just a classic design that rewards the good shot and punishes the bad.

DIRECTIONS: In Sacramento (about 15 miles east to the course): From I-80 take the Sunrise Avenue exit and drive east. Take a right on Douglas Avenue and a left onto Eagles Nest Road, to the course.

WINCHESTER COUNTRY CLUB (members only, 18 holes, r. trent jones sr. & jr. 1999) .

3030 Legends Drive
Meadow Vista, CA 95722
(530) 878-9585
winchestergolf.com

	YARDAGE	PAR	RATING	SLOPE	
FRONT	5289	72	70.8	129	**$65 - $150**
MIDDLE	6819	72	73.5	138	
BACK	7145	72	75.0	143	

WHAT TO EXPECT: This is a beautiful and rugged course set in the Sierra foothills. The fairways are rolling and flanked by mature native oaks. The course appears as if it has been there for years. From the back tees, the scratch golfer will be emotionally and physically drained, but will want to come back again. Soon.

OUR OPINION: There are any number of "Wow!" tee shots on this narrow, hilly layout. This course jumps to the top of the Sacramento area courses. – Bob

NOTES: Reciprocal play with other members only clubs is allowed.

DIRECTIONS: From Sacramento (about 45 miles northeast to the course): Drive east on I-80 to Auburn. Take the Clipper Gap/Meadow Vista exit and go north one mile. Turn west on Sugar Pine Road; the course is on the left.

FOREST MEADOWS GOLF COURSE (resort, 18 holes, robert trent jones jr. 1972) . . . . .

633 Forest Meadows Drive
Murphys, CA 95247
(209) 728-3439
forestmeadows.com

	YARDAGE	PAR	RATING	SLOPE	
FRONT	3221	60	58.8	99	**$15 - $37**
MIDDLE	3886	60	62.5	107	
BACK	3886	60	60.3	110	

WHAT TO EXPECT: The name Forest Meadows comes from the old Scottish term meaning "course with forest and meadows." Just kidding. This is a short, tricky course with meadows, hills, lakes, and trees. Break out your driver sparingly and put away your ego – there is little benefit for the long hitter. The golfer who can hit it straight and putt well will excel here.

OUR OPINION: You can find more expensive and slightly better-conditioned courses in the vicinity, but Forest Meadows is a fun, scenic, and challenging golf course. It is also one that the whole family can enjoy and the parents can afford. – Shaw

DIRECTIONS: From Sacramento (about 90 miles southeast to the course): Take Highway 99 south to Highway 4 east toward Murphys. The course is almost four miles above Murphys, right on Highway 4. It is in a gated community.

RIO LA PAZ GOLF CLUB (semi-private, 18 holes, peter jacobsen 2000) . . . .

201 Lee Road
Nicolaus, CA 95659
(530) 656-2182

	YARDAGE	PAR	RATING	SLOPE	
FRONT	4774	71	67.5	117	**$33 - $43**
MIDDLE	6003	71	69.3	125	
BACK	6494	71	71.3	126	

WHAT TO EXPECT: Rio la Paz is a meadow course. The landing areas are generous with trees, and water occasionally coming into play. With the exception of one hole, there was very little mounding or earth moved to produce this layout.

OUR OPINION: There is not much here to keep the better golfer entertained. Rio la Paz is better suited for family golf. – The Mole

DIRECTIONS: From Sacramento (about 25 miles north to the course): Take I-5 north to Highway 99 north. Take the Nicolaus exit, turn left onto Garden Highway, and follow that to the course.

OAKDALE GOLF & COUNTRY CLUB (members only, 18 holes, bob baldock 1961) . . . . .

243 North Stearns Road
Oakdale, CA 95361
(209) 847-2924

	YARDAGE	PAR	RATING	SLOPE	
FRONT	5715	72	73.6	127	**$35 - $55**
MIDDLE	6462	72	71.4	128	
BACK	6719	72	72.7	130	

WHAT TO EXPECT: This is a well-groomed traditional course with slight elevation changes. Oakdale is lined by trees, and many of the greens are elevated, putting an emphasis on accuracy.

NOTES: Reasonably priced memberships are still available. Reciprocal play with other member only clubs is allowed.

DIRECTIONS: From Modesto (about 18 miles northeast to the course): Take Highway 108 east from Highway 99. Turn left on Stearns Road, past Oakdale.

LAKE WILDWOOD COUNTRY CLUB (members only, 18 holes, billy bell, jr. 1971) . . . . .

11255 Cottontail Way
Penn Valley, CA 95946
(530) 432-1163

	YARDAGE	PAR	RATING	SLOPE	
FRONT	5230	72	69.7	124	**$22 - $55**
MIDDLE	6246	72	69.9	125	
BACK	6501	72	71.0	127	

WHAT TO EXPECT: Lake Wildwood is a straightforward course where most of the greens can be seen from the tee box. The green sites are fairly large and offer players many different ways to approach them. Most of the fairways are comfortable in width and are rolling, although the back nine does become hilly. Water will affect play on about one-third of the holes.

NOTES: Reciprocal play with other members only clubs is allowed.

DIRECTIONS: From Marysville (about 27 miles east to the course): Drive east on Highway 20. Follow Highway 20 about 27 miles. Turn left on Pleasant Valley Road. and then right onto Cottontail Way.

MACE MEADOW GOLF & COUNTRY CLUB (semi-private, 18 holes, jack fleming 1972) . .

26570 Fairway Drive
Pioneer, CA 95666
(209) 295-7020
macemeadow.com

	YARDAGE	PAR	RATING	SLOPE	
FRONT	5387	72	70.0	114	**$3 - $29**
MIDDLE	6010	72	68.7	122	
BACK	6285	72	70.0	125	

WHAT TO EXPECT: This sporty combination of meadow course meets forest course is compressed into small acreage. Though rustically attractive, bring your hard hat because "balls are a-flying."

NOTES: This is a semi-private course, but 80 percent of play is by the public.

DIRECTIONS: From Jackson (about 25 miles east to the course): Follow Highway 88 east. Take the Meadow Drive exit to Fairway Drive.

COLD SPRINGS GOLF & COUNTRY CLUB (members only, 18 holes, bert stamps 1961) .

6500 Clubhouse Drive
Placerville, CA 95667
(530) 622-4567

	YARDAGE	PAR	RATING	SLOPE	
FRONT	5597	725	73.0	128	**$30 - $45**
MIDDLE	5638	72	67.9	115	
BACK	6158	72	70.0	120	

WHAT TO EXPECT: This is a tight, hilly course with lots of trees, small greens, and a creek running throughout. The course favors the player who can hit the ball left to right.

NOTES: Reciprocal play with other members only clubs is allowed.

DIRECTIONS: From Sacramento (about 40 miles east to the course): Take US 50 east to Placerville. Exit at Placerville Road and go over the overpass. Turn left on Cold Springs Road. Turn left at Richard Avenue. Richard turns into Clubhouse.

SIERRA GOLF COURSE (public, 9 holes) . . . .

1822 Country Club Drive
Placerville, CA 95667
(530) 622-0760
sierragolf.net

	YARDAGE	PAR	RATING	SLOPE	
FRONT	1528	31	58.6	92	**$9 - $14**
MIDDLE	-	-	-	-	
BACK	1674	31	55.4	89	

WHAT TO EXPECT: Sloping greens make this short tree-lined course more than just a nice stroll in the woods. Just remember the greens tend to break toward Raley's.

DIRECTIONS: From Sacramento (about 40 miles east to the course): Take US 50 east to Placerville. Exit Bedford and turn right. Turn left on Main Street and then right on Cedar Ravine. Turn left on Country Club Drive to the course.

RANCHO MURIETA COUNTRY CLUB (members only, 36 holes, stamps & palmer 1971) .

7000 Alameda Drive
Rancho Murieta, CA 95683
(916) 354-2400

	YARDAGE	PAR	RATING	SLOPE	
FRONT	5608	73	73.5	135	**$45 - $85**
MIDDLE	6335	72	70.3	130	
BACK	6840	72	72.6	136	

WHAT TO EXPECT: The North Course, which has hosted Senior PGA Tour events, is scenic, well-bunkered and treed with large greens. Out-of-bounds are ever present on a layout that is among the best in the Sacramento area. Housing has encroached on the South Course, detracting from its natural beauty; however, the best holes on either course may be found farthest from the clubhouse on the South Course. This is an entertaining alternate course.

NOTES: The yardage listed is for the North Course. Reciprocal play with other private clubs is allowed.

DIRECTIONS: From Sacramento (about 25 miles east to the course): Drive east on US 50 and take the Bradshaw exit south. Turn left on Jackson Road (Highway 16) to the club, which is on the left.

GREEN VALLEY OAKS (public, 18 holes, gene thorne 1996) . . . .

3000 Alexandrite Drive
Rescue, CA 95672
(530) 677-4653

	YARDAGE	PAR	RATING	SLOPE	
FRONT	4525	72	68.8	110	**$20 - $25**
MIDDLE	5797	72	69.5	126	
BACK	6179	72	-	-	

WHAT TO EXPECT: The front nine is narrow and level, with plenty of oaks and pines. The eighth hole is a 200-yard par-3 over a lake. The back nine is more open, rolling and has a links feel. A word of advice: if you are going to miss the greens, be short rather than long. To really score well, course knowledge is key.

DIRECTIONS: From Sacramento (about 25 miles east to the course): Take US 50 east to Bass Lake Road. Go north on Bass Lake Road, which turns into Alexandrite Drive, and runs into the course.

SUNSET WHITNEY COUNTRY CLUB (members only, 18 holes) . . . .

4201 Midas Avenue
Rocklin, CA 95677
(916) 624-2610
sunsetwhitney.com

	YARDAGE	PAR	RATING	SLOPE	
FRONT	5511	72	72.9	132	**$30 - $40**
MIDDLE	6222	72	70.2	125	
BACK	6618	72	72.9	129	

WHAT TO EXPECT: There is a decided home-course advantage for members. The front nine is demanding off the tee, with lots of trees. The back nine is more roomy. The greens on both sides are fairly large.

NOTES: Reciprocal play with other members only clubs is allowed.

DIRECTIONS: From Sacramento (about 25 miles east to the course): Drive east on I-80 to Rocklin. Take the Taylor Road exit north. Turn left on Midas Avenue and drive to the course.

WHITNEY OAKS GOLF CLUB (public, 18 holes, miller & bliss 1997) . . . .

2305 Clubhouse Drive
Rocklin, CA 95765
(916) 632-8333
troongolf.com

	YARDAGE	PAR	RATING	SLOPE	
FRONT	4980	71	70.0	125	**$45 - $65**
MIDDLE	6383	71	72.2	134	
BACK	6794	71	74.2	138	

WHAT TO EXPECT: This course's reputation as a difficult one is well founded. Ancient oaks, wetlands, granite outcroppings, water, and narrow hitting areas are all part of the challenge here.

OUR OPINION: Although there are plenty of tee choices, novice golfers will leave frustrated. Come to think about it, so will the low handicapper. – Frank

DIRECTIONS: From Sacramento (about 25 miles east to the course): Take I-80 east toward Rocklin to Highway 65 north. Take the first right on Stanford Ranch Road and go three and one-half miles. Turn right on Park Drive. Make a left on Whitney Oaks Drive and then the first right, onto Clubhouse Drive.

DIAMOND OAKS GOLF COURSE (public, 18 holes, ted robinson 1963) . . . .

349 Diamond Oaks Road
Roseville, CA 95678
(916) 783-4947
golfroseville.com

	YARDAGE	PAR	RATING	SLOPE	
FRONT	5481	72	71.5	119	**$8 - $23**
MIDDLE	5885	72	67.8	115	
BACK	6179	73	69.1	118	

WHAT TO EXPECT: Diamond Oaks features rolling fairways with plenty of oak trees. The course is not punishing, but the trees can make club selection interesting. The course is very popular, so a quick afternoon round is not going to happen. For the amount of play Diamond Oaks sees, the course is usually in good condition.

DIRECTIONS: From Sacramento (about 20 miles east to the course): Take I-80 east to Highway 65 and go north toward Marysville. Take the Stanford Ranch/Galleria exit. Follow Galleria to Roseville Parkway. Make a right on Roseville Parkway and then a left on Reserve. Take a right on Diamond Oaks Road to the course.

ROSEVILLE ROLLING GREENS GOLF CLUB (public, 9 holes) . . . .

5572 Eureka Road
Roseville, CA 95746
(916) 797-9986

	YARDAGE	PAR	RATING	SLOPE	
FRONT	1530	29	56.6	92	**$9 - $15**
MIDDLE	-	-	-	-	
BACK	1530	27	56.6	84	

WHAT TO EXPECT: This short course has a little bit of everything, including rolling fairways, trees, a few traps, a creek, and two lakes. The wind can affect play.

DIRECTIONS: From Sacramento (about 20 miles northeast to the course): Take I-80 east, exit at Douglas Street and turn right. Make another right on Sierra College Boulevard and then a left on Eureka Road.

SIERRA VIEW COUNTRY CLUB (members only, 18 holes, jack fleming 1953) . . . .

105 Alta Vista Drive
Roseville, CA 95678
(916) 783-4600

	YARDAGE	PAR	RATING	SLOPE
FRONT	5168	72	64.6	105
MIDDLE	5936	72	68.0	113
BACK	6482	72	70.5	120

$35 - $75

WHAT TO EXPECT: This is a thinking person's course with rolling terrain, lots of trees, doglegs and elevated tees and greens. To score well at Sierra View, you will need to have a deft touch on these small, crowned greens with subtle breaks.

NOTES: Reciprocal play with other members only clubs is allowed.

DIRECTIONS: From Sacramento (about 20 miles east to the course): Drive east on I-80 to Roseville and get off at Atlantic/Eureka Road. exit. Take Atlantic to Yosemite Street and turn right. Follow to Alta Vista Drive and turn left. The entrance to the course is on the right.

SUN CITY GOLF CLUB (semi-private, 27 holes, greg nash/billy casper 1995) . . . .

7050 Del Webb Boulevard
Roseville, CA 95747
(916) 774-3850

	YARDAGE	PAR	RATING	SLOPE
FRONT	5182	72	70.4	119
MIDDLE	6007	71	68.7	118
BACK	6384	72	70.5	123

$45 - $50

WHAT TO EXPECT: The Lakes nine is open and plays among the homes. The Oaks nine is far more scenic and entertaining, as it veers away from the housing, back into the trees. The Sierra Pines Course is similiar to the Lakes Course.

NOTES: The yardage listed is for the Lake/Oak combination.

DIRECTIONS: From Sacramento (about 20 miles northeast to the course): Take I-80 east to Highway 65 north toward Lincoln/Marysville. Take the Blue Oaks exit and head west. Turn left on Del Webb Boulevard to the club.

WOODCREEK GOLF CLUB (municipal, 18 holes, robert muir graves 1995) . . . .

5880 Woodcreek Oaks Boulevard
Roseville, CA 95747
(916) 771-4653
golfroseville.com

	YARDAGE	PAR	RATING	SLOPE
FRONT	4739	70	66.2	112
MIDDLE	6043	72	70.2	123
BACK	6518	72	71.8	132

$25 - $40

WHAT TO EXPECT: At only 6,500 yards, this sprawling course is dominated by mature oaks and natural wetlands. Busy and tough, Woodcreek in some respects looks like a country club and can feel like a muni.

DIRECTIONS: From Sacramento (about 20 miles northeast to the course): Take I-80 east to Highway 65 north. Then take Blue Oaks west. Turn left on Woodcreek Oaks Boulevard to the course.

BARTLEY CAVANAUGH GOLF COURSE (public, 18 holes, perry dye 1994) . . . .

8301 Freeport Boulevard
Sacramento, CA 95832
(916) 665-2020
americangolf.com

	YARDAGE	PAR	RATING	SLOPE
FRONT	4714	71	66.3	107
MIDDLE	5734	71	67.3	113
BACK	6118	71	69.0	116

$10 - $25

WHAT TO EXPECT: This course is speed-bump city, as numerous berms separates the holes from each other. Nevertheless, bring your hard hat as the holes are dangerously close to one another.
DIRECTIONS: From within Sacramento: Off I-5, exit at Pocket Road and head east. Make a right on Freeport Boulevard and drive two miles to the course.

BING MALONEY GOLF COURSE (public, 27 holes, mac macdonald 1952) . . . .

6801 Freeport Boulevard
Sacramento, CA 95822
(916) 433-2283

	YARDAGE	PAR	RATING	SLOPE
FRONT	5839	72	67.5	114
MIDDLE	6292	72	70.0	119
BACK	6658	72	70.7	120

$13 - $25

WHAT TO EXPECT: This is your typical older municipal course with flat greens and fairways outlined by mature trees.
OUR OPINION: This is one of the few courses that offer separate tee boxes for juniors. We hope more people take up this cause. – Shaw
NOTES: There is an 18-hole Championship Course and a nine-hole Executive Course.
DIRECTIONS: From within Sacramento: Off I-5, exit at Florin Road and head east. Turn left on Freeport Boulevard. The course is on the right.

BRADSHAW RANCH GOLF COURSE (public, 9 holes) . . . .

7350 Bradshaw Road
Sacramento, CA 95829
(916) 363-6549

	YARDAGE	PAR	RATING	SLOPE
FRONT	-	-	-	-
MIDDLE	-	-	-	-
BACK	1096	27	-	-

$6 - $9

WHAT TO EXPECT: Bradshaw Ranch is a well-maintained short course that has increased its challenge by adding several new traps and mature trees. Players must also negotiate over two lakes.
DIRECTIONS: From within Sacramento: Off Highway 99, exit at Florin Road and drive east. Turn right on Bradshaw Road.

CAMPUS COMMONS GOLF COURSE (public, 9 holes, bill mcdowell 1972) . . . .

Two Cadillac Drive
Sacramento, CA 95825
(916) 922-5861

	YARDAGE	PAR	RATING	SLOPE
FRONT	1508	29	54.3	83
MIDDLE	-	-	-	-
BACK	1673	29	56.7	84

$8 - $10

WHAT TO EXPECT: This is a favorite among beginners and juniors. The course is slightly rolling with scattered trees. For the most part, the course big fairways. However, the American River does come into play on a few holes.
DIRECTIONS: From within Sacramento: Off US 50, take the Howe Avenue exit north. Make a left on Fair Oaks Boulevard then a right on Cadillac Drive.

CHAMPIONS GOLF LINKS (public, 9 holes, richard bigler 1996) . . . .

8915 Gerber Road
Sacramento, CA 95828
(916) 688-9120
championsgolf.com

	YARDAGE	PAR	RATING	SLOPE	
FRONT	1274	30	57.8	92	**$9 - $15**
MIDDLE	1660	30	58.6	94	
BACK	1946	30	59.1	94	

WHAT TO EXPECT: The layout is wide enough and short enough to accommodate players new to the game. In addition, with four lakes, two tiered greens, and plenty of trees, even lower handicaps will be entertained.

OUR OPINION: This is a well-crafted neigbhorhood practice center and golf course. – Shaw

DIRECTIONS: From within Sacramento: Off Highway 99, exit at Florin Road and head east. Turn right on Elk Grove-Florin Road for approximately one mile. The course is at the corner of Elk Grove and Gerber Road.

CORDOVA GOLF COURSE (public, 18 holes) . . . .

9425 Jackson Road
Sacramento, CA 95826
(916) 362-1196
crpd.com

	YARDAGE	PAR	RATING	SLOPE	
FRONT	4728	66	64.9	96	**$9 - $12**
MIDDLE	-	-	-	-	
BACK	4776	63	61.9	92	

WHAT TO EXPECT: This course is short in total yardage but is large in challenge. Cordova is flat and features relatively short par 4s, one par-5 and seven par 3s. The difficulty lies in the par 3s, where seven of the ten range from 170 yards to over 200 yards.

OUR OPINION: The only thing harder than playing this course might be getting on. This is a popular facility with the locals. – Bob

DIRECTIONS: From within Sacramento: Off US 50, take the Bradshaw exit and head south to Jackson Road. Make a left on Jackson Road. The golf course is on the right.

DEL PASO COUNTRY CLUB (members only, 18 holes, herbert fowler 1916) . . . .

3333 Marconi Avenue
Sacramento, CA 95821
(916) 483-0401

	YARDAGE	PAR	RATING	SLOPE	
FRONT	5828	74	73.8	129	**$50 - $85**
MIDDLE	-	-	-	-	
BACK	6323	72	70.6	122	

WHAT TO EXPECT: One of the area's oldest layouts, it is a traditional park-setting layout with small, well-bunkered greens.

NOTES: Reciprocal play with other members only clubs is allowed.

DIRECTIONS: From within Sacramento: Off I-80, take the Watt Avenue exit and head south. Turn right on Marconi Avenue to the course.

HAGGIN OAKS GOLF COMPLEX (municipal, 36 holes, alister mackenzie 1932) . . . .

3645 Fulton Avenue
Sacramento, CA 95821
(916) 481-4653
hagginoaks.com

	YARDAGE	PAR	RATING	SLOPE
FRONT	5786	72	71.1	111
MIDDLE	6552	72	69.9	110
BACK	6889	72	71.2	114

$18 - $35

WHAT TO EXPECT: The Mackenzie Course is the stronger of the two courses, and features a traditional tree-lined layout on flat terrain. It has recently been renovated to regain its luster; it once hosted the PGA Tour back in the late 1930s. The Arcade Course is a "grip-and-rip it" course that can boost your self-esteem.

OUR OPINION: This is a busy, well run complex. The earlier you can get out, the better. – Bob

NOTES: The yardage listed is for the Arcade Course.

DIRECTIONS: From within Sacramento: Off Business I-80, exit at Fulton Avenue. Follow Fulton Avenue north to the course.

SWALLOWS NEST GOLF COURSE (members only, 9 holes) . . . .

2245 Orchard Lane
Sacramento, CA 95833
(916) 927-6481

	YARDAGE	PAR	RATING	SLOPE
FRONT	1484	30	55.8	83
MIDDLE	-	-	-	-
BACK	1484	30	53.2	82

$5 - $5

WHAT TO EXPECT: This is a short executive course that is part of a residential community.

NOTES: There is no proshop phone number. The number listed is for the residential management group.

DIRECTIONS: From within Sacramento: Off Highway 99, take the El Camino exit and head west. Make a left on Orchard Lane to the course.

TEAL BEND GOLF CLUB (public, 18 holes, brad bell 1997) . . . .

7200 Garden Highway
Sacramento, CA 95837
(916) 922-5209
clubcorpgolf.com

	YARDAGE	PAR	RATING	SLOPE
FRONT	5077	72	68.8	112
MIDDLE	6532	72	71.7	129
BACK	7000	72	73.9	134

$28 - $55

WHAT TO EXPECT: With open greens that permit run-up shots, this course is a rarity among new facilities. Wetlands require accuracy off the tee, and the course can be stretched for the longer hitters.

DIRECTIONS: From within Sacramento: Off Highway 99, take Elverta Road west. Turn left on Garden Highway. The course is on the left.

WILDHAWK GOLF CLUB (public, 18 holes, j. michael poellot 1997) . . . .

7713 Vineyard Road
Sacramento, CA 95829
(916) 688-4653
wildhawkgolf.com

	YARDAGE	PAR	RATING	SLOPE	
FRONT	4847	72	67.2	109	**$20 - $49**
MIDDLE	6260	72	69.7	118	
BACK	6695	72	71.2	124	

WHAT TO EXPECT: Wildhawk offers plenty of mounding and ample opportunity to break out your driver. Beware of the creek and the bunkers, they definitely come into play.
OUR OPINION: This fun course is still maturing and should get even better with age. – Shaw
DIRECTIONS: From within Sacramento: Off US 50, take the Bradshaw Road exit. Follow Bradshaw south to Gerber Road. Make a left on Gerbar and a right on Vineyard.

WILLIAM LAND PARK GOLF COURSE (public, 9 holes, william lock 1924) . . . .

1701 Sutterville Road
Sacramento, CA 95822
(916) 277-1207

	YARDAGE	PAR	RATING	SLOPE	
FRONT	2579	34	68.4	106	**$9 - $10**
MIDDLE	-	-	-	-	
BACK	2599	34	63.4	102	

WHAT TO EXPECT: This is a busy executive course located in William Land Park with four par 4s and one par-5, with the rest being par 3s.
DIRECTIONS: From within Sacramento: Off I-5, take the Sutterville exit and head east to course.

MOUNTAIN SPRINGS GOLF CLUB (public, 18 holes, robert muir graves 1990) . . . . . .

17566 Lime Kiln Road
Sonora, CA 95370
(209) 532-1000
mountainspringsgolf.com

	YARDAGE	PAR	RATING	SLOPE	
FRONT	5084	72	70.2	120	**$25 - $36**
MIDDLE	6149	72	70.3	128	
BACK	6529	72	72.1	131	

WHAT TO EXPECT: This hilly layout has six lakes that come into play on seven holes. The fairways are broad, except for some well-placed sand traps. Maturing trees will eventually tighten things up. Enjoy the mountain vistas.
DIRECTIONS: From Modesto (about 50 miles northeast to the course): Take Highway 99 north then go east on Highway 120. From Highway 120, take Highway 108 toward Sonora. Make a right on Lime Kiln Road and drive two miles to the entrance.

PHOENIX LAKE GOLF COURSE (public, 9 holes, bert stamps 1968) . . . .

21448 Paseo de los Portales
Sonora, CA 95370
(209) 532-0111

	YARDAGE	PAR	RATING	SLOPE	
FRONT	2373	35	65.8	114	**$9 - $17**
MIDDLE	2702	35	66.4	115	
BACK	2711	35	67.0	116	

WHAT TO EXPECT: The longest hole on the course is a 437-yard par 5, but that doesn't mean Phoenix Lake is easy. Hitting your driver off the tee can be risky because the course is surrounded by trees and a creek runs through one-third of of the holes.
DIRECTIONS: From within Sonora: Off Highway 108, take Phoenix Lake Road north. The course is on the left.

SOUTHRIDGE GOLF COURSE (public, 18 holes, cal olson 1991) . . . .

9413 South Butte Road
Sutter, CA 95982
(530) 755-4653
southridge.com

	YARDAGE	PAR	RATING	SLOPE
FRONT	5541	72	71.3	122
MIDDLE	6611	72	71.6	126
BACK	7047	72	73.7	130

$14 - $29

WHAT TO EXPECT: This is two distinct golf courses in one. The front nine is a links-style course with plenty of water. The back nine is a punishing mountain course, with steep hills and narrow landing areas.

DIRECTIONS: From Yuba City (about 14 miles west to the course): Off Highway 99, take Highway 20 west. After Acacia and two big warehouses, turn right on Southridge. When this dead-ends, turn right on South Butte Road. The course entrance is on the left.

TWAIN HARTE GOLF CLUB (public, 9 holes, bob baldock 1961) . . . .

22909 Meadow Lane
Twain Harte, CA 95383
(209) 586-3131

	YARDAGE	PAR	RATING	SLOPE
FRONT	1674	32	58.7	95
MIDDLE	1674	29	58.1	89
BACK	1717	29	58.4	90

$9 - $18

WHAT TO EXPECT: This is a rolling, but easily walkable course, with narrow fairways and greens varying in size from small to large. Keep it straight or you will encounter one of the hundreds of trees that line the fairways. Water comes into play on a few holes.

DIRECTIONS: From Sonora (about ten miles northeast to the course): Take Highway 108 east. Take the Lower Twain Harte Drive exit into the town of Twain Harte. Turn left at the 7-11, right before the arch. Take the next left on Meadow Lane, and the parking lot is at the end of the road.

LA CONTENTA GOLF CLUB (semi-private, 18 holes, richard bigler 1973) . . . .

1653 Highway 26
Valley Springs, CA 95252
(209) 772-1081
empiregolf.com

	YARDAGE	PAR	RATING	SLOPE
FRONT	5203	71	70.2	125
MIDDLE	5749	71	68.5	130
BACK	6103	71	70.1	133

$21 - $33

WHAT TO EXPECT: Blind shots, narrow fairways, hills, small greens, uneven lies, out-of-bounds and lateral water hazards are just some of the things you will encounter at La Contenta. Somehow they have crafted all of the above into a challenging but fun course.

OUR OPINION: Off the beaten path, recent renovations and economical fees make this hilly layout worth playing. – Bob

DIRECTIONS: From Stockton (abut 30 miles northeast to the course): Off Highway 99, drive east on Highway 26 to Valley Springs.

LIGHTHOUSE GOLF COURSE (public, 18 holes, bert stamps 1990) . . . .

500 Douglas Street
West Sacramento, CA 95605
(916) 372-4949
lighthousegc.com

	YARDAGE	PAR	RATING	SLOPE	
FRONT	4521	70	65.6	116	**$11 - $27**
MIDDLE	5108	70	66.4	113	
BACK	5309	70	67.3	115	

WHAT TO EXPECT: With water affecting 13 holes, there should be a lighthouse here. The course is well treed, and accuracy off the tee is at a premium on this relatively short course. If you are looking for a place to play in the rainy season, Lighthouse is known as a course with excellent drainage.

DIRECTIONS: From within Sacramento: Take the Jefferson Boulevard exit north off I-80 Business Loop. Turn right on Sacramento Avenue and then a left on Douglas Street.

YOLO FLIERS COUNTRY CLUB (members only, 18 holes, baldock & mcdonagh 1950) . .

17980 Country Road 94B
Woodland, CA 95695
(530) 662-8050
yolofliers.com

	YARDAGE	PAR	RATING	SLOPE	
FRONT	5200	70	69.1	115	**$30 - $55**
MIDDLE	6459	72	70.2	118	
BACK	6783	72	71.7	121	

WHAT TO EXPECT: This flat, tree-lined layout, adjacent to an airport with the same name, is a fun, well-maintained and sporty layout.

NOTES: Reciprocal play with other members only clubs is allowed.

DIRECTIONS: From Sacramento (about 20 miles northeast to the course): Go north on I-5 and take the second Woodland exit, Main Street. Head west through town. Keep straight, and there are signs to the club.

MALLARD LAKE GOLF COURSE (public, 9 holes) . . . .

4238 South Highway 99
Yuba City, CA 95991
(530) 674-0475

	YARDAGE	PAR	RATING	SLOPE	
FRONT	2402	34	68.6	118	**$9 - $16**
MIDDLE	2600	34	65.4	117	
BACK	2694	34	66.2	119	

WHAT TO EXPECT: With water on every hole, there areplenty of places for mallards to land. Besides lots of water, you will find the course spacious and flat.

DIRECTIONS: From Sacramento (about 40 miles north to the course): Take Highway 99 north toward Yuba City. The course is on the right. If you reach Barry Road, you've gone too far north.

North Coast

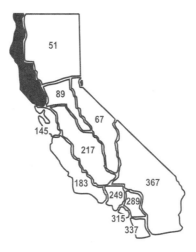

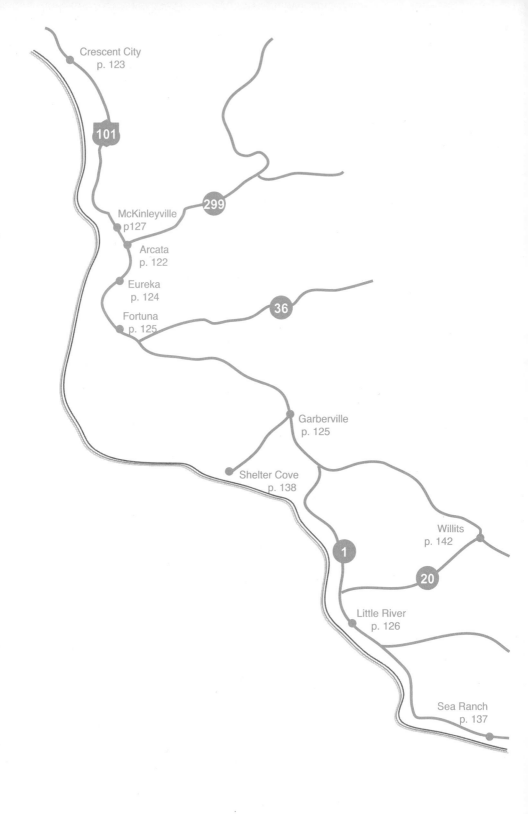

Crescent City
p. 123

101

299

McKinleyville
p127

Arcata
p. 122

Eureka
p. 124

Fortuna
p. 125

36

Garberville
p. 125

Shelter Cove
p. 138

1

Willits
p. 142

20

Little River
p. 126

Sea Ranch
p. 137

Map not to scale

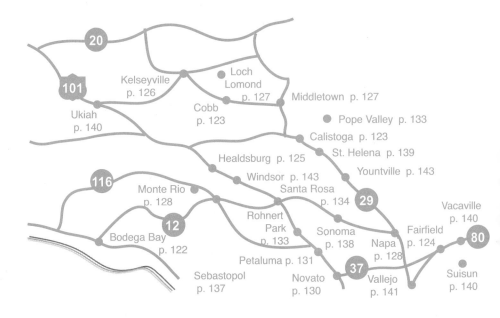

BAYWOOD GOLF & COUNTRY CLUB (members only, 18 holes, bob baldock 1958) . . . . .

3600 Buttermilk Lane
Arcata, CA 95521
(707) 822-3688

	YARDAGE	PAR	RATING	SLOPE
FRONT	5427	74	67.9	115
MIDDLE	5757	72	70.4	123
BACK	6150	72	71.6	125

$35 - $60

WHAT TO EXPECT: Near the coast and set among redwood trees, this is a scenic course that will test even the most capable golfer. Because of the dense air and fog, the ball will not carry as far as you think. Water comes into play on one-third of the holes. In general the course is tight, but the back nine fairways are especially slim, with trees protecting both sides.

NOTES: Reciprocal play with other members only clubs is allowed.

DIRECTIONS: From Eureka (about eight miles north to the course): Take US 101 north, exit at Sunny Brae, and turn right (east). At the second roundabout, Buttermilk Lane, follow it to the left, and the course.

BODEGA HARBOUR GOLF LINKS (semi-private, 18 holes, robert trent jones jr. 1977) .

21301 Heron Drive
Bodega Bay, CA 94923
(707) 875-3538
bodegaharbourgolf.com

	YARDAGE	PAR	RATING	SLOPE
FRONT	4749	71	67.7	123
MIDDLE	5685	70	69.3	125
BACK	6266	70	72.4	134

$40 - $90

WHAT TO EXPECT: The course is bipolar. The front nine is a demanding, hilly, links-style course with few flat lies. The back nine is more open off the tee, with subtle elevation changes. The course is well manicured, with spectacular ocean views, tricky greens and a coastal breeze.

OUR OPINION: This should be on everyone's must-play list. The last three holes are spectacular. However, on the front side, you can be penalized for hitting a good shot. Walking (climbing) the front nine is nearly impossible. The back side is just the opposite. You will either love or hate this course. Our prediction is that if you play it during the week, you will love Bodega, but if you pay $90 on the weekend, you will hate it. – Frank

NOTES: The course does not offer a driving range, but allows players to hit into nets.

DIRECTIONS: From San Francisco (about 65 miles northwest to the course): Take US 101 north to Petaluma. Exit at East Washington Street and head west toward Valley Ford, Bodega Bay and Highway 1. Go north on Highway 1. Make a left on South Harbor Way and then a right on Heron Drive. Drive time is about 30 minutes from Petaluma.

MOUNT ST. HELENA GOLF COURSE (public, 9 holes) . . . .

2025 Grant Street
Calistoga, CA 94515
(707) 942-9966

	YARDAGE	PAR	RATING	SLOPE
FRONT	2647	35	69.1	113
MIDDLE	-	-	-	-
BACK	2759	34	66.5	105

$11 - $20

WHAT TO EXPECT: This is a short, flat course set in the middle of the the Napa County Fairgrounds.
DIRECTIONS: From Napa (about 30 miles north to the course): Take Highway 29 to Calistoga. Turn right at Lincoln Avenue. Turn left on Stephenson, and then left again on Grant Street.

COBB MEADOWS GOLF COURSE (public, 9 holes, norman wren 1954) . . . .

10200 Golf Road
Cobb, CA 95426
(707) 928-5276

	YARDAGE	PAR	RATING	SLOPE
FRONT	2262	34	62.2	107
MIDDLE	-	-	-	-
BACK	2319	33	61.2	109

$10 - $22

WHAT TO EXPECT: This is a user-friendly layout with an alpine setting, situated 3,000 feet above sea level. The course has decent-sized fairways, but miss them, and you will find yourself in the trees, or worse yet, out-of-bounds. There is a creek running throughout and the greens are small.
NOTES: This course was formerly known as Hoberg's Forest Lake Golf & Country Club.
DIRECTIONS: From Napa (about 70 miles north to the course): Drive north on Highway 29 to Highway 175. Take Highway 175 north to Cobb. Golf Road is on the right.

DEL NORTE GOLF COURSE (public, 9 holes) . . . .

130 Club Drive
Crescent City, CA 95531
(707) 458-3214

	YARDAGE	PAR	RATING	SLOPE
FRONT	2996	36	71.8	122
MIDDLE	-	-	-	-
BACK	3121	35	67.4	114

$12 - $18

WHAT TO EXPECT: The course has several doglegs lined with redwood trees, but all in all, the fairways are fairly broad. A creek comes into play on two holes. The greens tend to break toward the clubhouse.
DIRECTIONS: From within Crescent City: Off US 101, take Highway 199 east. After the bridge, turn left on Highway 197. Club Drive and the course are on the right.

KINGS VALLEY GOLF COURSE (public, 9 holes) . . . .

3030 Lesina Road
Crescent City, CA 95531
(707) 464-2886

	YARDAGE	PAR	RATING	SLOPE
FRONT	1197	28	54.1	-
MIDDLE	-	-	-	-
BACK	1259	28	55.8	-

$7 - $11

WHAT TO EXPECT: This is a straightforward, flat, wide-open course. The greens are slightly crowned, and out-of-bounds comes into play on four holes.
DIRECTIONS: From within Crescent City: Off US 101, take Highway 199 east. Turn left on Kings Valley Road, and the left again on Lesina Road.

EUREKA GOLF LLC (municipal, 18 holes, bob baldock 1959) . . . .

4750 Fairway Drive
Eureka, CA 95503
(707) 443-4808

	YARDAGE	PAR	RATING	SLOPE
FRONT	5313	71	69.8	117
MIDDLE	5521	70	67.0	115
BACK	5713	70	68.0	117

$8 - $16

WHAT TO EXPECT: The course has magnificent coastal redwoods and Douglas firs throughout, but don't be afraid to hit your driver off the tee. The course offers ample room on most fairways. Because of the damp climate, the ball tends not to carry, so be careful not to under-club.

DIRECTIONS: From within Eureka: Off US 101, take the Herrick exit east. Drive to the course, which is on the left.

PARADISE VALLEY GOLF COURSE (public, 18 holes, robert muir graves 1993) . . . .

3950 Paradise Valley Drive
Fairfield, CA 94533
(707) 426-1600
paradisevalleygc.com

	YARDAGE	PAR	RATING	SLOPE
FRONT	5413	72	71.1	119
MIDDLE	6704	72	72.7	124
BACK	6993	72	73.9	129

$32 - $45

WHAT TO EXPECT: This is a level course where the wind can create a severe challenge. Although you will find water on half the holes, don't be afraid to use your driver. The greens have been designed to help receive the ball, rather than punish it.

OUR OPINION: An excellent value and a fun course, but what's up with the tenth hole? They must have run out of room. You have to hit a five iron, seven iron, and a wedge to the par 5. – Frank

NOTES: This course is known for its excellent drainage and has become a favorite in the winter months.

DIRECTIONS: From Vallejo (about 19 miles east to the course): Drive east on I-80 to Fairfield. Take the North Texas Street exit and turn right. Turn left on Dixon Hill Road and turn left again on Dover Street. Follow Dover Street a short distance to the course.

RANCHO SOLANO GOLF COURSE (public, 18 holes, gary roger baird 1990) . . . .

3250 Rancho Solano Parkway
Fairfield, CA 94533
(707) 429-4653
ranchosolanoclub.com

	YARDAGE	PAR	RATING	SLOPE
FRONT	5260	72	69.6	117
MIDDLE	6152	72	69.7	122
BACK	6638	72	72.1	128

$19 - $43

WHAT TO EXPECT: This course is the measuring stick for all courses that claim to have large greens. While most golfers complain about three putts, at Rancho Solano they complain about four putts and more. The rest of the course is dominated by rolling hills, five lakes, plenty of native oaks, and many bunkers.

OUR OPINION: All in all, the course is a good value but uninspiring. – Val

DIRECTIONS: From Vallejo (about 20 miles east to the course): Take I-80 east, exit at Waterman Boulevard, and head west for a couple of miles. Go right on Rancho Solano Parkway to the course.

REDWOOD EMPIRE GOLF & COUNTRY CLUB (members only, 18 holes, fred bliss 2000) .

352 Country Club Drive
Fortuna, CA 95540
(707) 725-5194

	YARDAGE	PAR	RATING	SLOPE
FRONT	5145	72	70.3	121
MIDDLE	5820	72	67.9	122
BACK	6129	72	69.2	125

$20 - $25

WHAT TO EXPECT: Forget about overpowering this short course. You have much more to worry about. The course is set on a ridge and surrounded by trees. The fairways are undulating, leaving golfers with squirrelly lies if they are not careful. The greens are the fastest in the county, and after midmorning, you will be contending with wind. Beware of holes 13 through 15 – they pose an extreme challenge.

NOTES: Reciprocal play with other members only clubs is allowed.

DIRECTIONS: From Eureka (about 20 miles south to the course): Drive south on US 101 to Fortuna. Take the Kenmar Road exit. Go east to Fortuna Boulevard/Mill Street and turn right. Stay to the right when the road forks, which then dead-ends at the course.

BENBOW VALLEY RV RESORT & GOLF COURSE (public, 9 holes) . . . .

7000 Benbow Drive
Garberville, CA 95542
(707) 923-2777
benbowrv.com

	YARDAGE	PAR	RATING	SLOPE
FRONT	2482	35	69.0	114
MIDDLE	2638	35	65.5	103
BACK	2674	35	65.8	103

$14 - $20

WHAT TO EXPECT: None of the fairways run side-by-side on this narrow, tree-lined, rolling golf course. The combination of trees, hazards, and homes make this course extremely unforgiving. A driver off the tee is not a wise choice on many of the holes.

DIRECTIONS: From Ukiah (about 90 miles north to the course): Head north on US 101, through Willits. Do not take the first Benbow Drive exit in Richardson Grove. Take the second Benbow Drive exit and turn right. Follow the signs for Benbow Lake Recreation Area.

HEALDSBURG TAYMAN PARK GOLF COURSE (public, 9 holes, w. h. tayman 1921) . . . .

927 South Fitch Mountain Road
Healdsburg, CA 95448
(707) 433-4275
taymanparkgolf.com

	YARDAGE	PAR	RATING	SLOPE
FRONT	2347	35	69.9	121
MIDDLE	2544	35	-	-
BACK	2615	34	66.4	118

$10 - $18

WHAT TO EXPECT: When this course was built, the term "moving earth" had not been coined. Courses were built on the natural terrain, and the terrain at Tayman Park is hilly. The course features postage-stamp-sized greens with plenty of trees and a few hazards.

OUR OPINION: Recent improvements have made this course much more playable. Tayman Park is worth a second look if you haven't played here in the last few years. – Frank

DIRECTIONS: From Santa Rosa (about 15 miles north to the course): Go north on US 101. Use the Central Healdsburg exit, which becomes Healdsburg Avenue. Turn right on Matheson. Matheson turns into Fitch Mountain Road. Follow this to the course, which is on the left.

BUCKINGHAM GOLF & COUNTRY CLUB (semi-private, 9 holes, james young 1960) . . .

2855 Eastlake Drive
Kelseyville, CA 95451
(707) 279-4863

	YARDAGE	PAR	RATING	SLOPE	
FRONT	2778	36	71.9	126	**$16 - $28**
MIDDLE	2932	36	69.2	121	
BACK	3021	36	70.0	122	

WHAT TO EXPECT: This is a short, level course that wraps counterclockwise around a small lake. Although not difficult, it's a fun course for someone who wants to play a quick nine holes.

DIRECTIONS: From Napa (about 80 miles north to the course): Take Highway 29 north to Lower Lake. Make a left (still on Highway 29) and drive seven miles to Soda Bay. Turn right on Soda Bay Road and drive one mile past Konocti Harbor Resort. The entrance is on the left.

CLEAR LAKE RIVIERA GOLF CLUB (public, 9 holes, ed defelice 1965) . . . .

10200 Fairway Drive
Kelseyville, CA 95451
(707) 277-7129

	YARDAGE	PAR	RATING	SLOPE	
FRONT	2563	36	69.9	125	**$16 - $22**
MIDDLE	-	-	-	-	
BACK	2910	35	67.3	122	

WHAT TO EXPECT: Put away the driver on this very hilly course, which is lined by houses. This creates plenty of out-of-bounds, but also creates separation between the holes. The greens are good sized and elevated. The views of Clear Lake are spectacular.

DIRECTIONS: From Napa (about 80 miles north to the course): Take Highway 29 north through Middletown to Lower Lake. Make a left (still on Highway 29) and drive seven miles to Soda Bay. Turn right on Soda Bay Road to Fairway Drive.

LITTLE RIVER INN GOLF CLUB (resort, 9 holes, ole hervilla 1957) . . . .

7901 North Highway 1
Little River, CA 95456
(707) 937-5667
littleriverinn.com

	YARDAGE	PAR	RATING	SLOPE	
FRONT	2712	35	67.8	120	**$20 - $35**
MIDDLE	2746	36	67.8	122	
BACK	5020	70	68.6	121	

WHAT TO EXPECT: This is a charming, hilly course with tight fairways lined by firs and redwoods. There are excellent ocean views from three of the holes. For a coastal course, you will notice little wind. The course actually has 11 greens that can be used to create an 18-hole layout.

OUR OPINION: This course is off the beaten path but a great place to sneak in some golf on your romantic getaway. With a reasonable price, you can't do much better. – Shaw

NOTES: Wildlife is everywhere. Don't be surprised if you see some wild turkeys roaming the course.

DIRECTIONS: From Santa Rosa (about 95 miles northwest to the course): Head north on US 101 to Cloverdale. Take Highway 128 west to cut over to Highway 1. Drive north on Highway 1 toward Mendocino. Another option is to just head north on Highway 1 from anywhere in Marin or Sonoma counties for a beautiful, but long, drive.

ADAMS SPRINGS GOLF COURSE (public, 9 holes, jack fleming 1962) . . . .

14347 Snead Court at Highway 175
Loch Lomond, CA 95426
(707) 928-9992

	YARDAGE	PAR	RATING	SLOPE
FRONT	2499	34	68.1	119
MIDDLE	-	-	-	-
BACK	2630	34	65.8	117

$10 - $20

WHAT TO EXPECT: This is a driver-friendly golf course with three lakes. Beware of the first hole – it is the hardest – a par 4 dogleg with a blind second shot.
DIRECTIONS: From Napa (about 72 miles north to the course): Take Highway 29 north to Middletown. Then go west on Highway 175. The course is just south of Loch Lomond.

BEAU PRE GOLF CLUB (semi-private, 18 holes, don harling 1967) . . . .

1777 Norton Road
McKinleyville, CA 95519
(707) 839-2342
beaupregc.com

	YARDAGE	PAR	RATING	SLOPE
FRONT	4869	72	68.4	122
MIDDLE	5328	71	66.8	111
BACK	5824	71	69.0	118

$7 - $30

WHAT TO EXPECT: Beau Pre combines mountainous hills with meadow golf, and most of the fairways are surrounded by tall trees. Although the course offers magnificent views of the ocean, you don't have to worry about hitting it into the Pacific. You do have to avoid the water that is found on half the holes. If you haven't guessed by now, the course requires precision on every shot.
DIRECTIONS: From Eureka (about 15 miles north to the course): Take US 101 north toward McKinleyville. Then exit onto Murray Road. Drive north on Central Avenue. The course is on Norton Road.

HIDDEN VALLEY LAKE COUNTRY CLUB (semi-private, 18 holes, billy bell, jr. 1970) . .

19210 Hartman Road
Middletown, CA 95461
(707) 987-3035
hiddenvalleylakegc.com

	YARDAGE	PAR	RATING	SLOPE
FRONT	5546	74	72.4	126
MIDDLE	6292	72	70.6	122
BACK	6667	72	72.5	124

$27 - $48

WHAT TO EXPECT: In Hollywood, they would describe Hidden Valley as Meadow Course meets Mountain Course. The front nine is open and flat, while the back nine is narrow and steep. On the 15th hole, you will find yourself 200 feet above the fairway. If you aim for the corner of the pool and hit a fade, you will be within 150 yards of the green.
DIRECTIONS: From Napa (about 40 miles north to the course): Take Highway 29 north, five miles past Middletown. The entrance to the course is on the right.

NORTHWOOD GOLF CLUB (public, 9 holes, alister mackenzie 1928) . . . .

19400 Highway 116
Monte Rio, CA 95462
(707) 865-1116
northwoodgolf.com

	YARDAGE	PAR	RATING	SLOPE
FRONT	2780	36	72.2	127
MIDDLE	-	-	-	-
BACK	2858	36	67.7	113

$16 - $37

WHAT TO EXPECT: Redwoods frame nearly every hole on this historic, Alister Mackenzie layout. Besides narrow fairways, you will encounter small greens, many of which have false fronts. Don't judge this course by what you see on the scorecard. Northwood does not give up low scores without some great shot-making.

OUR OPINION: It's not as easy as it looks. Did you know redwood trees make little sound when your ball hits them? If you love old-style courses and spectacular redwood trees, this is a must-play. – Brad

DIRECTIONS: From Santa Rosa (about 20 miles west to the course): Off US 101, at the north end of Santa Rosa, take the River Road exit. Head west on River Road to Highway 116 west, in Guerneville. The course is a couple of miles west of town, on Highway 116/River Road.

CHARDONNAY GOLF CLUB (public/private, 37 holes, jack barry) . . . .

2555 Jameson Canyon Road
Napa, CA 94558
(707) 257-1900
chardonnaygolfclub.com

	YARDAGE	PAR	RATING	SLOPE
FRONT	5223	72	70.7	124
MIDDLE	6450	72	72.1	126
BACK	6817	72	73.8	129

$45 - $130

WHAT TO EXPECT: The Vineyards Course uses the natural terrain, working vineyards, creeks, barrancas, and wind to create a substantial challenge. The course is distinguished with some of the quirkiest-shaped greens in existence. Club Shakespeare (the private club) has more of a country club feel, but also uses working vineyards. The challenge is compounded with many water hazards and deceptive greens.

OUR OPINION: Chardonnay is an excellent destination course. It is easy to get to from the Bay Area, Sacramento, and the Wine Country. However, maintenance on the Vineyards can be inconsistent. The course has some solid par 3s, but a few "what-were-they-thinking?" holes as well. If you could combine the best of Vineyards, with the best of Shakespeare, you would have one heck of a track. – Val

NOTES: The yardage listed is for the Vineyards Course. The Vineyards has an actual 19th hole – a tiny par 3. We're pretty sure you can substitute your score on that hole with any score you didn't like on the previous eighteen. Of course, we could be wrong.

DIRECTIONS: From within Napa: Off Highway 29, take Highway 12 east. Go about one and one-half miles, and the course is on the right . The course is located on Highway 12 between Highway 29 and I-80.

NAPA GOLF COURSE (municipal, 18 holes, fleming & baldock 1967) . . . .

2295 Streblow Drive
Napa, CA 94558
(707) 255-4333
playnapa.com

	YARDAGE	PAR	RATING	SLOPE	
FRONT	4958	68	68.5	120	**$8 - $40**
MIDDLE	6506	72	71.2	120	
BACK	6704	72	72.3	123	

WHAT TO EXPECT: This is long, parkland-style course with mature trees and water on 11 holes. The description maybe simple, but the course plays tough. A steady putter and proper club selection are the keys to shooting a low score.

OUR OPINION: Much-needed renovation over the last few years has improved course conditions considerably. – Bob

DIRECTIONS: From Vallejo (about 15 miles north to the course): Take Highway 29 north. Take the Lake Berryessa/Downtown Napa split to Streblow Drive. Make a left on Streblow Drive to the course.

NAPA VALLEY COUNTRY CLUB (members only, 18 holes, member built/front 9 1917)

3385 Hagen Road
Napa, CA 94558
(707) 252-1114
napavalleycc.com

	YARDAGE	PAR	RATING	SLOPE	
FRONT	5325	72	71.6	125	**$90 - $90**
MIDDLE	5696	72	68.5	121	
BACK	6149	72	70.6	125	

WHAT TO EXPECT: This is two courses in one. The original nine was built in 1917 and was designed by the members. The front nine features smaller greens and oak tree-lined fairways. The back nine was built in 1990 by Ron Fream and has a more modern feel, with an emphasis on target golf. This is a fun and interesting layout, but be careful if you wager with a member – local knowledge rules.

NOTES: Reciprocal play with other members only clubs is allowed.

DIRECTIONS: From San Francisco (about 60 miles northeast to the course): Take US 101 north to Highway 37 and go east to Highway 29. Follow Highway 29 north toward Highway 121. Take Highway 121 east. Turn right on Hagen Road, to the course.

SILVERADO COUNTRY CLUB & RESORT (resort, 36 holes, robert trent jones jr. 1975) .

1600 Atlas Peak Road
Napa, CA 94558
(707) 257-5460
silveradoresort.com

	YARDAGE	PAR	RATING	SLOPE	
FRONT	5642	72	72.7	127	**$70 - $130**
MIDDLE	6243	72	70.5	124	
BACK	6686	72	72.4	129	

WHAT TO EXPECT: There are two 18-hole golf courses. The North Course is longer and more straightforward. The South Course takes more course knowledge and allows less room for error. Both courses have plenty of oak trees, water, and large, well-thought-out greens.

OUR OPINION: We prefer the North Course for its more traditional and interesting layout. On the South Course, almost all the par 4s are dogleg rights and all the par 5s are dogleg lefts. – Val

DIRECTIONS: From within Napa: Take Highway 29 north to Trancas. Turn right on Trancas and follow the sign to Lake Berryessa, Highway 121. Turn left on Atlas Peak Road. Turn right at the traffic light and drive up to the resort.

INDIAN VALLEY GOLF CLUB (public, 18 holes, robert nyberg 1957) . . . .

3035 Novato Boulevard
Novato, CA 94947
(415) 897-1118
ivgc.com

	YARDAGE	PAR	RATING	SLOPE	
FRONT	5057	71	69.5	122	**$30 - $49**
MIDDLE	5842	72	68.3	116	
BACK	6253	72	68.4	119	

WHAT TO EXPECT: Indian Valley is a mature course with plenty of native oaks. Many of the fairways are rolling, and there are a few steep ones as well. Indian Valley boasts a 15,000-square-foot green, the largest in Marin County.

OUR OPINION: On the ninth green I putted three feet past the hole and made the putt. How? The ball rolled back down the hill into the cup, and along with it came five skins from my angry playing partners. Silly green site but hey, it works for me. This is not an easy walking course – trust me. – Frank

DIRECTIONS: From San Francisco (about 30 miles north to the course): Take US 101 north. Take the San Marin Drive exit west to Novato Boulevard. Turn right on Novato Boulevard. The course is on the left.

MARIN COUNTRY CLUB (members only, 18 holes, lawrence hughes 1959) . . . .

500 Country Club Drive
Novato, CA 94949
(415) 382-6707

	YARDAGE	PAR	RATING	SLOPE	
FRONT	5802	72	74.2	133	**$55 - $125**
MIDDLE	6194	72	71.1	131	
BACK	6441	72	72.0	133	

WHAT TO EXPECT: This was a nine-hole course expanded into an 18-hole course in the mid-'80s. You will find danger in the form of lateral hazards on 15 holes. The greens demand a steady hand, and wind can be a factor. The front nine is fairly level, with narrow fairways, while the back nine is hilly and a little more forgiving off the tee.

NOTES: Reciprocal play with other members only clubs is allowed.

DIRECTIONS: From San Francisco (about 30 miles north to the course): Drive north on US 101 to Novato. Take the Ignacio Boulevard exit west for approximately one and one-half miles. Turn left on Country Club Drive.

STONETREE GOLF CLUB (public, 18 holes, summers, tatum, miller and bliss 2000) . . .

9 StoneTree Lane
Novato, CA 94945
(415) 209-6090
stonetreegolf.com

	YARDAGE	PAR	RATING	SLOPE
FRONT	5232	72	71.2	127
MIDDLE	6295	72	70.0	132
BACK	6811	72	72.7	137

$85 - $115

WHAT TO EXPECT: This is two different golf courses. There are ten holes on the flats with forced carries, mounding, water hazards and drainage ditches. The other eight holes are up in the oak-covered hills with little water, lots of trees, severe elevations changes, small greens, and gorgeous views.

OUR OPINION: This is a new course that the golf enthusiasts will want to play at least once. Will they come back? Several of our staff played here and enjoyed the course, but at $115 can anyone play this course on a regular basis? – Shaw

NOTES: StoneTree has does not have a driving range.

DIRECTIONS: From San Francisco (about 30 miles north to the course): Take US 101 north to Highway 37 east for two and one-half miles. The course is on the right. Take the Black Point/Atherton Avenue exit. Take a right to the driveway.

ADOBE CREEK GOLF CLUB (public, 18 holes, robert trent jones jr. 1990) . . . .

1901 Frates Road
Petaluma, CA 94954
(707) 765-3000
adobecreek.com

	YARDAGE	PAR	RATING	SLOPE
FRONT	5085	72	?	120
MIDDLE	6290	72	71.3	125
BACK	6887	72	73.8	131

$17 - $57

WHAT TO EXPECT: This flat, open course is spotted with water, mounding, and bunkers. All of this makes accurate shot-making a must. The layout drains well for those who enjoy winter golf. In the summer time, afternoon wind will be a factor. If you make it through holes seven, eight, nine, and ten without any major disasters, a low score will be your reward.

OUR OPINION: The course is slightly more entertaining than nearby Rooster Run, but has suffered from neglect for several years. Adobe Creek is highly recommended for winter play, as it remains open and playable when others are not. – Frank

DIRECTIONS: From San Francisco (about 40 miles north to the course): Take US 101 north, through Marin County. Just before entereing Petaluma, exit at Highway 116 east. Make a left on Frates Road. The course is on the left.

PETALUMA GOLF & COUNTRY CLUB (members only, 9 holes, roger baird 1922) . . . . . .

1500 Country Club Drive
Petaluma, CA   94953
(707) 762-7041

	YARDAGE	PAR	RATING	SLOPE	
FRONT	2704	35	72.3	125	**$20 - $30**
MIDDLE	-	-	-	-	
BACK	2808	35	67.2	111	

WHAT TO EXPECT: What this course lacks in distance, it makes up for in elevation changes. If you are not used to walking hills, you might want to bring an oxygen tank and your own caddy to carry it.
NOTES: Reciprocal play with other members only clubs is allowed.
DIRECTIONS: From San Francisco (about 40 miles north to the course): Take US 101 north, exit on Petaluma Boulevard South and head downtown. Go south on McNear Avenue to Country Club Drive.

ROOSTER RUN GOLF CLUB (public, 18 holes, fred bliss 1998) . . . .

2301 East Washington Street
Petaluma, CA 94954
(707) 778-1211
roosterrun.com

	YARDAGE	PAR	RATING	SLOPE	
FRONT	5139	72	69.1	113	**$17 - $49**
MIDDLE	6462	72	71.2	124	
BACK	7001	72	73.9	128	

WHAT TO EXPECT: Rooster Run offers level, wide fairways, wind, and plenty of water hazards. The real story is the greens. They are large, quick, and sloping. If you can putt here, you can putt anywhere. The local airport is nearby and can provide some distraction.
OUR OPINION: For the conditioning of the golf course, this is a superb value. Rooster Run is also a great venue, along with Adobe Creek, for winter golf in the Wine Country. Our only complaint is the greens are not consistent with the rest of the layout. The course is friendly tee to green, then downright mean once you are on the greens. – Frank
DIRECTIONS: From San Francisco (about 40 miles north to the course): Take US 101 north to Petaluma, and take the East Washington Street exit. Drive about a mile east. The course is on the left.

AETNA SPRINGS GOLF COURSE (public, 9 holes) . . . .

1600 Aetna Springs Road
Pope Valley, CA 94567
(707) 965-2115
aetnasprings.com

	YARDAGE	PAR	RATING	SLOPE	
FRONT	2432	35	68.0	107	**$10 - $20**
MIDDLE	-	-	-	-	
BACK	2690	35	65.9	106	

WHAT TO EXPECT: This is one of the oldest courses in California, dating back to the 1890s. It's a cute course that features lots of native oaks, two creeks, and small, well-maintained greens.

OUR OPINION: Aetna Springs Golf Course is a great history lesson. Play it while you can. Rumor has it the course won't be around much longer. – Shaw

DIRECTIONS: From Napa (about 35 miles north to the course): Take Highway 29 north, past Saint Helena. Turn right on Deer Park Road and head east. Cross the Silverado Trail and drive 12 miles to Pope Valley. Pass through the town of Angwin. Turn left on Pope Valley Road. Drive three and one-half miles to Aetna Springs Road. Turn left and drive about a mile to the course.

MOUNTAIN SHADOWS GOLF RESORT (public, 36 holes, bob baldock 1963) . . . .

100 Golf Course Drive
Rohnert Park, CA 94928
(707) 584-7766
courseco.com

	YARDAGE	PAR	RATING	SLOPE	
FRONT	5761	72	72.1	122	**$16 - $35**
MIDDLE	6074	71	68.9	116	
BACK	6502	71	71.1	121	

WHAT TO EXPECT: There are two courses, the South Course and the North Course. Both courses are fairly flat and open, although houses do create out-of-bounds. The North Course is the newer, longer and more challenging of the two courses and winds through houses.

OUR OPINION: Save your money until renovations have been completed. Call the pro shop for details. – Shaw

NOTES: An new management group has won approval from the city to begin much needed renovations. The yardage listed is for the South Course.

DIRECTIONS: From Petaluma (about 11 miles north to the course): Take US 101 north to Rohnert Park and take the Golf Course Drive exit. Head east and follow Golf Course Drive to the facility.

BENNETT VALLEY GOLF COURSE (municipal, 18 holes, ben harmon 1969) . . . .

3330 Yulupa Avenue
Santa Rosa, CA 95405
(707) 528-3673

	YARDAGE	PAR	RATING	SLOPE	
FRONT	5958	72	72.5	116	**$14 - $25**
MIDDLE	6221	72	69.0	109	
BACK	6583	72	70.6	112	

WHAT TO EXPECT: Bennett Valley is nearly finished with the redesign of all the greens. They have been enlarged to allow for more pin placements and a better challenge. The fairways are driver friendly (more so on the back nine), and many of the holes run parallel to one another, but that doesn't take away from the interest or the beauty of the golf course.

OUR OPINION: You would be hard pressed to find a better value anywhere in the state. The course is fun, well maintained, and always improving. The only drawback is that there is not another course like this in Santa Rosa, so slow play is common in the afternoons. – Shaw

DIRECTIONS: From San Francisco (about 55 miles north to the course): Take US 101 north to Highway 12 and go east. Stay in the right lane and immediately take the Downtown Santa Rosa exit. Pass the fairgrounds and stay to the right to get on Bennett Valley Road. Bennett Valley Road runs into the course parking lot at the Yulupa Road intersection.

FAIRGROUNDS GOLF CENTER (public, 9 holes) . . . .

1350 Bennett Valley Road
Santa Rosa, CA 95405
(707) 577-0755
empiregolf.com

	YARDAGE	PAR	RATING	SLOPE	
FRONT	1735	30	57.1	79	**$5 - $16**
MIDDLE	-	-	-	-	
BACK	1735	30	57.2	86	

WHAT TO EXPECT: This is a short, flat course located in the center of the Santa Rosa Fairgrounds race track.

NOTES: The course is closed for two weeks, usually at the end of July, for the Sonoma County Fair.

DIRECTIONS: From Petaluma (about 20 miles north to the course): Drive north on US 101 to Highway 12 and go east. Stay in the right lane. That will lead to the course. The entrance is on the right, just before the main expo center of the fairgrounds.

FOUNTAINGROVE CLUB, THE (semi-private, 18 holes, ted robinson 1985) . . . .

1525 Fountaingrove Parkway
Santa Rosa, CA 95403
(707) 579-4653
fountaingrovegolf.com

	YARDAGE	PAR	RATING	SLOPE
FRONT	5325	72	70.9	126
MIDDLE	6439	72	71.5	131
BACK	6872	72	73.3	135

$75 - $95

WHAT TO EXPECT: This is a beautiful, demanding, hilly course, where the fairways seem to get smaller as the day goes along. A recent remodel has made this course more enjoyable, but no less challenging. Do everything in your power to stay in the fairway. Several elevated tee shots provide not only some special views, but blind shots as well.
OUR OPINION: Play it while you can, this course could go private at any moment. – Shaw
DIRECTIONS: From San Francisco (about 55 miles north to the course): Take US 101 north to Bicentennial Way and go east. Bicentennial Way merges into Fountaingrove Parkway. The entrance is up the hill, on the left.

MAYACAMA GOLF CLUB (members only, 18 holes, jack nicklaus 2001) . . . .

500 Shiloh Meadow Road
Santa Rosa, CA 95403
(707) 543-8040
mayacama.com

	YARDAGE	PAR	RATING	SLOPE
FRONT	4713	72	-	-
MIDDLE	6156	72	71.3	144
BACK	6761	72	74.3	150

WHAT TO EXPECT: This is a Jack Nicklaus classic design with a combination of risk-reward par 5s, long par 4s, and challenging par 3s. The greens are subtle but roll true and are pro-tour fast. The fairways are fairly wide, but the rough is thick. A wedge maybe your only answer for getting back on the fairway. This is a great-looking course that will favor a low handicapper who can hit straight tee shots and high, soft irons. Everybody else should bring dozens of balls and lots of patience.
DIRECTIONS: From San Francisco (about 60 miles north to the course): Take US 101 north to Santa Rosa, almost to Windsor. Exit onto Shiloh Road and head east.

OAKMONT GOLF CLUB (semi-private, 36 holes, ted robinson 1963) . . . .

7025 Oakmont Drive
Santa Rosa, CA 95409
(707) 539-0415
oakmontvillage.com

	YARDAGE	PAR	RATING	SLOPE
FRONT	5384	72	71.8	125
MIDDLE	6059	71	69.6	120
BACK	6379	71	71.1	124

$28 - $45

WHAT TO EXPECT: On the West Course, if you are hitting the ball remotely straight, expect to have a good time. Oakmont West is a well-conditioned, pleasant golf course with ample fairways and greens. However, if straight is not in your game plan, you will contend with native oaks, lakes, creeks, streams, and plenty of homes. The executive East Course is a demanding layout, with tough par 3s and short, tricky par 4s.

OUR OPINION: The West Course is fun, and the East Course maybe one of the best executive courses in the state. These courses are part of a retirement community, so mid-mornings can play slow, but during the afternoon nap time, things seem to speed up. – Frank

NOTES: The yardage listed is for the West Course.

DIRECTIONS: From within Santa Rosa: Take Highway 12 east approximately five miles toward Sonoma. Turn right on Oakmont Drive, where there is a stoplight. The course is on the left.

SANTA ROSA GOLF & COUNTRY CLUB (members only, 18 holes, ben harmon 1959) . .

5110 Oak Meadow Drive
Santa Rosa, CA 95401
(707) 546-6617
santarosagolf.com

	YARDAGE	PAR	RATING	SLOPE
FRONT	5798	73	72.7	123
MIDDLE	6321	72	70.4	125
BACK	6750	72	72.7	129

$40 - $85

WHAT TO EXPECT: What you see is what you get. There are no hidden agendas on this classic layout. Santa Rosa features tree-lined fairways and well-protected greens. Over the past several years, many of the greens have been successfully redesigned to increase the challenge.

NOTES: Reciprocal play with other members only clubs is allowed.

DIRECTIONS: In San Francisco (about 55 miles north to the course): Drive north on US 101 to Highway 12 and then go west. Off Highway 12, make a right at the light on Fulton Road. Turn left on Hall Road. Go two miles, then turn left on Country Club Drive, to the course.

WIKIUP GOLF COURSE (public, 9 holes, clark glasson 1963) . . . .

5001 Carriage Lane
Santa Rosa, CA 95403
(707) 546-8787

	YARDAGE	PAR	RATING	SLOPE
FRONT	1550	29	57.7	93
MIDDLE	-	-	57.7	91
BACK	1673	29		

$11 - $21

WHAT TO EXPECT: This is a short course that plays through the Wikiup subdivision. The course is suited for beginners and seniors. It winds along Mark West Springs Creek.
DIRECTIONS: From within Santa Rosa: Off US 101, at the north end of Santa Rosa, take the River Road/Mark West Springs exit. Drive east. At the stoplight turn left (north) on Old Redwood Highway for half a mile. Turn right on Wikiup Drive and make another right on Carriage Lane.

SEA RANCH GOLF LINKS, THE (public, 18 holes, robert muir graves 1973) . . . .

42000 Highway 1
Sea Ranch, CA 95497
(707) 785-2468
searanchvillage.com

	YARDAGE	PAR	RATING	SLOPE
FRONT	6601	72	70.2	120
MIDDLE	6219	72	71.9	130
BACK	6602	72	73.2	136

$30 - $70

WHAT TO EXPECT: Located along the coast, this is a challenging Scottish-style course with excellent ocean views. Sea Ranch is unprotected from the ocean breezes, and the fairways are outlined by native grasses and plants. Translation: bring lots of golf balls.
OUR OPINION: This course has a rustic charm and is well worth playing if you get the chance. It's one of the those layouts that evokes a strong opinion from everyone who plays it. The drive up the coast is winding and spectacular. – Shaw
DIRECTIONS: From Bodega Bay (about 40 miles north to the course): Follow Highway 1 north to Sea Ranch. The course is on the left.

SEBASTOPOL GOLF COURSE (public, 9 holes) . . . .

2881 Scotts Right-of-Way
Sebastopol, CA 95472
(707) 823-9852

	YARDAGE	PAR	RATING	SLOPE
FRONT	1663	33	57.8	81.0
MIDDLE	-	-	-	-
BACK	1663	31	57.8	84.0

$10 - $15

WHAT TO EXPECT: This is a short, but challenging, family-owned golf course that is a favorite of locals, beginners, and seniors.
DIRECTIONS: From Petaluma (about 20 miles northwest to the course): Take US 101 north to Highway 116 west. Follow Highway 116 west and pass through the town of Sebastopol. Turn right on Scotts Right-of-Way.

SHELTER COVE GOLF COURSE (public, 9 holes) . . . .

1555 Upper Pacific Drive
Shelter Cove, CA 95589
(707) 986-1464

	YARDAGE	PAR	RATING	SLOPE	
FRONT	-	-	-	-	**$10 - $18**
MIDDLE	-	-	-	-	
BACK	2380	32	-	-	

WHAT TO EXPECT: This is a links-style course that features ocean views on every hole. Although not long, it is not easy, either. Native vegetation lurks outside the fairways, happily consuming errant golf balls. If you land near the airstrip bordering the course, you receive a free drop.

DIRECTIONS: From Garberville (about 22 miles west to the course): Off US 101 head west 22 miles (to Shelter Cove) on Briceland/Shelter Cove Road. Turn right onto Upper Pacific Drive. The course is on the right.

LOS ARROYOS GOLF CLUB (public, 9 holes, unknown 1965) . . . .

5000 Stage Gulch Road
Sonoma, CA 95476
(707) 938-8835

	YARDAGE	PAR	RATING	SLOPE	
FRONT	-	-	-	-	**$7 - $17**
MIDDLE	-	-	-	-	
BACK	1600	29	-	-	

WHAT TO EXPECT: The executive course is flat and straightforward with some trees. The longest hole on the course is 305 yards. The pitch-and-putt course is 620 yards long. On the eighth hole, players begin out of the bunker.

DIRECTIONS: From Petaluma (about 15 miles east to the course): Off US 101, at the south end of Petaluma, take Highway 116 east toward Sonoma. The course is at the intersection of Highway 116 and Highway 121, three miles from downtown Sonoma.

SONOMA MISSION INN GOLF AND COUNTRY CLUB (resort, 18 holes, s. whiting 1926) .

17700 Arnold Drive
Sonoma, CA 95476
(707) 996-0300
sonomamissioninn.com

	YARDAGE	PAR	RATING	SLOPE	
FRONT	5511	72	66.6	132	**$80 - $130**
MIDDLE	6637	72	71.7	130	
BACK	7088	72	74.1	132	

WHAT TO EXPECT: This course is a very subtle traditional golf layout. The fairways seem wide enough, but they are easy to miss. The bunkers aren't very large, but are always in the right place. The greens seem straightforward, but they are deceptively undulating and quick. Even the elevation changes are subtle. The only thing that is not subtle is your score at the end of the day if you try to be to aggressive.

OUR OPINION: Sonoma Mission Inn should not be missed. The course is classic in design and will make you think at every turn. The course will reward good shots and punish bad ones. Every club in your bag will have remnants of grass on them. – Val

NOTES: This is soon to be a private resort for members, guests, and Sonoma Mission Inn patrons only.

DIRECTIONS: From San Francisco (about 45 miles north to the course): Drive north on US 101. Take Highway 37 east to Highway 121 north. Stay north on Highway 121 until Highway 116 west. Stay straight and the road turns into Highway 116 west. Follow Highway 116 west for a couple of miles. Take the right on Arnold Drive and follow to the course, which is five miles down, on the left.

MEADOWOOD RESORT HOTEL GOLF COURSE (members only, 9 holes, j. fleming 1964) .

900 Meadowood Lane
St. Helena, CA 94574
(707) 963-3646
meadowood.com

	YARDAGE	PAR	RATING	SLOPE	
FRONT	1777	32	60.8	97	**$35 - $35**
MIDDLE	-	-	-	-	
BACK	2021	31	60.9	100	

WHAT TO EXPECT: This is a quiet resort course that incorporates the natural terrain into its layout. The course is peaceful, but does provide some challenge with tree-lined fairways, a few hills and undulating greens. There are four par 4s, five par 3s, and water on one hole.

NOTES: Reciprocal play with other members only clubs is allowed.

DIRECTIONS: From Napa (about 20 miles north to the course): Drive north on Highway 29. Turn right on Pope Street and then left on the Silverado Trail. Soon after, go right onto Howell Mountain Road, to the course.

GREEN VALLEY COUNTRY CLUB (members only, 18 holes, elmer borders 1951) . . . . .

35 Country Club Drive
Suisun , CA 94585
(707) 864-0473
greenvalleycc.com

	YARDAGE	PAR	RATING	SLOPE	
FRONT	5866	72	73.7	131	**$40 - $70**
MIDDLE	6219	72	69.7	128	
BACK	6494	72	71.0	130	

WHAT TO EXPECT: Tricky greens are this course's best defense. They provide members with a distinct home-course advantage. The front nine is level, while the back nine provides some elevation changes. Wind is often a factor.

NOTES: Reciprocal play with other members only clubs is allowed.

DIRECTIONS: From Vallejo (about 16 miles northeast to the course): Travel east on I-80 and exit at Green Valley Road. Cross the over the freeway and follow the signs to Green Valley Road, which will lead to the club.

UKIAH MUNICIPAL GOLF COURSE (municipal, 18 holes, paul underwood 1953) . . . . .

599 Park Boulevard
Ukiah, CA 95482
(707) 467-2832

	YARDAGE	PAR	RATING	SLOPE	
FRONT	5312	70	71.1	117	**$6 - $21**
MIDDLE	5657	69	67.5	116	
BACK	5850	69	68.2	117	

WHAT TO EXPECT: If you have never played here before, expect to repeat the following phrase: "I didn't know that was there." Don't get excited by the short yardage, as course knowledge is to key your success on this quirky, hilly course surrounded by trees and hazards.

OUR OPINION: With plenty of blind spots, the first few times you play this course can be a painful experience. The more you play, the more enjoyable the course becomes. – Frank

DIRECTIONS: From Santa Rosa (about 60 miles north to the course): Drive north on US 101 to Ukiah. Take the Perkins Street exit. Make a left (west) on Perkins Street and drive to Dora Street and turn right. Follow Dora Street to Walnut Street and make a left. Walnut Street turns into Park Boulevard.

CYPRESS LAKES GOLF COURSE (military, 18 holes, joseph finger 1960) . . . .

5601 Meridian Road
Vacaville, CA 95687
(707) 448-7186

	YARDAGE	PAR	RATING	SLOPE	
FRONT	5809	73	73.0	120	**$9 - $25**
MIDDLE	6494	72	71.0	116	
BACK	6908	72	72.7	121	

WHAT TO EXPECT: This is a walkable course with seven lakes, plenty of trees, large greens and plenty of wind.

DIRECTIONS: From Vallejo (about 20 miles northeast to the course): Drive east on I-80 to the Elmira exit. Go east until Meridian Road. Turn right on Meridian Road and continue to the course.

GREEN TREE GOLF CLUB (public, 27 holes, billy bell, jr. 1963) . . . .

999 Leisure Town Road
Vacaville, CA 95687
(707) 448-1420

	YARDAGE	PAR	RATING	SLOPE	
FRONT	5262	71	69.9	118	
MIDDLE	6008	71	68.5	114	**$7 - $28**
BACK	6301	71	70.2	119	

WHAT TO EXPECT: Look up walkable in the dictionary and you will find a photo of Green Tree. The course is level, with wide fairways, lots of trees, and very little out-of-bounds. The greens have subtle breaks that favor the player with local knowledge.
DIRECTIONS: From Vallejo (about 20 miles northeast to the course): Drive east on I-80 to Vacaville. Take the Leisure Town Road exit and head south. The course is on the right.

BLUE ROCK SPRINGS GOLF COURSE (municipal, 36 holes, robert muir graves 1993) . .

655 Columbus Parkway
Vallejo, CA 94591
(707) 643-8476
bluerockspringsgolf.com

	YARDAGE	PAR	RATING	SLOPE	
FRONT	4851	70	68.2	117	
MIDDLE	5701	71	66.9	119	**$17 - $30**
BACK	5948	71	67.9	121	

WHAT TO EXPECT: The East Course is newer and has large, undulating greens. You will encounter many side-hill lies. The West Course is hilly with smallish greens and more trees than the East Course.
NOTES: The yardage listed is for the West Course.
DIRECTIONS: From San Francisco (about 30 miles northeast to the course): Travel east on I-80 and exit on Columbus Parkway. Go to the right about two miles. The course is on the right.

HIDDENBROOKE GOLF CLUB (public, 18 holes, arnold palmer & ed seay 1995) . . . . . .

1095 Hiddenbrooke Parkway
Vallejo, CA 94591
(707) 558-1140
hiddenbrookegolf.com

	YARDAGE	PAR	RATING	SLOPE	
FRONT	4648	72	66.4	117	
MIDDLE	5773	72	69.2	126	**$75 - $100**
BACK	6679	72	72.8	142	

WHAT TO EXPECT: Sandwiched in a scenic, secluded valley, this is a formidable layout. Hiddenbrooke features 125 bold bunkers, 12 lateral water hazards, rolling hills and large, challenging greens.
OUR OPINION: Hiddenbrooke is a well-conditioned course that will force you to hit a variety of shots. This makes the course interesting, as well as challenging, for the low handicapper. We only have one issue with this Palmer design. Why you are sometimes penalized for hitting the ball in the fairway? – Val
DIRECTIONS: From San Francisco (about 30 miles northeast to the course): Take I-80 east, exit at American Canyon Road in Vallejo. At the stop sign, turn right onto Hiddenbrooke Parkway.

JOE MORTARA GOLF COURSE (public, 9 holes, mortara, sr. & fleming 1981) . . . .

900 Fairgrounds Drive
Vallejo, CA 94590
(707) 642-5146

	YARDAGE	PAR	RATING	SLOPE	
FRONT	-	-	-	-	**$7 - $13**
MIDDLE	-	-	-	-	
BACK	1591	28	54.4	56	

WHAT TO EXPECT: Located on the inside of the Solano County Fairgrounds, this is a short, busy, open course where golf balls can come from any direction.

DIRECTIONS: From San Francisco (about 30 miles northeast to the course): Travel east on I-80 to Highway 37 west . Turn at Fairgrounds Drive. The course is located inside the fairgrounds.

MARE ISLAND GOLF CLUB (public, 18 holes, robin nelson (r) 2000) . . . .

1800 Club Drive/ Mare Island
Vallejo, CA 94592
(707) 562-4653
mareislandgolfclub.com

	YARDAGE	PAR	RATING	SLOPE	
FRONT	4832	70	-	-	**$20 - $45**
MIDDLE	5788	70	68.0	121	
BACK	6150	70	69.8	124	

WHAT TO EXPECT: This is a magnificent target golf course with small greens, plenty of trees, some water, and sloping fairways. If you can't hit a downhill, uphill, or side-hill lie, you will be in for a long day.

OUR OPINION: This is truly an undiscovered gem. The new nine has been incorporated to make a phenomenal golf course. Up until a few months ago, this course was only played by locals, but now Mare Island must be considered a topnotch destination course. – Bob

NOTES: A former military course, nine new holes have been intermixed with the original nine that date back to 1892.

DIRECTIONS: From San Francisco (about 35 miles northeast to the course): Take I-80 east, exit at Tennessee Street in Vallejo and head west. This will dead-end at the Mare Island Causeway. Go west. At the blue and white bridge, go to the guard gate, where the guard gives further directions.

BROOKTRAILS GOLF COURSE (public, 9 holes, robert muir graves 1961) . . . .

24860 Birch Street
Willits, CA 95490
(707) 459-6761

	YARDAGE	PAR	RATING	SLOPE	
FRONT	2574	58	55.4	88	**$10 - $14**
MIDDLE	-	-	-	-	
BACK	2574	56	55.7	86	

WHAT TO EXPECT: If you don't hit the ball straight, expect to see plenty of the 1,100 redwood trees that guard this short, beautiful golf course. If that wasn't challenge enough, there is a creek running throughout, and the greens are the size of dime. In the winter, you can catch the salmon run.

DIRECTIONS: From Ukiah (about 25 miles north to the course): Take US 101 north to the Sherwood Road exit. Turn left on Brooktrails Road. Brooktrails Road runs right into Birch Street.

WINDSOR GOLF CLUB (public, 18 holes, golf plan, fred bliss 1989) . . . .

1340 19th Hole Drive
Windsor, CA 95492
(707) 838-7888
windsorgolf.com

	YARDAGE	PAR	RATING	SLOPE	
FRONT	5116	72	69.3	125	**$26 - $44**
MIDDLE	6169	72	70.1	121	
BACK	6650	72	72.3	126	

WHAT TO EXPECT: This is a short, interesting, and challenging golf course. The fairways are generous, but miss them and you will find yourself in a creek, pond, or behind a native oak. If you can't hit the small greens, be prepared for a difficult chip to get up and down.

OUR OPINION: This a fun golf course at a reasonable price. A word of advice: weekend afternoon rounds can exceed the four-hour-15-minute requested time limit by well over an hour. – Brad

DIRECTIONS: From Santa Rosa (about five miles north to the course): Take US 101 north to the Shiloh exit. Drive west, over the freeway, and make a right on Golf Course Drive. Turn left on 19th Hole Drive, to the course.

VINTNER'S GOLF CLUB (public, 9 holes, casey o'callaghan 1999) . . . .

7901 Solano Avenue
Yountville, CA 94599
(707) 944-1992
vintnersgolfclub.com

	YARDAGE	PAR	RATING	SLOPE	
FRONT	2049	34	62.8	108	**$10 - $30**
MIDDLE	-	-	-	-	
BACK	2636	34	65.2	119	

WHAT TO EXPECT: Vintners is a modern, nine-hole layout with large greens, good sized fairways and mature trees. This is a family golf course, challenging enough for mom and dad, easy enough for children and beginners. The course also offers a large practice facility.

NOTES: The course is located next to the Domaine Chandon Winery and was formerly known as the Yountville Golf Course.

DIRECTIONS: From Napa (about 15 miles north to the course): Drive north on Highway 29, toward Saint Helena. Take the Yountville/Veterans Home exit and head west. Make a left on Solano Avenue, to the course.

Bay Area

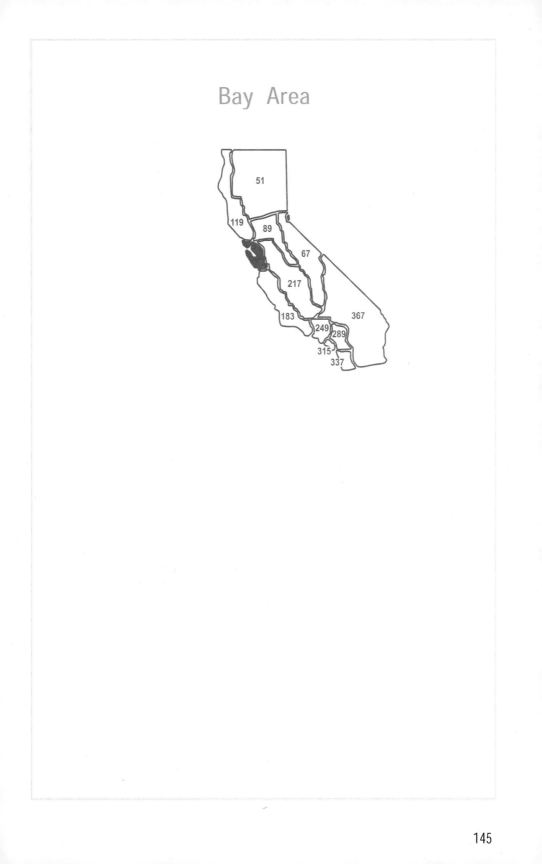

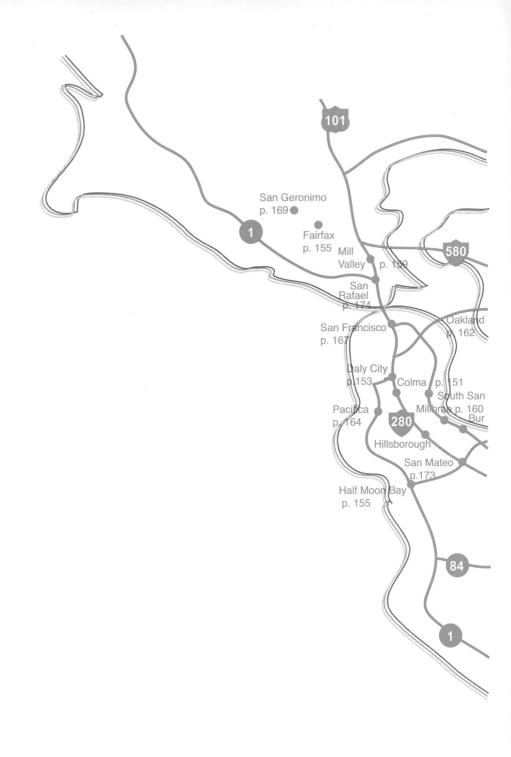

San Geronimo
p. 169

Fairfax
p. 155

Mill
Valley   p. 159

San
Rafael
p. 174

San Francisco
p. 167

Oakland
p. 162

Daly City
p. 153

Colma p. 151

South San

Pacifica
p. 164

Millbrae p. 160

Bur

280

Hillsborough

San Mateo
p.173

Half Moon Bay
p. 155

101

580

84

1

1

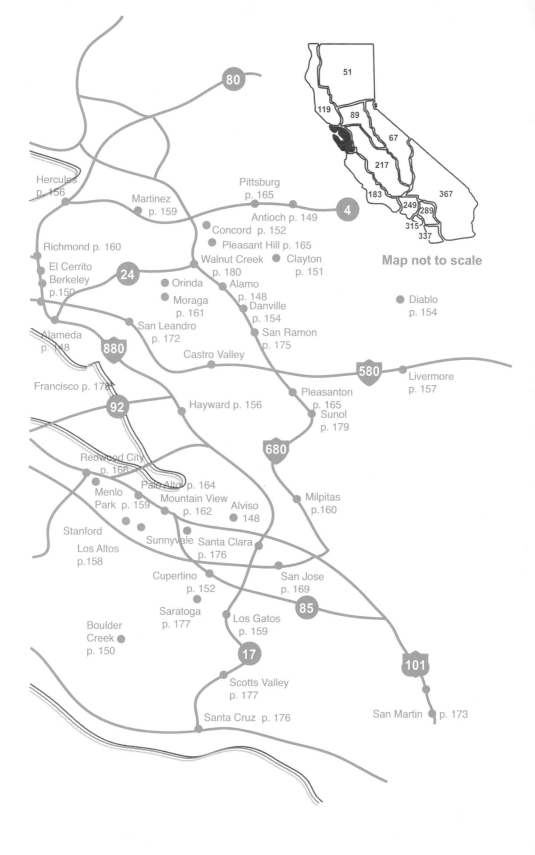

Hercules
p. 156

Pittsburg
p. 165

Martinez
p. 159

Antioch p. 149

Concord p. 152

Pleasant Hill p. 165

Richmond p. 160

Walnut Creek
p. 180

Clayton
p. 151

El Cerrito
Berkeley
p.150

Orinda

Alamo
p. 148

Moraga
p. 161

Danville
p. 154

San Leandro
p. 172

San Ramon
p. 175

Alameda
p. 148

Castro Valley

Diablo
p. 154

Francisco p. 178

Livermore
p. 157

Hayward p. 156

Pleasanton
p. 165

Sunol
p. 179

Redwood City
p. 166

Palo Alto p. 164

Milpitas
p.160

Menlo
Park p. 159

Mountain View
p. 162

Alviso
148

Stanford

Sunnyvale

Santa Clara
p. 176

Los Altos
p.158

Cupertino
p. 152

San Jose
p. 169

Saratoga
p. 177

Los Gatos
p. 159

Boulder
Creek
p. 150

Scotts Valley
p. 177

San Martin p. 173

Santa Cruz p. 176

Map not to scale

51

119

89

67

217

183

367

249

289

315

337

CHUCK CORICA GOLF COMPLEX (public, 36 holes, william bell 1922) . . . .

One Clubhouse Memorial Road
Alameda, CA 94502
(510) 522-4321

	YARDAGE	PAR	RATING	SLOPE
FRONT	5202	72	69.6	113
MIDDLE	5955	70	69.2	120
BACK	6310	70	70.9	123

$20 - $27

WHAT TO EXPECT: The North Course is considered the better and more interesting of the two courses. Its fairways are generally tighter with more water hazards. The South Course is flat and straightforward, with no forced carries. The fairways are tree-lined, but generous in width.

OUR OPINION: It's no secret that the North Course is the more interesting of the two. And it's no secret that any decent course in the Bay Area that charges a reasonable price is going to be crowded. – Shaw

NOTES: The yardage listed is for the North Course.

DIRECTIONS: From San Francisco (about 20 miles southeast to the course): Take I-80 east to I-880 south. Exit at High Street west. Turn left on Otis Drive and then turn right on Island Drive. The golf complex is on the left.

ROUND HILL COUNTRY CLUB (members only, 18 holes, lawrence hughes 1960) . . . . .

3169 Round Hill Road
Alamo, CA 94507
(925) 837-7424

	YARDAGE	PAR	RATING	SLOPE
FRONT	5632	72	73.0	129
MIDDLE	6233	71	70.7	128
BACK	6447	71	71.8	131

$50 - $100

WHAT TO EXPECT: This is a long, relatively open course that plays among upscale housing. It is forgiving off the tee and places a premium on the approaches to the subtle, immaculate greens.

NOTES: Reciprocal play with other members only clubs is allowed.

DIRECTIONS: From Walnut Creek (about 6 miles south to the course): Drive south on I-680. Exit at Stone Valley Road east. About one mile up, turn left onto Round Hill Road.

PIN HIGH FAMILY GOLF CENTER (public, 3 holes) . . . .

4701 North First Street
Alviso, CA 95002
(408) 934-1111

	YARDAGE	PAR	RATING	SLOPE
FRONT	1819	30	57.8	83
MIDDLE	1895	30	57.9	83
BACK	1974	30	57.9	83

$3 - $5

WHAT TO EXPECT: This is a three-hole course with two par 3s and one par 4. The longest hole is just under 300 yards.

DIRECTIONS: From San Jose (about five miles northwest to the course): Off I-880 north, go west on Highway 237 and take the North First Street exit. Turn right as you exit the freeway, to the course.

LONE TREE GOLF COURSE (public, 18 holes, bob baldock 1939) . . . .

4800 Golf Course Road
Antioch, CA 94509
(925) 706-4220
lonetreegolfcourse.com

	YARDAGE	PAR	RATING	SLOPE
FRONT	5667	72	71.9	121
MIDDLE	6098	72	68.9	121
BACK	6446	72	70.5	124

$16 - $30

WHAT TO EXPECT: Hang on there, partner; Lone Tree is just the name of the course. Chances are if you miss with your driver, you will hit several trees. Because of an abundance of slope, club selection can be tricky. The greens run average to small in size. Despite the hills, this layout is extremely walkable because of good placement of tees and greens.

OUR OPINION: For the price, it's well maintained and a good choice if you are in the area. – Frank

DIRECTIONS: From Walnut Creek (about 20 miles northeast to the course): Go north on I-680. Take Highway 242 east to Highway 4 and drive east. Exit on Lone Tree Way and turn right. Turn right on Golf Course Road.

RODDY RANCH, THE CLUB AT (public, 18 holes, j. michael poellot 2000) . . . .

One Tour Way
Antioch, CA 94509
(925) 978-4653
roddyranch.com

	YARDAGE	PAR	RATING	SLOPE
FRONT	5390	73	71.7	120
MIDDLE	6529	72	72.1	128
BACK	6946	72	74.3	131

$55 - $75

WHAT TO EXPECT: This is a links-style layout with rolling and treeless fairways. The challenge of the course comes from the wind, usually out of the west, and the large, quick greens that are well guarded by bunkers. With few trees, distances can be hard to judge. Beware of some of the pin placements – hitting directly at the flag could be a major mistake.

OUR OPINION: The perfect blend of service, reasonable price, and an outstanding layout, Roddy Ranch is a definite must-play. – Frank

DIRECTIONS: From Walnut Creek (about 22 miles northeast to the course): Go north on I-680. Take Highway 242 east to Highway 4 and drive east. Exit at Lone Tree Way. Go three to four miles and turn right on Deer Valley Road. The club is on the right.

TILDEN PARK GOLF COURSE (public, 18 holes, william p. bell 1937) . . . .

Grizzly Peak & Shasta Road
Berkeley, CA 94708
(510) 848-7373
americangolf.com

	YARDAGE	PAR	RATING	SLOPE	
FRONT	5399	71	71.1	122	**$26 - $42**
MIDDLE	5823	69	68.3	120	
BACK	6294	70	70.6	123	

WHAT TO EXPECT: This is a popular, hilly, tree-lined course that is not long in yardage but strong in personality. The course favors the player with local knowledge and a bit of luck. The greens can be very tricky.

OUR OPINION: American Golf has made many nice improvements on both the course and the facility. – Shaw

DIRECTIONS: From San Francisco (about 15 miles east to the course): Take I-80 east to Highway 24, toward Walnut Creek. Exit on Fish Ranch Road and head north. Turn right on Grizzly Peak. Turn right on Golf Course Road.

BOULDER CREEK GOLF & COUNTRY CLUB (resort, 18 holes, jack fleming 1961) . . . . . .

16901 Big Basin Way
Boulder Creek, CA 95006
(831) 338-2121
bouldercreekgolf.com

	YARDAGE	PAR	RATING	SLOPE	
FRONT	-	-	-	-	**$22 - $40**
MIDDLE	-	-	-	-	
BACK	4396	65	61.8	104	

WHAT TO EXPECT: This wavy course is carved out of a forest of redwood trees. The course is short, but narrow fairways and numerous par 3s that leave little room for error make this course a challenge. The front nine features five par 3s, while the back has three par 5s and four par 3s.

DIRECTIONS: From San Jose (about 40 miles southwest to the course): Take Highway 17 south, exit at Bear Creek Road, and turn right. This dead-ends in about nine miles on Highway 9. Turn left on Highway 9. Turn right on Big Basin Way. Boulder Creek is about three miles down, on the left.

CRYSTAL SPRINGS GOLF COURSE (public, 18 holes, herbert fowler 1924) . . . .

6650 Golf Course Drive
Burlingame, CA 94010
(650) 342-0603
playcrystalsprings.com

	YARDAGE	PAR	RATING	SLOPE	
FRONT	5667	72	72.5	126	**$40 - $79**
MIDDLE	6236	72	70.4	121	
BACK	6515	72	71.7	124	

WHAT TO EXPECT: The course is part of a federal reserve, and the holes range from flat to steep. For the most part, the course is revealing with no hidden tricks. However, you will encounter some side-hill lies, even if you hit the fairways. The greens are small and traditional.

OUR OPINION: The views of the adjoining reservoir are even better than the golf course. – Bob

DIRECTIONS: From San Francisco (about 16 miles south to the course): Take I-280 south. Exit on Black Mountain Road. Turn right, heading west to the stop sign. Turn right on Golf Course Drive.

WILLOW PARK GOLF COURSE (public, 18 holes, bob baldock 1967) . . . .

17007 Redwood Road
Castro Valley, CA 94546
(510) 537-8989

	YARDAGE	PAR	RATING	SLOPE	
FRONT	5241	71	69.6	121	
MIDDLE	5516	71	67.4	110	**$22 - $31**
BACK	5846	71	69.7	115	

WHAT TO EXPECT: In a beautiful, pristine valley, wildlife frequents this popular, busy layout. The relatively narrow fairways place a premium on driving accuracy.
DIRECTIONS: From San Francisco (about 25 miles southeast to the course): Take I-80 east to I-580 east. Exit on Redwood Road. Go left for approximately two and one-half miles.

OAKHURST COUNTRY CLUB (semi-private, 18 holes, ron fream 1990) . . . .

1001 Peacock Creek Drive
Clayton, CA 94517
(925) 672-9737
americangolf.com

	YARDAGE	PAR	RATING	SLOPE	
FRONT	5839	72	69.0	126	
MIDDLE	6283	72	71.1	132	**$50 - $80**
BACK	6747	72	73.4	137	

WHAT TO EXPECT: Don't look to yardage when picking your tees. Even at 6,275 yards, this is a challenging layout. Oakhurst is demanding off the tee, in the fairway, and on the greens. With plenty of homes and streets nearby, out-of-bounds is everywhere. The fairways are rolling to hilly, and uneven lies are common. You will be hitting into large, well-protected greens. The greens are big, quick, and sloping. The 18th hole is one of most feared in Northern California. Did we mention the wind?
OUR OPINION: Beginners will struggle here. Low handicappers will struggle here. The difference between the two is that low handicappers will love the challenge and want to return. The beginning golfer will yearn for the clubhouse bar and may be traumatized for life. At $90 on weekends, this course can not be considered a great value, but definitely worth playing. – Shaw
DIRECTIONS: From Walnut Creek (about nine miles east to the course): Off I-680, exit onto Ygnacio Valley Road and drive east for about eight miles. Turn right on Clayton Road. Turn left on Peacock Creek Drive.

CYPRESS GOLF COURSE (public, 9 holes, jack fleming 1961) . . . .

2001 Hillside Boulevard
Colma, CA 94014
(650) 992-5155
cypressgc.com

	YARDAGE	PAR	RATING	SLOPE	
FRONT	1674	29	59.8	84	
MIDDLE	-	-	-	-	**$10 - $15**
BACK	1710	29	59.6	105	

WHAT TO EXPECT: Cypress is under renovation but is playable. Two new holes are being created on the hill, as the course is are losing two holes on flats. Completion is expected sometime before 2002. The course is open and much improved.
DIRECTIONS: From San Francisco (about ten miles south to the course): Take I-280 south. Exit on Serramonte Boulevard and turn left. Turn right on Hillside Boulevard. The course is on the left.

BUCHANAN FIELDS GOLF COURSE (public, 9 holes, robert muir graves 1963) . . . . . .

1091 Concord Boulevard
Concord, CA 94520
(925) 682-1846

	YARDAGE	PAR	RATING	SLOPE
FRONT	1529	31	56.0	83
MIDDLE	1758	31	58.2	83
BACK	1932	31	59.2	85

$9 - $18

WHAT TO EXPECT: This is a popular executive course that is best suited for those who are learning the game or for those who want to brush up on their iron play.
NOTES: The practice facility is open until 9:30 p.m. and has over 76 hitting stations, many of which are covered.
DIRECTIONS: From Walnut Creek (about six miles north to the course): Take I-680 north. Exit at Concord Boulevard. Turn left at Diamond Avenue, and then right on Concord Boulevard.

DIABLO CREEK GOLF COURSE (municipal, 18 holes, bob baldock 1963) . . . .

4050 Port Chicago Highway
Concord, CA 94520
(925) 686-6262
ebgc.com

	YARDAGE	PAR	RATING	SLOPE
FRONT	5883	72	73.1	122
MIDDLE	6409	71	70.4	117
BACK	6830	71	72.4	123

$22 - $38

WHAT TO EXPECT: This popular municipal course features five lakes on the more open front side and then delves into the trees for a challenging back nine. Wind can also be a factor.
DIRECTIONS: From Walnut Creek (about six miles north to the course): Take I-680 north to Highway 242. Exit Port Chicago Highway north. Loop under freeway and the course is on the right.

BLACKBERRY FARM GOLF COURSE (municipal, 9 holes, robert muir graves 1964) . . . .

22100 Stevens Creek Boulevard
Cupertino, CA 95014
(408) 253-9200
blackberryfarm.org

	YARDAGE	PAR	RATING	SLOPE
FRONT	1571	29	58.5	83
MIDDLE	-	-	-	-
BACK	1571	29	57.0	89

$9 - $24

WHAT TO EXPECT: This is a short, nine-hole course, with two par 4s. The course is part of a popular recreation area used for picnics, barbecues and corporate retreats.
OUR OPINION: Great for kids, beginners and high handicappers. Why can't all staffs be this friendly? – Frank
DIRECTIONS: From San Jose (about ten miles northwest to the course): Go north on I-280 to Highway 85 south. Exit onto Stevens Creek Boulevard. Head northwest about one-half mile. The course is on the left.

DEEP CLIFF GOLF COURSE (public, 18 holes) . . . .

10700 Clubhouse Lane
Cupertino, CA 95014
(408) 253-5357
courseco.com

	YARDAGE	PAR	RATING	SLOPE
FRONT	2938	60	56.8	91
MIDDLE	3369	60	59.2	96
BACK	3369	60	59.2	101

$15 - $35

WHAT TO EXPECT: This short, par-60 course is popular for beginners, but its narrow fairways and small greens can be deceptively difficult for the better player.
OUR OPINION: Deep Cliff should be renamed Deep Sleep. It doesn't matter what day you play, your chances of finishing in less than five hours are remote. – Frank
DIRECTIONS: From San Jose (about 10 miles northwest to the course): Take I-280 north. Exit onto Foothill Expressway and turn left. Go one and one-half miles and turn left on McClellan Road. Turn right on Clubhouse Lane.

LAKE MERCED GOLF & COUNTRY CLUB (members only, 18 holes, william locke 1922) .

2300 Junipero Serra Boulevard
Daly City, CA 94015
(650) 755-2239

	YARDAGE	PAR	RATING	SLOPE
FRONT	5823	74	73.8	132
MIDDLE	6503	72	72.7	134
BACK	6863	72	74.4	138

$70 - $175

WHAT TO EXPECT: This long, undulating course is quietly one of Northern California's best and prettiest park-setting venues. Always a respected tournament site, it has been recently been renovated, making play more difficult.
NOTES: Call the pro for details on reciprocal play.
DIRECTIONS: From San Francisco (about 10 miles south to the course): Take I-280 south. Exit at Westlake District/Daly City. Go straight. The club is on the right.

OLYMPIC CLUB, THE (members only, 45 holes, sam whiting 1919) . . . .

Off Skyline Boulevard
Daly City, CA 94015
(415) 587-8338
olyclub.com

	YARDAGE	PAR	RATING	SLOPE
FRONT	5718	71	69.2	127
MIDDLE	6529	71	72.7	136
BACK	6842	71	74.4	140

$65 - $300

WHAT TO EXPECT: The Lakeside Course is one of the west's great championship layouts. This hillside course plays longer than the yardage. Overhanging trees and small bunkered greens make it penal in nature. While the Ocean Course is often overshadowed by its famous neighbor, the Ocean Course is perhaps more interesting and scenic. It can play deceptively difficult and should be considered among the state's best. The Cliffs Course features dramatic flashed bunkering, a vast array of floral background, and spectacular views of the Pacific. They combine to create an "All World," nine-hole par-3 layout.
NOTES: The yardage listed is for the Lakeside Course.
DIRECTIONS: From the Golden Gate Bridge southbound: Take the 19th Avenue exit. Turn right on Sloat and then left on Skyline Boulevard. The club is on the left, past Funston.

BLACKHAWK COUNTRY CLUB (members only, 36 holes, enviromental golf 2000) . . . .

599 Blackhawk Club Drive
Danville, CA 94506
(925) 736-6550

	YARDAGE	PAR	RATING	SLOPE
FRONT	5367	72	71.0	131
MIDDLE	6260	72	71.2	135
BACK	6738	72	73.6	136

$45 - $125

WHAT TO EXPECT: The Falls Course is cart-golf. The layout features some breathtaking views from the first and tenth tees and then meanders among upscale housing. The Lake Course is a stout test of golf with several very difficult holes. Like its sister course, carts are a necessity, and housing is the dominant visual feature. It features several outstanding holes.

NOTES: The yardage listed is for the Falls Course.

DIRECTIONS: From Walnut Creek (about 13 miles south to the course): Take I-680 south. Exit on Sycamore Valley Road and head east. Turn left on Blackhawk Road. Turn right on Blackhawk Drive to the security gate. The guard gives directions from there.

CROW CANYON COUNTRY CLUB (members only, 18 holes, ted robinson 1977) . . . . . .

711 Silverlake Drive
Danville, CA 94526
(925) 735-8300
crow-canyon.com

	YARDAGE	PAR	RATING	SLOPE
FRONT	5043	69	69.9	121
MIDDLE	5908	69	68.8	125
BACK	6032	69	69.4	126

$45 - $90

WHAT TO EXPECT: This sporty private course is always busy and plays among condominiums and homes, up and down hills. Because it is relatively short, you should be able to score well here, provided you can keep the ball in play.

NOTES: Reciprocal play with other members only clubs is allowed.

DIRECTIONS: From Walnut Creek (about 10 miles south to the course): Take I-680 south. Exit on Crow Canyon Road and turn left. Turn left on Tahiti. The club is on the right.

DIABLO COUNTRY CLUB (members only, 18 holes, jack neville 1914) . . . .

1700 Clubhouse Road
Diablo, CA 94528
(925) 837-9233
diablocc.com

	YARDAGE	PAR	RATING	SLOPE
FRONT	5752	72	73.2	129
MIDDLE	6277	71	70.3	126
BACK	6641	71	72.1	130

$45 - $120

WHAT TO EXPECT: Small greens and solid shot making are requirements at this venerable East Bay club, considered one of the area's best tracks.

NOTES: Reciprocal play with other members only clubs is allowed.

DIRECTIONS: From Walnut Creek (about 14 miles south to the course): Take I-680 south. Exit on El Cerro Boulevard and head east about three miles. The brick wall entrance is on the left.

MIRA VISTA COUNTRY CLUB (members only, 18 holes, willie watson 1924) . . . .

7901 Cutting Boulevard
El Cerrito, CA 94530
(510) 237-7045
miravistagc.com

	YARDAGE	PAR	RATING	SLOPE
FRONT	5053	72	69.7	122
MIDDLE	6158	71	71.1	127
BACK	6488	71	72.7	131

$45 - $60

WHAT TO EXPECT: When the sky is clear, this old, traditional-style East Bay course provides some gorgeous views of the San Francisco Bay. It is an engaging, traditional layout situated on hilly terrain. Its small, elevated greens require accurate approaches.
NOTES: Reciprocal play with other members only clubs is allowed.
DIRECTIONS: From San Francisco (about 15 miles east to the course): Take I-80 east. Exit on Potrero and turn right. Turn left on Richmond, which turns into Cutting Boulevard. The club is at the top of the hill.

MEADOW CLUB (members only, 18 holes, alister mackenzie 1927) . . . .

1001 Bolinas Road
Fairfax, CA 94930
(415) 456-9393

	YARDAGE	PAR	RATING	SLOPE
FRONT	5942	73	75.2	135
MIDDLE	6324	71	71.4	128
BACK	6603	71	72.7	131

$150 - $150

WHAT TO EXPECT: You are in for a treat. This is an immaculately kept Alister Mackenzie design. The fairways are lined with trees and the greens are well protected and challenging. The yardage is no indication of the challenge.
NOTES: Reciprocal play with other members only clubs is allowed.
DIRECTIONS: From San Francisco (about 23 miles north to the course): Take US 101 north. Exit at Sir Francis Drake and go left (west). Veer to the left in Fairfax. Turn right on Broadway (parallel to Sir Francis Drake). Turn left on Bolinas Road.

HALF MOON BAY GOLF LINKS (public, 36 holes, francis duane 1973) . . . .

2000 Fairway Drive
Half Moon Bay, CA 94019
(650) 726-4438
halfmoonbaygolf.com

	YARDAGE	PAR	RATING	SLOPE
FRONT	4877	71	67.7	108
MIDDLE	6623	71	70.4	123
BACK	6629	72	72.5	128

$95 - $145

WHAT TO EXPECT: The two courses at Half Moon Bay are the Old Course (formerly known as the Links Course) and the Ocean Course. The Old Course plays among the pines and homes before heading to the Pacific for a dramatic three-hole finish. The Ocean Course is a wonderfully crafted links-style course with excellent views of the ocean. With the wind, this course will put up quite a fight.
OUR OPINION: For the golf enthusiast the Ocean Course is a must-play. – Bob
NOTES: The yardage listed is for the Ocean Course. A world-class resort now graces the property.
DIRECTIONS: From San Francisco (about 25 miles south to the course): Take I-280 or US 101 south to Highway 92 west. Turn left at Highway 1 south. The entrance is approximately two and one-half miles south on the right. Another option is to take Highway 1 down from San Francisco.

MISSION HILLS GOLF COURSE (public, 9 holes, rainville-bye 2000) . . . .

275 Industrial Boulevard
Hayward, CA 94544
(510) 888-0200

	YARDAGE	PAR	RATING	SLOPE	
FRONT	1644	60	59.2	90	**$11 - $18**
MIDDLE	-	-	-	-	
BACK	1720	30	57.2	93	

WHAT TO EXPECT: Mission Hills has six par 3s and three par 4s. The par 4s may not be long, but they have water on one side and traps on the other. On the par 3s, don't go after the pins; instead, hit to the center of the greens. Environmentally Sensitive Areas surround many of the holes.

OUR OPINION: This is a nice little course, where young people do not need to be intimated and the better player doesn't need to be bored. – Frank

DIRECTIONS: From Fremont (about ten miles north to the course): Take I-880 north. Exit on Industrial Boulevard and head east. The course is on the right corner of Industrial Boulevard and Mission.

SKYWEST GOLF COURSE (public, 18 holes, bob baldock 1964) . . . .

1401 Golf Course Road
Hayward, CA 94541
(510) 317-2300

	YARDAGE	PAR	RATING	SLOPE	
FRONT	6171	73	74.3	123	**$25 - $33**
MIDDLE	6540	72	71.0	117	
BACK	6930	72	72.9	121	

WHAT TO EXPECT: There is nothing tricky about Skywest. What you see is what you get. The fairways are level, tree-lined, and wide. The greens are large with slope. You can definitely bring out your $600 driver and have some fun.

DIRECTIONS: From Oakland (about 15 miles south to the course): Take I-880 south. Exit on A Street and head west. Turn right on Hesperian Boulevard. Turn left on Golf Course Road.

FRANKLIN CANYON GOLF COURSE (public, 18 holes, john muir graves 1968) . . . .

94547 Highway 4
Hercules, CA 94547
(510) 799-6191
americangolf.com

	YARDAGE	PAR	RATING	SLOPE	
FRONT	5516	72	71.2	123	**$19 - $48**
MIDDLE	6201	72	69.2	122	
BACK	6761	72	71.8	127	

WHAT TO EXPECT: This course flows through a valley and ventures up against a pristine hillside. The wooded holes and the back nine in general make for pleasant, scenic play.

DIRECTIONS: From San Francisco (about 24 miles northeast to the course): Take I-80 east to Highway 4 east, toward Stockton. The course is on the right side after about four miles.

BURLINGAME COUNTRY CLUB (members only, 18 holes, robert trent jones jr.) . . . . .

80 New Place Road
Hillsborough, CA 94010
(650) 342-0750

	YARDAGE	PAR	RATING	SLOPE
FRONT	5743	72	73.2	125
MIDDLE	6394	73	75.6	130
BACK	6182	70	70.9	127

$40 - $80

WHAT TO EXPECT: This old, exclusive, private course receives little play and features large eucalyptus trees and smallish greens.
DIRECTIONS: From San Francisco (about 18 miles south to the course): Go south on US 101, exit at Burlingame Avenue and turn right. Turn left on El Camino Real. Turn right on Floribunda and then left on Eucalyptus. Turn right on New Place Road and stay to the right.

LAS POSITAS GOLF COURSE (municipal, 18 holes, robert muir graves 1966) . . . .

917 Clubhouse Drive
Livermore, CA 94550
(925) 455-7820

	YARDAGE	PAR	RATING	SLOPE
FRONT	5275	72	70.1	120
MIDDLE	6331	72	70.8	123
BACK	6677	72	72.1	127

$28 - $36

WHAT TO EXPECT: This popular layout features both wooded and open areas. Its large, well-bunkered greens, water, and wind form the challenge. A sporty, nine-hole executive course adjoins.
DIRECTIONS: From Dublin (about 12 miles east to the course): Take I-580 east and exit at Airway Boulevard. The course is visible, on the south side of the freeway.

POPPY RIDGE GOLF COURSE (public, 27 holes, rees jones 1996) . . . .

4280 Greenville Road
Livermore, CA 94550
(925) 456-8202
ncga.org

	YARDAGE	PAR	RATING	SLOPE
FRONT	5212	72	70.6	129
MIDDLE	6259	72	72.8	136
BACK	7106	72	74.8	141

$35 - $70

WHAT TO EXPECT: There are three courses at Poppy Ridge that are played in 18-hole combinations. They are the Chardonnay, Zinfandel, and Merlot. The 27 holes here have been artfully blended to be similar in challenge and attractiveness. Bold, artistic bunkering is a highlight. Although this course is long, make accuracy off the tee a priority. Wind will almost always be a factor.
OUR OPINION: People pay $100 for courses that aren't half this nice. The only disappointment is that the course is not easily walkable. – Frank
NOTES: This is one of the two homes of the NCGA.
DIRECTIONS: From Dublin (about 15 miles east to the course): Take I-580 east to Livermore. Take the Greenville Road exit and head south about seven minutes to the course.

SPRINGTOWN GOLF COURSE (public, 9 holes, billy bell, jr. 1964) . . . .

939 Larkspur Drive
Livermore, CA 94550
(925) 455-5695

	YARDAGE	PAR	RATING	SLOPE
FRONT	2563	35	68.8	110
MIDDLE	2769	35	71.4	114
BACK	2862	35	67.0	116

$14 - $25

WHAT TO EXPECT: This is a open, level course with elevated and undulating greens. There are plenty of out-of-bounds, but you almost have to work to hit out.
DIRECTIONS: From Dublin (about 12 miles east to the course): Drive east on I-580 to the Springtown Boulevard exit and go north. Turn right on to Bluebell Drive. Bluebell Drive turns into Larkspur Drive.

WENTE VINEYARDS, THE COURSE AT (public, 18 holes, greg norman 1998) . . . .

5050 Arroyo Road
Livermore, CA 94550
(925) 456-2475
wentegolf.com

	YARDAGE	PAR	RATING	SLOPE
FRONT	4971	72	69.4	122
MIDDLE	6241	72	71.3	130
BACK	6941	72	74.5	142

$85 - $115

WHAT TO EXPECT: Well-framed greens and some wonderful holes and views highlight Greg Norman's first California project, which to date is the class of East Bay golf. Before you head out, get a feel for the greens; newcomers tend to over-read the break. Off the tee remember, "keep it straight"; there is a lot of out-of-bounds.
OUR OPINION: This is a difficult Greg Norman layout, with plenty of visual mind games and distractions. Wente is an every-club-in-the-bag course. The switchback trail up to the 11th hole makes the course unwalkable, but the view from the top is spectacular. The price is steep, but you have to play it at least once. – Frank
DIRECTIONS: From Dublin (about 12 miles east to the course): Take I-580 east. Exit on Portola Avenue in Livermore. Turn right on North L Street. This will change from North L Street to South L Street, then into Arroyo Road. The course is on the left.

LOS ALTOS GOLF & COUNTRY CLUB (members only, 18 holes, tom nichol 1923) . . . . .

1560 Country Club Drive
Los Altos, CA 94024
(650) 947-3110
lagcc.com

	YARDAGE	PAR	RATING	SLOPE
FRONT	5911	73	75.0	132
MIDDLE	6250	71	70.4	129
BACK	6534	71	71.7	132

$70 - $150

WHAT TO EXPECT: Noted as one of the country's most expensive clubs to join, the course is interesting with lots of hills, narrow fairways, and challenging green sites.
NOTES: Reciprocal play with other members only clubs is allowed.
DIRECTIONS: From San Jose (about 15 miles northwest to the course): Take I-280 north. Exit on Foothill Expressway and turn right. Take the Loyola Corners/Fremont Avenue exit and immediately take the first two lefts.

LA RINCONADA COUNTRY CLUB (members only, 18 holes, brad benz 1936) . . . .

14595 Clearview Drive
Los Gatos, CA 95032
(408) 395-4220

	YARDAGE	PAR	RATING	SLOPE	
FRONT	5098	71	68.9	121	**$50 - $95**
MIDDLE	5918	70	68.9	130	
BACK	6123	70	69.8	131	

WHAT TO EXPECT: This mature course features rolling, narrow fairways, and an abundance of mature oaks that seem to move directly into the flight of your ball. The undulating greens are well protected by mounding and traps.
NOTES: Reciprocal play with other members only clubs is allowed.
DIRECTIONS: From San Jose (about ten miles southwest to the course): Take Highway 17 south, exit at Lark Avenue, and turn right. Turn left on Winchester Boulevard and then right on La Rinconada Drive. Follow this to Clearview Drive and turn left.

PINE MEADOWS GOLF COURSE (public, 9 holes, james coward 1966) . . . .

451 Vine Hill Way
Martinez, CA 94553
(925) 228-2881

	YARDAGE	PAR	RATING	SLOPE	
FRONT	-	-	-	-	**$8 - $11**
MIDDLE	-	-	-	-	
BACK	1500	28	57.5	86	

WHAT TO EXPECT: This is a family golf course with tricky greens.
DIRECTIONS: From San Francisco (about 30 miles northeast to the course): Take I-80 east to Highway 4 and drive east. Exit at Morello Avenue and turn right. Turn left at Center Avenue and then left on Vine Hill Way.

SHARON HEIGHTS GOLF & COUNTRY CLUB (members only, 18 holes, j. fleming 1962)

2900 Sand Hill Road
Menlo Park, CA 94025
(650) 854-6429

	YARDAGE	PAR	RATING	SLOPE	
FRONT	5734	72	73.7	132	**$60 - $145**
MIDDLE	6476	72	71.7	134	
BACK	6837	72	73.4	138	

WHAT TO EXPECT: Tall redwoods, hilly terrain, and excellent greens mark this challenging and well-regarded course.
NOTES: Reciprocal play with other members only clubs is allowed.
DIRECTIONS: From San Francisco (about 30 miles south to the course): Take I-280 south. Exit on Sand Hill Road. and turn left to head east. The course will quickly be on the left.

MILL VALLEY GOLF COURSE (municipal, 9 holes) . . . .

280 Buena Vista Avenue
Mill Valley, CA 94941
(415) 388-9982
mvgolf.com

	YARDAGE	PAR	RATING	SLOPE	
FRONT	2159	34	62.8	104	**$7 - $23**
MIDDLE	2177	34	63.5	107	
BACK	2178	33	63.1	107	

WHAT TO EXPECT: This is a steep course surrounded by redwoods. Because of the short yardage, the course is very walkable.
NOTES: The course has no driving range.
DIRECTIONS: From San Francisco (about 13 miles north to the course): Go north on US 101. Exit on East Blithedale Avenue and head west. Turn right on Carmelita. Turn right on Buena Vista Avenue.

GREEN HILLS COUNTRY CLUB (members only, 18 holes, alister mackenzie 1930) . . . .

500 End of Ludeman Lane
Millbrae, CA   94030
(650) 583-0882
greenhillscc.com

	YARDAGE	PAR	RATING	SLOPE
FRONT	4482	69	66.1	116
MIDDLE	6032	71	70.2	136
BACK	6306	71	71.5	139

$70 - $146

WHAT TO EXPECT: The club has done an excellent job of bringing back the original Alister Mackenzie design. None of the challenges are hidden on this short layout, yet course knowledge is key to scoring well. Don't miss the greens; getting up and down is no easy task, and may be one reason this 6,300-yard track carries a slope of 139 from the back tees.

NOTES: Reciprocal play with other members only clubs is allowed.

DIRECTIONS: From San Francisco (about 15 miles south to the course): Take US 101 south. Exit on to Millbrae Avenue, heading west. Turn right on El Camino Real. After two or three miles, turn left on Ludeman Lane. There is no light for Ludeman Lane, but there is a left turn lane.

SPRING VALLEY GOLF COURSE (public, 18 holes) . . . .

3441 East Calaveras Boulevard
Milpitas, CA 95035
(408) 262-1722
springvalleygolfcourse.com

	YARDAGE	PAR	RATING	SLOPE
FRONT	5503	72	70.4	114
MIDDLE	5866	70	67.7	110
BACK	6099	70	68.8	112

$10 - $47

WHAT TO EXPECT: Set in the quiet Milpitas foothills, this busy layout relies on trees and sloping greens as its primary challenges.

OUR OPINION: If you haven't played here lately, you will be surprised by the improvements of the recent remodel. – Frank

DIRECTIONS: From San Jose (about eight miles northeast to the course): Drive north on I-680 to Milpitas. Take the Calaveras Boulevard exit and drive east. The course is on the left.

SUMMITPOINTE GOLF CLUB (public, 18 holes) . . . .

1500 Country Club Drive
Milpitas, CA 95035
(408) 262-8813
americangolf.com

	YARDAGE	PAR	RATING	SLOPE
FRONT	5519	72	70.6	121
MIDDLE	6061	72	69.7	130
BACK	6329	72	71.1	131

$17 - $80

WHAT TO EXPECT: This is a very hilly course with some great views of the Silicon Valley. The front nine is open and built on the side of a hill, while the back nine is tighter, with water frequently coming into play.

OUR OPINION: This is a wacky layout with hidden hazards that penalize good shots. – Frank

DIRECTIONS: From San Jose (about eight miles northeast to the course): Take I-680 north to the Jacklin Road exit and head east to North Park Victoria. Turn left on North Park Victoria and then right on Country Club Drive.

MORAGA COUNTRY CLUB (members only, 18 holes, robert muir graves 1974) . . . . . .

1600 Saint Andrews Drive
Moraga, CA 94556
(925) 376-2253

	YARDAGE	PAR	RATING	SLOPE
FRONT	5114	71	70.8	129
MIDDLE	5654	70	69.4	123
BACK	6073	71	71.4	128

$45 - $60

WHAT TO EXPECT: Moraga Country Club plays among the Contra Costa Hills and housing. The course is not easy to walk. It is very tight and hilly in spots, level in other places, but wherever you are, a premium is placed on accuracy. The best way to describe this course is quirky.

NOTES: Reciprocal play with other members only clubs is allowed.

DIRECTIONS: From San Francisco (about 25 miles east to the course): Take I-80 east to Highway 24 toward Walnut Creek. Take the Moraga Way exit and head southeast. Go about five miles on Moraga Way. Turn right on Saint Andrews Drive.

COYOTE CREEK GOLF CLUB (public, 36 holes, jack nicklaus 1999) . . . .

One Coyote Creek Golf Drive
Morgan Hill, CA 95037
(408) 463-1400
coyotecreekgolf.com

	YARDAGE	PAR	RATING	SLOPE
FRONT	5184	71	70.4	124
MIDDLE	6633	72	73.4	130
BACK	7027	72	75.5	141

$35 - $95

WHAT TO EXPECT: The Tournament Course plays on both sides of the freeway and is a stout test of your skills. Off the tee, the course gives you plenty of room, but the greens are surrounded by overly protective, deep traps. The greens are undulating and can unnerve the weak putter. The Valley Course routing is confusing, but the playability and improved conditions make it a much-needed addition to the area. It is flatter and somewhat easier than the neighboring Tournament Course.

OUR OPINION: Along with Cinnabar Hills, this is your best bet for an upscale golf experience in San Jose. – Shaw

NOTES: The Tournament Course hosts the Siebel Classic, a Senior PGA Tour event. The yardage listed is for the Tournament Course.

DIRECTIONS: From San Jose (about 20 miles south to the course): Drive south on US 101. Exit at Coyote Creek Golf Drive. The course is visible from the freeway.

SHORELINE GOLF LINKS (municipal, 18 holes, robert trent jones jr. 1981 & 1984) . .

2940 North Shoreline Boulevard
Mountain View, CA 94043-1347
(650) 969-2041

	YARDAGE	PAR	RATING	SLOPE
FRONT	5400	72	66.4	111
MIDDLE	6061	72	69.3	117
BACK	6576	72	71.9	124

$35 - $50

WHAT TO EXPECT: Shoreline is a level course with narrow fairways, large greens, and plenty of sand. Water comes into play on several holes. To score well, spend some time on the putting surface to get a feel for the greens – they can be fast.

NOTES: Shoreline offers a separate scorecard for low index players. They play to over 7,000 yards.

DIRECTIONS: From San Jose (about 13 miles northwest to the course): Take US 101 north to Mountain View and exit at Shoreline Boulevard. Drive northeast on Shoreline Boulevard, through the park entry gate. Go two miles to the parking lot.

CLAREMONT COUNTRY CLUB (members only, 18 holes, alister mackenzie 1904) . . . . .

5295 Broadway Terrace
Oakland, CA 94618
(510) 655-2431

	YARDAGE	PAR	RATING	SLOPE
FRONT	5372	71	71.7	127
MIDDLE	5449	72	72.2	128
BACK	5450	68	67.3	121

$40 - $55

WHAT TO EXPECT: This well-maintained old layout features some excellent holes. Its tree lined fairways are compressed into a small plot of land. An unusual feature is that three holes cross each other.

DIRECTIONS: From San Francisco (about 15 miles east to the course): Take I-80 east to Highway 24 toward Walnut Creek. Exit at Broadway and turn right. Go two miles and then turn left on Broadway Terrace. The club is on the right.

LAKE CHABOT GOLF COURSE (public, 18 holes, william lock 1927) . . . .

11450 Golf Links Road
Oakland, CA 94605
(510) 351-5812

	YARDAGE	PAR	RATING	SLOPE
FRONT	5234	71	69.7	115
MIDDLE	6018	70	68.1	119
BACK	5976	70	69.4	123

$18 - $23

WHAT TO EXPECT: This hilly course is sporty and fun, especially when it is in good condition. Notable is the long downhill par 6 finishing hole that is reachable in three shots.

OUR OPINION: Lake Chabot has a lot of personality, a friendly disposition, and a price most people can afford. The course does come with the usual muni drawbacks, but it is well worth the price. – Shaw

DIRECTIONS: From within Oakland: Off I-880 south, exit at 98th Avenue and head east. Turn left at Golf Links Road. Bear right at the fork.

MONTCLAIR GOLF COURSE (public, 9 holes) . . . .

2477 Monterey Boulevard
Oakland, CA 94611
(510) 482-0422

	YARDAGE	PAR	RATING	SLOPE
FRONT	-	-	-	-
MIDDLE	-	-	-	-
BACK	567	27	-	-

$3 - $6

WHAT TO EXPECT: If you're not pitching, you're putting.
DIRECTIONS: From within Oakland: Off Highway 13, take the Park Boulevard exit west.
Follow Park Boulevard to Monterey Boulevard and the course.

SEQUOYAH COUNTRY CLUB (members only, 18 holes) . . . .

4550 Heafey Road
Oakland, CA 94605
(510) 632-4069
sequoyahcc.com

	YARDAGE	PAR	RATING	SLOPE
FRONT	5608	72	73.3	131
MIDDLE	5901	70	69.7	128
BACK	6056	70	70.4	129

$65 - $105

WHAT TO EXPECT: Sequoyah is best known for its hilly terrain, sloping tree-lined fairways
and lightning-fast greens. The course has no parallel fairways. To score well here, you
need more then a deft putting touch – you need course knowledge.
NOTES: Reciprocal play with other members only clubs is allowed.
DIRECTIONS: From San Francisco (about 15 miles east to the course): Take I-80 east to
I-580 east. Exit on Golf Links Road and go left. Turn left on Mountain Boulevard. Turn
right on Sequoyah Road and then right on Heafey Road.

MONTANERA GOLF CLUB (members only, 18 holes, jack nicklaus) . . . .

Physical Address Not Available
Orinda, CA 94563
(925) 258-1020

	YARDAGE	PAR	RATING	SLOPE
FRONT				
MIDDLE				
BACK				

WHAT TO EXPECT: This is an often-talked-about, but yet-to-be-built, private club in the
Orinda hills.
NOTES: This course is due to open in 2003.
DIRECTIONS: Directions to the course were not available at time of press. Please check
our website www.InTheLoopGolf.com for updates.

ORINDA COUNTRY CLUB (members only, 18 holes, willie watson 1926) . . . .

315 Camino Sobrante
Orinda, CA 94563
(925) 254-0811
orindacc.org

	YARDAGE	PAR	RATING	SLOPE
FRONT	5323	72	70.8	125
MIDDLE	6123	72	70.1	130
BACK	6351	72	71.2	132

$45 - $125

WHAT TO EXPECT: You can pretty much give your driver the day off. This is a short,
narrow, tree-lined course with diminutive greens. Orinda will give up low scores provided
you keep it in the fairway.
NOTES: Reciprocal play with other members only clubs is allowed.
DIRECTIONS: From San Francisco (about 17 miles east to the course): Take I-80 east to
Highway 24 toward Walnut Creek. Take the Orinda exit and go left. Turn right on Camino
Sobrante. At the end, turn left on El Robero. Turn left to get onto Camino Sobrante
again.

SHARP PARK GOLF COURSE (public, 18 holes, alister mackenzie 1929) . . . .

Highway 1, Foot of Sharp Park Road
Pacifica, CA 94044
(650) 359-3380

	YARDAGE	PAR	RATING	SLOPE
FRONT	6095	72	73.0	120
MIDDLE	-	-	-	-
BACK	6299	72	70.6	119

$23 - $27

WHAT TO EXPECT: Not much is left of the original Alister Mackenzie design, which is situated alongside the ocean. The front nine proceeds inland, while the back nine runs along the ocean.

OUR OPINION: Sharp Park provides some engaging ambience, even if somewhat rough around the edges. – Bob

DIRECTIONS: From San Francisco (about 12 miles south to the course): Take I-280 south to Highway 1. Head south toward Pacifica, about three miles. Take the Sharp Park Road/Fairway Drive exit, which leads directly to the golf course.

PALO ALTO GOLF COURSE (public, 18 holes, william bell, jr. 1956) . . . .

1875 Embarcadero Road
Palo Alto, CA 94303
(650) 856-0881
city.palo-alto.ca.us/golf

	YARDAGE	PAR	RATING	SLOPE
FRONT	5679	72	71.8	118
MIDDLE	6580	72	71.1	117
BACK	6820	72	72.4	118

$28 - $39

WHAT TO EXPECT: If every course were this driver friendly, the world would be beautiful place. The layout features super-size fairways. Palo Alto has benefited from a recent remodel, with improved conditioning and some more interesting rolling fairways. The greens are large with subtle breaks. To score well, you will have to carry a big stick and club up when hitting into the greens. The course plays long, and you will encounter plenty of wind.

OUR OPINION: Public courses like this one are good for the community and fun to play. We wish there were more of them, especially in this area. – Shaw

DIRECTIONS: From San Francisco (about 35 miles south to the course): Take US 101 south to Palo Alto and exit at Embarcadero Road east. Follow Embarcadero Road east to the golf course.

PALO ALTO HILLS GOLF & COUNTRY CLUB (members only, 18 holes, c. glasson 1958) .

3000 Alexis Drive
Palo Alto, CA 94304
(650) 948-2320

	YARDAGE	PAR	RATING	SLOPE
FRONT	5147	71	70.7	128
MIDDLE	5980	71	70.5	131
BACK	6239	71	71.7	133

$55 - $125

WHAT TO EXPECT: This tight, hilly course is more challenging than its relatively short yardage would suggest. There are some wonderful views of the San Francisco Bay.

DIRECTIONS: From San Jose (about 20 miles northwest to the course): Take I-280 north. Exit on Page Mill Road, and head west toward the mountains. Turn right on Alexis Drive and the club is on the right.

PITTSBURG'S DELTA VIEW GOLF COURSE (municipal, 18 holes, r. muir graves 1947) . .

2242 Golf Club Road
Pittsburg, CA 94565
(925) 439-4040
deltaviewgolf.com

	YARDAGE	PAR	RATING	SLOPE
FRONT	5328	72	71.1	124
MIDDLE	5775	70	68.1	122
BACK	6333	70	70.7	127

$12 - $26

WHAT TO EXPECT: This course can get windy, and together with some dramatic elevations changes, makes par more elusive than you would imagine. Pittsburg is an extremely popular course with the locals, so a four hour round in the afternoon is not realistic.
OUR OPINION: Don't miss the tri-tip sandwich at Zandonella's, the on-course restaurant. – Shaw
DIRECTIONS: From Martinez (about 13 miles east to the course): Take Highway 4 east. Exit on Bailey Road and go south. Turn left on Leland. Turn right on Golf Club Road after about one and one-half miles.

CONTRA COSTA COUNTRY CLUB (members only, 18 holes, members 1925) . . . .

801 Golf Club Road
Pleasant Hill, CA 94523
(925) 685-8288
contracostacc.org

	YARDAGE	PAR	RATING	SLOPE
FRONT	5300	72	71.3	125
MIDDLE	6230	72	70.2	127
BACK	6527	72	71.6	132

$60 - $75

WHAT TO EXPECT: A short course with no water, how hard can it be? Not very, if you hit the ball perfectly straight and avoid the trees and rough. Even if you hit it straight, you may encounter some difficult lies on undulating fairways. Oh, make sure you don't hit the ball above the hole, or you'll rarely make the putt. One last thing, the course tends to play much longer than the scorecard indicates.
NOTES: Reciprocal play with other members only clubs is allowed.
DIRECTIONS: From Walnut Creek (about 5 miles north to the course): Take I-680 north. Exit on Concord Avenue. Turn left on Diamond and then left again on Concord Avenue. Turn left on Contra Costa Road and then turn right onto Golf Club Road.

CASTLEWOOD COUNTRY CLUB (members only, 36 holes, william bell 1923) . . . .

707 Country Club Circle
Pleasanton, CA 94566
(925) 485-2250

	YARDAGE	PAR	RATING	SLOPE
FRONT	5919	74	74.5	131
MIDDLE	6374	72	71.1	126
BACK	6678	72	72.4	128

$75 - $100

WHAT TO EXPECT: The Valley Course, unlike its sister course, is a flat, straightforward layout. This is a good test of golf crammed into a minimum amount of space. The Hill Course is the older of the two and plays along a relatively steep hillside around homes. It boasts several interesting, tough holes.
NOTES: The yardage listed is for Valley Course.
DIRECTIONS: From Walnut Creek (about 20 miles south to the course): Take I-680 south and exit at Castlewood Drive/Sunol Boulevard. Go right and stay to the right at the fork. The club is at the top.

PLEASANTON FAIRWAYS GOLF COURSE (public, 9 holes, roland curtola 1974) . . . . . .

Alameda County Fairgrounds
Pleasanton, CA 94566
(925) 462-4653

	YARDAGE	PAR	RATING	SLOPE
FRONT	1714	30	57.7	88
MIDDLE	-	-	-	-
BACK	1714	30	58.0	84

$11 - $27

WHAT TO EXPECT: This is a small course in the infield of the Alameda County Fairgrounds that has elevated greens and actually will make you work for a par.
NOTES: One of the area's best driving ranges is located just a half mile away.
DIRECTIONS: From within Pleasanton: Off I-680, exit at Bernal Avenue and drive east. Turn left at Pleasanton Avenue and enter the fairgrounds.

RUBY HILL GOLF CLUB (members only, 18 holes, jack nicklaus 1996) . . . .

3404 West Ruby Hill Drive
Pleasanton, CA 94566
(925) 417-5850
rubyhill.com

	YARDAGE	PAR	RATING	SLOPE
FRONT	5279	72	71.3	123
MIDDLE	7017	72	74.6	130
BACK	7448	72	76.7	134

$75 - $125

WHAT TO EXPECT: This is a long, relatively open course that plays among upscale housing. It is forgiving off the tee and places a premium on the approaches to the subtle, immaculate greens.
DIRECTIONS: From Walnut Creek (about 25 miles south to the course): Take I-680 south. Take the Bernal Avenue exit and go east about three miles. Turn right on Vineyard Avenue and go almost three miles. Turn right into the golf club.

EMERALD HILLS GOLF CLUB (public, 9 holes, van gorder 1960) . . . .

938 Wilmington Way
Redwood City, CA 94062
(650) 368-7820
emeraldhillsgolf.com

	YARDAGE	PAR	RATING	SLOPE
FRONT	1205	27	52.9	71
MIDDLE	-	-	-	-
BACK	1205	27	54.2	88

$9 - $13

WHAT TO EXPECT: Emerald Hills is a hilly, par-3 course with small greens and a few ponds.
DIRECTIONS: From San Francisco (about 30 miles south to the course): Take I-280 south, exit at Edgewood Road, and go west. Turn left on Canada and then left on Jefferson. Turn right on Wilmington.

MENLO COUNTRY CLUB (members only, 18 holes, thomas nicoll 1906) . . . .

2300 Woodside Road
Redwood City, CA 94064
(650) 366-9910

	YARDAGE	PAR	RATING	SLOPE
FRONT	5641	72	72.5	123
MIDDLE	6034	70	69.3	124
BACK	6315	70	70.5	126

$35 - $40

WHAT TO EXPECT: Accuracy is at a premium as old oaks line Menlo's narrow fairways. This exclusive club is a short but stout test of golf and receives little play.
DIRECTIONS: From San Francisco (about 30 miles south to the course): Take I-280 south and exit on Woodside Road. Head west, and the club is on the left.

RICHMOND COUNTRY CLUB (members only, 18 holes, pat j. markovich 1924) . . . . . .

One Markovich Lane
Richmond, CA 94806
(510) 232-7815
richmondcc.com

	YARDAGE	PAR	RATING	SLOPE	
FRONT	5214	72	69.1	116	**$65 - $100**
MIDDLE	6313	72	70.9	125	
BACK	6572	72	72.0	127	

WHAT TO EXPECT: This old course is short, with large eucalyptus and pine trees, tight fairways, and tiny, sloping greens. Making par is more difficult than meets the eye.
NOTES: Reciprocal play with other members only clubs is allowed.
DIRECTIONS: From San Francisco (about 20 miles northeast to the course): Take I-80 east and exit at Richmond Parkway. Go about four miles, exit on Giant Highway and turn right. Turn on Markovich Lane.

GLENEAGLES INTERNATIONAL GOLF COURSE (public, 9 holes, john fleming 1962) . . .

2100 Sunnydale Avenue
San Francisco, CA 94134
(415) 587-2425

	YARDAGE	PAR	RATING	SLOPE	
FRONT	2930	36	75.6	136	**$11 - $24**
MIDDLE	-	-	-	-	
BACK	3195	36	72.8	140	

WHAT TO EXPECT: Prepare for battle. This rugged (unkempt) nine-hole course will push your game to the limit. You will be fighting against hilly, narrow, tree-lined terrain, uneven lies and hitting onto little greens. If you play in the morning, you must brave the elements San Francisco is famous for – fog and wind. How many nine-hole courses have you seen with a slope of 140?
OUR OPINION: This is not in the best part of town. Like most courses in San Francisco, the facility is badly in need of renovation. This course is a diamond in the rough, and could be a showplace. – Bob
DIRECTIONS: From San Francisco: Take US 101 south. Exit at Paul Avenue. Take Mansell straight up the hill. Stay to the left and turn left on Sunnydale Avenue. The driveway is on the left and has no signage.

GOLDEN GATE PARK GOLF COURSE (public, 9 holes, jack fleming 1950) . . . .

47th Avenue and Fulton Street
San Francisco, CA 94117
(415) 751-8987

	YARDAGE	PAR	RATING	SLOPE	
FRONT	-	-	-	-	**$7 - $15**
MIDDLE	-	-	-	-	
BACK	1357	27	-	-	

WHAT TO EXPECT: This pitch-and-putt course is located in Golden Gate Park.
DIRECTIONS: From the Golden Gate Bridge southbound: Take the 19th Avenue exit. Off Park Presidio, turn right on Fulton. Turn left on 47th Avenue into Golden Gate Park.

HARDING PARK GOLF COURSE (public, 27 holes, willie watson 1925) . . . .

Harding Road @ Skyline Boulevard
San Francisco, CA 94132
(415) 661-1865

	YARDAGE	PAR	RATING	SLOPE	
FRONT	6195	72	73.9	122	
MIDDLE	6471	72	70.3	119	**$7 - $31**
BACK	6743	72	71.7	124	

WHAT TO EXPECT: This venerable public layout with its tree-lined look is reminiscent of its famous nearby neighbor, the Olympic Club.

OUR OPINION: The best thing about Harding Park is its potential. Conditioning has been a problem, and the course still awaits extensive improvements. For the golfer looking for the country club setting, don' t play here. For any golfer who wants to play an excellent layout and can ignore sub-par conditioning, go for it. – Shaw

DIRECTIONS: From the Golden Gate Bridge southbound: Take the 19th Avenue exit. Off Park Presidio, turn right on Fulton. Turn left at the beach onto Skyline Boulevard. The course is on the right.

LINCOLN PARK GOLF COURSE (municipal, 18 holes, tom bendelow 1910) . . . .

34th & Clement Streets
San Francisco, CA 94121
(415) 221-9911

	YARDAGE	PAR	RATING	SLOPE	
FRONT	4732	70	66.0	105	
MIDDLE	4948	68	65.1	107	**$23 - $27**
BACK	5146	68	66.0	109	

WHAT TO EXPECT: The course provides some of the best views in the Bay Area. Beneath the beauty you will find a fun course with rolling hills, side-hill lies, and blind shots.

OUR OPINION: Lincoln Park is worth playing for the views; just don't expect much in the way of conditioning or fast play. We continually hear rumors that upgrades are coming soon. Let's hope so. – Shaw

DIRECTIONS: From the Golden Gate Bridge southbound: Take the 19th Avenue exit. Off Park Presidio, turn right on Geary. Turn right on 34th Avenue. The parking lot is on the left, and the clubhouse on the right.

PRESIDIO GOLF COURSE (public, 18 holes, robert johnstone 1895) . . . .

300 Finley Road/ Arguello Gate
San Francisco, CA   94129
(415) 561-4661
presidiogolf.com

	YARDAGE	PAR	RATING	SLOPE	
FRONT	5785	73	74.2	131	
MIDDLE	6141	72	70.8	131	**$42 - $99**
BACK	6478	72	72.2	136	

WHAT TO EXPECT: Renovations have kept this former military course in the forefront of San Francisco golf. Tall, tree-lined fairways surround each hole on this challenging, hilly layout.

OUR OPINION: With green fees of $42 for weekday golf, this course is still a bargain. Of course, that fact is not unknown by area golfers. This is a must-play for any golfer who likes a great challenge. – Shaw

DIRECTIONS: From Stonestown in San Francisco: Go north on 19th Avenue, toward the Golden Gate Bridge. Make a right turn on Lake Street and a left on Arguello Boulevard to the course. The course is ten minutes from downtown.

SAN FRANCISCO GOLF CLUB (members only, 18 holes, a. w. tillinghast 1895) . . . . . .

Brotherhood Way & Thomas More
San Francisco, CA 94132
(415) 469-4122

	YARDAGE	PAR	RATING	SLOPE	
FRONT	6015	73	75.8	137	**$50 - $150**
MIDDLE	6400	71	71.7	131	
BACK	6716	71	73.0	134	

WHAT TO EXPECT: This is one of America's finest courses, known for its distinctive, flashed Tillinghast bunkering. When they speed up the greens, the course can play much more difficult, despite its relatively modest length.
DIRECTIONS: From the Golden Gate Bridge southbound: Take the 19th Avenue exit. After Stonestown, turn right on Junipero Serra and then right on Brotherhood Way. Then take a left on Thomas Moore.

SAN GERONIMO GOLF COURSE (public, 18 holes, arthur vernon mc kahn 1965) . . . . .

5800 Sir Francis Drake Boulevard
San Geronimo, CA 94963
(415) 488-4030
bayinsider.com

	YARDAGE	PAR	RATING	SLOPE	
FRONT	5140	72	69.9	125	**$15 - $60**
MIDDLE	6439	72	72.3	132	
BACK	6781	72	73.8	135	

WHAT TO EXPECT: The front nine is a forgiving and open course. The back nine is longer and has more elevation. If you miss left on most of the holes on the back, you will find yourself out-of-bounds or in a water hazard. An afternoon wind is common.
OUR OPINION: They say its links but the front nine is more a muni-style layout. The back nine is a real challenge. – Frank
DIRECTIONS: From San Francisco (about 30 miles northwest to the course): Go north on US 101. Exit Kentfield/San Anselmo to Sir Francis Drake Boulevard. Take Sir Francis Drake Boulevard west for 13.5 miles. The course is on the left.

ALMADEN GOLF & COUNTRY CLUB (members only, 18 holes, jack fleming 1955) . . . . .

6663 Hampton Drive
San Jose, CA 95120
(408) 268-3959

	YARDAGE	PAR	RATING	SLOPE	
FRONT	5591	72	71.9	125	**$50 - $110**
MIDDLE	6550	72	72.4	126	
BACK	6945	72	74.1	132	

WHAT TO EXPECT: Almaden meanders amongst rolling terrain and homes. It has been a popular site for both the LPGA and Nike Tours, as well as local pro events.
NOTES: Reciprocal play with other members only clubs is allowed.
DIRECTIONS: From north of San Jose: From US 101 or I-280, exit Highway 85 heading south. Exit onto Almaden Expressway and turn left. Take Almaden Expressway to Crown Boulevard and turn right to Hampton Drive. Follow Hampton Drive to the course.

BOULDER RIDGE, THE GOLF CLUB AT (members only, 18 holes, bradford benz 2001)

6039 Crossview Circle
San Jose, CA 95120
(408) 323-9900
troongolf.com

	YARDAGE	PAR	RATING	SLOPE
FRONT	-	-	-	-
MIDDLE	-	-	-	-
BACK	6930	72	-	-

WHAT TO EXPECT: Boulder Ridge was once slated to be a public facility. The course features dramatic elevation changes and views of San Jose and beyond. Once the quarry that helped build Stanford, the rocks left over are now obstacles that should be avoided.
DIRECTIONS: Directions were not available at time of press. Please check our website, www.InTheLoopGolf.com for updates.

CINNABAR HILLS GOLF CLUB (public, 27 holes, john harbottle 1998) . . . .

23600 McKean Road
San Jose, CA 95141
(408) 323-7815
cinnabarhills.com

	YARDAGE	PAR	RATING	SLOPE
FRONT	5070	72	68.1	120
MIDDLE	6397	72	70.8	130
BACK	6854	72	73.1	135

$35 - $120

WHAT TO EXPECT: There are three nines, the Lake, Canyon, and Mountain Courses. Terrific views, abundant bunkering, and lightning-quick greens characterize the 27 holes of this welcome new addition to the San Jose golf scene.
OUR OPINION: Even if there were a bountiful supply of upscale daily fee facilities in San Jose (there is not), you would still want to play Cinnabar. The course to watch out for is the Mountain Course. Do not pick your tees based on yardage. Save yourself some strokes; ask the pro-shop for some assistance. The golf memorabilia in the clubhouse is worth checking out. – Shaw
NOTES: The yardage listed is for the Lake and Mountain nines.
DIRECTIONS: From within San Jose: Off US 101, take the Bernal Avenue exit and head west. Turn left on Santa Teresa and travel about four miles. Turn right on Bailey Avenue. Turn left when it dead-ends.

PLEASANT HILLS GOLF COURSE (public, 18 holes, henry duino, joseph soto 1959) . . .

2050 South White Road
San Jose, CA 95148
(408) 238-3485

	YARDAGE	PAR	RATING	SLOPE
FRONT	5800	73	71.5	115
MIDDLE	6198	72	69.2	120
BACK	6510	72	70.6	123

$22 - $30

WHAT TO EXPECT: This is a level, easily walkable course with over 4,500 trees. Out-of-bounds comes into play on six holes. The greens are large and do not punish the average putter. Course conditions are fair, but it's a good price point and nice place for juniors and beginners.
NOTES: There is a nine-hole pitch-and-putt course called Cypress Greens at the same location.
DIRECTIONS: From within San Jose: Off US 101, exit at Tully Road and head east. Turn left on White Road.

RANCHO DEL PUEBLO (public, 9 holes, damian pascuzzo 2001) . . . .

1649 Hermocilla Way
San Jose, CA 95116
(408) 347-0990
ranchodelpueblo.com

	YARDAGE	PAR	RATING	SLOPE	
FRONT	1122	28	-	-	**$9 - $13**
MIDDLE	-	-	-	-	
BACK	1418	28	-	-	

WHAT TO EXPECT: The course incorporates three ponds and multiple sand bunkers.
NOTES: Bilingual PGA professionals are on staff. Twice a week the driving range features grass, a rarity in the area.
DIRECTIONS: From within San Jose: Take US 101 south, exit Alum Rock, and turn left. Turn right on King Road. The course is visible from there.

SAN JOSE COUNTRY CLUB (members only, 18 holes, tom nichol 1906) . . . .

15571 Alum Rock Avenue
San Jose, CA 95127
(408) 258-3636

	YARDAGE	PAR	RATING	SLOPE	
FRONT	5474	72	71.9	126	**$55 - $100**
MIDDLE	5926	70	69.4	124	
BACK	6200	70	70.5	127	

WHAT TO EXPECT: This old course, with some hilly lies and small, sloped greens, plays more difficult than the yardage would suggest. A highlight is the view from the fourth tee; you can see most of the golf course and San Francisco.
NOTES: Reciprocal play with other members only clubs is allowed.
DIRECTIONS: From within San Jose: Off I-680, exit on Alum Rock Avenue and head east. Go about two and one-half miles and the club is on the left, just past a narrow bridge.

SAN JOSE MUNICIPAL GOLF COURSE (municipal, 18 holes, robert muir graves 1968) .

1560 Oakland Road
San Jose, CA 95131
(408) 441-4653

	YARDAGE	PAR	RATING	SLOPE	
FRONT	5504	72	69.7	112	**$29 - $40**
MIDDLE	6362	72	68.7	105	
BACK	6659	72	70.1	108	

WHAT TO EXPECT: This busy, clean, well-maintained course is not particularly interesting, but rather designed to accommodate heavy play. San Jose is one of the better, more aggressive operations around.
DIRECTIONS: From within San Jose: Off US 101, take the North 13th Street exit and head east to Old Oakland Road. The course is on the right.

SANTA TERESA GOLF CLUB (public, 18 holes, george santana 1962) . . . .

260 Bernal Road
San Jose, CA 95119
(408) 225-2650

	YARDAGE	PAR	RATING	SLOPE	
FRONT	6032	73	73.5	125	**$11 - $44**
MIDDLE	6419	71	70.6	122	
BACK	6738	71	72.1	124	

WHAT TO EXPECT: Planted adjacent to hilly, wild terrain, this playable, park-setting layout is very popular with the local golfers.
DIRECTIONS: From within San Jose: Off US 101, take the Bernal Road exit and drive west. Go about one and one-half miles and the course is on the left.

SILVER CREEK VALLEY COUNTRY CLUB (members only, 18 holes, ted robinson 1992) .

5460 Country Club Parkway
San Jose, CA 95138
(408) 239-5775
scvcc.com

	YARDAGE	PAR	RATING	SLOPE	
FRONT	5289	72	71.1	127	**$70 - $115**
MIDDLE	6439	72	72.2	134	
BACK	6868	72	74.0	140	

WHAT TO EXPECT: Built in the hill, this development course is scenic, but really requires a golf cart to play it. With the elevation changes and hazards, local knowledge comes in handy.

NOTES: Reciprocal play with other members only clubs is allowed.

DIRECTIONS: From within San Jose: Off US 101, exit at Blossom Hill/Silver Creek and head east. Drive about three miles. The entrance is on the right.

VILLAGES GOLF & COUNTRY CLUB, THE (members only, 27 holes, r. m. graves 1970) .

5000 Cribari Lane
San Jose, CA 95135
(408) 274-3220
the-villages.com

	YARDAGE	PAR	RATING	SLOPE	
FRONT	5851	73	72.2	120	**$32 - $55**
MIDDLE	6338	72	69.7	120	
BACK	6707	72	71.6	122	

WHAT TO EXPECT: There is nothing particularly easy or short about this senior community golf course, which measures over 6,700 yards from the tips. The club also has a nine-hole, par-27 course.

NOTES: Reciprocal play with other members only clubs is allowed.

DIRECTIONS: From within San Jose: Off US 101, exit at Yerba Buena Road and head east. Turn right on San Felipe Road, and follow into the Villages.

MONARCH BAY GOLF CLUB (public, 27 holes, john harbottle) . . . .

13800 Neptune Drive
San Leandro, CA   94577
(510) 895-2162
americangolf.com

	YARDAGE	PAR	RATING	SLOPE	
FRONT	6061	71	68.8	115	**$30 - $83**
MIDDLE	6937	71	73.2	121	
BACK	7015	71	73.5	121	

WHAT TO EXPECT: The Tony Lema Course has been renovated with great care. The course is Scottish-links in style, right down to the tons of deep bunkers, with three-to-four-foot faces. The greens are fairly level with subtle breaks. On the back nine, holes 15 through 17 play along the water's edge. Wind can be a factor. Native areas allow players a free drop. The popular executive course is lined with mature trees.

OUR OPINION: The improvements have not only given this course a new body, but also a new soul. Well worth checking out.

NOTES: There are two courses, the 18-hole Tony Lema Course and a nine-hole executive course. The yardage listed is for the Tony Lema Course.

DIRECTIONS: From San Francisco (about 20 miles southeast to the course): Take I-80 east to I-880 south. Exit on Marina Boulevard and head west. Marina Boulevard becomes Neptune Drive.

CORDEVALLE GOLF CLUB (members only, 18 holes, robert trent jones jr. 1999) . . . . .

One Cordevalle Club Drive
San Martin, CA 95046
(408) 695-4590
cordevalle.com

	YARDAGE	PAR	RATING	SLOPE
FRONT	5385	72	71.0	120
MIDDLE	6703	72	72.7	136
BACK	7170	72	75.0	142

$75 - $350

WHAT TO EXPECT: This walkable links-style course features water on nine holes and concludes with very difficult par 4s on each nine. The course features awesome bunkering, no housing, and is set in oak-dotted, rolling hills.

OUR OPINION: This is one of the Robert Trent Jones' groups best layouts anywhere. A must-play if you can. – Bob

DIRECTIONS: From San Jose (about 25 miles south to the course): Go south on US 101 to Morgan Hill. Exit at San Martin and head west. Make a left on Santa Teresa and a right on Cordevalle Club Drive.

PENINSULA GOLF & COUNTRY CLUB, THE (members only, 18 holes, d. ross 1911) . . .

701 Madera Drive
San Mateo, CA 94403
(650) 638-2239

	YARDAGE	PAR	RATING	SLOPE
FRONT	5782	74	73.5	131
MIDDLE	6345	71	71.7	130
BACK	6578	71	72.8	132

$50 - $135

WHAT TO EXPECT: Noted as one of the few courses west of the Mississippi that famed architect Donald Ross built, this mature hillside layout is dominated by large pines and eucalyptus and distant views of Mount Diablo across the bay to the east.

NOTES: Reciprocal play with other members only clubs is allowed.

DIRECTIONS: From San Francisco (about 20 miles south to the course): Take US 101 south to Highway 92 west. Take the Alameda de las Pulgas exit and drive south. Turn right on Madera Drive.

POPLAR CREEK GOLF COURSE (public, 18 holes, remodeled 2000) . . . .

1700 Coyote Point Drive
San Mateo, CA 94401
(650) 522-4653
poplarcreekgolf.com

	YARDAGE	PAR	RATING	SLOPE
FRONT	4768	70	67.6	113
MIDDLE	5645	70	67.3	111
BACK	6042	70	69.0	113

$10 - $38

WHAT TO EXPECT: Poplar Creek has recently been renovated. Gone are the constant parallel fairways. The greens have been elevated and are now undulating. Miss the greens and you will have a challenge getting up and down. There are no hidden agendas on this layout.

DIRECTIONS: From San Francisco (about 20 miles south to the course): Take US 101 south to San Mateo and exit at Poplar Avenue. Turn right on North Humboldt and then right on Peninsula Avenue to go back over the freeway. Follow the signs to Coyote Point Drive by taking two lefts to get to the course.

MCINNIS PARK GOLF CENTER (public, 9 holes, fred bliss 1993) . . . .

350 Smith Ranch Road
San Rafael, CA 94903
(415) 492-1800
mcinnisparkgolfacademy.com

	YARDAGE	PAR	RATING	SLOPE	
FRONT	1458	31	60.0	94	**$12 - $18**
MIDDLE	1695	31	60.2	94	
BACK	1842	31	61.0	96	

WHAT TO EXPECT: This is a modern nine-hole course with water on two holes. There is out-of-bounds throughout, but the challenge at McInnis Park is fairway to green. The green sites are mounded and the greens are undulating. To score well, you must hit the greens in regulation because getting up and down from off the greens is not easy.

OUR OPINION: The food and service at the restaurant rate high among local and visiting golfers. – Shaw

NOTES: This is a golf and entertainment complex that includes a driving range, miniature golf, and batting cages.

DIRECTIONS: From San Francisco (about 20 miles north to the course): Take US 101 north and exit at Smith Ranch Road/Lucas Valley Road. Stay to the right. Smith Ranch Road dead-ends in the golf center's lot.

PEACOCK GAP GOLF & COUNTRY CLUB (semi-private, 18 holes, william bell 1960) . . .

333 Biscayne Drive
San Rafael, CA 94901
(415) 453-4940

	YARDAGE	PAR	RATING	SLOPE	
FRONT	5629	73	71.9	126	**$32 - $60**
MIDDLE	6001	71	68.3	116	
BACK	6355	71	70.0	118	

WHAT TO EXPECT: Avoiding lateral water hazards, fourteen of them, and trees will be your biggest challenge. Twelve holes run parallel to a small creek. There is one lake, and the San Francisco Bay comes into play on one hole. On some holes, if you miss the fairways far enough, you will land in another; however, the mature trees won't make your return shot easy. The greens are straightforward with little break.

NOTES: Reciprocal play with other members only clubs is allowed.

DIRECTIONS: From San Francisco (about 20 miles north to the course): Go north on US 101. Take the Central San Rafael exit. Turn right on Second Street. Turn left on Biscayne Drive.

BRIDGES GOLF CLUB, THE (public, 18 holes, damian pascuzzo 1999) . . . .

9000 South Gale Ridge Road
San Ramon, CA 94583
(925) 735-4253
thebridgesgolf.com

	YARDAGE	PAR	RATING	SLOPE
FRONT	6342	73	71.3	130
MIDDLE	6733	73	73.0	132
BACK	7082	73	74.5	134

$55 - $95

WHAT TO EXPECT: The Bridges is situated in a valley bisected by a creek and surrounded by houses above. It features bold, attractive bunkering and is a very demanding layout from tee to green with plenty of forced carries and challenging lies.

OUR OPINION: If you want to push your game to the limit, you want to play The Bridges; however, don't bring younger or less experienced golfers, as they will struggle throughout the round. – Frank

DIRECTIONS: From Walnut Creek (about 18 miles south to the course): Take I-680 south. Exit at Bollinger Canyon Road and turn left (east). Drive for approximately three miles. Turn right on Gale Ridge Road.

CANYON LAKES COUNTRY CLUB (public, 18 holes, ted robinson 1987) . . . .

640 Bollinger Canyon Way
San Ramon, CA 94583
(925) 735-6511

	YARDAGE	PAR	RATING	SLOPE
FRONT	5230	71	69.9	121
MIDDLE	5966	71	69.7	126
BACK	6370	71	71.4	129

$65 - $80

WHAT TO EXPECT: This is one of the East Bay's better and tougher tracks. The course plays among housing, around water and creeks, and up and down the hilly terrain.

DIRECTIONS: From Walnut Creek (about 15 miles south to the course): Take I-680 south. Take the Bollinger Canyon exit and head east. Turn left on Canyon Lakes Drive. Immediately turn left on Bollinger Canyon Way, into the shopping center.

SAN RAMON ROYAL VISTA GOLF CLUB (public, 18 holes, clark glasson 1962) . . . .

9430 Fircrest Lane
San Ramon, CA 94583
(925) 828-6100

	YARDAGE	PAR	RATING	SLOPE
FRONT	5781	72	73.5	124
MIDDLE	6163	72	70.1	119
BACK	6425	72	71.1	122

$15 - $39

WHAT TO EXPECT: This level course has been renovated, and an island green has been added. Trees and homes frame the layout, which features many doglegs, most of which favor the player who can work the ball left to right.

DIRECTIONS: From Walnut Creek (about 15 miles south to the course): Take I-680 south. Exit at Alcosta Boulevard and go east. Turn left on Fircrest Lane.

PRUNERIDGE GOLF CLUB (public, 9 holes, jack fleming, robert trent jones jr. 1964) .

400 North Saratoga Avenue
Santa Clara, CA 95050
(408) 248-4424

	YARDAGE	PAR	RATING	SLOPE	
FRONT	1628	31	60.0	75	**$16 - $16**
MIDDLE	1628	31	57.2	86	
BACK	1814	31	58.0	92	

WHAT TO EXPECT: Pruneridge has only two holes that run side by side, and the course is well maintained. The fairways are narrow and most are lined by town homes, so out-of-bounds does come into play.

DIRECTIONS: From San Jose (about five miles north to the course): Take I-280 north. Exit on Saratoga Avenue and turn right. The course is on the left, after Pruneridge Avenue.

SANTA CLARA GOLF & TENNIS CLUB (public, 18 holes, robert muir graves 1987) . . . .

5155 Stars and Stripes Drive
Santa Clara, CA 95054
(408) 980-9515
americangolf.com

	YARDAGE	PAR	RATING	SLOPE	
FRONT	5492	72	70.4	112	**$28 - $36**
MIDDLE	6329	72	70.9	122	
BACK	6704	72	72.8	125	

WHAT TO EXPECT: One of Northern California's busiest courses, Santa Clara features mildly rolling fairways, large greens and is open and susceptible to the wind.

DIRECTIONS: From San Jose (about 6 miles north to the course): Take US 101 north and exit onto Great America Parkway. Make a right on Tasman Drive and the course is on the left.

DE LAVEAGA GOLF COURSE (public, 18 holes, bert stamps 1970) . . . .

401 Upper Park Road, Box A
Santa Cruz, CA 95065
(831) 423-7212
delaveagagolf.com

	YARDAGE	PAR	RATING	SLOPE	
FRONT	5322	72	71.2	124	**$35 - $45**
MIDDLE	-	-	-	-	
BACK	6005	72	70.0	136	

WHAT TO EXPECT: This is a hilly and interesting layout that features two very challenging opening par 5s, the 1st and 10th holes. Accurate shot-making is essential, as there is an abundance of trouble to the sides. The course plays much tougher than it looks.

OUR OPINION: De Laveaga is an interesting track, an excellent value and a well run facility. We recommend it. The course can be a little rough around the edges because its popularity makes it hard to maintain consistently. – The Mole

DIRECTIONS: From San Jose (about 35 miles southwest to the course): Take Highway 17 south to Highway 1, driving south to the Morrisey exit. Turn right on Fairmount and then another right on Branciforte. Turn left on Upper Park Road to the course.

PASATIEMPO GOLF COURSE (semi-private, 18 holes, alister mackenzie 1929) . . . .

20 Clubhouse Road
Santa Cruz, CA 95060
(831) 459-9155
pasatiempo.com

	YARDAGE	PAR	RATING	SLOPE
FRONT	5646	72	73.4	132
MIDDLE	6128	70	71.2	135
BACK	6493	70	72.6	139

$125 - $140

WHAT TO EXPECT: This Alister Mackenzie masterpiece opened in 1929 and annually is included among America's best. Though relatively short, it features some of the best green sites in American golf, making it a beautiful, classic challenge.

OUR OPINION: Alister Mackenzie retired to Pasatiempo. To get a sense of what golf was, and unfortunately no longer is, this is a must-play. The 16th hole is one of the toughest par 4s you'll ever play. – Andy

NOTES: The club stays private until 10:30 a.m. on Saturday and 9:30 a.m. on Sunday.

DIRECTIONS: From San Jose (about 35 miles southwest to the course): Take Highway 17 south toward Santa Cruz. Take the Pasatiempo Drive exit. Follow the signs to the clubhouse. The clubhouse is on the right.

SARATOGA COUNTRY CLUB (members only, 9 holes) . . . .

21990 Prospect Road
Saratoga, CA 95070
(408) 253-5494
saratogacc.com

	YARDAGE	PAR	RATING	SLOPE
FRONT	2390	35	69.6	118
MIDDLE	-	-	-	-
BACK	2390	34	65.0	123

$22 - $54

WHAT TO EXPECT: Extremely short, tight and hilly, this is definitely a "local knowledge" course.

DIRECTIONS: From Cupertino (about five miles south to the course): Off I-280, take Highway 85 south. Exit on De Anza Boulevard and turn right. Turn right on Prospect Road. Keep to the left to stay on Prospect Road and head up into the hills.

VALLEY GARDENS GOLF COURSE (public, 9 holes, bob baldock 1971) . . . .

263 Mount Hermon Road
Scotts Valley, CA 95066
(831) 438-3058
valleygardens.com

	YARDAGE	PAR	RATING	SLOPE
FRONT	1534	32	55.0	82
MIDDLE	-	-	-	-
BACK	1782	31	58.0	85

$11 - $15

WHAT TO EXPECT: This is a flat, short nine-holer that features small greens and a variety of trees.

DIRECTIONS: From San Jose (about 25 miles southwest to the course): Take Highway 17 south. Exit onto Mount Hermon Road and turn right. The course is on the left.

CALIFORNIA GOLF CLUB (members only, 18 holes, locke & macan 1918) . . . .

844 West Orange Avenue
South San Francisco, CA 94080
(650) 589-0144

	YARDAGE	PAR	RATING	SLOPE
FRONT	5969	72	75.9	136
MIDDLE	6477	72	72.0	137
BACK	6735	72	73.2	139

$80 - $160

WHAT TO EXPECT: This is a hilly, tight, well-bunkered course that is often damp and windy. It will provide most anyone with all the challenge they can handle. Quietly, California Golf Club is one of Northern California's premier courses.

DIRECTIONS: From San Francisco (about 8 miles south to the course): Go south on I-280, exit on Westborough Boulevard and head east. Turn right at West Orange Avenue. The club is on the right.

STANFORD UNIVERSITY GOLF COURSE (members only, 18 holes, william bell 1930) . .

198 Junipero Serra Boulevard
Stanford, CA 94305
(650) 323-0944
stanfordgolfcourse.com

	YARDAGE	PAR	RATING	SLOPE
FRONT	5697	73	72.5	130
MIDDLE	6344	71	71.5	130
BACK	6778	71	73.4	136

$75 - $150

WHAT TO EXPECT: Considered one of America's top college courses, Stanford boasts many striking oaks, as well as eucalyptus, with a creek often coming into play and large greens. Sufficiently long, it is a stalwart test of golf.

DIRECTIONS: From San Francisco (about 35 miles south to the course): Take I-280 south. Exit onto Alpine Road and head east. Turn right on Junipero Serra Boulevard. Turn right on West Campus Drive and follow it up the hill to the course.

MOFFETT FIELD GOLF COURSE (military, 18 holes) . . . .

1080 Lockheed Way, Box 35
Sunnyvale, CA 94089
(650) 603-8026

	YARDAGE	PAR	RATING	SLOPE
FRONT	6003	73	74.3	122
MIDDLE	6344	72	70.2	123
BACK	6524	72	71.0	126

$5 - $23

WHAT TO EXPECT: This is a flat, easily walkable and not-too-difficult course adjoining the airfield. The biggest obstacle is noise as pilots practice landings in low-flying cargo planes.

DIRECTIONS: From San Jose (about 10 miles north to the course): Take US 101 north. Exit on Moffett Boulevard and proceed to the main gate. The guard will give directions from there.

SUNKEN GARDENS GOLF COURSE (public, 9 holes, clark glasson 1959) . . . .

1010 South Wolfe Road
Sunnyvale, CA 94086
(408) 739-6588

	YARDAGE	PAR	RATING	SLOPE	
FRONT	-	-	-	-	**$13 - $16**
MIDDLE	-	-	-	-	
BACK	1501	29	56.8	86	

WHAT TO EXPECT: A good place for beginners to take up the game, this is an executive course with two par 4s.

NOTES: They are often able to accommodate walk-ons.

DIRECTIONS: From San Jose (about 10 miles north to the course): Drive north on I-280 to Sunnyvale, take the Wolfe Road exit, and head northeast toward El Camino Real. The course is on the right, one block north of El Camino Real.

SUNNYVALE GOLF COURSE (municipal, 18 holes, clark glasson 1969) . . . .

605 Macara Lane
Sunnyvale, CA   94086
(408) 738-3666

	YARDAGE	PAR	RATING	SLOPE	
FRONT	5292	70	69.7	116	**$18 - $37**
MIDDLE	5764	70	67.6	114	
BACK	6255	70	70.1	121	

WHAT TO EXPECT: The course features wide fairways lined by trees and greens that can be approached by air or land.

OUR OPINION: For a muni course, it is in good shape and an average-to-good player can score well. Play can be slow, especially around the eighth hole, which features water to the right and left of the fairway and in front of the green. – Shaw

DIRECTIONS: From San Jose (about 10 miles north to the course): Go north on US 101. Exit on South Mathilda and head over the freeway. Turn right on Maude Avenue and then right on Macara Lane.

SUNOL VALLEY GOLF CLUB (public, 36 holes, clark glasson 1968) . . . .

6900 Mission Road
Sunol, CA 94586
(925) 862-0414
sunolvalley.com

	YARDAGE	PAR	RATING	SLOPE	
FRONT	5997	72	74.8	126	**$10 - $52**
MIDDLE	6406	72	70.4	120	
BACK	6830	72	72.4	126	

WHAT TO EXPECT: There are two 18-hole golf courses, the Cypress and Palm. The Cypress is short and narrow, with sloping greens. The Palm Course is longer and more spacious, with hazards on nearly half the course. Wind is a factor on both courses.

OUR OPINION: Fun layouts, but If you were expecting anything more than typical muni golf – you will be disappointed. – The Mole

NOTES: Sunol Valley does not have a driving range. Be cautious coming in and out of the property, as the beginning holes of each course closely adjoin the driveway. The yardage listed is for the Palm Course.

DIRECTIONS: From San Jose (about 20 miles north to the course): Take I-680 north to Andrade Road. Make a left over the freeway to the course.

BOUNDARY OAK GOLF COURSE (public, 18 holes, robert muir graves 1969) . . . .

3800 Valle Vista Road
Walnut Creek, CA 94598
(925) 934-4775
boundaryoak.com

	YARDAGE	PAR	RATING	SLOPE
FRONT	5699	72	72.0	120
MIDDLE	6739	72	72.2	128
BACK	7063	72	73.8	132

$18 - $30

WHAT TO EXPECT: Few municipal golf courses are longer in yardage from the back tees than Boundary Oak. Set in the rolling hills just below Mount Diablo, the fairways are roomy off the tee, but trees and water (six holes) do come into play. The greens are sloped and quick.

OUR OPINION: This is a nice course and a solid value, but its nemesis has always been the pace of play. – Shaw

NOTES: Home of the Stead Motors Shoot-Out.

DIRECTIONS: From within Walnut Creek: Off I-680, exit at Ygnacio Valley Road and head east. At Oak Grove Boulevard, turn right. Turn right on Valle Vista Road.

DIABLO HILLS GOLF COURSE (public, 9 holes, robert muir graves 1975) . . . .

1551 Marchbanks Drive
Walnut Creek, CA 94598
(925) 939-7372
diablohills.com

	YARDAGE	PAR	RATING	SLOPE
FRONT	2302	34	65.4	106
MIDDLE	-	-	-	-
BACK	2302	34	61.8	105

$14 - $17

WHAT TO EXPECT: This walkable short course is not too fancy, but may be just the ticket for affordability and the novice golfer. The course winds through hills and condos.

DIRECTIONS: From within Walnut Creek: Off I-680, exit on Ygnacio Valley Road and head east. Go about two miles and turn left on Marchbanks Drive.

ROSSMOOR GOLF COURSE (members only, 27 holes, robert muir graves 1965) . . . . . .

1010 Stanley Dollar Drive
Walnut Creek, CA 94595
(925) 933-2607

	YARDAGE	PAR	RATING	SLOPE
FRONT	5628	72	70.6	117
MIDDLE	5845	72	68.2	120
BACK	6177	72	69.5	125

$11 - $40

WHAT TO EXPECT: There is a nine-hole course and an 18-hole regulation course. Both courses wind through the retirement community of Rossmoor. Although the fairways are ample, housing can come into play. The nine-hole South Course has more slope. All the greens can be tricky to read.

NOTES: The yardage listed is for the 18-hole regulation course.

DIRECTIONS: From within Walnut Creek: Off Highway 24, exit on Pleasant Hill Road and head south. Turn left on Olympic and then turn right on Tice Valley. Turn right on Rossmoor Parkway and then right again on Stanley Dollar Drive.

Central Coast

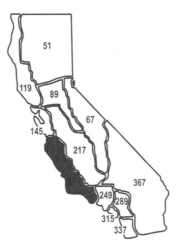

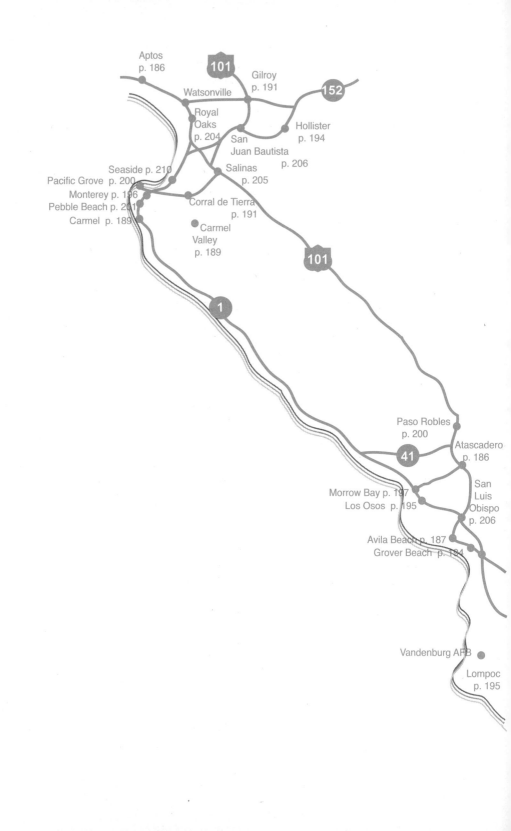

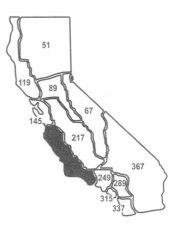

Map not to scale

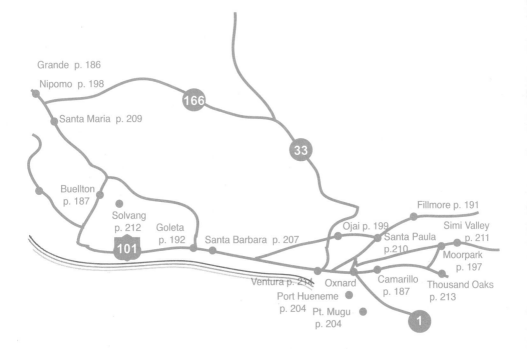

166

33

101

1

SEASCAPE GOLF CLUB (resort, 18 holes) . . . .

610 Clubhouse Drive
Aptos, CA 95003
(831) 688-3213
americangolf.com

	YARDAGE	PAR	RATING	SLOPE	
FRONT	5514	71	67.0	120	**$45 - $70**
MIDDLE	5813	71	69.2	127	
BACK	6084	71	70.2	129	

WHAT TO EXPECT: Seascape plays in the shadows of tall cypress trees. Diminutive in length by today's standards, the course's tight fairways and small greens require precision over distance.

OUR OPINION: Seascape's improvements over the last few years have really helped. – Frank

DIRECTIONS: From San Jose (about 35 miles south to the course): Take Highway 17 south toward Santa Cruz. Go south on Highway 1. Exit west on Rio del Mar. Veer left on Clubhouse Drive.

CYPRESS RIDGE GOLF COURSE (public, 18 holes, peter jacobsen 1999) . . . .

780 Cypress Ridge Parkway
Arroyo Grande, CA 93420
(805) 474-7979
cypressridge.com

	YARDAGE	PAR	RATING	SLOPE	
FRONT	5087	72	70.3	120	**$30 - $55**
MIDDLE	6443	72	71.3	129	
BACK	6804	72	73.0	133	

WHAT TO EXPECT: Set on a mesa overlooking the ocean, this is rolling course. Cypress Ridge affords excellent ocean views, but keep your head down. This is a rigorous course with deep fairway bunkers, sliding greens (hidden breaks) and Environmentally Sensitive Areas that devour golf balls. The wind picks up in the afternoon.

OUR OPINION: Interesting layout + reasonable rates + helpful staff = a course you want to play. – Shaw

NOTES: The course is walkable, but not recommended for the faint of legs. This is an Audubon International Signature Sanctuary.

DIRECTIONS: From San Luis Obispo (about 20 miles southeast to the course): Take US 101 north and exit at El Campo. Stay on El Campo until crossing Los Berros Road. The next intersection is Halcyon. Turn left and the course is on the right.

CHALK MOUNTAIN GOLF CLUB (public, 18 holes, robert muir graves 1980) . . . .

10000 El Bordo Road
Atascadero, CA 93422
(805) 466-8848

	YARDAGE	PAR	RATING	SLOPE	
FRONT	5330	72	71.4	119	**$24 - $29**
MIDDLE	5926	72	69.2	122	
BACK	6299	72	70.9	126	

WHAT TO EXPECT: Canyons, oak trees, narrow fairways, and sloping greens are just a few of the obstacles at Chalk Mountain. The course is not long in today's graphite and titanium world, but provides ample challenge, especially for golfers with little course experience.

DIRECTIONS: From San Luis Obispo (about 17 miles north to the course): Drive north on US 101. Exit at Santa Rosa and turn right. At El Camino Real, turn left. Then make an immediate right onto El Bordo Road. The golf course is at the end.

EAGLE CREEK GOLF & LEARNING CENTER (public, 9 holes) . . . .

13000 Atascadero Road
Atascadero, CA 93422
(805) 461-7500

	YARDAGE	PAR	RATING	SLOPE
FRONT	-	-	-	-
MIDDLE	-	-	-	-
BACK	1300	27	-	-

$5 - $7

WHAT TO EXPECT: This is a par-3 course with lots of water.
DIRECTIONS: From San Luis Obispo (about 17 miles north to the course): Drive north on US 101. Take the Santa Barbara Road exit in Atascadero. The course is next to the freeway.

AVILA BEACH RESORT (public, 18 holes, desmond muirhead 1968) . . . .

Avila Beach Road
Avila Beach, CA 93424
(805) 595-4000
avilabeachresort.com

	YARDAGE	PAR	RATING	SLOPE
FRONT	5116	71	69.9	126
MIDDLE	6048	71	69.0	116
BACK	6443	71	70.9	122

$12 - $52

WHAT TO EXPECT: This is a scenic resort course that places the emphasis on fun, rather than punishing golf. The front nine plays up into the hills and through the canyons. The back nine is flat and navigates around a tidal lagoon.
NOTES: Avila Beach Resort is also home to many concerts and festivals. There are not a lot of places you can golf and then go to a Beers n' Blues fest.
DIRECTIONS: From San Luis Obispo (about eight miles south to the course): Take US 101 south and exit at Avila Beach. Travel west for approximately four miles. The resort is on the right.

ZACA CREEK GOLF COURSE (public, 9 holes) . . . .

223 Shadow Mountain Drive
Buellton, CA 93427
(805) 688-2575

	YARDAGE	PAR	RATING	SLOPE
FRONT	1544	31	56.5	-
MIDDLE	-	-	-	-
BACK	1560	29	54.1	

$9 - $12

WHAT TO EXPECT: Zaca Creek is a level nine-hole course with two par 4s. The greens slope front to back, with subtle breaks.
DIRECTIONS: From Santa Barbara (about 40 miles northwest to the course): Go north on US 101 to Highway 246 west. Drive to the Avenue of Flags and turn left. Go to Shadow Mountain Drive and turn right.

LAS POSAS COUNTRY CLUB (members only, 18 holes, lawrence hughes 1958) . . . . . .

955 Fairway Drive
Camarillo, CA 93010
(805) 482-4518

	YARDAGE	PAR	RATING	SLOPE
FRONT	5614	71	73.1	126
MIDDLE	5931	71	68.9	122
BACK	6213	71	70.1	124

$70 - $100

WHAT TO EXPECT: Las Posas is a residential course with fairways bordered by homes, creating out-of-bounds on nearly every hole. The front nine is fairly level, while the back nine is hilly and the greens are medium in size.
DIRECTIONS: From Ventura (about 17 miles southeast to the course): Take US 101 south to Camarillo. Exit at Las Posas Road and go north. Turn right on Crestview Avenue and then right again on Valley Vista Drive. Continue one mile to Fairway Drive and turn left to the club.

SATICOY COUNTRY CLUB (members only, 18 holes, billy bell, jr. 1964) . . . .

4450 Clubhouse Drive
Camarillo, CA 93010
(805) 485-5216
saticoycountryclub.com

	YARDAGE	PAR	RATING	SLOPE	
FRONT	5847	72	74.3	128	**$50 - $100**
MIDDLE	6407	72	71.0	124	
BACK	6924	72	74.5	138	

WHAT TO EXPECT: Narrow tree-lined fairways and hilly terrain characterize this classic design, which ranks among Southern California's best courses.

NOTES: Reciprocal play with other members only clubs is allowed.

DIRECTIONS: From Ventura (about 17 miles southeast to the course): Take US 101 south to the Central Avenue exit. Drive north two miles to Santa Clara Avenue. Turn right and travel just over a mile to Los Angeles Avenue and turn left. Proceed one-half mile to the club.

SPANISH HILLS GOLF & COUNTRY CLUB (members only, 18 holes, robert cupp 1993)

999 Crestview Avenue
Camarillo, CA 93010
(805) 389-1644
spanishhillscc.com

	YARDAGE	PAR	RATING	SLOPE	
FRONT	4993	71	69.6	121	**$60 - $150**
MIDDLE	6310	71	70.8	126	
BACK	6749	71	72.9	132	

WHAT TO EXPECT: Huge amounts of earth were moved to make this difficult site playable. The result is an aesthetically pleasing venue with abundant bunkering and floral beds, which also serve as lateral hazards.

NOTES: Reciprocal play with other members only clubs is allowed.

DIRECTIONS: From Ventura (about 17 miles southeast to the course): Take US 101 south toward Camarillo. Exit at Las Posas and head north. Turn left on Ponderosa. At the top of hill, turn left on Crestview Avenue, to the club.

STERLING HILLS GOLF CLUB (public, 18 holes, graves and pascuzzo 1999) . . . .

901 Sterling Hills Drive
Camarillo, CA 93010
(805) 987-3446
sterlinghillsgolf.com

	YARDAGE	PAR	RATING	SLOPE	
FRONT	5445	71	72.0	120	**$39 - $54**
MIDDLE	6395	71	71.1	125	
BACK	6814	71	72.7	131	

WHAT TO EXPECT: Sterling Hills is a rarity among newer golf courses. You can actually walk this course. The fairways give you plenty of room for error, and the greens are big and sweeping. The course is interesting and entertaining, but not punishing.

OUR OPINION: A great value all things considered. Of course, to offer lower fees, the club has to put out more golfers, so it can get a touch crowded. The greens are still exceedingly firm, more in line with a course that just opened, not one open for nearly two years. – Andy

DIRECTIONS: From Ventura (about 17 miles southeast to the course): Take US 101 south to Camarillo. Exit at Central Avenue and drive east one mile to Beardsley. Make a right and drive another mile. The course is on the right.

CAMARILLO SPRINGS GOLF COURSE (public, 18 holes, ted robinson 1972) . . . .

791 Camarillo Springs Road
Camarillo Springs, CA 93012
(805) 484-1075
americangolf.com

	YARDAGE	PAR	RATING	SLOPE
FRONT	5224	72	69.3	118
MIDDLE	5931	72	67.9	108
BACK	6375	72	70.2	115

$24 - $45

WHAT TO EXPECT: Plenty of water, with an abundance of trees, demands golfers to be accurate. The course sits attractively at the base of the Santa Monica Mountains.
DIRECTIONS: From Ventura (about 20 miles southeast to the course): Take US 101 south to Camarillo. Turn left (south) on Camarillo Springs Road.

CARMEL VALLEY RANCH (semi-private, 18 holes, pete dye 1981) . . . .

One Old Ranch Road
Carmel, CA 93923
(831) 626-2510
troongolf.com

	YARDAGE	PAR	RATING	SLOPE
FRONT	5046	70	65.2	120
MIDDLE	5563	70	67.5	123
BACK	6234	70	70.5	132

$90 - $180

WHAT TO EXPECT: This Pete Dye layout is more forgiving than many of his others. The back nine plays above the front nine, and features picturesque views and memorable shots.
OUR OPINION: Carmel Valley Ranch is a well maintained but a little quirky, due to the hillside layout. There are some nice holes, but the course can be pricey if you are not staying at the resort. The resort is excellent, so play if you are staying there; otherwise, we'd pass on this one. – Frank
DIRECTIONS: From Monterey (about 15 miles southeast to the course): Head south on Highway 1. Turn left on Carmel Valley Road. Go about eight miles. Merge to the right on Robinson Canyon Road. Go about 100 yards to the entrance to the resort on the left.

GOLF CLUB AT QUAIL LODGE, THE (resort, 18 holes, robert muir graves 1964) . . . . . .

8000 Valley Greens Drive
Carmel, CA 93923
(831) 620-8808
quail-lodge-resort.com

	YARDAGE	PAR	RATING	SLOPE
FRONT	5451	71	71.8	124
MIDDLE	6140	71	70.4	125
BACK	6516	71	72.1	129

$65 - $175

WHAT TO EXPECT: Like most resorts, Quail Lodge is user-friendly, but not a pushover. Use the driver early, but as you make the turn, think twice. The course tightens off the tee, the greens seem to shrink, and lateral hazards are more apparent. On the green, double check your line. The greens don't break half as much as you think.
OUR OPINION: A prototypical classy resort course, not too tough, but pretty and peaceful. Playing among homes does detract some from the ambience. – Bob
DIRECTIONS: From Monterey (about ten miles south to the course): Take Highway 1 south. Turn left on Carmel Valley Road and travel three and one-half miles to Valley Greens Drive, and the course.

PRESERVE GOLF CLUB, THE (members only, 18 holes, tom fazio 2001) . . . .

19 Pronghorn Run
Carmel, CA 93923
(831) 626-6584

	YARDAGE	PAR	RATING	SLOPE
FRONT	5148	72	69.9	123
MIDDLE	6548	72	72.2	137
BACK	6996	72	74.5	146

WHAT TO EXPECT: This isolated, exclusive course enjoys one of the most beautiful pristine sites in American golf. Rolling hills and flat meadow holes, with restrained bunkering, combine for a very playable course that can bare its teeth if you play from the tips.
DIRECTIONS: From Monterey (about 15 miles south to the course): Go south on Highway 1. Turn left on Carmel Valley Road. After about two and one-half miles, turn right on Rancho San Carlos Road. The club is about 20 minutes past the security gate.

RANCHO CAÑADA GOLF CLUB (public, 36 holes, robert dean putman 1970) . . . .

4860 Carmel Valley Road
Carmel, CA 93922
(800) 536-9459
ranchocanada.com

	YARDAGE	PAR	RATING	SLOPE	
FRONT	5568	72	71.9	118	**$35 - $80**
MIDDLE	6116	71	69.3	123	
BACK	6349	71	70.4	125	

WHAT TO EXPECT: The West Course is the longer and tougher of the two courses. On the shorter East Course, the front nine is tighter, while the back nine opens up. Both of these scenic courses share other similarities. The greens are large, so hitting them in regulation does not guarantee par. A river comes into play three times on the West Course and five times on the East. Most of the fairways are well protected by a variety of trees. Trade accuracy for distance.
OUR OPINION: Don't choose your course solely by the yardage. We feel the East Course is just as enjoyable as the West Course. – Bob
NOTES: The West Course yardage is listed.
DIRECTIONS: From Monterey (about ten miles south to the course): Go south on Highway 1. Turn left on Carmel Valley Road. The club is one mile east, on the right.

TEHAMA GOLF CLUB (members only, 18 holes, jay morrish 1999) . . . .

101 Via Malpaso
Carmel Valley, CA 93924
(831) 624-5549
tehamainc.com

	YARDAGE	PAR	RATING	SLOPE	
FRONT	5085	72	71.2	123	**$75 - $200**
MIDDLE	6183	72	71.3	134	
BACK	6458	72	72.7	137	

WHAT TO EXPECT: This exclusive club boasts terrific views of the surrounding Monterey area. Since this is a very hilly site that is artistically bunkered and has smallish greens, expect Tehama to play more difficult than the yardage would suggest.
DIRECTIONS: From Monterey (about 15 miles south to the course): Off Highway 1, take Highway 68 east toward Salinas. Turn right on Olmstead Road. Turn left on Via Malpaso to the front gate.

CORRAL DE TIERRA COUNTRY CLUB (members only, 18 holes, bob baldock 1960) . . . .

81 Corral de Tierra Road
Corral de Tierra, CA 93908
(831) 484-1325

	YARDAGE	PAR	RATING	SLOPE	
FRONT	5392	72	71.7	125	**$50 - $90**
MIDDLE	6340	72	70.9	130	
BACK	6677	72	72.4	134	

WHAT TO EXPECT: Corral de Tierra, situated between Salinas and Monterey, is hilly with small putting surfaces. The course typically plays more difficult than it appears.
NOTES: Reciprocal play with other members only clubs is allowed.
DIRECTIONS: From Monterey (about ten miles east to the course): Off Highway 1, take Highway 68 east. Turn right on Corral de Tierra Road. The club is on the left.

ELKINS RANCH GOLF COURSE (public, 18 holes, rawleigh thomas 1961) . . . .

1386 Chambersburg Road
Fillmore, CA 93015
(805) 524-1440

	YARDAGE	PAR	RATING	SLOPE	
FRONT	5700	72	72.7	123	**$16 - $34**
MIDDLE	6019	71	68.3	112	
BACK	6303	71	69.9	117	

WHAT TO EXPECT: Slightly rolling, tree-lined fairways and five lakes can be found at Elkins Ranch. Located in a quiet canyon setting, the course has few parallel fairways. It has elevated tees with greens that tend to break toward the town of Fillmore, due north.
DIRECTIONS: From Valencia (about 17 miles west to the course): Take I-5 north to Highway 126 west. Go 19 miles to Fillmore, and make a left at the third traffic light (Highway 23). Travel one and one-half miles to the golf course on the left.

EAGLE RIDGE GOLF CLUB (public, 18 holes, fream & miller 1999) . . . .

2951 Club Drive
Gilroy, CA 95020
(408) 846-4531
eagleridgegc.com

	YARDAGE	PAR	RATING	SLOPE	
FRONT	5102	72	69.6	119	**$35 - $95**
MIDDLE	6665	72	72.2	136	
BACK	6972	72	74.0	138	

WHAT TO EXPECT: The holes against the hillside are breathtaking and the bunkering is distinctively bold and attractive. The greens, with their speed and undulations, are perhaps the most challenging of any public course in Northern California.
DIRECTIONS: From San Jose (about 30 miles south to the course): Go south on US 101. Exit on Masten and turn right. Go about one mile and turn left on Santa Teresa Boulevard. Go about four miles south and Club Drive is on the right.

GAVILAN GOLF COURSE (public, 9 holes) . . . .

5055 Santa Teresa Boulevard
Gilroy, CA 95020
(408) 846-4920

	YARDAGE	PAR	RATING	SLOPE
FRONT	1795	30	59.5	92
MIDDLE	-	-	-	-
BACK	1835	30	59.1	94

$11 - $20

WHAT TO EXPECT: This is a short, executive course with small, fast greens. A pond comes into play on one hole.
DIRECTIONS: From San Jose (about 30 miles south to the course): Take US 101 south to Gilroy. Take the Monterey Street exit and turn left. Take a left on Thomas Road and then another left on Santa Theresa Boulevard. Turn right in to the second entrance to Gavilan College.

GILROY GOLF COURSE (public, 11 holes) . . . .

2695 Hecker Pass Highway
Gilroy, CA 95020
(408) 848-0490
gilroygolfcourse.com

	YARDAGE	PAR	RATING	SLOPE
FRONT	2680	36	70.5	114
MIDDLE	-	-	-	-
BACK	2988	35	69.0	110

$14 - $30

WHAT TO EXPECT: This old course is not as easy as you might imagine. Gilroy Golf Course was built on a hillside in the early 1920s. There are constant elevation changes, which can create some unique lies, even if your ball is in the fairway. The small greens leave little margin for error.
NOTES: The two extra holes change the configuration of the front and back nines.
DIRECTIONS: From San Jose (about 30 miles south to the course): Go south on US 101. Exit on Masten and go right. Turn left on Santa Teresa Boulevard. Turn right on Hecker Pass Highway. The course is on the right.

GLEN ANNIE GOLF CLUB (public, 18 holes, graves & pascuzzo 1997) . . . .

405 Glen Annie Road
Goleta, CA 93117
(805) 968-6400
glenanniegolf.com

	YARDAGE	PAR	RATING	SLOPE
FRONT	5036	71	69.5	118
MIDDLE	5940	71	68.8	117
BACK	6420	71	71.1	122

$70 - $85

WHAT TO EXPECT: This is a player-friendly course with some excellent ocean views. Several of the par 4s are drivable for the long hitter. If you miss the fairway, you may find yourself in fescue rough, which can be quite irritating but not disastrous. The Environmentally Sensitive Areas, on the other hand, can cost you several strokes. Be prepared for a breeze.
OUR OPINION: You'll have a good time. The views are excellent, the layout is fun, even for the less gifted golfer, and the price is reasonable. A couple of the holes are kind of funky, but it's typical with new courses. They are forced to cram 18 holes into a small space. – Brad
NOTES: The golf carts are equipped with Par View GPS systems.
DIRECTIONS: From Santa Barbara (about 17 miles northwest to the course): Take US 101 north to the Glen Annie Road off-ramp, heading north. Go for one-half mile to the entry gate on the left.

OCEAN MEADOWS GOLF COURSE (public, 9 holes, harry rainville 1964) . . . .

6925 Whittier Drive
Goleta, CA 93117
(805) 968-6814

	YARDAGE	PAR	RATING	SLOPE
FRONT	2657	36	65.1	102
MIDDLE	3000	36	68.2	108
BACK	3196	36	70.0	115

$15 - $30

WHAT TO EXPECT: This is a family-oriented golf course. The fairways are lined by oak and pine trees, but are generous in width. A creek runs through all nine holes. The greens are small and flat, with subtle breaks. Place the ball in the middle of the greens and birdies will be your reward.

DIRECTIONS: From Santa Barbara (about 17 miles northwest to the course): Take US 101 north to the Glen Annie/Storke exit. Drive south one mile to Whittier Drive and turn right.

SANDPIPER GOLF COURSE (public, 18 holes, billy bell, jr. 1971) . . . .

7925 Hollister Avenue
Goleta, CA 93117
(805) 968-1541

	YARDAGE	PAR	RATING	SLOPE
FRONT	5725	73	73.3	125
MIDDLE	6597	72	71.7	123
BACK	7068	72	74.5	134

$40 - $100

WHAT TO EXPECT: Dubbed "the mid income man's Pebble Beach," by In The Loop Golf, this layout plays on a coastal plateau high above the Pacific, with gorgeous views of the ocean and the mountains.

OUR OPINION: The back nine is the story. Holes ten through 14 are set along the ocean and are better than anything Ocean Trails and Pelican Hill can offer. – Andy

DIRECTIONS: From Santa Barbara (about 17 miles northwest to the course): Take US 101 north. Take the Winchester Canyon Road/Hollister Avenue exit. Turn left at the stop sign and go over the freeway. Drive one-half mile on Hollister Avenue to the course, which is on the right.

TWIN LAKES GOLF COURSE (public, 9 holes) . . . .

6034 Hollister Avenue
Goleta, CA 93117
(805) 964-1414
twinlakes.com

	YARDAGE	PAR	RATING	SLOPE
FRONT	1292	29	53.6	73
MIDDLE	-	-	-	-
BACK	1474	29	53.6	73

$9 - $15

WHAT TO EXPECT: This par-29 course is lined with trees that can affect your shots. The pro shop gives sound advice on how to play this course: "Keep up with the group in front of you."

DIRECTIONS: From Santa Barbara (about 17 miles northwest to the course): Drive north on US 101 to the Fairview exit. Drive west to the course.

PISMO STATE BEACH GOLF COURSE (public, 9 holes) . . . .

25 Grand Avenue
Grover Beach, CA 93433
(805) 481-5215

	YARDAGE	PAR	RATING	SLOPE	
FRONT	1315	30	-	-	**$7 - $9**
MIDDLE	-	-	-	-	
BACK	1465	27	-	-	

WHAT TO EXPECT: This a challenging, level course with water coming into play on three holes. There are plenty of trees and ocean views to keep you entertained.
DIRECTIONS: From San Luis Obispo (about 15 miles south to the course): Take Highway 1 south to Grover City. Go right on Grand Avenue, toward the beach, and follow the signs to the course.

RIDGEMARK COUNTRY CLUB RESORT (semi-private, 36 holes, richard bigler 1972) . . .

3800 Airline Highway
Hollister, CA 95023
(831) 634-2222
ridgemark.com

	YARDAGE	PAR	RATING	SLOPE	
FRONT	5542	72	71.6	118	**$58 - $70**
MIDDLE	6336	72	71.0	123	
BACK	6721	72	72.7	126	

WHAT TO EXPECT: This popular, semi-private resort boasts two fun courses. The Gabilan Course plays mainly among homes, while the Diablo Course extends into the countryside. The area enjoys a mild, dry microclimate, and the two layouts are eminently playable.
OUR OPINION: Ridgemark offers reasonable prices and good services, along with some nice golf. All of that makes this a genuine value. – Bob A great experience and a must-play for women golfers. – Loralei
NOTES: Each day one of the two courses is for members only. The reserved course alternates each day. The yardage listed is for the Gabilan Course.
DIRECTIONS: From San Jose (about 50 miles south to the course): Take US 101 south. Take Highway 25 east to Hollister. Go right onto Main Street. Turn left on Union. Turn right on Airline Highway.

LA PURISIMA GOLF COURSE (public, 18 holes, robert muir graves 1986) . . . .

3455 State Highway 246
Lompoc, CA 93436
(805) 735-8395
lapurisimagolf.com

	YARDAGE	PAR	RATING	SLOPE
FRONT	5763	72	74.3	131
MIDDLE	6657	72	72.8	132
BACK	7106	72	75.4	142

$30 - $60

WHAT TO EXPECT: La Purisima is built into the hills of the Lompoc. Do you have trouble keeping the ball straight? Beware – miss the fairways or greens and you will find yourself in trees, brush, creeks, ponds, or a well-placed trap. With elevated tees and greens, chances are you will be hitting at an angle at some point during the round. Wind can be a factor in the afternoon.

OUR OPINION: You're going to have to take our word on this. Factoring in the quality of the course, the ambience and the cost, this is the best course in California. Words don't do it justice. Play in the morning – it can get windy in the afternoon. – Andy

NOTES: The PGA and US Open used this as a qualifying site from 1995 to 2001. The LPGA Santa Barbara Open was held here in 1987 and 1988.

DIRECTIONS: From Santa Barbara (about 55 miles northwest to the course): Travel north on US 101 to Highway 246 west. Follow Highway 246 west about 13 miles to the entrance.

VILLAGE COUNTRY CLUB (members only, 18 holes, ted robinson 1963) . . . .

4300 Clubhouse Road
Lompoc, CA 93436
(805) 733-3537
impulse.net/~vcc

	YARDAGE	PAR	RATING	SLOPE
FRONT	5199	72	71.1	121
MIDDLE	6269	72	69.6	118
BACK	6564	72	71.5	126

$25 - $60

WHAT TO EXPECT: Ted Robinson used the natural surroundings to create a playable and fun course. The tree-lined fairways keep you honest, and the tiered greens reward golfers who are willing to take the risk.

NOTES: Reciprocal play with other members only clubs is allowed.

DIRECTIONS: From Santa Barbara (about 55 miles northwest to the course): Travel north on US 101 to Highway 1, into Lompoc. Stay on the road (it changes names and becomes Harris Grade Road). Travel north on Harris Grade Road. (continue past La Purisma Road) to Burton Mesa Boulevard and turn left. Follow to Clubhouse Road and make a right to the club.

SEA PINES GOLF RESORT (resort, 9 holes, unknown 1953) . . . .

1945 Solano Street
Los Osos, CA 93402
(805) 528-1788
seapinesgolfresort.com

	YARDAGE	PAR	RATING	SLOPE
FRONT	3800	34	-	-
MIDDLE	-	-	-	-
BACK	3800	31	-	-

$7 - $20

WHAT TO EXPECT: Sea Pines is an executive course with excellent ocean views. One of the unique features of the course is the many different redwood carved animals you will find along the way. The animals give you information about the holes to be played.

DIRECTIONS: From San Luis Obispo (about 11 miles west to the course): Off US 101, take the Los Osos Valley Road exit. Go west almost 11 miles to Pecho Road. Turn right on Pecho Road and drive one-quarter mile to Skyline Drive. Turn left to the course.

DEL MONTE GOLF COURSE (public, 18 holes, charles maud 1897) . . . .

1300 Sylvan Road
Monterey, CA 93940
(831) 373-2700
pebblebeach.com

	YARDAGE	PAR	RATING	SLOPE	
FRONT	5526	74	71.0	120	**$75 - $80**
MIDDLE	6052	72	69.5	121	
BACK	6357	72	70.8	123	

WHAT TO EXPECT: Depending on who you talk to, this 100-year-old layout may be the oldest in the state. Owned by the Pebble Beach Resort, this flat but charming course uses its natural simplicity to create an enjoyable round of golf.

OUR OPINION: If you are spending any length of time in Monterey, you should plan on adding this fun course to your mix if for nothing else, to give your wallet a rest. – Shaw

DIRECTIONS: From within Monterey: Take Highway 1 south and take the two exit-only lanes toward Monterey. Make a left on Aguajito Road and head back under the freeway. Turn left at Mark Thomas Drive, then turn right Joslyn Canyon and finally, right on Sylvan Road to the course.

LAGUNA SECA GOLF CLUB (public, 18 holes, robert trent jones sr. & jr. 1970) . . . . . .

10520 York Road
Monterey, CA 93940
(831) 373-3701
lagunasecagolf.com

	YARDAGE	PAR	RATING	SLOPE	
FRONT	5204	72	70.8	121	**$35 - $65**
MIDDLE	5726	71	68.9	122	
BACK	6157	71	70.7	127	

WHAT TO EXPECT: Laguna Seca is short, but very scenic and hilly. The layout is a change of pace from the nearby flatter, cooler, coastal courses.

OUR OPINION: Laguna Seca is a fun and interesting layout. We wouldn't describe it as a destination course, but it is a solid alternative to the high-end courses in the area.

DIRECTIONS: From within Monterey: Off Highway 1, take Highway 68 toward Salinas. Make a left on York Road and follow to the course.

PASADERA COUNTRY CLUB (members only, 18 holes, jack nicklaus 2000) . . . .

100 Pasadera Drive
Monterey, CA 93940
(831) 647-2421
pasadera.com

	YARDAGE	PAR	RATING	SLOPE	
FRONT	5015	72	69.6	124	**$185 - $250**
MIDDLE	6348	71	71.0	132	
BACK	6752	71	72.8	142	

WHAT TO EXPECT: From the back tees this is a difficult, but beautiful, course. Pasadera incorporates the hills, canyons, and oak groves to forge a classic design. The use of native grasses and the natural surroundings creates a peaceful atmosphere. The peacefulness is only interrupted by an occasional screaming, crying or whimpering low handicapper who decided to play it from the tips.

NOTES: This is a members only course, but is open to the public on Mondays.

DIRECTIONS: From within Monterey: Off Highway 1, take Highway 68 toward Salinas. Make a left on Pasadera Road. The course is past the Monterey Airport.

TIERRA REJADA GOLF CLUB (public, 18 holes, robert cupp 1999) . . . .

15187 Tierra Rejada Road
Moorpark, CA 93021
(805) 531-9300
tierrarejada.com

	YARDAGE	PAR	RATING	SLOPE	
FRONT	5829	72	68.5	121	**$75 - $100**
MIDDLE	6340	72	71.0	126	
BACK	6793	72	73.3	132	

WHAT TO EXPECT: The front nine is mountainous — players will be hitting down to fairways and up to greens. The back nine is more level, with little room for error off the tee. Watch out for the greens; many of them have false fronts and are well guarded by traps.
OUR OPINION: This is built on the same kind of land as Cascades (that is not a compliment). The driving range, first hole, ninth hole and 13th hole are all squeezed together. This is preposterous layout for an upscale daily fee course. – Andy
DIRECTIONS: From downtown Los Angeles (about 47 miles northwest to the course): Take US 101 north to Highway 23 north. Exit at Tierra Rejada Road. Turn right to the entrance of the club, which is about one-quarter mile away, on the left side.

MORRO BAY GOLF COURSE (public, 18 holes, russell neyes 1929) . . . .

201 State Park Road
Morro Bay, CA 93442
(805) 782-8060
slocountyparks.com/golf.html

	YARDAGE	PAR	RATING	SLOPE	
FRONT	5633	69	67.3	110	**$28 - $36**
MIDDLE	6107	71	69.6	112	
BACK	6360	71	70.7	115	

WHAT TO EXPECT: This Audubon-certified course was hit hard by a disease that affected many of the pine trees that lined the fairways. A tree planting effort is already underway. With that said, Morro Bay actually affords even more spectacular views of the ocean than before. This hilly course is best known for its small, tricky greens. Optical illusions often have golfers playing the breaks in the opposite direction.
OUR OPINION: This course has some excellent par 4s and tough par 3s. You won't regret playing this course. – The Mole
DIRECTIONS: From San Luis Obispo (about 15 miles northwest to the course): From US 101, exit Highway 1 toward Morro Bay. Exit Morro Bay Boulevard. Turn left on Main Street. After entering the park, turn left on State Park Road. The course is on the left.

BLACKLAKE GOLF COURSE (public, 27 holes, ted robinson 1965) . . . .

1490 Golf Course Lane
Nipomo, CA 93444
(805) 343-1214
blacklake.com

	YARDAGE	PAR	RATING	SLOPE	
FRONT	5628	72	72.9	126	**$30 - $68**
MIDDLE	6056	72	69.2	118	
BACK	6401	72	70.9	123	

WHAT TO EXPECT: The Lake nine is user friendly with level, open fairways. Miss a fairway here and chances are you will land in another. The Canyon nine has elevation changes, houses and more out-of-bounds. The Oaks nine, the shortest and most challenging of the three courses, features target golf. Keep your driver in your bag to score well, as out-of-bounds and Environmentally Sensitive Areas abound.

OUR OPINION: This is a 27-hole facility with 18 really strong holes. The Oaks nine, although fairly new and more challenging, is my least favorite. Call ahead to see which combination is in play. – Brad

NOTES: The yardage listed is for the Lake and Canyon nines.

DIRECTIONS: From Santa Maria (about nine miles north to the course): Head north on US 101. Take the Tefft Street exit in Nipomo. Turn left over the highway and make a right on Pomeroy. Then turn left on Willow and right to the course.

MONTEREY PINES GOLF COURSE (public, 18 holes, robert muir graves 1963) . . . .

1250 Garden Road
NPS Monterey, CA 93943
(831) 656-2167
golfmonterey.com

	YARDAGE	PAR	RATING	SLOPE	
FRONT	5250	71	69.3	110	**$12 - $26**
MIDDLE	5247	69	65.7	117	
BACK	5675	69	67.8	123	

WHAT TO EXPECT: As its name would suggest, the Monterey pines are the distinguishing feature for this flattish, relatively simple, layout. Small, well-maintained greens make scoring more of a challenge than the yardage might suggest.

DIRECTIONS: From within Monterey: From Highway 1 north take the Casa Verde exit and turn left. Turn right on Fairgrounds Road. Turn left at the light on Mark Thomas/Garden Road.

OJAI VALLEY INN & SPA (resort, 18 holes, george c. thomas 1923) . . . .

905 Country Club Drive
Ojai, CA 93023
(805) 646-2420
ojairesort.com

	YARDAGE	PAR	RATING	SLOPE	
FRONT	5225	71	71.0	129	**$115 - $135**
MIDDLE	5892	70	68.5	117	
BACK	6236	70	70.2	122	

WHAT TO EXPECT: Not particularly long, Ojai is a beautiful George Thomas design, set in the country mountainside. The course is well maintained and extremely playable.

OUR OPINION: Small greens and distinctive bunkering make this course more difficult that its 6,200 length would indicate. A great place to get away. – Bob

NOTES: Ojai also has a world-class spa. The course has been the site of 7 Senior PGA Tour events.

DIRECTIONS: From downtown Los Angeles (about 83 miles northwest to the course): Drive north on US 101 to Ventura. Travel north on Highway 33 to Ojai. In Ojai, don't make the turn to stay on Highway 33, at the Von's. Continue straight and then turn right on Country Club Drive.

SOULE PARK GOLF COURSE (public, 18 holes, william p. bell 1962) . . . .

1033 East Ojai Avenue
Ojai, CA 93023
(805) 646-5633

	YARDAGE	PAR	RATING	SLOPE	
FRONT	5639	72	71.8	121	**$11 - $34**
MIDDLE	6209	72	69.4	118	
BACK	6475	72	70.5	121	

WHAT TO EXPECT: This is a pretty course nestled in the Ojai Valley. For the lower handicapper, there is little in the way of challenge, although a creek does come into play on four holes. For the rest of us, this friendly course has sloping terrain, wide tree-lined fairways, and good sized greens.

DIRECTIONS: From Ventura (about 15 miles north to the course): Off US 101, take Highway 33 east to Ojai. Turn right on East Ojai Avenue, and drive to the course.

RIVER RIDGE GOLF CLUB (public, 18 holes, william bell 1986) . . . .

2401 West Vineyard Avenue
Oxnard, CA 93030
(805) 983-4653

	YARDAGE	PAR	RATING	SLOPE	
FRONT	5351	72	71.3	124	**$25 - $35**
MIDDLE	6104	72	69.3	114	
BACK	6718	72	72.3	121	

WHAT TO EXPECT: Hit your driver on the front nine, because there is water on six holes on the back. The greens are good sized and undulating. For the player who constantly hits left, expect your ball to land out-of-bounds. Wind can be a constant companion.

DIRECTIONS: From Ventura (about 10 miles southeast to the course): Take US 101 south. Take the Vineyard Avenue exit and drive west two miles to the course.

PACIFIC GROVE GOLF COURSE (public, 18 holes, jack neville 1932) . . . .

77 Asilomar Boulevard
Pacific Grove, CA 93950
(831) 648-5777

	YARDAGE	PAR	RATING	SLOPE	
FRONT	5305	72	70.1	112	
MIDDLE	5571	70	66.9	117	**$18 - $38**
BACK	5732	70	67.7	119	

WHAT TO EXPECT: Often referred to as a "poor man's Pebble Beach," Pacific Grove has magnificent ocean views and a ton of personality. The front nine is tree-lined and requires accuracy; the back nine is more revealing and plays like a links-style course.
OUR OPINION: For those of you who have been punished both in spirit and wallet by many of the high-end Monterey courses, take refuge here; this is a fun course. Expect play to be on the slow side. – Brad
DIRECTIONS: From Monterey (about four miles northwest to the course): From Highway 1 take the Pebble Beach/Pacific Grove/Highway 68 west exit. Turn right onto Highway 68. In Pacific Grove, take the Highway 68/Sunset Avenue exit. Turn right on Asilomar Avenue.

HUNTER RANCH GOLF COURSE (public, 18 holes, hunter resources 1994) . . . .

4041 Highway 46 East
Paso Robles, CA 93446
(805) 237-7444
hunterranchgolf.com

	YARDAGE	PAR	RATING	SLOPE	
FRONT	5639	72	72.0	128	
MIDDLE	6292	72	70.7	131	**$35 - $60**
BACK	6716	72	72.6	136	

WHAT TO EXPECT: Hunter Ranch will punish the impatient golfer. On the front nine of this rolling course, players can hit a driver off most holes, but on the back nine, a driver is not always your best choice. Many fairways and greens are guarded by oak trees and sand traps. The greens are undulating and fast.
OUR OPINION: This is a solid test of golf at a reasonable price. – Shaw
DIRECTIONS: From San Luis Obispo (about 35 miles north to the course): Drive north on US 101 to Highway 46 east. Take Highway 46 for over three miles. The course is on the right.

LINKS COURSE AT PASO ROBLES, THE (public, 18 holes, rudy duran 1996) . . . .

5151 Jardine Road
Paso Robles, CA 93446
(805) 227-4567

	YARDAGE	PAR	RATING	SLOPE	
FRONT	5610	72	72.1	121	
MIDDLE	6642	72	71.3	113	**$15 - $21**
BACK	7056	72	73.3	118	

WHAT TO EXPECT: The Links at Paso Robles is a vast, open, links-style golf course. The greens are subtle, so players tend to read more break than is actually there. Afternoon winds are common.
DIRECTIONS: From San Luis Obispo (about 35 miles north to the course): Take US 101 north to Highway 46 east. Turn left at the flashing light on Jardine Road. The course is on the left, after one and one-half miles.

PASO ROBLES GOLF CLUB (public, 18 holes, bert stamps 1960) . . . .

1600 Country Club Drive
Paso Robles, CA 93446
(805) 238-4722
pasoroblesgolfclub.com

	YARDAGE	PAR	RATING	SLOPE
FRONT	5766	73	73.5	126
MIDDLE	6011	71	70.1	121
BACK	6218	71	71.0	123

$9 - $18

WHAT TO EXPECT: Save your driver for the back nine; the front side requires a surgeon's touch, with an abundance of water, and homes lining both sides of the fairways. On the back nine, the course becomes a little less severe — you lose the homes, but still have plenty of chances to hit it in the drink.

DIRECTIONS: From San Luis Obispo (about 35 miles north to the course): Travel north on US 101 and exit at Spring Street. Turn right at the light on Niblick Road. After about one and one-half miles, turn right on Country Club Drive.

CYPRESS POINT CLUB (members only, 18 holes, alister mackenzie 1928) . . . .

3150 17-Mile Drive
Pebble Beach, CA 93953
(831) 624-2223

	YARDAGE	PAR	RATING	SLOPE
FRONT	5816	75	74.1	139
MIDDLE	6332	72	71.2	130
BACK	6536	72	72.3	134

WHAT TO EXPECT: Part meadow, forest, and oceanside course, this is simply one of the best, most enjoyable courses on earth. Sadly, it is fiercely private and only a few get to appreciate its beauty.

DIRECTIONS: From within Monterey: Take the Pebble Beach exit off Highway 1. Follow the signs to the Pebble Beach gate. The guard gives further directions from there.

MONTEREY PENINSULA COUNTRY CLUB (members only, 36 holes, bob baldock 1926) .

3000 Club Road
Pebble Beach, CA 93953
(831) 372-8141

	YARDAGE	PAR	RATING	SLOPE
FRONT	5935	73	74.4	130
MIDDLE	6466	72	72..9	129
BACK	6762	72	74.1	132

$60 - $225

WHAT TO EXPECT: The Dunes Course combines the best of forest and oceanside golf to make what is one of the state's most underrated layouts. Recent renovations have made the course more difficult, especially for the average golfer. The Shore Course plays in the open, adjacent to 17-Mile Drive. The layout is simple and understated.

NOTES: The yardage listed is for the Dunes Course.

DIRECTIONS: From within Monterey: Take the Pebble Beach exit off Highway 1. Follow the signs to the Pebble Beach gate. The guard gives further directions from there.

PEBBLE BEACH GOLF LINKS (resort, 18 holes, jack neville 1919) . . . .

17-Mile Drive
Pebble Beach, CA 93953
(831) 624-3811
pebblebeach.com

	YARDAGE	PAR	RATING	SLOPE
FRONT	5267	71	71.9	130
MIDDLE	6352	72	72.3	137
BACK	6726	72	73.8	142

$300 - $325

WHAT TO EXPECT: America's premier public access course affords gorgeous views, and a walk through golfing lore. Its small putting surfaces, together with the weather, provide most of the golfing challenge to a course that everyone will want to play at least once.
OUR OPINION: Can you believe people are paying $325 to play one round of golf? The truth is, at $325 it may be a bargain. Getting a tee time a Pebble is the real challenge. You might want add staying at the Lodge to your once-in-a-lifetime experience. – Shaw
DIRECTIONS: From within Monterey: Take the Pebble Beach exit off Highway 1. Follow the signs to the Pebble Beach gate. The guard gives further directions from there.

PETER HAY GOLF COURSE (public, 9 holes, peter hay 1957) . . . .

17-Mile Drive
Pebble Beach, CA 93953
(831) 625-8518
pebblebeach.com

	YARDAGE	PAR	RATING	SLOPE
FRONT	-	-	-	-
MIDDLE	-	-	-	-
BACK	820	27	-	-

$17 - $17

WHAT TO EXPECT: This is a short pitch-and-putt course located on a small hillside, inside the grounds of Pebble Beach.
OUR OPINION: This course is $300 dollars cheaper than Pebble Beach and is not quite as challenging. Take the entire family to play here and then go home and tell everyone back home that you took the entire family to play Pebble. Technically you are not lying.
DIRECTIONS: From within Monterey: Take the Pebble Beach exit off Highway 1. Follow the signs to the Pebble Beach gate. The guard gives further directions from there.

POPPY HILLS GOLF COURSE (public, 18 holes, robert trent jones jr. 1986) . . . .

3200 Lopez Road
Pebble Beach, CA 93953
(831) 622-8239
ncga.org

	YARDAGE	PAR	RATING	SLOPE
FRONT	5403	72	72.1	131
MIDDLE	6237	72	71.5	138
BACK	6833	72	74.6	144

$45 - $150

WHAT TO EXPECT: Home of the NCGA and a host course to the AT&T, Poppy Hills is scenic, challenging and well maintained. Longer hitters will need to throttle back and be patient on this layout that rewards accuracy.
OUR OPINION: Poppy Hills is a great test of golf. You will use every club in your bag and maybe a few in someone else's. Join the NCGA, if for nothing else, to play this course once a year at a discount. – Frank
NOTES: Not only is Poppy Hills one the three courses that the AT&T calls home, the NCGA also makes a home there.
DIRECTIONS: From within Monterey: Take the Pebble Beach exit off Highway 1. Follow the signs to the Pebble Beach gate. The guard gives further directions from there.

SPANISH BAY, THE LINKS AT (resort, 18 holes, r.t. jones jr., watson & tatum 1987) .

2700 17-Mile Drive
Pebble Beach, CA 93953
(831) 647-7495
pebblebeach.com

	YARDAGE	PAR	RATING	SLOPE	
FRONT	5287	72	70.6	129	
MIDDLE	6408	72	72.9	141	**$185 - $185**
BACK	6820	72	74.8	146	

WHAT TO EXPECT: Golfers seem to either love or hate this links-style course, which affords wonderful views. The problem for some is that most of the holes are not framed by trees and give no perspective or easy clues where to hit. If you prefer dial-it-in park-setting golf, the mystery and host of shot options at Spanish Bay will frustrate and bedevil you.

OUR OPINION: It's not cheap, but play it at least once if you can. The service is first rate, and we enjoy the fact that the course evokes such strong emotions. – Bob

DIRECTIONS: From within Monterey: Take the Pebble Beach exit off Highway 1. Follow the signs to the Pebble Beach gate. The guard gives further directions from there.

SPYGLASS HILL GOLF COURSE (semi-private, 18 holes, robert trent jones, sr. 1966) .

Spyglass Hill Road at Stevenson Drive
Pebble Beach, CA 93953
(831) 625-8563
pebblebeach.com

	YARDAGE	PAR	RATING	SLOPE	
FRONT	5618	74	73.7	133	
MIDDLE	6347	72	72.8	141	**$225 - $250**
BACK	6855	72	75.3	148	

WHAT TO EXPECT: This is an exacting, demanding, and exigent golf course. It's really hard. After opening with five holes out in the ocean view and sand, the course retreats quietly back into the forest. Back there, the only sounds you hear are the cries of desperate golfers trying to make par. Ok, we are exaggerating, just a little bit. The truth is, this is a spectacular layout, set on rolling terrain, with ocean holes, forest holes, and elevated, sloping greens.

OUR OPINION: There are more than a few golfers who regard Spyglass Hill as a better course than Pebble Beach. It certainly tends to play more difficult. Spyglass is definitely a must-play for any golf fanatic. – Bob

NOTES: Members only for tee times before 10:00 a.m.

DIRECTIONS: From within Monterey: Take the Pebble Beach exit off Highway 1. Follow the signs to the Pebble Beach gate. The guard gives further directions from there.

POINT MUGU GOLF CLUB (military, 9 holes, marlin cox 1963) . . . .

NAWS, Building 153
Point Mugu, CA 93042
(805) 989-7109

	YARDAGE	PAR	RATING	SLOPE	
FRONT	2929	36	72.6	119	**$10 - $15**
MIDDLE	-	-	-	-	
BACK	2991	35	68.1	113	

WHAT TO EXPECT: Located on an air base, this is a meadow course with nine holes, but 18 sets of tee boxes.
NOTES: Reciprocal play with other members only clubs is allowed.
DIRECTIONS: From west Los Angeles (about 47 miles northwest to the course): Take the Santa Monica Freeway (I-10) west to the Pacific Coast Highway. Take the Pacific Coast Highway (Highway 1) north toward Camarillo. Take the Wood Road/USN Point Mugu exit. Proceed to the gate for a pass and directions.

SEABEE GOLF COURSE OF PORT HUENEME, THE (military, 18 holes, jack daray 1957)

Building 1537
Port Hueneme, CA 93043-4300
(805) 982-2620

	YARDAGE	PAR	RATING	SLOPE	
FRONT	5453	72	71.3	118	**$9 - $24**
MIDDLE	5971	71	68.6	118	
BACK	6278	71	70.1	122	

WHAT TO EXPECT: Seabee is a level, friendly course that will reward a good putter. Beware of the first hole. Many a golfer with the first-hole jitters, has busted one right into the driving range and started their round by re-teeing and adding two strokes. Of course you could always just take a mulligan.
NOTES: Public play is accepted.
DIRECTIONS: From downtown Los Angeles (about 66 miles northwest to the course): Take US 101 north, exit at Wagon Wheel/Ventura Road and turn left. This leads to Ventura Road heading west. Take at right at the Sunkist Gate.

PAJARO VALLEY GOLF CLUB (public, 18 holes, floyd mcfarland 1922) . . . .

967 Salinas Road
Royal Oaks, CA 95076
(831) 724-3851
pvgolf.com

	YARDAGE	PAR	RATING	SLOPE	
FRONT	5696	72	72.3	123	**$16 - $60**
MIDDLE	6005	72	68.3	116	
BACK	6211	72	69.3	118	

WHAT TO EXPECT: This is an often overlooked gem — scenic, with a few challenges, but not too difficult. The fairways are generous and the length modest, allowing the average golfer a chance at a good score.
DIRECTIONS: From Monterey (about 25 miles north to the course): Take Highway 1 north. Turn right at the blinking light at Salinas Road. The clubhouse is on the right.

SALINAS FAIRWAYS GOLF COURSE (municipal, 18 holes, jack fleming 1956) . . . .

45 Skyway Boulevard
Salinas, CA 93905
(831) 758-7300
golfsalinas.com

	YARDAGE	PAR	RATING	SLOPE
FRONT	5121	71	67.9	105
MIDDLE	6230	71	68.7	113
BACK	6479	71	69.8	115

$20 - $28

WHAT TO EXPECT: The new greens provide much of the challenge on Salinas Fairways. They are now well protected by traps and undulating. The front nine is roomy but does have some actual rough for those who cannot hit the ball straight. Water comes into play on four holes.

DIRECTIONS: From San Jose (about 60 miles south to the course): Go south on US 101. Exit on Airport Boulevard in Salinas and travel approximately one mile east to the course.

SALINAS GOLF & COUNTRY CLUB (members only, 18 holes, sherwin smith 1925) . . . .

475 San Juan Grade Road
Salinas, CA 93906
(831) 449-1526
salinasgcc.com

	YARDAGE	PAR	RATING	SLOPE
FRONT	5621	72	72.4	129
MIDDLE	6017	72	69.0	122
BACK	6102	72	69.4	123

$40 - $70

WHAT TO EXPECT: This is a short but interesting and hilly course that often requires precision over power. Many trees and small greens make up the challenge.

NOTES: Reciprocal play with other members only clubs is allowed.

DIRECTIONS: From San Jose (about 60 miles south to the course): Take US 101 south to Salinas. Exit Crazy Horse Canyon Turnoff, drive to San Juan Grade Road and go right. The club is on the right.

TWIN CREEKS GOLF COURSE (public, 9 holes, steve halsey 2000) . . . .

1551 Beacon Hill Drive
Salinas, CA 93905
(831) 758-7333
golfsalinas.com

	YARDAGE	PAR	RATING	SLOPE
FRONT	1616	31	57.4	86
MIDDLE	1676	31	58.3	84
BACK	1859	31	58.8	86

$10 - $20

WHAT TO EXPECT: With large fairways and immature trees, Twin Creeks is suited for all skill levels. There is one huge lake; otherwise, there is very little in the way of hazards. The greens are well-kept and undulating.

NOTES: The course has an excellent practice facility.

DIRECTIONS: From San Jose (about 60 miles south to the course): Take US 101 south. Exit Laurel Drive and head east. Turn left on Constitution. Turn right on Beacon Hill Drive.

SAN JUAN OAKS GOLF CLUB (public, 18 holes, fred couples & gene bates 1996) . . . .

3825 Union Road
San Juan Bautista, CA 95045
(831) 636-6115
sanjuanoaks.com

	YARDAGE	PAR	RATING	SLOPE
FRONT	4770	69	67.1	116
MIDDLE	6712	72	73.3	139
BACK	7133	72	75.6	145

$50 - $75

WHAT TO EXPECT: A good design, challenge, scenery and ambience all contribute to what has become one of Northern California's more popular public-access courses.

OUR OPINION: If you are near Monterey or San Jose, it's well worth the trip. – The Mole

DIRECTIONS: From San Jose (about 45 miles south to the course): Go south on US 101. Exit onto Highway 156 east toward Hollister. About seven miles east, turn right on Union Road. The club is on the right.

DAIRY CREEK GOLF COURSE (public, 18 holes, john harbottle 1997) . . . .

2990 Dairy Creek Road
San Luis Obispo, CA 93405
(805) 782-8060

	YARDAGE	PAR	RATING	SLOPE
FRONT	4965	71	69.0	121
MIDDLE	6108	71	69.8	123
BACK	6548	71	71.9	127

$26 - $30

WHAT TO EXPECT: Many a golf ball has given up its life at Dairy Creek. The course has three large lakes that come into play and a creek (Dairy Creek) that appears on nearly every hole. The greens are large, but subtle in slope. Off the tee, aiming for the cart path could save you many strokes. The cart paths run away from hazards, and balls hit in that direction tend to funnel back into the middle of the fairway.

OUR OPINION: These are the types of courses that are in short supply in California. Dairy Creek won't "blow you away" from a design standpoint, but it is a user friendly layout with good service at a reasonable price. – Bob

DIRECTIONS: From within San Luis Obispo: From US 101, exit onto Highway 1 toward Morro Bay. After about six miles, at the light, turn right onto Dairy Creek Road. Stay to the left.

SAN LUIS OBISPO COUNTRY CLUB (members only, 18 holes, bert stamps 1957) . . . . .

255 Country Club Drive
San Luis Obispo, CA 93401
(805) 543-4035

	YARDAGE	PAR	RATING	SLOPE
FRONT	5901	74	74.9	129
MIDDLE	6365	72	72.0	127
BACK	6671	72	73.3	129

$30 - $40

WHAT TO EXPECT: This is a hilly course with scattered trees and plenty of rough. There are homes around the course, but they do not usually come into play. The greens are undulating.

NOTES: Reciprocal play with other members only clubs is allowed.

DIRECTIONS: From within San Luis Obispo: From US 101 north, exit Los Osos Valley and go right. Turn left on South Higuera. Turn right at Farm Road. Turn right on Broad Street. Turn right on Los Rancho Road. Turn right on Country Club Drive.

BIRNAM WOOD GOLF CLUB (members only, 18 holes, robert trent jones, sr. 1967) ..

2031 Packing House Road
Santa Barbara, CA 93108
(805) 969-0919

	YARDAGE	PAR	RATING	SLOPE
FRONT	5904	70	68.7	121
MIDDLE	-	-	-	-
BACK	5365	71	72.1	127

$40 - $95

WHAT TO EXPECT: There are only two or three holes where the smart player uses their driver on this course, which is riddled with out-of-bounds and hazards. Birnam Wood is made even more challenging because barrancas guard the front of many greens. Players must hit the ball over the hazard, but keep it below the hole for any chance of scoring well.
NOTES: Reciprocal play with other members only clubs is allowed.
DIRECTIONS: From within Santa Barbara: Off US 101, exit at Sheffield Drive. Follow Sheffield Drive until it dead-ends. Turn left on East Valley Road and drive to the top of the hill. At the top, there is a stone gatehouse and the club entrance.

HIDDEN OAKS GOLF COURSE (public, 9 holes, billy casper 1975) ....

4760-G Calle Camarada
Santa Barbara, CA 93110
(805) 967-3493

	YARDAGE	PAR	RATING	SLOPE
FRONT	854	27	-	-
MIDDLE	-	-	-	-
BACK	1118	27	-	-

$10 - $11

WHAT TO EXPECT: Designed by the former PGA professional Billy Casper, this is an undulating course with mature trees, where players are hitting either up or down to greens.
NOTES: The course does not accept credit cards.
DIRECTIONS: From within Santa Barbara: Off US 101, take the Turnpike exit toward the Pacific. Turn left on Hollister. Then turn right on Puente and follow it to Calle Camarada. Then turn right to get to the course.

LA CUMBRE COUNTRY CLUB (members only, 18 holes, william p. bell, jr. 1954) .....

4015 Via Laguna
Santa Barbara, CA 93110
(805) 682-3131

	YARDAGE	PAR	RATING	SLOPE
FRONT	5701	72	74.0	134
MIDDLE	6092	71	69.1	120
BACK	6406	71	70.8	128

$135 - $135

WHAT TO EXPECT: La Cumbre is surrounded by homes. The front nine features narrow fairways guarded by native oaks. The back nine has a lake that comes into play on five holes.
NOTES: Reciprocal play with other members only clubs is allowed.
DIRECTIONS: From within Santa Barbara: Off US 101, exit at La Cumbre Road. Continue past the arched entrance to the Hope Ranch Park and Via Laguna. Turn left to the club.

MONTECITO COUNTRY CLUB (members only, 18 holes, max behr 1922) . . . .

820 Summit Road
Santa Barbara, CA 93108
(805) 969-0800

	YARDAGE	PAR	RATING	SLOPE
FRONT	5897	74	75.0	131
MIDDLE	-	-	-	-
BACK	6184	71	70.2	123

$60 - $100

WHAT TO EXPECT: This is a tight, rolling course cut out of a hillside. With hilly, tree-lined fairways and small undulating greens, the key to scoring well is the ability to hit a variety of shots from different angles and to keep the ball below the hole. It doesn't hurt if you putt well, either. At the end of your round, you will swear that this course is far longer than scorecard indicates.

NOTES: Reciprocal play with other members only clubs is allowed.

DIRECTIONS: From within Santa Barbara: Off US 101 north, take the Cabrillo Boulevard exit north, through the underpass, bearing right to Hot Springs Road. Turn left and drive one-quarter mile to Summit Road. Turn left to the club.

RANCHO SAN MARCOS GOLF COURSE (public, 18 holes, robert trent jones jr. 1998) . .

4600 Highway 154
Santa Barbara, CA 93105
(805) 683-6334
rsm1804.com

	YARDAGE	PAR	RATING	SLOPE
FRONT	5018	71	69.2	117
MIDDLE	6290	71	70.2	127
BACK	6803	71	73.1	135

$56 - $139

WHAT TO EXPECT: Inland from Santa Barbara on the site of the an old stagecoach trail, this beautifully rustic setting affords stunning views of the Santa Ynez River Valley. The front nine is situated on a flat plains, while the back nine plays on and around a ridge.

OUR OPINION: Psychologically, the tees fill you with confidence, as many of the fairways are wide and there are not many hazards. However, don't be fooled. If you don't have a decent short game, it will be reflected in your score. If you are carrying your own bag, the back nine is a hike, not a walk. – Andy

DIRECTIONS: From downtown Los Angeles (about 105 miles northwest to the course): Take US 101 north to Santa Barbara and take the State Street/San Marcos Pass exit; Cross State Street and turn toward the mountains on San Marcos Pass, Highway 154. The course is 13 miles on the right.

SANTA BARBARA GOLF CLUB (public, 18 holes, lawrence hughes 1958) . . . .

3500 McCaw Avenue
Santa Barbara, CA 93105
(805) 687-7087

	YARDAGE	PAR	RATING	SLOPE
FRONT	5541	72	64.9	105
MIDDLE	5782	70	66.3	109
BACK	6014	70	67.6	113

$27 - $36

WHAT TO EXPECT: This popular muni course is open and rolling with scattered trees. The greens vary in size and slope and are guarded by traps that can easily be avoided. There is out-of-bounds that can come into play around the perimeter of the course. Kikuyu grass in the fairways makes this course play longer.

DIRECTIONS: From within Santa Barbara: Exit US 101 at Las Positas Road and drive east for almost a mile to McCaw Avenue. Turn left and go one-quarter mile to the club.

VALLEY CLUB OF MONTECITO, THE (members only, 18 holes, alister mackenzie 1929)

1901 East Valley Road
Santa Barbara, CA 93150
(805) 969-4681

	YARDAGE	PAR	RATING	SLOPE	
FRONT	5813	73	74.3	134	**$35 - $150**
MIDDLE	6333	72	70.0	122	
BACK	6603	72	72.1	133	

WHAT TO EXPECT: If you are fortunate enough to play here, you will experience the quintessential Members Course. It is interesting but not too difficult and possesses some of the finest green sites in the game.

NOTES: They are currently remodeling all the bunkers back to Alister Mackenzie's original specifications.

DIRECTIONS: From within Santa Barbara: Off US 101, take the San Ysidro Road exit. Travel north to East Valley Road. Turn right one mile to Valley Club Road, then turn right again to the club.

RANCHO MARIA GOLF CLUB (public, 18 holes, bob baldock 1965) . . . .

1950 State Highway 1
Santa Maria, CA 93455
(805) 937-2019
ranchomariagolf.com

	YARDAGE	PAR	RATING	SLOPE	
FRONT	5504	73	71.3	123	**$19 - $30**
MIDDLE	6150	72	68.8	114	
BACK	6390	72	70.2	119	

WHAT TO EXPECT: Head for the putting green. There are plenty of trees on Rancho Maria, which is set in the foothills, but it is the small greens that are sometimes lightning fast that will give you fits. There are no parallel fairways, and an afternoon breeze is common.

DIRECTIONS: From Santa Barbara (about 70 miles northwest to the course): Take US 101 north toward Santa Maria. Take the Clark Avenue exit west to Highway 1 and turn right for two miles. The course is on the left.

SANTA MARIA COUNTRY CLUB (members only, 18 holes) . . . .

505 West Waller Lane
Santa Maria, CA 93455
(805) 937-2027

	YARDAGE	PAR	RATING	SLOPE	
FRONT	5907	72	74.3	127	**$35 - $75**
MIDDLE	6270	72	70.0	122	
BACK	6495	72	71.8	129	

WHAT TO EXPECT: Santa Maria is a level layout, with fairways guarded by trees. The greens are fairly large and range from flat to undulating. Water comes into play on four holes, and there is out-of-bounds on the holes that outline the course.

NOTES: Reciprocal play with other members only clubs is allowed.

DIRECTIONS: From Santa Barbara (about 70 miles northwest to the course): Head north on US 101 to the Betteravia exit. Turn west and drive to Broadway, then south to Waller Lane. Turn right on Waller Lane to the club.

SUNSET RIDGE GOLF COURSE (public, 9 holes, larry popoff 1994) . . . .

1424 Fairway Drive
Santa Maria, CA 93455
(805) 347-1070

	YARDAGE	PAR	RATING	SLOPE	
FRONT	1526	28	56.1	84	**$5 - $12**
MIDDLE	-	-	-	-	
BACK	1526	28	56.1	84	

WHAT TO EXPECT: This is a level course with one par 4 and the rest par 3s. With wind, small elevated greens, and plenty of out-of-bounds, Sunset Ridge can put up a fight. Beware of the last four holes.

DIRECTIONS: From within Santa Maria: Off US 101, take the Betteravia exit and head west to Skyway Drive. Turn left on Skyway Drive.

MOUNTAIN VIEW GOLF CLUB (public, 18 holes, anthony pawlak 1969) . . . .

16799 South Mountain Road
Santa Paula, CA 93060
(805) 525-1571

	YARDAGE	PAR	RATING	SLOPE	
FRONT	4710	72	69.4	117	**$16 - $21**
MIDDLE	-	-	-	-	
BACK	5378	69	64.8	103	

WHAT TO EXPECT: Mountain View has many short par 4s and five par 3s. With trees along the fairways and ponds that come into play on a few holes, Mountain View keeps the long hitters honest by requiring some semblance of accuracy.

DIRECTIONS: From Ventura (about 17 miles east to the course): Drive south on US 101 and take Highway 126 east to the Tenth Street exit. Turn left to Harvard Boulevard and then make a right on 12th Street. Go over the bridge and turn right on South Mountain Road, to the course.

BAYONET/BLACKHORSE GOLF COURSE (public, 36 holes, gen. robert mc clure 1954) .

One McClure Way
Seaside, CA 93955
(831) 899-7271
bayonetblackhorse.com

	YARDAGE	PAR	RATING	SLOPE	
FRONT	6496	72	72.4	129	**$45 - $95**
MIDDLE	6817	72	73.8	135	
BACK	7095	72	75.1	139	

WHAT TO EXPECT: Good players have long recognized that the Bayonet Course is one of the most demanding in the entire state. Closely tree lined, its sloping fairways and smallish greens are intimidating to the careless shot-maker. Blackhorse is similar in nature, but does not have the distance of Bayonet. The course affords many excellent ocean views.

OUR OPINION: Both courses are a must-play. For those with higher handicaps, we recommend Blackhorse. The layout is not easy, but less severe and is in excellent condition – even better than its more famous brother, Bayonet. – Frank

NOTES: Yardage listed is for Bayonet. Bayonet hosted a PGA Tour Qualifier in 2000 and Blackhorse in 2001.

DIRECTIONS: From Monterey (about five miles northeast to the course): Go north on Highway 1. Take the Fort Ord main entrance exit. Go straight when exiting the freeway. There are signs to the right.

LOST CANYONS GOLF CLUB (public, 36 holes, pete dye & fred couples 2000 & 2001) .

3301 Lost Canyons Drive
Simi Valley, CA 93063
(805) 522-4653
lostcanyons.com

	YARDAGE	PAR	RATING	SLOPE
FRONT	6162	72	70.3	133
MIDDLE	6789	72	73.6	143
BACK	7290	72	76.1	149

$50 - $145

WHAT TO EXPECT: Any course that requires you to take a fore caddy to guide you around and help you find golf balls is going to be difficult. Both courses are pristine, and we could spend two pages describing elevation changes, canyons, undulating greens, wind, and beautiful scenery, but you are just going to have to experience it for yourself. We will give you some advice. One, if you are a good golfer, you may not want to play from the tips, but don't play too far up. Your landing areas for long drives shrinks. Two, spend time on the putting green. Three, give your fore caddie a lift now and then. I know it's probably against the rules, but hunting for hackers' golf balls on the sides of canyons is no easy task.

OUR OPINION: Located a few miles away in Simi Valley, it delivers on the promise of upscale daily fee golf. Holes 11 through 17 on the Sky Course are an amazing experience. – Andy

NOTES: At Lost Canyons, you can play either the Shadow Course or the Sky Course. The yardage listed is for the Sky Course.

DIRECTIONS: From west Los Angeles (about 35 miles northwest to the course): Take the San Diego Freeway (I-405) north to Highway 118 west. Take the Tapo Canyon exit and head north almost two miles. Turn left on Lost Canyons Drive.

SIMI HILLS GOLF COURSE (public, 18 holes, ted robinson 1981) . . . .

5031 Alamo Street
Simi Valley, CA 93063
(805) 522-0803

	YARDAGE	PAR	RATING	SLOPE
FRONT	5392	71	71.1	120
MIDDLE	6062	71	69.1	121
BACK	6411	71	70.6	125

$22 - $34

WHAT TO EXPECT: This is a popular, rolling course with a good variety of holes. With lots of trees and rough, hitting it in the fairway is imperative. The greens are slower than they appear, and many golfers make the mistake of reading too much break. The course can get windy.

DIRECTIONS: From within Simi Valley: Off Highway 118 , exit at Stearns and drive north. Make a left on Alamo Street, to the course.

SINALOA GOLF COURSE (public, 9 holes, geoff shackelford 1994) . . . .

980 Madera Road
Simi Valley, CA 93065
(805) 581-2662

	YARDAGE	PAR	RATING	SLOPE
FRONT	-	-	-	-
MIDDLE	-	-	-	-
BACK	1084	27	-	-

$6 - $15

WHAT TO EXPECT: This is a pitch-and-putt course.

DIRECTIONS: From within Simi Valley: Off Highway 118, take the Madera Road exit and travel south about two miles to the course.

WOOD RANCH GOLF CLUB (members only, 18 holes, ted robinson 1985) . . . .

301 Wood Ranch Parkway
Simi Valley, CA 93065
(805) 522-7262
americangolf.com

	YARDAGE	PAR	RATING	SLOPE	
FRONT	5392	72	65.9	115	**$65 - $90**
MIDDLE	6552	72	72.1	131	
BACK	6972	72	74.4	137	

WHAT TO EXPECT: This is a demanding links-style layout with rolling terrain, menacing bunkers and water on more than half the holes. The fairways are good sized, but miss them and you will find yourself in some nasty rough. Wind will be a factor. The course provides breathtaking views of the Conejo Valley.

NOTES: Wood Ranch has hosted two GTE Senior Tour Classics and the 2000 LPGA Los Angeles Open. Reciprocal play with other member only clubs is allowed.

DIRECTIONS: From downtown Los Angeles (about 40 miles northwest to the course): Take US 101 north to Highway 23 north. Exit at Olsen Road and turn right. Turn right again on Wood Ranch Parkway. The club is less than a mile away.

RANCH COURSE AT THE ALISAL (resort, 18 holes, billy bell, jr. 1955) . . . .

1054 Alisal Road
Solvang, CA 93463
(805) 688-4215
alisal.com

	YARDAGE	PAR	RATING	SLOPE	
FRONT	5752	73	74.5	133	**$75 - $90**
MIDDLE	6122	72	70.1	127	
BACK	6551	72	72.0	133	

WHAT TO EXPECT: To score well at the picturesque valley course, it is imperative that your ball stay in the fairway. Just beyond the short grass is an abundance of trees and Kikuyu rough, which will stop a ball dead in its tracks. If you safely negotiate the fairways, you will find the greens medium-sized and undulating, yet very puttable.

DIRECTIONS: From Santa Barbara (about 35 miles north to the course): Take US 101 north to Highway 246 east. Go three miles into Solvang. Then turn right on Alisal Road.

RIVER COURSE AT THE ALISAL (public, 18 holes, halsey/daray design 1992) . . . .

150 Alisal Road
Solvang, CA 93463
(805) 688-6042
rivercourse.com

	YARDAGE	PAR	RATING	SLOPE	
FRONT	5710	72	73.1	122	**$25 - $55**
MIDDLE	6451	72	70.6	120	
BACK	6830	72	73.1	126	

WHAT TO EXPECT: A riverbed sandwiched between hillsides provides the setting for this 1992 course. The noted hole is the 397-yard seventh, with a lake on the left and out-of-bounds on the right. Because the trees are still immature, the River Course is far more revealing than its counterpart, the Ranch Course.

DIRECTIONS: From Santa Barbara (about 35 miles north to the course): Take US 101 north to Highway 246 east. Go three miles into Solvang. Then turn right on Alisal Road. The course is on the left.

LOS ROBLES GOLF COURSE (public, 18 holes) . . . .

299 South Moorpark Road
Thousand Oaks, CA 91361
(805) 495-6421
golfthousandoaks.com

	YARDAGE	PAR	RATING	SLOPE	
FRONT	5184	69	69.0	115	**$22 - $27**
MIDDLE	5858	69	66.5	108	
BACK	6264	69	68.7	116	

WHAT TO EXPECT: Because the course has three par 3s on each side, the total distance is deceiving. For the most part, Los Robles is driver friendly, even though the fairways are sloping and tree lined. The greens are fairly large and will reward the good putter. There are four lakes that come into play.

NOTES: The course has recently been renovated.

DIRECTIONS: From downtown Los Angeles (about 40 miles northwest to the course): Take US 101 north, exit at Moorpark Road and turn left. Go about 300 yards and turn right to the course.

SHERWOOD COUNTRY CLUB (members only, 18 holes, jack nicklaus 1989) . . . .

320 West Stafford Road
Thousand Oaks, CA   91361
(805) 496-3036
sherwoodcc.com

	YARDAGE	PAR	RATING	SLOPE	
FRONT	5278	72	72.3	132	**$90 - $90**
MIDDLE	6577	72	72.3	136	
BACK	7008	72	74.3	142	

WHAT TO EXPECT: Opened in 1989 on the site of the original Robin Hood movie and the M.A.S.H. TV show, this Nicklaus design is dominated by its oaks, surrounding homes, and hillside views. It has been the scene of several TV-oriented golf competitions.

DIRECTIONS: From downtown Los Angeles (about 40 miles northwest to the course): Take US 101 north into the Valley. Exit at Westlake Boulevard, turn left and go about two miles. Turn right on Potrero Road and go about another two miles. Turn left into the brick entrance at Trentwood Drive.

SUNSET HILLS COUNTRY CLUB (members only, 18 holes, ted robinson 1974) . . . . . .

4155 Erbes Road North
Thousand Oaks, CA 91360
(805) 495-5407

	YARDAGE	PAR	RATING	SLOPE	
FRONT	5543	71	72.2	124	**$50 - $70**
MIDDLE	5804	71	68.0	118	
BACK	6066	71	69.3	121	

WHAT TO EXPECT: Sunset Hills is short in distance but not in challenge. The undulating fairways are flanked by trees and bordered by rough. You will encounter uneven lies on the fairways and elevated greens on some holes, which make your ability to judge distances paramount.

NOTES: Reciprocal play with other members only clubs is allowed.

DIRECTIONS: From downtown Los Angeles (about 44 miles northwest to the course): Take US 101 north, to Highway 23 north. Exit on Olsen Road and turn left. Turn left on Erbes Road at the flashing red light. The club is on the right.

MARSHALLIA RANCH GOLF COURSE (military, 18 holes, bob baldock 1959) . . . .

Vandenberg AFB
Vandenberg AFB, CA 93437
(805) 734-1333

	YARDAGE	PAR	RATING	SLOPE
FRONT	5404	72	72.5	124
MIDDLE	6388	72	71.1	122
BACK	6845	72	74.1	130

$16 - $45

WHAT TO EXPECT: The course is surrounded by eucalyptus trees. The front nine is flat, while the back nine is rolling with small greens and plenty of ice plant. Be prepared for the wind and keep the ball below the hole at all costs.

OUR OPINION: It's almost worth joining the military. – Bob

NOTES: Civilian play is allowed on a limited basis.

DIRECTIONS: From Santa Barbara (about 60 miles northwest to the course): Take US 101 north to Highway 1 north. Take the Lompoc-Vandenberg exit north to Vandenberg AFB. Drive past the main gate about four miles to the exit for Marshallia Ranch. The course is on the left.

BUENAVENTURA GOLF COURSE (public, 18 holes, billy bell, jr. 1932) . . . .

5882 Olivas Park Drive
Ventura, CA 93003
(805) 642-2231
eaglegolf.com

	YARDAGE	PAR	RATING	SLOPE
FRONT	5443	73	71.8	123
MIDDLE	6146	72	69.1	124
BACK	6412	72	70.7	126

$18 - $26

WHAT TO EXPECT: This popular course has six lakes, tree-lined fairways, and small greens. At 6,400 yards, the key to scoring well is leaving your ego in the clubhouse and using your driver sparingly.

DIRECTIONS: From downtown Los Angeles (about 65 miles northwest to the course): Take US 101 north and exit at Victoria. Go southwest about one and one-half miles to Olivas Park Drive. Turn left to the entrance on the right.

OLIVAS PARK GOLF COURSE (public, 18 holes, billy bell, jr. 1969) . . . .

3750 Olivas Park Drive
Ventura, CA 93003
(805) 677-6771
eaglegolf.com

	YARDAGE	PAR	RATING	SLOPE
FRONT	5501	72	72.4	119
MIDDLE	6353	72	70.7	119
BACK	6758	72	72.6	124

$14 - $29

WHAT TO EXPECT: This is a wide-open layout with plenty of parallel fairways and large undulating greens. You will find water on about one-third of the holes. Olivas Park is nothing fancy, just straightforward golf.

DIRECTIONS: From Santa Barbara (about 33 miles southeast to the course): Drive south on US 101 to the Seaward exit in Ventura. Turn left on Harbor Road and go five miles to Olivas Park Drive. Turn left and drive 100 yards toward the course.

SATICOY GOLF COURSE (public, 9 holes, george thomas 1921) . . . .

1025 South Wells Road
Ventura, CA 93004
(805) 647-6678

	YARDAGE	PAR	RATING	SLOPE	
FRONT	2557	34	67.9	112	**$11 - $20**
MIDDLE	-	-	-	-	
BACK	2723	34	65.4	109	

WHAT TO EXPECT: If the the words "out-of-bounds" give you the jitters, this may not be your course; fences can be found on nearly every hole. When you mix in some trees and old-school, level greens, it means accuracy is the name of the game at Saticoy.
DIRECTIONS: From downtown Los Angeles (about 65 miles northwest to the course): Take US 101 north to Highway126 east. Exit onto Wells Road and turn right.

CASSERLY GOLF COURSE (public, 9 holes, robert sanford 1966) . . . .

626 Casserly Road
Watsonville, CA 95076
(831) 724-1654

	YARDAGE	PAR	RATING	SLOPE	
FRONT	1158	27	-	-	**$5 - $5**
MIDDLE	-	-	-	-	
BACK	1264	27	-	-	

WHAT TO EXPECT: This is a hilly par-3 course with small greens. Miss the green and chances are you will not have a level lie. Water comes into play on a couple of holes.
NOTES: No alcoholic beverages are allowed on the premises.
DIRECTIONS: From San Jose (about 45 miles south to the course): Take US 101 south. Take Highway 152 west toward Watsonville. Turn right at the stop sign at Casserly Road. Drive two miles to the course.

SPRING HILLS GOLF COURSE (public, 18 holes, hank schimpeler 1965) . . . .

501 Spring Hills Drive
Watsonville, CA 95076
(831) 724-1404

	YARDAGE	PAR	RATING	SLOPE	
FRONT	5397	71	70.8	114	**$18 - $40**
MIDDLE	5883	71	68.8	115	
BACK	6015	71	69.4	117	

WHAT TO EXPECT: Club selection is key to scoring well at Spring Hills. The front nine is hilly and tight. The back nine allows more room for error and offers panoramic views of the surrounding area. Both nines feature small, elevated greens with subtle breaks.
DIRECTIONS: From San Jose (about 45 miles south to the course): Take US 101 south. Take Highway 152 west. Turn right at the stop sign at Casserly Road and go two miles. Turn right on Smith Road. Turn left on Spring Hills Drive.

Central Valley

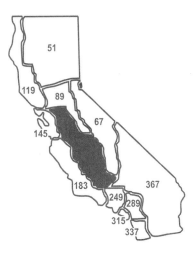

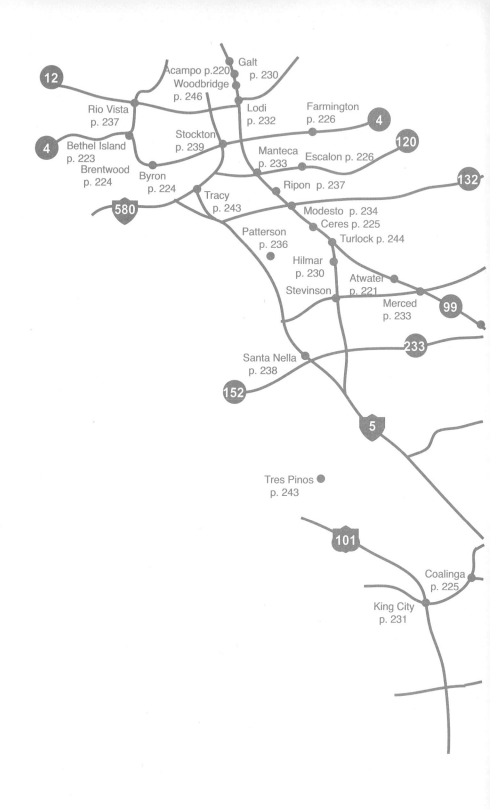

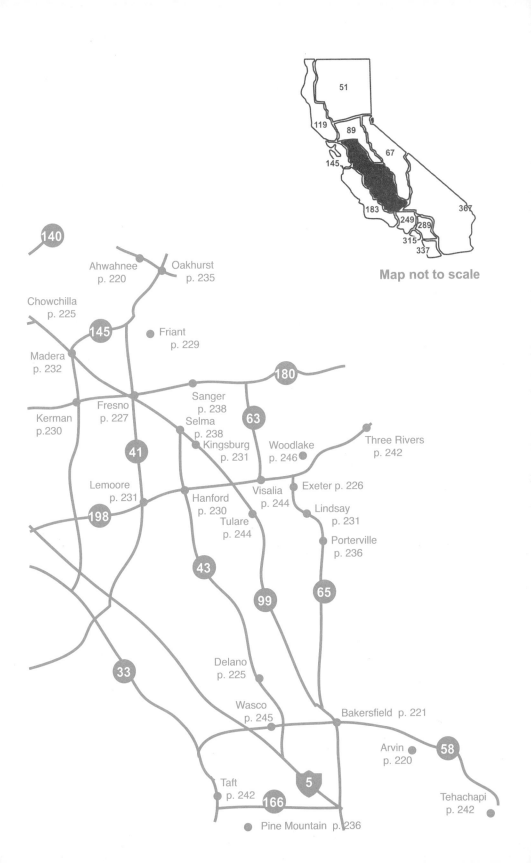

140

Ahwahnee
p. 220

Oakhurst
p. 235

Chowchilla
p. 225

145

Friant
p. 229

Madera
p. 232

180

Kerman
p. 230

Sanger
p. 238

Fresno
p. 227

Selma
p. 238

63

Kingsburg
p. 231

Woodlake
p. 246

Three Rivers
p. 242

41

Exeter p. 226

Lemoore
p. 231

Hanford
p. 230

Visalia
p. 244

Lindsay
p. 231

198

Tulare
p. 244

Porterville
p. 236

43

99

65

33

Delano
p. 225

Wasco
p. 245

Bakersfield p. 221

Arvin
p. 220

58

5

Taft
p. 242

166

Tehachapi
p. 242

Pine Mountain p. 236

51

119

89

67

145

183

249

289

315

337

367

Map not to scale

FOREST LAKE GOLF CLUB (public, 18 holes, unknown 1980) . . . .

2450 East Woodson Road
Acampo, CA 95220
(209) 369-5451

	YARDAGE	PAR	RATING	SLOPE	
FRONT	3517	60	57.4	85	**$13 - $16**
MIDDLE	-	-	-	-	
BACK	4622	66	61.1	97	

WHAT TO EXPECT: The course is diminutive in length, but the fairways are protected by trees that have no empathy for the struggling golfer. Miss the short grass, and you have little chance of placing your next shot on the green.

NOTES: This course actually has 24 holes. On Monday and Tuesday, par is 60. During the rest of the week, par is 66.

DIRECTIONS: From Lodi (about seven miles north to the course): Take Highway 99 north to the Jahant Road exit and go west. Jahant Road turns into Woodson Road. The course is on the left.

SIERRA MEADOWS - RIVER CREEK COURSE (public, 9 holes, john hilborn 1991) . . . . .

41709 Road 600
Ahwahnee, CA 93601
(559) 683-3388

	YARDAGE	PAR	RATING	SLOPE	
FRONT	2562	36	67.8	118	**$11 - $22**
MIDDLE	3014	36	68.3	123	
BACK	3152	36	69.4	125	

WHAT TO EXPECT: The undulating, breaking greens are the course's trademark, but you will also encounter plenty of trees, rocks, and the Fresno River along the way.

NOTES: This course was formerly known as the River Creek Golf Course.

DIRECTIONS: From Fresno (about 50 miles north to the course): Take Highway 41 north toward Oakhurst. Go left on Highway 49 toward Mariposa. After about five miles, turn left on Road 600 toward the course.

SYCAMORE CANYON GOLF CLUB (public, 18 holes, robert dean putnam 1989) . . . . . .

500 Kenmar Lane
Arvin, CA 93203
(661) 854-3163

	YARDAGE	PAR	RATING	SLOPE	
FRONT	5744	72	71.6	120	**$13 - $21**
MIDDLE	6428	72	69.9	117	
BACK	7100	72	74.2	123	

WHAT TO EXPECT: Although landing on the level fairways should be easy for the player who can hit the ball semi-straight, you can't ignore the water which comes into play on 14 holes. The greens are average size and undulating.

DIRECTIONS: From Bakersfield (about 18 miles southeast to the course): Drive south on Highway 99 to Bear Mountain Boulevard (Highway 223). Drive east 10 miles to South Derby. Go south approximately four miles to Kenmar Lane. Turn left to the course.

RANCHO DEL REY GOLF CLUB (public, 18 holes, bob baldock 1962) . . . .

5250 Green Sands Avenue
Atwater, CA 95301
(209) 358-7131

	YARDAGE	PAR	RATING	SLOPE
FRONT	5927	75	73.6	125
MIDDLE	6314	72	70.6	121
BACK	6702	72	72.5	124

$10 - $25

WHAT TO EXPECT: This flat valley course possesses enough trees, water, and challenge to
be interesting.
DIRECTIONS: From Merced (about eight miles northwest to the course): Take Highway 99
north and exit at Buchach Road, toward the Castle Air Museum. Turn left on Ashby and
then left on Green Sands Avenue.

BAKERSFIELD COUNTRY CLUB (members only, 18 holes, william bell 1950) . . . .

4200 Country Club Drive
Bakersfield, CA 93306
(661) 871-4121
bakersfieldcountryclub.com

	YARDAGE	PAR	RATING	SLOPE
FRONT	6156	77	75.8	129
MIDDLE	6458	72	70.8	123
BACK	6819	72	72.6	127

$100 - $100

WHAT TO EXPECT: This traditional layout is built on a hillside. With four par 4s over 400
yards and several long par 5s, accurate and long drives are a good start. The course,
however, is not one dimensional and requires golfers to be adept at every aspect of their
game.
NOTES: Reciprocal play with other members only clubs is allowed.
DIRECTIONS: From within Bakersfield: Off Highway 99, take Highway 178 east for six
miles. Take the Oswell Street exit and then turn right to Country Club Drive.

KERN RIVER GOLF COURSE (public, 18 holes, william bell 1953) . . . .

Lake Ming Road
Bakersfield, CA 93306
(661) 872-5128

	YARDAGE	PAR	RATING	SLOPE
FRONT	5971	73	72.3	123
MIDDLE	6258	70	69.6	118
BACK	6458	70	70.7	120

$15 - $15

WHAT TO EXPECT: Landing in the fairway on this rolling layout is not a problem, but
accuracy is a must from the fairway to the small, plateau greens. Miss them, and you will
struggle to get up and down.
DIRECTIONS: From within Bakersfield: Off Highway 99, take Highway 178 east to Alfred
Harrell Highway. Then head north and follow the signs to Lake Ming.

NORTH KERN GOLF COURSE (public, 18 holes, kermit styber 1953) . . . .

17412 Quality Road
Bakersfield, CA 93308
(661) 399-0347

	YARDAGE	PAR	RATING	SLOPE
FRONT	6182	76	72.7	116
MIDDLE	6461	72	69.9	109
BACK	6769	72	71.4	115

$12 - $15

WHAT TO EXPECT: This is a traditional, straightforward course with level fairways,
mature trees, and small greens. What you see is what you get.
DIRECTIONS: From within Bakersfield: Off Highway 99 exit Shafter/Lerdo Highway and
head east. Turn left (north) on Quality Road to the course.

RIO BRAVO COUNTRY CLUB (members only, 18 holes, robert muir graves 1981) . . . .

15200 Casa Club Drive
Bakersfield, CA 93306
(661) 871-4653

	YARDAGE	PAR	RATING	SLOPE
FRONT	5704	72	72.5	123
MIDDLE	6555	72	70.9	122
BACK	7018	72	74.4	138

$35 - $50

WHAT TO EXPECT: Set near the Sierra foothills, this course has constant elevation changes and considerable mounding, so level lies are far and few between. The greens are odd shapes and surrounded by angles and rough. Miss them and you'll need luck to get up and down. On the putting surface, you will find the greens can break any direction, including uphill. If you hit the ball long and wrong, (left to right) you might as well stay at home; you will out-of-bounds all day.

NOTES: Reciprocal play with other members only clubs is allowed.

DIRECTIONS: From within Bakersfield: Off Highway 99, take Highway 178 east and drive 15 miles to the Rio Bravo Resort. Go past the airport and turn right on Mira Monte.

RIVERLAKES RANCH, THE LINKS AT (public, 18 holes, ron fream 1999) . . . .

5201 RiverLakes Drive
Bakersfield, CA 93312
(661) 587-5465
riverlakesranchgolf.com

	YARDAGE	PAR	RATING	SLOPE
FRONT	5180	72	70.4	120
MIDDLE	6379	72	70.6	128
BACK	6800	72	72.6	133

$30 - $45

WHAT TO EXPECT: The Links at River Lakes is a contoured course with many well-placed bunkers and water hazards. The greens are fairly large and undulating, requiring a good touch. The front nine is more forgiving, while the back nine roams through an almond orchard. RiverLakes will make you think on every shot.

OUR OPINION: RiverLakes is a good value and a fun layout. We recommend it. When we played, there were no homes on the course. How they will impact play remains to be seen. – Shaw

DIRECTIONS: From within Bakersfield: Off Highway 99, take the Olive Street exit and head west to Riverlakes Drive. Go left on RiverLakes Drive.

SEVEN OAKS COUNTRY CLUB (members only, 18 holes, robert muir graves 1991) . . .

2000 Grand Lakes Avenue
Bakersfield, CA 93311
(661) 664-6474
sevenoaks.com

	YARDAGE	PAR	RATING	SLOPE
FRONT	5970	72	67.8	109
MIDDLE	6578	72	71.0	119
BACK	7119	72	73.7	128

$35 - $60

WHAT TO EXPECT: The test is bold at Seven Oaks. Sand, water, and considerable length combine with wind to push your skills to the limit on this flat layout.

NOTES: Reciprocal play with other member only clubs is accepted on a limited basis.

DIRECTIONS: From within Bakersfield: Off Highway 99, take the Ming Avenue exit and go west. Turn left on Grand Lakes Avenue, to the club.

STOCKDALE COUNTRY CLUB (members only, 18 holes, lloyd tevis 1925) . . . .

7001 Stockdale Highway
Bakersfield, CA 93309
(661) 832-0587

	YARDAGE	PAR	RATING	SLOPE
FRONT	5764	71	74.0	124
MIDDLE	6172	71	69.2	116
BACK	6327	71	70.4	120

$30 - $60

WHAT TO EXPECT: Built in the 1920s, this is a classic, level course with narrow, tree-lined fairways and small greens with subtle slopes.
NOTES: Reciprocal play with other members only clubs is allowed.
DIRECTIONS: From within Bakersfield: Off Highway 99, take the Stockdale Highway exit and go west two miles.

SUNDALE COUNTRY CLUB (semi-private, 18 holes, del webb 1963) . . . .

6218 Sundale Avenue
Bakersfield, CA 93309
(661) 831-5224

	YARDAGE	PAR	RATING	SLOPE
FRONT	5743	72	72.7	122
MIDDLE	6589	72	70.7	115
BACK	6800	72	71.8	120

$25 - $36

WHAT TO EXPECT: This is a park-setting course with tree-lined fairways and large, level greens. Water can be found on three holes.
DIRECTIONS: From within Bakersfield: Off Highway 99, take the Ming Avenue exit and go west to New Stine Road. Turn north one-quarter mile to Sundale Avenue and then proceed west one-half mile to the club.

VALLE GRANDE GOLF COURSE (public, 18 holes, william p. bell 1952) . . . .

1119 Watts Drive
Bakersfield, CA 93307
(661) 832-2259

	YARDAGE	PAR	RATING	SLOPE
FRONT	5318	72	68.4	109
MIDDLE	6070	72	67.5	109
BACK	6331	72	68.7	112

$13 - $16

WHAT TO EXPECT: Keep the ball in play. Short and flat, Valle Grande is anything but easy. You will find out-of-bounds on 12 of the 18 holes, water on six holes, and fairways boarded by trees. With small greens and tight fairways the patient player who can hit greens will be rewarded with a low score.
DIRECTIONS: From within Bakersfield: Off Highway 99, drive east on Highway 58. Turn right on Cottonwood Road for a little over a mile. Turn left on Watts Drive to the club.

BETHEL ISLAND GOLF COURSE (public, 18 holes, bob baldock 1966) . . . .

3303 Gateway Road
Bethel Island, CA 94511
(925) 684-2654

	YARDAGE	PAR	RATING	SLOPE
FRONT	5839	74	72.2	117
MIDDLE	6292	72	69.7	115
BACK	6592	72	71.2	118

$11 - $26

WHAT TO EXPECT: If you hit the ball to the right off the tee, you will most likely be forgiven. If you go left off the tee, you will be be disciplined by canals. The fairways are level, but give little roll. The greens are level, quick, and they break. Drainage is fantastic, so this is a good place for winter golf. Wind can be a factor.
DIRECTIONS: From Walnut Creek (about 32 miles northeast to the course): Go north on I-680. Take Highway 242 east to Highway 4 east and go through Oakley. Go left on Cypress Road, which becomes Bethel Island Road. Turn right on to Gateway Road.

BRENTWOOD GOLF CLUB (public, 27 holes, ted robinson 1994) . . . .

100 Summerset Drive
Brentwood, CA 94513
(925) 516-3400
brentwoodgolf.com

	YARDAGE	PAR	RATING	SLOPE	
FRONT	5992	72	69.8	126	**$45 - $60**
MIDDLE	6413	72	71.7	130	
BACK	6824	72	73.6	132	

WHAT TO EXPECT: This 27-hole golf courses features wide fairways, several water holes, some blind shots, and large, sloping greens. On a few holes, housing and large power lines do come into play.

OUR OPINION: You actually play under power lines for a few holes. That's not the problem. What you need to be aware of is the holes with blind drives over a hill. There are lakes sitting on the other side. You think you toasted one in the fairway and the next thing you know, you're hitting three. – Frank

NOTES: Yardage shown is for the Creekside/Hillside combination.

DIRECTIONS: From San Francisco (about 55 miles east to the course): Take I-80 east to I-580 east to Livermore. Take the Vasco Road North exit and head north about 20 miles to Brentwood. Turn left on Balfour Road and follow to Summerset Drive. Turn left on Summerset Drive to the clubhouse.

SHADOW LAKES GOLF CLUB (public, 18 holes, gary roger baird 2001) . . . .

401 West Country Club Drive
Brentwood, CA 94513
(888) 876-6687
troongolf.com

	YARDAGE	PAR	RATING	SLOPE	
FRONT	-	-	-	-	**$60 - $80**
MIDDLE	-	-	-	-	
BACK	6711	72	-	-	

WHAT TO EXPECT: This is a hilly course that uses the natural terrain to create its challenge. Throughout the course you will find native grasses, deep bunkers, big greens, and water on six holes.

NOTES: Shadow Lakes is part of a housing development.

DIRECTIONS: Directions were not available at time of press. Please check our website, www.InTheLoopGolf.com for updates.

DISCOVERY BAY COUNTRY CLUB (members only, 18 holes, ted robinson 1986) . . . . . .

1475 Clubhouse Drive
Byron, CA 94514
(925) 634-0704
discoverybaycc.com

	YARDAGE	PAR	RATING	SLOPE	
FRONT	5266	71	71.1	125	**$28 - $65**
MIDDLE	6042	71	69.7	122	
BACK	6518	71	72.2	128	

WHAT TO EXPECT: Although water is a dominant feature appearing on all but two holes, there is room for error while remaining in play. Your shot into the green may cause you more headaches than the water. The greens are sloping and slick. Put the ball on the wrong side of the pin and a three putt will be your punishment.

NOTES: Reciprocal play with other members only clubs is allowed.

DIRECTIONS: From San Francisco (about 60 miles east to the course): Take I-80 east to Highway. 4 and go east to Discovery Bay. Take the Discovery Bay Boulevard exit. Make a right on Clubhouse Drive.

RIVER OAKS GOLF COURSE (public, 18 holes, jim phipps 1979) . . . .

3441 East Hatch Road
Ceres, CA 95307
(209) 537-4653

	YARDAGE	PAR	RATING	SLOPE
FRONT	2855	58	54.3	75
MIDDLE	-	-	-	-
BACK	2855	58	55.5	83

$12 - $15

WHAT TO EXPECT: Located along the Tuolumne River, this is a user-friendly executive course. There are trees scattered throughout and many parallel fairways. All the par 4s are on the back nine.

DIRECTIONS: From Modesto (about five miles south to the course): Take Highway 99 south, and take the Hatch Road turnoff. Go east approximately two and one-half miles. The course is on the left.

PHEASANT RUN GOLF CLUB (public, 18 holes, richard bigler 1998) . . . .

3125 Arcadian Street
Chowchilla, CA 93610
(559) 665-3411
pheasantrungolfclub.com

	YARDAGE	PAR	RATING	SLOPE
FRONT	6253	69	69.9	115
MIDDLE	6815	72	72.6	119
BACK	7244	72	74.8	126

$12 - $25

WHAT TO EXPECT: This flat, residential development course boasts some challenging putting surfaces and lots of length. Water and sand add to the challenge, with the par-4 18th one of the toughest finishing holes around. Wind can make this course much more imposing.

DIRECTIONS: From Fresno (about 40 miles northwest to the course): Drive north on Highway 99 to Chowchilla. Take the Chowchilla/Robertson exit. Make a right on Robertson and follow to the course.

POLVADERO GOLF COURSE (public, 9 holes, bob baldock 1963) . . . .

41605 Sutter Avenue
Coalinga, CA 93210
(559) 935-3578

	YARDAGE	PAR	RATING	SLOPE
FRONT	2901	36	73.1	124
MIDDLE	-	-	-	-
BACK	3185	36	70.4	119

$5 - $14

WHAT TO EXPECT: This is a tight driving course with plenty of trees and out-of-bounds surrounding the fairways. The terrain is rolling and the greens are undulating.

DIRECTIONS: From within Coalinga: Off I-5, take the Jayne Avenue exit and head west to Sutter Avenue. Turn left to the course.

DELANO GOLF COURSE (public, 9 holes, bert stamps 1962) . . . .

104 South Lexington
Delano, CA 93216
(661) 725-7527

	YARDAGE	PAR	RATING	SLOPE
FRONT	1993	32	63.1	108
MIDDLE	-	-	-	-
BACK	2177	32	60.8	94

$8 - $11

WHAT TO EXPECT: This is a straightforward course with rolling fairways flanked by trees.

DIRECTIONS: From Bakersfield (about 33 miles north to the course): Go north on Highway 99 and exit at Wollomes Avenue. Go east to Lexington and turn left.

ESCALON GOLF COURSE (public, 9 holes, kenneth roberts 1984) . . . .

17051 South Escalon Bellota Hwy.
Escalon, CA 95320
(209) 838-1277

	YARDAGE	PAR	RATING	SLOPE
FRONT	1520	29	55.1	70
MIDDLE	1520	28	56.1	77
BACK	1598	28	56.6	78

$6 - $12

WHAT TO EXPECT: This is a short course with generous fairways and mature trees.
DIRECTIONS: From Modesto (about 12 miles north to the course): From Highway 99, go north on McHenry Avenue, which becomes Escalon Bellota Highway. After passing through Escalon, the course is on the left.

EXETER GOLF COURSE (public, 9 holes, bob baldock 1963) . . . .

510 West Visalia
Exeter, CA 93211
(559) 592-4783

	YARDAGE	PAR	RATING	SLOPE
FRONT	1602	30	56.8	82
MIDDLE	-	-	-	-
BACK	1602	30	56.8	80

$6 - $8

WHAT TO EXPECT: This is a straightforward executive course with mature and slightly sloping greens.
DIRECTIONS: From Visalia (about 11 miles east to the course): Take Highway 99 south and go east on Caldwell Avenue, through Farmersville. Caldwell turns into Visalia. The course is on the right in Exeter.

J.B. GOLF COURSE (public, 9 holes, ken roberts 1990) . . . .

24305 East Highway 4
Farmington, CA 95230
(209) 886-5670

	YARDAGE	PAR	RATING	SLOPE
FRONT	-	-	-	-
MIDDLE	-	-	-	-
BACK	889	27	-	-

$6 - $6

WHAT TO EXPECT: This is a short par-3 course, with no hole longer than 135 yards.
NOTES: Kids are welcomed.
DIRECTIONS: From Stockton (about 33 miles east to the course): Off Highway 99, take Highway 4 east into Farmington.

AIRWAYS GOLF COURSE (public, 18 holes, bert stamps 1949) . . . .

5440 Airways Boulevard
Fresno, CA 93727
(559) 291-6254
airways-golf.com

	YARDAGE	PAR	RATING	SLOPE
FRONT	5263	69	69.2	115
MIDDLE	-	-	-	-
BACK	5288	68	64.2	108

$8 - $18

WHAT TO EXPECT: Airways is a level course with tight fairways. It is guarded by trees and small, flat greens.
OUR OPINION: This course will never make any major or minor publication's top ten list, but there is always a need for a place to learn the game. – Shaw
DIRECTIONS: From within Fresno: From Highway 99, take the Shaw Avenue exit and head east. Make a right on Peach Avenue. Follow Peach Avenue to the course.

BELMONT COUNTRY CLUB (members only, 18 holes) . . . .

8253 East Belmont
Fresno, CA 93727
(559) 251-5076
belmontccfresno.com

	YARDAGE	PAR	RATING	SLOPE
FRONT	5018	73	68.5	113
MIDDLE	6234	72	69.5	121
BACK	6445	72	70.4	124

$35 - $50

WHAT TO EXPECT: Belmont is a short, tree-dominated course with water on five holes. Keep it in the fairway and low scores are a real possibility.
NOTES: Reciprocal play with other members only clubs is allowed.
DIRECTIONS: From within Fresno: Off Highway 99, exit at Jensen Avenue and head east for about ten minutes. Turn left on Clovis Avenue and then right on Belmont. The club is approximately three and one-half miles east.

COPPER RIVER COUNTRY CLUB (members only, 18 holes, david pfaff 1995) . . . .

11500 North Friant Road
Fresno, CA 93720
(559) 434-5200
copperriverranch.com

	YARDAGE	PAR	RATING	SLOPE
FRONT	5374	72	70.5	120
MIDDLE	6620	72	72.0	126
BACK	7043	72	74.3	132

$35 - $45

WHAT TO EXPECT: You will find flowing, open fairways, quick greens, and water that comes into play on half the holes. Play in the afternoon and you will encounter a prevailing wind.
DIRECTIONS: From within Fresno: Off Highway 99, take Highway 41 north. Take the Friant exit and head east about four and one-half miles. The club is on the right.

FIG GARDEN GOLF COURSE (semi-private, 18 holes, nick d. lombardo 1958) . . . .

7700 North Van Ness Boulevard
Fresno, CA 93711
(559) 439-2928
psnw.com/-fggc

	YARDAGE	PAR	RATING	SLOPE
FRONT	5510	72	70.4	117
MIDDLE	6305	72	69.6	119
BACK	6701	72	71.6	124

$14 - $57

WHAT TO EXPECT: This is a flat, narrow course with lots of trees, two lakes, and a river that comes into play on three holes.
NOTES: Carts are $15 for nine holes and $26 for 18 holes.
DIRECTIONS: From within Fresno: Off Highway 99, take the Herndon exit east. Turn left on North Van Ness Boulevard, which leads to the course.

FT. WASHINGTON GOLF & COUNTRY CLUB (members only, 18 holes, w. watson 1923)

10272 North Millbrook
Fresno, CA 93720
(559) 434-9120

	YARDAGE	PAR	RATING	SLOPE
FRONT	5603	72	72.0	123
MIDDLE	6461	72	71.8	126
BACK	6729	72	73.0	130

$35 - $125

WHAT TO EXPECT: Though not the toughest course, this walkable course meanders along rolling terrain.
DIRECTIONS: From within Fresno: Take Highway 41 north and exit on Friant Road (still head north). Take another right on Fort Washington Road, which leads to the club.

HANK'S SWANK PAR 3 (public, 9 holes, henry bocchini, jr. 1983) . . . .

6101 East Olive Avenue
Fresno, CA 93727
(559) 252-7077

	YARDAGE	PAR	RATING	SLOPE
FRONT	-	-	-	-
MIDDLE	-	-	-	-
BACK	1305	27	-	-

$7 - $12

WHAT TO EXPECT: The course features plenty of sand, and the greens are big enough to support different pin placements for the front and back nine.
DIRECTIONS: In Fresno (about 60 miles south to the course): Take Highway 99 to East Olive Avenue. The course is one mile east of the airport.

PALM LAKES GOLF COURSE (public, 18 holes, richard bigler 1986) . . . .

5025 East Dakota Avenue
Fresno, CA 93727
(559) 291-4050

	YARDAGE	PAR	RATING	SLOPE
FRONT	4462	62	62.8	97
MIDDLE	-	-	-	-
BACK	4100	62	60.2	93

$7 - $13

WHAT TO EXPECT: This is an open course with one lake.
DIRECTIONS: From within Fresno: Off Highway 99, exit onto Shaw Avenue, and head east. Turn right on Blackstone and then left on Dakota Avenue.

RIVERSIDE GOLF COURSE (public, 18 holes, william p. bell 1939) . . . .

7672 North Josephine Avenue
Fresno, CA 93722
(559) 275-5900
playriverside.com

	YARDAGE	PAR	RATING	SLOPE
FRONT	5924	75	73.6	123
MIDDLE	6425	72	70.1	121
BACK	6645	72	71.1	123

$14 - $16

WHAT TO EXPECT: You will find plenty of trees and subtle, sloping greens throughout the course, but what catches your attention is the fairway moguls. Even the straightest of shots will end up with an uneven lie.
NOTES: Riverside is the host site of the Fresno City Amateur Championship.
DIRECTIONS: From within Fresno: Off Highway 99, exit Herndon Avenue, and head east. Turn left on Weber (after the railroad tracks) and follow the signs to the course.

SAN JOAQUIN COUNTRY CLUB (members only, 18 holes, bob baldock 1961) . . . .

3484 West Bluff Avenue
Fresno, CA 93711
(559) 439-3359

	YARDAGE	PAR	RATING	SLOPE
FRONT	5717	72	73.4	129
MIDDLE	6346	72	71.6	129
BACK	6847	72	73.4	133

$35 - $75

WHAT TO EXPECT: This lengthy traditional course has long been considered one of Fresno's best.
NOTES: San Joaquin hosted the 2001 Mid-Amateur Championship. Reciprocal play with other member only clubs is allowed.
DIRECTIONS: From within Fresno: Off Highway 99, take the West Herndon exit and head east. Make a left on North Marks Avenue and follow it to the course.

SUNNYSIDE COUNTRY CLUB (members only, 18 holes, william p. bell 1906) . . . .

5704 East Butler
Fresno, CA 93727
(559) 255-6871

	YARDAGE	PAR	RATING	SLOPE
FRONT	5548	72	71.9	126
MIDDLE	64668	72	71.2	128
BACK	6801	72	72.5	130

$35 - $75

WHAT TO EXPECT: This flat, well-treed, well-bunkered course is the oldest in the San Joaquin Valley and still considered one of the very best. It is a shot-maker's course that also possesses some tricky putting surfaces.

NOTES: Reciprocal play with other members only clubs is allowed.

DIRECTIONS: From within Fresno: Off Highway 99, take Kings Canyon Road east. Turn right, to head south on Clovis Avenue and then turn left on Butler. The club is on the right.

VILLAGE GREEN GOLF COURSE (public, 9 holes, robert dean putnam 1959) . . . .

236 South Clovis Avenue
Fresno, CA 93727
(559) 456-4653

	YARDAGE	PAR	RATING	SLOPE
FRONT	1631	30	59.6	93
MIDDLE	-	-	-	-
BACK	1798	30	58.2	99

$6 - $12

WHAT TO EXPECT: The course winds in and around an apartment complex. The longest hole on the course is 350 yards.

DIRECTIONS: From within Fresno: Off Highway 99, take Kings Canyon east. Turn left on Clovis Avenue. The course is on the left.

BRIGHTON CREST GOLF & COUNTRY CLUB (semi-private, 18 holes, j. miller 1991) . . .

21722 Fairway Oaks Lane
Friant, CA 93626
(559) 299-8586
brightoncrest.com

	YARDAGE	PAR	RATING	SLOPE
FRONT	5195	72	71.2	124
MIDDLE	6298	72	70.9	129
BACK	6788	72	73.0	134

$35 - $55

WHAT TO EXPECT: This is Johnny Miller's first golf course designed in California, and maybe one of his most tame. That doesn't mean it isn't challenging. The course features plenty of native oaks and creeks to keep you honest off the tee. The greens vary in size, but all are undulating and require a soft touch.

DIRECTIONS: From Fresno (about 25 miles north to the course): Take Highway 41 north to the Friant off-ramp. Go north on Friant, and the club is just past town.

DRY CREEK RANCH GOLF CLUB (public, 18 holes, jack fleming 1962) . . . .

809 Crystal Way
Galt, CA 95632
(209) 745-2330

	YARDAGE	PAR	RATING	SLOPE	
FRONT	5892	74	74.5	134	**$20 - $34**
MIDDLE	6454	72	71.1	129	
BACK	6720	72	72.4	131	

WHAT TO EXPECT: Dry Creek is a classic layout that plays among towering oaks, ponds, and creeks. It will provide an excellent test of your skills.

OUR OPINION: This is a fun, overlooked course, definitely one of the best public layouts in the Valley and a great value. – Bob

DIRECTIONS: From Sacramento (about 25 miles south to the course): Drive south on Highway 99 and take the Central Galt exit. Turn left over the freeway and take the first right on Crystal Way.

KINGS COUNTRY CLUB (members only, 18 holes, william lock 1923) . . . .

3529 12th Avenue
Hanford, CA 93230
(559) 582-0740

	YARDAGE	PAR	RATING	SLOPE	
FRONT	5983	73	74.4	129	**$35 - $50**
MIDDLE	6411	72	71.1	126	
BACK	6656	72	72.2	128	

WHAT TO EXPECT: Kings Country Club is a narrow tree-lined course, with water coming into play on four holes. The greens are on the small side and have subtle breaks. If you hit your driver well, you will do ok.

NOTES: Reciprocal play with other members only clubs is allowed.

DIRECTIONS: From Fresno (about 37 miles south to the course): Take Highway 99 south to Highway 43 south. Turn right on Dover Avenue and right again on 12th Avenue.

MEADOW LAND (public, 9 holes) . . . .

19920 First Street
Hilmar, CA 95324
(209) 669-6777

	YARDAGE	PAR	RATING	SLOPE	
FRONT	1500	29	56.3	84	**$6 - $14**
MIDDLE	-	-	-	-	
BACK	1500	29	55.0	82	

WHAT TO EXPECT: The is a short course with holes ranging from 96 to 277 yards. There are two par 4s.

DIRECTIONS: From Modesto (about 20 miles south to the course): Take Highway 99 south past Hilmar. Take the Bloss Street exit and head west. Make a right on Lander Avenue and another right on First Street to the course.

JAVIER'S FRESNO WEST GOLF COURSE (public, 18 holes, bob baldock 1966) . . . .

23986 West Whitesbridge Road
Kerman, CA 93630
(559) 846-8655

	YARDAGE	PAR	RATING	SLOPE	
FRONT	5486	72	71.3	116	**$13 - $16**
MIDDLE	6607	72	70.8	116	
BACK	6959	72	72.5	119	

WHAT TO EXPECT: Although there are plenty of trees and some rough, the fairways are spacious and the greens large. The challenge from Fresno West comes from wind and water. The water comes into play both off the tee and around the greens.

DIRECTIONS: From Fresno (about 30 miles west to the course): Off Highway 99, take Highway 180 west past Kerman. The golf course is on the right.

KING CITY GOLF COURSE (public, 9 holes, bob baldock 1958) . . . .

613 South Vanderhurst Street
King City, CA 93930
(831) 385-4546

	YARDAGE	PAR	RATING	SLOPE
FRONT	2675	35	69.0	112
MIDDLE	-	-	-	-
BACK	2817	35	67.3	111

$8 - $17

WHAT TO EXPECT: This is a cute course lined with trees and mounding. Notice we didn't say easy. Miss the fairway and you will find yourself in actual rough. The greens are tiny and slick. The par 3s are on the long side and all are exposed to wind.
DIRECTIONS: From Salinas (about 45 miles southeast to the course): Take US 101 south, exit at Canal Street, and turn left. Turn right on Division and right on Vandenhurst Street.

KINGS RIVER GOLF & COUNTRY CLUB (members only, 18 holes, bob baldock 1955) . .

3100 Avenue 400
Kingsburg, CA 93631
(559) 897-2077

	YARDAGE	PAR	RATING	SLOPE
FRONT	6022	72	75.1	129
MIDDLE	6431	72	70.7	126
BACK	6695	72	71.9	128

$24 - $100

WHAT TO EXPECT: Snap hookers beware: Kings River has 14 holes with out-of-bounds left. For golfers who can keep it in play, they will find level, tight fairways that give way to small greens.
NOTES: Reciprocal play with other members only clubs is allowed.
DIRECTIONS: From Fresno (about 25 miles north to the course): Go south on Highway 99 and then exit at Conejo Avenue. Head east on Avenue 400 to the club.

LEMOORE GOLF COURSE (public, 18 holes, bob baldock 1963) . . . .

350 West Iona Avenue
Lemoore, CA 93245
(559) 924-9658

	YARDAGE	PAR	RATING	SLOPE
FRONT	5126	72	69.7	118
MIDDLE	5978	72	67.8	112
BACK	6431	72	69.8	115

$17 - $20

WHAT TO EXPECT: The front and the back nines at Lemoore were built some 30 years apart. The front side has mature trees, is much shorter, and has smaller greens. The back nine is 400 yards longer, with freeway-wide fairways and larger greens. Chances are your game will be suited for a least half of this course.
DIRECTIONS: From Visalia (about 30 miles west to the course): Take Highway 198 west to the 18th Avenue exit. Take 18th Avenue south to Iona Avenue. Turn right on Iona Avenue to the course.

LINDSAY MUNICIPAL GOLF COURSE (municipal, 9 holes, bob baldock 1961) . . . .

801 North Elmwood
Lindsay, CA 93247
(559) 562-1144

	YARDAGE	PAR	RATING	SLOPE
FRONT	1090	27	50.0	-
MIDDLE	-	-	-	-
BACK	1090	27	50.0	-

$4 - $8

WHAT TO EXPECT: This pitch-and-putt course is set in a well established city park.
DIRECTIONS: From Visalia (about 50 miles southeast to the course): Off Highway 99, take Highway 198 east to Highway 65 south. The course is in the city park of Lindsay, eight blocks east of Highway 65. It is between Exeter and Porterville.

LOCKEFORD SPRINGS GOLF COURSE (public, 18 holes, tatum & summers 1995) . . . . .

16360 North Highway 88
Lodi, CA 95240
(209) 333-6275

	YARDAGE	PAR	RATING	SLOPE
FRONT	5542	72	71.6	118
MIDDLE	6482	72	71.4	125
BACK	6858	72	73.0	130

$13 - $33

WHAT TO EXPECT: This is a level course with some mounding, scattered trees and wetlands. First time players, beware of some hidden hazards on the course. It can be confusing on a few holes to find the correct green.
OUR OPINION: Critics will point out that this flat course has some goofy holes that detract from the solid ones. Play it and decide for yourself. – Bob
DIRECTIONS: From Stockton (about ten miles north to the course): Off I-5 take Eight Mile Road east to Highway 88. Turn left and head to Lockeford. The course is on the right, a few miles before Lockeford.

MICKE GROVE GOLF LINKS (public, 18 holes, bob dorham 1990) . . . .

11401 North Micke Grove Road
Lodi, CA 95240
(209) 369-4410
americangolf.com

	YARDAGE	PAR	RATING	SLOPE
FRONT	5296	72	70.0	116
MIDDLE	6020	72	68.0	115
BACK	6572	72	71.0	118

$19 - $29

WHAT TO EXPECT: This is a flat, valley course that is more fun and challenging than you would expect. Man-made lakes and mounding, combined with a natural wind, make this layout anything but a pushover.
DIRECTIONS: From Stockton (about ten miles north to the course): Take Highway 99 north, exit Armstong Road and head west. Turn left on Micke Grove Road. The course is at the south end of the park.

MADERA GOLF & COUNTRY CLUB (members only, 18 holes, bob baldock 1953) . . . . . .

19297 Road 26
Madera, CA 93638
(559) 674-2682

	YARDAGE	PAR	RATING	SLOPE
FRONT	5900	73	74.3	126
MIDDLE	6450	72	70.2	122
BACK	6647	72	71.0	123

$25 - $30

WHAT TO EXPECT: This is a classic design with two long par 3s, par 4s, and par 5s.
NOTES: Reciprocal play with other members only clubs is allowed.
DIRECTIONS: From Fresno (about 30 miles northwest to the course): Head north on Highway 99 to Madera. Exit Avenue 17 and head east. Turn left on Road 26.

MADERA MUNICIPAL GOLF COURSE (municipal, 18 holes, dean putman 1991) . . . . . .

23200 Avenue 17
Madera, CA 93637
(559) 675-3504
maderagolf.com

	YARDAGE	PAR	RATING	SLOPE
FRONT	5513	112	70.6	112
MIDDLE	6369	118	69.7	118
BACK	6831	121	72.0	121

$14 - $19

WHAT TO EXPECT: Maturity and better conditioning have really improved this flat, treed valley course. While not particularly long and fairly open off the tee, there is enough bunkering to keep your attention.
DIRECTIONS: From Fresno (about 27 miles northwest to the course): Drive north on Highway 99, take the Avenue 17 exit and go west to the course. It is on the left.

RIVERBEND GOLF CLUB (public, 18 holes, gary roger baird 1997) . . . .

43369 Avenue 12
Madera, CA 93638
(559) 432-3020
riverbendgolfcourse.com

	YARDAGE	PAR	RATING	SLOPE
FRONT	5720	72	66.8	110
MIDDLE	6366	72	69.9	117
BACK	6967	72	72.8	124

$50 - $80

WHAT TO EXPECT: This is a tight course with water coming into play on a third of the holes. The greens are large, with an abundance of slope. Putting your tee shot on the correct side of the fairway can make all the difference.
DIRECTIONS: From Fresno (about 30 miles northwest to the course): Take Highway 41 north to Avenue 12. Go east on Avenue 12 for two and one-half miles to the clubhouse.

FRENCH CAMP GOLF COURSE & RV PARK (public, 18 holes, lloyd zastre 1995) . . . . . .

3919 East French Camp Road
Manteca, CA 95336
(209) 234-3030
frenchcamp.com

	YARDAGE	PAR	RATING	SLOPE
FRONT	5804	70	68.8	118
MIDDLE	6059	70	70.1	122
BACK	6314	70	71.4	126

$8 - $20

WHAT TO EXPECT: This is a long, nine-hole golf course with plenty of water. Out-of-bounds comes into play on four holes. The greens are on the small side and range from flat to sloping.
DIRECTIONS: From Stockton (about 13 miles south to the course): Drive south on Highway 99. The course is at the intersection of Highway 99 and French Camp Road. If you reach the town of Manteca, you have gone too far.

MANTECA PARK GOLF COURSE (public, 18 holes, jack fleming 1966) . . . .

305 North Union Road
Manteca, CA 95337
(209) 825-2500

	YARDAGE	PAR	RATING	SLOPE
FRONT	4982	70	68.1	115
MIDDLE	6131	72	69.7	117
BACK	6478	72	71.3	121

$15 - $24

WHAT TO EXPECT: This flat, park-setting course is better than you might imagine. Possessing a number of trees, this course is attractive and fair.
DIRECTIONS: From Stockton (about 15 miles south to the course): Take I-5 south, exit at Louise Avenue, and head east. Turn right (south) on Union Road, and the course is on the right.

MERCED GOLF & COUNTRY CLUB (members only, 18 holes, bob baldock 1926) . . . . . .

6333 North Golf Road
Merced, CA 95340
(209) 722-3357

	YARDAGE	PAR	RATING	SLOPE
FRONT	5696	72	72.9	129
MIDDLE	6206	72	70.0	129
BACK	6519	72	71.4	131

$35 - $50

WHAT TO EXPECT: Originally built in the 1920s but recently redesigned, the course still carries much of its original flavor. Merced is a peaceful layout with narrow fairways, water on six holes and small greens. Drive well and you have a chance to score well.
NOTES: Reciprocal play with other members only clubs is allowed.
DIRECTIONS: From Fresno (about 55 miles north to the course): Take Highway 99 north, exit at R Street, and turn right. Go right on Yosemite Avenue and then left on G Street. Take a right on Bellevue and then a left on Golf Road.

MERCED HILLS GOLF CLUB (public, 18 holes, charles howard 1995) . . . .

5320 North Lake Road
Merced, CA 95340
(209) 383-4943
mercedhills.com

	YARDAGE	PAR	RATING	SLOPE	
FRONT	5316	72	70.6	115	**$15 - $24**
MIDDLE	6358	72	70.5	120	
BACK	6831	72	72.8	128	

WHAT TO EXPECT: With no trees and fairly level terrain, Merced Hills is a challenging, Scottish-style course where judging distances can be an adventure. The greens are open in front to allow a variety of shots, and you will encounter wetlands along the way. Wind is a strong possibility.

DIRECTIONS: From Fresno (about 55 miles north to the course): Take Highway 99 north, exit at R Street, and turn right. Go right on Yosemite Avenue and then left on G Street. Take a right on Bellevue and then a left on North Lake Road.

CREEKSIDE GOLF COURSE (public, 18 holes, steve halsey 1991) . . . .

701 Lincoln Avenue
Modesto, CA 95354
(209) 571-5123

	YARDAGE	PAR	RATING	SLOPE	
FRONT	5496	72	69.5	108	**$20 - $30**
MIDDLE	6021	72	68.5	115	
BACK	6610	72	71.2	118	

WHAT TO EXPECT: The newer of Modesto's two 18-hole courses, Creekside features some artistic green-side bunkering, as well as some very testing, tiered putting surfaces. The two holes that play creekside are the most engaging.

DIRECTIONS: From within Modesto: Off Highway 99, take Highway 132 east. It turns into Yosemite Boulevard. About a mile and one-half past Mitchell, turn left on Lincoln Avenue to the course.

DEL RIO COUNTRY CLUB (members only, 27 holes, william bell 1947) . . . .

801 Stewart Road
Modesto, CA 95356
(209) 545-0013
delriocountryclub.com

	YARDAGE	PAR	RATING	SLOPE	
FRONT	6027	71	69.5	120	**$30 - $120**
MIDDLE	6537	72	72.0	127	
BACK	6928	72	73.9	133	

WHAT TO EXPECT: This classic, private club has gently rolling, tree-lined fairways with subtle greens. Del Rio is a fixture among the Central Valley's best layouts.

NOTES: Reciprocal play with other members only clubs is allowed.

DIRECTIONS: From within Modesto: Go north on Highway 99 Take the Salida/Kerinin Road exit and head east. Turn left on McHenry and then left on Stewart Road.

DRYDEN PARK GOLF COURSE (public, 18 holes, billy bell, jr. 1959) . . . .

920 Sunset Boulevard
Modesto, CA 95351
(209) 577-5359

	YARDAGE	PAR	RATING	SLOPE	
FRONT	5910	74	73.4	121	**$7 - $23**
MIDDLE	6238	72	69.5	120	
BACK	6531	72	70.9	122	

WHAT TO EXPECT: This is a flat, pine-tree lined traditional layout that features wide fairways, but with relatively challenging green sites. The course is easily walkable. The Tuolumne River flows adjacent.

DIRECTIONS: From within Modesto: Off Highway 99, take the Tuolumne Boulevard exit, heading west. Turn left on Roselawn and left again on Sunset Boulevard.

MODESTO MUNICIPAL GOLF COURSE (municipal, 9 holes) . . . .

400 Tuolumne Boulevard
Modesto, CA 95351
(209) 577-5360

	YARDAGE	PAR	RATING	SLOPE	
FRONT	2904	36	72.0	112	**$5 - $12**
MIDDLE	-	-	-	-	
BACK	2997	35	68.6	116	

WHAT TO EXPECT: Modesto Municipal is tight, flat, and walkable. Narrow fairways, guarded by tall, mature trees, make the course deceptively challenging and one of the area's better nine-hole layouts.
DIRECTIONS: From within Modesto: Off Highway 99, exit at Tuolumne Boulevard. Head west on Tuolumne Boulevard.

ST. STANISLAUS GOLF CLUB (public, 9 holes, robert muir graves 1995) . . . .

5000 Crows Landing Road
Modesto, CA 95358
(209) 538-2828

	YARDAGE	PAR	RATING	SLOPE	
FRONT	1533	28	55.8	73	**$8 - $14**
MIDDLE	-	-	-	-	
BACK	1533	28	56.0	70	

WHAT TO EXPECT: This is a short, executive course with elevated tee boxes. Many immature trees line the fairways, making accuracy less of an issue now than it will be in ten years.
DIRECTIONS: From within Modesto: Off Highway 99, exit at Crows Landing Road and head east. The course is on the left corner of Crows Landing Road and Grayson.

SIERRA MEADOWS - RANCH COURSE (semi-private, 18 holes, allan thomas 1988) . . .

46516 Opah Drive
Oakhurst, CA 93644
(559) 642-1343

	YARDAGE	PAR	RATING	SLOPE	
FRONT	4823	70	68.0	123	**$15 - $25**
MIDDLE	6087	70	70.1	133	
BACK	6391	70	71.5	136	

WHAT TO EXPECT: You will find tree-lined fairways and small greens at Sierra Meadows. There is also a creek that wanders throughout, coming into play on 10 of the 18 holes. Although not a long course, the Ranch Course requires accuracy off the tee.
NOTES: This course was formerly known as Ahwahnee Golf Club.
DIRECTIONS: From Mariposa (about 25 miles southeast to the course): Take Highway 49 east toward Oakhurst. Pass throught the little town of Ahwahnee. Turn left on Harmony Lane Continue straight, and the the road becomes Opah Drive. Drive another two and one-half miles to the course. There is signage.

DIABLO GRANDE GOLF CLUB (resort/private, 36 holes, nicklaus & sarazen 1996) . . . .

10001 Oak Flat Road
Patterson, CA 95363
(209) 892-4653
diablogrande.com

	YARDAGE	PAR	RATING	SLOPE
FRONT	6378	72	71.4	129
MIDDLE	6915	72	73.5	136
BACK	7243	72	75.1	141

$50 - $80

WHAT TO EXPECT: The Legends Course features generous landing areas and becomes more of an approach-shot course. It is very playable for the average golfer, but a challenge to break par for the scratch player. The Ranch Course is tighter and the more difficult of the two courses. A good tee to green game is required to score well. You will encounter several difficult holes from the tips.

OUR OPINION: Ok, it's not the easiest course to get to, but well worth the effort. The Legends course is fantastic. – Frank

NOTES: The yardage listed is for the Ranch Course. The Legends Course is private.

DIRECTIONS: From Stockton (about 40 miles south to the course): Take I-5 south, exit at Patterson, and turn left on to Sperry. Turn right on Ward and go about three miles. Turn right on Oak Flat Road for about eight miles to the club.

PINE MOUNTAIN CLUB (members only, 9 holes, billy bell, jr. 1971) . . . .

2524 Beechwood Way
Pine Mountain, CA 93222
(805) 242-3734
frazmtn.com/pmcpoa

	YARDAGE	PAR	RATING	SLOPE
FRONT	1585	30	57.0	95
MIDDLE	-	-	-	-
BACK	1819	30	58.7	92

$9 - $16

WHAT TO EXPECT: This is an attractive mountain course cut out of a pine forest — hence the name, Pine Mountain.

DIRECTIONS: From Bakersfield (about 48 miles south to the course): Drive south about 40 miles on I-5 and take the Frazier Park exit to Frazier Mountain Road. Drive west and continue west on Cuddy Valley Road. Turn right on Mill Potrero Road and drive to the course.

PORTERVILLE GOLF COURSE (municipal, 9 holes) . . . .

702 East Isham Avenue
Porterville, CA 93257
(559) 784-9468

	YARDAGE	PAR	RATING	SLOPE
FRONT	2751	35	70.7	115
MIDDLE	-	-	-	-
BACK	2811	34	67.0	112

$5 - $14

WHAT TO EXPECT: For the low handicapper, the hardest thing about Porterville Golf Course may be finding the first and second tee boxes. This is a level course with a few hilly holes and gently sloping greens. The nearby road creates out-of-bounds on at least three holes.

DIRECTIONS: From within Porterville: Off Highway 190, drive north on Plano Street. When the road zigs, turn right on Corona and follow it to the course. Turn on to Isham Avenue when the range.

RIVER ISLAND COUNTRY CLUB (semi-private, 18 holes, robert dean putman 1965) . .

31989 River Island Drive
Porterville, CA 93257
(559) 784-9425

	YARDAGE	PAR	RATING	SLOPE
FRONT	5277	72	73.0	128
MIDDLE	6364	72	69.9	119
BACK	6910	72	72.8	127

$45 - $45

WHAT TO EXPECT: The course is generous and dotted with oak trees. The greens tend to be fast, so you would be wise to spend some time on the putting green. The Tule River and several lakes come into play.
NOTES: Outside play is allowed after 10 a.m.
DIRECTIONS: From within Porterville: Take Highway 190 east for 13 miles. River Island Drive, and the entrance to the course, are on the right.

RIO VISTA GOLF CLUB (public, 18 holes, ted robinson 1996) . . . .

1000 Summerset Drive
Rio Vista, CA 94571
(707) 374-2900
riovistagolf.com

	YARDAGE	PAR	RATING	SLOPE
FRONT	5330	72	72.4	124
MIDDLE	6393	72	71.9	126
BACK	6800	72	73.9	131

$34 - $49

WHAT TO EXPECT: For the low handicapper with nerves of steel, there are plenty of opportunities for birdies. For those with Jell-O legs, we suggest you think twice before hitting a driver off the tee. Why? Because if you miss the fairways, you could be depleting your stash of golf balls. You will find water on 14 of the 18 holes. Besides plenty of water, you will encounter well-placed traps around the greens and in the fairway. Afternoon wind is usually a factor.
OUR OPINION: Reasonably priced and fun, Rio Vista is worth playing. Our only gripe is that some of the houses are a bit close. – Shaw
DIRECTIONS: From Vallejo (about 40 miles east to the course): Take I-80 east to Highway 12 east. The course is two miles west of Rio Vista. Make a left on Summerset Drive to the course.

JACK TONE GOLF (public, 18 holes, george buzzini 1997) . . . .

1500 Ruess Road
Ripon, CA 95366
(209) 599-2973
jacktonegolf.com

	YARDAGE	PAR	RATING	SLOPE
FRONT	3292	62	57.0	79
MIDDLE	3510	62	57.6	80
BACK	3715	62	58.2	82

$10 - $19

WHAT TO EXPECT: This is a short executive course with one par 5.
DIRECTIONS: From Modesto (about 10 miles north to the course): Take Highway 99 north, exit Jack Tone Road and head west. The road dead-ends in the parking lot.

SPRING CREEK GOLF & COUNTRY CLUB (members only, 18 holes, jack fleming 1964) .

16436 Spring Creek Drive
Ripon, CA 95366
(209) 599-3630

	YARDAGE	PAR	RATING	SLOPE	
FRONT	5626	73	72.4	122	**$50 - $50**
MIDDLE	6144	72	69.8	123	
BACK	6380	72	70.9	125	

WHAT TO EXPECT: This is a short, tight course with plenty of oak trees. To score well, simply hit the ball straight and don't read too much break in the greens. Sounds easy enough, doesn't it?

NOTES: Reciprocal play with other members only clubs is allowed.

DIRECTIONS: From Modesto (about 10 miles north to the course): Take Highway 99 north to the Ripon exit. Turn east on Main Street, left on Manley and then make a right on Spring Creek Drive to the club.

SHERWOOD FOREST GOLF COURSE (public, 18 holes, bob baldock 1968) . . . .

79 North Frankwood Avenue
Sanger, CA 93657
(559) 787-2611

	YARDAGE	PAR	RATING	SLOPE	
FRONT	5597	72	71.4	118	**$19 - $23**
MIDDLE	6181	71	68.5	116	
BACK	6345	71	69.2	118	

WHAT TO EXPECT: With hundreds of trees, many which line the fairways, Sherwood Forest demands accuracy off the tee. Besides narrow landing areas, you will also encounter the Kings River on several holes.

DIRECTIONS: From Fresno (about 19 miles east to the course): Off Highway 99, take Kings Canyon (Highway 180) east. Turn left on Frankwood Avenue and drive one mile to the club.

FOREBAY GOLF COURSE (public, 9 holes, joe setnor 1963) . . . .

29500 Bayview Road
Santa Nella, CA 95322
(209) 826-3637

	YARDAGE	PAR	RATING	SLOPE	
FRONT	2697	37	68.7	109	**$10 - $19**
MIDDLE	-	-	-	-	
BACK	3302	36	70.2	112	

WHAT TO EXPECT: This is a parkland-style course with wide fairways and large level greens.

DIRECTIONS: From Gilroy (about 40 miles east to the course): Head east on Highway 152 and then head north on Highway 33 (Santa Nella Boulevard). Just before I-5, turn left on Bayview Road.

SELMA VALLEY GOLF COURSE (public, 18 holes, bob baldock 1963) . . . .

12389 East Rose Avenue
Selma, CA 93662
(559) 896-2424

	YARDAGE	PAR	RATING	SLOPE	
FRONT	5170	70	69.6	118	**$14 - $18**
MIDDLE	5327	70	70.5	119	
BACK	5332	69	65.3	112	

WHAT TO EXPECT: This a short, level course, with plenty of trees lining the fairways. Water comes into play on several holes.

DIRECTIONS: From Fresno (about 20 miles southeast to the course): Take Highway 99 south, exit at Floral Avenue and head east. Turn right to head south at the dead-end at Bethel. Turn left to go east on Rose Avenue. The course is on the right.

STEVINSON RANCH (public, 18 holes, john harbottle 1995) . . . .

2700 North Van Clief
Stevinson, CA 95374
(209) 668-8200
stevinsonranch.com

	YARDAGE	PAR	RATING	SLOPE
FRONT	5461	72	71.9	124
MIDDLE	7060	72	73.9	137
BACK	7135	72	74.3	140

$35 - $85

WHAT TO EXPECT: Stevinson's landscape is distinct for its vast open areas of grasslands, scattered trees and marsh areas. Its exceptional bunkering and links-feel make for an excellent test of your skills.

OUR OPINION: This has been one of the most popular and highly regarded courses in the San Joaquin Valley. It has excelled in service as well as playability. – Shaw

DIRECTIONS: From Modesto (about 30 miles south to the course): Drive south on Highway 99, take Lander Avenue exit, and turn right. Drive about nine miles on Lander Avenue. Turn left on Westside Boulevard and follow the signs.

BROOKSIDE COUNTRY CLUB (members only, 18 holes, robert trent jones jr. 1991) . .

3603 Saint Andrews Drive
Stockton, CA 95219
(209) 956-7888

	YARDAGE	PAR	RATING	SLOPE
FRONT	5022	72	69.1	118
MIDDLE	6108	72	69.5	123
BACK	6595	72	72.1	126

$35 - $75

WHAT TO EXPECT: Even without the usual wind, this course has plenty of water, bunkers, and severe rough. Overall, this is a very engaging test, especially the par 5s. You need to keep the ball in the fairway to have any chance of scoring well.

NOTES: Reciprocal play with other members only clubs is allowed.

DIRECTIONS: From within Stockton: Off I-5, exit on March Lane and drive west. Turn left at the fifth light, which is Saint Andrews Drive.

ELKHORN COUNTRY CLUB (members only, 18 holes, bert stamps 1963) . . . .

1050 Elkhorn Drive
Stockton, CA 95209
(209) 477-0252
elkhorncc.com

	YARDAGE	PAR	RATING	SLOPE
FRONT	5794	73	?	127
MIDDLE	6125	71	70.6	126
BACK	6559	71	72.5	129

$25 - $50

WHAT TO EXPECT: This is a flat, tree-lined and well-conditioned valley course with elevated greens. Do not miss the greens, or you will find yourself with a difficult chip or pitch.

NOTES: Reciprocal play with other members only clubs is allowed.

DIRECTIONS: From within Stockton: Off I-5, exit on Eight Mile Road and head east about three miles. Turn south on Davis Road. Go east on Elkhorn Drive to the course.

LYONS GOLF COURSE (public, 9 holes, captain lyons 1968) . . . .

3303 Navy Drive
Stockton, CA 95203
(209) 937-7905

	YARDAGE	PAR	RATING	SLOPE	
FRONT	1897	32	60.4	99	**$9 - $17**
MIDDLE	2047	32	60.0	93	
BACK	2107	32	60.4	94	

WHAT TO EXPECT: This executive course is an excellent place for beginners, seniors, and juniors.

DIRECTIONS: From within Stockton: Off I-5, take the Fresno Avenue/Downtown Exit and head north on Fresno Avenue. Turn left on Washington Street and go over the bridge onto Rough and Ready Island. The course is on the right.

OAKMOORE GOLF COURSE (tournaments only, 9 holes, donald crump 1960) . . . .

3737 North Wilson Way
Stockton, CA 95205
(209) 462-6712

	YARDAGE	PAR	RATING	SLOPE	
FRONT	3281	37	74.5	-	**$26 - $37**
MIDDLE	3281	36	72.0	122	
BACK	3236	36	72.0	-	

WHAT TO EXPECT: This is a level course with lots of trees, long par 3s, and small elevated greens. Water comes into play on several holes.

NOTES: This course is only open for tournament play. It books one tournament per day. Think of it as your own private course for a day. A 48-player minimum is needed. It is a nine-hole layout, but you play 18.

DIRECTIONS: From within Stockton: Off Highway 99, take the Business 99/Wilson Way exit and drive a little less than a mile to the course.

SPANOS PARK, THE RESERVE AT   (semi-private, 18 holes, andy raugust 1999) . . . . .

6301 West Eight Mile Road
Stockton, CA 95219
(209) 477-4653
americangolf.com

	YARDAGE	PAR	RATING	SLOPE	
FRONT	5294	72	69.9	118	**$16 - $70**
MIDDLE	6550	72	71.8	130	
BACK	7001	72	74.2	133	

WHAT TO EXPECT: Considering that the course is built upon deadpan flat ground, it is an interesting, challenging layout. Ponds have been cut out and the fill was used to provide mounding.

OUR OPINION: They moved a lot of dirt to make a nice layout on a flat venue. I have played here three times, and the staff was excellent each time. The course drains exceptionally, so it's a good place to come if you need your fix of golf during the stormy season. – Frank

DIRECTIONS: From within Stockton: Off I-5, exit at Eight Mile Road and head west.

STOCKTON GOLF & COUNTRY CLUB (members only, 18 holes, alister mackenzie 1914)

3800 West Country Club Boulevard
Stockton, CA 95204
(209) 466-6221

	YARDAGE	PAR	RATING	SLOPE	
FRONT	6011	73	75.6	129	**$25 - $75**
MIDDLE	6261	71	70.1	122	
BACK	6432	71	70.8	124	

WHAT TO EXPECT: Don't worry about hitting the ball long; keep the ball in the fairway. This Alister Mackenzie design is set along the Delta. Three holes actually run up against the Delta. The fairways are surrounded by tall eucalyptus trees. The greens feature subtle breaks that can drive an average putter crazy.
NOTES: Reciprocal play with other members only clubs is allowed.
DIRECTIONS: From within Stockton: Off I-5, take the Country Club exit. Drive west a couple of miles to the course.

SWENSON PARK GOLF COURSE (municipal, 27 holes, jack fleming 1952) . . . .

6803 Alexandria Place
Stockton, CA 95207
(209) 937-7360

	YARDAGE	PAR	RATING	SLOPE	
FRONT	6266	74	75.2	125	**$9 - $22**
MIDDLE	6407	75	76.0	127	
BACK	6407	72	69.6	114	

WHAT TO EXPECT: Though this flat course boasts few bunkers and just two water holes, its wooded park-like setting makes for enjoyable golf.
NOTES:
DIRECTIONS: From within Stockton: Off I-5, exit Benjamin Holt and head east. Turn left on Alexandria Place. Swenson Park is on the left across from the high school.

VAN BUSKIRK GOLF COURSE (public, 18 holes, larry nordstrom 1961) . . . .

1740 Houston Avenue
Stockton, CA 95206
(209) 937-7357

	YARDAGE	PAR	RATING	SLOPE	
FRONT	5927	73	73.0	122	**$18 - $23**
MIDDLE	6502	72	70.1	116	
BACK	6928	72	72.2	118	

WHAT TO EXPECT: From the back tees this is a long, free-flowing golf course. There is lots of water on the front nine and elevated tees and greens on the back nine. Although the front nine has the hazards, the long finishing holes on the back side make it the more difficult nine.
DIRECTIONS: From within Stockton: Off I-5, take the Eighth Street exit west to Fresno Avenue. Turn left on Fresno Avenue and drive to the course.

BUENA VISTA GOLF COURSE (public, 18 holes, george mifflin 1953) . . . .

10256 Golf Course Road
Taft, CA 93268
(661) 398-9720

	YARDAGE	PAR	RATING	SLOPE
FRONT	5581	72	71.8	117
MIDDLE	6318	72	69.8	113
BACK	6668	72	71.0	118

$11 - $15

WHAT TO EXPECT: A prevailing wind from the north makes club selection tricky on this open course. It has wide fairways and large greens. A few palm trees and some out-of-bounds do come into play.

DIRECTIONS: From Valencia (about 89 miles northwest to the course): Take I-5 north to Highway 119 west. Drive west on Highway 119 for about five miles and turn left onto Golf Course Road.

HORSE THIEF COUNTRY CLUB (resort, 18 holes, bob baldock 1974) . . . .

28930 Horse Thief Drive
Tehachapi, CA 93561
(661) 823-8571
stallionsprings.com

	YARDAGE	PAR	RATING	SLOPE
FRONT	5677	72	72.1	124
MIDDLE	6347	72	69.9	117
BACK	6735	72	72.1	124

$30 - $50

WHAT TO EXPECT: This is not the course for those who can't hit where they aim. Horse Thief features rolling terrain, out-of-bounds on half the holes, 300-year-old oaks and granite rock piles. The good news is that at 4,000 feet above sea level, you'll get a few extra yards as you watch your ball sail out of play.

DIRECTIONS: From Bakersfield (about 56 miles east to the course): Drive east on Highway 58 for about 40 miles and take Highway 202 exit. Follow the signs for 16 miles to the Stallion Springs resort.

OAK TREE COUNTRY CLUB (members only, 9 holes, ted robinson 1972) . . . .

29541 Rolling Oak Drive
Tehachapi, CA 93561
(661) 821-5144

	YARDAGE	PAR	RATING	SLOPE
FRONT	3076	36	72.1	126
MIDDLE	-	-	-	-
BACK	3249	36	70.3	122

$10 - $28

WHAT TO EXPECT: This is a user-friendly, level course lined by houses (out-of-bounds) with medium-sized, elevated greens.

NOTES: Reciprocal play with other members only clubs is allowed.

DIRECTIONS: From Bakersfield (about 55 miles southeast to the course): Drive east on Highway 58 for approximately 40 miles and take the Highway 202 exit. Follow the signs for 14 miles to Bear Valley Springs.

THREE RIVERS GOLF COURSE (public, 9 holes, robert dean putman 1962) . . . .

41117 Sierra Drive
Three Rivers, CA 93271
(559) 561-3133

	YARDAGE	PAR	RATING	SLOPE
FRONT	2021	34	63.6	97
MIDDLE	2636	35	65.8	107
BACK	2731	35	66.8	109

$13 - $28

WHAT TO EXPECT: The course was completely renovated back in 1999. Except for one hole, Three Rivers is a fairly level course, with water coming into play on two holes.

DIRECTIONS: From Visalia (about 33 miles northeast to the course): Take Highway 198 east to Three Rivers. The course is adjacent to the highway.

OLD RIVER GOLF COURSE (public, 9 holes, tom donahue 1999) . . . .

18007 MacArthur Drive
Tracy, CA 95376
(209) 830-8585

	YARDAGE	PAR	RATING	SLOPE
FRONT	2265	35	67.4	108
MIDDLE	2935	36	69.6	117
BACK	3104	36	71.2	123

$8 - $22

WHAT TO EXPECT: There are a lot of parallel holes on Old River, yet each hole has a unique challenge. This is not an easy course, with water coming into play on all but one hole. Around the greens, there is little room for error. The greens are various shapes and sizes, many with lots of undulations.

NOTES: Old River is currently a nine-hole course but is building a new nine, due to open in Spring 2002.

DIRECTIONS: From Stockton (about 20 miles southwest to the course): Take I-5 south to I-205 west. Exit at MacArthur Drive and head north. Follow MacArthur Drive to the course.

TRACY GOLF & COUNTRY CLUB (members only, 18 holes, robert trent jones, sr. 1956)

35200 South Chrisman Road
Tracy, CA 95376
(209) 835-9463
tracygolfandcc.com

	YARDAGE	PAR	RATING	SLOPE
FRONT	5776	74	72.9	126
MIDDLE	6034	72	70.5	122
BACK	6616	72	72.3	124

$25 - $50

WHAT TO EXPECT: This flat, treed course is bisected by Hwy. 580. The wind can be tough, and all of the out-of-bounds to the left can make it a hooker's nightmare.

NOTES: Reciprocal play with other members only clubs is allowed.

DIRECTIONS: From within Tracy: The course is right off I-580, at the Chrisman Road exit.

BOLADO PARK GOLF COURSE (public, 9 holes, w.i. hawkins 1928) . . . .

7777 Airline Highway 25
Tres Pinos, CA 95075
(831) 628-9995

	YARDAGE	PAR	RATING	SLOPE
FRONT	2818	36	70.2	111
MIDDLE	-	-	-	-
BACK	2991	35	68.3	116

$15 - $20

WHAT TO EXPECT: This is a level course with tree-lined fairways, a creek running through a couple of holes and well-conditioned greens. There are no water hazards, but there is two-inch rough outside the fairways.

DIRECTIONS: From San Jose (about 55 miles southeast to the course): Take US 101 south to Highway 25 east, into Hollister. Go through Hollister. The course is on Airline Highway 25.

TULARE GOLF COURSE (public, 18 holes, bob baldock 1957)

5310 South Laspina
Tulare, CA 93274
(559) 686-5300

	YARDAGE	PAR	RATING	SLOPE
FRONT	120	72	71.9	120
MIDDLE	6565	72	71.0	120
BACK	6784	72	71.8	124

$17 - $22

WHAT TO EXPECT: This is a level, open course. The front nine has elevated greens that make a good wedge essential. The greens throughout the course are on the smaller side, and water comes into play on ten holes.
DIRECTIONS: From within Tulare: Off Highway 99, take Avenue 200 east. Turn left on South Laspina. The course is on the right.

TURLOCK GOLF & COUNTRY CLUB (members only, 18 holes)

10532 Golf Link Road
Turlock, CA 95380
(209) 634-4976

	YARDAGE	PAR	RATING	SLOPE
FRONT	5309	73	70.6	123
MIDDLE	6345	72	71.0	122
BACK	6673	72	72.4	125

$30 - $40

WHAT TO EXPECT: This is a placement course with narrow fairways, difficult rough, and greens that do not accommodate a weak putter. The course is underrated and plays longer than the yardage on the scorecard.
NOTES: Reciprocal play with other members only clubs is allowed.
DIRECTIONS: From Modesto (about 15 miles south to the course): Take Highway 99 south, exit at Bradbury, and turn right. At the second stop sign, turn left onto Golf Link Road. The course is on the left.

OAK PATCH GOLF COURSE (public, 9 holes)

30400 Road 158
Visalia, CA 93291
(559) 733-5000

	YARDAGE	PAR	RATING	SLOPE
FRONT	1227	29	58.2	72
MIDDLE	-	-	-	-
BACK	1314	29	55.2	84

$6 - $13

WHAT TO EXPECT: Oak Patch is an open, walkable course with two par 4s.
DIRECTIONS: From within Visalia: Take Highway 198 east. Turn left on Road 158. Cross the canal and then follow the signs to the course.

SIERRA VIEW GOLF COURSE OF VISALIA (public, 18 holes, robert dean putnam 1957)

12608 Avenue 264
Visalia, CA 93277
(559) 732-2078

	YARDAGE	PAR	RATING	SLOPE
FRONT	5886	73	72.5	118
MIDDLE	6169	72	68.7	112
BACK	6388	72	69.7	114

$17 - $22

WHAT TO EXPECT: This solid, rolling, tree-lined course features excellent greens and a nice variety of par 4s ranging from 300 to 459 yards from the tips.
NOTES: Reciprocal play with other members only clubs is allowed.
DIRECTIONS: From within Visalia: Off Highway 99, take the Avenue 264 (Tagus) exit east. This will dead-end into the course.

VALLEY OAKS GOLF COURSE (public, 27 holes, robert putnam 1972) . . . .

1800 South Plaza Drive
Visalia, CA 93277
(559) 651-1441

	YARDAGE	PAR	RATING	SLOPE
FRONT	5500	72	72.4	123
MIDDLE	6200	72	70.0	117
BACK	6500	72	71.2	121

$20 - $24

WHAT TO EXPECT: There are three courses: the Valley Course, the Oaks Course, and the Lakes Course. They are rotated in 18-hole combinations every day. The Valley and Oaks courses are the original and are traditional in design, with large greens. The Lakes Course is more of a links-style course.

OUR OPINION: The Lakes Course is the best layout of the three. – Bob

NOTES: The yardage's listed below are the approximate distances for any of the 18-hole combinations.

DIRECTIONS: From within Visalia: Off Highway 198, take the Plaza Drive exit and follow the signs to the course.

VISALIA COUNTRY CLUB (members only, 18 holes, desmond muirhead 1964) . . . . . .

625 Ranch Road
Visalia, CA 93291
(559) 734-1458

	YARDAGE	PAR	RATING	SLOPE
FRONT	5823	72	73.6	128
MIDDLE	6298	72	69.7	122
BACK	6634	72	71.9	127

$30 - $60

WHAT TO EXPECT: The front nine is a tight, stadium-style course, where accurate drives are at a premium. The back nine dates back to the 1920s. It is more user friendly, so an accurate driver is not as critical. However, the greens tend to be smaller and are deceptive. The real key to scoring well at Visalia is course knowledge.

NOTES: Reciprocal play with other members only clubs is allowed.

DIRECTIONS: From within Visalia: Off Highway 99, take the Visalia exit east. Go three stoplights and turn left onto West Main. Turn left again on Ranch Road, and follow it to the end.

WASCO VALLEY ROSE GOLF COURSE (public, 18 holes, robert dean putman 1991) . . .

301 North Leonard Avenue
Wasco, CA 93280
(661) 758-8301

	YARDAGE	PAR	RATING	SLOPE
FRONT	5356	72	70.5	119
MIDDLE	6230	72	70.8	122
BACK	6862	72	74.1	126

$9 - $14

WHAT TO EXPECT: "Unleash the Big Dog." What does that mean? It is just another way of saying hit your driver. Maturing tees will some day change that strategy here. To score well, your emphasis should be placed on your short game. Wasco features plenty of water, traps, and quick greens that range from flat to undulating.

DIRECTIONS: From Bakersfield (about 35 miles northwest to the course): Drive north on Highway 99 and take the Highway 46 exit west. Two miles west of Wasco head north on Leonard Avenue, to the course.

WOODBRIDGE GOLF & COUNTRY CLUB (members only, 27 holes, h. sampson 1923) . .

800 East Woodbridge Road
Woodbridge, CA 95258
(209) 369-2371

	YARDAGE	PAR	RATING	SLOPE	
FRONT	6066	73	75.6	134	**$40 - $50**
MIDDLE	6401	73	71.5	128	
BACK	6611	73	72.4	130	

WHAT TO EXPECT: This 27-hole layout features plenty of trees and water. Together with its small greens, accurate shot making is a must.
NOTES: Reciprocal play with other members only clubs is allowed.
DIRECTIONS: From Sacramento (about 35 miles south to the course): Drive south on Highway. 99 and take Woodbridge Road in Woodbridge. Go west and the course is on the left.

SAWTOOTH ON THE ST. JOHNS (public, 18 holes) . . . .

21730 Avenue 332
Woodlake, CA 93286
(559) 564-1503

	YARDAGE	PAR	RATING	SLOPE	
FRONT	6117	71	68.9	118	**$9 - $15**
MIDDLE	-	-	-	-	
BACK	6407	71	70.2	122	

WHAT TO EXPECT: This is a narrow course surrounded by trees. With a creek running through five holes and small greens, Sawtooth on the St. John's is a shot-maker's delight.
DIRECTIONS: From Visalia (about 22 miles northeast to the course): Take Highway 198 east. Turn left on Road 245. Turn right at the blue church on to Avenue 332. Follow Avenue 332 to the course.

Los Angeles

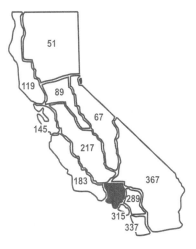

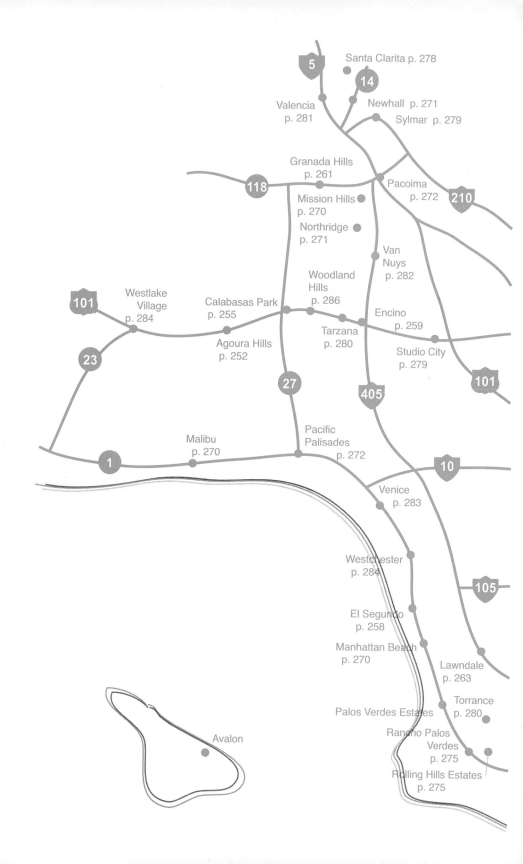

Santa Clarita p. 278

Valencia p. 281

Newhall p. 271

Sylmar p. 279

Granada Hills p. 261

Pacoima p. 272

Mission Hills p. 270

Northridge p. 271

Van Nuys p. 282

Woodland Hills p. 286

Westlake Village p. 284

Calabasas Park p. 255

Encino p. 259

Tarzana p. 280

Studio City p. 279

Agoura Hills p. 252

Pacific Palisades p. 272

Malibu p. 270

Venice p. 283

Westchester p. 284

El Segundo p. 258

Manhattan Beach p. 270

Lawndale p. 263

Torrance p. 280

Palos Verdes Estates

Rancho Palos Verdes p. 275

Avalon

Rolling Hills Estates p. 275

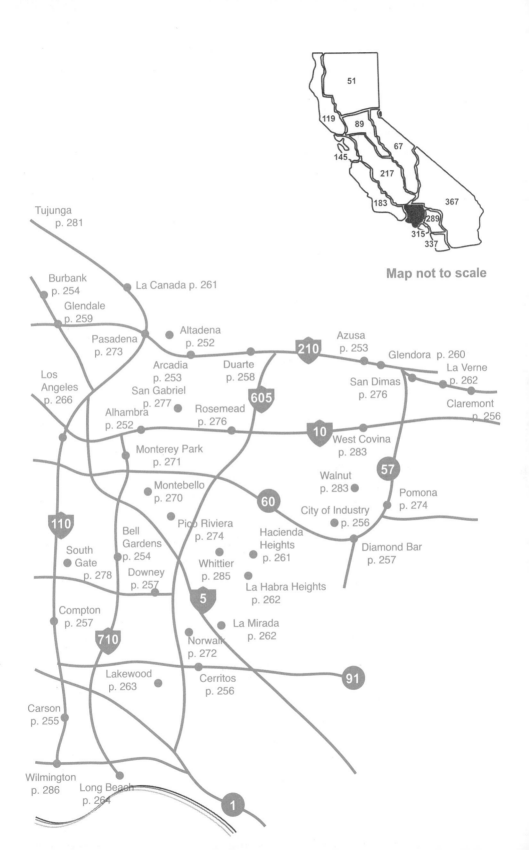

Map not to scale

Tujunga p. 281

Burbank p. 254

La Canada p. 261

Glendale p. 259

Altadena p. 252

Azusa p. 253

Glendora p. 260

Pasadena p. 273

Arcadia p. 253

Duarte p. 258

210

La Verne p. 262

Los Angeles p. 266

San Gabriel p. 277

Rosemead p. 276

605

San Dimas p. 276

Claremont p. 256

Alhambra p. 252

Monterey Park p. 271

10

West Covina p. 283

Walnut p. 283

57

Montebello p. 270

Pomona p. 274

110

South Gate p. 278

Pico Riviera p. 274

60

City of Industry p. 256

Bell Gardens p. 254

Hacienda Heights p. 261

Diamond Bar p. 257

Downey p. 257

Whittier p. 285

La Habra Heights p. 262

Compton p. 257

5

La Mirada p. 262

710

Norwalk p. 272

Lakewood p. 263

Cerritos p. 256

91

Carson p. 255

Wilmington p. 286

Long Beach p. 264

1

LINDERO COUNTRY CLUB (semi-private, 9 holes, ted robinson 1976) . . . .

5719 Lake Lindero Drive
Agoura Hills, CA 91301
(818) 889-1158

	YARDAGE	PAR	RATING	SLOPE
FRONT	1612	29	58.1	94
MIDDLE	-	-	-	-
BACK	1667	29	58.4	95

$14 - $16

WHAT TO EXPECT: With trees, traps, and water, tee to green can be a challenge. For those who can hit the greens in regulation, low scores will be your reward.

DIRECTIONS: From downtown Los Angeles (about 36 miles north to the course): Take US 101 north, exit at Reyes Adobe, and turn right. Turn left on Thousand Oaks Boulevard and then left again on Lake Lindero Drive.

ALHAMBRA GOLF COURSE (municipal, 18 holes, billy bell, jr. 1956) . . . .

630 South Almansor Street
Alhambra, CA 91801
(626) 570-5059

	YARDAGE	PAR	RATING	SLOPE
FRONT	4501	71	64.7	105
MIDDLE	4863	70	63.1	102
BACK	5197	70	64.3	107

$20 - $24

WHAT TO EXPECT: Alhambra is a walkable course with narrow fairways and small, level greens. Because of its relatively short length, the course is well suited for juniors and players new to the game.

DIRECTIONS: From downtown Los Angeles (about 12 miles east to the course): Take I-10 east and take the Garfield North exit, toward Alhambra. Turn right on Valley Boulevard and go about one-half mile. Turn left on Almansor Street, which will dead-end at the course.

ALTADENA GOLF COURSE (public, 9 holes, william p. bell) . . . .

1456 East Mendocino Street
Altadena, CA 91001
(626) 797-3821

	YARDAGE	PAR	RATING	SLOPE
FRONT	2840	36	66.0	104
MIDDLE	-	-	-	-
BACK	2995	36	67.4	108

$13 - $15

WHAT TO EXPECT: Altadena has plenty of trees, but with many parallel holes and wide landing areas, missing the short grass is nearly impossible. Chipping or pitching onto the elevated and crowned greens requires a deft touch.

NOTES: With an extensive practice facility, this is a great place to take up the game.

DIRECTIONS: From downtown Los Angeles (about 16 miles northeast to the course): Take the Pasadena Freeway (I-110) north to the I-210 east. Exit at Lake Avenue, and go north about two and one-half miles. Turn right on Mendocino Street. The course is on the right.

ARCADIA GOLF COURSE (public, 18 holes) . . . .

620 East Live Oak Avenue
Arcadia, CA 91006
(626) 443-9367
americangolf.com

	YARDAGE	PAR	RATING	SLOPE
FRONT	-	-	-	-
MIDDLE	-	-	-	-
BACK	1947	54	-	-

$9 - $12

WHAT TO EXPECT: This is an 18-hole night-lit golf course, where players hit off mats. The longest hole is 153 yards. With no sand or water to contend with, this is a good place for beginners to learn the game.
DIRECTIONS: From downtown Los Angeles (about 19 miles northeast to the course): Take the Pasadena Freeway (I-110) north to I-210 east. Exit on Santa Anita and turn right. Turn left on Live Oak Avenue; the course is on the right.

SANTA ANITA GOLF COURSE (public, 18 holes, william f. bell) . . . .

405 South Santa Anita Avenue
Arcadia, CA 91006
(626) 447-7156

	YARDAGE	PAR	RATING	SLOPE
FRONT	5904	74	73.3	122
MIDDLE	5904	70	68.1	113
BACK	6398	71	70.4	122

$20 - $25

WHAT TO EXPECT: Level lies are hard to come by on this open, undulating course. Although Santa Anita is not long, there are places where length off the tee is beneficial to stay out of trouble. The end result is that players often think the course plays much longer than the yardage indicates.
DIRECTIONS: From downtown Los Angeles (about 20 miles northeast to the course): Take the I-10 east, exit at Santa Anita Avenue, and head north.

CATALINA ISLAND GOLF COURSE (resort, 9 holes, perry dye) . . . .

One Country Club Road
Avalon, CA 90704
(310) 510-0530
santacatalinaislandcompany.com

	YARDAGE	PAR	RATING	SLOPE
FRONT	2065	32	62.6	105
MIDDLE	-	-	-	-
BACK	2155	32	61.2	102

$25 - $45

WHAT TO EXPECT: Often rumored to be expanding to 18 holes, this is a tricky executive layout with small greens.
DIRECTIONS: This course is located on Catalina Island. Make it over there, and you can get to the course.

AZUSA GREENS COUNTRY CLUB (public, 18 holes, bob baldock 1963) . . . .

919 West Sierra Madre Avenue
Azusa, CA 91702
(626) 969-1727
directoryofgolf.com

	YARDAGE	PAR	RATING	SLOPE
FRONT	5601	72	70.9	115
MIDDLE	6010	70	67.9	109
BACK	6220	70	69.1	112

$27 - $36

WHAT TO EXPECT: This is a level, straight-away golf course with narrow fairways, many of which are protected by trees and homes. The condition of the fairways have been improved by the addition of cement cart paths.
DIRECTIONS: From downtown Los Angeles (about 25 miles northeast to the course): Take the Pasadena Freeway (I-110) north to I-210 east. Exit Azusa Avenue, and head north. Turn left on Sierra Madre Avenue. The course is on the right.

FORD PARK GOLF COURSE (public, 9 holes) . . . .

8000 Park Lane
Bell Gardens, CA 90201
(562) 927-8811

	YARDAGE	PAR	RATING	SLOPE
FRONT	-	--	-	-
MIDDLE	-	-	-	-
BACK	2034	54	-	-

$2 - $4

WHAT TO EXPECT: Set in the back of a park, this is a pitch-and-putt course. For those who are not accurate off the tee, this is a pitch, chip, and putt course.

DIRECTIONS: From downtown Los Angeles (about 17 miles southeast to the course): Take I-5 south to the Long Beach Freeway (I-710) south. Exit on Florence and go east. Turn right on Scout and then make a quick left on Park Lane.

DE BELL GOLF COURSE (public, 27 holes, william f. bell 1958) . . . .

1500 Walnut Avenue
Burbank, CA 91504
(818) 845-5052
debellgolf.com

	YARDAGE	PAR	RATING	SLOPE
FRONT	5362	71	71.6	123
MIDDLE	5420	71	67.1	104
BACK	5633	71	67.7	108

$2 - $23

WHAT TO EXPECT: De Bell is Short, tight, hilly, with no water and few bunkers. On a rare, clear day, you can see all the way to the Pacific Ocean.

NOTES: The yardage listed is for the regulation-length course. They also have a nine-hole par-3 course.

DIRECTIONS: From downtown Los Angeles (about 10 miles north to the course): Take I-5 north, exit on Olive Avenue, and head east . Turn left on Sunset Canyon Boulevard and then right on Walnut Avenue.

LAKESIDE GOLF CLUB (members only, 18 holes, max behr 1926) . . . .

4500 Lakeside Drive
Burbank, CA 91505
(818) 985-3335

	YARDAGE	PAR	RATING	SLOPE
FRONT	5983	74	75.3	134
MIDDLE	6272	70	70.6	123
BACK	6534	70	71.9	127

$55 - $65

WHAT TO EXPECT: Gently rolling terrain, mature trees and some strong bunkering make this private club course one of the true quiet gems of Southern California.

DIRECTIONS: From downtown Los Angeles (about 12 miles north to the course): Take US 101 north, exit at Barham, and go right. Turn left at Lakeside Drive. Follow Lakeside Drive to the course.

CALABASAS GOLF & COUNTRY CLUB (members only, 18 holes, r.t. jones sr. & jr. 1968)

4515 Park Entrada
Calabasas Park, CA 91302
(818) 222-3222

	YARDAGE	PAR	RATING	SLOPE
FRONT	5602	72	74.0	135
MIDDLE	6082	72	69.2	122
BACK	6323	72	70.4	125

$55 - $85

WHAT TO EXPECT: The tight Bermuda fairways take some getting used to, but if you play from the fairways, the Calabasas will give up low scores. Houses can be found throughout the course, but really only affect the severe slicer or duck hooker (of course that is probably about 85 percent of all golfers).

DIRECTIONS: From downtown Los Angeles (about 29 miles northwest to the course): Take the Ventura Freeway (US 101) north and exit on Parkway Calabasas. Make a couple of lefts to cross over the freeway. Turn right on Park Entrada. The club is on the left.

DOMINGUEZ GOLF COURSE & PRACTICE CENTER (public, 18 holes) . . . .

19800 South Main Street
Carson, CA 90745
(310) 719-1942
americangolf.com

	YARDAGE	PAR	RATING	SLOPE
FRONT	-	-	-	-
MIDDLE	-	-	-	-
BACK	2053	54	-	-

$12 - $14

WHAT TO EXPECT: This is a pitch-and-putt course with no hole longer than 135 yards.

DIRECTIONS: The course is about 14 miles south of downtown Los Angeles. Go south on the Harbor Freeway (I-10), exit at Torrance Boulevard, and go right. Turn right on Delano and left on Main Street. The course is on the right.

VICTORIA, THE LINKS OF (public, 18 holes, edwin h. ripperdan 1966) . . . .

340 East 192nd Street
Carson, CA 90746
(310) 323-6981

	YARDAGE	PAR	RATING	SLOPE
FRONT	6098	74	73.0	115
MIDDLE	6616	72	71.4	117
BACK	6847	72	72.5	119

$20 - $25

WHAT TO EXPECT: This is a an open, links-style layout with lots of contour in the fairways.

NOTES: This was once one of the poorest-maintained courses in California, but Arnold Palmer Golf Management Company literally brought in thousands of tons of dirt and remodeled the entire layout.

DIRECTIONS: From west Los Angeles (about 18 miles southeast to the course): Take the San Diego Freeway (I-405) south. Exit on Avalon and head north. Turn left on 192nd Street.

IRON-WOOD NINE GOLF COURSE (public, 9 holes) . . . .

16449 Piuma Avenue
Cerritos, CA 90703
(562) 916-8400

	YARDAGE	PAR	RATING	SLOPE
FRONT	-	-	-	-
MIDDLE	-	-	-	-
BACK	1468	29	-	-

$7 - $8

WHAT TO EXPECT: Iron-Wood probably should be named Iron-Iron, since there are not many occasions to use a wood. Even if the course were long enough to be called Iron-Wood, nobody uses real woods anymore. On second thought, maybe it should be called Iron-Wood, because the course is tree-lined, with two lakes. We may never know.
DIRECTIONS: From downtown Los Angeles (about 16 miles southeast to the course): Take I-5 south to I-605 south. Exit Alondra and go straight. It turns into Piuma and dead-ends at the course.

INDUSTRY HILLS GOLF CLUB (public, 36 holes, william f. bell) . . . .

One Industry Hills Parkway
City of Industry, CA 91744
(626) 810-4653
industryhills.com

	YARDAGE	PAR	RATING	SLOPE
FRONT	5589	72	74.1	139
MIDDLE	6735	72	72.9	136
BACK	7181	72	75.3	143

$70 - $85

WHAT TO EXPECT: The Eisenhower Course is one of the toughest layouts in California. The course is hilly and long. The large greens are tiered and undulating. The Zaharias Course is shorter, but still hilly with plenty of trouble. If you have an A game, bring it to Zaharias.
OUR OPINION: Any course that provides a tram to get you and your cart back up to the clubhouse is worth playing. Even without the tram, Industry Hills should not be overlooked in your golf journeys. – Shaw
NOTES: The yardage is for the Eisenhower Course.
DIRECTIONS: From downtown Los Angeles (about 22 miles east to the course): Take I-10 east, exit Azusa Avenue, turn right, and head south a few miles. Turn right on Industry Hills Parkway. That leads to the Sheraton, where the course is located.

CLAREMONT GOLF COURSE (public, 9 holes) . . . .

1550 North Indian Hill Boulevard
Claremont, CA 91711
(909) 624-2748
claremontgolf.com

	YARDAGE	PAR	RATING	SLOPE
FRONT	1685	32	60.5	90
MIDDLE	1685	32	55.2	79
BACK	1915	32	57.4	86

$10 - $12

WHAT TO EXPECT: This is a short, nine-hole course with two par 4s.
NOTES: Check Claremont's web site—you may get lucky and find a coupon.
DIRECTIONS: From downtown Los Angeles (about 36 miles east to the course): Take I-10 east and exit at Indian Hill Boulevard and go north. The course is a few blocks past Foothill, on the right, across from the high school.

COMPTON GOLF COURSE (public, 9 holes) . . . .

6400 East Compton Boulevard
Compton, CA 90221
(562) 633-6721

	YARDAGE	PAR	RATING	SLOPE
FRONT	-	-	-	-
MIDDLE	-	-	-	-
BACK	1300	27	-	-

$4 - $5

WHAT TO EXPECT: Some of the best courses have nothing to do with course layout or conditioning. This nine-hole course provides junior golfers a chance to learn the game and improve themselves on and off the course.

DIRECTIONS: From downtown Los Angeles (about 20 miles southeast to the course): Take I-5 south to the Long Beach Freeway (I-710) south. Exit at Alondra and turn right. Turn right on Atlantic and right again on Compton Boulevard.

DIAMOND BAR GOLF COURSE (public, 18 holes, william bell) . . . .

22751 East Golden Springs Drive
Diamond Bar, CA 91765
(909) 861-8282
americangolf.com

	YARDAGE	PAR	RATING	SLOPE
FRONT	6009	72	74.3	122
MIDDLE	6475	72	70.4	119
BACK	6801	72	72.8	125

$20 - $25

WHAT TO EXPECT: This is a reasonably priced course that will allow you to use every club in your bag. Diamond Bar features generous, yet tree-lined, fairways. For the really erratic and long hitter who misses the fairways and clears the trees, a nearby freeway can be a factor.

DIRECTIONS: From downtown Los Angeles (about 28 miles east to the course): Take the Pomona Freeway (Highway 60) east. Exit on Grand and head south. Turn left on Golden Springs Drive and the course is on the left.

LOS AMIGOS COUNTRY CLUB (public, 18 holes) . . . .

7295 Quill Drive
Downey, CA 90242
(562) 862-1717

	YARDAGE	PAR	RATING	SLOPE
FRONT	5653	71	71.5	117
MIDDLE	5763	70	67.4	113
BACK	5937	70	68.1	116

$20 - $25

WHAT TO EXPECT: With its relatively short yardage, honest fairways and super-sized greens, this is a popular course with the seniors. The back nine features water on four holes.

DIRECTIONS: From downtown Los Angeles (about 20 miles southeast to the course): Take the Harbor Freeway (I-110) south to the Imperial Freeway (I-105) east. Exit onto Old River School Road and turn left. Make another left on Quill Drive.

RIO HONDO GOLF & COUNTRY CLUB (public, 18 holes, gerald pirkl) . . . .

10627 Old River School Road
Downey, CA 90241
(562) 927-2329

	YARDAGE	PAR	RATING	SLOPE
FRONT	5633	71	72.5	124
MIDDLE	6010	71	68.9	118
BACK	6344	71	70.5	122

$35 - $45

WHAT TO EXPECT: This is a flat course with water coming into play on four holes. Many trees line the fairway, and the crowned greens are average in size.
DIRECTIONS: From downtown Los Angeles (about 18 miles southeast to the course): Take I-5 south to the Long Beach Freeway (I-710) south. Exit at Firestone and go east. Turn left on Old River School Road. The course is on the left.

RANCHO DUARTE GOLF CLUB (public, 9 holes, william f. bell) . . . .

1000 Las Lomas Road
Duarte, CA 91010
(626) 357-9981

	YARDAGE	PAR	RATING	SLOPE
FRONT	1341	31	56.2	81
MIDDLE	-	-	-	-
BACK	1559	31	53.8	76

$10 - $13

WHAT TO EXPECT: This is a straight, flat, wide-open executive course.
DIRECTIONS: From downtown Los Angeles (about 24 miles northeast to the course): Take the Pasadena Freeway (I-110) north to the Foothill Freeway (I-210) east. Exit at Mount Olive Drive and head north. Turn right on Huntington and then left at Las Lomas.

EL SEGUNDO, THE LAKES AT (public, 9 holes) . . . .

400 South Sepulveda Boulevard
El Segundo, CA 90245
(310) 322-0202

	YARDAGE	PAR	RATING	SLOPE
FRONT	-	-	-	-
MIDDLE	-	-	-	-
BACK	1430	29	-	-

$9 - $11

WHAT TO EXPECT: This is a short, level, executive course with large greens, water, and sand traps.
NOTES: The course offers an extensive program for junior golfers.
DIRECTIONS: From west Los Angeles (about 12 miles south to the course): Take the San Diego Freeway (I-405) south, exit at Rosecrans, and head west. Turn right on Sepulveda.

SEPULVEDA GOLF COMPLEX (public, 36 holes, william p. bell 1953) . . . .

16821 Burbank Boulevard
Encino, CA 91436
(818) 986-4560

	YARDAGE	PAR	RATING	SLOPE	
FRONT	6192	75	74.3	118	**$20 - $25**
MIDDLE	6458	72	70.0	112	
BACK	6789	72	71.5	116	

WHAT TO EXPECT: Sepulveda has two 18-hole courses, the Encino and the Balboa. If you are looking for a nice walk in the park, pick the longer, but more forgiving, Encino Course. For players seeking more excitement, try the Balboa Course. With tighter fairways and smaller greens, this course forces you to make better shots.
OUR OPINION: The biggest elevation change on the Encino course is from the 10th green to the snack bar near the 11th tee. Still, half the golfers find the need to ride a cart. – Andy
NOTES: The yardage listed is for the Encino Course.
DIRECTIONS: From downtown Los Angeles (about 19 miles northwest to the course): Take US 101 north, exit at Havenhurst, and take a right. Then take a left on Burbank Boulevard, to the course.

CHEVY CHASE COUNTRY CLUB (members only, 9 holes, william f. bell 1925) . . . .

3067 East Chevy Chase Drive
Glendale, CA 91206
(818) 244-8461

	YARDAGE	PAR	RATING	SLOPE	
FRONT	2288	34	67.0	110	**$30 - $40**
MIDDLE	2288	33	62.6	113	
BACK	2460	33	64.2	116	

WHAT TO EXPECT: This private course, nestled in the foothills of old Glendale, features two sets of tees and ten greens that form 18 holes. The course's main challenge is the out-of-bounds found on nearly every hole.
DIRECTIONS: From downtown Los Angeles (about 10 miles north to the course): Take the Glendale Freeway (Highway 2) north, exit onto Holly, and go west. Turn right on Harvey Drive. Go north on Chevy Chase Drive and then left on Golf Club Drive.

OAKMONT COUNTRY CLUB (members only, 18 holes, w.p. bell, m. behr, k. killian) . .

3100 Country Club Drive
Glendale, CA 91208
(818) 542-4292
oakmontcc.com

	YARDAGE	PAR	RATING	SLOPE	
FRONT	5785	72	74.6	134	**$55 - $65**
MIDDLE	6413	72	71.2	127	
BACK	6736	72	72.8	131	

WHAT TO EXPECT: Oakmont is a perennial favorite of the LPGA. The course is flat but interesting, with narrow trees guarding hitting areas and deceptive, well-maintained putting surfaces.
DIRECTIONS: From downtown Los Angeles (about 11 miles north to the course): Take the Glendale Freeway (Highway 2) north, exit at Mountain Street and turn left. Go downhill and turn right on Verdugo. Bear to the left onto Cañada. Turn left on Country Club Drive and go uphill to the club.

SCHOLL CANYON GOLF & TENNIS CLUB (public, 18 holes, george williams) . . . .

3800 East Glenoaks Boulevard
Glendale, CA 91206
(818) 243-4100
americangolf.com

	YARDAGE	PAR	RATING	SLOPE
FRONT	-	-	-	-
MIDDLE	-	-	-	-
BACK	3039	60	56.6	81

$8 - $32

WHAT TO EXPECT: Built on top of a canyon, this executive course has excellent views of the surrounding area. On a good day (especially if the Santa Ana winds have been through), you can see the ocean. While the less-skilled players can enjoy themselves, the course is made interesting for the better golfer with constant elevation changes.

DIRECTIONS: From downtown Los Angeles (about 10 miles north to the course): Take the Glendale Freeway (Highway 2) north. Exit at Holly Drive and turn right down Mount Carmel Drive. Turn right on Glenoaks Boulevard, then travel three miles to the club entrance.

GLENDORA COUNTRY CLUB (members only, 18 holes, robert trent jones jr. (r)) . . . .

310 South Amelia Avenue
Glendora, CA 91741
(626) 335-3713
glendoracountryclub.com

	YARDAGE	PAR	RATING	SLOPE
FRONT	5992	74	75.5	135
MIDDLE	6377	72	71.1	125
BACK	6597	72	72.2	128

$50 - $50

WHAT TO EXPECT: Don't worry about distance; concentrate on hitting your targets, which can be narrow (fairways) or small (greens). If you can't hit your mark or avoid hitting the ball in one of the four lakes, enjoy the scenery and the flowing, traditional layout.

DIRECTIONS: From downtown Los Angeles (about 32 miles northeast to the course): Take I-10 east to Highway 57 north. Exit at Auto Center Drive and turn right, heading east. Turn left on Amelia Avenue. The clubhouse is on the right. Turn right on Country Club Drive.

GLENOAKS GOLF CLUB (public, 9 holes) . . . .

200 West Dawson Avenue
Glendora, CA 91740
(626) 335-7565

	YARDAGE	PAR	RATING	SLOPE
FRONT	-	-	-	-
MIDDLE	-	-	-	-
BACK	1120	27	-	-

$4 - $6

WHAT TO EXPECT: With several holes under 100 yards, this course is a good place to learn the game or perfect your short-iron game.

DIRECTIONS: From Pasadena (about 19 miles east to the course): Take the Foothill Freeway (I-210) east, exit on Grand and head south on Grand. Turn left on Dawson Avenue. The range is on the right, but parking lot is on the left.

KNOLLWOOD COUNTRY CLUB (public, 18 holes, william f. bell 1956) . . . .

12040 Balboa Boulevard
Granada Hills, CA 91344
(818) 363-8161
americangolf.com

	YARDAGE	PAR	RATING	SLOPE
FRONT	5714	72	73.1	126
MIDDLE	5963	72	68.9	119
BACK	6313	72	70.8	124

$20 - $25

WHAT TO EXPECT: Knollwood is part of a housing development, so out-of-bounds stakes can be found throughout. The greens are protected by traps and run from small to medium in size. This is a hilly course, so take some extra time with your club selection.
DIRECTIONS: From downtown Los Angeles (about 23 miles northwest to the course): Go north on US 101, exit at Balboa Boulevard, and head north to the course.

WILDWOOD MOBILE COUNTRY CLUB (members only, 9 holes) . . . .

901 South 6th Avenue
Hacienda Heights, CA 91745
(626) 968-2338

	YARDAGE	PAR	RATING	SLOPE
FRONT	1162	27	-	-
MIDDLE	-	-	-	-
BACK	1190	27	-	-

WHAT TO EXPECT: From the name, it sounds like you could pick up the course and move it, but this is not the case. Instead, you will find a short par-3 course in a mobile home park with out-of-bounds everywhere.
DIRECTIONS: From downtown Los Angeles (about 20 miles east to the course): Take Highway 60 east and exit at Seventh Street heading north. At the second light, turn left on Clark. This leads right into Wildwood.

LA CAÑADA–FLINTRIDGE COUNTRY CLUB (members only, 18 holes, lawrence hughes)

5500 Godbey Drive
La Cañada, CA 91011
(818) 790-0155

	YARDAGE	PAR	RATING	SLOPE
FRONT	5219	70	70.9	127
MIDDLE	5606	70	67.4	122
BACK	5771	70	68.5	125

$38 - $48

WHAT TO EXPECT: Why should you fear this 5,700 yard course? First, hilly, narrow fairways will have the smart player thinking twice about hitting driver. Second, Kikuyu grass on the fairway gives little roll and forces you to fly the ball to the green. Third, there is not third, but aren't the other two enough?
NOTES: Reciprocal play with other members only clubs is allowed.
DIRECTIONS: From downtown Los Angeles (about 18 miles north to the course): Take Pasadena Freeway (I-110) north to I-210 west. Exit onto Angeles Crest Highway and go north just over a mile. Turn right on Starlight and then right on Godbey Drive.

HACIENDA GOLF CLUB (members only, 18 holes, max behr) . . . .
718 East Road
La Habra Heights, CA 90631
(562) 697-3610

	YARDAGE	PAR	RATING	SLOPE	
FRONT	5833	72	74.9	138	**$50 - $60**
MIDDLE	6379	71	71.3	129	
BACK	6660	71	72.7	133	

WHAT TO EXPECT: Dubbed as Little Riviera, the course packs plenty of challenge, though not especially long on the card. Small greens, narrow fairways and strategic bunkering all create a deceptively difficult challenge.

DIRECTIONS: From downtown Los Angeles (about 23 miles southeast to the course): Take the Pomona Freeway (Highway 60) east. Exit at Hacienda and head south about four miles. Turn left on East Road to get to the club.

LA MIRADA GOLF COURSE (public, 18 holes, w.f. bell 1960) . . . .
15501 East Alicante Road
La Mirada, CA 90638
(562) 943-7123
americangolf.com

	YARDAGE	PAR	RATING	SLOPE	
FRONT	5652	71	71.8	117	**$20 - $25**
MIDDLE	5806	70	67.4	111	
BACK	6083	70	68.6	114	

WHAT TO EXPECT: This is a slightly rolling course with trees, but the player is still left with plenty of fairway. The greens range in size from small to medium.

NOTES: La Mirada was named municipal course of the year by the county of Los Angeles.

DIRECTIONS: From downtown Los Angeles (about 20 miles southeast to the course): Take I-5 south to La Mirada. Exit on Rosecrans and head east. Turn left on La Mirada Boulevard and then right on Alicante Road.

MARSHALL CANYON GOLF CLUB (public, 18 holes) . . . .
6100 North Stephens Ranch Road
La Verne, CA 91750
(909) 593-8211
marshallcanyon.com

	YARDAGE	PAR	RATING	SLOPE	
FRONT	5627	71	71.8	118	**$20 - $25**
MIDDLE	5896	71	68.3	118	
BACK	6110	71	69.5	120	

WHAT TO EXPECT: Located in a canyon, this is a hilly course where golfers will encounter some forced carries. They will also have to deal with trees and rough. For the first-time player, it should be noted that putts tend to break toward the Valley.

DIRECTIONS: From downtown Los Angeles (about 35 miles east to the course): Take the Pasadena Freeway (I-110) north to I-210 east. When I-210 ends, it becomes Foothill Boulevard. Turn left (north) at Wheeler. At the top of the hill, turn right on Golden Hills and then left on Stephens Ranch Road.

SIERRA LA VERNE COUNTRY CLUB (members only, 18 holes, dan murray) . . . .

6300 Country Club Drive
La Verne, CA 91750
(909) 596-2100

	YARDAGE	PAR	RATING	SLOPE	
FRONT	5602	72	74.4	138	**$40 - $60**
MIDDLE	5996	71	69.0	122	
BACK	6337	71	70.6	126	

WHAT TO EXPECT: The front nine winds through a housing development but is fairly open. The back nine has more trees, out-of-bounds, and hazards. For those interested in shooting a low number, opt for accuracy over distance and keep the ball below the hole.

NOTES: Reciprocal play with other members only clubs is allowed.

DIRECTIONS: From downtown Los Angeles (about 35 miles east to the course): Take the Pasadena Freeway (I-110) north to the Foothill Freeway (I-210) east. Stay on it until it ends and becomes Foothill Boulevard. After about a mile on Foothill Boulevard, turn left on Wheeler. Turn right on Birdie Lane and then left at the dead-end to the club.

LAKEWOOD COUNTRY CLUB (public, 18 holes, william p. bell) . . . .

3101 East Carson Street
Lakewood, CA 90712
(562) 429-9711
americangolf.com

	YARDAGE	PAR	RATING	SLOPE	
FRONT	5920	72	74.1	121	**$20 - $25**
MIDDLE	6739	72	71.2	119	
BACK	7045	72	73.2	121	

WHAT TO EXPECT: From the back tees, this is a long course, with wide, generous fairways and plenty of water. The front nine plays among an industrial complex, while the back nine plays among homes. To score well, you must get past the long par 3s. Afternoon wind can be a factor.

DIRECTIONS: From west Los Angeles (about 27 miles southeast to the course): Take the San Diego Freeway (I-405) south, exit at Lakewood Boulevard, and head north. Take a left on Carson Street to the club.

ALONDRA PARK GOLF COURSE (municipal, 36 holes, william p. bell) . . . .

16400 South Prairie
Lawndale, CA 90260
(310) 217-9919

	YARDAGE	PAR	RATING	SLOPE	
FRONT	5976	73	74.4	117	**$11 - $25**
MIDDLE	6224	72	69.5	117	
BACK	6450	72	70.6	120	

WHAT TO EXPECT: This course can boost your ego. Alondra is a walkable course, with little trouble off the tee and slightly elevated greens. Wind can be a factor. There is also a 18-hole par-3 course.

NOTES: The yardage listed is for the regulation-length course.

DIRECTIONS: From west Los Angeles (about 13 miles south to the course): Take the San Diego Freeway (I-405) south to Redondo Beach Boulevard exit. Go left, back under the freeway, and continue on Redondo Beach Boulevard. Turn left on Prairie, which leads to the course.

BIXBY VILLAGE GOLF COURSE (public, 9 holes, ron fream) . . . .

6180 Bixby Village Drive
Long Beach, CA 90803
(562) 498-7003

	YARDAGE	PAR	RATING	SLOPE
FRONT	1417	29	55.1	82
MIDDLE	-	-	-	-
BACK	1573	29	57.5	86

$5 - $11

WHAT TO EXPECT: For golfers who play here thinking they will be able to shoot Tiger-like numbers, think again. The course is rolling, with rough and bunkers guarding undulating greens.

DIRECTIONS: Bixby is about 30 miles southeast of the course from Los Angeles. Drive south on I-405 to Bellflower Boulevard. Head south to the Pacific Coast Highway. Go south on the Pacific Coast Highway. Make a left on Loynes and another left on Bixby Village Drive.

EL DORADO PARK GOLF COURSE (public, 18 holes, cal olson) . . . .

2400 Studebaker Road
Long Beach, CA 90815
(562) 430-5411
americangolf.com

	YARDAGE	PAR	RATING	SLOPE
FRONT	5986	72	74.3	126
MIDDLE	6461	72	70.9	126
BACK	6900	72	72.6	130

$27 - $32

WHAT TO EXPECT: This is a mature parkland-style course with water coming into play on several holes.

NOTES: The course is home to the Long Beach Open.

DIRECTIONS: From west Los Angeles (about 30 miles southeast to the course): Take the San Diego Freeway (I-405) south. Exit at Studebaker Road and head north to the course. It is less than a mile from the freeway.

HEARTWELL GOLF COURSE (public, 18 holes, william f. bell) . . . .

6700 East Carson Street
Long Beach, CA 90808
(562) 421-8855
americangolf.com

	YARDAGE	PAR	RATING	SLOPE
FRONT	-	-	-	-
MIDDLE	-	-	-	-
BACK	2143	54	-	-

$11 - $12

WHAT TO EXPECT: This is a night-lit course with little out-of-bounds and nice greens. For the good golfer, your greatest challenge maybe trying to pick up the flight of the ball at night.

DIRECTIONS: From west Los Angeles (about 30 miles southeast to the course): Take the San Diego Freeway (I-405) south. Exit at Palo Verde and head north. Turn right on Carson to the course.

RECREATION PARK GOLF COURSE (public, 27 holes, william f. bell) . . . .

5001 Deukmejian Drive
Long Beach, CA 90804
(562) 494-5000
americangolf.com

	YARDAGE	PAR	RATING	SLOPE	
FRONT	5930	74	72.6	120	**$7 - $27**
MIDDLE	6155	72	68.8	108	
BACK	6405	72	69.9	111	

WHAT TO EXPECT: Off the first tee, the driving range creates out-of-bounds. Once you get past that, the fairways have plenty of trees, but are generous. Make your mistakes early, because holes 6, 7 and 8 are monster par 4s. The greens are mostly elevated and have subtle breaks that tend to move toward the ocean.

NOTES: Recreation Park South is the short nine-hole course, located across the street.

DIRECTIONS: From west Los Angeles (about 29 miles southeast to the course): Take the San Diego Freeway (I-405) south, exit at Seventh Street and go west about five miles. Turn right on Federation into the park and then right at the stop sign to the course.

SKYLINKS GOLF COURSE (public, 18 holes, william f. bell) . . . .

4800 East Wardlow Road
Long Beach, CA 90808
(562) 429-0030

	YARDAGE	PAR	RATING	SLOPE	
FRONT	5933	74	74.0	121	**$15 - $23**
MIDDLE	6136	72	69.3	115	
BACK	6379	72	70.5	119	

WHAT TO EXPECT: This is a player-friendly course, with wide fairways that can accommodate every type of skill level. For the better player, the par 3s can present a challenge.

DIRECTIONS: From west Los Angeles (about 27 miles southeast to the course): Take the San Diego Freeway (I-405) south, exit at Lakewood Boulevard and head north about a half mile.

VIRGINIA COUNTRY CLUB (members only, 18 holes, a.w. tillinghast) . . . .

4602 Virginia Road
Long Beach, CA 90807
(562) 424-5211

	YARDAGE	PAR	RATING	SLOPE	
FRONT	5754	72	74.7	130	**$50 - $65**
MIDDLE	6240	71	69.7	125	
BACK	6505	71	70.9	128	

WHAT TO EXPECT: This is a classic, pretty course, with rolling terrain and tree-lined fairways. The greens are small and tiered. It's one of those courses that will have you shaking your head at the end of the day, wondering how your round turned out to look like a good bowling score.

NOTES: All 18 greens are being replaced and should be completed by the end of 2001.

DIRECTIONS: From west Los Angeles (about 25 miles southeast to the course): Take the San Diego Freeway (I-405) south. Exit at Long Beach Boulevard and make two rights to go left on Long Beach Boulevard, heading north, away from the ocean. Turn left on San Antonio Boulevard and then right on Virginia Road to the club.

BEL AIR COUNTRY CLUB (members only, 18 holes, george c. thomas 1926) . . . .

10768 Bellagio Road
Los Angeles, CA 90077
(310) 440-2423

	YARDAGE	PAR	RATING	SLOPE
FRONT	5778	70	74.7	134
MIDDLE	6482	70	72.0	134
BACK	6772	70	73.8	137

WHAT TO EXPECT: Bel Air is one of the premier private courses in Southern California. It has been greatly altered from its original George Thomas design, but remains a favorite of celebrities and movers and shakers.

DIRECTIONS: From west Los Angeles: Off the San Diego Freeway (I-405), exit at Sunset Boulevard and head east. Turn left on Bellagio Road. This leads to the Bel Air West Gate. At the fork, bear to the right.

BRENTWOOD COUNTRY CLUB (members only, 18 holes, willie watson) . . . .

590 South Burlingame Avenue
Los Angeles, CA 90049
(310) 451-8011

	YARDAGE	PAR	RATING	SLOPE	
FRONT	5534	73	73.7	128	**$55 - $70**
MIDDLE	6500	72	70.5	120	
BACK	6757	72	71.9	124	

WHAT TO EXPECT: This traditional-style course is flat, fairly long, and attractively manicured and maintained. The fairways are tight with lots of trees.

DIRECTIONS: From west Los Angeles: Off the San Diego Freeway (I-405), exit onto Wilshire Boulevard and go west. Turn right on San Vicente and then left on Burlingame Avenue.

CHESTER WASHINGTON GOLF COURSE (public, 18 holes, unknown 1920) . . . .

1930 West 120th Street
Los Angeles, CA 90047
(323) 756-6975
americangolf.com

	YARDAGE	PAR	RATING	SLOPE	
FRONT	5673	73	72.2	120	**$20 - $25**
MIDDLE	6007	73	68.3	115	
BACK	6321	73	69.8	119	

WHAT TO EXPECT: The fairways are super-sized and lined with mature trees. The terrain is rolling and the greens are sloping.

DIRECTIONS: From downtown Los Angeles (about 10 miles south to the course): Take the Harbor Freeway (I-110) south and exit at El Segundo. Turn right and then make another right on Western. Chester Washington is just up the hill.

GRIFFITH PARK GOLF CLUB (public, 36 holes, george c. thomas, jr. 1920) . . . .

4730 Crystal Springs Drive
Los Angeles, CA 90027
(323) 664-2255
griffithpark.com

	YARDAGE	PAR	RATING	SLOPE
FRONT	6489	73	76.6	128
MIDDLE	6678	72	70.7	114
BACK	6947	72	72.7	117

$20 - $25

WHAT TO EXPECT: There are two popular (crowded) courses at Griffith Park, the Harding Course and the Wilson Course. The Wilson Course is the more preferred and respected of the two. Both are classic in design. They are tree-lined, rolling courses that are located at the base of the Hollywood Hills
OUR OPINION: Not exactly as inspiring as Rancho Park, but the Wilson Course comes pretty close. Wonderful location in Griffith Park. – Andy
NOTES: The yardage listed is for the Wilson Course.
DIRECTIONS: From downtown Los Angeles: Take I-5 north, take the exit to Griffith Park and turn right. Make a left at the second stop sign and follow the road about a mile.

HILLCREST COUNTRY CLUB (members only, 18 holes, willie watson 1920) . . . .

10000 West Pico Boulevard
Los Angeles, CA 90064
(310) 553-8911

	YARDAGE	PAR	RATING	SLOPE
FRONT	5817	73	74.6	130
MIDDLE	6068	71	69.0	119
BACK	6480	71	70.4	123

$30 - $45

WHAT TO EXPECT: Hillcrest is well-conditioned and hilly. With an abundance of trees, it is more interesting than it is difficult and long.
NOTES: At press time, they are renovating the course.
DIRECTIONS: From west Los Angeles: Off the San Diego Freeway (I-405), exit at Olympic Boulevard/Pico Boulevard and head east on Pico Boulevard to the club.

LOS ANGELES COUNTRY CLUB, THE (members only, 36 holes, george c. thomas 1921)

10101 Wilshire Boulevard
Los Angeles, CA 90024
(310) 276-6104

	YARDAGE	PAR	RATING	SLOPE
FRONT	6205	71	77.7	148
MIDDLE	6601	71	72.3	131
BACK	6909	71	74.0	135

$55 - $75

WHAT TO EXPECT: The North Course is one of the country's top three dozen courses and among the most publicity shy. Its strong rolling fairways are highlighted by superb bunkering, great flow, and balance of holes. The South Course is similar in style, but much less demanding and not as long.
NOTES: The yardage listed is for the North Course.
DIRECTIONS: From west Los Angeles: Off the San Diego Freeway (I-405), exit Wilshire Boulevard and head east. The club is on Wilshire Boulevard, between Comstock and Whittier.

LOS FELIZ MUNICIPAL GOLF COURSE (public, 9 holes) . . . .

3207 Los Feliz Boulevard
Los Angeles, CA 90039
(323) 663-7758

	YARDAGE	PAR	RATING	SLOPE	
FRONT	-	-	-	-	**$4 - $5**
MIDDLE	-	-	-	-	
BACK	1065	27	-	-	

WHAT TO EXPECT: If you are expecting a lot, you obviously haven't seen the price.
OUR OPINION: Ok, we have never played this course, but for $5, it's got to be worth it.
DIRECTIONS: From downtown Los Angeles: Take I-5 north, exit onto Los Feliz Boulevard, and head east.

MAGGIE HATHAWAY GOLF COURSE (public, 9 holes) . . . .

1921 West 98th Street
Los Angeles, CA 90047
(323) 755-6285

	YARDAGE	PAR	RATING	SLOPE	
FRONT	-	-	-	-	**$6 - $7**
MIDDLE	-	-	-	-	
BACK	1008	27	-	-	

WHAT TO EXPECT: This is a short nine-hole, par 3 course. The longest hole is 132 yards.
DIRECTIONS: From Los Angeles (about nine miles south to the course): Take the Harbor Freeway (I-110) south, exit onto Century Boulevard, and head west. Turn right on Western Avenue, and then left on West 98th Street.

MOUNTAINGATE COUNTRY CLUB (members only, 27 holes, ted robinson) . . . .

12445 MountainGate Drive
Los Angeles, CA 90049
(310) 476-2800
americangolf.com

	YARDAGE	PAR	RATING	SLOPE	
FRONT	5667	72	74.0	123	**$80 - $125**
MIDDLE	6358	72	69.8	120	
BACK	6719	72	71.8	126	

WHAT TO EXPECT: The three courses are played in 18-hole combinations. They are the North, South, and Lake. The North Course is a wooded layout that hugs the mountain and is the easiest and most picturesque of the three. The South Course is the newest nine and is open but the most challenging. The first three holes are hell, but get by them in par and you are on your way to a good score. The Lake Course is straightforward, with water coming into play on two holes. It has three par 5s and three par 3s. All courses do have similarities—undulating greens and plenty of hills.
NOTES: Reciprocal play with other members only clubs is allowed.
DIRECTIONS: From west Los Angeles: Off the San Diego Freeway (I-405), exit at Getty Center Drive and head north on Sepulveda. Turn left at the third light, which is MountainGate Drive.

RANCHO PARK GOLF COURSE (public, 27 holes, william p. bell) . . . .

10460 West Pico Boulevard
Los Angeles, CA 90064
(310) 839-4374

	YARDAGE	PAR	RATING	SLOPE
FRONT	6001	73	74.4	124
MIDDLE	6300	71	70.1	123
BACK	6628	71	71.7	126

$5 - $25

WHAT TO EXPECT: This is a scenic, hilly park-setting course, with mature trees and new, modern-style greens.

OUR OPINION: Great course, great waits. Plan on five hours plus and be thrilled if you finish in less. It is worth the entire hassle to play. By the way, how do all the same old guys go out the same time every week? When they score 120 for the round, is it time for them to go play Encino or Woodley? We know, one day we'll get old, but at least we'll have the sense to go play an appropriate course. – Andy

NOTES: A city reservation card is needed to book a tee time. The yardage listed is for the regulation-length course. There is also a par-3 nine-hole course.

DIRECTIONS: From west Los Angeles: Off the Santa Monica Freeway (I-10), exit on Overland and head north. Turn right on Pico Boulevard.

ROOSEVELT EXECUTIVE GOLF COURSE (public, 9 holes) . . . .

2650 North Vermont Avenue
Los Angeles, CA 90027
(323) 665-2011

	YARDAGE	PAR	RATING	SLOPE
FRONT	2244	33	61.4	102
MIDDLE	2357	33	62.2	106
BACK	2478	33	63.4	110

$11 - $14

WHAT TO EXPECT: Located in Griffith Park, this is a nine-hole executive course is set on rolling hills with mature trees and small greens.

OUR OPINION: Roosevelt is a fun nine-holer in Griffith Park. Good for all levels. – Andy

DIRECTIONS: From downtown Los Angeles: Take the I-5 north, exit at Los Feliz,and head west. Turn right on Vermont to the course.

WILSHIRE COUNTRY CLUB, THE (members only, 18 holes, norman macbeth 1919) . .

301 North Rossmore Avenue
Los Angeles, CA 90004
(323) 934-1121

	YARDAGE	PAR	RATING	SLOPE
FRONT	6008	71	75.6	140
MIDDLE	6295	71	70.0	120
BACK	6531	71	71.5	126

$45 - $60

WHAT TO EXPECT: This old, classic tree-lined course has hosted the Senior PGA Tour. A barranca runs through fourteen of its fairways. The par-4 finishing hole has long been considered on of the area's best.

DIRECTIONS: From downtown Los Angeles: Take the Santa Monica Freeway (I-10) west, exit at Crenshaw and head north. Turn left on Wilshire and then right on Rossmore. The entrance is at the first driveway on the left just past Beverly Boulevard.

MALIBU COUNTRY CLUB (public, 18 holes, william f. bell 1977) . . . .

901 Encinal Canyon Road
Malibu, CA 90265
(818) 889-6680
malibucountryclub.net

	YARDAGE	PAR	RATING	SLOPE
FRONT	6090	72	70.0	125
MIDDLE	-	-	-	-
BACK	6589	72	72.5	132

$55 - $80

WHAT TO EXPECT: You will find the front nine narrow with lots of trees, undulation, and out-of-bounds. The back nine is much more forgiving.
DIRECTIONS: From west Los Angeles (about 23 miles west to the course): Head north on the Pacific Coast Highway six miles past Pepperdine. Turn right on Kanan Dume Road. Go about six miles, and turn left on Mulholland Highway. Bear left at the fork onto Encinal Canyon Road.

MARRIOTT HOTEL GOLF COURSE - MANHATTAN BEACH (public, 9 holes) . . . .

1400 Parkview Avenue
Manhattan Beach, CA 90266
(310) 546-4551
marriott.com

	YARDAGE	PAR	RATING	SLOPE
FRONT	-	-	-	-
MIDDLE	-	-	-	-
BACK	1220	27	-	-

$7 - $9

WHAT TO EXPECT: This is a short par-3 course with one lake and no holes over 180 yards.
DIRECTIONS: From west Los Angeles (about 12 miles south to the course): Take the San Diego Freeway (I-405) south, exit at Rosecrans and go west. The hotel is visible. Make a left on Nash/Parkview Avenue. The course is behind the hotel, on the north side.

MISSION HILLS LITTLE LEAGUE GOLF COURSE (public, 9 holes) . . . .

Mission Hills, CA 91343
(818) 892-3019

	YARDAGE	PAR	RATING	SLOPE
FRONT	-	-	-	-
MIDDLE	-	-	-	-
BACK	1140	27	-	-

$8 - $12

WHAT TO EXPECT: This is a pitch-and-putt golf course located on the grounds behind the VA Hospital.
DIRECTIONS: From west Los Angeles (about 17 miles north to the course): Go north on the San Diego Freeway (I-405), exit Nordoff and turn left. Turn right on Haskell and then left on Plummer. Enter at the VA Hospital. The course is at the back of the grounds of the hospital.

MONTEBELLO COUNTRY CLUB, THE (public, 18 holes, max behr 1928) . . . .

901 Via San Clemente
Montebello, CA 90640
(323) 725-0892
themontebellocc.com

	YARDAGE	PAR	RATING	SLOPE
FRONT	5624	71	71.8	121
MIDDLE	6030	71	68.9	119
BACK	6616	71	71.6	124

$28 - $38

WHAT TO EXPECT: This level course has recently been renovated with new greens and three new lakes. Keep out of the fairway bunkers; they can be hazardous to your score.
DIRECTIONS: From downtown Los Angeles (about ten miles east to the course): Take the Pomona Freeway (Highway 60) east, exit on Garfield Avenue, and drive south for one block. Turn right on Via San Clemente, where there is a sign.

MONTEREY PARK GOLF COURSE (public, 9 holes) . . . .

3600 Ramona Boulevard
Monterey Park, CA 91754
(323) 266-2241

	YARDAGE	PAR	RATING	SLOPE
FRONT	-	-	-	-
MIDDLE	-	-	-	-
BACK	1400	29	-	-

$7 - $8

WHAT TO EXPECT: You will find no hole over 300 yards on this wavy layout with small greens.

DIRECTIONS: From downtown Los Angeles (about nine miles east to the course): Take I-10 east, exit at Eastern Avenue and go straight. After passing Corporate Center Drive, turn right up the driveway that is marked golf/restaurant.

FRIENDLY VALLEY GOLF LAUNCH (members only, 9 holes) . . . .

19345 Avenue of the Oaks
Newhall, CA 91321
(661) 252-9859

	YARDAGE	PAR	RATING	SLOPE
FRONT	1200	28	-	-
MIDDLE	-	-	-	-
BACK	1400	28	-	-

WHAT TO EXPECT: This is a short course with one par 4 and the rest par 3s. This is a private club that doesn't want you there and you don't want to be there.

OUR OPINION: For this being "Friendly Valley" the definition of "friendly" must be different than mine. – Nancy

DIRECTIONS: From downtown Los Angeles (about 29 miles north to the course): Take I-5 north to Highway 14, and exit at Golden Valley Road. This leads to Friendly Valley Parkway. Turn right into the complex and enter the parking lot for the course.

PORTER VALLEY COUNTRY CLUB (members only, 18 holes, ted robinson 1968) . . . . . .

19216 Singing Hills Drive
Northridge, CA 91326
(818) 368-2919
portervalley.com

	YARDAGE	PAR	RATING	SLOPE
FRONT	5462	70	72.5	128
MIDDLE	5788	70	69.2	126
BACK	6086	70	70.6	129

$50 - $70

WHAT TO EXPECT: This is a traditional course set on a hill. The fairways are rolling, but the course is walkable. Visually, the fairways appear tight, but you can hit a driver on most of the holes. The greens are medium in size and undulating. Excellent views of the valley can be had throughout the round.

DIRECTIONS: From west Los Angeles (about 23 miles north to the course): Take the San Diego Freeway (I-405) north to Highway 118 west. Exit at Reseda and get in the left lane to turn left on Rinaldi. Turn right on Porter Valley Drive. The ninth green comes into view.

NORWALK GOLF CENTER (public, 9 holes) . . . .

13717 Shoemaker Avenue
Norwalk, CA 90650
(562) 921-6500

	YARDAGE	PAR	RATING	SLOPE
FRONT	-	--	-	-
MIDDLE	-	-	-	-
BACK	2000	27	-	-

$5 - $6

WHAT TO EXPECT: This is a short, lighted par-3 course with parallel fairways.
DIRECTIONS: From downtown Los Angeles (about 16 miles southeast to the course): Take I-5 south, exit at Rosecrans, turn right off the exit. Make a left on Shoemaker Avenue, and the course is on the left.

RIVIERA COUNTRY CLUB (members only, 18 holes, george c. thomas 1926) . . . .

1250 Capri Drive
Pacific Palisades, CA 90272
(310) 459-5395

	YARDAGE	PAR	RATING	SLOPE
FRONT	5716	74	74.7	137
MIDDLE	6505	71	71.9	130
BACK	6950	71	74.3	139

$85 - $300

WHAT TO EXPECT: The Riviera is one of the West's true championship layouts. This historic course plays in a canyon among the eucalyptus and features the tough, thick Kikuyu grass and high-lipped George Thomas bunkers.
NOTES: Reciprocal play with other members only clubs is allowed.
DIRECTIONS: From west Los Angeles (about six miles northwest to the course): Take the San Diego Freeway (I-405) north. Exit at Sunset Boulevard and head west. Turn left on Capri Drive. If you hit the ocean, you have gone too far.

HANSEN DAM GOLF COURSE (municipal, 18 holes) . . . .

10400 Glenoaks Boulevard
Pacoima, CA 91331
(818) 896-0050

	YARDAGE	PAR	RATING	SLOPE
FRONT	6084	75	74.1	123
MIDDLE	6361	72	68.5	114
BACK	6662	72	71.1	118

$18 - $23

WHAT TO EXPECT: This is a flowing, open, high traffic course that sends out about 105,000 golfers per year.
OUR OPINION: A definite step up from the tarmacs that double as Woodley, Encino, and Balboa. An excellent front nine. – Andy
DIRECTIONS: From downtown Los Angeles (about 18 miles north to the course): Take I-5 north, exit at Osborne, and take a right on Osborne. Turn right on Glenoaks Boulevard. A left on Montague leads to the course.

PALOS VERDES GOLF CLUB (semi-private, 18 holes, george c. thomas 1924) . . . .

3301 Via Campesina
Palos Verdes Estates, CA 90274
(310) 375-2759

	YARDAGE	PAR	RATING	SLOPE
FRONT	4696	71	63.6	111
MIDDLE	5118	71	68.2	123
BACK	6219	71	70.5	129

$45 - $205

WHAT TO EXPECT: This is a traditional golf course with beautiful views, wide tree-lined fairways, and small greens that require a surgeon's touch. Wind does come into play. Although the obstacles are straightforward, course knowledge is the key to scoring well. The placement of your shots off the tee and fairway to green may be the difference between birdie and bogey.
NOTES: This is a member-only course on weekends.
DIRECTIONS: From west Los Angeles (about 20 miles south to the course): Take the San Diego Freeway (I-405) south to the Hawthorne Boulevard exit. Go south about six miles and turn right on Palos Verde Drive North. Turn left at Via Campesina. Go one-quarter mile to the club on the right.

ANNANDALE GOLF COURSE (members only, 18 holes, william p. bell 1910) . . . .

One North San Rafael Avenue
Pasadena, CA 91105
(626) 795-8253

	YARDAGE	PAR	RATING	SLOPE
FRONT	5732	73	75.6	138
MIDDLE	6103	70	70.2	129
BACK	6448	70	71.9	132

$50 - $65

WHAT TO EXPECT: This is an old-school course. With mature trees framing the fairways, natural rolling terrain, and smallish but straightforward greens, Annadale offers no hidden agendas.
DIRECTIONS: From downtown Los Angeles (about 11 miles northeast to the course): Take Pasadena Freeway (I-110) north. Exit at 64th and Marmion Way. Immediately loop over the freeway and go north on 64th. When it dead-ends at Colorado, turn right, then turn left on San Rafael.

BROOKSIDE GOLF CLUB (public, 36 holes, william p. bell) . . . .

1133 North Rosemont Avenue
Pasadena, CA 91103
(626) 796-8151
americangolf.com

	YARDAGE	PAR	RATING	SLOPE
FRONT	6120	72	74.7	128
MIDDLE	6732	72	72.0	123
BACK	7037	72	73.6	128

$30 - $40

WHAT TO EXPECT: The C.W. Koiner Course features traditional styling and long par 4s, making this one of the best municipal tests in the Los Angeles area. Expect it to be crowded. The E.O. Nay Course is shorter and easier of the two, but shares the same attractive scenery and popularity.
NOTES: The yardage listed is for the C.W. Koiner Course.
DIRECTIONS: From downtown Los Angeles (about 12 miles northeast to the course): Take the Pasadena Freeway (I-110) north. Exit onto Orange Grove and turn left. Go about five miles and turn left on Rosemont Avenue.

EATON CANYON GOLF COURSE (public, 9 holes, william f. bell) . . . .

1150 North Sierra Madre Villa Avenue
Pasadena, CA 91107
(626) 794-6773

	YARDAGE	PAR	RATING	SLOPE	
FRONT	2563	35	69.3	114	**$13 - $15**
MIDDLE	2680	35	65.2	110	
BACK	2862	35	67.0	115	

WHAT TO EXPECT: The course heads downhill for the first two holes, then works it way back up the hill to the clubhouse. Tree-lined with lateral water hazards on two holes, Eaton Canyon requires accuracy around and on the greens. The greens tend to break away from the mountain.

DIRECTIONS: From downtown Los Angeles (about 17 miles northeast to the course): Take the Pasadena Freeway (I-110) north to I-210 east. Exit at Madre and head north one mile. Turn right on Sierra Madre Villa Avenue. There are signs.

RIVER RIDGE GOLF COURSE (public, 9 holes) . . . .

3260 Fairway Drive
Pico Rivera, CA 90660
(562) 692-9933

	YARDAGE	PAR	RATING	SLOPE	
FRONT	1300	29	-	-	**$7 - $8**
MIDDLE	-	-	-	-	
BACK	1529	29	-	-	

WHAT TO EXPECT: River Ridge is part pitch-and-putt, part executive course. There are two par 4s, but the rest are short par 3s.

DIRECTIONS: From downtown Los Angeles (about 14 miles east to the course): Take Highway 60 east to I-605 south. Exit at Beverly West (Rose Hills Road) and go straight off the exit. Turn right on Fairway Drive, to the course.

MOUNTAIN MEADOWS GOLF COURSE (public, 18 holes, william p. bell) . . . .

1875 Fairplex Drive
Pomona, CA 91768
(909) 623-3704
americangolf.com

	YARDAGE	PAR	RATING	SLOPE	
FRONT	5519	72	71.4	122	**$20 - $25**
MIDDLE	6113	72	68.7	113	
BACK	6440	72	70.4	120	

WHAT TO EXPECT: Constant elevations changes (hilly), large greens, and excellent mountain views characterize this golf course.

DIRECTIONS: From downtown Los Angeles (about 31 miles east to the course): Take I-10 east, exit onto Fairplex Drive, and head north to the course.

PALM LAKE GOLF COURSE (public, 9 holes) . . . .

1300 West Phillips Boulevard
Pomona, CA 91766
(909) 629-2852

	YARDAGE	PAR	RATING	SLOPE	
FRONT	-	-	-	-	**$6 - $7**
MIDDLE	-	-	-	-	
BACK	1044	27	-	-	

WHAT TO EXPECT: If you are looking for a challenge, try playing with only two clubs on this short par-3 course.

DIRECTIONS: From downtown Los Angeles (about 32 miles east to the course): Take Highway 60 east to Highway 71 north. Turn right at the light at Ninth Street. Take a quick right on Butterfield. Curve around and the course is on the right.

LOS VERDES GOLF COURSE (public, 18 holes, william f. bell 1964) . . . .

7000 West Los Verdes Drive
Rancho Palos Verdes, CA 90275
(310) 377-7888
americangolf.com

	YARDAGE	PAR	RATING	SLOPE
FRONT	5756	72	73.6	123
MIDDLE	6248	71	69.9	117
BACK	6626	71	71.7	122

$20 - $25

WHAT TO EXPECT: This L.A. County-owned layout is one of the best values in Southern California. A fun track with plenty of challenge from the tips, it features generally wide hitting areas, but several stout par-4 and par-3 holes. Its hilly terrain is walkable and affords many wonderful views of the ocean.

OUR OPINION: The back nine does have some astounding views of the ocean, but six hour rounds are not uncommon. Putting out fivesomes doesn't help. Course conditioning is inconsistent, not surprising since it's the busiest course in Southern California. – Andy

DIRECTIONS: From west Los Angeles (about 24 miles south to the course): Take the San Diego Freeway (I-405) south, exit at Hawthorne Boulevard south and head south about 13 miles into Palos Verdes. Just after passing Crest, turn right on Los Verdes Drive.

OCEAN TRAILS GOLF CLUB (public, 18 holes, pete dye 1999) . . . .

One Ocean Trails Drive
Rancho Palos Verdes, CA 90275
(877) 799-GOLF
oceantrails.com

	YARDAGE	PAR	RATING	SLOPE
FRONT	6056	72	68.9	133
MIDDLE	6369	72	70.3	138
BACK	6822	72	72.6	146

$150 - $220

WHAT TO EXPECT: This is the best 15-hole course in the world and soon to be an outstanding 18-hole layout. Dynamic ocean views, dramatic bunkering, and an interesting layout will soon make Ocean Trails a classic.

OUR OPINION: Ocean Trails offers amazing views of the Pacific Ocean on every hole. For a course set on only 110 acres, The club should allow walking. Not in the same class as Pete Dye's other L.A. course (Lost Canyons), due to a limited amount of land, but still a great golf experience. – Andy

DIRECTIONS: From downtown Los Angeles (about 27 miles south to the course): Take the Harbor Freeway (I-110) south until it ends. Turn left on Gaffey Street and right on First Street. Turn left on Western and then right on 25th. Go two and one-half miles to Ocean Trails Drive.

ROLLING HILLS COUNTRY CLUB (members only, 18 holes, ted robinson 1969) . . . .

27000 Palos Verdes Drive
Rolling Hills Estates, CA 90274
(310) 326-7731
rollinghillscc.com

	YARDAGE	PAR	RATING	SLOPE
FRONT	5432	70	73.3	131
MIDDLE	5809	70	67.9	119
BACK	6094	70	69.4	122

$75 - $100

WHAT TO EXPECT: The course was appropriately named. The fairways are rolling and tight, with lots of trees. The greens are large and undulating.

DIRECTIONS: From downtown Los Angeles (about 22 miles south to the course): Take the Harbor Freeway (I-110) south to the Pacific Coast Highway and head west. Turn left on Narbonne, which becomes Palos Verdes Drive. Follow Palos Verdes Drive to the club.

WHITTIER NARROWS GOLF COURSE (public, 27 holes, william f. bell) . . . .

8640 East Rush Street
Rosemead, CA 91770
(626) 288-1044
whittiernarrows.com

	YARDAGE	PAR	RATING	SLOPE	
FRONT	6294	72	73.6	113	**$20 - $25**
MIDDLE	6647	72	71.4	119	
BACK	6809	72	72.3	121	

WHAT TO EXPECT: Whittier Narrows has three nine-hole courses (Mountain, Pine, River) played in 18-hole combinations. The names given to each course are not necessarily a description. All three layouts are similar, although the Mountain Course greens tend to be a bit smaller. For the most part the courses are level and surrounded by trees, but allow players plenty of room to hit a driver. The greens are elevated on the smaller side and protected by sand.

NOTES: The yardage listed is for the River and Pines nines.

DIRECTIONS: From downtown Los Angeles (about 14 miles east to the course): Take Highway 60 east. Exit at San Gabriel Boulevard and make an immediate right on Walnut Grove. Turn right on Rush Street. alternatively, take I-10 east, exit at Walnut Grove, and turn right. Turn left on Rush Street.

SAN DIMAS CANYON GOLF COURSE (public, 18 holes, jeff brauer) . . . .

2100 Terrebonne Avenue
San Dimas, CA 91773
(909) 599-2313
americangolf.com

	YARDAGE	PAR	RATING	SLOPE	
FRONT	5546	74	73.0	127	**$23 - $32**
MIDDLE	5939	72	68.3	113	
BACK	6320	72	70.3	118	

WHAT TO EXPECT: Seventy-five-year-old men can shoot par here, while 25 year-old men struggle to break 100. Why? With narrow tree-lined fairways, rough that is constantly over two inches and a hilly back nine that creates uneven lies, the emphasis is on accuracy. Also, those 75-year-old men probably won't tell you, but the greens tend to break away from the mountains and will punish the player who leaves the ball above the hole.

DIRECTIONS: From downtown Los Angeles (about 33 miles east to the course): Take the Pasadena Freeway (I-110) north to the Foothill Freeway (I-210) east, almost to the end. Take the San Dimas Avenue exit and turn left. Turn right on Foothill Boulevard and left on San Dimas Canyon Road. Take a left on Terrebonne Avenue to the club.

VIA VERDE COUNTRY CLUB (members only, 18 holes, lawrence hughes) . . . .

1400 Avenida Entrada
San Dimas, CA 91773
(909) 599-8486
vvcountryclub.com

	YARDAGE	PAR	RATING	SLOPE	
FRONT	5729	72	74.6	130	**$35 - $55**
MIDDLE	6215	72	69.3	120	
BACK	6433	72	70.9	124	

WHAT TO EXPECT: Barrancas throughout the course make accuracy a must. Although they don't create many forced carries, they create a severe punishment for the golfer who can't hit straight. The course roams through the hillside of a residential community. The quick, smaller greens will make two-putting a challenge for those who leave the ball above the hole.

DIRECTIONS: From downtown Los Angeles (about 33 miles east to the course): Take I-10 east, exit at Via Verde, and go left at the stop sign. Turn right onto Via Verde. Turn left on Avenida Entrada. Make another left at the fourth stop sign, to the club.

SAN GABRIEL COUNTRY CLUB (members only, 18 holes, norman macbeth) . . . .

411 East Las Tunas Drive
San Gabriel, CA 91776
(626) 287-6052

	YARDAGE	PAR	RATING	SLOPE	
FRONT	5615	73	73.8	131	**$45 - $60**
MIDDLE	6254	71	70.3	124	
BACK	6518	71	71.7	129	

WHAT TO EXPECT: An abundance of bunkers and trees make this older layout a challenge. Kikuyu grass in the fairways gives up little roll, making the holes play longer than the card would suggest.

DIRECTIONS: From downtown Los Angeles (about 13 miles east to the course): Take I-10 east, exit Del Mar, and head north. Turn right on Las Tunas. Turn left into the club. There is a left-hand turn lane.

ROBINSON RANCH (public, 36 holes, ted robinson sr. & jr.) . . . .

27734 Sand Canyon Road
Santa Clarita, CA 91351
(661) 252-7666
RobinsonRanchGolf.com

	YARDAGE	PAR	RATING	SLOPE	
FRONT	5408	72	72.2	126	**$95 - $130**
MIDDLE	6469	72	72.2	136	
BACK	6904	72	74.5	140	

WHAT TO EXPECT: The Mountain Course is not long, but is undulating and demands accuracy off the tee. The short hitter who can hit it straight will do well here. Well-placed bunkers and oak trees are everywhere. From the 11th tee, you get a bird's-eye view of the Valley Course. The Valley Course is almost 400 yards longer and classic in design, with lots of sage, chaparral and trees. From the back tees, this rolling layout is demanding. The last third of this course has been dubbed "Death Row."
OUR OPINION: The Valley is more pleasing than the Mountain Course. The Valley ends with five holes that will severely beat you down. Not as memorable as Lost Canyons and not as pleasing to the eye as Ocean Trails, it's in the same class. Robinson Ranch also has one of the better websites that we have seen. – Andy
NOTES: The yardage is for the Valley Course.
DIRECTIONS: From downtown Los Angeles (about 33 miles northwest to the course): Take the I-5 north to Highway 14. Take Highway 14 to Sand Canyon Road and head south. Turn left on Robinson Ranch Road to the course.

SOUTH GATE GOLF COURSE (public, 9 holes) . . . .

9615 Pinehurst Avenue
South Gate, CA 90280
(323) 357-9613

	YARDAGE	PAR	RATING	SLOPE	
FRONT	-	-	-	-	**$5 - $6**
MIDDLE	-	-	-	-	
BACK	1010	27	-	-	

WHAT TO EXPECT: With lots of trees to get in your way, this pitch-and-putt course has some bite.
DIRECTIONS: From downtown Los Angeles (about 12 miles southeast to the course): Take I-5 south to I-710 south, exit at Imperial and head west. Go north on Atlantic to Tweedy and then go west on Tweedy. Make a quick right on Pinehurst to the course.

ARROYO SECO GOLF COURSE (public, 18 holes, william b. johnson) . . . .

1055 Lohman Lane
South Pasadena, CA 91030
(323) 255-1506

	YARDAGE	PAR	RATING	SLOPE	
FRONT	-	-	-	-	**$8 - $12**
MIDDLE	-	-	-	-	
BACK	2185	54	-	-	

WHAT TO EXPECT: This is a par-3 course, where players can get around in around two and a half hours. The greens are usually in good shape.
OUR OPINION: There should be more of these courses. No, it's not Pebble Beach, and it doesn't pretend to be. This is a great place for beginners and a place where families can afford to play. – Shaw
DIRECTIONS: From downtown Los Angeles (about ten miles northeast to the course): Take the Pasadena Freeway (I-110) north. Turn right on Orange Grove, then right again on Mission. Stay in the right lane and continue straight. This leads right to the course.

STUDIO CITY GOLF COURSE (public, 9 holes) . . . .

4141 Whitsett Avenue
Studio City, CA 91604
(818) 761-3250

	YARDAGE	PAR	RATING	SLOPE
FRONT	-	-	-	-
MIDDLE	-	-	-	-
BACK	935	27	-	-

$6 - $8

WHAT TO EXPECT: For every pitch, there should be a putt.
DIRECTIONS: From downtown Los Angeles (about 12 miles northwest to the course): Take US 101 north, exit at Coldwater Canyon, and turn left. Turn left on Ventura Boulevard and then left on Whitsett Avenue.

CASCADES GOLF CLUB, THE (public, 18 holes, timm & cupp 1998) . . . .

16325 Silver Oaks Drive
Sylmar, CA 91342
(818) 833-8900
cascadesgolf.com

	YARDAGE	PAR	RATING	SLOPE
FRONT	5080	71	69.4	124
MIDDLE	5654	71	68.1	127
BACK	6611	71	72.6	139

$60 - $85

WHAT TO EXPECT: This is a very steep course with excellent greens (some with false fronts), and fairways that reward golfers with level lies. The front nine is packed in tight, and you will encounter an unusual hazard, power lines. The back nine is more spacious and provides an excellent test of your golf skills. Be conservative your first time out; lack of course knowledge can hurt your score.
OUR OPINION: A new course for under $100 with good service? What a novelty. The front nine is a little cramped, the back nine is solid. We recommend weekday play, or maybe an early nine hole tee time off the back. – Andy
DIRECTIONS: From west Los Angeles (about 24 miles north to the course): Take the San Diego Freeway (I-405) north to I-210 east. Exit at Yarnell Avenue and turn south. Make a right on Foothill Boulevard and another right on Balboa Boulevard. Make a right on Silver Oaks Drive. The entrance to the club is on the right.

EL CARISO GOLF COURSE (public, 18 holes, robert muir graves 1977) . . . .

13100 Eldridge Avenue
Sylmar, CA 91342
(818) 367-6157

	YARDAGE	PAR	RATING	SLOPE
FRONT	3540	62	58.9	87
MIDDLE	4065	62	59.7	92
BACK	4493	62	61.1	97

$17 - $22

WHAT TO EXPECT: There are no "gimme" holes on this level, executive course. With plenty of water, trees, and wind, just being on the fairway does not guarantee an easy shot to the green. The greens are flat, but they tend to break away toward the ocean.
DIRECTIONS: From west Los Angeles (about 24 miles north to the course): Take the San Diego Freeway (I-405) north to I-210 east. Take the Hubbard exit and head north. Turn right on Eldridge to the course.

BRAEMAR COUNTRY CLUB (members only, 36 holes, ted robinson 1963) ....

4001 Reseda Boulevard
Tarzana, CA 91357
(818) 345-6520
braemarclub.com

	YARDAGE	PAR	RATING	SLOPE	
FRONT	5360	71	72.2	132	**$50 - $70**
MIDDLE	5772	70	68.4	128	
BACK	6061	70	69.8	131	

WHAT TO EXPECT: The East Course is longer and more open. The West Course is shorter, but tighter. Both courses are hilly and golfers must traverse their way over and around barrancas, water, and small sloped greens. Homes around the course create out-of-bounds.

NOTES: The yardage listed is for the East Course.

DIRECTIONS: From downtown Los Angeles (about 21 miles northwest to the course): Take the Ventura Freeway (US 101) north to Reseda Boulevard exit. Turn left and drive about two and one-half miles, toward the Santa Monica Mountains, up the hill.

EL CABALLERO COUNTRY CLUB (members only, 18 holes, robert trent jones, sr.) ....

18300 Tarzana Drive
Tarzana, CA 91356
(818) 345-2221

	YARDAGE	PAR	RATING	SLOPE	
FRONT	5904	72	74.9	137	**$55 - $90**
MIDDLE	6418	71	70.9	125	
BACK	6830	71	73.2	132	

WHAT TO EXPECT: Tight, tree-lined fairways, fast greens, and water make this a challenging course tee to fairway and fairway to green.

DIRECTIONS: From downtown Los Angeles (about 21 miles northwest to the course): Take US 101 north, exit on Reseda Boulevard, and go south. After crossing Ventura Boulevard, turn left on Tarzana Drive. The club is on the right.

NEW HORIZONS GOLF COURSE (members only, 9 holes) ....

22727 Maple Avenue
Torrance, CA 90505
(310) 325-3080

	YARDAGE	PAR	RATING	SLOPE
FRONT	-	-	-	-
MIDDLE	-	-	-	-
BACK	1104	27	-	-

WHAT TO EXPECT: Expect to pitch and putt. Of course if you miss the green, expect to chip and putt.

DIRECTIONS: From west Los Angeles (about 17 miles south to the course): Take the San Diego Freeway (I-405) south, exit at Hawthorne Boulevard and turn right. Make a left on Sepulveda and then a right on Maple Avenue.

SEA AIRE GOLF COURSE (public, 9 holes) ....

22730 Lupine Drive
Torrance, CA 90503
(310) 316-9779

	YARDAGE	PAR	RATING	SLOPE	
FRONT	-	-	-	-	**$2 - $4**
MIDDLE	-	-	-	-	
BACK	1020	27	-	-	

WHAT TO EXPECT: This short chip-and-jab course is a great place for juniors to learn the game.

DIRECTIONS: From west Los Angeles (about 17 miles south to the course): Take the San Diego Freeway (I-405) south, exit at Hawthorne Boulevard and go south. Turn right on Sepulveda. Turn left on Reynolds and then left on Lupine Drive.

VERDUGO HILLS GOLF COURSE (public, 18 holes) . . . .

6433 La Tuna Canyon Road
Tujunga, CA 91042
(818) 352-3282

	YARDAGE	PAR	RATING	SLOPE
FRONT	-	-	-	-
MIDDLE	-	-	-	-
BACK	1805	54	-	-

$8 - $10

WHAT TO EXPECT: This is an attractive, rolling par-3 course with no sand or water.
DIRECTIONS: From downtown Los Angeles (about 18 miles north to the course): Take Highway 2 north to I-210 west. Take the Lowell exit and go straight. By continuing straight, this will run right into the course.

VALENCIA COUNTRY CLUB (members only, 18 holes, robert trent jones, sr. 1965) . . .

27330 North Tourney Road
Valencia, CA 91355
(661) 287-1880

	YARDAGE	PAR	RATING	SLOPE
FRONT	5702	74	74.4	133
MIDDLE	6723	72	72.8	123
BACK	7076	72	74.7	138

$75 - $100

WHAT TO EXPECT: This course is vintage Robert Trent Jones style, with long tees, and bold fairway and green bunkering. This solid layout is situated in the trees and requires good play to achieve par, but is not too difficult for the bogey golfer.
NOTES: Valencia Country Club hosted the 1998 Nissan Open. It is the current host of the SBC Senior Classic on the Senior PGA Tour.
DIRECTIONS: From downtown Los Angeles (about 33 miles north to the course): Take I-5 north to the Valencia Boulevard exit. Turn right at the first light, North Tourney Road. Go left to the club.

VALENCIA, THE GREENS AT (public, 27 holes, ted robinson 1999) . . . .

26501 McBean Parkway
Valencia, CA 91355
(661) 222-2900
thegreens.com

	YARDAGE	PAR	RATING	SLOPE
FRONT				
MIDDLE				
BACK				

$12 - $15

WHAT TO EXPECT: Imagine a spectacular island green with a waterfall. Imagine stepping up to the tee box and having to tee off with your putter, because that is what you will have to do here. The Greens at Valencia is a 27-hole putting course, complete with water and sand.
OUR OPINION: Do putting greens bore you? This is a great place to sharpen your putting skills while relieving the boredom of practicing on your local putting green. A must-play for the serious putter.
NOTES: Only 18 holes are used at one time.
DIRECTIONS: From downtown Los Angeles (about 33 miles north to the course): Drive north on I-5. Take the Valencia Boulevard exit and turn right. Make a left on McBean Parkway. The course is right across from the Valencia Town Center.

VISTA VALENCIA GOLF COURSE (public, 18 holes) . . . .

24700 West Trevino Drive
Valencia, CA 91355
(661) 253-1870
americangolf.com

	YARDAGE	PAR	RATING	SLOPE
FRONT	3758	64	64.1	103
MIDDLE	4064	64	60.5	102
BACK	4376	61	61.4	104

$20 - $28

WHAT TO EXPECT: With lots of trees, water, and traps, Vista Valencia is an executive course with a bite. The 11 par 3s demand accuracy. Miss the greens and you will have a difficult time getting up and down for par.
DIRECTIONS: From downtown Los Angeles (about 33 miles north to the course): Go north on I-5 and exit at Lyons Avenue. Travel east one-half mile and turn left on Wiley Canyon Road. Turn left on Tourney Road, then drive another one-half mile to make another left, onto Trevino Road. Drive yet another one-half mile to the course.

VAN NUYS GOLF COURSE (public, 27 holes) . . . .

6550 Odessa Avenue
Van Nuys, CA 91406
(818) 785-3685
vngc.org

	YARDAGE	PAR	RATING	SLOPE
FRONT	-	-	-	-
MIDDLE	-	-	-	-
BACK	1574	30	56.4	81

$7 - $16

WHAT TO EXPECT: Van Nuys has an 18-hole pitch-and-putt course and a nine-hole executive course. Both are excellent starter courses.
NOTES: Yardage listed is for the nine-hole executive course.
DIRECTIONS: From west Los Angeles (about 15 miles north to the course): Take the San Diego Freeway (I-405) north. Exit at Victory Boulevard and go west. Turn right on Odessa Avenue, to the course.

WOODLEY LAKES GOLF COURSE (public, 18 holes, ray goates) . . . .

6331 Woodley Avenue
Van Nuys, CA 91406
(818) 787-8163

	YARDAGE	PAR	RATING	SLOPE
FRONT	6224	72	74.6	120
MIDDLE	6523	72	70.3	111
BACK	6803	72	71.7	114

$20 - $25

WHAT TO EXPECT: Although there is water on seven holes, players will find the fairways large. The greens are expansive and straightforward.
DIRECTIONS: From west Los Angeles (about 15 miles north to the course): Take the San Diego Freeway (I-405) north. Exit at Victory and head west. Turn left on Woodley to the course.

PENMAR GOLF COURSE (public, 9 holes) . . . .

1233 Rose Avenue
Venice, CA 90291
(310) 396-6228

	YARDAGE	PAR	RATING	SLOPE
FRONT	2311	34	66.0	104
MIDDLE	2311	33	61.9	94
BACK	2496	33	63.4	99

$9 - $12

WHAT TO EXPECT: This is a short, easy-to-walk, nine-hole layout. Penmar is a favorite for beginners, seniors, and locals.

OUR OPINION: Tasty waves in the morning, a breakfast burrito on the Venice Beach boardwalk, and nine holes before lunch with the eccentric denizens of Venice. Do it a couple times and you'll see why longtime locals never travel east of the 405. Good for beginners. – Andy

DIRECTIONS: From west Los Angeles (about four miles southwest to the course): Take the San Diego Freeway (I-405) south, exit on Venice Boulevard, and head west. Turn right on Lincoln and then right on Rose Avenue.

LOS ANGELES ROYAL VISTA GOLF COURSE (semi-private, 27 holes, billy bell, jr. 1965)

20055 East Colima Road
Walnut, CA 91789
(909) 595-7441
larv.com

	YARDAGE	PAR	RATING	SLOPE
FRONT	5528	71	71.3	118
MIDDLE	5989	71	68.0	114
BACK	6589	71	70.6	121

$24 - $35

WHAT TO EXPECT: This club has three nine-hole courses, which make up three different 18-hole combinations. the East/North, North/South, and South/East. All the courses have moderate elevation changes, and plenty of mature trees line the fairways. Water comes into play on several holes, and many of the greens are elevated. There are quite a few doglegs, so tee-shot placement is key to scoring well.

NOTES: The yardage listed is for the East/North nines.

DIRECTIONS: From downtown Los Angeles (about 27 miles east to the course): Take Highway 60 east, exit onto Fairway Drive, and turn right. Drive one mile to Colima Drive and turn left. The entry is one-quarter mile on the left.

SOUTH HILLS COUNTRY CLUB (members only, 18 holes, william p. bell) . . . .

2655 South Citrus Avenue
West Covina, CA 91791
(626) 332-3222

	YARDAGE	PAR	RATING	SLOPE
FRONT	5603	72	73.4	133
MIDDLE	6301	72	77.7	142
BACK	6301	71	69.7	120

$50 - $50

WHAT TO EXPECT: Off the tee this is a narrow course with fairways bordered by trees. The front nine is flat, while the back nine has several elevation changes. There are two lakes and a pond that cover four holes. The greens are medium in size and range from crowned to sloping.

DIRECTIONS: From downtown Los Angeles (about 25 miles east to the course): Take I-10 east, past I-605. Take the Citrus Avenue exit and head south about one and one-half miles. The club is on the left.

WESTCHESTER GOLF COURSE (public, 15 holes) . . . .

6900 West Manchester Avenue
Westchester, CA 90045
(310) 649-9166
americangolf.com

	YARDAGE	PAR	RATING	SLOPE	
FRONT	-	-	-	-	
MIDDLE	-	-	-	-	$7 - $19
BACK	3470	53	-	-	

WHAT TO EXPECT: If you are about to tee off on the 16th, run like crazy, because you are probably in the middle of the street. Winchester lost three holes to airport construction, but has still thrived as a 15-hole, night-lit, executive course.

DIRECTIONS: From west Los Angeles (about eight miles south to the course): Take the San Diego Freeway (I-405) south, exit Manchester Avenue, and go west about three miles.

NORTH RANCH COUNTRY CLUB (members only, 27 holes, ted robinson 1975) . . . . . .

4761 Valley Spring Drive
Westlake Village, CA 91362
(818) 889-9421

	YARDAGE	PAR	RATING	SLOPE	
FRONT	5345	72	71.7	124	
MIDDLE	6407	72	70.7	125	$55 - $75
BACK	6879	72	73.1	130	

WHAT TO EXPECT: There are three nine-hole courses played in 18-hole combinations. They are the Valley, Oaks, and Lake Courses. The Valley and Oaks Courses were the original layout. They are both rolling courses with narrow landing areas, above-average-sized-greens, and several lateral water hazards. The Lake Course has 80 percent fewer oak tress, so it is more forgiving off the tee, but you will find water on five of the nine holes.

NOTES: The yardage listed is for the Oaks and Lakes nines.

DIRECTIONS: From downtown Los Angeles (about 41 miles northwest to the course): Head north on US 101, exit at Westlake Boulevard, and turn right (north). Turn right on Valley Spring Drive. Take a left at the first stop sign to enter.

WESTLAKE GOLF COURSE (public, 18 holes, ted robinson 1967) . . . .

4812 Lakeview Canyon Road
Westlake Village, CA 91361
(818) 889-0770

	YARDAGE	PAR	RATING	SLOPE	
FRONT	4641	67	66.0	111	
MIDDLE	4641	67	61.2	95	$21 - $31
BACK	5053	67	63.4	99	

WHAT TO EXPECT: Forget using your driver on many of the holes, just put it in the fairway and you will do ok. The course is flat, flanked by trees and has several lakes and views of the Santa Monica Mountains.

DIRECTIONS: From downtown Los Angeles (about 41 miles northwest to the course): Take US 101 north, exit at Lindero Canyon, and turn left. Turn right on Agoura Road and then right on Lakeview Canyon Road. The course is on the right.

CALIFORNIA COUNTRY CLUB (members only, 18 holes, william f. bell 1956) . . . .

1509 South Workman Mill Road
Whittier, CA 90601
(626) 968-4222

	YARDAGE	PAR	RATING	SLOPE
FRONT	6098	74	75.7	136
MIDDLE	6531	72	70.9	121
BACK	6804	72	72.7	128

$48 - $77

WHAT TO EXPECT: This is a traditional layout with spacious, tree-lined fairways and smaller crowned greens. From morning to afternoon, the wind will change directions from west to east.

NOTES: Reciprocal play with other members only clubs is allowed.

DIRECTIONS: The course is located about 17 miles east of downtown Los Angeles. Drive east on the Pomona Freeway (Highway 60). Take the Crossroads exit and go left. Turn left on Crossroads Parkway North and then make a right on Workman Mill Road. Turn left on Coleford to the club.

CANDLEWOOD COUNTRY CLUB (members only, 18 holes, mix 1928) . . . .

14000 Telegraph Road
Whittier, CA 90604
(562) 941-5310
candlewood.com

	YARDAGE	PAR	RATING	SLOPE
FRONT	5708	70	74.7	135
MIDDLE	5899	70	68.1	117
BACK	6177	70	69.3	120

$45 - $55

WHAT TO EXPECT: Candlewood dates back to the late 1920s. Extremely short by today's standards, this traditional course, with lots of trees and lateral water hazards, can cause problems for the golfer who tends to hit the ball long and wrong.

NOTES: Reciprocal play with other members only clubs is allowed.

DIRECTIONS: From downtown Los Angeles (about 18 miles southeast to the course): Take Highway 60 east to I-605 south. Exit on Telegraph Road and turn left (east). The club is down three to four miles, past Florence.

FRIENDLY HILLS COUNTRY CLUB (members only, 18 holes, james wilfred hines 1968)

8500 Villaverde Drive
Whittier, ca 90605
(562) 698-0331
friendlyhillscc.com

	YARDAGE	PAR	RATING	SLOPE
FRONT	5639	71	74.9	134
MIDDLE	6136	70	70.3	133
BACK	6412	70	71.5	136

$55 - $75

WHAT TO EXPECT: Located in the hills, this a short and demanding course where driver is rarely your best option. To score well here, you need to keep in the fairway and be skilled with your flat stick.

DIRECTIONS: From downtown Los Angeles (about 20 miles southeast to the course): Take Highway 60 east, exit onto Hacienda Boulevard and travel south for three miles. Turn right on Colima Road for two and one-quarter miles. Turn left on Mar Vista and then right on Villaverde Drive. The club is on the right.

HARBOR PARK GOLF COURSE (public, 9 holes, william f. bell) . . . .

1235 North Figueroa Place
Wilmington, CA 90744
(310) 549-4953

	YARDAGE	PAR	RATING	SLOPE
FRONT	3010	36	74.0	126
MIDDLE	3161	36	70.4	115
BACK				

$11 - $14

WHAT TO EXPECT: This nine-hole course has some spunk. Harbor Park has narrow fairways, water hazards, and tricky greens.

DIRECTIONS: From downtown Los Angeles (about 18 miles south to the course): Take the Harbor Freeway (I-110) south, and exit at Anaheim Street. Take an immediate right from the off-ramp onto Figueroa Place. The course is on the left.

WOODLAND HILLS COUNTRY CLUB (members only, 18 holes, william p. bell 1925) . .

21150 Dumetz Road
Woodland Hills, CA 91364
(818) 347-1476
woodlandhills.com

	YARDAGE	PAR	RATING	SLOPE
FRONT	5291	72	71.5	129
MIDDLE	5975	70	69.3	124
BACK	6217	70	70.5	126

$45 - $75

WHAT TO EXPECT: Woodland Hills is an undulating layout with narrow fairways outlined by trees. Although keeping the ball in the fairway is imperative, the greens are the real story. They are small quick and slope front to back. Short and demanding, this is a shot-maker's paradise.

DIRECTIONS: From downtown Los Angeles (about 25 miles northwest to the course): Take US 101 north. Take the Canoga exit and turn left, going under the freeway. Cross over Ventura Boulevard. Turn left at Dumetz Road. The club is on the right.

Inland Empire

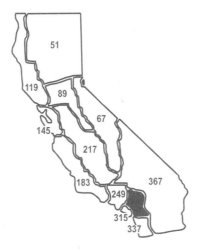

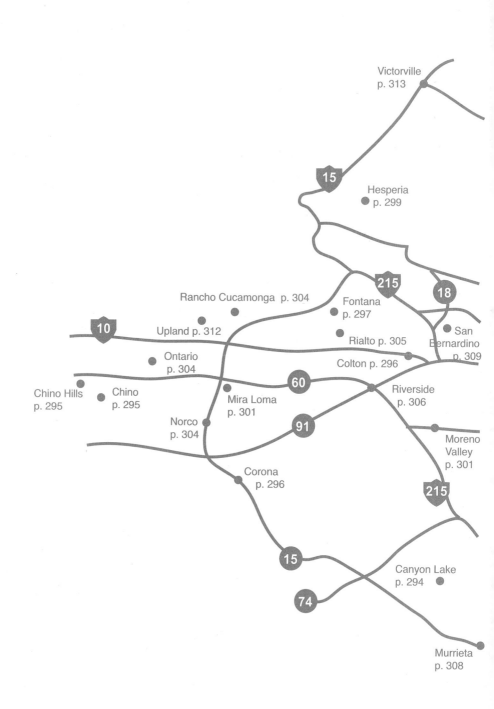

Victorville
p. 313

15

Hesperia
p. 299

215

18

Rancho Cucamonga p. 304

Fontana
p. 297

Upland p. 312

10

Rialto p. 305

San
Bernardino
p. 309

Ontario
p. 304

Colton p. 296

60

Chino Hills
p. 295

Chino
p. 295

Mira Loma
p. 301

Riverside
p. 306

Norco
p. 304

91

Moreno
Valley
p. 301

Corona
p. 296

215

15

Canyon Lake
p. 294

74

Murrieta
p. 308

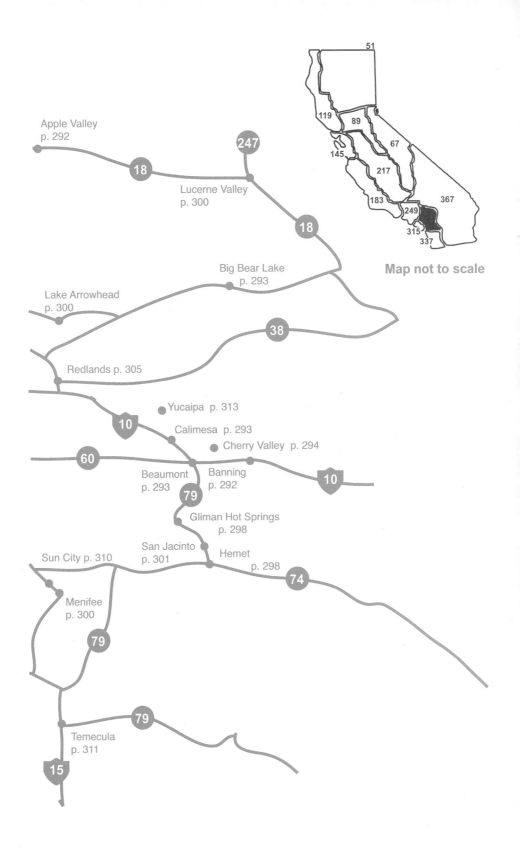

Apple Valley
p. 292

247

18

Lucerne Valley
p. 300

18

Big Bear Lake
p. 293

Lake Arrowhead
p. 300

38

Redlands p. 305

Yucaipa p. 313

10

Calimesa p. 293

Cherry Valley p. 294

60

Beaumont
p. 293

Banning
p. 292

79

10

Gliman Hot Springs
p. 298

San Jacinto
p. 301

Hemet
p. 298

Sun City p. 310

74

Menifee
p. 300

79

79

Temecula
p. 311

15

51

119

89

67

145

217

183

249

367

315

337

Map not to scale

APPLE VALLEY COUNTRY CLUB (members only, 18 holes, william f. bell 1949) . . . .

15200 Rancherias Road
Apple Valley, CA 92307
(760) 242-3125

	YARDAGE	PAR	RATING	SLOPE	
FRONT	5929	73	73.8	127	
MIDDLE	6477	71	70.5	119	**$41 - $57**
BACK	6805	71	72.3	123	

WHAT TO EXPECT: This is a flat course with tightly mowed, extensive fairways and hard, slick greens. Two lakes come into play.

DIRECTIONS: From San Bernardino (about 44 miles north to the course): Take I-15 north, and exit on D Street (Highway 18 east). Follow Highway 18 east about four miles; turn right on Rancherias Road.

JESS RANCH GOLF CLUB (public, 18 holes, david rainville) . . . .

10885 Apple Valley Road
Apple Valley, CA 92308
(760) 240-1800
americangolf.com

	YARDAGE	PAR	RATING	SLOPE	
FRONT	3699	65	61.8	101	
MIDDLE	4446	65	62.7	105	**$15 - $20**
BACK	4873	65	64.0	110	

WHAT TO EXPECT: This is a short course with views of the Southern California desert. There is water on seven holes.

DIRECTIONS: From San Bernardino (about 44 miles north to the course): Take I-15 north. Exit Bear Valley Road, and head east about eight miles. Turn right on Apple Valley Road to the course.

SUN LAKES COUNTRY CLUB (members only, 18 holes, david rainville) . . . .

850 South Country Club Drive
Banning, CA 92220
(909) 845-2135

	YARDAGE	PAR	RATING	SLOPE	
FRONT	5542	72	72.4	121	
MIDDLE	6523	72	71.0	120	**$50 - $50**
BACK	7006	72	73.6	129	

WHAT TO EXPECT: From the back tees, this is course stretches out to over 7,000 yards. A classic design, Sun Lakes throws no hidden punches, just good old-fashioned golf.

NOTES: Reciprocal play with other members only clubs is allowed.

DIRECTIONS: From San Bernardino (about 30 miles east to the course): Take I-10 east, exit onto Highland Springs and go south. Turn left at the stop sign (Sun Lakes) and then make the first right. The club is on the left.

OAK VALLEY GOLF CLUB (public, 18 holes, landmark design 1993) . . . .

1888 Golf Club Drive
Beaumont, CA 92223
(909) 769-7200
oakvalleygolf.com

	YARDAGE	PAR	RATING	SLOPE
FRONT	5332	72	72.0	122
MIDDLE	6372	72	71.0	131
BACK	7003	72	74.0	138

$32 - $75

WHAT TO EXPECT: There is no gray area at Oak Valley. This is a links-style course with constant elevation changes that give you ample opportunity to keep it on the short grass. However, if you miss the fairways, chances are you will never find your ball among the natural surroundings. If you can't handle the wind, early mornings would be your best bet.

OUR OPINION:

DIRECTIONS: From San Bernardino (about 26 miles east to the course): Take I-10 east, exit at Oak Valley Parkway, and turn left. Make the first left on Golf Club Drive.

BEAR MOUNTAIN GOLF COURSE (public, 9 holes) . . . .

43101 Goldmine Street
Big Bear Lake, CA 92315
(909) 585-8002
bearmountain.com

	YARDAGE	PAR	RATING	SLOPE
FRONT	2208	36	65.2	107
MIDDLE	2601	35	64.2	105
BACK	2730	35	65.4	108

$22 - $35

WHAT TO EXPECT: If you cannot hit the ball straight, you will receive little advantage from the mountain location—7,000 feet above sea level. Instead, your ball will find itself among the many pine trees, homes, or in the creek. Although located in the mountains, the course is set in gently rolling hills and is easily walkable.

DIRECTIONS: From downtown Los Angeles (about 98 miles northeast to the course): Take I-10 east. Exit at Orange Avenue in Redlands. Turn left toward Highway 38. Turn right on Ligonia Avenue, which becomes Highway 38. Turn left at Highway 18, which turns into Big Bear Boulevard. Turn left on Moonridge Road. Follow the signs to Big Bear Mountain.

CALIMESA COUNTRY CLUB (public, 18 holes, william f. bell) . . . .

1300 South Third Street
Calimesa, CA 92320
(909) 795-2488

	YARDAGE	PAR	RATING	SLOPE
FRONT	5293	72	70.8	117
MIDDLE	5608	70	67.1	106
BACK	5970	70	68.3	115

$15 - $22

WHAT TO EXPECT: Short and tricky, Calimesa Country Club has more doglegs than a kennel. There are blind shots and lots of ups and downs. Mature trees, together with its canyon setting, make this a picturesque course.

DIRECTIONS: From downtown Los Angeles (about 73 miles east to the course): Head out east on I-10. Take the first Calimesa exit, County Line Road, and go left. Take a right on Third Street to the club.

PGA OF SOUTHERN CALIFORNIA AT OAK VALLEY (public, 36 holes, curley & schmidt) .

36211 Champions Drive
Calimesa, CA 92320
(877) PGA-2500
scpgagolf.com

	YARDAGE	PAR	RATING	SLOPE
FRONT	5169	72	70.9	130
MIDDLE	6803	72	73.4	136
BACK	7443	72	76.6	144

$50 - $75

WHAT TO EXPECT: There are two courses, the Champions and Legends Courses. The Champions Course is open, native in appearance, with rolling terrain and rugged bunkering. The Legends Course has constant elevation changes and is classic in design, with oak-studded fairways.

OUR OPINION: People in Los Angeles will sit in traffic for an hour to get some milk at the corner market and think nothing of it, yet driving anywhere that isn't right in Los Angeles seems too far. Make the drive, you will not be disappointed. – Brad

NOTES: The yardage listed is for the Legends Course.

DIRECTIONS: From downtown Los Angeles (about 73 miles east to the course): Take I-10 east to Calimesa. Exit at Cherry Valley and head south. Turn left at Desert Lawn. The entrance is just over a mile east.

CANYON LAKE GOLF CLUB (members only, 18 holes, ted robinson) . . . .

32001 Railroad Canyon Road
Canyon Lake, CA 92587
(909) 246-1782

	YARDAGE	PAR	RATING	SLOPE
FRONT	5153	71	72.0	131
MIDDLE	5708	71	67.6	117
BACK	5949	71	68.7	121

$35 - $35

WHAT TO EXPECT: Leave the driver in the bag; this is a short course with several blind shots to small greens. Play with someone you trust; this layout is all about course knowledge.

NOTES: Reciprocal play with other members only clubs is allowed.

DIRECTIONS: From downtown Los Angeles (about 75 miles southeast to the club): Take Highway 60 east to I-15 south. Take the Railroad Canyon Road exit and turn left. The club is on the left. Go to the light, just past the club, and make a U-turn.

HIGHLAND SPRINGS VILLAGE GOLF COURSE (members only, 9 holes) . . . .

10370 1/2 Chisholm Trail
Cherry Valley, CA 92223
(909) 845-3060

	YARDAGE	PAR	RATING	SLOPE
FRONT	-	-	-	-
MIDDLE	-	-	-	-
BACK	1654	28	56.1	94

$4 - $8

WHAT TO EXPECT: This is basically a par-3 course, except for one hole. With that said, the par 3s here are not that easy. Five of the eight are over 170 yards.

DIRECTIONS: From San Bernardino (about 25 miles east to the course): Take I-10 east. Exit at Highland Springs Avenue and head north three miles. Turn left on Cherry Valley and then right to the course.

EL PRADO GOLF COURSES (public, 36 holes, harry rainville) . . . .

6555 Pine Avenue
Chino, CA 91710
(909) 597-1753

	YARDAGE	PAR	RATING	SLOPE
FRONT	5596	72	72.1	121
MIDDLE	6296	72	69.3	114
BACK	6617	72	71.5	119

$24 - $32

WHAT TO EXPECT: The Butterfield Stage course is much more patient with the erratic golfer. It has more water than the Chino Creek Course, but is not as long and more forgiving. The Chino Creek Course is the more challenging of the two layouts. The course requires accuracy off the tee, due to numerous trees, a creek, and out-of-bounds.
NOTES: The yardage listed is for the Chino Creek Course.
DIRECTIONS: From downtown Los Angeles (about 37 miles east to the course): Take the Pomona Freeway (Highway 60) east to Highway 71 south. Exit on Euclid and turn left. Turn left again on Pine Avenue. Resist the temptation to take the Pine exit. Trust us.

LOS SERRANOS COUNTRY CLUB (public, 36 holes, dunn 1925, kramer & eaton 1964)

15656 Yorba Avenue
Chino Hills, CA 91709
(909) 597-1711
losserranoscountryclub.com

	YARDAGE	PAR	RATING	SLOPE
FRONT	5954	74	73.9	128
MIDDLE	7104	74	74.0	134
BACK	7470	74	76.1	135

$23 - $43

WHAT TO EXPECT: These scenic courses have punished many golfers over the years. Unfortunately, due to disease, over 3,000 trees have been eliminated, with more to come. The South Course is a par 74 and features six par 5s, constant elevation changes, and can be breezy. The North Course is much shorter and less demanding.
NOTES: The yardage listed is for the South Course.
DIRECTIONS: From downtown Los Angeles (about 34 miles east to the course): Take Highway 60 east to Highway 71 south. Exit onto Central Avenue and turn right. Make another right on Los Serranos to the club.

WESTERN HILLS GOLF & COUNTRY CLUB (members only, 18 holes, david rainville) . .

1800 Carbon Canyon Road
Chino Hills, CA 91709
(714) 528-6400

	YARDAGE	PAR	RATING	SLOPE
FRONT	5882	72	75.9	136
MIDDLE	6401	72	71.0	128
BACK	6746	72	72.8	132

$35 - $60

WHAT TO EXPECT: Located in the Carbon Canyon, the front nine is tight and changes elevation constantly. The back nine is more forgiving.
DIRECTIONS: From downtown Los Angeles (about 34 miles east to the course): Take I-10 east to Highway 71 south. Take the Chino Hills Parkway and turn right. Turn left on Carbon Canyon Road/142. The club is on the right.

COLTON GOLF CLUB (public, 18 holes, robert trent jones, sr.) . . . .

1901 West Valley Boulevard
Colton, CA 92324
(909) 877-1712

	YARDAGE	PAR	RATING	SLOPE
FRONT	-	-	-	-
MIDDLE	-	-	-	-
BACK	3109	57	54.2	82

$10 - $20

WHAT TO EXPECT: This is a roomy course with small greens and water coming into play on two holes. Play to the middle of the greens and life will be good. Well, maybe not life, but at least your score.

NOTES: This course was once known as Sam Snead Golf Club. The legendary golfer used to visit and play often, giving lessons to the young children.

DIRECTIONS: From downtown Los Angeles (about 55 miles east to the course): Go east on I-10, exit on Riverside Avenue, and turn left. Turn right on Valley Boulevard. The course is on the left.

CRESTA VERDE GOLF CLUB (public, 18 holes, michael scott 1927) . . . .

1295 Cresta Road
Corona, CA 92879
(909) 737-2255

	YARDAGE	PAR	RATING	SLOPE
FRONT	5003	72	69.7	115
MIDDLE	5454	71	65.3	102
BACK	5822	71	67.3	111

$17 - $28

WHAT TO EXPECT: Slicers and lefties who duck-hook beware, the fairways are rolling and ample, but most of the out-of-bounds runs along the right side of the course.

DIRECTIONS: From Riverside (about 12 miles southwest to the course): Take Highway 91 west to I-15 north. Exit at Hidden Valley Parkway and head east. Go one mile and turn right on Parkridge. Then go another mile to turn left on Cresta Road. Turn left into the club.

EAGLE GLEN GOLF CLUB (public, 18 holes, gary roger baird 1999) . . . .

1800 Eagle Glen Parkway
Corona, CA 92883
(909) 272-4653
troongolf.com

	YARDAGE	PAR	RATING	SLOPE
FRONT	4998	72	67.7	113
MIDDLE	6290	72	69.7	121
BACK	6931	72	73.0	129

$60 - $115

WHAT TO EXPECT: Eagle Glen is a scenic, well-conditioned course featuring elevation changes along the fairways and on the greens. The fairways are wide, accommodating golfers who don't have complete control of their oversized, stiff-shafted, $600 drivers.

OUR OPINION: The course is great fun, but the last three golfers who attempted to walk this course have not been back seen since. Ok, that's a lie, but this is not a course where any sane individual would want to carry his bag. – Andy

NOTES: The course has the largest all-grass driving range in Southern California.

DIRECTIONS: From Riverside (about 17 miles southwest to the course): Take Highway 91 west to I-15 south. Exit on Cajalco Road and go right up the hill. Go about two miles and follow the signs to the clubhouse.

GREEN RIVER GOLF CLUB (public, 36 holes, lawrence hughes) . . . .

5215 Green River Road
Corona, CA 92880
(714) 970-8411

	YARDAGE	PAR	RATING	SLOPE	
FRONT	5717	72	72.8	125	**$30 - $37**
MIDDLE	6256	72	70.0	124	
BACK	6470	72	71.1	126	

WHAT TO EXPECT: There are two courses, the Orange and the Riverside. The Santa Ana River runs through both courses about nine times. The Orange Course, with its tighter tree-lined fairways, is the more challenging of the two courses. The Riverside Course features rolling terrain and many elevated greens.
NOTES: The yardage listed is for the Orange Course.
DIRECTIONS: From Riverside (about 15 miles southwest to the course): Take Highway 91 west. Exit at Green River Road and head north about a mile.

MOUNTAIN VIEW COUNTRY CLUB (public, 18 holes, william f. bell 1958) . . . .

2121 Mountain View Drive
Corona, CA 92882
(909) 737-9798

	YARDAGE	PAR	RATING	SLOPE	
FRONT	5432	72	71.7	120	**$34 - $45**
MIDDLE	6167	72	70.0	126	
BACK	6433	72	70.9	129	

WHAT TO EXPECT: The player who can pitch and putt will score well at Mountain View. Most of the greens are small, quick, and elevated. The fairways are narrow, tree lined and framed by homes. The back nine features a lot more elevation than the front.
NOTES: Once a private club, the course was nicknamed "home of the pros", because many professional golfers used to live near the course.
DIRECTIONS: From Riverside (about 15 miles southwest to the course): Take Highway 91 west. Exit at Serfas Club Drive and go south. Take the first left on Pinecrest and then an immediate left on Mountain View Drive.

SIERRA LAKES GOLF CLUB (public, 18 holes, ted robinson 2000) . . . .

16600 Clubhouse Road
Fontana, CA 92336
(909) 350-2500
sierralakes.com

	YARDAGE	PAR	RATING	SLOPE	
FRONT	6090	72	69.7	117	**$38 - $62**
MIDDLE	6435	72	71.2	121	
BACK	6806	72	73.0	125	

WHAT TO EXPECT: This is a very broad course where you seldom get an even lie. Errant tee shots will find the fairways due to a half-pipe effect on many of the fairways. There are palm trees on the course, but strong winds in the afternoon will cause problems for even the low handicapper.
OUR OPINION: If you put this course in Orange County, the rates would be double. Sierra Lakes is well worth playing. – Andy
DIRECTIONS: From downtown Los Angeles (about 50 miles east to the course): Take I-10 east to I-15 north. Exit onto Summit Avenue and turn left (east). Go about two miles to Clubhouse Drive. Turn right and go to the end of the street.

GOLDEN ERA GOLF COURSE (public, 9 holes) . . . .

19871 Highway 79
Gilman Hot Springs, CA 92583
(909) 654-0130
book4golf.com

	YARDAGE	PAR	RATING	SLOPE
FRONT	3004	36	72.1	128
MIDDLE	3004	36	73.4	130
BACK	3004	36	68.8	116

$18 - $32

WHAT TO EXPECT: This is an easily walkable course, set at the base of the mountains. Although there are plenty of trees along the way, the fairways are driver friendly. If you have golf balls that tend to gravitate toward water, beware. From the fourth hole on, you will encounter water on all but one hole.
DIRECTIONS: From Riverside (about 29 miles southeast to the club): Take Highway 60 east. Take Highway 79 (Gilman Road) south for about 12 miles to the course.

ARROYO FAIRWAYS MOBILE HOME CLUB & GOLF COURSE (members only, 11 holes) . . .

42751 East Florida
Hemet, CA 92544
(909) 927-1610

	YARDAGE	PAR	RATING	SLOPE
FRONT	-	-	-	-
MIDDLE	-	-	-	-
BACK	1114	27	-	-

$3 - $4

WHAT TO EXPECT: This par-3 course allows members to play an additional two holes.
DIRECTIONS: From Riverside (about 40 miles southeast to the course): Take I-215 south. Go east on Highway 74, into Hemet. Florida and Highway 74 are the same. The course is between Lake and New Chicago.

COLONIAL COUNTRY CLUB (members only, 18 holes) . . . .

601 North Kirby Street
Hemet, CA 92545
(909) 925-2664

	YARDAGE	PAR	RATING	SLOPE
FRONT	2046	54	-	-
MIDDLE	-	-	-	-
BACK	2420	54	-	-

$9 - $16

WHAT TO EXPECT: If you are looking up this course solely for the purpose of reading a course description, you are the definition of a golf addict.
DIRECTIONS: From Riverside (about 40 miles southeast to the course): Take I-215 south. Go east on Highway 74 into Hemet. Turn left on Kirby Street.

DIAMOND VALLEY GOLF CLUB (public, 18 holes, magnuson & martin 1999) . . . .

31220 Sage Road
Hemet, CA 92543
(909) 767-0828
diamondvalleygolf.com

	YARDAGE	PAR	RATING	SLOPE
FRONT	5313	72	70.5	124
MIDDLE	6118	72	70.2	128
BACK	6721	72	73.0	135

$20 - $60

WHAT TO EXPECT: If you arrive a half hour before your tee time and can't decide between the range and the putting green, choose the putting green. The course uses the natural, rolling terrain to create a layout that is not long, but challenges your shot making, golf management, and patience. The greens are undulating and fast, and if you miss off the edges, getting up and down will be no easy task.
DIRECTIONS: From San Bernardino (about 48 miles southeast to the course): Take I-10 east to Highway 79 south. Highway 79 turns into Sanderson. Turn left on Domenigoni and then right on State. There are signs from there.

ECHO HILLS GOLF CLUB (public, 9 holes) . . . .

545 East Thornton Avenue
Hemet, CA 92543
(909) 652-2203

	YARDAGE	PAR	RATING	SLOPE
FRONT	-	-	-	-
MIDDLE	-	-	-	-
BACK	2229	35	58.4	92

$7 - $10

WHAT TO EXPECT: This is a scenic course with plenty of oaks and other trees crowding the fairways.
DIRECTIONS: From Riverside (about 40 miles southeast to the course): Take I-215 south. Then take Highway 74 east, toward Hemet. Turn left on Santa Fe and then right on Thornton Avenue.

SEVEN HILLS GOLF CLUB (public, 18 holes, harry rainville) . . . .

1537 South Lyon Avenue
Hemet, CA 92545
(909) 925-4815

	YARDAGE	PAR	RATING	SLOPE
FRONT	5416	72	70.6	115
MIDDLE	6312	72	69.0	113
BACK	6557	72	70.2	116

$18 - $25

WHAT TO EXPECT: This course is level, in a park-like setting with friendly tree-lined fairways. Water comes into play on a few holes. The course can be managed by golfers of all skill levels.
DIRECTIONS: From Riverside (about 40 miles southeast to the course): Take I-10 east to Highway 79 south. Go through the town of Hemet and turn left on Stetson. Turn right on Lyon Avenue, to the course.

HESPERIA GOLF & COUNTRY CLUB (semi-private, 18 holes, william f. bell 1955) . . . .

17970 Bangor Avenue
Hesperia, CA 92345
(760) 244-9301
hesperiagolf.com

	YARDAGE	PAR	RATING	SLOPE
FRONT	6136	72	74.5	128
MIDDLE	6695	72	71.9	128
BACK	6996	72	73.5	131

$20 - $25

WHAT TO EXPECT: From the back tees this is a tough course; the desert lines the right side of the fairways and trees line the left. The greens are small and well protected by traps. To take your mind off your score, you will encounter an abundance of wildlife, including coyotes and 700 different types of birds.
NOTES: From 1957 to 1963, this course played host to a PGA Tour event.
DIRECTIONS: From San Bernardino (about 34 miles north to the course): Take I-15 north, into Hesperia. Take Main Street and turn right. Make another right on I Avenue. Turn left on Bangor Avenue, to the club.

LAKE ARROWHEAD COUNTRY CLUB (members only, 18 holes, william f. bell) . . . . . .

250 Golf Course Road
Lake Arrowhead, CA 92352
(909) 337-3515
lakearrowheadcc.com

	YARDAGE	PAR	RATING	SLOPE	
FRONT	4933	73	69.9	128	**$75 - $75**
MIDDLE	6035	71	68.5	125	
BACK	6231	71	69.6	128	

WHAT TO EXPECT: The front nine is fairly open, with plenty of water in the form of lakes and streams. The back nine is a mountain course with many trees and drop-offs that will come into play for the golfer who can't hit it straight. You will find some excellent views of the surrounding area along the way.

DIRECTIONS: From downtown Los Angeles (about 90 miles northeast to the course): Go I-10 east to I-215 north and exit onto Highway 30 (Mountain Resorts). Go to Highway 18 (Waterman Avenue) and turn left. Go through Rimforest to Blue Jay and bear left. At the stop sign, turn left. Go to Grass Valley Road and bear right, staying on Grass Valley Road. Turn left on Golf Course Road.

LEGENDS GOLF CLUB AT RANCHO LUCERNE (public, 27 holes, david edsall 2001) . . . .

33400 Rabbit Springs Road
Lucerne Valley, CA 92356
(760) 955-5976
rancholucerne.com

	YARDAGE	PAR	RATING	SLOPE
FRONT	-	-	-	-
MIDDLE	-	-	-	-
BACK	-	-	-	-

WHAT TO EXPECT: Scheduled to open in Fall 2001, the course will incorporate holes from famous golf courses throughout the world.

NOTES: The course will be part of a recreational area.

DIRECTIONS: Directions were not available at time of press. Please check our website, www.InTheLoopGolf.com for updates.

MENIFEE LAKES COUNTRY CLUB (semi-private, 27 holes, ted robinson 1989) . . . .

29875 Menifee Lakes Drive
Menifee, CA 92584
(909) 672-3090
menifee-lakes.com

	YARDAGE	PAR	RATING	SLOPE	
FRONT	6001	72	68.0	115	**$24 - $58**
MIDDLE	5368	72	71.5	120	
BACK	6393	72	70.5	120	

WHAT TO EXPECT: The three nine-hole courses are the Lakes, Falls, and Palms. Water plays a prominent role on all three nines. You will find the fairways snug and the traps well positioned for errant shots. Accurate left-to-right shots come in handy on all three courses.

NOTES: Carts are included in the price of green fees. The yardage listed is for the Palms/Lakes Course.

DIRECTIONS: From downtown Los Angeles (about 83 miles southeast to the club): Take Highway 60 east to I-15. Drive south to the Railroad Canyon Road exit. Turn left and travel five miles to Newport Road. Turn right on Newport Road for about five and one-half miles. Make a left on Menifee Lakes Drive and follow it to the clubhouse.

COUNTRY VILLAGE GOLF COURSE, THE (members only, 9 holes) . . . .

10301 Country Club Drive
Mira Loma, CA 91752
(909) 685-7466

	YARDAGE	PAR	RATING	SLOPE	
FRONT	878	27	-	-	**$5 - $5**
MIDDLE	-	-	-	-	
BACK	1073	27	-	-	

WHAT TO EXPECT: At a little over 1,000 yards from the back tees, expect your short game to get a workout.
DIRECTIONS: From downtown Los Angeles (about 47 miles east to the course): Take Highway 60 east, past I-15. Exit at Country Village Road and turn left back over the freeway. Turn left at the guardhouse into Country Village.

GOOSE CREEK GOLF CLUB (public, 18 holes, brian curley 1999) . . . .

11418 68th Street
Mira Loma, CA 91752
(909) 735-3982

	YARDAGE	PAR	RATING	SLOPE	
FRONT	5052	72	69.4	115	**$40 - $60**
MIDDLE	6128	70	69.4	121	
BACK	6521	70	71.1	127	

WHAT TO EXPECT: Goose Creek has dual personalities. The front nine plays through a marsh, and is a risk-and-reward course where golfers have several options to hitting into the greens. The back nine is much longer and straightforward. You finish your round with a 466-yard par 4 around a lake. All the greens have subtle breaks.
OUR OPINION: Good service makes this course a welcome addition to the Riverside County golf scene. – Bob
DIRECTIONS: From Riverside (about 10 miles west to the course): Take Highway 60 west to I-15 south. Exit at Limonite and turn left. Take the first right on Wineville. When Wineville ends, there is a choice of either a sharp left or an oblique left. Take the oblique left on 68th Street, to the course.

LJS GOLF CLUB (public, 9 holes) . . . .

13671 Frederick Street
Moreno Valley, CA 92553
(909) 413-3290

	YARDAGE	PAR	RATING	SLOPE	
FRONT	-	-	-	-	**$4 - $10**
MIDDLE	-	-	-	-	
BACK	1189	28	-	-	

WHAT TO EXPECT: LJS is a pitch-and-putt course with one par 4.
DIRECTIONS: From Riverside (about 11 miles east to the course): Take Highway 60 east. Exit at Frederick Street and turn right (south). It is on the right side, after the fifth light.

MORENO VALLEY RANCH GOLF COURSE (public, 27 holes, pete dye 1988) . . . .

28095 John F. Kennedy Drive
Moreno Valley, CA 92555
(909) 924-4444
mvrgolf.com

	YARDAGE	PAR	RATING	SLOPE	
FRONT	5264	72	70.1	122	**$25 - $65**
MIDDLE	6497	72	71.5	129	
BACK	6930	72	74.1	138	

WHAT TO EXPECT: Moreno Valley has three courses, the Mountain, Valley, and Lake Courses. There are some very demanding, scary holes at this 27-hole complex, which includes lakes, flat and mountainous terrain, and fast, sloping greens. Accuracy off the tee is a must.

OUR OPINION: We were invited to play Moreno Valley several times over the past few years but because of scheduling difficulties we were not able too. When we finally could play the courses, a new manager had taken over and was not only rude but uninvited us. Being uninvited is not uncommon but being rude is just bad for business. What goes around comes around. So we played these courses. And as much as we would like to say bad things about them, we can't. These are fun and rugged layouts, well worth the price of admission. Oh well, maybe next time. – The mole.

NOTES: The course was home to a Nike Tour event for several years. The yardage listed is for the Lake/Valley nines.

DIRECTIONS: From Riverside (about 15 miles east to the course): Take Highway 60 east. Exit at Moreno Beach Drive and turn right to head south. Turn left on John F. Kennedy Drive.

QUAIL RANCH GOLF CLUB (public, 18 holes, desmond muirhead) . . . .

15960 Gilman Springs Road
Moreno Valley, CA 92555
(909) 654-2727

	YARDAGE	PAR	RATING	SLOPE	
FRONT	5320	71	71.9	122	**$20 - $45**
MIDDLE	6191	72	70.4	129	
BACK	6842	72	73.4	135	

WHAT TO EXPECT: Carved out of the badlands, this course features hilly, open terrain with water hazards that come into play on six holes. To score well at Quail Ranch, you need to be aware that the greens are undulating and tricky. The ball tends to be pulled back to the west.

DIRECTIONS: From Riverside (about 15 miles east to the course): Take Highway 60 east. Take the Hemet/San Jacinto exit and go south about four miles on Gilman Springs Road.

BEAR CREEK GOLF CLUB (members only, 18 holes, jack nicklaus) . . . .

22640 Bear Creek Drive North
Murrieta, CA 92562
(909) 677-8631
bearcreekgc.com

	YARDAGE	PAR	RATING	SLOPE	
FRONT	5230	72	72.3	134	**$55 - $65**
MIDDLE	6422	72	71.8	135	
BACK	6985	72	74.7	141	

WHAT TO EXPECT: This is one of Jack Nicklaus's early designs in California. Water, strategically placed trees, bunkers and large, deceptive greens compose a complete challenge.

DIRECTIONS: From downtown Los Angeles (about 80 miles southeast to the club): Take I-10 east to I-15 south. Exit at Clinton Keith Road and turn right. The entrance is on the right after about one and one-half miles.

COLONY COUNTRY CLUB, THE (public, 18 holes, david rainville) . . . .

40603 Colony Drive
Murrieta, CA 92562
(909) 677-2221

	YARDAGE	PAR	RATING	SLOPE	
FRONT	3843	65	62.0	100	**$28 - $35**
MIDDLE	4308	65	60.5	104	
BACK	4649	65	62.3	108	

WHAT TO EXPECT: This is an executive-length golf course with a championship course attitude. With six lakes, narrow tree-lined fairways, and greens well protected by bunkers and other hazards, you will have to manage your game with great care. Players with an excessive left-to-right game will find trouble awaiting them on almost every hole.

DIRECTIONS: From downtown Los Angeles (about 80 miles southeast to the club): Take I-10 east to I-15 south. Exit at California Oaks Road and head east. Turn left on Jackson, and the course is on the right.

SCGA MEMBERS' CLUB (public, 18 holes, robert trent jones, sr.) . . . .

38275 Murrieta Hot Springs Road
Murrieta, CA 92563
(909) 677-7446
scgamembersclub.com

	YARDAGE	PAR	RATING	SLOPE	
FRONT	6294	72	71.0	128	**$45 - $75**
MIDDLE	6724	72	73.0	134	
BACK	7060	72	74.4	137	

WHAT TO EXPECT: The Members' Club is home of the Southern California Golf Association. This lengthy Robert Trent Jones Sr. layout features sculptured bunkers that guard both fairways and greens. Add in several lakes and large undulating greens, and you have a challenging course that will keep you coming back for more.

OUR OPINION: This is what reasonable golf was meant to be. – Bob

DIRECTIONS: From downtown Los Angeles (about 80 miles southeast to the club): Take I-10 east to I-15 south. Exit at Murrieta Hot Springs Road and turn left. Make the first left after Margarita, into the club.

HIDDEN VALLEY GOLF CLUB (public, 18 holes, casey o'callaghan 1999) . . . .

10 Clubhouse Drive
Norco, CA 92860
(909) 737-1010
hiddenvalleygolf.com

	YARDAGE	PAR	RATING	SLOPE
FRONT	4649	71	66.6	116
MIDDLE	6330	72	70.9	137
BACK	6722	72	73.3	140

$70 - $95

WHAT TO EXPECT: Though carts are essential because of dramatic elevation changes, the spectacular views make up for the fact that the course is not walker friendly. This is a target course, with rock outcroppings and small undulating greens.

OUR OPINION: If you are in the area, you are going to want to play this course. – Bob

DIRECTIONS: From Riverside (about 15 miles west to the course): Take Highway 60 west to I-15 south. Exit onto Hidden Valley Parkway, turn left, and head east about one and one-half miles. Turn left on Norco Hills Road. This leads to the course.

WHISPERING LAKES GOLF COURSE (public, 18 holes, william tucker, jr. 1950) . . . . . .

2525 Riverside Drive
Ontario, CA 91761
(909) 923-3673

	YARDAGE	PAR	RATING	SLOPE
FRONT	6006	72	73.0	118
MIDDLE	6310	72	69.0	114
BACK	6726	72	71.4	120

$12 - $23

WHAT TO EXPECT: This is a wide-open golf course with large greens and water that comes into play on several holes. There are plenty of opportunities to score well if you can make your approach shots count.

DIRECTIONS: From downtown Los Angeles (about 40 miles east to the course): Drive east on the Pomona Freeway (Highway 60) to Ontario. Exit at Vineyard Avenue. Go south to Riverside Drive and turn left to the club.

EMPIRE LAKES GOLF COURSE (public, 18 holes, arnold palmer 1996) . . . .

11015 Sixth Street
Rancho Cucamonga, CA 91730
(909) 481-6663
empirelakes.com

	YARDAGE	PAR	RATING	SLOPE
FRONT	5200	72	70.5	125
MIDDLE	6628	72	71.9	130
BACK	6923	72	73.4	133

$35 - $80

WHAT TO EXPECT: Arnold Palmer has created a relatively flat course that is interestingly mounded and bunkered. A strong accurate driver will make your round much more manageable.

OUR OPINION: Another worthy choice if you happen to be in the Inland Empire. With an abundant amount of competition in the region, it maybe a little pricey on weekends.

DIRECTIONS: From downtown Los Angeles (about 45 miles east to the course): Take I-10 east, exit at Haven, and turn left to head north. Turn right on Sixth Street and the course is on the right.

RED HILL COUNTRY CLUB (members only, 18 holes, george c. thomas) . . . .

8358 Red Hill Country Club Drive
Rancho Cucamonga, CA 91730
(909) 982-4559

	YARDAGE	PAR	RATING	SLOPE
FRONT	6019	74	75.6	137
MIDDLE	6463	72	70.9	123
BACK	6611	72	71.6	124

$50 - $50

WHAT TO EXPECT: Red Hill is a traditional, rolling, tree-lined layout with small, undulating greens. The course was designed by George Thomas, who is known for his work on such clubs as L.A. Country Club, Ojai, and Riviera Country Club.
DIRECTIONS: From downtown Los Angeles (about 45 miles east to the course): Take I-10 east, exit at Vineyards, and go north. Turn left on Red Hill Country Club Drive to the course.

REDLANDS COUNTRY CLUB (members only, 18 holes, alister mackenzie) . . . .

1749 Garden Street
Redlands, CA 92373
(909) 793-1295

	YARDAGE	PAR	RATING	SLOPE
FRONT	5738	73	73.7	127
MIDDLE	6082	70	68.9	118
BACK	6276	70	70.0	122

$50 - $60

WHAT TO EXPECT: This is a short, hilly course where course knowledge is key. The fairways are tree lined and narrow; the greens are small and some of the oldest in California.
NOTES: Reciprocal play with other members only clubs is allowed.
DIRECTIONS: From San Bernardino (about 12 miles east to the course): Take I-10 east, exit onto Ford Street, and go right for over two miles. Go left when it dead-ends at Garden Street.

EL RANCHO VERDE ROYAL VISTA GOLF CLUB (semi-private, 18 holes, rainville 1958) .

355 East Country Club Drive
Rialto, CA 92377
(909) 875-5346

	YARDAGE	PAR	RATING	SLOPE
FRONT	5563	72	72.0	124
MIDDLE	6596	72	71.3	122
BACK	6822	72	72.8	126

$16 - $42

WHAT TO EXPECT: This is a park-setting layout, with mature trees dotting the fairways on the front nine and orange groves on the back. A new lake has been added and now comes into play on the 11th hole. The greens are large and sloping. Three holes have out-of-bounds.
DIRECTIONS: From downtown Los Angeles (about 55 miles northeast to the course): Take I-10 east to I-15 and drive north. Take the Sierra Avenue off ramp. Make a right turn on Riverside Avenue and then a left on Country Club Drive.

CANYON CREST COUNTRY CLUB (members only, 18 holes, olin dutra 1968) . . . .

975 Country Club Drive
Riverside, CA 92506
(909) 274-7906
canyoncrestcc.com

	YARDAGE	PAR	RATING	SLOPE
FRONT	5855	72	74.9	130
MIDDLE	6267	72	70.2	121
BACK	6565	72	71.4	124

$37 - $57

WHAT TO EXPECT: Homes line this hilly course and create out-of-bounds on nearly every hole. The greens can create as much of a problem as the homes. The smart player will leave the ball below the hole if par or better is what they are after.
NOTES: Reciprocal play with other members only clubs is allowed.
DIRECTIONS: From within Riverside: Off Highway 60, exit at Martin Luther King and head west. Turn left on Canyon Crest Drive. After Central Avenue, the course can be seen to the right. Turn right on Country Club Drive.

EL RIVINO COUNTRY CLUB (public, 18 holes) . . . .

5530 El Rivino Road
Riverside, CA 92519
(909) 684-8905

	YARDAGE	PAR	RATING	SLOPE
FRONT	5863	73	71.8	116
MIDDLE	6132	73	69.0	111
BACK	6422	73	70.3	115

$20 - $33

WHAT TO EXPECT: El Rivino starts out with a 626-yard par six. If you can get past the first hole, you will find the rest of the course is not too long and relatively flat.
DIRECTIONS: From within Riverside: Off I-10, exit at Cedar Avenue and head south about three miles. Turn left on El Rivino Road.

FAIRMOUNT GOLF COURSE (public, 9 holes) . . . .

2681 Dexter Drive
Riverside, CA 92507
(909) 682-2202
fairmountgolfcourse.com

	YARDAGE	PAR	RATING	SLOPE
FRONT	-	-	-	-
MIDDLE	-	-	-	-
BACK	3126	36	69.1	108

$6 - $13

WHAT TO EXPECT: This is a flat course where each fairway is separated by trees.
DIRECTIONS: From within Riverside: Off Highway 60, exit on Market Street. Follow Market Street down to Dexter Drive to the course.

GENERAL OLD GOLF COURSE (public, 18 holes) . . . .

6104 Village West Drive
Riverside, CA 92518
(909) 697-6690

	YARDAGE	PAR	RATING	SLOPE
FRONT	5923	72	73.1	120
MIDDLE	6482	72	70.5	115
BACK	6757	72	71.9	118

$13 - $29

WHAT TO EXPECT: Except for four holes, this is a relatively level course with many doglegs, which favors the golfer who works the ball left to right. Water comes into play on four holes, and there are plenty of out-of-bounds and trees to keep you entertained – or frustrated.
DIRECTIONS: From within Riverside: Off I-215 south, exit at Van Buren and head west. Turn left on Village West Drive. The course is on the left.

INDIAN HILLS GOLF CLUB (public, 18 holes, harold heers) . . . .

5700 Club House Drive
Riverside, CA 92509
(909) 360-2090
indianhillsgolf.com

	YARDAGE	PAR	RATING	SLOPE	
FRONT	5562	72	72.5	120	**$25 - $47**
MIDDLE	5918	70	68.3	117	
BACK	6191	70	70.0	126	

WHAT TO EXPECT: This is a hilly course with homes lining both sides of the fairway and array of trees to keep your ball from reaching its final destination. The tee boxes are elevated, and the ball tends to kick toward the river, so missing the fairway on the wrong side could prove costly. There are two lakes that come into play.

DIRECTIONS: From within Riverside: Off the Pomona Freeway (Highway 60), exit at Pedley Street and go south about four to five miles. Turn left on Limonite and again left on Clay Street. Turn right on Lakeside and look for signs.

JURUPA HILLS COUNTRY CLUB (public, 18 holes, william f. bell) . . . .

6161 Moraga Avenue
Riverside, CA 92509
(909) 685-7214

	YARDAGE	PAR	RATING	SLOPE	
FRONT	5773	71	73.4	123	**$23 - $44**
MIDDLE	-	-	-	-	
BACK	6022	70	69.5	122	

WHAT TO EXPECT: Spend your pre-game warm-up on the putting green. The greens here provide the majority of the challenge; they are large, fast, and tricky to read. The fairways are rolling and forgiving, but a river and houses do create some hazards. Afternoon wind can increase the course difficulty.

DIRECTIONS: From within Riverside: Off Highway 60, take I-15 south. Exit at Limonite and head east about five and one-half miles. Turn right on Camino Real and then left when it dead-ends.

LANDMARK GOLF CLUB AT OAK QUARRY (public, 18 holes, schmidt-curley 2000) . . . .

7151 Sierra Avenue
Riverside, CA 92509
(909) 685-1440
oakquarry.com

	YARDAGE	PAR	RATING	SLOPE	
FRONT	5408	72	71.9	121	**$55 - $85**
MIDDLE	6500	72	71.9	133	
BACK	7003	72	73.9	137	

WHAT TO EXPECT: This stunning layout routes lush green fairways right through an old quarry. Landmark features steep-sided bunkering that can intimidate even the most confident golfer. The contrast of the white-faced mountains and natural surroundings with the green fairways is dramatic, but don't let it divert your attention. This is a challenging layout that makes you think on every shot.

OUR OPINION: Landmark at Oak Quarry is an inspiring layout. The contrast between the course and the old quarry is spectacular. This course is a must-play. – Bob

DIRECTIONS: From within Riverside: Off I-10, exit onto Sierra Avenue. Drive south a few miles to the club.

PARADISE KNOLLS GOLF COURSE (public, 18 holes) . . . .

9330 Limonite
Riverside, CA 92509
(909) 685-7034

	YARDAGE	PAR	RATING	SLOPE	
FRONT	5841	72	73.4	120	**$18 - $27**
MIDDLE	6050	72	68.6	113	
BACK	6278	72	69.6	116	

WHAT TO EXPECT: This is a popular course with lots of trees and fast greens. The front nine has parallel fairways, while the back nine is hilly.
DIRECTIONS: From within Riverside: Off Highway 60, take I-15 south. Exit onto Limonite and turn left. Drive about two and one-half miles, and the course is on the right.

RIVERSIDE GOLF COURSE (public, 18 holes, brunton/smith) . . . .

1011 North Orange Street
Riverside, CA 92501
(909) 682-3748

	YARDAGE	PAR	RATING	SLOPE	
FRONT	6262	72	74.8	120	**$17 - $22**
MIDDLE	6491	72	70.0	113	
BACK	6773	72	71.5	115	

WHAT TO EXPECT: The is an old muni course, built more for function than form. You will find wide fairways, mature trees, and flat greens.
DIRECTIONS: From within Riverside: Off Highway 91, exit onto Columbia Avenue and head west. Turn right on Orange Street, to the course.

VAN BUREN GOLF CENTER (public, 18 holes, murray nonhoff) . . . .

6720 Van Buren Boulevard
Riverside, CA 92503
(909) 688-2563
vanburengolf.com

	YARDAGE	PAR	RATING	SLOPE	
FRONT	-	-	-	-	**$14 - $15**
MIDDLE	-	-	-	-	
BACK	2644	57	-	-	

WHAT TO EXPECT: The course is part of a learning center dedicated to the education and instruction of junior golfers and first-time golfers. The course is made up of mostly par 3s, but does have four par 4s.
DIRECTIONS: From within Riverside: Off Highway 60, exit at Limonite and head east. Turn right on Van Buren Boulevard to the course.

VICTORIA CLUB (members only, 18 holes, charles e. maud 1903) . . . .

2521 Arroyo Drive
Riverside, CA 92506
(909) 684-5035

	YARDAGE	PAR	RATING	SLOPE	
FRONT	5849	72	74.3	127	**$65 - $65**
MIDDLE	6256	72	70.2	128	
BACK	6483	72	71.3	130	

WHAT TO EXPECT: This is an old course, built around 1903. Set in a canyon, the course has rolling terrain and plays up and down. There is a ditch running throughout the course. The greens are good sized.
NOTES: Reciprocal play with other members only clubs is allowed.
DIRECTIONS: From within Riverside: Off Highway 91, exit at Central and head east about one and one-half miles. Turn left on Victoria and then right on Arroyo Drive to the club.

ARROWHEAD COUNTRY CLUB (members only, 18 holes) . . . .

3433 Parkside Drive
San Bernardino, CA 92404
(909) 882-1638
arrowheadcountryclub.org

	YARDAGE	PAR	RATING	SLOPE	
FRONT	5752	72	68.0	119	**$45 - $55**
MIDDLE	6252	72	70.2	124	
BACK	6588	72	71.8	127	

WHAT TO EXPECT: This is a parkland-style course set in the desert. The fairways are level and are surrounded by mature trees and rough. The greens are small, quick, and sloping.
DIRECTIONS: From downtown Los Angeles (about 65 miles east to the course): Take I-10 east, to I-215. Go north to Highway 30 and go east to Waterman. Exit at Waterman, and turn left (north). Turn right on Marshall, and then left into the parking lot.

PALM MEADOWS GOLF COURSE (public, 18 holes, william f. bell) . . . .

1964 East Palm Meadows Drive
San Bernardino, CA 92408
(909) 382-2002

	YARDAGE	PAR	RATING	SLOPE	
FRONT	5851	73	73.0	124	**$17 - $25**
MIDDLE	6404	72	70.4	120	
BACK	6674	72	71.5	124	

WHAT TO EXPECT: The advice from the pro shop is fairly straightforward: "Stay out of the trees if you want to make par." This is a level course with plenty of trees and some doglegs.
NOTES: The course was once part of the Norton Air Force Base.
DIRECTIONS: From downtown Los Angeles (about 60 miles east to the course): Take I-10 east, exit at Tippacanoe, and turn left. Go one and one-half miles and then turn right on Palm Meadows Drive.

SAN BERNARDINO GOLF COURSE (public, 18 holes, dan brown) . . . .

1494 South Waterman Avenue
San Bernardino, CA 92408
(909) 885-2414

	YARDAGE	PAR	RATING	SLOPE	
FRONT	5356	73	69.9	114	**$16 - $26**
MIDDLE	5543	70	66.4	109	
BACK	5778	70	67.5	111	

WHAT TO EXPECT: This is short, straightaway course with level terrain. A few water holes make it interesting for the better player.
DIRECTIONS: From downtown Los Angeles (about 60 miles east to the course): Take I-10 east to San Bernardino. Exit at Waterman Avenue and head north. The course is on the left.

SHANDIN HILLS GOLF CLUB (public, 18 holes, cary bickler) . . . .

3380 Little Mountain Drive
San Bernardino, CA 92407
(909) 886-0669
americangolf.com

	YARDAGE	PAR	RATING	SLOPE	
FRONT	5592	72	71.6	122	**$22 - $29**
MIDDLE	6192	72	70.4	122	
BACK	6517	72	71.9	129	

WHAT TO EXPECT: The fairway bunkers on this narrow course are not for show; they have killed more than their fair share of good golf rounds. Water is only a factor on one hole. The course is bisected by the highway.

OUR OPINION: Shandin Hills is a nice course with a reasonable price – Brad

DIRECTIONS: From downtown Los Angeles (about 75 miles east to the course): Take I-10 east to I-215 north. Exit at Mount Vernon/27th Street and turn right on 27th Street. Turn left onto Little Mountain Drive.

SOBOBA SPRINGS ROYAL VISTA GOLF COURSE (public, 18 holes, desmond muirhead) .

1020 Soboba Road
San Jacinto, CA 92583
(909) 654-9354
sobobasprings.com

	YARDAGE	PAR	RATING	SLOPE	
FRONT	5777	74	73.1	126	**$35 - $50**
MIDDLE	6366	73	70.1	125	
BACK	6846	73	72.7	130	

WHAT TO EXPECT: You will need little advice to enjoy golfing at Soboba Springs. This is an old-style course with revealing fairways, lots of trees and water on half the holes (mainly on the front nine). This level course rests at the base of the San Jacinto mountains.

NOTES: Soboba Casino is located a mile and a half up the road.

DIRECTIONS: From Riverside (about 32 miles southeast to the club): Take Highway 60 east to Highway 79 south. Turn left on Gilman Springs Road and then left on Soboba Road.

CHERRY HILLS GOLF CLUB (semi-private, 18 holes, del webb 1965) . . . .

26583 Cherry Hills Boulevard
Sun City, CA 92586
(909) 679-1182

	YARDAGE	PAR	RATING	SLOPE	
FRONT	5801	72	68.1	115	**$18 - $35**
MIDDLE	6483	72	70.5	120	
BACK	6908	72	72.6	124	

WHAT TO EXPECT: Cherry Hills is part of a senior community. The fairways are lined with homes and dotted with trees. The greens are large and user friendly.

DIRECTIONS: From Riverside (about 25 miles southeast to the club): Take I-215 south. Take the McCall exit. Turn left on Bradley and then right on Cherry Hills Boulevard. The club is on the left.

NORTH GOLF COURSE (semi-private, 18 holes, del webb) . . . .

26660 McCall Boulevard
Sun City, CA 92586
(909) 679-9668

	YARDAGE	PAR	RATING	SLOPE	
FRONT	3467	61	59.0	89	**$17 - $20**
MIDDLE	-	-	-	-	
BACK	4000	61	58.2	90	

WHAT TO EXPECT: This is a straightforward executive course. North Golf Course is a good place to learn or become reacquainted with the game.

DIRECTIONS: From Riverside (about 25 miles southeast to the club): Take I-215 south. Exit at McCall Boulevard and turn right. The course is on the right just past Sun City Boulevard.

CROSS CREEK GOLF CLUB (semi-private, 18 holes, arthur hills 2001) . . . .

43860 Glen Meadows Road
Temecula, CA 92590
(909) 506-3402
crosscreekgolfclub.com

	YARDAGE	PAR	RATING	SLOPE
FRONT	4811	71	-	-
MIDDLE	6387	71	-	-
BACK	6822	71	-	-

$60 - $85

WHAT TO EXPECT: Cross Creek uses the rolling landscape and mature oaks, lakes, and natural hazards to create a classic course that appears to have been around for decades. NOTES: Don't be surprised if you see some of golf's greatest players roaming around the clubhouse. No, they aren't ghosts, just staff, each dressed to play the part of a famous, legendary golfer.
DIRECTIONS: From downtown Los Angeles (about 90 miles southeast to the course): Take Highway 60 east to I-15 south. Exit at Rancho California Road and head west. Turn left on De Luz Road, and then left again on Via Vaquero Road, to the course.

REDHAWK GOLF CLUB (public, 18 holes, ron fream) . . . .

45100 Redhawk Parkway
Temecula, CA 92592
(909) 302-3850
redhawkgolfcourse.com

	YARDAGE	PAR	RATING	SLOPE
FRONT	5515	72	72.0	124
MIDDLE	6310	72	69.5	125
BACK	6755	72	72.7	137

$49 - $69

WHAT TO EXPECT: Flowers and elevation changes added to an abundance of water and bunkering make this one of the premier public access layouts in Southern California.
OUR OPINION: Men may love this course, but the women's tees are poorly placed and the pace of play reminds me of a Los Angeles freeway during rush hour. – Loralei
DIRECTIONS: From downtown Los Angeles (about 90 miles southeast to the course): Take Highway 60 east to I-15 south to Temecula. Exit onto Highway 79 southeast toward Indio, go left, and drive about two and one-half miles. Turn right on Redhawk Parkway, to the club.

TEMECULA CREEK INN GOLF RESORT (resort, 27 holes, dick rossen 1969) . . . .

44501 Rainbow Canyon Road
Temecula, CA 92592
(800) 642-4653
temeculacreekinn.com

	YARDAGE	PAR	RATING	SLOPE
FRONT	5737	72	72.8	118
MIDDLE	6344	72	70.3	121
BACK	6757	72	72.2	126

$60 - $90

WHAT TO EXPECT: There are three nine-hole courses, the Oaks, Creek, and Stonehouse. The Creek Course is flat and tree lined. The Oaks Course has constant elevation changes and is bordered by trees. The Stonehouse is the most difficult of the three and features steeper grades, more trees, and a few blind shots.

OUR OPINION: All three nines are "feel good" resort golf. You won't be talking about any of the holes at the water cooler the next day, but you will recommend Temecula Creek to your friends. – Shaw

NOTES: The yardage listed is for the Creek and Oaks nines.

DIRECTIONS: From downtown Los Angeles (about 90 miles southeast to the course): Take Highway 60 east to I-15 south. Exit onto Highway 79 south and turn left at the end of the ramp. Turn right on Pala Road and then another right on Rainbow Canyon Road. Temecula Creek Inn is on the right.

TEMEKU HILLS GOLF & COUNTRY CLUB (public, 18 holes, ted robinson 1990) . . . . . .

41687 Temeku Drive
Temecula, CA 92591
(909) 694-9998

	YARDAGE	PAR	RATING	SLOPE
FRONT	5113	72	70.5	123
MIDDLE	6175	72	70.3	126
BACK	6636	72	72.4	131

$24 - $58

WHAT TO EXPECT: Yes, there is plenty of water, bunkers (sand and grass) and the course is hilly (carts are required), but its the greens that will get you in your score. Most of them are either two- or three-tiered and a couple of them are four-tiered. Getting your ball on the greens in regulation means little, if you find yourself two or three tiers from the cup.

NOTES: Temeku Hills prides themselves on being a friendly learning facility, with a top staff.

DIRECTIONS: From downtown Los Angeles (about 90 miles southeast to the course): Take Highway 60 east to I-15 south. Exit at Rancho California Road and head east. Almost a mile past Margarita Road, the entrance to Temeku Hills on the left. Make an immediate right on Temeku Drive, to the clubhouse.

UPLAND HILLS COUNTRY CLUB (semi-private, 18 holes, david rainville) . . . .

1231 East 16th Street
Upland, CA 91784
(909) 946-4711
americangolf.com

	YARDAGE	PAR	RATING	SLOPE
FRONT	4921	70	68.3	110
MIDDLE	5549	70	66.7	118
BACK	5938	70	68.6	121

$22 - $47

WHAT TO EXPECT: This is a short, user-friendly course with large greens, which is part of a housing community.

DIRECTIONS: From downtown Los Angeles (about 41 miles east to the course): Take I-10 east, exit at Euclid Avenue, and head north. Turn right on 16th Street to the club.

GREEN TREE GOLF COURSE (public, 18 holes, william f. bell 1962) . . . .

14144 Green Tree Boulevard
Victorville, CA 92392
(760) 245-4860

	YARDAGE	PAR	RATING	SLOPE
FRONT	5874	73	72.5	124
MIDDLE	6332	72	69.8	120
BACK	6643	72	71.3	123

$19 - $23

WHAT TO EXPECT: Out-of-bounds is the major challenge on this high-desert, level, traditional layout.
DIRECTIONS: From San Bernardino (about 36 miles north to the course): Take I-15 Victorville. Take the Palmdale Road exit and turn left. Turn right on Seventh Street, then right onto Green Tree Boulevard.

SPRING VALLEY LAKE COUNTRY CLUB (members only, 18 holes, jones sr. & jr. 1971) .

13229 Spring Valley Parkway
Victorville, CA 92392
(760) 245-7921

	YARDAGE	PAR	RATING	SLOPE
FRONT	5083	72	70.6	121
MIDDLE	6184	72	69.7	126
BACK	6541	72	71.3	130

$35 - $50

WHAT TO EXPECT: One of the few Trent Jones, Sr. and Jr. designs in the state, this is a course that can be enjoyed by all skill levels. At Spring Valley, all the obstacles are in plain view and easily avoided by a semi-accurate shot-maker. The front is fairly level, while the back has some undulation.
NOTES: Reciprocal play with other members only clubs is allowed.
DIRECTIONS: From San Bernardino (about 36 miles north to the course): Take I-15 north. Exit at Bear Valley Road, and turn right. Drive about five miles and turn left on Spring Valley Parkway. The club is on the right.

YUCAIPA VALLEY GOLF CLUB (public, 18 holes, gary bye) . . . .

33725 Chapman Heights Road
Yucaipa, CA 92399
(909) 790-6522
yvgc.com

	YARDAGE	PAR	RATING	SLOPE
FRONT	6066	72	69.4	120
MIDDLE	6446	72	71.2	124
BACK	6804	72	72.8	128

$26 - $36

WHAT TO EXPECT: This is a fairly level, open course. Yucaipa Valley has four lakes that come into play around many of the greens. There are plenty of traps, and the greens vary in shape and size. Immature trees should pose little problem for the inaccurate golfer.
DIRECTIONS: From San Bernardino (about 20 miles east to the course): Take I-10 east, exit onto Oak Glen Road, and turn left. Cross Yucaipa Boulevard, and the driving range comes into view. Make two lefts to the parking lot.

Orange County

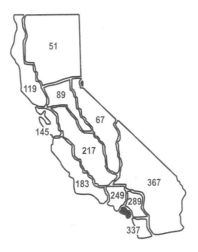

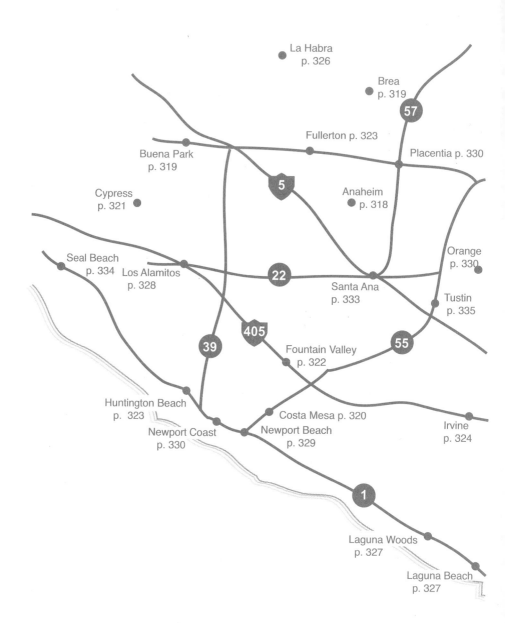

La Habra
p. 326

Brea
p. 319

57

Fullerton p. 323

Placentia p. 330

Buena Park
p. 319

5

Anaheim
p. 318

Cypress
p. 321

Orange
p. 330

Seal Beach
p. 334 Los Alamitos
p. 328

22

Santa Ana
p. 333

Tustin
p. 335

405

39

Fountain Valley
p. 322

55

Huntington Beach
p. 323

Costa Mesa p. 320

Irvine
p. 324

Newport Coast
p. 330

Newport Beach
p. 329

1

Laguna Woods
p. 327

Laguna Beach
p. 327

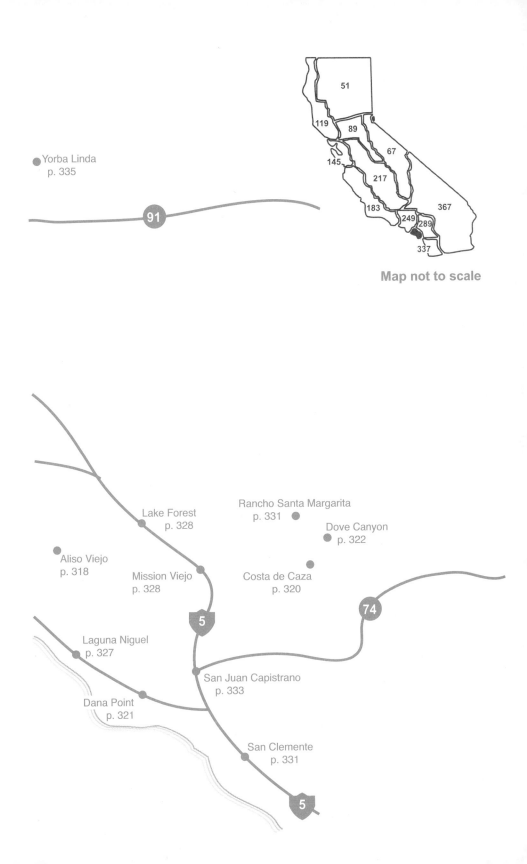

Yorba Linda
p. 335

91

51

119

89

67

145

217

183

249

289

367

337

Map not to scale

Rancho Santa Margarita
p. 331

Dove Canyon
p. 322

Lake Forest
p. 328

Aliso Viejo
p. 318

Mission Viejo
p. 328

Costa de Caza
p. 320

74

5

Laguna Niguel
p. 327

San Juan Capistrano
p. 333

Dana Point
p. 321

San Clemente
p. 331

5

ALISO VIEJO GOLF CLUB (public, 27 holes, nicklaus & nicklaus jr. 1999) . . . .

25002 Golf Drive
Aliso Viejo, CA 92656
(949) 598-9200
alisogolf.com

	YARDAGE	PAR	RATING	SLOPE
FRONT	5928	71	68.9	126
MIDDLE	6251	71	70.5	129
BACK	6436	71	71.3	131

$35 - $125

WHAT TO EXPECT: Aliso Viejo consists of three nine-hole courses that are played in 18-hole combinations. Wildly undulating greens, some with false fronts, are the distinguishing features on these rolling, but open, Jack Nicklaus layouts. It is well-maintained, but not overly long.

OUR OPINION: This course offers variable, seasonal pricing. Fun golf courses, but not worth $125 during any season. The good news: if you stay away from peak times, there are some very reasonable rates. – Shaw

NOTES: The yardage listed is for the Creek/Valley combination.

DIRECTIONS: From Irvine (about 11 miles south to the course): Take the San Diego Freeway (I-405) south to I-5 south and exit at El Toro Road. Turn west toward the ocean. Turn left on Moulton Parkway and then right on Glenwood Drive. Turn right at the second light, Golf Drive, into the property.

ANAHEIM "DAD MILLER" GOLF COURSE (public, 18 holes, dick miller) . . . .

430 North Gilbert Street
Anaheim, CA 92801
(714) 765-3481

	YARDAGE	PAR	RATING	SLOPE
FRONT	5362	72	70.2	116
MIDDLE	5756	71	66.4	105
BACK	6025	71	68.0	108

$15 - $32

WHAT TO EXPECT: This is a short, level course with mature trees. There are five par 3s, and the course finishes with two par 5s, one long and one short.

DIRECTIONS: From downtown Los Angeles (about 25 miles southeast to the course): Go south on I-5. Exit at Brookhurst Street and travel south. Turn right on Crescent Avenue. Turn left again on Gilbert Street. Follow Gilbert Street to the course.

ANAHEIM HILLS GOLF CLUB (public, 18 holes, richard bigler) . . . .

6501 Nohl Ranch Road
Anaheim, CA 92807
(714) 998-3041

	YARDAGE	PAR	RATING	SLOPE
FRONT	5361	72	71.0	119
MIDDLE	6005	71	68.4	114
BACK	6245	71	69.6	117

$26 - $50

WHAT TO EXPECT: The "Hills" in Anaheim Hills is there for a good reason. This is a short, fun course with fantastic elevation changes and few fairways running side by side. First-time players would be wise to hook up with a local to help them negotiate this tricky course. First-time players would be foolish to hook up with a local and decide to wager.

OUR OPINION: Anaheim Hills offers an enjoyable round of golf at a reasonable price. – Shaw

DIRECTIONS: From downtown Los Angeles (course is about 30 miles southeast): Take the Harbor Freeway (I-110) south to Highway 91 east. Take the Imperial Highway exit and turn right. Turn left at Nohl Ranch Road. The course is on the left.

BIRCH HILLS GOLF COURSE (public, 18 holes) . . . .

2250 East Birch Street
Brea, CA 92621
(714) 990-0201

	YARDAGE	PAR	RATING	SLOPE
FRONT	3000	59	55.9	85
MIDDLE	3319	59	57.3	90
BACK	3481	59	57.7	91

$18 - $26

WHAT TO EXPECT: This is a miniature championship-style course with tree-lined fairways and plenty of sand and water. The greens are usually in fair shape. Most of the out-of-bounds can be found along the left side of the fairway.

DIRECTIONS: From Anaheim (about six miles north to the course): Take Highway 57 north. Exit on Imperial Highway and turn right. Turn left on Associated and left again on Birch Street.

BREA GOLF COURSE (public, 9 holes) . . . .

501 West Fir Street
Brea, CA 92621
(714) 529-3003
seniorpro.com

	YARDAGE	PAR	RATING	SLOPE
FRONT	-	-	-	-
MIDDLE	-	-	-	-
BACK	3466	58	-	-

$7 - $12

WHAT TO EXPECT: Besides a storm creek that runs through the middle of the course, you will find few obstacles on this short layout.

NOTES: Currently, these are the lowest green fees in Orange County.

DIRECTIONS: From Anaheim (about six miles north to the course): Take Highway 57 (Orange Freeway) north. Exit at Imperial Highway and head west. Turn left on Brea Boulevard and then right on Fir Street.

BUENA PARK GOLF CENTER (public, 9 holes) . . . .

5151 Beach Boulevard
Buena Park, CA 90621
(714) 562-0840

	YARDAGE	PAR	RATING	SLOPE
FRONT	-	-	-	-
MIDDLE	-	-	-	-
BACK	1098	27	-	-

$7 - $7

WHAT TO EXPECT: This is a short, night-lit par-3 course.

DIRECTIONS: From Anaheim (about six miles northwest to the course): Take I-5 north, exit at Beach Boulevard, and drive north. It is about one and one-half miles up.

LOS COYOTES COUNTRY CLUB (members only, 27 holes, william f. bell) . . . .

8888 Los Coyotes Drive
Buena Park, CA 90621
(714) 994-7777

	YARDAGE	PAR	RATING	SLOPE
FRONT	6053	72	76.2	134
MIDDLE	6638	72	71.8	120
BACK	6940	72	73.4	124

$75 - $125

WHAT TO EXPECT: This 27-hole private complex is set on rolling terrain. There are the
Valley Course, Vista Course and Lake Course. With plenty of trees and thick Kikuyu grass,
the rough is, well, rough. The Valley/Vista nines combine for the longer and better test of
your skills.
NOTES: Los Coyotes once hosted an LPGA Tour event. The yardage listed is for the
Valley/Vista nines. Reciprocal play with other member only clubs is allowed.
DIRECTIONS: From Anaheim (about eight miles northwest to the course): Take I-5 north,
exit onto Beach Boulevard, and head north. Go a few miles and turn right on Los Coyotes
Drive.

COSTA MESA COUNTRY CLUB (public, 36 holes, william f. bell) . . . .

1701 Golf Course Drive
Costa Mesa, CA 92626
(714) 540-7500

	YARDAGE	PAR	RATING	SLOPE
FRONT	5907	72	73.1	124
MIDDLE	6233	72	68.9	111
BACK	6542	72	70.5	117

$18 - $33

WHAT TO EXPECT: These sporty, park-setting courses are fun and just challenging enough
to keep your attention. Fortunately, they are not so tough that a beginner can't enjoy
them, too.
NOTES: The yardage listed is for the Los Lagos Course.
DIRECTIONS: From Irvine (about six miles northwest to the course): Take the San Diego
Freeway (I-405) north. Exit on Harbor Boulevard, and head south. Turn right on Mesa Verde
Drive east and then left on Golf Course Drive.

MESA VERDE COUNTRY CLUB (members only, 18 holes, william f. bell) . . . .

3000 Club House Road
Costa Mesa, CA 92626
(714) 549-0522

	YARDAGE	PAR	RATING	SLOPE
FRONT	5467	71	72.0	130
MIDDLE	6256	71	69.9	124
BACK	6733	71	72.4	130

$70 - $90

WHAT TO EXPECT: Relatively narrow fairways give the power hitter little advantage on
this engaging and underrated layout that has hosted both the Senior Tour and the LPGA.
It finishes with a strong par 3 that has out-of-bounds to the left and water to the right.
The hole often drowns a promising round.
DIRECTIONS: From Irvine (about six miles northwest to the course): Take the San Diego
Freeway (I-405) north, exit at Harbor Boulevard, and head south. Turn right on Baker,
right on Mesa Verde, and finally, again right on Club House Road.

COTO DE CAZA GOLF & RACQUET CLUB (members only, 36 holes, robert trent jones jr.

25291 Vista del Verde
Coto de Caza, CA 92679
(949) 858-2770
lennarhomes.com

	YARDAGE	PAR	RATING	SLOPE
FRONT	5338	72	71.7	130
MIDDLE	6745	72	73.6	140
BACK	7089	72	75.5	147

$90 - $150

WHAT TO EXPECT: The South Course is the shorter, less difficult of the club's courses, provided you are accurate. It is, nonetheless, fun and tough enough to keep your attention. The formidable North Course begins with one of the toughest opening par 5s in America, and the challenge never lets up. Diabolic greens, narrow fairways, and length will push you to your limits.
NOTES: The yardage listed is for the North Course.
DIRECTIONS: From Irvine (about 22 miles southeast to the course): Off the San Diego Freeway (I-405), exit on Highway 133 northeast, heading away from the ocean. Take Highway 241 southeast, veering right toward Santa Margarita. Exit at Antonio and turn left. Turn right into the gates of Coto de Caza.

NAVY GOLF COURSE - SEAL BEACH (military, 27 holes) . . . .

5660 Orangewood Avenue
Cypress, CA 90630
(714) 527-4401

	YARDAGE	PAR	RATING	SLOPE
FRONT	5914	72	73.6	126
MIDDLE	6505	72	71.2	123
BACK	6819	72	72.7	126

$24 - $27

WHAT TO EXPECT: The Cruiser Course is a short nine-hole course. The Destroyer Course is a championship layout with plenty of water that affects mostly your tee shots. The real challenge from the Destroyer comes from the slick greens.
NOTES: The yardage listed is for the Destroyer Course.
DIRECTIONS: From Irvine (about 17 miles northwest to the course): Take the San Diego Freeway (I-405) north to Highway 22 east. Immediately take the Valley View exit and head north, away from the ocean. Turn left on Orangewood Avenue.

MONARCH BEACH GOLF LINKS (resort, 18 holes, robert trent jones jr.) . . . .

33033 Niguel Road
Dana Point, CA 92629
(949) 240-8247
troongolf.com

	YARDAGE	PAR	RATING	SLOPE
FRONT	5046	70	70.3	119
MIDDLE	5705	70	68.1	126
BACK	6344	70	71.4	134

$115 - $145

WHAT TO EXPECT: This is a target golf course with great views, rolling hills, trees, and an abundance of fairway and green-side bunkers. The course may appear short from a yardage standpoint, but remember it is a par-70. Don't under-club unless you brought lots of golf balls.
OUR OPINION: There is not too terribly much to distinguish this hilly course from the other area layouts. That is until you get in sight of the ocean, where the view is spectacular. All in all, an enjoyable resort course. – Bob
DIRECTIONS: From Irvine (about 25 miles south to the course): Take I-405 south to I-5 south, exit at Crown Valley Parkway, and head west. Turn left on Niguel Road. Monarch Beach is on the right, after about three and one-half miles.

DOVE CANYON COUNTRY CLUB (members only, 18 holes, jack nicklaus) . . . .

22682 Golf Club Drive
Dove Canyon, CA 92679
(949) 858-2888
americangolf.com

	YARDAGE	PAR	RATING	SLOPE	
FRONT	5265	71	71.9	129	**$70 - $110**
MIDDLE	6660	71	72.4	133	
BACK	6902	71	73.7	136	

WHAT TO EXPECT: Playing along ridgelines and into canyons forms the setting for this housing development course. Depending on the tees you choose, the course can be playable or very challenging. The elevated tee shots from the tenth and 17th holes are spectacular.

DIRECTIONS: From Irvine (about 20 miles southeast to the course): Take the San Diego Freeway (I-405) south to I-5 south, exit onto Alicia Parkway, and turn left. At the end, turn right on Santa Margarita Parkway until that ends. Turn right on Plano Trabuco. Turn left into Dove Canyon, to the gate.

DAVID L. BAKER MEMORIAL GOLF CENTER (public, 18 holes) . . . .

10410 Edinger Avenue
Fountain Valley, CA 92708
(714) 418-2152
americangolf.com

	YARDAGE	PAR	RATING	SLOPE	
FRONT	2960	62	54.6	93	**$16 - $22**
MIDDLE	-	-	-	-	
BACK	3825	62	57.7	91	

WHAT TO EXPECT: This is a reasonably priced, level, executive course with plenty of water and bunkers.

DIRECTIONS: From Irvine (about 9 miles northwest to the course): Take the San Diego Freeway (I-405) north. Exit on Brookhurst and go north. Turn right on Edinger Avenue and then turn right into the course.

MILE SQUARE GOLF CLUB (public, 36 holes, david rainville 1970) . . . .

10401 Warner Avenue
Fountain Valley, CA 92708
(714) 968-4556
scga.org\clubs\milesquare

	YARDAGE	PAR	RATING	SLOPE	
FRONT	5747	72	73.3	125	**$27 - $36**
MIDDLE	6834	72	70.5	119	
BACK	6759	72	72.3	125	

WHAT TO EXPECT: There are two courses at Mile Square, the Classic and the Players. The Classic Course is a traditional parkland-style course lined by trees, parallel fairways, and flattish greens. The Players Course features snug fairways, mounding, water, lots of natural brush, and greens with considerable break.

OUR OPINION: The Players Course is the easy choice between the two courses. – Shaw

DIRECTIONS: From Irvine (about nine miles northwest to the course): Take the San Diego Freeway (I-405) north, exit on Brookhurst, and go north. Turn right on Warner Avenue. The club is on the left.

COYOTE HILLS GOLF COURSE (semi-private, 18 holes, olson & stewart) . . . .

1440 East Bastanchury Road
Fullerton, CA 92835
(714) 672-6800
CoyoteHillsGC.com

	YARDAGE	PAR	RATING	SLOPE
FRONT	4437	70	65.0	115
MIDDLE	6007	70	68.6	120
BACK	6510	70	71.1	128

$40 - $105

WHAT TO EXPECT: Trouble awaits you immediately off the fairways on this attractive, hilly and well-bunkered course.
OUR OPINION: From the tips, the course boasts some exhilarating, and sometimes intimidating, tee shots. This is a good, challenging layout. – Bob
NOTES: This layout was designed in part by the late Payne Stewart.
DIRECTIONS: From Anaheim (about six miles north to the course): Take Highway 57 north. Exit at Yorba Linda Boulevard and go west. Turn right on State College Boulevard. Turn left on Bastanchury Road and then left on Payne Stewart Drive.

FULLERTON GOLF COURSE (public, 18 holes) . . . .

2700 North Harbor Boulevard
Fullerton, CA 92635
(714) 871-5141
americangolf.com

	YARDAGE	PAR	RATING	SLOPE
FRONT	5008	68	69.0	118
MIDDLE	5008	67	64.3	114
BACK	5174	67	65.2	116

$20 - $28

WHAT TO EXPECT: Fullerton is a short, traditional-style course with mature trees and a creek running through 14 holes. The greens are large and fairly level.
DIRECTIONS: From Anaheim (about six miles north to the course): Take Highway 57 (Orange Freeway) north. Exit at Imperial Highway and head west. Drive three miles and turn left on Harbor Boulevard. The course is on the left.

MEADOWLARK GOLF COURSE (public, 18 holes, william f. bell) . . . .

16782 Graham Street
Huntington Beach, CA 92649
(714) 846-1364

	YARDAGE	PAR	RATING	SLOPE
FRONT	5251	71	69.9	117
MIDDLE	5251	70	65.1	109
BACK	5609	70	66.8	113

$25 - $35

WHAT TO EXPECT: The hilly topography, along with well-placed water holes, makes this a tight course. The scorecard indicates short yardage, and the course layout dictates that you must think accuracy before distance. The result is the course seems much longer. Pace of play can be slow.
DIRECTIONS: From Irvine (about 14 miles west to the course): Take the San Diego Freeway (I-405) north, exit at Springdale, and head south. Turn right on Warner. The course is at the corner of Warner and Graham Street.

SEACLIFF COUNTRY CLUB (members only, 18 holes, ron fream) . . . .

6501 Palm Avenue
Huntington Beach, CA 92648
(714) 536-7575
americangolf.com

	YARDAGE	PAR	RATING	SLOPE
FRONT	6079	72	70.1	125
MIDDLE	6567	72	72.3	130
BACK	6935	72	73.9	136

$65 - $85

WHAT TO EXPECT: From the back tees, this is a long, tree-lined, real estate development course with tricky, undulating greens.

DIRECTIONS: From Irvine (about 12 miles west to the course): Take the San Diego Freeway (I-405) north, exit at Golden West, and head south. Head toward the ocean about seven miles. Turn right on Palm Avenue toward the course.

EL TORO GOLF COURSE (public, 18 holes, william p. bell) . . . .

7000 Trabuco Road
Irvine, CA 92619
(949) 726-2577

	YARDAGE	PAR	RATING	SLOPE
FRONT	5657	72	71.8	117
MIDDLE	6468	72	69.7	111
BACK	6750	72	71.5	114

$15 - $32

WHAT TO EXPECT: This former military course is level with no water and few bunkers. However, there are plenty of trees that can get in your way.

DIRECTIONS: From downtown Los Angeles (about 45 miles southeast): Take I-5 south, exit at Sand Canyon, and turn left. Turn right at Trabuco Road and head to the gate. The guard will give further directions.

OAK CREEK GOLF CLUB (public, 18 holes, tom fazio) . . . .

One Golf Club Drive
Irvine , CA 92620
(949) 653-7300
oakcreekgolfclub.com

	YARDAGE	PAR	RATING	SLOPE
FRONT	5605	71	71.2	121
MIDDLE	6410	71	71.3	129
BACK	6730	71	72.7	132

$70 - $135

WHAT TO EXPECT: Rolling, wide fairways, meandering creeks, towering eucalyptus trees, and stylized Tom Fazio bunkering combine for a pleasant experience at this upscale daily fee facility.

OUR OPINION: This is a fun golf course with excellent service. The $135 weekend green fee is steep, but on Sunday after 11:30 a.m., juniors are only $20 accompanied by an adult. Spend some quality time with your children and save money. Is that an oxymoron? (Things change quickly, so call the pro shop for further details) – Shaw

DIRECTIONS: From within Irvine: Off the San Diego Freeway (I-405), exit onto Jeffrey Road and head north. Turn right on Irvine Center Drive and then left on Golf Club Drive.

PARK PLACE, THE GREENS AT (public, 18 holes, ted robinson) . . . .

3301 Michelson Drive
Irvine, CA 92612
(949) 250-7888
thegreens.com

	YARDAGE	PAR	RATING	SLOPE
FRONT	-	-	-	-
MIDDLE	-	-	-	-
BACK	1678	56	-	-

$10 - $13

WHAT TO EXPECT: "Putt for the show and putt for the dough." This is a well crafted, 18-hole putting course designed by Ted Robinson. It comes complete with sand traps, water, and other hazards.

OUR OPINION: Truly miniature golf at its best. – Shaw

DIRECTIONS: From west Los Angeles (about 50 miles southeast): Take the San Diego Freeway (I-405) south, exit at Jamboree, and turn right. Turn left on Michelson Drive and then left on Carlson, into the Park Place Shopping Center. It is on the right corner.

RANCHO SAN JOAQUIN GOLF COURSE (public, 18 holes, william f. bell) . . . .

One Sandburg Way
Irvine, CA 92715
(949) 786-5522
americangolf.com

	YARDAGE	PAR	RATING	SLOPE
FRONT	5763	72	73.5	109
MIDDLE	6180	72	68.9	112
BACK	6438	72	70.6	118

$28 - $69

WHAT TO EXPECT: The greens are the story at Rancho San Joaquin. If you are going to conquer this relatively short course, it will mean putting well on its large, undulating greens. Expect slow play, especially on weekends.

OUR OPINION: For whatever (snobbish?) reason, pull carts are not allowed. Good price break for locals, so come with a fake ID or be prepared to bluff. Rancho San Joaquin is definitely worth a round. – Andy

DIRECTIONS: From within Irvine: Off the San Diego Freeway (I-405), exit at Culver and head west. Turn right on Sandburg Way to the course.

SHADY CANYON GOLF CLUB (members only, 18 holes, tom fazio 2001) . . . .

Irvine, CA

troongolf.com

	YARDAGE	PAR	RATING	SLOPE
FRONT	-	-	-	-
MIDDLE	-	-	-	-
BACK	7000	71	-	-

WHAT TO EXPECT: This long, par-71 Fazio design is routed behind crops of boulders. Shady Creek and East Shady Creek run through Shady Canyon. The course changes elevations throughout. It is a habitat-sensitive course located on 299 acres.

NOTES: At time of press, the course was not yet open. Check www.InTheLoopGolf.com for updates.

DIRECTIONS: From within Irvine: Off the San Diego Freeway (I-405), exit at Shady Canyon Drive and head west to the golf club.

STRAWBERRY FARMS GOLF CLUB (public, 18 holes, jim lipe 1997) . . . .

11 Strawberry Farms Road
Irvine, CA 92612
(949) 551-1811
strawberryfarmsgolf.com

	YARDAGE	PAR	RATING	SLOPE
FRONT	4832	72	68.7	114
MIDDLE	5805	72	70.4	129
BACK	6701	72	72.7	134

$85 - $145

WHAT TO EXPECT: This upscale, daily fee course plays mostly in a valley. There are wetlands and hazards constantly to the golfer's left, a hooker's nightmare. Afternoon wind is common. This is an attractive, difficult layout.

OUR OPINION: Environmentally Sensitive Areas make this beautiful course quite difficult. The nines are dramatically different. The back nine seems tougher because of the water, but it's actually easier. The waterfall on the 18th hole is dramatic, but is it worth $145 for weekend play? Leave the weekend play for golfers who are cash heavy. For the rest of us, play Strawberry Farms during the week. – Andy

DIRECTIONS: From within Irvine: Off the San Diego Freeway (I-405), exit at University/Jeffrey and head west to the course.

WESTRIDGE GOLF CLUB (public, 18 holes, graves & pascuzzo) . . . .

1400 South La Habra Hills Drive
La Habra, CA 90631
(562) 690-4200
westridgegolf.com

	YARDAGE	PAR	RATING	SLOPE
FRONT	5860	72	68.6	128
MIDDLE	-	-	-	-
BACK	6343	72	71.1	134

$58 - $85

WHAT TO EXPECT: The front nine of Westridge is very difficult, which may be the result of not enough land. You seem to be punished for the slightest error, especially around the green. Cut out of the hillside, the holes are narrow off the tee and continue to narrow the closer you get to the greens. Miss the fairway and you might find yourself out-of-bounds and in Environmentally Sensitive Areas. The back nine is more open, hilly and scenic. Both nines afford some good views of the surrounding area.

OUR OPINION: The staff was friendly, the course was well maintained, and the price was reasonable during the week. Although we thought the front nine was funky and a little extreme, it's worth playing to form your own opinion. – Shaw

DIRECTIONS: From Anaheim (about eight miles north to the course): Take I-5 north, exit onto Beach Boulevard, and head north. Turn right at Imperial Highway. Make another right on South La Habra Hills Drive to the club.

ALISO CREEK GOLF COURSE (public, 9 holes, gary roger baird) . . . .

31106 Pacific Coast Highway
Laguna Beach, CA 92651
(949) 499-1919

	YARDAGE	PAR	RATING	SLOPE
FRONT	1669	32	65.4	109
MIDDLE	-	-	-	-
BACK	2221	32	59.7	104

$15 - $25

WHAT TO EXPECT: Aliso Creek features recently renovated tees, fairways, and greens. This is a short course, with the water of Aliso Creek coming into play on six holes. The fairways are narrow, but the greens are large, elevated, and tiered.
OUR OPINION: This is a cool, laid back, fun, and scenic course. If you are tired of forking out high fees and fighting for tee times, this may be a good alternative. – Brad
DIRECTIONS: From within Irvine (about 15 miles south to the course): Off the San Diego Freeway (I-405), take Laguna Canyon Road south (Highway 133 west). Keep heading southwest, eventually reaching the Pacific Coast Highway. Go south on the Pacific Coast Highway about two and one-half miles. The course is on the left.

EL NIGUEL COUNTRY CLUB (members only, 18 holes) . . . .

23700 Clubhouse Drive
Laguna Niguel, CA 92677
(949) 496-5767

	YARDAGE	PAR	RATING	SLOPE
FRONT	5733	72	74.2	134
MIDDLE	6629	72	72.1	128
BACK	7010	72	73.8	134

$50 - $70

WHAT TO EXPECT: Tricky greens, Kikuyu grass, lots of trees and bunkers are the challenge for this respected course. Wind, especially El Niguel winds around the canyon floors, can be a factor.
DIRECTIONS: From Irvine (about 16 miles south to the course): Take the San Diego Freeway (I-405) south to I-5 south and exit at Crown Valley Parkway. Drive west about five miles to Clubhouse Drive and turn left. The club is on the right.

LAGUNA WOODS GOLF CLUB (members only, 27 holes, david rainville) . . . .

24112 Moulton Parkway Leisure World - Gate 12
Laguna Woods, CA 92653
(949) 597-4336

	YARDAGE	PAR	RATING	SLOPE
FRONT	5534	71	71.3	120
MIDDLE	6002	71	68.8	115
BACK	6070	71	69.1	116

$25 - $25

WHAT TO EXPECT: There are three separate nines with pars of 34, 35, and 36. The hardest of the three is the short par 34, which features elevated greens and lots of trees. Right-handed golfers who slice will find themselves punching out of trees all day long.
NOTES: The yardage listed is for the Course 1 & 2 combo.
DIRECTIONS: From within Irvine (about 12 miles south to the course): Off the San Diego Freeway (I-405) south, exit on Irvine Center Drive and head south. This turns into Moulton Parkway. Turn left into Leisure World Gate 12 to the course.

LAKE FOREST GOLF & PRACTICE CENTER (public, 9 holes) . . . .

23308 Cherry Avenue
Lake Forest, CA 92630
(949) 859-1455
americangolf.com

	YARDAGE	PAR	RATING	SLOPE
FRONT	-	-	-	-
MIDDLE	-	-	-	-
BACK	1115	29	-	-

$13 - $15

WHAT TO EXPECT: This is an executive-style course with two par 4s.
DIRECTIONS: From Irvine (about 10 miles southeast to the course): Take I-405 south to I-5 south and exit at El Toro Road. Turn left on El Toro Road and then right on Geronimo. Take a right on Cherry Avenue to the course.

CYPRESS GOLF CLUB (public, 18 holes, perry dye) . . . .

4921 Katella Avenue
Los Alamitos, CA 90720
(714) 527-1800
cypressgolfclub.com

	YARDAGE	PAR	RATING	SLOPE
FRONT	5188	71	70.8	129
MIDDLE	6039	71	69.0	122
BACK	6510	71	71.4	129

$25 - $75

WHAT TO EXPECT: Cone-shaped mounds, nine lakes, and clusters of eucalyptus trees make for a very formidable course. Cypress is scenic and imaginatively crammed into a very small property.
DIRECTIONS: From downtown Los Angeles (about 23 miles south to the course): Take I-5 south to I-605 south. Exit on Katella Avenue and head east to the club.

CASTA DEL SOL GOLF COURSE (public, 18 holes, ted robinson) . . . .

27601 Casta del Sol Road
Mission Viejo, CA 92692
(949) 581-0940
americangolf.com

	YARDAGE	PAR	RATING	SLOPE
FRONT	3397	60	60.0	98
MIDDLE	3670	60	61.8	102
BACK	3670	60	58.1	96

$20 - $31

WHAT TO EXPECT: Recent renovations have improved this popular executive course. Upgrades have been made to the tee boxes, greens, and cart paths. New traps have been added. Putting is the key to scoring well here.
DIRECTIONS: From Irvine (about 17 miles southeast to the course): Take the San Diego Freeway (I-405) south to I-5 south, exit on Alicia Parkway, and head east. Turn right on Marguerite and then left on Casta del Sol Road. The club is on the left.

MISSION VIEJO COUNTRY CLUB (members only, 18 holes, robert trent jones, sr.) . . . .

26200 Country Club Drive
Mission Viejo, CA 92691
(949) 582-1020
missionviejocc.com

	YARDAGE	PAR	RATING	SLOPE
FRONT	5659	72	75.0	140
MIDDLE	6456	72	71.7	130
BACK	6814	72	73.6	136

$75 - $85

WHAT TO EXPECT: This is a hilly, demanding course that requires long, precise drives and a good touch on and around the greens. Water comes into play on a few holes.
DIRECTIONS: From Irvine (about 13 miles southeast to the course): Take the San Diego Freeway (I-405) south to I-5 south, exit Oso Parkway and turn right off the freeway. Turn right on Country Club Drive. The course is visible from both sides of Oso Parkway.

BIG CANYON COUNTRY CLUB (members only, 18 holes, desmond muirhead 1970) . . .

One Big Canyon Drive
Newport Beach, CA 92660
(949) 644-5404

	YARDAGE	PAR	RATING	SLOPE	
FRONT	5605	72	75.1	137	**$75 - $75**
MIDDLE	6617	72	72.7	130	
BACK	6876	72	73.9	135	

WHAT TO EXPECT: This upscale private, course plays among the hills and homes of
Newport Beach. The course features many blind shots into greens, so course knowledge is
imperative to score well.
DIRECTIONS: From west Los Angeles (about 50 miles southeast to the course): Take the San
Diego Freeway (I-405) south to the 73 Toll Road south. Exit at MacArthur Boulevard and
head south. Turn right on San Joaquin Hills Road. The next right is Big Canyon Drive. The
guard at the gate will give further instructions.

HYATT NEWPORTER (public, 9 holes) . . . .

1107 Jamboree Road
Newport Beach, CA 92660
(949) 729-6193

	YARDAGE	PAR	RATING	SLOPE	
FRONT	-	-	-	-	**$8 - $12**
MIDDLE	-	-	-	-	
BACK	1200	27	-	-	

WHAT TO EXPECT: This is a pitch-and-putt located at the hotel.
DIRECTIONS: From Irvine (about six miles west to the course): Off the San Diego Freeway
(I-405), exit at Jamboree Road and head west.

NEWPORT BEACH COUNTRY CLUB, THE (members only, 18 holes, william f. bell) . . .

1600 East Pacific Coast Highway
Newport Beach, CA 92660
(949) 644-9680

	YARDAGE	PAR	RATING	SLOPE	
FRONT	5702	71	74.4	134	**$80 - $95**
MIDDLE	6240	71	70.2	122	
BACK	6588	71	71.8	126	

WHAT TO EXPECT: This Senior PGA Tour stop is not especially difficult, but its rolling
wooded terrain is easily walked, and the layout is enjoyable.
DIRECTIONS: From west Los Angeles (about 50 miles southeast to the course): Take the San
Diego Freeway (I-405) south to the 73 Toll Road south. Exit onto MacArthur Boulevard and
take it down to the Pacific Coast Highway. Turn right and the country club is at the third
light on the right.

NEWPORT BEACH GOLF COURSE (public, 18 holes) . . . .

3100 Irvine Avenue
Newport Beach, CA 92660
(949) 852-8681
newportbeachgolf.com

	YARDAGE	PAR	RATING	SLOPE	
FRONT	3216	59	57.2	84	**$15 - $22**
MIDDLE	-	-	-	-	
BACK	3216	59	54.7	81	

WHAT TO EXPECT: This executive-length layout is lighted for night play. The holes
measure between 89 and 316 yards. Expect to tee off artificial mats.
DIRECTIONS: From west Los Angeles (about 50 miles southeast to the course): Take the San
Diego Freeway (I-405) south to Highway 55 south. Immediately get on the 73 Toll Road
south and take the first exit, Irvine Avenue. Turn right on Irvine Avenue, and the course
is on the left.

PELICAN HILL GOLF CLUB (public, 36 holes, tom fazio) . . . .

22651 Pelican Hill Road South
Newport Coast, CA 92657
(949) 760-0707
PelicanHill.com

	YARDAGE	PAR	RATING	SLOPE
FRONT	4950	71	67.6	112
MIDDLE	6516	71	71.7	129
BACK	6857	71	73.3	133

$99 - $250

WHAT TO EXPECT: The South Course is located immediately above the Pacific, and most consider this the premier course in Orange County. Without the wind, it is not overly difficult. The canyon-crossing tee shots and oceanside holes are spectacular. The North Course is located farther and higher above the Pacific than the South Course. The North Course features many views of the Pacific. It plays around 300 yards longer and leaves less room for error.

OUR OPINION: The ocean views are great. The layouts are extremely playable. The courses are in immaculate condition. The staff treats you like a million dollars, which, by the way, is nearly the green fees on weekends. We highly recommend this course for weekday play. If you're looking for a place to play on the weekend and can live without the ocean views, try the PGA Courses at Oak Valley. Great tracks and $150 cheaper. – Brad

NOTES: The yardage listed is for the Ocean North Course.

DIRECTIONS: From west Los Angeles (about 50 miles southeast to the course): Take the San Diego Freeway (I-405) south to 73 Toll Road south. Exit at Newport Coast Drive, heading west toward the ocean. Turn right on Pelican Hill Road South. The clubhouse is on the left.

RIDGELINE EXECUTIVE GOLF COURSE (public, 9 holes) . . . .

1051 North Meads Avenue
Orange, CA 92869
(714) 538-5030

	YARDAGE	PAR	RATING	SLOPE
FRONT	-	-	-	-
MIDDLE	-	-	-	-
BACK	1831	32	-	-

$12 - $18

WHAT TO EXPECT: Set in the hills, Ridgeline actually has few steep inclines or declines, but many of the holes have gentle slopes. The greens are fairly small throughout.

DIRECTIONS: From Anaheim (about 10 miles southeast to the course): Take Highway 91 east to Highway 55 south. Exit at Katella, turn east and drive about three and one-half miles. Turn right on Meads Avenue, and the course is on the left.

ALTA VISTA COUNTRY CLUB (members only, 18 holes, david rainville) . . . .

777 East Alta Vista Street
Placentia, CA 92870
(714) 528-1103

	YARDAGE	PAR	RATING	SLOPE
FRONT	5408	72	72.6	124
MIDDLE	6199	72	70.1	127
BACK	6474	72	71.2	129

$50 - $60

WHAT TO EXPECT: This is a member-friendly course that rewards the accurate driver. Avoiding the homes that border the fairways creates plenty of challenge.

NOTES: Reciprocal play with other members only clubs is allowed.

DIRECTIONS: From Anaheim (about eight miles northeast to the course): Go east on Highway 91. Exit at Tustin Avenue. Turn left on Tustin Avenue and then left on Alta Vista Street. The club is on the right, at the corner of Alta Vista Street and Sue.

TIJERAS CREEK GOLF CLUB (public, 18 holes, ted robinson) . . . .

29082 Tijeras Creek Road
Rancho Santa Margarita, CA 92688
(949) 589-9793
tijerascreek.com

	YARDAGE	PAR	RATING	SLOPE
FRONT	5130	72	69.8	120
MIDDLE	6220	72	69.5	120
BACK	6613	72	71.7	126

$50 - $115

WHAT TO EXPECT: Tijeras Creek is the tale of two styles. The front is real estate golf, winding through a development. The back nine heads out along ridges and valleys for an exhilarating finish.

OUR OPINION: Tijeras Creek is a nice course, and the price is pretty reasonable for this area. The pace of play was excellent. The pace was so good that on one hole, where there was a par with a big oak on the side of the green, we played it twice. Greens and fairways are usually in good shape. Due to the heat and dry conditions in the summer, it would be wise to play early and bring a lot of water. – Frank

DIRECTIONS: From Irvine (about 20 miles southeast to the course): Take the San Diego Freeway (I-405) south to I-5 south, exit onto Oso Parkway, and head east. Turn left on Antonio Parkway and then left on Tijeras Creek Road.

PACIFIC GOLF & COUNTRY CLUB (members only, 27 holes, gary player) . . . .

200 Avenida la Pata
San Clemente, CA 92673
(949) 498-3771
pacificgc.com

	YARDAGE	PAR	RATING	SLOPE
FRONT	4531	72	67.9	124
MIDDLE	6411	72	71.7	136
BACK	6847	72	73.8	142

$45 - $65

WHAT TO EXPECT: There are three courses played in 18-hole combinations. They are the Carnoustie, Muirfield, and Royal Courses. This 27-hole layout features a links-like theme that unfolds through sloping meadows. Wind and rough can be factors here.

NOTES: The yardage listed is for the Carnoustie and Muirfield combination.

DIRECTIONS: From Irvine (about 25 miles south to the course): Take the San Diego Freeway (I-405) south to I-5 south, exit at Avenida Pico, and turn left. Go about three miles and turn right on Avenida la Pata.

SAN CLEMENTE GOLF COURSE (public, 18 holes, william f. bell) . . . .

150 East Magdalena
San Clemente, CA 92672
(949) 361-8380

	YARDAGE	PAR	RATING	SLOPE
FRONT	5722	73	73.0	120
MIDDLE	6114	72	68.9	117
BACK	6447	72	70.6	121

$27 - $33

WHAT TO EXPECT: This popular course is a pleasant walk and not too difficult. This is an older course, but all the greens have been redone and have a modern feel. There are six greens with severe undulations. The back nine is more challenging and interesting. The best feature of the course is the ocean views.

NOTES: The course leaves open tee times for walk-on play – usually three times per hour.

DIRECTIONS: From Irvine (about 25 miles south to the course): Take the San Diego Freeway (I-405) south to I-5 south and exit at Avenida Califia in San Clemente. Make the first three rights and then the first left to get to the course.

SHORECLIFFS GOLF COURSE (public, 18 holes, joe williams) . . . .

501 Avenida Vaquero
San Clemente, CA 92672
(949) 492-1177

	YARDAGE	PAR	RATING	SLOPE
FRONT	5231	72	66.4	115
MIDDLE	5704	72	69.3	124
BACK	6160	72	71.3	130

$32 - $52

WHAT TO EXPECT: Bogey isn't always a bad score, especially here. Shorecliffs is a tight, difficult course, which winds in and out of canyons. The trick to scoring here is keeping the ball in play and out of the lateral hazards. Distance is not an issue (but check out the slope rating), so use your favorite 200-yard club off the tee, the one you can hit straight. There are no green-side bunkers. If you can hit the small greens in regulation, birdie is a real possibility.

NOTES: A few of the holes have been reconstructed to provide more landing areas.

DIRECTIONS: From Irvine (about 25 miles south to the course): Take the San Diego Freeway (I-405) south to I-5 south, exit at Camino Estrella, and turn left. Turn right on Avenida Vaquero. The course is on the right.

TALEGA GOLF CLUB (public, 18 holes, schmidt-curley & couples 2001) . . . .

990 Avenida Talega
San Clemente, CA 92673
(949) 369-6226
talegagolfclub.com

	YARDAGE	PAR	RATING	SLOPE
FRONT	5245	72	71.1	121
MIDDLE	6583	72	71.8	130
BACK	6952	72	73.6	137

$45 - $115

WHAT TO EXPECT: There are no ocean holes, but plenty of white sand to keep you busy if you happen to find yourself in one of the many large traps. The front nine is more forgiving with many parallel holes. Although the back nine fairways are just as generous, miss them and you will be hard pressed to find your ball. The back side runs through a canyon, so you will encounter forced carries off the tee and natural vegetation lining the fairways.

OUR OPINION: Talega is a tough, upscale residential course with severe greens. There is nothing ground breaking about the layout, but it is attractive and well conditioned. – The Mole

NOTES: Green fees are temporary.

DIRECTIONS: From Irvine (about 25 miles south to the course): Take the San Diego Freeway (I-405) south to I-5 to the Avenida Pico exit and head east for about three miles. Turn left on Avenida Vista Hermosa and then again left on Avenida Talega.

MARBELLA GOLF & COUNTRY CLUB (members only, 18 holes, j. morrish & t. weiskopf)

30800 Golf Club Drive
San Juan Capistrano, CA 92675
(949) 248-8590

	YARDAGE	PAR	RATING	SLOPE
FRONT	5296	70	72.2	128
MIDDLE	6199	70	69.6	125
BACK	6563	70	71.7	130

$90 - $90

WHAT TO EXPECT: This private, residential course is mostly hilly and features some bold bunkering. Keep the ball in play if you want to score well. The downhill 18th is a dramatic finishing hole.
DIRECTIONS: From Irvine (about 20 miles south to the course): Take the San Diego Freeway (I-405) south to I-5 and go south to the Ortega Highway (Highway 74) east. Take the first left on Rancho Viejo. The club is on the right.

SAN JUAN HILLS COUNTRY CLUB (public, 18 holes, david rainville) . . . .

32120 San Juan Creek Road
San Juan Capistrano, CA 92675
(949) 493-1167

	YARDAGE	PAR	RATING	SLOPE
FRONT	5402	71	71.4	122
MIDDLE	5960	71	67.7	111
BACK	6295	71	69.5	116

$40 - $55

WHAT TO EXPECT: This is a straightforward and fairly hilly course, with plenty of trees and some water. To score well here, you will need to remember to use one extra club on the uphill holes, or you will find yourself in one of the many green-side bunkers. Wind on the back nine can be a factor.
DIRECTIONS: From Irvine (about 20 miles south to the course): Take the San Diego Freeway (I-405) south to I-5 south to San Juan Capistrano. Exit at Camino Capistrano and turn right. Take another right on San Juan Creek Road. The course is on the right.

RIVER VIEW GOLF CLUB (public, 18 holes) . . . .

1800 West 22nd Street
Santa Ana, CA 92706
(714) 543-1115
riverviewgolf.com

	YARDAGE	PAR	RATING	SLOPE
FRONT	5360	70	71.0	121
MIDDLE	5790	70	65.7	110
BACK	6176	70	67.8	115

$18 - $26

WHAT TO EXPECT: This is an open course with a waterway river bed running throughout. It comes into play off the tee during the winter and spring months. Many of your approach shots will be uphill.
DIRECTIONS: From downtown Los Angeles (about 30 miles southeast to the course): Take I-5 south, exit at Bristol, and go south. Turn right on Santa Clara to the course.

SANTA ANA COUNTRY CLUB (members only, 18 holes, john dunn) . . . .

20382 Newport Boulevard
Santa Ana, CA 92707
(714) 545-7260

	YARDAGE	PAR	RATING	SLOPE
FRONT	5399	72	73.0	128
MIDDLE	6175	72	69.9	123
BACK	6536	72	71.7	128

$55 - $80

WHAT TO EXPECT: Santa Ana is relatively unknown outside the area. Interesting bunkering, slightly rolling terrain, and an abundance of trees combine to make this a very enjoyable and deceptively challenging layout.

DIRECTIONS: From Irvine (about six miles northwest to the course): Take the San Diego Freeway (I-405) north to Highway 55 south. Take the first exit, Del Mar/Fair. Take a quick left on Mesa and another quick left on Newport Boulevard. The club is on the right.

WILLOWICK GOLF CLUB (public, 18 holes, william p. bell) . . . .

3017 West Fifth Street
Santa Ana, CA 92703
(714) 554-0672

	YARDAGE	PAR	RATING	SLOPE
FRONT	5481	72	70.5	116
MIDDLE	6061	72	74.1	126
BACK	6061	71	67.7	110

$20 - $30

WHAT TO EXPECT: Easily walkable, with expansive fairways, this is a straightforward course with lots of trees.

NOTES: Recent overseeding has dramatically improved fairway play.

DIRECTIONS: From Irvine (about ten miles northwest to the course): Take the San Diego Freeway (I-405) north, exit onto Harbor Boulevard and head north. Turn right on Fifth Street.

OLD RANCH COUNTRY CLUB (members only, 18 holes, ted robinson (r) 2001) . . . . . .

3901 Lampson Avenue
Seal Beach, CA 90740
(562) 596-4611
oldranch.com

	YARDAGE	PAR	RATING	SLOPE
FRONT	5346	72	66.0	117
MIDDLE	6384	72	70.9	129
BACK	6835	72	72.9	135

$70 - $95

WHAT TO EXPECT: Recently redesigned by Ted Robinson, Old Ranch features 28 acres of water, open fairways, and well-bunkered and mounded green sites. Getting your ball up and down from a missed approach shot could be hazardous to your score. The one thing that has not changed at Old Ranch is the prevailing wind.

NOTES: Reciprocal play with other members only clubs is allowed.

DIRECTIONS: From west Los Angeles (about 33 miles southeast to the course): Take the San Diego Freeway (I-405) south. Exit at Seal Beach Boulevard and turn right. Turn right again on Lampson Avenue to the club.

TUSTIN RANCH GOLF CLUB (public, 18 holes, ted robinson 1989) . . . .

12442 Tustin Ranch Road
Tustin, CA 92782
(714) 730-1611
tustinranchgolf.com

	YARDAGE	PAR	RATING	SLOPE	
FRONT	6064	72	68.7	119	**$55 - $135**
MIDDLE	6446	72	70.6	124	
BACK	6803	72	72.4	129	

WHAT TO EXPECT: Tustin Ranch has undulating fairways and multi-tiered greens. There is an abundance of sand and water, including waterfalls. All of this contributes to making this one of the most popular courses in Orange County.

OUR OPINION: A little pricey, but a solid Ted Robinson design that will be enjoyed by golfers who like a good challenge, fairway through green. – Bob

NOTES: This is the only public course in Orange County with a world-class caddy program.

DIRECTIONS: From Anaheim (about 13 miles south to the course): Take I-5 south to Tustin Ranch Road. Turn left and proceed one and one-half miles to Township Drive. Turn right to the course.

BLACK GOLD GOLF CLUB (public, 18 holes, arthur hills 2001) . . . .

17681 Lakeview Avenue
Yorba Linda, CA 92886
(714) 961-0060
blackgoldgolf.com

	YARDAGE	PAR	RATING	SLOPE	
FRONT	4936	72	-	-	**$40 - $105**
MIDDLE	6439	72	-	-	
BACK	6757	72	-	-	

WHAT TO EXPECT: Sitting 750 feet above sea level, Black Gold offers excellent views of Orange County and Catalina Island. The course, bordered by the Chino Hills State Park, is rolling with a traditional feel. Not overly long, the course has strategically placed bunkers. The greens are medium-sized with some undulation. You will find water on eight holes. The golfer who is patient and can manage their game will score well at Black Gold.

NOTES: Black Gold is scheduled to open September 28, 2001.

DIRECTIONS: From Anaheim (about 10 miles northeast to the course): Take Highway 91 east to Imperial Highway north. Exit at Lakeview Avenue. Follow the signs (northeast) to the clubhouse.

YORBA LINDA COUNTRY CLUB (members only, 18 holes, harry rainville 1957) . . . .

19400 Mountain View Drive
Yorba Linda, CA 92886
(714) 779-2461

	YARDAGE	PAR	RATING	SLOPE	
FRONT	5830	73	75.3	138	**$82 - $92**
MIDDLE	6527	71	71.2	123	
BACK	6834	71	73.2	130	

WHAT TO EXPECT: Yorba Linda is a park-setting layout that is part of a housing development. The homes are on the edge of the course, leaving ample space along the rolling fairways to keep the ball in play.

DIRECTIONS: From Anaheim (about ten miles northeast to the course): Take Highway 91 east to the Imperial Highway north. Take the Kellogg exit and turn right. Make another right on Mountain View Drive, which will dead-end at the club.

San Diego

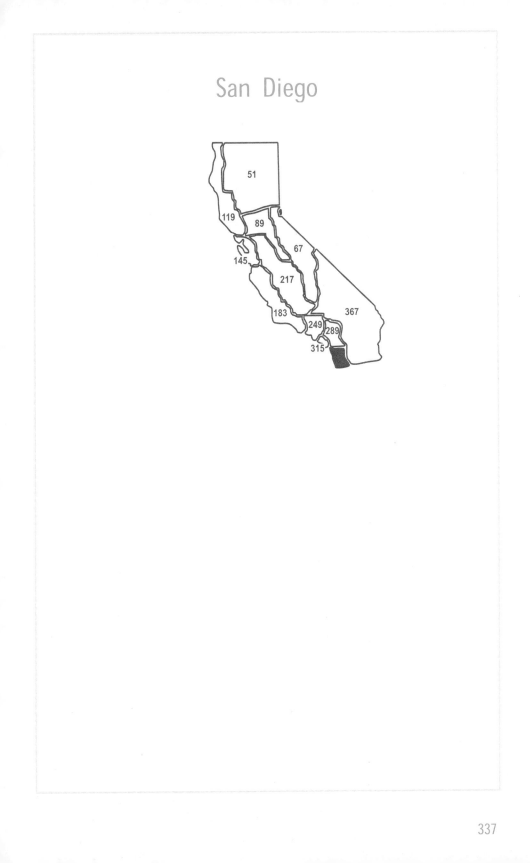

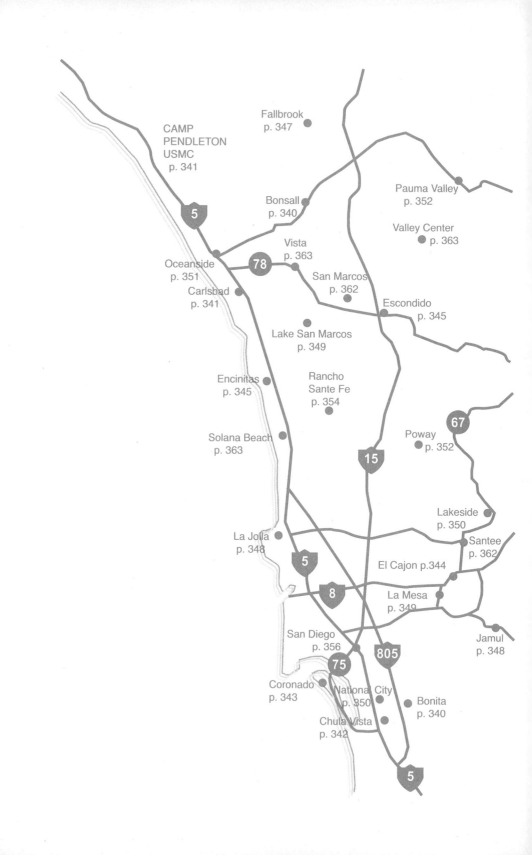

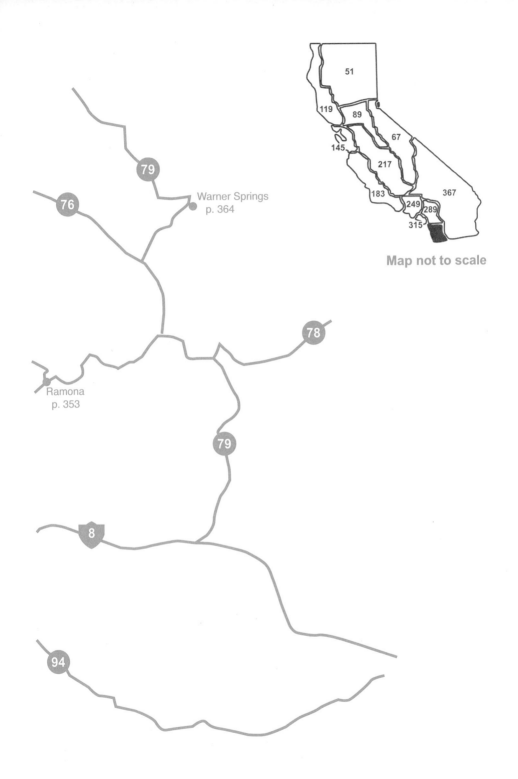

Warner Springs
p. 364

Ramona
p. 353

Map not to scale

51

119

89

67

145

217

183

367

249

289

315

79

76

78

79

8

94

BONITA GOLF CLUB (public, 18 holes, william f. bell) . . . .

5540 Sweetwater Road
Bonita, CA 91902
(619) 267-1103
bonitagolfclub.com

	YARDAGE	PAR	RATING	SLOPE	
FRONT	5442	71	71.0	119	**$21 - $31**
MIDDLE	5832	71	67.3	114	
BACK	6287	71	68.8	117	

WHAT TO EXPECT: This is a level, straightforward, tree-lined course. There is a river that comes into play on five holes and one lake that comes into play on another two. The greens are flat and there are no blind shots.

DIRECTIONS: From San Diego (about ten miles south to the course): Take I-5 south to Highway 54 east. Turn right on Sweetwater Road.

CHULA VISTA MUNICIPAL GOLF COURSE (public, 18 holes, billy casper) . . . .

4475 Bonita Road
Bonita, CA 91902
(619) 479-4141
americangolf.com

	YARDAGE	PAR	RATING	SLOPE	
FRONT	5419	72	70.8	120	**$21 - $28**
MIDDLE	6520	73	71.0	123	
BACK	6759	73	72.3	128	

WHAT TO EXPECT: Two lakes and a creek run throughout the course. These create hazards on 16 holes, but it is the wind that can create the most problems on this wide-open course.

DIRECTIONS: From San Diego (about 10 miles south to the course): Take I-805 south and exit at Bonita Road/E Street. Go east about two miles and the course is on the left.

SAN LUIS REY DOWNS (public/resort, 18 holes, william p. bell) . . . .

31474 Golf Club Drive
Bonsall, CA 92003
(800) 783-6967
slrd.com

	YARDAGE	PAR	RATING	SLOPE	
FRONT	5493	72	72.1	124	**$34 - $56**
MIDDLE	6365	72	71.2	132	
BACK	6850	72	73.0	136	

WHAT TO EXPECT: San Luis Rey Downs is a scenic course with many trees. Accuracy isn't critical, but it will definitely help. What is critical is making par or better on the five par 5s, because you will need that cushion when playing the five long par 3s.

DIRECTIONS: From San Diego (about 45 miles north to the course): Head north on I-15 and then west on Highway 76. In Bonsall, turn left on Camino del Rey. Follow Camino del Rey to Golf Club Drive and turn left.

MARINE MEMORIAL GOLF COURSE (military, 27 holes, william p. bell 1950) . . . .

Building 18415
Camp Pendleton, CA 92055
(760) 725-4704

	YARDAGE	PAR	RATING	SLOPE
FRONT	5716	72	73.1	125
MIDDLE	6443	72	70.1	117
BACK	6711	72	72.3	127

$6 - $27

WHAT TO EXPECT: There is an 18-hole championship golf course and a nine-hole par-3 golf course. The championship course is set in a valley and is friendly for most skill levels. The fairly large greens require a good touch on long putts.

NOTES: All guests must be accompanied by military personnel. The yardage listed is for the 18-hole championship golf course.

DIRECTIONS: From San Diego (about 46 miles north to the course): Take I-5 north for about 40 miles. Then take Highway 76 east for three and one-half miles. Turn left on Douglas Drive. Turn right on North River Road and drive to the Camp Pendleton gate. Follow the signs to the course.

FOUR SEASONS RESORT AVIARA (public/resort, 18 holes, arnold palmer) . . . .

7447 Batiquitos Drive
Carlsbad, CA 92009
(760) 603-6900
fshr.com

	YARDAGE	PAR	RATING	SLOPE
FRONT	5007	72	69.1	119
MIDDLE	6591	72	71.8	130
BACK	7007	72	74.2	137

$175 - $195

WHAT TO EXPECT: This is considered among the best courses that Arnold Palmer has designed and one of the the best in the San Diego region. The waterscaping and bunkering make for a beautiful challenge.

OUR OPINION: Attached to the Four Seasons Hotel in Carlsbad, this is for when the non-golfer in your life wants to "be with you." Everything about the hotel is top-notch and luxurious, though the course, while top-notch, is certainly not worth the money. But you don't go to Aviara simply to play golf; it's a mini-vacation or you've done something wrong and you're trying to make up. It's also notorious among Hollywood types for being the locale the husband says he's getting away to for a couple days of golf with the boys, but then spends nights in Tijuana checking out the local strip clubs, et al. – Andy

DIRECTIONS: From San Diego (about 30 miles north to the course): Take I-5 north, exit at Poinsettia/Aviara Parkway, and turn right. Take another right on Batiquitos Drive. The club is up about two miles on the right.

LA COSTA RESORT AND SPA (resort/private, 36 holes, joe lee) . . . .

2100 Costa del Mar Road
Carlsbad, CA 92009
(760) 438-9111
lacosta.com

	YARDAGE	PAR	RATING	SLOPE	
FRONT	5939	72	76.3	137	**$140 - $140**
MIDDLE	6608	72	72.1	128	
BACK	6988	72	74.8	137	

WHAT TO EXPECT: Perimeter housing now dominates the landscape of these very playable, park-setting golf courses, one of Southern California's most famous golf destinations. There are two courses, the North and South. Play either of the two, as they are comparable. Neither individually is as good a test as the original composite course that the touring pros have played.

OUR OPINION: Even though the new holes don't mesh well, La Costa is still an excellent facility with fun golf courses. If you want to get a feel of what the pros played, you need to bring a wad of cash and play both courses. – Bob

NOTES: The yardage listed is for the North Course.

DIRECTIONS: From San Diego (about 30 miles north to the course): Take I-5 north, exit at La Costa Avenue, and head east. Turn left on El Camino Real and right on Costa del Mar Road.

RANCHO CARLSBAD GOLF COURSE (public, 18 holes) . . . .

5200 El Camino Real
Carlsbad, CA 92008
(760) 438-1772

	YARDAGE	PAR	RATING	SLOPE	
FRONT	2000	56	-	-	**$13 - $16**
MIDDLE	2100	56	-	-	
BACK	2396	56	-	-	

WHAT TO EXPECT: This is a short executive course with only two par 4s and the rest par 3s. The terrain is flat, the trees are tall, and the greens can be on the slick side.

DIRECTIONS: From San Diego (about 30 miles north to the course): Take I-5 north, exit at Palomar and head inland. Turn left on El Camino Real. The course is up El Camino Real about one and one-half miles, on the right.

AULD COURSE, THE (public, 18 holes, bickler & cook 2001) . . . .

525 Hunte Parkway
Chula Vista, CA 91915
(619) 482-4666
theauldcourse.com

	YARDAGE	PAR	RATING	SLOPE	
FRONT	5525	72	67.2	116	**$25 - $78**
MIDDLE	6525	72	71.7	131	
BACK	6856	72	73.4	135	

WHAT TO EXPECT: Set among the foothills of Mount San Miguel, The Auld Course is patterned in the style of a traditional Scottish links course. With no trees, rolling fairways, undulating greens that allow a variety of shots, and native grasses that have an appetite for stray golf balls, mission accomplished.

DIRECTIONS: From San Diego (about 15 miles south to the course): Take I-805 to Chula Vista, exit at H Street, and head east almost seven miles. Turn left at Hunte Parkway. It will dead-end at the course.

EASTLAKE COUNTRY CLUB (public, 18 holes, ted robinson) . . . .

2375 Clubhouse Drive
Chula Vista, CA 91915
(619) 482-5757
americangolf.com

	YARDAGE	PAR	RATING	SLOPE
FRONT	5118	72	70.9	120
MIDDLE	6225	72	68.4	113
BACK	6606	72	70.1	116

$50 - $65

WHAT TO EXPECT: This is a grip-it-and-rip-it test that boasts multi-tiered greens and becomes much more challenging with the afternoon breezes.

DIRECTIONS: From San Diego (about 15 miles south to the course): Take I-805 south, exit on Telegraph Canyon Road, and head east about six miles. Turn right on EastLake Parkway and take the second left on Clubhouse Drive. The clubhouse is on the left.

SAN DIEGO COUNTRY CLUB (members only, 18 holes, william p. bell 1921) . . . .

88 L Street
Chula Vista, CA 91911
(619) 422-0108

	YARDAGE	PAR	RATING	SLOPE
FRONT	4956	70	69.1	118
MIDDLE	6630	72	70.2	122
BACK	6885	72	74.2	137

$60 - $60

WHAT TO EXPECT: Endlessly rolling fairways and interesting, well-conditioned greens make this one of California's quiet gems.

DIRECTIONS: From San Diego (about 12 miles south to the course): Take I-5 south to the L Street exit. Go east just over a mile to the club. From I-805 heading south, take the Telegraph Canyon Road/L Street exit. Drive west one mile to the club.

CORONADO MUNICIPAL GOLF COURSE (public, 18 holes, jack daray) . . . .

2000 Visalia Row
Coronado, CA 92118
(619) 435-3121

	YARDAGE	PAR	RATING	SLOPE
FRONT	5742	72	73.0	126
MIDDLE	6276	72	70.0	117
BACK	6590	72	71.5	120

$15 - $25

WHAT TO EXPECT: This is a picturesque course that runs along Coronado Bay. The course is roomy, easy to walk, and the greens are level, yet putt well. The last three holes run along the water.

OUR OPINION: Great value and great fun. The most difficult feature about the course may be getting a tee time. – Shaw

DIRECTIONS: From within San Diego: Take I-5 south, and head across the Coronado Bay Bridge to the toll plaza. Turn left at Orange Avenue, and left on Sixth Street. At the dead-end, turn right to the course.

SEA 'N' AIR GOLF COURSE (military, 18 holes) . . . .

NAS North Island, Building 800
Coronado, CA 92135
(619) 545-9659

	YARDAGE	PAR	RATING	SLOPE
FRONT	5462	72	72.7	121
MIDDLE	6066	72	69.2	113
BACK	6275	72	70.3	117

$15 - $20

WHAT TO EXPECT: This is a level course with fairways dotted by trees. On the back nine, the course runs along the ocean for four holes. Do not miss the fairways on these holes; they are outlined by ice plant. The strength of Sea 'N' Air is the small, crowned greens.
DIRECTIONS: From within San Diego: Take I-5 south and exit to cross the Coronado Bay Bridge. Go until it dead-ends and turn left. Go through the gate and take a left on the fourth street down. Turn left at the car wash to the course. We suggest asking at the main gate for further clarification.

COTTONWOOD AT RANCHO SAN DIEGO (public, 36 holes, o.w. morman 1962) . . . . . .

3121 Willow Glen Road
El Cajon, CA 92019
(800) 455-1902
cottonwoodgolf.com

	YARDAGE	PAR	RATING	SLOPE
FRONT	5686	72	72.4	121
MIDDLE	6523	72	70.5	116
BACK	6873	72	72.6	126

$11 - $42

WHAT TO EXPECT: The Ivanhoe is the more interesting and preferred of the two courses. It is spacious, but several doglegs, Kikuyu rough, and trees will test your skills. The Monte Vista Course is shorter and tighter and has excellent, soft greens that allow players to go after pins.
NOTES: The yardage listed is for the Ivanhoe Course. The course allows fivesomes if they take a cart.
DIRECTIONS: From San Diego (about 20 miles east to the course): Take I-8 east to the Second Street exit. Turn right and head south about four miles. Turn left on Willow Glen.

SINGING HILLS RESORT (resort, 54 holes, ted robinson) . . . .

3007 Dehesa Road
El Cajon, CA 92019
(619) 442-3425
singinghills.com

	YARDAGE	PAR	RATING	SLOPE
FRONT	5585	82	72.5	127
MIDDLE	6207	72	69.5	113
BACK	6605	72	72.0	124

$37 - $45

WHAT TO EXPECT: There are two regulation 18-hole courses, plus a par-3 course. Oak Glen is the shorter of the two full-length courses. This park-setting layout is playable and walkable. Willow Glen is a scenic layout that is challenging enough to keep your attention. It is also one of the reasons that this complex is popular and busy.
OUR OPINION: Singing Hills has been, and continues to be, a leader in promoting and educating women about the game of golf. The courses are fun and playable for the entire family.
NOTES: The yardage listed is for the Willow Glen Course.
DIRECTIONS: From San Diego (about 20 miles east to the course): Take I-8 east, exit at Second Street, and turn right. Turn left on Washington Avenue. Drive about three miles; the club is on the right.

ENCINITAS RANCH GOLF COURSE (public, 18 holes, cary bickler 1998) . . . .

1275 Quail Gardens Drive
Encinitas, CA 92024
(760) 944-1936
jcresortsgolf.com

	YARDAGE	PAR	RATING	SLOPE	
FRONT	4690	72	67.0	109	**$24 - $73**
MIDDLE	5820	72	67.9	118	
BACK	6524	72	71.2	127	

WHAT TO EXPECT: This is a flowing, open course near the coast and affords excellent views. To score well at Encinitas, you will need to do two things. First, play in the morning – the afternoon wind will add several strokes to your score. Second, don't go left unless you like re-teeing. The greens are on the stiff side, but putt extremely true and you can attack them in a variety of different ways.

OUR OPINION: A fun course that is only going to get better with time. – Shaw

DIRECTIONS: From San Diego (about 23 miles north to the course): Head north on I-5, exit at Leucadia, and drive east one mile. Turn left on Quail Gardens Drive.

CASTLE CREEK GOLF COURSE (semi-private, 18 holes, jack daray) . . . .

8797 Circle R Drive
Escondido, CA 92026
(760) 749-2422

	YARDAGE	PAR	RATING	SLOPE	
FRONT	4813	72	67.4	114	**$30 - $40**
MIDDLE	5958	72	68.3	116	
BACK	6396	72	70.8	124	

WHAT TO EXPECT: This short, tree-lined course plays through Castle Creek on six holes. The back nine is far more demanding than the front.

DIRECTIONS: From San Diego (about 30 miles north to the course): Take I-15 north to exit onto Gopher Canyon Road and go right. Turn left at the first light. Then take the next right on Circle R Drive.

EAGLE CREST GOLF CLUB (public, 18 holes, david rainville) . . . .

2492 Old Ranch Road
Escondido, CA 92027
(760) 737-9762
americangolf.com

	YARDAGE	PAR	RATING	SLOPE	
FRONT	4941	72	69.9	123	**$37 - $60**
MIDDLE	6035	72	69.3	125	
BACK	6417	72	71.6	136	

WHAT TO EXPECT: Each hole at Eagle Crest is individually framed on this succinct layout. With plenty of hills and several lakes, trade distance for accuracy.

DIRECTIONS: From San Diego (about 27 miles north to the course): Take I-15 north, exit Via Rancho Parkway, and turn right. Drive about one and one-half miles to San Pasqual and turn right. Go four miles, and cross Highway 78, where San Pasqual changes into Cloverdale. Go about one mile and turn right on Rockwood. Go about two and one-half miles to the guard gate. The guard gives further directions.

ESCONDIDO COUNTRY CLUB (members only, 18 holes, harry rainville 1967) . . . .

1800 West Country Club Lane
Escondido, CA 92026
(760) 746-4212
americangolf.com

	YARDAGE	PAR	RATING	SLOPE
FRONT	5593	70	74.2	130
MIDDLE	6012	70	70.0	123
BACK	6140	70	70.3	124

$50 - $55

WHAT TO EXPECT: Nestled in the foothills of North San Diego County, this is a rolling course with mature trees found throughout. Although not long, some of the holes require precise shot making. Your driver may not always be the answer. Hazards in the form of a creek come into play on several holes. The greens are not severely undulating, but can be tricky.

DIRECTIONS: From San Diego (about 30 miles north to the course): Head north on I-15, exit at El Norte, and turn left. Drive just over a mile and turn right on Country Club Lane.

MEADOW LAKE GOLF CLUB (semi-private, 18 holes) . . . .

10333 Meadow Glen Way East
Escondido, CA 92026
(760) 749-1620

	YARDAGE	PAR	RATING	SLOPE
FRONT	5610	73	73.3	133
MIDDLE	6147	71	69.9	127
BACK	6409	71	71.2	130

$30 - $58

WHAT TO EXPECT: This is a tight course that has you playing every direction except upside down. There are many blind shots, so the smart player will drive ahead to see the greens. The break of the greens can be tricky for those who have never played here.

DIRECTIONS: From San Diego (about 30 miles north to the course): Take I-15 north, exit at Deer Spring/Mountain Meadow Road. From the four-way stop, go up the hill to the club.

VINEYARD GOLF CLUB, THE (public, 18 holes, david rainville) . . . .

925 San Pasqual Road
Escondido, CA 92025
(760) 735-9545
americangolf.com

	YARDAGE	PAR	RATING	SLOPE
FRONT	5073	70	70.3	117
MIDDLE	6160	70	68.3	119
BACK	6531	70	70.3	125

$23 - $60

WHAT TO EXPECT: On the front nine, you can spray the ball off the tee and find another fairway. On the back nine, you will most likely find out-of-bounds. Bunkers, five lakes, and stunning mountain backdrops form the ingredients for this popular course that meanders among wildlife preserves.

DIRECTIONS: From San Diego (about 25 miles north to the course): Take I-15 north, exit at Via Rancho Parkway, and head east. Turn right on San Pasqual Road. The club is on the right.

WELK RESORT (resort, 36 holes, david rainville 1964) . . . .

8860 Lawrence Welk Drive
Escondido, CA 92026
(760) 749-3225
welkresort.com

	YARDAGE	PAR	RATING	SLOPE	
FRONT	3111	62	57.7	90	**$14 - $42**
MIDDLE	3567	62	56.8	93	
BACK	4041	62	59.1	99	

WHAT TO EXPECT: There are two courses: the Oaks is par-3 course and the Fountains is an executive course. The Fountains Executive Course is mountainous with good-sized greens and water that comes into play on three holes. If you miss the fairways, think twice about going after your ball – rattlesnakes have been known to lurk in the brush. The Oaks Course is level and well maintained, with lots trees guarding the fairways. You will have to contend with a creek on three holes.

NOTES: The yardage listed is for the Fountains Executive Course. The Welk Resort hosted the Junior World 11-12 age division in 2000 and 2001.

DIRECTIONS: From San Diego (about 30 miles north to the course): Take I-15 north, exit Mount Meadow Road and turn right. Turn left on Champagne Boulevard, to the resort. From north of the resort: Take I-15 south, exit onto Gopher Canyon Road, and turn left. At the stop sign, turn right on Champagne Boulevard to the resort.

FALLBROOK GOLF CLUB (public, 18 holes, harry rainville 1962) . . . .

2757 Gird Road
Fallbrook, CA 92088
(760) 728-8334
fallbrookgolfclub.com

	YARDAGE	PAR	RATING	SLOPE	
FRONT	5597	72	73.8	130	**$25 - $35**
MIDDLE	-	-	-	-	
BACK	6223	72	69.9	119	

WHAT TO EXPECT: Set in the Gird Valley, this is a scenic and playable rural course. The fairways are lined by mature live oaks, sycamores, and a variety of other trees. Trees make some of the holes extremely narrow and will catch any shot that is slightly off course. The greens are traditionally crowned, with subtle breaks. Traps and creeks will come into play for those who miss to the left or the right.

DIRECTIONS: From San Diego (about 50 miles north to the course): Take I-15 north to Highway 76 west. Go about two miles and turn right on Gird Road. Go another two miles to the club.

PALA MESA RESORT (resort, 18 holes, dick rossen) . . . .

2001 Old Highway 395
Fallbrook, CA 92028
(800) 722-4700
palamesa.com

	YARDAGE	PAR	RATING	SLOPE	
FRONT	5632	72	74.0	134	**$60 - $80**
MIDDLE	6172	72	70.2	127	
BACK	6461	72	72.0	131	

WHAT TO EXPECT: You might want to practice a few putts before you head out. This is a tight course off the tee, where you find yourself driving out of tree-lined chutes to the fairway. Keeping it straight doesn't not guarantee you an easy day or a low score. Unlike many resort courses, the greens here are fast, challenging, and will punish a weak putter.

DIRECTIONS: From San Diego (about 48 miles north to the course): Take I-15 north to Highway 76 west. Soon after, turn right (north) on Old Highway 395. Follow Old Highway 395 for a couple of miles. The resort is on the left.

STEELE CANYON GOLF CLUB (semi-private, 27 holes, gary player) . . . .

3199 Stonefield Drive
Jamul, CA 91935
(619) 441-6900
steelecanyon.com

	YARDAGE	PAR	RATING	SLOPE	
FRONT	4818	71	67.9	124	**$30 - $95**
MIDDLE	6283	71	69.9	124	
BACK	6794	71	72.6	130	

WHAT TO EXPECT: This popular 27-hole complex features three distinct nines. The Canyon nine is the most scenic but the most intimidating for the average player. The Meadows and Ranch nines are equally entertaining, yet less formidable.

NOTES: The yardage listed is for the Ranch and Meadow nines.

DIRECTIONS: From San Diego (about 17 miles east to the course): Go east on Highway 94. This turns into a surface street, Highway 54. Turn right on Willow Glen Drive and then again right on Steele Canyon Road. Turn left on Jamul Drive and follow the signs.

LA JOLLA COUNTRY CLUB (members only, 18 holes, william p. bell) . . . .

7301 High Avenue Extension
La Jolla, CA 92038
(858) 454-2505

	YARDAGE	PAR	RATING	SLOPE	
FRONT	5320	74	72.5	130	**$60 - $80**
MIDDLE	6260	72	65.0	112	
BACK	6685	72	72.9	129	

WHAT TO EXPECT: Another quiet gem, this rolling layout is fairly tight with some challenging targets and several outstanding holes.

DIRECTIONS: From San Diego (about ten miles north to the course): Take I-5 north and exit onto Ardath, which turns into Torrey Pines Road. Turn left on Girard Street, then left again on Pearl. Turn right on High Avenue to the club.

TORREY PINES GOLF COURSE (public, 36 holes, william p. bell) . . . .

11480 North Torrey Pines Road
La Jolla, CA 92037
(858) 452-3226
torreypinesgolfcourse.com

	YARDAGE	PAR	RATING	SLOPE
FRONT	6117	72	75.4	134
MIDDLE	6691	72	73.1	130
BACK	6986	72	74.6	135

$24 - $60

WHAT TO EXPECT: The North Course is the shorter and the easier of the two courses. The South Course is probably the best known of San Diego courses, due to the PGA Tour stop. The course is relatively roomy, exposed to the wind, with small, well-guarded greens and sweeping vistas of the Pacific.

OUR OPINION: This is a busy course, and its reputation as an excellent facility is well deserved. Getting onto Torrey Pines, however, is no easy task. – Bob

NOTES: The yardage listed is for the South Course.

DIRECTIONS: From San Diego (about 12 miles north to the course): Take I-5 north, exit at Genesee Avenue and head west. Keep to the right; this turns into North Torrey Pines Road. Stay on this and follow the green signs for the golf course.

SUN VALLEY GOLF COURSE (public, 9 holes) . . . .

5080 Memorial Drive
La Mesa, CA 91941
(619) 466-6102
sunvalleygolfclub.com

	YARDAGE	PAR	RATING	SLOPE
FRONT	-	-	-	-
MIDDLE	-	-	-	-
BACK	1013	27	-	-

$5 - $12

WHAT TO EXPECT: This pitch-and-putt course is part of a complex that includes a recreation center and a pool.

NOTES: All day on Mondays, you can play for $5.

DIRECTIONS: From San Diego (about 13 miles east to the course): Take I-8 east, exit onto Jackson Drive and turn right. Turn right on La Mesa Boulevard and then again right on Memorial Drive.

LAKE SAN MARCOS COUNTRY CLUB (resort/private, 18 holes, david rainville) . . . . . .

1750 San Pablo Drive
Lake San Marcos, CA 92069
(760) 744-1310
lakesanmarcosresort.com

	YARDAGE	PAR	RATING	SLOPE
FRONT	5929	73	75.2	131
MIDDLE	6272	72	71.1	125
BACK	6515	72	72.2	128

$45 - $55

WHAT TO EXPECT: This is a level, parkland-style course with plenty of trees that run through a housing community. The lake does not come into play, but there are ponds that affect three holes. Conquer the large greens, and you can score well here.

NOTES: This is a private course, open to guests of the resort.

DIRECTIONS: From San Diego (about 30 miles north to the course): Take I-5 north, exit at Palomar Airport Road, and head east. Turn right on Rancho Santa Fe Road and then left at the first light, which is Lake San Marcos Drive. There are signs from there.

BARONA CREEK GOLF CLUB (public, 18 holes, baird & eckenrode 2001) . . . .

1932 Wildcat Canyon Road
Lakeside , CA 92040
(619) 387-7018
barona.com

	YARDAGE	PAR	RATING	SLOPE	
FRONT	5813	72	68.3	124	**$45 - $75**
MIDDLE	6590	72	72.1	133	
BACK	7089	72	74.5	139	

WHAT TO EXPECT: You find yourself hitting either uphill or downhill on this roller-coaster course, with extra wide fairways. Although you are given plenty of room for error off the tee, the player who fails to hit the fairways or the first cut of rough will find their ball (or not find their ball) in the three-foot high native grasses. Good iron play is a must from fairways to green. A ball on the wrong side of the green or in a green-side bunker will have you scrambling for par or worse.

OUR OPINION: The first returns are in and they are all positive. We will keep you posted as the course matures.

NOTES: This course is located on the southwest corner of the Barona Indian Reservation.

DIRECTIONS: From San Diego (about 25 miles north to the course): Take I-8 to Highway 67 north. Turn right on Willow Road and then left on Wildcat Canyon Road. Travel six miles to the course.

WILLOWBROOK GOLF COURSE (public, 9 holes, jack daray) . . . .

11905 Riverside Drive
Lakeside, CA 92040
(619) 561-1061

	YARDAGE	PAR	RATING	SLOPE	
FRONT	2740	36	70.5	116	**$17 - $22**
MIDDLE	-	-	-	-	
BACK	2945	36	68.5	123	

WHAT TO EXPECT: Most of the greens are guarded by either water or traps. Bring on some wind and this flat nine-hole course can be a considerable challenge even for the most arrogant golfer.

DIRECTIONS: From San Diego (about 22 miles north to the course): Take I-8 east to Highway 67 north. Take the Riverford exit and get in the left lane to go under the freeway. Turn right on Riverside Drive.

NATIONAL CITY GOLF COURSE (public, 9 holes) . . . .

1439 Sweetwater Road
National City, CA 91950
(619) 474-1400
americangolf.com

	YARDAGE	PAR	RATING	SLOPE	
FRONT	-	-	-	-	**$9 - $12**
MIDDLE	-	-	-	-	
BACK	2220	34	-	-	

WHAT TO EXPECT: National City starts out narrow and ends narrow. Sandwiched between hillsides, this is a tight, short, level course that will punish the right-handed golfer who tends to hook the ball off the tee. Why? Most of the out-of-bounds run along the left side of the course.

DIRECTIONS: From San Diego (about six miles south to the course): Take I-805 south, exit at Sweetwater Road, and head west.

EL CAMINO COUNTRY CLUB (members only, 18 holes, billy bell 1958) . . . .

3202 Vista Way
Oceanside, CA 92056
(760) 757-0321
americangolf.com

	YARDAGE	PAR	RATING	SLOPE	
FRONT	5814	72	75.0	130	**$64 - $79**
MIDDLE	6527	72	71.7	129	
BACK	6734	72	72.8	131	

WHAT TO EXPECT: There are generous landing areas at El Camino, but there is trouble in the form of trees and out-of-bounds if you can't hit the ball fairly straight. The good news is the out-of-bounds generally does not affect the golfer who hits the ball left to right. The greens are big and undulating. Get by the long par 4s and the rest is downhill.
NOTES: Reciprocal play with other members only clubs is allowed.
DIRECTIONS: From San Diego (about 36 miles north to the course): Take I-5 north to Highway 78 east in Oceanside. Take the El Camino Real exit and head north. Turn right (east) on Vista Way. Turn into the Days Inn parking lot. The club is located behind Days Inn.

EMERALD ISLE GOLF COURSE (public, 18 holes, mike gandy 1986) . . . .

660 South El Camino Real
Oceanside, CA 92057
(760) 721-4700

	YARDAGE	PAR	RATING	SLOPE	
FRONT	2700	56	-	-	**$19 - $22**
MIDDLE	2400	56	54.5	-	
BACK	2150	56	55.4	-	

WHAT TO EXPECT: Emerald Isle has two par 4s, while the rest are par 3s. The course has water on several holes and plays tougher than it looks.
DIRECTIONS: From San Diego (about 40 miles north to the course): Take I-5 north to Oceanside. Then take Highway 76 (Mission) east and then turn left on El Camino Real. Turn left at Vista Oceana to the course.

OCEANSIDE CENTER CITY GOLF COURSE (public, 18 holes, william johnson 1955) . . . .

2323 Greenbrier Drive
Oceanside, CA 92054
(760) 433-8590

	YARDAGE	PAR	RATING	SLOPE	
FRONT	3872	66	61.8	99	**$12 - $15**
MIDDLE	4146	66	60.3	93	
BACK	4443	66	61.2	94	

WHAT TO EXPECT: This is a mature executive course with lots of trees and rolling terrain.
DIRECTIONS: From San Diego (about 38 miles north to the course): Take I-5 north, exit at Oceanside Boulevard, and turn left. Pay attention not to miss the left turn on Saratoga. Go up the hill to the course.

OCEANSIDE GOLF COURSE (public, 18 holes) . . . .

825 Douglas Drive
Oceanside, CA 92054
(760) 433-1360
americangolf.com

	YARDAGE	PAR	RATING	SLOPE
FRONT	5398	72	71.6	121
MIDDLE	6043	72	68.8	117
BACK	6402	72	70.6	122

$21 - $28

WHAT TO EXPECT: This is a short, challenging layout with ocean breezes and water coming into play on 12 holes.

DIRECTIONS: From San Diego (about 38 miles north to the course): Take I-5 north to Highway 76 east for about four miles. Make a left on Douglas Drive, right after the drive-in. Go about two miles to the course.

PAUMA VALLEY COUNTRY CLUB (members only, 18 holes, robert trent jones, sr.) . . .

15835 Pauma Valley Drive
Pauma Valley, CA 92061
(760) 742-1230
paumacc.com

	YARDAGE	PAR	RATING	SLOPE
FRONT	5891	72	74.7	130
MIDDLE	6811	71	73.1	130
BACK	7077	71	74.4	133

$100 - $100

WHAT TO EXPECT: Long a fixture of America's top 100 courses by the leading golf publications, the layout boasts large greens and tons of length. But what most people remember about Pauma Valley are the bunkers. You'll have plenty of opportunity to use your 56 degree, 60 degree, 85 degree wedges. This course remains one of the premier layouts in Southern California.

DIRECTIONS: From San Diego (about 55 miles north to the course): Take I-15 north to Highway 76 and drive east for 14 miles. Pay attention! On the left is the post office and a market. The club entrance is directly across the street. It is very easy to drive right by.

MADERAS GOLF CLUB (semi-private, 18 holes, johnny miller/robert muir graves) . . .

17750 Old Coach Road
Poway, CA 92064
(858) 726-4653
maderasgolf.com

	YARDAGE	PAR	RATING	SLOPE
FRONT	6057	72	69.9	129
MIDDLE	6654	72	72.8	139
BACK	7116	72	75.2	143

$85 - $135

WHAT TO EXPECT: Maderas is one of the longer San Diego area courses from the tips. This scenic layout plays through cliffs, trees, and creeks of the inland hill country. It also features dramatic rock outcroppings.

DIRECTIONS: From San Diego (about 18 miles north to the course): Take I-15 north, exit at Rancho Bernardo Road, and head east for three miles. Turn left on Old Coach Road to the club.

STONERIDGE COUNTRY CLUB (members only, 18 holes, ted robinson) . . . .

17166 Stoneridge Country Club Lane
Poway, CA 92064
(858) 487-2117

	YARDAGE	PAR	RATING	SLOPE
FRONT	5696	73	74.5	133
MIDDLE	6042	72	68.5	111
BACK	6286	72	69.9	118

$70 - $70

WHAT TO EXPECT: This course is part of a housing development, so players who tend to hit the ball long and wrong will find themselves in the trees or out-of-bounds on all but a few holes. The front nine is fairly level but the back nine is mountain goat territory. The greens are average size and undulating.

NOTES: Reciprocal play with other members only clubs is allowed.

DIRECTIONS: From San Diego (about 18 miles north to the course): Take I-15 north, exit at Rancho Bernardo Road, and head east. The entrance is on the left, after about two and one-half miles.

MOUNT WOODSON GOLF CLUB (semi-private, 18 holes, schmidt-curley) . . . .

16422 North Woodson Drive
Ramona, CA 92065
(760) 788-3555
mtwoodson.com

	YARDAGE	PAR	RATING	SLOPE
FRONT	4441	70	65.9	116
MIDDLE	5265	70	65.7	124
BACK	6089	70	68.3	130

$39 - $80

WHAT TO EXPECT: Despite its modest length, this is an entertaining and popular layout with no parallel fairways. The views and unique bridges are worth the price of admission. Tight and tough.

DIRECTIONS: From San Diego (about 32 miles northeast to the course): Take I-15 north. Exit Scripps-Poway Parkway and head east eight miles. At the end, turn left and go north on Highway 65. After five miles, turn left on Archie Moore Road. Turn left again into the entrance.

SAN VICENTE INN & GOLF CLUB (semi-private, 18 holes, ted robinson 1972) . . . . . .

24157 San Vicente Road
Ramona, CA 92065
(760) 789-3477
sanvicenteresort.com

	YARDAGE	PAR	RATING	SLOPE
FRONT	5543	72	72.8	128
MIDDLE	6228	72	69.3	116
BACK	6633	72	71.5	123

$24 - $59

WHAT TO EXPECT: The course is surrounded by homes. They can be a factor, mostly on the front nine. Many of the fairways are lined by trees, and four lakes come into play on 14 holes. The narrow landing areas on a few holes require accurate tee shots. The greens can be on the fast side.

DIRECTIONS: From San Diego (about 32 miles northeast to the course): Take I-8 east to Highway 67 north. Follow Highway 67 to Dye Road. Turn right on Dye Road and take another right on San Vicente Road. Drive another two miles to the club, on the left.

BRIDGES AT RANCHO SANTA FE, THE (members only, 18 holes, r.t. jones jr. 2001) . .

18550 Seven Bridges Road
Rancho Santa Fe, CA 92067
(858) 759-7200
thebridgesrsf.com

	YARDAGE	PAR	RATING	SLOPE	
FRONT	5740	71	68.6	122	**$90 - $90**
MIDDLE	6561	71	72.4	139	
BACK	6902	71	74.0	145	

WHAT TO EXPECT: From the back tees, this is a demanding course with many forced carries. Although the landing areas are generous, miss the fairways and you will most likely end up in a natural vegetation area. Translation: you will be reaching in your bag for another ball. The only hole where you really have to think about water is on eighteen. The front nine is rolling, while on the back nine you will encounter dramatic elevation changes.

DIRECTIONS: From San Diego (about 20 miles north to the course): Take I-5 north, exit at Via de la Valle, and turn right. Turn right at Paseo Delicias, which turns into Del Dios Highway. Turn left on El Camino del Norte and then right on Aliso Canyon Road. Turn right at the T, and then make a quick left into the club.

CROSBY NATIONAL GOLF CLUB, THE (members only, 18 holes) . . . .

8001 Del Dios Highway
Rancho Santa Fe, CA 92067
(858) 756-6300
troongolf.com

	YARDAGE	PAR	RATING	SLOPE
FRONT	-	-	-	-
MIDDLE	-	-	-	-
BACK	-	-	-	-

WHAT TO EXPECT: A description was not available at time of press.

DIRECTIONS: From San Diego (about 20 miles north to the course): Take I-5 north to Via de la Valle. Take Via de la Valle east to Paseo Delicias. Turn right to Del Dios Highway. The property is on the right side. Make another right on Bing Crosby Boulevard.

DEL MAR COUNTRY CLUB (members only, 18 holes, joe lee) . . . .

6001 Clubhouse Drive
Rancho Santa Fe, CA 92067
(858) 759-5520

	YARDAGE	PAR	RATING	SLOPE	
FRONT	5381	72	72.5	128	**$70 - $85**
MIDDLE	6508	72	71.8	134	
BACK	6950	72	74.0	138	

WHAT TO EXPECT: Most of this attractive layout is situated in a valley, with water and strong bunkering coming into play.

DIRECTIONS: From San Diego (about 20 miles north to the course): Take I-5 north, exit onto Del Mar Heights Road, and go east. Turn left on El Camino Real and then right on San Dieguito Road. Turn right on Camino Santa Fe to the gate.

FAIRBANKS RANCH COUNTRY CLUB (members only, 18 holes, ted robinson) . . . .

15150 San Dieguito Road
Rancho Santa Fe, CA 92067
(858) 259-8819
fairbanksranch.com

	YARDAGE	PAR	RATING	SLOPE
FRONT	5034	72	70.5	123
MIDDLE	6769	72	73.1	131
BACK	7225	72	75.0	135

$70 - $90

WHAT TO EXPECT: This immaculate layout is set in a flat valley. Fairbanks Ranch features lots of water, bunkering, and terraced putting surfaces, which are framed by mounds and palm trees. It can be a formidable test of golf, especially when the wind picks up in the afternoon.

DIRECTIONS: From San Diego (about 20 miles north to the course): Take I-5 north, exit at Del Mar Heights Road, turn right, and head east. Turn left on El Camino Real and right on San Dieguito Road. Go about one and one-half miles, and the club is on the left.

FARMS GOLF CLUB, THE (members only, 18 holes, pete dye & perry dye 1988) . . . . .

8500 Saint Andrews Road
Rancho Santa Fe, CA 92067
(858) 756-5585

	YARDAGE	PAR	RATING	SLOPE
FRONT	4847	72	69.2	124
MIDDLE	6645	72	72.8	141
BACK	6860	72	73.9	143

$75 - $200

WHAT TO EXPECT: Not only is this private course visually intimidating, it is also difficult to play. Long rough, water, bunkering, and diabolical putting surfaces provide more challenge than most can handle.

DIRECTIONS: From San Diego (about 20 miles north to the course): Take I-5 north, exit at Del Mar Heights, and head east. Turn left on El Camino Real and then right on San Dieguito. Turn right on Rancho Diegueno. At the T, turn left on Rancho Santa Fe Farms Road and then right on Rancho Santa Fe Farms Drive. The guardhouse is on the left.

MORGAN RUN RESORT AND CLUB (members only, 27 holes, jay morrish) . . . .

5690 Cancha de Golf
Rancho Santa Fe, CA 92091
(858) 756-3255
morganrun.com

	YARDAGE	PAR	RATING	SLOPE
FRONT	5505	71	71.2	123
MIDDLE	6096	71	69.6	119
BACK	6469	71	71.2	123

$85 - $110

WHAT TO EXPECT: There are three courses at Morgan Run: the East, North, and South. They are played in 18-hole combinations. If you come to Morgan Run for an extreme challenge, you are missing the point of being at a resort. All three courses are level, short, and player friendly.

NOTES: You must be a resort guest to play the course. The yardage listed is for the South and North nines.

DIRECTIONS: From San Diego (about 20 miles north to the course): Take I-5 north, exit at Via de la Valle, and head east about three miles. Driving down the backside of the hill, turn right on Cancha de Golf.

RANCHO SANTA FE GOLF CLUB (members only, 18 holes, max behr) . . . .

5827 Via de la Cumbre
Rancho Santa Fe, CA 92067
(858) 756-3094

	YARDAGE	PAR	RATING	SLOPE	
FRONT	5012	72	70.0	126	**$70 - $85**
MIDDLE	6452	72	71.8	129	
BACK	6911	72	73.9	133	

WHAT TO EXPECT: This residential park-setting layout is rolling with strategic bunkering. The incoming nine one of the best tests of golf anywhere in California.

NOTES: Reciprocal play with other members only clubs is allowed.

DIRECTIONS: From San Diego (about 20 miles north to the course): Take I-5 north, exit Via de la Valle, and head east until it ends. Turn left on Paseo Delicias and then right on La Granada. Turn right on Avenida de Acasias and then take the first left on Via de la Cumbre.

3-PAR AT FOUR POINTS SHERATON (resort, 9 holes) . . . .

8110 Aero Drive
San Diego, CA 92123
(858) 715-1763
sd4points.com

	YARDAGE	PAR	RATING	SLOPE	
FRONT	-	-	-	-	**$3 - $8**
MIDDLE	-	-	-	-	
BACK	1200	24	-	-	

WHAT TO EXPECT: All you need for this short par-3 course is your putter and six wedges.

NOTES: This is right in the center of San Diego's business area.

DIRECTIONS: From within San Diego: Take I-805 north to Highway 163 and go north. Exit at Kearny Villa Road and turn right. Follow to Aero Drive, which is on the right. The course is located at the Four Points Sheraton.

ADMIRAL BAKER GOLF COURSE (military, 36 holes, jack daray) . . . .

Friars and Admiral Baker Roads
San Diego, CA 92190
(619) 556-5520

	YARDAGE	PAR	RATING	SLOPE	
FRONT	5844	72	74.4	124	**$17 - $29**
MIDDLE	6486	72	70.8	124	
BACK	6801	72	72.4	127	

WHAT TO EXPECT: The North Course is the longer and more difficult of the two courses. Deep rough, trees, and out-of-bounds await the the player who can't keep it in the fairway on this hilly course. The South Course is narrow but is much shorter and less punishing than the North Course.

NOTES: The yardage listed is for the North Course.

DIRECTIONS: From within San Diego: Go north on I-15 to the Friars Road exit. Head east after exiting the freeway. Turn left on Santos Road and then right on Admiral Baker Road.

BALBOA PARK GOLF COURSE (public, 27 holes) . . . .

2600 Golf Course Drive
San Diego, CA 92102
(619) 239-1632
americangolf.com

	YARDAGE	PAR	RATING	SLOPE
FRONT	5464	72	71.4	119
MIDDLE	5811	72	67.5	114
BACK	6267	72	69.8	119

$32 - $38

WHAT TO EXPECT: Balboa is a hilly, walkable course. The fairways on the front nine are fairly tight with small greens. On the back nine, errant drives will usually find another fairway. The nine-hole executive course is short and presents little challenge for the low handicapper.

OUR OPINION: The executive course is recommended for beginners and for golfers who have had the shanks and are in need of rehab. – Shaw

DIRECTIONS: From within San Diego: Off I-5, take the Pershing Drive exit and head east to 26th Street. Turn right and then turn left on Golf Course Drive, to the club.

BERNARDO HEIGHTS COUNTRY CLUB (members only, 18 holes, ted robinson 1982) . .

16066 Bernardo Heights Parkway
San Diego, CA 92128
(858) 487-3440
bhcc.net

	YARDAGE	PAR	RATING	SLOPE
FRONT	5617	72	73.2	127
MIDDLE	6221	72	69.7	119
BACK	6679	72	71.9	124

WHAT TO EXPECT: This is a prototypical country club with well manicured greens, level fairways, undulating greens, and water coming into play on four holes. Surrounded by homes, slicing golfers may want to review their insurance policies.

NOTES: Reciprocal play with other members only clubs is allowed.

DIRECTIONS: From San Diego (about 20 miles north to the course): Take I-15 north. Exit at Bernardo Center Drive and go right. Turn right on Bernardo Heights Parkway. The small, easy-to-miss driveway is on the right, at the top of the hill.

CARMEL MOUNTAIN RANCH (public, 18 holes, ron fream 1985) . . . .

14050 Carmel Ridge Road
San Diego, CA 92128
(858) 487-9224
americangolf.com

	YARDAGE	PAR	RATING	SLOPE
FRONT	5006	71	71.0	122
MIDDLE	5934	71	69.7	123
BACK	6296	71	71.9	131

$20 - $85

WHAT TO EXPECT: This steep and rugged course plays through homes, so there are no parallel fairways. Carmel Mountain Ranch features barrancas, pot bunkers, streams, and natural rock formations. It usually receives high marks from local golfers, but is not walkable.

DIRECTIONS: From San Diego (about 20 miles north to the course): Take I-15 north, exit on Carmel Mountain Road and proceed east. Turn right on Highland Ranch Road and turn right again on Carmel Ridge Road.

COLINA PARK GOLF COURSE (public, 18 holes) . . . .

4085 52nd Street
San Diego, CA 92105
(619) 582-4704
prokidsgolf.com

	YARDAGE	PAR	RATING	SLOPE	
FRONT	-	-	-	-	$2 - $5
MIDDLE	-	-	-	-	
BACK	1525	54	-	-	

WHAT TO EXPECT: This is short, tree-lined, par-3 course, set in the inner city. Colina Park is home to one of the most dynamic junior programs in the country.
NOTES: This is the home of the Pro Kids Golf Academy. Pro Kids is a non-profit organization dedicated to the educational and over-all advancement of junior golfers.
DIRECTIONS: From within San Diego: Off I-8, exit on College Avenue and head south. Turn right on University. The course is on the corner of University and 52nd Street, on the right.

COUNTRY CLUB OF RANCHO BERNARDO (members only, 18 holes, ted robinson 1967)

12280 Greens East Road
San Diego, CA 92128
(858) 487-1212
ccofrb.com

	YARDAGE	PAR	RATING	SLOPE	
FRONT	5546	72	76.3	134	$50 - $60
MIDDLE	6163	72	69.5	121	
BACK	6428	72	70.7	124	

WHAT TO EXPECT: This is a well-conditioned golf course with wide rolling fairways and medium-sized greens that have mild undulations. To shoot a low number at Rancho Bernardo, you must be selective on which holes you want to be aggressive.
DIRECTIONS: From San Diego (about 20 miles north to the course): Travel north on I-15. Take the Rancho Bernardo Road exit east. Drive one mile to Bernardo Oaks Drive. Turn left and follow to the entrance of the Inn; bear right to the country club.

DOUBLETREE CARMEL GOLF RESORT (resort, 18 holes, billy bell, jr. 1964) . . . .

14455 Penasquitos Drive
San Diego, CA 92129
(858) 485-4145
doubletreehotels.com

	YARDAGE	PAR	RATING	SLOPE	
FRONT	5361	72	71.9	125	$35 - $70
MIDDLE	6018	72	68.4	116	
BACK	6429	72	70.7	123	

WHAT TO EXPECT: Mature trees and excellent greens provide most of the challenge on this well-maintained, fairly short, resort course.
DIRECTIONS: From San Diego (about 15 miles north to the course): Take I-15 north to the Carmel Mountain Road exit. Drive west for a quarter mile off the freeway to Penasquitos Drive. Turn right on Penasquitos Drive, to the resort.

MEADOWS DEL MAR GOLF CLUB, THE (resort, 18 holes, tom fazio 1999) . . . .

5300 Meadows Del Mar
San Diego, CA 92130
(877) 530-0636
meadowsdelmargc.com

	YARDAGE	PAR	RATING	SLOPE
FRONT	4929	71	68.3	116
MIDDLE	6353	71	71.2	131
BACK	6886	71	73.7	138

$110 - $160

WHAT TO EXPECT: This hilly site is spectacular with many views, but essentially requires a cart to play it. Expansive fairways with mounded bunkering look dramatic but play slightly easier. There is nothing easy about the par 3 17th that has to rank with the most demanding in America. To score well, keep it in play and trust the yardage – it's accurate.
OUR OPINION: Putting the cost aside, this upscale layout is one of your best choices to play in the San Diego area. With the Meadows Del Mar, San Diego has added another quality course to its repertoire. – Bob
DIRECTIONS: From within San Diego: Take I-5, exit at the Route 56 East/Carmel Valley Road Junction. Proceed one and one-half miles to the Carmel Country Road exit. Turn right, then proceed one-quarter mile to Meadows Del Mar. Turn left to the club.

MIRAMAR MEMORIAL GOLF CLUB (military, 18 holes, jack daray) . . . .

MCAS Miramar
San Diego, CA 92145
(858) 577-4155

	YARDAGE	PAR	RATING	SLOPE
FRONT	5900	72	67.4	115
MIDDLE	6399	72	70.0	120
BACK	6816	72	72.2	126

$21 - $26

WHAT TO EXPECT: Hitting fairways won't be an issue, even with many mature trees. Putting the tricky greens that seem to always break toward the runway and getting in before the wind picks up will be the challenge.
DIRECTIONS: From within San Diego: Take I-15 north, exit at Miramar Way, and head west to the main gate.

MISSION BAY GOLF COURSE (public, 18 holes, ted robinson) . . . .

2702 North Mission Bay Drive
San Diego, CA 92109
(858) 490-3370

	YARDAGE	PAR	RATING	SLOPE
FRONT	-	-	-	-
MIDDLE	-	-	-	-
BACK	2719	58	-	-

$13 - $20

WHAT TO EXPECT: This is a night-lit executive course with four par 4s and the rest par 3s. This is a good family course because it is not too taxing for the beginning or junior golfer, and interesting enough for the more sophisticated player.
DIRECTIONS: From within San Diego: Take I-5 north, exit at Clairemont Drive/Mission Bay Drive. Turn left on Clairemont and then right on East Mission Bay. Go straight to the course.

MISSION TRAILS GOLF COURSE (public, 18 holes, william p. bell) . . . .

7380 Golfcrest Place
San Diego, CA 92119
(619) 460-5400
americangolf.com

	YARDAGE	PAR	RATING	SLOPE
FRONT	5175	71	71.1	120
MIDDLE	5601	71	66.4	107
BACK	6004	71	68.6	114

$22 - $32

WHAT TO EXPECT: This is a traditional course with mature trees. The front nine traverses the valley, while the back nine plays close to the shores of Lake Murray. The course has many short par 4s, so think accuracy over distance.

DIRECTIONS: From within San Diego: Take I-8 east, exit on College Avenue, and turn left. Go about one and one-half miles and turn right on Navajo. Turn right on Golfcrest Drive and then left on Golfcrest Place.

OAKS NORTH EXECUTIVE COURSE (public, 27 holes, ted robinson) . . . .

12602 Oaks North Drive
San Diego, CA 92128
(858) 487-3021
jcresortsgolf.com

	YARDAGE	PAR	RATING	SLOPE
FRONT	3234	60	57.8	87
MIDDLE	3577	60	59.4	93
BACK	3577	60	56.8	89

$12 - $40

WHAT TO EXPECT: Oaks North has three courses, played in 18-hole combinations. They are the North, South and East Courses. These are well-conditioned executive courses, with short par 4s that will tempt you to use your driver. If you are interested in scoring well, leave your ego at home and the driver in your bag. The par 3s range from just over a hundred yards to just over 200 yards.

NOTES: The yardage listed is for the South/East Combination.

DIRECTIONS: From San Diego (about 20 miles north to the course): Take I-15 north, exit at Rancho Bernardo Road, and turn right. Turn left on Pomerado Road and then right on Oaks North Drive.

PRESIDIO HILLS GOLF COURSE (public, 18 holes) . . . .

4136 Wallace Street
San Diego, CA 92110
(619) 295-9476

	YARDAGE	PAR	RATING	SLOPE
FRONT	-	-	-	-
MIDDLE	-	-	-	-
BACK	1325	54	-	-

$9 - $10

WHAT TO EXPECT: A pitch-and-putt with personality.

OUR OPINION: Want to play golf with the entire family and not go broke? Presidio Hills is worth playing, just for a chance to check out the scrapbook of all the famous juniors who have played here. The list includes Tiger, Mickelson, Price, and many others. – Shaw

NOTES: Presidio Hills is home to the Junior (eight and under) World Championship. The clubhouse was built in the 1820s and is the oldest adobe building in San Diego.

DIRECTIONS: From within San Diego: Take the I-8 east, exit on Taylor Street and go south. Turn left on Juan and the course is on the left.

RANCHO BERNARDO INN (resort, 18 holes, william f. bell 1962) . . . .

17550 Bernardo Oaks Drive
San Diego, CA 92128
(858) 675-8500
ranchobernardoinn.com

	YARDAGE	PAR	RATING	SLOPE	
FRONT	5721	72	68.0	124	**$38 - $100**
MIDDLE	6233	72	70.4	129	
BACK	6631	72	72.3	133	

WHAT TO EXPECT: This is an attractive resort course, set in a valley and surrounded by homes. Rancho Bernardo is extremely playable with generous fairways. It is dotted with trees and has an occasional lateral water hazard. This is a traditional layout without gimmicks and is conveniently located next to the hotel.

OUR OPINION: Pretty, fun, and well conditioned. If you're lucky an occasional hawk may buzz past. – Frank

NOTES: The course is the only one in San Diego that has hosted both PGA and LPGA events.

DIRECTIONS: From San Diego (about 20 miles north to the course): Take I-15 north to Rancho Bernardo. Take the Rancho Bernardo Road exit east. Turn left on Bernardo Oaks Drive.

RIVERWALK GOLF CLUB (public, 27 holes, ted robinson, sr. & jr. 1998) . . . .

1150 Fashion Valley Road
San Diego, CA 92108
(619) 296-4653
americangolf.com

	YARDAGE	PAR	RATING	SLOPE	
FRONT	5532	72	70.9	115	**$19 - $96**
MIDDLE	6277	72	70.0	119	
BACK	6627	72	71.6	123	

WHAT TO EXPECT: There are three nines: Mission, Presidio and Friars. All three nines feature rolling fairways, the San Diego River, waterfalls, and well-protected, undulating greens. The longest combination is the Friars-Presidio nines.

OUR OPINION: The courses won't knock your socks off, but they are nice middle-of-the-road layouts. – Frank

NOTES: The yardage listed is for the Friars-Presidio nines. Formerly the Stardust Country Club, the course once hosted the PGA Tour in the '50s and '60s.

DIRECTIONS: From within San Diego: Take I-8 east, exit on Hotel Circle and head east. Go north on Fashion Valley Road. The club is on the left.

SAIL HO GOLF COURSE (public, 9 holes) . . . .

2960 Sellars Plaza, NTC
San Diego, CA 92138
(619) 523-5003

	YARDAGE	PAR	RATING	SLOPE	
FRONT	-	-	-	-	**$9 - $14**
MIDDLE	-	-	-	-	
BACK	1480	29	-	-	

WHAT TO EXPECT: The is a short executive course with two par 4s and seven par 3s. The course is open, with bunkers on every hole but one and extremely small greens.

DIRECTIONS: From downtown San Diego: Take I-5 north and exit on the Pacific Coast Highway. Exit the Pacific Coast Highway onto Barnett and turn left. Turn left on Rosecrans. Turn left into Gate 3 on Roosevelt Drive. At the second stop sign, turn left to the course. This is on the old navy training center base.

TECOLOTE CANYON GOLF CLUB (public, 18 holes, robert trent jones, sr. 1965) . . . . .

2755 Snead Avenue
San Diego, CA 92111
(858) 279-1600
americangolf.com

	YARDAGE	PAR	RATING	SLOPE	
FRONT	2625	58	57.0	93	**$17 - $23**
MIDDLE	-	-	-	-	
BACK	3166	58	55.6	91	

WHAT TO EXPECT: This is an easily walkable executive course designed by Robert Trent Jones II and Sam Snead. There are four par 4s, and the longest hole is 340 yards. The greens can be lightning fast.

DIRECTIONS: From within San Diego: Off I-5, exit at Clairemont/Mission Bay and go east on Clairemont Drive. Turn right on Burgener and then left on Field. Turn right on Snead Avenue to the course.

TWIN OAKS GOLF COURSE (public, 18 holes, ted robinson 1993) . . . .

1425 North Twin Oaks Valley Road
San Marcos, CA 92069
(760) 591-4653
jcresortsgolf.com

	YARDAGE	PAR	RATING	SLOPE	
FRONT	5423	72	71.7	128	**$25 - $69**
MIDDLE	6146	72	70.1	126	
BACK	6536	72	71.9	130	

WHAT TO EXPECT: Elevation changes, undulating greens, and water make this a very playable and entertaining course.

OUR OPINION: Twin Oaks was tough enough for us to enjoy ourselves and easy enough for the high handicapper. Watch out for the ninth hole – it is on the side of the hill. – Frank

DIRECTIONS: From San Diego (about 30 miles north to the course): Take I-15 north to Highway 78 west. Exit at Twin Oaks Valley Road and head north for three miles. The course is on the right.

CARLTON OAKS COUNTRY CLUB (resort, 18 holes, pete dye) . . . .

9200 Inwood Drive
Santee, CA 92071
(619) 448-8500
carltonoaksgolf.com

	YARDAGE	PAR	RATING	SLOPE	
FRONT	4548	71	67.1	114	**$55 - $75**
MIDDLE	6534	72	71.3	127	
BACK	7088	72	74.6	137	

WHAT TO EXPECT: This challenging course plays on flat terrain, but has all the ingredients of a solid course: water, rough, strong bunkering, and length. Phil Mickelson terms the 18th hole one of the best in golf.

DIRECTIONS: From San Diego (about 14 miles northeast to the course): Take Highway 52 east off either I-5, I-805 or I-15. Exit on Mast Boulevard and head north. Turn right on West Hills Boulevard and then left on Carlton Oaks. Turn right on Inwood Drive, to the club.

LOMAS SANTA FE COUNTRY CLUB (members only, 18 holes, billy bell 1967) . . . .

1505 Lomas Santa Fe Drive
Solana Beach, CA 92075
(858) 755-1547
americangolf.com

	YARDAGE	PAR	RATING	SLOPE
FRONT	5830	72	76.1	138
MIDDLE	6400	72	71.4	126
BACK	6607	72	72.3	128

$70 - $90

WHAT TO EXPECT: Two miles from the Pacific Ocean, Lomas Santa Fe has rolling hills, tree-lined fairways, and plenty of ocean views.
DIRECTIONS: From San Diego (about 18 miles north to the course): Take I-5 north, exit onto Lomas Santa Fe Drive, and head east a mile to Highland. Turn right to club entry.

LOMAS SANTA FE EXECUTIVE GOLF COURSE (public, 18 holes) . . . .

1580 Sun Valley Road
Solana Beach, CA 92075
(858) 755-0195
americangolf.com

	YARDAGE	PAR	RATING	SLOPE
FRONT	-	-	-	-
MIDDLE	-	-	-	-
BACK	2500	28	-	-

$11 - $24

WHAT TO EXPECT: This is a short executive course well suited for juniors and beginners.
DIRECTIONS: From San Diego (about 18 miles north to the course): Take I-5 north, exit at Lomas Santa Fe Drive, and head east. Turn left on Highland and then left on Sun Valley Road.

SKYLINE COUNTRY CLUB RANCH (members only, 9 holes) . . . .

18218 Paradise Mountain Road
Valley Center, CA 92082
(760) 749-3233

	YARDAGE	PAR	RATING	SLOPE
FRONT	1500	30	56.7	87
MIDDLE	-	-	-	-
BACK	1500	29	54.5	85

$2 - $3

WHAT TO EXPECT: Skyline is pitch-and-putt meets executive course.
DIRECTIONS: From San Diego (about 37 miles north to the course): Take I-15 north, exit at Via Rancho Parkway and turn right to head east. This turns into Bear Valley Road. Turn right at the stop sign at Valley Center. Turn right at Woods Valley and then left on Paradise Mountain Road.

SHADOWRIDGE COUNTRY CLUB (members only, 18 holes, david rainville) . . . .

1980 Gateway Drive
Vista, CA 92083
(760) 727-7706
shadowridgecc.com

	YARDAGE	PAR	RATING	SLOPE
FRONT	5693	72	74.9	135
MIDDLE	6650	72	73.9	125
BACK	6984	72	74.4	129

$55 - $70

WHAT TO EXPECT: Generous fairways and large, bold bunkering is purposely reminiscent of the great sand-belt course of Australia.
NOTES: The Faldo Golf Institute adjoins the facility.
DIRECTIONS: From San Diego (about 38 miles north to the course): Take I-5 north to Highway 78 east and drive toward Vista. Exit Sycamore and turn right. Turn right on Shadowridge Drive and then right at Gateway Drive.

VISTA VALLEY COUNTRY CLUB (members only, 18 holes, ted robinson) . . . .

29354 Vista Valley Drive
Vista, CA   92084
(760) 758-5275
vistavalley.org

	YARDAGE	PAR	RATING	SLOPE	
FRONT	5192	71	65.5	115	**$50 - $80**
MIDDLE	6035	71	69.6	125	
BACK	6345	71	71.1	130	

WHAT TO EXPECT: Surrounded by mountains, hundreds of mature oak and sycamore trees, and a small creek, this tree-lined course features a fairly flat front nine and a rolling, but more driver-friendly, back nine.

NOTES: Reciprocal play with other members only clubs is allowed.

DIRECTIONS: From San Diego (about 40 miles north to the course): Take I-15 north to Gopher Canyon Road. Exit and drive west for two miles to Valley Vista Drive. Turn left and drive to the club.

WARNER SPRINGS RANCH GOLF COURSE (semi-private, 18 holes, h. & d. rainville) . .

31652 Highway 79
Warner Springs, CA 92086
(760) 782-4270
warnersprings.com

	YARDAGE	PAR	RATING	SLOPE	
FRONT	5470	72	65.7	112	**$25 - $50**
MIDDLE	6701	72	71.9	126	
BACK	6892	72	72.7	128	

WHAT TO EXPECT: This is a driver-friendly, park-setting course, surrounded by trees and excellent views of the nearby mountains.

NOTES: The course is open to outside play Monday through Thursday, excluding holidays.

DIRECTIONS: From San Diego (about 83 miles northeast to the course): Drive north on I-15. Make a right turn on Scripps-Poway Parkway and a left on Highway 67. Take Highway 67 to Santa Ysabel, Highway 79, and turn left.

Desert

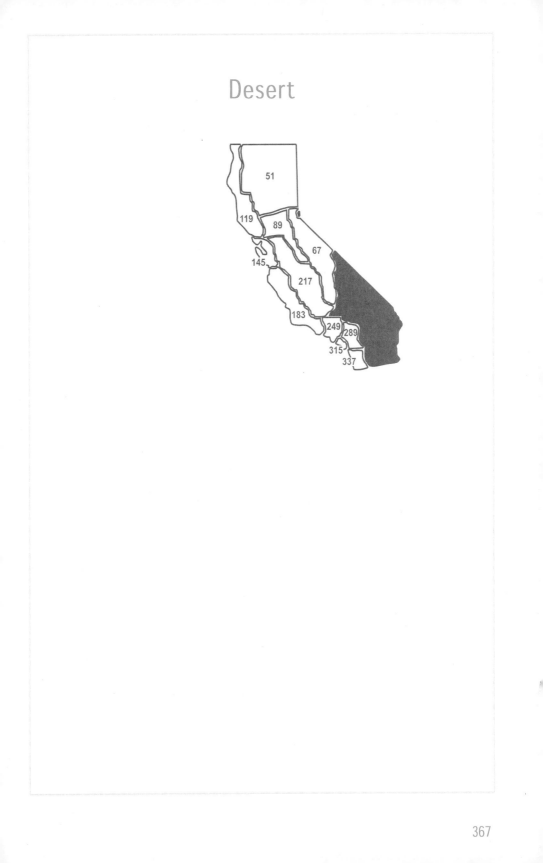

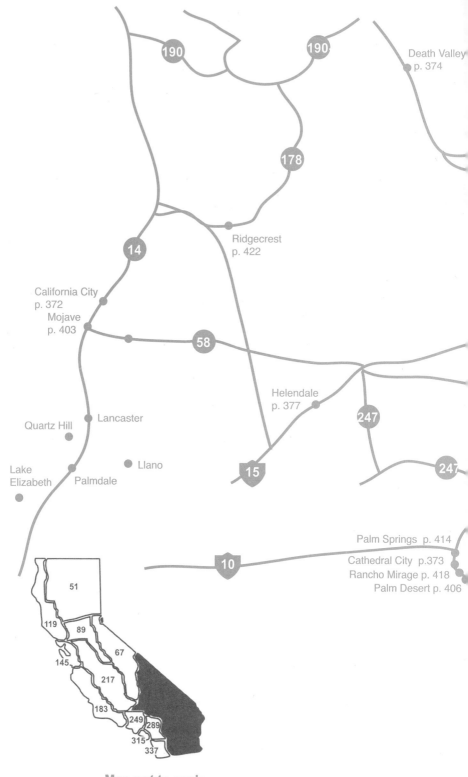

190

190

Death Valley
p. 374

178

14

Ridgecrest
p. 422

California City
p. 372
Mojave
p. 403

58

Helendale
p. 377

247

Quartz Hill

Lancaster

Lake
Elizabeth

Llano

15

247

Palmdale

Palm Springs p. 414

10

Cathedral City p.373
Rancho Mirage p. 418
Palm Desert p. 406

51

119

89

67

145

217

183

249

289

315

337

Map not to scale

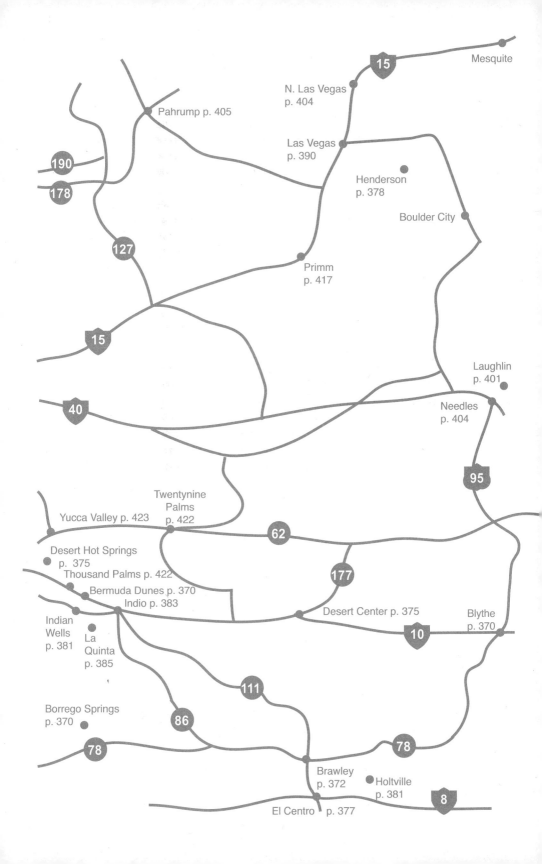

BERMUDA DUNES COUNTRY CLUB (members only, 27 holes, william f. bell) . . . .

42-360 Adams Street
Bermuda Dunes, CA 92201
(760) 345-2771
bermudadunescc.com

	YARDAGE	PAR	RATING	SLOPE	
FRONT	5484	72	72.2	123	**$80 - $80**
MIDDLE	6542	72	70.6	117	
BACK	6927	72	72.9	122	

WHAT TO EXPECT: Long one of the PGA Tour courses, Bermuda Dunes is located in a park-like setting with numerous trees and smallish greens. Not too easy, not too hard, this is a splendid members' course.

NOTES: The yardage listed is for the Classic Course.

DIRECTIONS: From Los Angeles (about 130 miles east to the course): Take I-10 east toward Palm Springs. Exit on Washington Street and turn right. Go about a miles and one-half, then turn left on Avenue 42. Turn right on Adams Street to the entrance gate.

BLYTHE GOLF COURSE (public, 18 holes, william f. bell) . . . .

4708 Wells Road
Blythe, CA 92225
(760) 922-7272

	YARDAGE	PAR	RATING	SLOPE	
FRONT	5684	73	72.6	117	**$20 - $20**
MIDDLE	6447	73	70.4	117	
BACK	6866	73	72.4	121	

WHAT TO EXPECT: Located on a mesa overlooking the Palo Verde Valley, this wide-open course features rolling hills on the front nine, while the back nine is relatively flat. The greens are small and level. If hitting fairways isn't part of your game, you're in luck, there is little trouble outside the short grass.

DIRECTIONS: From within Blythe: Off I-10, take the Lovekin exit and go north. Turn left on Hobson Way and right on Defrain. The course is on top of the hill.

BORREGO SPRINGS GOLF RESORT & COUNTRY CLUB (resort, 18 holes, cary bickler) . .

1112 Tilting T Drive
Borrego Springs, CA 92004
(760) 767-3330
borregospringsresort.com

	YARDAGE	PAR	RATING	SLOPE	
FRONT	4726	71	66.7	104	**$54 - $64**
MIDDLE	5954	72	67.6	112	
BACK	6480	72	70.4	117	

WHAT TO EXPECT: Known for its generous fairways and large, tiered greens, Borrego Springs is accented with palm trees and bunkers. Water comes into play on five holes.

DIRECTIONS: From San Diego (about 90 miles northeast to the course): Take I-8 east to Highway 67, go north to Highway 78, and go east. In Santa Ysabel, turn left on to Highway 79. Turn right onto S-2, then left onto S-22. Once in Borrego Springs, pass the roundabout and then turn left at the only stop sign.

DE ANZA COUNTRY CLUB (members only, 18 holes, lawrence hughes 1955) . . . .

509 Catarina Drive
Borrego Springs, CA 92004
(760) 767-5577
deanzacc.com

	YARDAGE	PAR	RATING	SLOPE
FRONT	5557	72	71.4	118
MIDDLE	6373	72	69.8	117
BACK	6778	72	72.1	123

$60 - $60

WHAT TO EXPECT: Part of a housing development, this is an old, level, traditional course with tree-lined fairways and medium-sized crowned greens.

DIRECTIONS: From San Diego (about 90 miles northeast to the course): Take I-8 east to Highway 67 and go north to Highway 78 and go east. In Santa Ysabel, turn left on to Highway 79. Turn right onto S-2, then left on to S-22. Once in Borrego Springs, from Christmas Tree Circle on the north side of town, take Borrego Springs Road. Turn left on San Ysidro and then right on Catarina.

RAMS HILL COUNTRY CLUB (semi-private, 18 holes, ted robinson) . . . .

1881 Rams Hills Road
Borrego Springs, CA 92004
(760) 767-5124

	YARDAGE	PAR	RATING	SLOPE
FRONT	5694	72	73.4	127
MIDDLE	6328	72	70.1	123
BACK	6866	72	72.9	130

$40 - $105

WHAT TO EXPECT: Being in the fairways is not that difficult here. But staying out of the traps is a must. This area receives constant wind that blows sand continually out of the traps, causing them to be on the hard side. If you can avoid the traps and hit the large greens, you will be rewarded. They are mildly sloping, roll true, and usually kept in good shape.

NOTES: The course is currently under new ownership and changes are on the way.

DIRECTIONS: From San Diego (about 90 miles northeast to the course): Take I-8 east to Highway 67 go north to Highway 78 east. Past Ramona, take S-3 north to Borrego Springs.

ROAD RUNNER CLUB (public, 18 holes) . . . .

1010 Palm Canyon Drive
Borrego Springs, CA 92004
(760) 767-5373

	YARDAGE	PAR	RATING	SLOPE
FRONT	-	-	-	-
MIDDLE	-	-	-	-
BACK	2500	54	-	-

$15 - $15

WHAT TO EXPECT: This par-3 course is part of a residential community. The longest hole is 170 yards, and there is water on one hole. The greens are generous in size. With homes lining the course, semi-accurate iron play is a must.

NOTES: The course is closed to the public Tuesday and Thursday morning until noon, but open for resident golfers.

DIRECTIONS: From San Diego (about 90 miles northeast to the course): Take I-8 east to Highway 67, go north to Highway 78 and go east. In Santa Ysabel, turn left onto Highway 79. Turn right on to S-2, then left onto S-22.

BOULDER CITY GOLF COURSE (public, 18 holes) . . . .

One Clubhouse Drive
Boulder City, NV 89005
(702) 293-9236
bcgolf.com

	YARDAGE	PAR	RATING	SLOPE
FRONT	5458	72	66.4	110
MIDDLE	6120	72	68.0	103
BACK	6542	72	70.2	110

$25 - $45

WHAT TO EXPECT: Boulder City is a roomy course with numerous bunkers and large flat greens.
NOTES: Water is currently being added to the course.
DIRECTIONS: From the Las Vegas Airport (about 23 miles southeast to the course): Take Sunset Road to the 95 Expressway and head south. In Boulder City, take a right at the second light, which is Buchanan. The course is about one mile down, on the left.

DEL RIO COUNTRY CLUB (semi-private, 18 holes, william p. bell) . . . .

102 East Del Rio Road
Brawley, CA 92227
(760) 344-0085

	YARDAGE	PAR	RATING	SLOPE
FRONT	5738	73	72.3	117
MIDDLE	-	-	-	-
BACK	6001	70	67.6	115

$38 - $41

WHAT TO EXPECT: The player who can effectively bump and run the ball will score well at Del Rio. The greens here are small and open in the front. During the summer months they are extremely firm, so flying the ball at the pin is not wise. This tree-lined course, with many doglegs, will also favor the player who can hit the ball left to right.
DIRECTIONS: From Brawley: Take Highway 111 north. The course is a mile north of Brawley.

TIERRA DEL SOL GOLF CLUB (public, 18 holes, r. von hagge & b. devlin 1977) . . . . . .

10300 North Loop Drive
California City, CA 93505
(760) 373-2384

	YARDAGE	PAR	RATING	SLOPE
FRONT	5225	72	68.0	122
MIDDLE	6300	72	70.6	121
BACK	6908	72	74.0	130

$15 - $22

WHAT TO EXPECT: This is not your typical desert course. There are plenty of elevation changes, with most greens elevated and guarded by traps. Rolling the ball up to the green is not an option. You will find little out-of-bounds to get in your way, but water can be found off the tee and on your second shot. The greens are fairly level and crowned. Wind can be a factor.
DIRECTIONS: From Mojave (about 15 miles northeast to the course): Take Highway 14 north. Drive five miles to California City Boulevard and head east. Travel about nine miles and turn left on North Loop Drive. Follow the signs to the clubhouse.

CATHEDRAL CANYON COUNTRY CLUB (semi-private, 27 holes, david rainville) . . . . . .

68-311 Paseo Real
Cathedral City, CA 92234
(760) 328-6571
cathedralcity.com

	YARDAGE	PAR	RATING	SLOPE
FRONT	5423	72	70.8	124
MIDDLE	6177	72	69.5	128
BACK	6510	72	71.1	130

$20 - $85

WHAT TO EXPECT: Cathedral Canyon is three distinct courses played in 18-hole combinations. The Lake Course is target golf, with water hazards on every hole. The Mountain Course is hilly, with tree-lined fairways. It has the longest yardage of the three courses. The Arroyo Course is Scottish links in style with bountiful fairways and no trees.
OUR OPINION: Beware of the trees on the Lake and Mountain Courses. They are not for show and should command your full attention. – Bob
NOTES: The yardage listed is for the Lake and Mountain nines.
DIRECTIONS: From downtown Los Angeles (about 115 miles east to the course): Take I-10 east. Exit at Date Palm Drive, turn right, and drive about five miles. Turn right on Dinah Shore Drive and then left on Cathedral Canyon Drive. The club is on the left.

CIMARRON GOLF RESORT (public, 36 holes, john fought 2000) . . . .

67-603 30th Avenue
Cathedral City, CA 92234
(760) 770-6060
cimarrongolf.com

	YARDAGE	PAR	RATING	SLOPE
FRONT	5879	71	67.9	114
MIDDLE	6474	71	70.7	119
BACK	6859	71	72.4	123

$55 - $115

WHAT TO EXPECT: The mountains provide an excellent backdrop for both the Short Course and the Long Course. Both layouts are similar in design, combining desert golf with European-like characteristics. You will find strategically placed sod-wall bunkers, mounding, and expansive greens with subtle undulations.
OUR OPINION: If you can score well on the Short Course, you can score well anywhere. The is one of the best executive courses in America. – Bob
NOTES: The yardage listed is for the Long Course.
DIRECTIONS: From downtown Los Angeles (about 115 miles east to the course): Take I-10 east and exit on Date Palm Drive. Head south and turn right on 30th Avenue. It will dead-end at the club.

DATE PALM COUNTRY CLUB (semi-private, 18 holes, ted robinson) . . . .

36-200 Date Palm Drive
Cathedral City, CA 92234
(760) 328-1315

	YARDAGE	PAR	RATING	SLOPE
FRONT	3083	58	57.2	93
MIDDLE	-	-	-	-
BACK	3083	58	54.0	85

$40 - $45

WHAT TO EXPECT: Narrow tree-lined fairways and small greens, many of which are guarded by water, make up the challenge on this executive course.
DIRECTIONS: From downtown Los Angeles (about 115 miles east to the course): Take I-10 east, exit on Date Palm Drive, and head south about three miles. The entrance is on the left.

DESERT PRINCESS COUNTRY CLUB (resort, 27 holes, david rainville) . . . .

28-555 Landau Boulevard
Cathedral City, CA 92234
(760) 322-2280
desertprincesscc.com

	YARDAGE	PAR	RATING	SLOPE	
FRONT	5303	72	71.0	119	**$45 - $120**
MIDDLE	6300	72	70.0	121	
BACK	6734	72	72.5	126	

WHAT TO EXPECT: There are three courses, the Cielo, Lagos, and Vista. The Cielo and Lagos courses are very similar, winding through condominiums, with water coming into play on 15 of the 18 holes. The Vista Course is a more wide-open, links-style course. The greens on all the courses are very large and undulating. They tend to break toward Indio. Putting will be the key to a low score.

NOTES: This is a private resort for members and guests of the resort only. The yardage listed is for the Cielo-Vista Courses.

DIRECTIONS: From downtown Los Angeles (about 115 miles east to the course): Take I-10 east, exit at Date Palm Drive, and head south. Turn right on Vista Chino and then left on Landau Boulevard.

OUTDOOR RESORT & COUNTRY CLUB (members only, 27 holes) . . . .

69-411 Ramon Road
Cathedral City, CA 92234
(760) 328-3834

	YARDAGE	PAR	RATING	SLOPE	
FRONT	-	-	-	-	**$10 - $20**
MIDDLE	-	-	-	-	
BACK	1900	54	-	-	

WHAT TO EXPECT: There are two courses at the Outdoor Resort. A short 500 yard par-3 course (as opposed to a long 500 yard par-3 course) and an 18-hole executive course.

DIRECTIONS: From downtown Los Angeles (about 115 miles east to the course): Take I-10 east. Exit at Date Palm and go to Ramon Road. Turn left at Ramon Road. The club is down about two lights, on the right.

FURNACE CREEK GOLF COURSE (resort, 18 holes, william p. bell 1939) . . . .

Highway 190
Death Valley, CA 92328
(760) 786-2301
furnacecreekresort.com

	YARDAGE	PAR	RATING	SLOPE	
FRONT	4724	70	66.0	109	**$30 - $50**
MIDDLE	5856	70	67.8	111	
BACK	6215	70	69.6	114	

WHAT TO EXPECT: Furnace Creek is 214 feet below sea level and is the lowest course in the world. Because of the lack of altitude, the ball does not carry well, so remember to club up. Believe it or not, there are plenty of trees on the course, and water comes into play on six holes.

OUR OPINION: If you truly want to educate yourself on the variety of courses available to you in California, you must play the lowest course in the world. – Bob

DIRECTIONS: From Las Vegas (about 120 miles northwest to the course): Take Blue Diamond Highway 160 to Pahrump. Pass through Pahrump and take a left on Bellevista Avenue, to the Death Valley junction. Follow this to Stateline Road 190; it's 30 miles to Furnace Creek Ranch Resort.

LAKE TAMARISK GOLF CLUB (public, 9 holes, robert trent jones) . . . .

26-251 Parkview Drive
Desert Center, CA 92239
(760) 227-3203

	YARDAGE	PAR	RATING	SLOPE
FRONT	2786	37	69.9	104
MIDDLE	-	-	-	-
BACK	2965	35	66.9	100

$15 - $20

WHAT TO EXPECT: Although oleanders and many other shade trees are scattered along the fairways, Lake Tamarisk is still driver friendly. For the player who hits it long and wrong, your ball will be bouncing off the highway. The greens vary in size, and the lake comes into play on two fairways.
DIRECTIONS: From Palm Springs: Take I-10 east for about 60 miles. Exit at Desert Center Road and head north. Go left on Kaiser Road to the course.

DESERT CREST COUNTRY CLUB (semi-private, 9 holes) . . . .

69400 South Country Club Drive
Desert Hot Springs, CA 92241
(760) 329-8711

	YARDAGE	PAR	RATING	SLOPE
FRONT	-	-	-	-
MIDDLE	-	-	-	-
BACK	889	27	-	-

$12 - $14

WHAT TO EXPECT: This is a friendly pitch-and-putt course.
NOTES: The course is not open to the public on Tuesday, Wednesday, and Friday.
DIRECTIONS: In Palm Springs: Go north on Gene Autry Drive, which turns into Palm Drive. Stay on Palm Drive until Dillion Road. Go east on Dillon Road four and one-half miles, to the course.

DESERT DUNES GOLF CLUB (semi-private, 18 holes, robert trent jones jr.) . . . .

19-300 Palm Drive
Desert Hot Springs, CA 92240
(760) 251-5366
book4golf.com

	YARDAGE	PAR	RATING	SLOPE
FRONT	5250	72	72.1	125
MIDDLE	6529	72	71.5	126
BACK	7005	72	73.7	132

$79 - $110

WHAT TO EXPECT: Often included by the large golf magazines in their national rankings, this tough layout somehow still remains undiscovered. The course is beautifully framed with sand dunes and the natural desert and is very playable , with one exception. At times Desert Dunes can be extremely windy.
OUR OPINION: No wind checks are allowed. That is the sign you are greeted with when you enter the pro shop. Forget about no wind checks (unless its really windy). This is a fabulous Scottish links course with hard greens and no homes. All you see is golf course and desert. – Frank
DIRECTIONS: From downtown Los Angeles (about 110 miles east to the course): Take I-10 east, exit at Palm Drive, and head left over the freeway. Desert Dunes is on the right a mile or two up the road.

HIDDEN SPRINGS COUNTRY CLUB (public, 9 holes) . . . .

15-500 Bubbling Wells Road
Desert Hot Springs, CA 92240
(760) 329-8816

	YARDAGE	PAR	RATING	SLOPE
FRONT	-	-	-	-
MIDDLE	-	-	-	-
BACK	1506	29	-	-

$15 - $15

WHAT TO EXPECT: This is a short executive course, with two par 4s.
DIRECTIONS: From downtown Los Angeles (about 110 miles east to the course): Take I-10 east, exit at Palm Drive/Gene Autry Trail, and head north on Palm Drive. Turn right (east) on Dillon Road, and then left on Bubbling Wells Road.

MISSION LAKES COUNTRY CLUB (semi-private, 18 holes, ted robinson) . . . .

8484 Clubhouse Drive
Desert Hot Springs, CA 92240
(760) 329-8061

	YARDAGE	PAR	RATING	SLOPE
FRONT	5390	72	70.6	115
MIDDLE	6396	71	70.5	121
BACK	6742	71	72.1	124

$55 - $75

WHAT TO EXPECT: Mission Lakes is not a long course, but it is imperative that you have a good score on the front nine since the back nine is a beast. Holes 10 through 12 play up, along and down the mountain. You finish your round with a 234-yard par 3, a 608-yard par 5, a 209-yard par 3 and a 418-yard par 4, uphill. Good Luck.
DIRECTIONS: From downtown Los Angeles (about 110 miles east to the course): Take I-10 east, exit at Indian Avenue, and turn left to head north. Go about five miles and turn right on Mission Lakes Boulevard. Take the first left on Clubhouse Drive, to the course.

SANDS R.V. RESORT (public, 9 holes) . . . .

16-400 Bubbling Wells Road
Desert Hot Springs, CA 92240
(760) 251-1173

	YARDAGE	PAR	RATING	SLOPE
FRONT	1832	32	57.7	-
MIDDLE	-	-	-	-
BACK	2127	32	57.7	-

$12 - $17

WHAT TO EXPECT: Sands is a great place for beginners and those who want to break 80 but don't have the game to do it on a regulation course. The course is short, with few trees and generous fairways. We must report, despite the name, there is no sand.
DIRECTIONS: From downtown Los Angeles (about 110 miles east to the course): Take I-10 east, exit at Palm Drive, and head north. Make a right on Dillon Road and drive one mile to Bubbling Wells Road. The course is on the corner.

MUROC LAKE GOLF COURSE (military, 18 holes, william f. bell) . . . .

36 North Wolfe Avenue
Edwards, CA 93523
(661) 277-3469

	YARDAGE	PAR	RATING	SLOPE
FRONT	5561	72	72.2	123
MIDDLE	6446	72	71.3	125
BACK	6915	72	73.5	129

$10 - $17

WHAT TO EXPECT: This is a long, older desert course with mature trees and rolling fairways. Many of the fairways are parallel to each other, so chances are if you don't hit your fairway, you will hit someone else's. The greens are on the smaller side, and Muroc Lake comes into play on one hole.
NOTES: This course is limited to military personnel and guests only.
DIRECTIONS: From Palmdale (about 50 miles north to the course): Take Highway 14 north to the Rosamond exit, to Edwards AFB. Turn right and head to the Edwards AFB gate. The guard has further directions.

BROKEN SPOKE GOLF COURSE (public, 9 holes, jack kirby) . . . .

225 Wake Avenue
El Centro, CA 92243
(760) 353-4653

	YARDAGE	PAR	RATING	SLOPE
FRONT	-	-	-	-
MIDDLE	-	-	-	-
BACK	1740	30	-	-

$14 - $14

WHAT TO EXPECT: The course is open, yet tree-lined with a couple of lakes.
DIRECTIONS: From within El Centro: Off I-8, exit at Fourth Street and head south. Turn left on Wake Avenue, and go until it ends.

LAKEVIEW GOLF CLUB (public, 9 holes) . . . .

1589 Drew Road
El Centro, CA 92243
(760) 352-6638

	YARDAGE	PAR	RATING	SLOPE
FRONT	-	-	-	-
MIDDLE	-	-	-	-
BACK	2182	33	60.6	102

$10 - $17

WHAT TO EXPECT: Don't be surprised if you see some coyotes on this short, executive course. Lakeview has a lake that comes into play on two holes. The greens are good sized and mildly sloped. The road nearby creates out-of-bounds.
DIRECTIONS: From El Centro: Take I-8 west, exit on Drew Road, and head south. This is west of the town of El Centro.

SILVER LAKES COUNTRY CLUB (members only, 27 holes, ted robinson 1974) . . . .

14814 Clubhouse Drive
Helendale, CA 92342
(760) 245-7435

	YARDAGE	PAR	RATING	SLOPE
FRONT	5564	72	72.3	122
MIDDLE	6455	72	70.3	123
BACK	6851	72	72.4	128

$25 - $35

WHAT TO EXPECT: There are three courses, the North, South, and East. They are played in 18-hole combinations.   All three courses at Silver Lakes are member friendly with wide fairways and good-sized greens. The South Course has the most water.
NOTES: The yardage listed is for the North/South nines.
DIRECTIONS: From San Bernardino (about 55 miles north to the course): Drive north on I-15 to the D Street/Apple Valley exit, north of Victorville. Turn left on National Trails Highway and continue 14 miles to Vista Road. Make a left to the club.

ANTHEM, THE REVERE AT (public, 18 holes, billy casper) . . . .

2600 Evergreen Oaks Drive
Henderson, NV 89052
(702) 259-4653
revereatanthem.com

	YARDAGE	PAR	RATING	SLOPE
FRONT	5305	72	69.9	117
MIDDLE	6590	72	70.8	131
BACK	7144	72	73.6	139

$55 - $215

WHAT TO EXPECT: Set in three separate canyons, this course has dramatic elevation changes (from 2500' to 3000'), open fairways and large greens. Even more impressive than the course may be the views of the Las Vegas skyline.

DIRECTIONS: From the Las Vegas Airport (about eight miles south to the course): Take I-215 east. Exit on Eastern Avenue and turn right. Veer to the left on Anthem Parkway. There are signs to the course from there.

BLACK MOUNTAIN COUNTRY CLUB (semi-private, 18 holes, bob baldock 1957) . . . . .

500 Greenway Road
Henderson, NV 89009
(702) 565-7933
golfblackmountain.com

	YARDAGE	PAR	RATING	SLOPE
FRONT	5509	73	71.1	120
MIDDLE	5939	72	69.8	120
BACK	6551	72	71.2	123

$40 - $100

WHAT TO EXPECT: The front nine is fairly clear of obstacles, while the back narrows, with trees coming into play. The greens are on the small side, and experienced players have learned that they break toward town.

NOTES: The public is allowed to play after 11 a.m. , earlier if there are cancellations.

DIRECTIONS: From the Las Vegas Airport (about 14 miles southeast to the course): Take I-215 east to US 95 south. Exit on Horizon and go left to Greenway Road.

DESERT WILLOW GOLF CLUB (public, 18 holes, greg nash 1996) . . . .

2020 West Horizon Ridge Parkway
Henderson, NV 89012
(702) 263-4653

	YARDAGE	PAR	RATING	SLOPE
FRONT	-	-	-	-
MIDDLE	-	-	-	-
BACK	3876	60	-	-

$55 - $60

WHAT TO EXPECT: This is an open desert course with medium-sized, flat greens and executive in length.

DIRECTIONS: From the Las Vegas Airport (about 11 miles southeast to the course): Take I-215 east, exit on Green Valley Parkway, and turn right. At the end of the road, turn left on Horizon Ridge Parkway.

DRAGONRIDGE GOLF CLUB (semi-private, 18 holes, morrish & druzisky 2000) . . . . . .

552 South Stephanie Street
Henderson, NV 89012
(702) 614-4444
dragonridgegolfclub.com

	YARDAGE	PAR	RATING	SLOPE	
FRONT	5040	72	68.2	118	**$60 - $195**
MIDDLE	6481	72	70.4	131	
BACK	7040	72	72.9	143	

WHAT TO EXPECT: With split fairways and blind tee and approach shots, don't wager with a member if you have not played this course. Course knowledge is key. Friendly off the tee, this course will challenge you fairway to green. DragonRidge is located in a natural desert surrounding with plenty of scenic outcroppings and well-placed traps.
DIRECTIONS: From the Las Vegas Airport (about 11 miles southeast to the course): Take I-215 east. Take Exit 2/Valle Verde. Go south on Valle Verde until it dead ends. Cross the dead-end to the gate. This is 15 to 20 minutes from the Strip.

LEGACY GOLF CLUB, THE (public, 18 holes, arthur hills) . . . .

130 Par Excellence Drive
Henderson, NV 89014
(702) 897-2187
thelegacygolf.com

	YARDAGE	PAR	RATING	SLOPE	
FRONT	5340	72	71.0	120	**$55 - $165**
MIDDLE	6744	72	72.1	128	
BACK	7234	72	74.9	136	

WHAT TO EXPECT: The Legacy Golf Course features extensive mounding in the fairways and elevated greens where players can use their creativity with their approach shots.
OUR OPINION: A decent Arthur Hills course that plays among the housing. – Andy
DIRECTIONS: From the Las Vegas Airport (about seven miles southeast to the course): Take I-215 east. Exit at Green Valley Parkway and go left. Turn right on Wigwam, and the club is on the left.

REFLECTION BAY GOLF CLUB (public, 18 holes, jack nicklaus) . . . .

75 Monte Lago Boulevard
Henderson, NV 89011
(702) 740-4653
lakelasvegas.com

	YARDAGE	PAR	RATING	SLOPE	
FRONT	5891	72	68.1	124	**$190 - $250**
MIDDLE	6862	72	73.2	135	
BACK	7262	72	74.8	138	

WHAT TO EXPECT: The course features plenty of elevation changes. Each nine has players starting uphill and finishing downhill. For those who have an aversion to water, you might want to skip the last five holes, which play along a large lake.
OUR OPINION: This is a terrific layout, with the only drawbacks being that a few greens are not deep enough for the length of the approach shots and the price is out of reach for most golfers. – Bob
DIRECTIONS: From the Las Vegas Airport (about 19 miles east to the course): Take I-215 east. This turns in to Lake Mead Drive. Drive about 10 miles and turn left at the Lake Las Vegas Resort sign. There are signs from there.

RIO SECCO GOLF CLUB (resort, 18 holes, rees jones 1997) . . . .

2851 Grand Hills Drive
Henderson, NV 89012
(888) 867-3226
playrio.com

	YARDAGE	PAR	RATING	SLOPE
FRONT	5778	72	70.0	127
MIDDLE	6375	72	71.0	125
BACK	7333	72	75.7	142

$125 - $290

WHAT TO EXPECT: This is a hilly, well-conditioned course with large greens that are surrounded by mounding and protected by traps. Although the course affords excellent views, keep your attention on the generous fairways – outside the fairways the view is not so pretty.

OUR OPINION: This is a spectacular Rees Jones desert course, but the price is too steep. – Bob

NOTES: Primarily for guests of the Rio Hotel, guests of other hotels are welcome.

DIRECTIONS: From the Las Vegas Airport (about ten miles south to the course): Take I-215 east, exit onto Eastern Avenue and go south. Stay on Eastern Avenue, don't turn off into Anthem. Turn right at the stop sign on Grand Hills Drive to the course.

SOUTHSHORE GOLF CLUB (members only, 18 holes, jack nicklaus 1995) . . . .

29 Grand Mediterranean Drive
Henderson, NV 89011
(702) 558-0022
lakelasvegas.com

	YARDAGE	PAR	RATING	SLOPE
FRONT	-	-	-	-
MIDDLE	-	-	-	-
BACK	6926	71	-	-

$115 - $115

WHAT TO EXPECT: Views of the lake and mountains, plus a solid challenge, make this one of the better private club layouts in the Las Vegas area.

DIRECTIONS: From the Las Vegas Airport (about 19 miles east to the course): Take I-215 east, which turns into Lake Mead Drive. Turn left at the Lake Las Vegas sign. Turn right at the first stop sign, to the security gate.

WILDHORSE GOLF CLUB (public, 18 holes, hubert green) . . . .

2100 West Warm Springs Road
Henderson, NV 89014
(702) 434-9000
americangolf.com

	YARDAGE	PAR	RATING	SLOPE
FRONT	5311	72	71.3	125
MIDDLE	6465	72	72.2	129
BACK	7042	72	75.2	135

$75 - $150

WHAT TO EXPECT: From the back tees, this is a long course with undulating greens that can wreak havoc on the weak putter. With mature trees everywhere, WildHorse is more traditional than desert in style.

DIRECTIONS: From the Las Vegas Airport (about 7 miles southeast to the course): Take I-215 east. Exit on Warm Springs Road and turn left. WildHorse is just past the intersection of Green Valley Parkway.

BARBARA WORTH GOLF RESORT (semi-private, 18 holes) . . . .

2050 Country Club Drive
Holtville, CA 92250
(760) 356-5842
bwresort.com

	YARDAGE	PAR	RATING	SLOPE
FRONT	5827	73	72.9	125
MIDDLE	6302	71	70.0	119
BACK	6580	71	71.8	122

$25 - $30

WHAT TO EXPECT: This is a horizontal course with generous fairways and mid-sized greens. Although several ponds and trees line the course, missing the fairways does not penalize you unfairly. The course is walkable and suited for family golf.

DIRECTIONS: From San Diego (about 125 miles east to the course): Take I-8 east and go through El Centro. Pass Dogwood, and take the Highway 111 exit north to Brawley. At the only light, which is a large intersection, turn right on Evan Hughes.

DESERT HORIZONS COUNTRY CLUB (members only, 18 holes, ted robinson) . . . .

44-900 Desert Horizons Drive
Indian Wells, CA 92210
(760) 340-4651
deserthorizonscountryclub.com

	YARDAGE	PAR	RATING	SLOPE
FRONT	5417	72	71.9	121
MIDDLE	6150	72	68.9	116
BACK	6567	72	71.7	125

$85 - $85

WHAT TO EXPECT: This is a narrow, easily walkable course bordered by palms and a variety of other trees. The greens are medium sized and flat. Water comes into play on six holes.

DIRECTIONS: From downtown Los Angeles (about 125 miles east to the course): Take I-10 east, exit on Cook Street, and head south. Turn left on Highway 111 and then left on Desert Horizons Drive. Check in at the gate.

ELDORADO COUNTRY CLUB (members only, 18 holes, lawrence hughes) . . . .

46-000 Fairway Drive
Indian Wells, CA 92210
(760) 346-8081

	YARDAGE	PAR	RATING	SLOPE
FRONT	5280	72	71.7	120
MIDDLE	6346	72	70.2	125
BACK	6808	72	72.5	131

$150 - $150

WHAT TO EXPECT: One of the desert's older courses, it has hosted the Bob Hope Desert Classic. This charming layout is based on the flats adjoining the mountains. With a host of palm trees and out-of-bounds, it is essential to get off the tee well. That accomplished, this well-manicured course is not too difficult.

DIRECTIONS: From downtown Los Angeles (about 125 miles east to the course): Go east on Freeway I-10, take the Cook Street exit, and head south. Drive about ten minutes and then turn left on Fairway Drive to the club.

GOLF RESORT AT INDIAN WELLS, THE (resort, 36 holes, ted robinson) . . . .

44-500 Indian Wells Lane
Indian Wells, CA 92210
(760) 346-4653
americangolf.com

	YARDAGE	PAR	RATING	SLOPE	
FRONT	6135	72	69.0	115	**$70 - $140**
MIDDLE	6254	72	69.5	117	
BACK	6681	72	71.7	122	

WHAT TO EXPECT: Indian Wells could be the definition of a resort course: aesthetically pleasing and user friendly. Sure, there is water on 14 of the 36 holes, but in most spots the water can be easily avoided. Hit the ball well and you will score well. Hit the ball poorly and you will be surprised at how many good bounces you receive.

OUR OPINION: During prime season, $140 is a lot of money to boost your ego. – Shaw

DIRECTIONS: From downtown Los Angeles (about 125 miles east to the course): Take I-10 east, exit at Washington Avenue and head south. Go west on Highway 111, then north on Indian Wells Lane to the club. The club is on the right, just past the Hyatt.

INDIAN WELLS COUNTRY CLUB (members only, 27 holes, eddie sussalla) . . . .

46-000 Club Drive
Indian Wells, CA 92210
(760) 360-0861
indianwellsclub.com

	YARDAGE	PAR	RATING	SLOPE	
FRONT	5607	72	73.2	131	**$190 - $190**
MIDDLE	6095	72	69.3	118	
BACK	6478	72	71.0	124	

WHAT TO EXPECT: There are three nine-hole courses, none of which is exceedingly long. The course can be configured as 18-hole combinations or as a compilation 18-hole course. All the courses are desert layouts that require precise iron play.

NOTES: The yardage is for the Classic Course. Reciprocal play with other member only clubs is allowed.

DIRECTIONS: From downtown Los Angeles (about 125 miles east to the course): Take I-10 east, exit at Cook Street and head south. Turn left on Highway 111 and then right on Club Drive.

RESERVE, THE (members only, 18 holes, tom weiskopf & jay morrish 1998) . . . .

74-001 Reserve Drive
Indian Wells, CA 92210
(760) 674-2240

	YARDAGE	PAR	RATING	SLOPE	
FRONT	5243	72	71.1	129	**$100 - $200**
MIDDLE	6575	72	71.1	133	
BACK	7052	72	73.5	137	

WHAT TO EXPECT: Set at the base of the mountains, this is a long, challenging course. The length from the back tees is imposing, but is not as much a factor on your scorecard as course knowledge. Slight elevation changes and deceptive pin locations give the decided advantage to the member golfer.

DIRECTIONS: From downtown Los Angeles (about 125 miles east to the course): Take I-10 east, exit at Monterey Avenue, and turn right. Stay on this past Highway 111. It will turn into Highway 74. Turn left on Haystack and then right on Portola. Take the second left into the iron gates.

VINTAGE CLUB, THE (members only, 36 holes, tom fazio) . . . .

75-001 Vintage Drive West
Indian Wells, CA 92210
(760) 862-2076

	YARDAGE	PAR	RATING	SLOPE
FRONT	5166	72	69.7	121
MIDDLE	6422	72	70.6	122
BACK	6830	72	73.3	132

$100 - $100

WHAT TO EXPECT: The Mountain Course is the Augusta National of Palm Springs: manicured with open driving areas, understated strategy and lots of native color. The 16th hole is one of the most beautiful and memorable you will ever play. The Desert Course, with its very small greens, abundant bunkering, and more narrow landing areas, is a fresh and attractive alternative to its sister course, the Mountain.

NOTES: The yardage listed is for the Mountain Course.

DIRECTIONS: From downtown Los Angeles (about 125 miles east to the course): Take the I-10 east, exit at Cook Street, and drive south into Indian Wells. Cook Street dead-ends at The Vintage.

HERITAGE PALMS GOLF CLUB (semi-private, 18 holes, arthur hills 1996) . . . .

44291 Heritage Palms Drive South
Indio, CA 92201
(760) 772-7334
heritagepalms.com

	YARDAGE	PAR	RATING	SLOPE
FRONT	4885	72	67.4	110
MIDDLE	6293	72	69.9	119
BACK	6727	72	71.9	124

$50 - $120

WHAT TO EXPECT: Heritage Palms has subtle sloping fairways and greens. If you are interested in scoring well, you will have to get past the par 3s, which are aesthetically pleasing and formidable.

OUR OPINION: The course is solid but nothing fancy. However, Heritage Palms has a reputation for immaculate conditioning and views, and it does not dissappoint. – The Mole

DIRECTIONS: From Los Angeles (about 130 miles east to the course): Take I-10 east, exit at Jefferson Street and head south. Turn left on Fred Waring Drive and then right on Heritage Palms Drive.

INDIAN PALMS COUNTRY CLUB (semi-private, 27 holes, jackie cochran 1945) . . . . . .

48-630 Monroe Street
Indio, CA 92201
(760) 347-2326
indianpalms.com

	YARDAGE	PAR	RATING	SLOPE
FRONT	5859	73	74.1	119
MIDDLE	6359	72	70.5	120
BACK	6710	72	72.7	131

$20 - $70

WHAT TO EXPECT: All three nines feature mature trees, plenty of water, and subtle elevation changes.

NOTES: Once a citrus ranch, this course was developed by Jackie Cochran. She took over the mantle as the leading woman pilot after the disappearance of Amelia Earhart. The course played host to many celebrities and dignitaries of the time. A wall in the clubhouse is dedicated to the history of the course. The yardage listed is for the Indian/Mountain Course.

DIRECTIONS: From Los Angeles (about 130 miles east to the course): Take I-10 east toward Palm Springs. Take the Monroe Street exit south. The course is one-quarter mile past 48th Street, on the left.

INDIO GOLF COURSE (public, 18 holes, lawrence hughes 1964) . . . .

83-040 Avenue 42
Indio, CA 92201
(760) 347-9156

	YARDAGE	PAR	RATING	SLOPE
FRONT	2662	54	56.3	80
MIDDLE	-	-	-	-
BACK	3005	54	54.1	77

$12 - $15

WHAT TO EXPECT: This is one of the longest par-3 courses in California. This night-lit, mature layout features small, well-kept, undulating greens and fairways guarded by mature trees. On busy days, balls can come from every direction, so if you hear someone yell, "Fore!", duck; it is not a drill.

DIRECTIONS: From Los Angeles (about 130 miles east to the course): Take I-10 east, exit at Jackson Street, and head north. Turn right on Avenue 42. The course is on the right.

LANDMARK GOLF CLUB (public, 36 holes, landmark, schmidt - curley 1999) . . . .

84-000 Landmark Parkway
Indio, CA 92203
(760) 347-2326
landmarkgc.com

	YARDAGE	PAR	RATING	SLOPE
FRONT	5094	72	70.9	128
MIDDLE	6500	72	68.9	123
BACK	7230	72	75.1	136

$55 - $135

WHAT TO EXPECT: Desert links golf is the best way to describe Landmark's two courses. Both layouts incorporate constant elevation changes, perfectly manicured fairways, large undulating greens, and fantastic views of the surrounding desert mountains. A word of advice: the greens fall off around the edges, so play to the center. A good wedge game is key to scoring well at either course.

OUR OPINION: Not a blade of grass out of shape, as good a conditioned course as you will ever find. We played for $70, well worth the price. If you can only play one, pick the North Course. – Frank

NOTES: Landmark Golf Club is home to the Skins Game. The yardage listed is for Skins South.

DIRECTIONS: From Los Angeles (about 130 miles east to the course): Take I-10 east and exit at Golf Center Parkway. Go north one mile; the course is on the right.

PLANTATION GOLF CLUB, THE (members only, 18 holes, curley & couples 1998) . . . .

50994 Monroe Street
Indio, CA 92253
(760) 775-3688

	YARDAGE	PAR	RATING	SLOPE
FRONT	6196	72	69.6	124
MIDDLE	6597	72	71.7	127
BACK	7042	72	73.9	134

WHAT TO EXPECT: Plantation features some of the best bunkering in many years. Located at an old orchard, the flat layout appears more mature than its actual age.

DIRECTIONS: From downtown Los Angeles (about 130 miles east to the course): Take I-10 east toward Palm Springs. Take the Monroe Street exit. Turn right on Monroe Street. The main entrance is located between 50th and 52nd Avenue.

INDIAN SPRINGS COUNTRY CLUB (semi-private, 18 holes, david ginkel) . . . .

46-080 Jefferson Street
La Quinta, CA 92253
(760) 775-3360

	YARDAGE	PAR	RATING	SLOPE
FRONT	5601	72	71.1	115
MIDDLE	6052	72	68.6	118
BACK	6225	72	71.3	110

$50 - $75

WHAT TO EXPECT: A new clubhouse, eight lakes affecting 11 holes, and 300 extra yards are some of the changes on this completely refurbished and affordable La Quinta layout. NOTES: Play it while you can; word has it they eventually want to go private. DIRECTIONS: From downtown Los Angeles (about 130 miles east to the course): Take I-10 east, exit at Jefferson Street, and head south to the club. The club is on the left.

LA QUINTA COUNTRY CLUB (members only, 18 holes, lawrence hughes) . . . .

77-750 Avenue 50
La Quinta, CA   92253
(760) 564-4151
lqcc.org

	YARDAGE	PAR	RATING	SLOPE
FRONT	5338	72	71.5	124
MIDDLE	6554	72	71.8	131
BACK	7060	72	74.2	136

$75 - $75

WHAT TO EXPECT: The course has hosted both the Bob Hope and Old CBS Golf Classic when there were few trees or houses around. Now the course has matured into one of the best in the area. It combines narrow fairways, smallish greens, and sufficient length to challenge any player. DIRECTIONS: From downtown Los Angeles (about 130 miles east to the course): Take I-10 east, exit on Washington Street, and go south. After crossing Highway 111, turn right on Avenue 50. The club is on the right.

LA QUINTA RESORT & CLUB: CITRUS COURSE (members only, 18 holes, pete dye) . . .

50-503 Jefferson Street
La Quinta, CA 92253
(760) 564-7620
laquintaresort.com

	YARDAGE	PAR	RATING	SLOPE
FRONT	5326	72	70.9	126
MIDDLE	6509	72	71.0	123
BACK	7127	72	74.3	135

$90 - $90

WHAT TO EXPECT: Of the three La Quinta courses, this is the easiest to conquer. Cut out of an orchard, the course has plenty of trees, but they do not make the fairways narrow enough to take the driver out of your hands. Citrus has lots of water and sand, which make it picturesque; but neither the water nor the sand will intimidate golfers who have any command of their swing. DIRECTIONS: From downtown Los Angeles (about 130 miles east to the course): Take I-10 east, exit on Jefferson Street, and head south.

LA QUINTA RESORT & CLUB: DUNES & MOUNTAIN (resort, 36 holes, pete dye) . . . . .

50-200 Avenida Vista
La Quinta, CA 92253
(760) 564-7686
laquintaresort.com

	YARDAGE	PAR	RATING	SLOPE
FRONT	5219	72	70.7	125
MIDDLE	5752	72	67.1	114
BACK	6922	72	74.1	140

$140 - $235

WHAT TO EXPECT: The Dunes Course is the least attractive of La Quinta Resort's layouts, but it is fun and challenging. The Mountain Course has long been considered one of the Desert's leading courses. It combines spectacular mountainside vistas with a desert environment.

OUR OPINION: Both layouts offer you the classic Pete Dye experience. Of course, if you can play during the shoulder or off seasons, you can get the same experience for a lot less money. – Val

NOTES: The yardage listed is for the Mountain Course.

DIRECTIONS: From downtown Los Angeles (about 130 miles east to the course): Take I-10 east, exit at Washington Street, and go south. Turn right on Eisenhower to the resort, which is on the right. Shuttle service is provided to the courses.

PALM ROYALE GOLF COURSE (public, 18 holes, ted robinson 1984) . . . .

78-259 Indigo Drive
La Quinta , CA 92253
(760) 345-9701

	YARDAGE	PAR	RATING	SLOPE
FRONT	-	-	-	-
MIDDLE	-	-	-	-
BACK	1984	54	-	-

$15 - $27

WHAT TO EXPECT: This is a par-3 course with lakes and nice greens and is part of a gated community.

OUR OPINION: Palm Royale is a great place to bring the kids for fun day of golf. For the lower handicappers, it is also a chance to work on your short game. – Frank

DIRECTIONS: From downtown Los Angeles (about 130 miles east to the course): Take I-10 east, exit at Washington Street, and head south. Turn left on Fred Waring Drive to the course entrance.

PALMS GOLF CLUB, THE (members only, 18 holes, couples & curley) . . . .

81-771 Airport Boulevard
La Quinta, CA 92253
(760) 771-2606

	YARDAGE	PAR	RATING	SLOPE
FRONT	5560	71	72.6	130
MIDDLE	6617	70	72.0	129
BACK	7020	70	74.0	134

WHAT TO EXPECT: An artfully crafted design that is both playable and challenging. The routing is fairly flat and plays among the many palms, water, and bunkers.

DIRECTIONS: From downtown Los Angeles (about 130 miles east to the course): Take the I-10 east, exit on Monroe Street, and turn right. The course is at the corner of Monroe Street and Airport Boulevard.

PGA WEST: GREG NORMAN COURSE (semi-private, 18 holes, greg norman) . . . .

81-405 Kingston Heath
La Quinta, CA 92253
(760) 564-3900
pgawest.com

	YARDAGE	PAR	RATING	SLOPE	
FRONT	6227	72	69.7	121	**$75 - $235**
MIDDLE	6671	72	71.8	128	
BACK	7157	72	74.0	134	

WHAT TO EXPECT: This flat course is getting good reviews due to the stunning white bunkering and rugged-looking tall reed grass that surrounds the fairways.

OUR OPINION: Men have raved about this course, but it deserves even more praise from a women's perspective. The two sets of forward tees are well thought out. For the better women golfers, they will encounter some reasonable forced carries. For the novice golfer, they can avoid the forced carries by playing the correct tees. – Loralei

DIRECTIONS: From downtown Los Angeles (about 130 miles east to the course): Take I-10 east, exit at Washington, and turn right. Go about ten miles until it dead-ends. Turn left on 52nd Street and then right on Jefferson Street. Turn left on 54th (do NOT go into PGA West). Turn right on Madison and the course is on the left.

PGA WEST: PRIVATE COURSES (members only, 54 holes, palmer, nicklaus, weiskopf)

55-955 PGA Boulevard
La Quinta, CA   92253
(760) 564-7100
pgawest.com

	YARDAGE	PAR	RATING	SLOPE	
FRONT	6129	72	68.3	117	**$105 - $250**
MIDDLE	6654	72	71.6	123	
BACK	7164	72	74.2	130	

WHAT TO EXPECT: The private courses consist of the Nicklaus, Palmer, and Weiskoph. There is nothing subtle about the Nicklaus Private Course. Cavernous bunkers, flowers, and tall grasses are among the challenges that can make this layout play among the toughest of any course in the Desert. The real thrill to the Palmer Course is the holes adjacent to the mountain. Otherwise, this is a solid park-setting layout in a desert atmosphere. The Weiskopf is a long course, but tee to fairway and fairway to green, it is quite manageable. For those who want to score well, you need to master the large greens.

NOTES: The yardage listed is for the Tom Weiskopf Private Course.

DIRECTIONS: From downtown Los Angeles (about 130 miles east to the course): Take I-10 east, exit at Jefferson Street, and turn right. Turn into the PGA West entrance.

PGA WEST: TPC STADIUM & NICKLAUS (semi-private, 36 holes, dye '86, nicklaus ' 87)

56-150 PGA Boulevard
La Quinta, CA 92253
(760) 564-7170
pgawest.com

	YARDAGE	PAR	RATING	SLOPE	
FRONT	5092	72	70.0	124	**$100 - $235**
MIDDLE	6739	72	73.0	142	
BACK	7266	72	75.9	150	

WHAT TO EXPECT: The Nicklaus Course is a slightly tamer version of the other private Nicklaus and Dye creations at PGA West. Deep bunkers, forced carries, and curvaceous greens make this layout play tough. Since its opening in 1986, the TPC Stadium Course's fabled challenge has made it one of America's must-play golf courses. Ample bailout areas around the water and cavernous bunkers make the course surprisingly playable, provided you choose the right tee.

OUR OPINION: The average golfer will crash and burn at the Nicklaus Tournament course. It has more of a Pete Dye severity. The TPC course received a bum rap from pros when it first opened, but is actually a playable course and a superb test of your golfing ability. – BobThe Staduim Course has two sets of foward tees that are thoughtfully designed by Alice Dye. This is a must-play for the avid woman golfer. – Loralei

NOTES: The yardage listed is for the TPC Stadium Course.

DIRECTIONS: From downtown Los Angeles (about 130 miles east to the course): Take I-10 east, exit Jefferson Street and turn right. Follow this to the PGA West entrance.

QUARRY AT LA QUINTA, THE (members only, 18 holes, tom fazio 1994) . . . .

One Quarry Lane
La Quinta, CA 92253
(760) 777-1100

	YARDAGE	PAR	RATING	SLOPE	
FRONT	5226	72	70.3	120	**$100 - $100**
MIDDLE	6852	72	72.5	132	
BACK	7083	72	73.7	135	

WHAT TO EXPECT: This exclusive layout features Tom Fazio's attractive bunkering and, with its expansive fairways and collecting greens, plays easier than it looks. Beware of the finishing four.

DIRECTIONS: From downtown Los Angeles (about 130 miles east to the course): Take the I-10 east, exit on Monroe and turn right. Take it all the way to 58th Avenue and turn right. This leads to the guard gate.

RANCHO LA QUINTA COUNTRY CLUB (members only, 36 holes, robert trent jones jr.)

79-325 Cascades Circle Street
La Quinta, CA 92253
(760) 777-7799

	YARDAGE	PAR	RATING	SLOPE	
FRONT	5941	72	68.8	125	**$175 - $175**
MIDDLE	6474	72	71.3	130	
BACK	6972	72	73.6	135	

WHAT TO EXPECT: Built from the desert floor, the layout is both attractive and challenging. Great care must be taken to avoid the numerous bunkers and water hazards.

NOTES: The yardage listed is for the Pate Course.

DIRECTIONS: From downtown Los Angeles (about 130 miles east to the course): Take the I-10 east, exit at Washington Street, and head south. Turn left on Eisenhower to the gate.

TRADITION GOLF CLUB (members only, 18 holes, palmer & seay) . . . .

78-505 Old Avenue 52
La Quinta, CA 92253
(760) 564-1067

	YARDAGE	PAR	RATING	SLOPE
FRONT	5540	72	72.5	131
MIDDLE	6541	72	70.0	136
BACK	6910	72	72.8	140

$90 - $90

WHAT TO EXPECT: This is one of Arnold Palmer's best designs. Not only is it scenically set against the mountains, but the conditioning is immaculate, and the course is playable and challenging.
DIRECTIONS: From downtown Los Angeles (about 130 miles east to the course): Take I-10 east, exit Washington, and turn right. The club is at the end of Washington.

LAKE ELIZABETH GOLF & RANCH CLUB (public, 18 holes) . . . .

42505 Ranch Club Road
Lake Elizabeth, CA   93532
(661) 724-1221

	YARDAGE	PAR	RATING	SLOPE
FRONT	5074	70	72.9	115
MIDDLE	5658	70	67.1	114
BACK	6037	70	68.8	118

$25 - $35

WHAT TO EXPECT: Except for the par 3s, this is not a long course. Lake Elizabeth features small greens and several elevation changes. Water comes into play on nearly half the holes.
DIRECTIONS: From Los Angeles (about 85 miles north to the course): Take I-5 north, exit at Magic Mountain Parkway and head east. Go north on McBean Parkway. Turn on San Francisquito and drive northeast almost 20 miles. Turn left on Elizabeth Lake Road. Turn left on Ranch Club Drive.

LANCASTER GOLF CENTER (public, 9 holes) . . . .

431 East Avenue K
Lancaster, CA 93535
(661) 726-3131

	YARDAGE	PAR	RATING	SLOPE
FRONT	-	-	-	-
MIDDLE	-	-	-	-
BACK	800	27	-	-

$6 - $9

WHAT TO EXPECT: This is a pitch-and-putt course that specializes in teaching and promoting golf to juniors.
DIRECTIONS: From within Lancaster: Off Highway 14, exit at Avenue K and go east about four miles. They are on the right.

RANCHO SIERRA GOLF CLUB (public, 9 holes, jack roesinger 1963) . . . .

47205 60th Street East
Lancaster, CA 93535
(661) 946-1080

	YARDAGE	PAR	RATING	SLOPE
FRONT	2600	35	70.7	115
MIDDLE	-	-	-	-
BACK	2600	35	63.4	100

$17 - $19

WHAT TO EXPECT: This is an unusual course; you will find no sand, just grass bunkers throughout. The course is mature with lots of trees but with short par 4s and par 3s and one par 5.
DIRECTIONS: From within Lancaster: Off Highway 14, exit at Avenue G and drive east. Take that all the way down to 60th Street East and turn right.

ANGEL PARK GOLF CLUB (resort, 48 holes, arnold palmer 1989) . . . .

100 South Rampart Boulevard
Las Vegas , NV 89145
(888) 446-5358
angelpark.com

	YARDAGE	PAR	RATING	SLOPE
FRONT	5751	71	67.8	116
MIDDLE	6235	71	70.3	117
BACK	6723	71	72.4	128

$45 - $155

WHAT TO EXPECT: You will find the Mountain Course and the Palm Course set at 2,500 feet above sea level. When it isn't windy, both courses can be very pleasant to play. Both are desert-style courses with subtle mounding, a few trees, some water, and generous landing areas. You will also find Cloud 9 at Angel Park. Cloud 9 is a 12-hole, lighted, par-3 course featuring famous par 3s from around the world. Angel Park also has an 18-hole putting course.

OUR OPINION: This is a reasonably priced (for Vegas) alternative to the other local courses. – Andy

NOTES: The yardage listed is for the Mountain Course.

DIRECTIONS: From the Las Vegas Airport (about 15 miles northwest to the course): Take I-15 to US 95 north. Take Summerlin Parkway, Exit 81A, and merge onto East Summerlin Parkway. Take the Rampart Boulevard exit and stay left. Turn left on to Rampart Boulevard.

ANTHEM COUNTRY CLUB (members only, 18 holes, irwin & foster 1999) . . . .

One Anthem Club Drive
Las Vegas, NV 89012
(702) 914-7888
delwebblive.com

	YARDAGE	PAR	RATING	SLOPE
FRONT	5284	72	69.6	117
MIDDLE	6730	72	71.4	126
BACK	7268	72	73.6	133

$200 - $200

WHAT TO EXPECT: Anthem is generous from tee to fairway. The challenge on this desert course plays out fairway to green. Placing the ball in proper position on these large, undulating greens is the difference between birdie and bogey. Although you can hit a variety of shots into the greens, there are plenty of traps and water on 12 holes to make you think twice about running the ball up. Keep in mind, most greens break toward the Las Vegas strip, which you can see throughout your round.

NOTES: Reciprocal play with other members only clubs is allowed.

DIRECTIONS: From the Las Vegas Airport (about 11 miles southeast to the course): Take I-215 east. Exit at Eastern Avenue and drive south. Past Saint Rose Parkway, the road will split. Take Anthem Parkway. This will lead to the security gate.

BADLANDS GOLF CLUB (semi-private, 27 holes, johnny miller) . . . .

9119 Alta Drive
Las Vegas, NV 89145
(702) 363-0754
americangolf.com

	YARDAGE	PAR	RATING	SLOPE	
FRONT	-	-	-	-	**$140 - $205**
MIDDLE	-	-	-	-	
BACK	6927	72	73.0	133	

WHAT TO EXPECT: This is a spectacular course cut out of gullies. The course plays through deep washes, so if you are not in the fairway, you are in the badlands. The greens are fairly small by today's standards, but in excellent shape.

OUR OPINION: Johnny Miller's name is synonymous with extreme challenge. The Badlands is no different. We liked this course better when there were no homes, and the price hurts, ouch! With that said, we recommend the Badlands if your budget affords it. You may love it, you may hate it, but you won't forget it. – Shaw

NOTES: The course warns of snakes outside the fairways. By the looks of all the golf balls lying around in plain sight, they must be telling the truth.

DIRECTIONS: From the Las Vegas Airport (about 15 miles northwest to the course): Take I-15 north to US 95 north. Exit onto Summerlin Parkway. Take the Rampart Boulevard exit and go left (south). Turn right on Alta Drive. The club is on the left.

BALI HAI GOLF CLUB (public, 18 holes, schmidt & curley 2000) . . . .

5160 Las Vegas Boulevard South
Las Vegas, NV 89119
(888) 397-2499
waltersgolf.com

	YARDAGE	PAR	RATING	SLOPE	
FRONT	6174	71	68.6	113	**$150 - $300**
MIDDLE	6619	71	70.2	125	
BACK	7003	71	73.0	130	

WHAT TO EXPECT: Can't afford to go to the South Pacific? Don't worry; Las Vegas brings the South Pacific to you. This is a tropical course with an abundance of water, palm trees, and tropical plants. Even the out-of-bounds has been transformed with beach sand and volcanic rock. Resort in nature, the course is not overpowering, but golfers will notice that the challenge increases with each passing hole.

OUR OPINION: The course was in great condition and the service was first rate, but the Environmentally Sensitive Areas were annoying because you have to take a stroke, even when you could easily hit the ball out. – Brad

DIRECTIONS: Bali Hai is right on the Strip, just south of the Mandalay Bay Hotel & Resort.

BEAR'S BEST (public, 18 holes, jack nicklaus 2001) . . . .

11111 West Flamingo Road
Las Vegas, NV 89134
(702) 804-8500

	YARDAGE	PAR	RATING	SLOPE	
FRONT	-	-	-	-	**$175 - $250**
MIDDLE	-	-	-	-	
BACK	7101	72	-	-	

WHAT TO EXPECT: Bear's Best is a compilation of Jack Nicklaus' favorite holes. At Bear's Best, you can play courses that Jack has designed all over the United States and Mexico. The unique thing about this course is that each hole is built to the exact specifications of the original, right down to the placement of trees. Located next to the Red Rock Canyon National Conservation Area, the course should afford some excellent views.

OUR OPINION: At the time of press, this course was not available for play, but our guess is that it will be worth playing. Yes, the green fees are astronomical, but just think how much money you saved by not gambling all afternoon. – Shaw

NOTES: At time of press the course is not yet rated and is scheduled to open November 2001.

DIRECTIONS: From the Las Vegas Airport (about 20 miles northwest to the course): Take I-215 west, exit at Town Center and make a right. Turn left at Desert Inn. When that ends, turn left. The course is on the right.

CALLAWAY GOLF CENTER (public, 9 holes) . . . .

6730 South Las Vegas Boulevard
Las Vegas, NV 89119
(702) 897-9500
callawaygolfcenter.com

	YARDAGE	PAR	RATING	SLOPE	
FRONT	-	27	-	-	**$12 - $30**
MIDDLE	-		-	-	
BACK	-	27	-	-	

WHAT TO EXPECT: The Divine Nine is a fully lit, par-3 course featuring lakes, rapids, and waterfalls. The course maybe small, but the greens are regulation size.

NOTES: The course has a 113-station lit driving range. The proshop carries a wide selection of Callaway Clubs; just don't ask for a set of Pings.

DIRECTIONS: The center is located on the corner of Sunset and Las Vegas Boulevard, south of the airport.

CANYON GATE COUNTRY CLUB (members only, 18 holes) . . . .

2001 Canyon Gate Drive
Las Vegas, NV 89117
(702) 363-0303
canyon-gate.com

	YARDAGE	PAR	RATING	SLOPE	
FRONT	5141	72	-	-	**$70 - $100**
MIDDLE	6259	72	-	-	
BACK	6743	72	-	-	

WHAT TO EXPECT: This private club features water on 11 of 18 holes. Three greens are guarded by water, and plenty more are protected by traps. Beware of the finishing hole—it has fairway traps right and left, as well as a lake just off the left side of the green.

DIRECTIONS: From the Las Vegas Airport (about 12 miles northwest to the course): Take I-215 west to the Sahara exit. The entrance is on the left on the 8700 block of Sahara.

DESERT INN GOLF CLUB (resort, 18 holes, lawrence hughes 1952) . . . .

3145 Las Vegas Boulevard South
Las Vegas, NV 89109
(702) 733-4290
thedesertinn.com

	YARDAGE	PAR	RATING	SLOPE	
FRONT	5884	72	72.7	121	**$125 - $225**
MIDDLE	6732	72	72.1	121	
BACK	7194	72	73.9	124	

WHAT TO EXPECT: This is an older, level, desert-style course with palm trees, fairway bunkers, and water. The course has a rich history of hosting PGA events.

OUR OPINION: Insanely overpriced. But then again, eat enough at the casino buffets and you'll have saved enough to dough to mitigate the cost. – Andy

NOTES: At time of press, the hotel is closed, but the golf club remains open.

DIRECTIONS: This is located right on the Strip.

DESERT PINES GOLF CLUB (public, 18 holes, perry dye) . . . .

3415 Bonanza Road
Las Vegas, NV 89101
(702) 388-4400
waltersgolf.com

	YARDAGE	PAR	RATING	SLOPE	
FRONT	5873	71	69.4	116	**$85 - $165**
MIDDLE	6464	71	66.8	112	
BACK	6811	71	70.4	122	

WHAT TO EXPECT: Fashioned after a classic layout you might find in the Carolinas, this desert course features fairways dotted with maturing pines, large lakes, manicured flower beds, and white sand.

OUR OPINION: From the back tees, it ain't that easy. – Frank

DIRECTIONS: From the Las Vegas Airport (about 10 miles north to the course): Take I-15 north to US 95 south. Take the Eastern exit and go left on Eastern. Turn right on Bonanza. The club is on the right.

DESERT ROSE GOLF COURSE (public, 18 holes, joe lee) . . . .

5483 Clubhouse Drive
Las Vegas, NV 89122
(702) 431-4653
americangolf.com

	YARDAGE	PAR	RATING	SLOPE	
FRONT	5458	71	71.0	119	**$25 - $89**
MIDDLE	6135	71	69.0	114	
BACK	6512	71	69.6	117	

WHAT TO EXPECT: Desert Rose is a friendly course with mature palm trees, crowned greens, and water. There is nothing deceiving about the layout; hit the ball well, score well.

DIRECTIONS: From the Strip (about 12 miles northeast to the course): Go east on Sahara. After crossing Nellis, take the third right onto Winterwood. Follow Winterwood to the course.

EAGLE CREST GOLF CLUB (semi-private, 18 holes, billy casper) . . . .

2203 Thomas Ryan Boulevard
Las Vegas, NV 89134
(702) 240-1320

	YARDAGE	PAR	RATING	SLOPE
FRONT	3259	60	-	-
MIDDLE	3668	60	58.7	90
BACK	4068	60	60.0	92

$40 - $59

WHAT TO EXPECT: With generous landing areas and large, undulating greens the course is a favorite of the senior set. There are no par 5s, but there are plenty of bunkers.
NOTES: Eagle Crest is located in a retirement community.
DIRECTIONS: From the Las Vegas Airport (about 20 miles northwest to the course): Take I-15 north to US 95 north. Exit at Summerlin Parkway. Take Anasazi to the right. Take the next left to the club.

HIGHLAND FALLS GOLF CLUB (resort, 18 holes, billy casper 1992) . . . .

10201 Sun City Boulevard
Las Vegas, NV 89134
(702) 254-7010

	YARDAGE	PAR	RATING	SLOPE
FRONT	5099	72	68.8	110
MIDDLE	6017	72	68.6	116
BACK	6513	72	71.2	126

$75 - $145

WHAT TO EXPECT: Although the course accommodates the senior population with wide fairways and large greens, the undulating and tricky greens will challenge even the low handicapper. Locals know to always play the break to move toward the Las Vegas Strip. The course makes its way around a housing development, giving it a links feel.
DIRECTIONS: From the Las Vegas Airport (about 22 miles northwest to the course): Take I-215 west to the last exit (until they build I-215 out farther), which is Summerlin Parkway, and turn right. Turn left on Anasazi. The club is on the right, past Lake Mead Boulevard.

LAS VEGAS COUNTRY CLUB (members only, 18 holes, ron garl 1967) . . . .

3000 Joe W. Brown Drive
Las Vegas, NV 89109
(702) 734-1122

	YARDAGE	PAR	RATING	SLOPE
FRONT	5641	72	-	-
MIDDLE	-	-	-	-
BACK	7162	72	-	-

WHAT TO EXPECT: This is a venerable old course with a rich tradition reaching all the way back to the 1960s. In Las Vegas terms, that's old. The course is well maintained and classic in nature, with pristine fairways and well-protected greens.
NOTES: The course has played host to the PGA Tour Las Vegas Invitational.
DIRECTIONS: From the Las Vegas Airport (about five miles north to the course): Take Paradise heading north. Turn right at Desert Inn and then left on Joe W. Brown Drive. The club is on the right.

LAS VEGAS GOLF CLUB (public, 18 holes, casey o'callaghan) . . . .

4300 West Washington Avenue
Las Vegas, NV 89107
(702) 646-3003
americangolf.com

	YARDAGE	PAR	RATING	SLOPE	
FRONT	5210	72	69.9	112	**$49 - $89**
MIDDLE	5918	72	68.1	105	
BACK	6320	72	70.0	112	

WHAT TO EXPECT: This is one of the more user-friendly courses in the area. Las Vegas Golf Club has plenty of trees, but the fairways are spacious. Water comes into play on a few holes, and the greens are gently sloped.

DIRECTIONS: From the Las Vegas Airport (about 10 miles northwest to the course): Take I-15 north to US 95 north. Take the second exit, Valley View, and turn right. Turn left when it dead-ends at Washington. The club is on the right, just past the little school.

LAS VEGAS NATIONAL GOLF CLUB (public, 18 holes, bert stamps 1960) . . . .

1911 East Desert Inn Road
Las Vegas, NV 89109
(702) 734-1796
americangolf.com

	YARDAGE	PAR	RATING	SLOPE	
FRONT	5741	71	72.9	127	**$35 - $185**
MIDDLE	6418	71	70.2	121	
BACK	6816	71	72.1	130	

WHAT TO EXPECT: Las Vegas National is traditional in design, with fairways lined with palm, olive, and pine trees. Off the tee, the course is forgiving, but the greens are well bunkered. Wind can increase the challenge dramatically.

OUR OPINION: A four-and-a-half-hour round is the exception, not the rule. – Shaw

NOTES: This club was formerly known as Sahara Country Club, Stardust Country, Del Webb Country Club, and the Las Vegas Hilton. It has hosted PGA and LPGA Tour events, including the Tournament of Champions and 1996 Las Vegas Invitational. Tiger Woods won his first professional event on this course.

DIRECTIONS: From the Las Vegas Airport (about five miles north to the course): Take Paradise Road heading north. Turn right on Desert Inn Road and the course is on the right.

LAS VEGAS PAIUTE GOLF RESORT (resort, 36 holes, pete dye 1995, 1996 & 2001) . . .

10325 Nu-Wav Kaiv Boulevard
Las Vegas, NV 89124
(800) 711-2833
lvpaiutegolf.com

	YARDAGE	PAR	RATING	SLOPE	
FRONT	5340	72	70.4	123	**$55 - $160**
MIDDLE	-	-	-	-	
BACK	7159	72	73.4	130	

WHAT TO EXPECT: Snow Mountain is a classic Pete Dye design complete with railroad ties, pot bunkers, and numerous natural hazards. There are no parallel fairways on this course. The greens will allow you to play a variety of shots (if you have them). The Sun Mountain Course has many similarities with Snow Mountain but has its own personality, including wild flowers, water, and large greens.

OUR OPINION: Word is out that the third course is even better than the previous two, and even more demanding. The courses are excellent, and the service was even better. Beware of the wind. – Shaw

NOTES: A third course is scheduled to open November 2001.

DIRECTIONS: From the Las Vegas Airport (about 25 miles east to the course): Take US 95 north. Use Exit 95, Snow Mountain, and turn right. Pauite can't be missed, It is the only thing out there.

LOS PRADOS GOLF COURSE (semi-private, 18 holes, jeff hardin 1986) . . . .

5150 Los Prados Circle
Las Vegas, NV 89130
(702) 645-5696
losprados.com

	YARDAGE	PAR	RATING	SLOPE	
FRONT	4500	70	66.6	104	**$35 - $45**
MIDDLE	5350	70	63.2	107	
BACK	5500	70	65.5	115	

WHAT TO EXPECT: Except for a few tight fairways, this is a short, uncomplicated course that is part of a gated community. Los Prados is suited for all skill levels.

OUR OPINION: If you are tired of being punished by the green fees and demanding courses of Las Vegas, this may be the course for you. – Shaw

DIRECTIONS: From the Las Vegas Airport (about 15 miles north to the course): Take I-15 north to US 95 north. Turn right on Rancho and right again on Decater. Turn left on Lone Mountain and then right on Los Prados to the guard gate.

PAINTED DESERT GOLF COURSE (public, 18 holes, jay morrish) . . . .

5555 Painted Mirage Road
Las Vegas, NV 89129
(702) 645-2880
americangolf.com

	YARDAGE	PAR	RATING	SLOPE	
FRONT	5711	72	73.0	127	**$80 - $170**
MIDDLE	6323	72	71.0	128	
BACK	6841	72	73.7	136	

WHAT TO EXPECT: This is a target course with extensive mounding, grass bunkers, and sloping greens that can be difficult to read for the golfer with little course knowledge.

OUR OPINION: The challenge wasn't so much in the course as it was in avoiding the homes and condos along the fairways. If you are interested in a new facade for your home, just check out the cool look of stucco peppered with dimples created by errant shots. – Val

DIRECTIONS: From the Las Vegas Airport (about 20 miles northwest to the course): Take I-15 north to US 95 north. Exit on Ann Road and go left. Take the first left after crossing the highway, into the complex.

PALM VALLEY GOLF CLUB (semi-private, 18 holes) . . . .

9201 Del Webb Boulevard
Las Vegas, NV 89134
(702) 363-4373

	YARDAGE	PAR	RATING	SLOPE	
FRONT	5502	72	71.5	124	**$75 - $145**
MIDDLE	6341	72	69.8	124	
BACK	6870	72	72.3	127	

WHAT TO EXPECT: Part of the Del Webb retirement community, this course features many elevation changes. An average ball striker with a good putter will do well here. A good ball striker with an average putter will struggle on these fast greens.
DIRECTIONS: From the Las Vegas Airport (about 18 miles northwest to the course): Take I-15 north to US 95 north. Exit onto Summerlin Parkway. Take Rampart and go right. Turn left on Lake Mead and right on Del Webb Boulevard. The course is on the right.

RED ROCK COUNTRY CLUB (members only, 36 holes, arnold palmer 1999) . . . .

2250A Red Springs Road
Las Vegas, NV 89135
(702) 304-5600
redrockcountryclub.com

	YARDAGE	PAR	RATING	SLOPE	
FRONT	5039	72	-	-	**$75 - $116**
MIDDLE	6450	72	-	-	
BACK	6847	72	-	-	

WHAT TO EXPECT: There are two 18-hole courses. Palm trees, great views, water, and solid greens tell you most of what you need to know about both courses.
DIRECTIONS: From the Las Vegas Airport (about 12 miles northwest to the course): Take I-15 north to US 95 north. Exit Summerlin Parkway. Turn left on I-215. Turn right on Sahara and then take the next left.

RHODES RANCH GOLF CLUB (public, 18 holes, ted robinson) . . . .

20 Rhodes Ranch Parkway
Las Vegas, NV 89148
(888) 311-8337
rhodesranch.com

	YARDAGE	PAR	RATING	SLOPE	
FRONT	4967	72	64.8	110	**$85 - $160**
MIDDLE	6403	72	71.1	120	
BACK	6856	72	73.0	122	

WHAT TO EXPECT: Rhodes Ranch is part of a golf community. The course has elevated tee boxes and fairly wide fairways dotted with palm trees, and sand traps. Outside the fairways you will actually find some rough. Low scores are possible for the golfer who takes risks.
DIRECTIONS: From the Las Vegas Airport (about 13 miles west to the course): Take I-215 west. Take Durango exit and turn left. Go south, past Warm Springs, to the entrance of Rhodes Ranch. The entrance is gated with palm trees and is on the right.

ROYAL LINKS GOLF CLUB (public, 18 holes) . . . .

5995 East Vegas Valley Road
Las Vegas, NV 89122
(702) 450-8000
waltersgolf.com

	YARDAGE	PAR	RATING	SLOPE
FRONT	5142	72	-	-
MIDDLE	6602	72	-	-
BACK	7030	72	-	-

$135 - $275

WHAT TO EXPECT: In the land of theme, why should the golf courses be any different? Many of the holes were inspired by famous holes of various British Open courses. The course even offers that traditional blistering heat in summer, so well known at the British Open.

OUR OPINION: A refreshingly different motif, but with soft turf and Las Vegas as a backdrop, the course may not quite measure up to the hype. If you can't afford Royal Links, you might want to try Angel Park Golf Club instead. – Bob

NOTES: The pro shop is a castle.

DIRECTIONS: From the Las Vegas Airport (about eight miles east to the course): Take I-15 north to US 95 south. Exit at Flamingo Road and turn left. Turn left on Nellis Boulevard and right on Vegas Valley Road.

SIENA GOLF CLUB (public, 18 holes, schmidt & curley 2000) . . . .

10575 Siena Monte Avenue
Las Vegas, NV 89135
(888) 689-6469
sienagolfclub.com

	YARDAGE	PAR	RATING	SLOPE
FRONT	4978	72	68.0	112
MIDDLE	6538	72	70.2	126
BACK	6817	72	71.5	129

$35 - $160

WHAT TO EXPECT: Siena Golf Club is wide-open, incorporating water, sand, and the natural desert into a visually appealing layout. Sand traps guard the greens, making players think twice about hitting at the pins.

OUR OPINION: Great shaping and bunkering make this one of the most enjoyable new layouts in Vegas. – Bob

DIRECTIONS: From the Las Vegas Airport (about 12 miles northwest to the course): Take I-215 west. Exit at Town Center Drive and turn left. Head south to Siena Monte Avenue and turn left.

SILVERSTONE GOLF CLUB (resort, 27 holes, robert cupp 2001) . . . .

8317 Mount Geneva Court
Las Vegas, NV 89131
(877) 888-2127
silverstonegolf.com

	YARDAGE	PAR	RATING	SLOPE
FRONT	5986	72	67.1	115
MIDDLE	6552	72	70.2	128
BACK	7160	72	73.3	145

$145 - $180

WHAT TO EXPECT: There are three nines that will be played in 18-hole combinations. All the courses are spacious, with an abundance of mounding, long par 5s, plenty of water, and views of Sheep Mountain. Wind will be a factor.

NOTES: The yardage shown is for the Mountain and Desert Course combination. At time of press, the course was not yet open.

DIRECTIONS: From the Las Vegas Airport (about 23 miles north to the course): Take I-15 north to US 95 north. Exit on Centennial Parkway and follow the signs.

SOUTHERN HIGHLANDS GOLF CLUB (members only, 18 holes, jones sr. & jr. 2000) . .

One Robert Trent Jones Lane
Las Vegas, NV 89141
(702) 263-1000
southernhighlandsgolf.com

	YARDAGE	PAR	RATING	SLOPE	
FRONT	5430	72	-	-	**$110 - $130**
MIDDLE	6945	72	-	-	
BACK	7382	72	-	-	

WHAT TO EXPECT: This is one of only three collaborations between Robert Trent Jones, Sr. and Jr. With their knowledge of golf course design and a budget that most facilities only dream of, they have turned Southern Highlands into an elegant facility. There are constant elevation changes and creeks lined with rocks that guard several greens. For the good player, the is a risk-and-reward layout. For the regular country club player, the course looks intimidating, but allows players many bail-out areas.

DIRECTIONS: From the Las Vegas Airport (about nine miles southwest to the course): Go south on I-15 and then west on Saint Rose Parkway. Follow the signs north to the Southern Highlands entrance.

SPANISH TRAIL GOLF & COUNTRY CLUB (members only, 27 holes, r. trent jones jr.) .

5050 Spanish Trail Lane
Las Vegas, NV 89102
(702) 364-0357
spanishtrailcc.com

	YARDAGE	PAR	RATING	SLOPE	
FRONT	-	-	-	-	**$87 - $87**
MIDDLE	-	-	-	-	
BACK	-	-	-	-	

WHAT TO EXPECT: Spanish Trail is part of a gated community, and you will find three nine-hole courses: Lakes, Canyon, and Sunrise. All the courses are similar, with big fairways surrounded by homes, generous greens, and wind. With six holes having water, the Lakes Course is the most challenging.

DIRECTIONS: From the Las Vegas Airport (about eight miles west to the course): Take I-215 west to Rainbow and take a right. Turn left on Tropicana and the entrance is on the left.

STALLION MOUNTAIN COUNTRY CLUB (members only, 54 holes) . . . .

5500 East Flamingo Road
Las Vegas, NV 89122
(702) 450-8044
waltersgolf.com

	YARDAGE	PAR	RATING	SLOPE	
FRONT	5405	72	70.3	118	**$80 - $95**
MIDDLE	6579	72	70.2	121	
BACK	7224	72	73.6	127	

WHAT TO EXPECT: This is a 54-hole private resort that has hosted the Las Vegas Invitational and the Frank Sinatra Celebrity Classic.

NOTES: Reciprocal play with other members only clubs is allowed.

DIRECTIONS: From the Las Vegas Airport (about nine miles east to the course): Take I-15 north to US 95 south. Exit on Flamingo Road and turn left. The course is past Nellis Boulevard.

SUNRISE VISTA GOLF CLUB (military, 36 holes) . . . .

2841 Kinley Drive (Nellis AFB)
Las Vegas, NV 89191
(702) 652-2602

	YARDAGE	PAR	RATING	SLOPE
FRONT	5476	72	-	-
MIDDLE	6608	72	-	-
BACK	7024	72	-	-

$10 - $49

WHAT TO EXPECT: Sunrise Vista consists of the Eagle Falcon and the Phantom Thunderbird courses. They are similar in nature, although the back nine of the Phantom Thunderbird is new and not quite as mature. These are traditional desert-style courses with plenty of mature trees and smallish greens. There are no tricks here – hit it long and straight and you will score well.

NOTES: The course is open to guests of the military. Sunrise Vista is open to the general public on a standby basis. The yardage listed is for the Eagle Falcon Course.

DIRECTIONS: From the Las Vegas Airport (about 18 miles northeast to the course): Take I-15 north to Exit 48, Craig Road. Turn right and go about five miles to the entrance of Nellis Air Force Base.

TPC AT SUMMERLIN (members only, 18 holes, fuzzy zoeller 1991) . . . .

1700 Village Center Circle
Las Vegas, NV 89134
(702) 256-0222
pgatour.com

	YARDAGE	PAR	RATING	SLOPE
FRONT	5395	72	71.0	122
MIDDLE	6292	72	70.6	118
BACK	6867	72	73.0	127

$95 - $240

WHAT TO EXPECT: Generous fairways are offset by long, forced carries over desert and well-positioned bunkers. Around the greens a deft touch and a keen eye are needed to avoid three putts and worse. Water comes into play on four holes.

NOTES: Tiger Woods won his first PGA Tour event here back in 1995.

DIRECTIONS: From the Las Vegas Airport (about 20 miles northwest to the course): Take I-15 north to US 95 north. Exit at Summerlin Parkway. Turn right on Town Center Drive to the roundabout. The first right exit off the roundabout leads to the TPC, on the right.

TPC AT THE CANYONS (public, 18 holes, weed & floyd 1996) . . . .

9851 Canyon Run Drive
Las Vegas, NV 89144
(702) 256-2000
pgatour.com

	YARDAGE	PAR	RATING	SLOPE	
FRONT	5039	71	67.0	109	**$55 - $235**
MIDDLE	6110	71	67.7	118	
BACK	6773	71	70.9	128	

WHAT TO EXPECT: The TPC uses the lay of the land and incorporates the natural wash areas, barrancas, arroyos, and native desert plants to create a rugged but visually appealing course. Pick your tees carefully; the course may not only be longer, but also play differently.

OUR OPINION: The average golfer should not expect the same results as the pros, who regularly post low numbers here when the PGA Tour comes to town. The course is much tougher than they make it look. – Bob

NOTES: Call for current green fees; they vary widely with the seasons.

DIRECTIONS: From the Las Vegas Airport (about 17 miles northwest to the course): Take I-15 north to US 95 north. Exit at Summerlin Parkway. Go three miles, exit at Rampart Drive, then turn left. Take the first right at Canyon Run Drive. TPC is one and one-half miles on the left.

EMERALD RIVER GOLF COURSE (public, 18 holes) . . . .

1155 West Casino Drive
Laughlin, NV 89029
(702) 298-4653
americangolf.com

	YARDAGE	PAR	RATING	SLOPE	
FRONT	5205	72	71.3	129	**$50 - $80**
MIDDLE	6502	72	69.1	131	
BACK	6573	72	73.6	144	

WHAT TO EXPECT: Running through the desert and red foothills of the Colorado River, this is a short, yet demanding, target course. With narrow fairways and little rough, players will be hitting either from the short grass or the desert. The greens are large and undulating, so merely being on them does not guarantee your troubles are over.

DIRECTIONS: From Laughlin (about 90 miles south of Las Vegas): Stay on Casino Drive south toward Harrahs. The course is on Casino Drive, on the left, about five to ten minutes past Harrah's.

MOJAVE RESORT GOLF COURSE (resort, 18 holes, schmidt/curley) . . . .

9905 Aha Macav Parkway
Laughlin, NV 89029
(702) 535-4653
mojaveresort.com

	YARDAGE	PAR	RATING	SLOPE	
FRONT	5520	72	72.3	124	**$62 - $72**
MIDDLE	6435	72	70.9	122	
BACK	6940	72	73.2	126	

WHAT TO EXPECT: No matter which sets of tees you choose, you will find this to be a handicap-friendly course surrounded by native vegetation, wind-shaped sand dunes, and lots of water.

DIRECTIONS: From Laughlin (this is about 90 miles south of Las Vegas): Take Needles Highway south. Exit at Aha Macav Parkway and head east. The course is across from the Avi Hotel and Casino.

CRYSTALAIRE COUNTRY CLUB (members only, 18 holes, william f. bell 1956) . . . . . .

15701 Boca Raton Avenue
Llano, CA 93544
(661) 944-2111
crystalairecc.com

	YARDAGE	PAR	RATING	SLOPE	
FRONT	5275	72	71.5	123	**$30 - $56**
MIDDLE	6629	72	71.4	122	
BACK	6962	72	73.1	131	

WHAT TO EXPECT: Long and pretty, this is an open, sloping course with lots of trees. Besides the length, the biggest challenge may come from the greens, which are difficult to read. When in doubt, play the breaks toward Palmdale.

DIRECTIONS: From Los Angeles (about 80 miles northeast to the course): Take I-5 north to Highway 14 toward Lancaster. Take Highway 138 (Pearlblossom Highway). Stay on Highway 138 toward Palmdale. Turn right on 165th Street and then right again on Crystalaire. Turn right on Boca Raton Avenue to the club.

CASABLANCA GOLF CLUB (resort, 18 holes, cal olson) . . . .

950 West Mesquite Boulevard
Mesquite, NV 89027
(888) 711-4653
casablancaresort.com

	YARDAGE	PAR	RATING	SLOPE	
FRONT	5161	72	68.8	119	**$29 - $110**
MIDDLE	6600	72	70.7	126	
BACK	7012	72	72.5	130	

WHAT TO EXPECT: CasaBlanca is a rolling layout, which contrasts beautifully with the desert floor. The course features ample fairways, water on nearly every hole and plenty of sand. The bunkers are unique in the fact that many of them are bail-out areas that will stop your ball from rolling into the lakes. This is a classic risk-reward course.

DIRECTIONS: From the Las Vegas Airport (about 90 miles northeast to the course): Take I-15 north to Mesquite. Take Exit 120, and the resort is on the right.

OASIS GOLF CLUB, THE (resort/semi-private, 27 holes, arnold palmer (oasis)) . . . . .

100 Palmer Lane
Mesquite, NV 89027
(702) 346-7820
theoasisgolfclub.com

	YARDAGE	PAR	RATING	SLOPE	
FRONT	4627	71	65.7	110	**$55 - $135**
MIDDLE	5711	71	70.2	130	
BACK	6738	71	73.2	141	

WHAT TO EXPECT: The Oasis Course, a Palmer design, has a rugged feel with the scenic desert as a back-drop. The course plays through canyons and requires a good touch around the greens. The Vistas Course is a long nine-hole course (3,500), par 37. It can be a beast.

OUR OPINION: This is a spectacular golf course, one of Palmer Group's best, and easily worth the drive from Vegas. – Shaw

NOTES: The yardage listed is for the Oasis Course.

DIRECTIONS: From the Las Vegas Airport (about 90 miles northeast to the course): Take I-15 north to Mesquite. Take the second Mesquite exit, Exit 122. Take the first right.

PALMS GOLF CLUB, THE (resort, 18 holes) . . . .

711 Palms Boulevard
Mesquite, NV 89024
(800) 621-0187
casablancaresort.com

	YARDAGE	PAR	RATING	SLOPE	
FRONT	5016	72	70.4	122	**$50 - $140**
MIDDLE	6284	72	71.1	130	
BACK	7009	72	74.9	137	

WHAT TO EXPECT: The front nine is fairly level with long fairways; the back nine is more of a mountain course with a premium on good shot making. Along the way, you will find plenty of palm trees, water and traps.

DIRECTIONS: From the Las Vegas Airport (about 90 miles norttheast to the course): Take I-15 north to Mesquite. Take the second Mesquite exit, Exit 122. Take a right and then a left at the light, which is Hillside. Drive about one and one-half miles to the course.

WOLF CREEK AT PARADISE CANYON (public, 18 holes, d. rider & j. rider 2000) . . . . . .

401 Paradise Parkway
Mesquite, NV 89027
(866) 252-GOLF
playthewolf.com

	YARDAGE	PAR	RATING	SLOPE	
FRONT	4169	72	61.0	106	**$100 - $150**
MIDDLE	5820	72	68.2	134	
BACK	7074	72	75.4	154	

WHAT TO EXPECT: Wolf Creek is a canyon course constructed atop the natural desert terrain. This creates a visually appealing layout. The course winds, up, down, through, around, and over deserts and canyons to create some unique and challenging holes.

OUR OPINION: At time of press, this course has not been reviewed by a staff member. Word on the street, or in this case, the desert, is that Wolf Creek is a winner. We will keep you posted. – Shaw

NOTES: Don't be surprised if you see jackrabbits, road runners, gila monsters and many other forms of wildlife.

DIRECTIONS: From the Las Vegas Airport (about 90 miles northeast to the course): Take I-15 north to Mesquite. Take the second Mesquite exit, Exit 122, and turn left under the freeway. Turn right on Oasis and then right again on Kittyhawk.

CAMELOT GOLF COURSE (public, 9 holes) . . . .

3430 Camelot Boulevard
Mojave, CA 93501
(661) 824-4107

	YARDAGE	PAR	RATING	SLOPE	
FRONT	2731	36	72.7	125	**$12 - $15**
MIDDLE	-	-	-	-	
BACK	3080	36	70.4	124	

WHAT TO EXPECT: Narrow tree-lined fairways, tricky greens with considerable break, and an ever-present wind make this course a challenge.

DIRECTIONS: From within Mojave: Off Highway 14, turn west onto Camelot Boulevard. Travel one and one-half miles to the course.

NEEDLES MUNICIPAL GOLF COURSE (public, 18 holes, david rainville 1964) . . . .

144 Marina Drive
Needles, CA 92363
(760) 326-3931
needlesgolf.com

	YARDAGE	PAR	RATING	SLOPE	
FRONT	5574	70	71.4	114	**$30 - $35**
MIDDLE	6220	70	70.1	112	
BACK	6513	70	71.3	117	

WHAT TO EXPECT: If you hit the ball well, you will score well. This traditional course has no hidden agendas.

DIRECTIONS: From within Needles (this is about 115 miles south of Las Vegas): Heading east on I-40, exit at J Street and turn left. Turn right when it dead-ends on Front Street. Turn left across the railroad tracks to the course.

CRAIG RANCH GOLF COURSE (public, 18 holes) . . . .

628 West Craig Road
North Las Vegas, NV 89032
(702) 642-9700

	YARDAGE	PAR	RATING	SLOPE	
FRONT	-	-	-	-	**$19 - $27**
MIDDLE	-	-	-	-	
BACK	6000	70	-	-	

WHAT TO EXPECT: One of the oldest courses in Las Vegas, this is a rolling, tree-lined course with a few water holes and small greens.

DIRECTIONS: From the Las Vegas Airport (about 17 miles north to the course): Take I-15 north, exit onto Craig Road and turn left.

NORTH LAS VEGAS PAR-3 (public, 9 holes) . . . .

324 East Brooks Avenue
North Las Vegas, NV 89030
(702) 633-1833
cityofnorthlasvegas.com

	YARDAGE	PAR	RATING	SLOPE	
FRONT	-	-	-	-	**$6 - $8.5**
MIDDLE	-	-	-	-	
BACK	1100	27	-	-	

WHAT TO EXPECT: This is a short night-lit course with excellent views of the Las Vegas skyline. The course can be enjoyed by all skill levels.

DIRECTIONS: From the Las Vegas Airport (about 13 miles north to the course): Take I-15 north and take the Cheyenne exit. Go west to the Losee and make a left. The first right is Brooks. Make a right, and the course is one-quarter mile on the right.

SHADOW CREEK GOLF CLUB (resort, 18 holes, tom fazio 1990) . . . .

Three Shadow Creek Drive
North Las Vegas, NV 89031
(866) 260-0069
shadowcreek.com

	YARDAGE	PAR	RATING	SLOPE	
FRONT	6701	72	-	-	**$500 - $500**
MIDDLE	-	-	-	-	
BACK	7240	72	-	-	

WHAT TO EXPECT: The course wins rave reviews for beauty and style, with mature trees, flowers, and imported wildlife. Shadow Creek's course conditioning is second to none.

OUR OPINION: Legitimately a "Top 50" course with a classic design, but not worth a king's ransom to play it. – Bob

NOTES: This is open only to guests of MGM Mirage properties.

DIRECTIONS: A limousine takes you from your hotel to the course. This is included in your green fees.

LAKE VIEW EXECUTIVE COURSE (public, 18 holes, william bell 1979) . . . .

1471 Mount Charleston
Pahrump, NV 89048
(775) 727-6388
wcgolf.com

	YARDAGE	PAR	RATING	SLOPE	
FRONT	-	-	-	-	**$10 - $25**
MIDDLE	-	-	-	-	
BACK	3587	59	58.6	82	

WHAT TO EXPECT: This should not be considered an executive course, but instead a diminutive championship layout. With long par 3s, two of which are over 200 yards, and narrow par 4s, making par will be no easier here than on a course with several thousand more yards.

DIRECTIONS: From the Las Vegas Airport (about 60 miles northwest to the course): Take I-15 south. Take Exit 3/Blue Diamond Road/Highway 160 for 55 miles to Pahrump. Turn left at Calvada. At the first stop sign, Pahrump Valley Road, turn left. Make another left on Mount Charleston.

WILLOW CREEK GOLF COURSE (public, 36 holes, william bell 1979) . . . .

1500 South Red Butte Street
Pahrump, NV 89048
(877) 779-4653
wcgolf.com

	YARDAGE	PAR	RATING	SLOPE	
FRONT	5923	73	68.5	110	**$25 - $60**
MIDDLE	6514	71	71.2	122	
BACK	7026	71	73.7	127	

WHAT TO EXPECT: The course recently changed its name from Calvada to Willow Creek. Thought was taken in choosing a name, as the course has many willow trees and water on nearly every hole. This is a long course, but golfers should focus on placement over distance. The extra 20 yards will not do you much good if you are pulling your ball out of the water.

DIRECTIONS: From the Las Vegas Airport (about 60 miles northwest to the course): Take I-15 south. Take Exit 3/Blue Diamond Road/Highway 160 for 55 miles to Pahrump. Turn left at Highway 372 and go about one and one-half miles. Turn left on Red Butte Street.

AVONDALE GOLF CLUB (members only, 18 holes, jimmy hines 1970) . . . .

75-800 Avondale Drive
Palm Desert, CA 92211
(760) 345-3712

	YARDAGE	PAR	RATING	SLOPE	
FRONT	5781	72	74.7	125	**$80 - $110**
MIDDLE	6400	72	70.5	122	
BACK	6782	72	72.4	127	

WHAT TO EXPECT: This is a traditional course set in the desert. Narrow, tree-lined fairways and water make it important to be accurate off the tee. The greens are medium-sized and defended by trees.

NOTES: Reciprocal play with other members only clubs is allowed.

DIRECTIONS: From downtown Los Angeles (about 130 miles east to the course): Take I-10 east. Exit at Cook Street and turn right. Turn left on Frank Sinatra Drive and then right on El Dorado.

BIGHORN GOLF CLUB (members only, 36 holes, tom fazio) . . . .

255 Palowet Drive
Palm Desert, CA 92260
(760) 341-4653
bighorngolf.com

	YARDAGE	PAR	RATING	SLOPE	
FRONT	5162	72	69.2	123	**$100 - $100**
MIDDLE	6673	72	72.1	136	
BACK	7084	72	74.1	139	

WHAT TO EXPECT: The Canyons Course appears challenging, but plays easier than its sister course, which is very difficult. The Hills Course boasts splendid views of the Coachella Valley and some demanding desert holes. The course meanders among housing. A cart is required because of long distances between holes.

NOTES: The yardage listed is for the Canyons Course.

DIRECTIONS: From downtown Los Angeles (about 120 miles east to the course): Go east on I-10 toward Palm Springs. Exit on Monterey Avenue and turn right. This turns into Highway 74. The club is visible from Highway 74.

CHAPARRAL COUNTRY CLUB (members only, 18 holes, ted robinson 1978) . . . .

100 Chaparral Drive
Palm Desert, CA 92260
(760) 340-1501

	YARDAGE	PAR	RATING	SLOPE	
FRONT	3103	60	57.6	89	**$35 - $35**
MIDDLE	3667	60	57.9	90	
BACK	3913	60	59.0	94	

WHAT TO EXPECT: If you can't hit a green to save your life, miss long rather than short. You will find water on 13 of the 18 holes of this short executive course. Most of the water can be found on the front of the greens, along with well-placed bunkers.

DIRECTIONS: From downtown Los Angeles (about 120 miles east to the course): Take I-10 east, exit at Monterey Avenue, and head south. Turn left on Country Club Drive and then right on Portola Avenue. The course is at 42555 Portola Avenue.

DESERT FALLS COUNTRY CLUB (semi-private, 18 holes, ron fream) . . . .

1111 Desert Falls Parkway
Palm Desert, CA 92211
(760) 340-4653

	YARDAGE	PAR	RATING	SLOPE	
FRONT	5250	72	72.1	125	**$115 - $140**
MIDDLE	6529	72	71.5	126	
BACK	7005	72	73.7	132	

WHAT TO EXPECT: Desert Falls is a long, European-style course. It will give you little trouble in front of the greens, but lots of sand for those who miss left or right. Water comes into play on seven holes. On the par 3s, you will find the water around the green; on the par 5s the water will be along the fairway. Wind can be a factor in the afternoon. The greens vary in shapes and sizes.

OUR OPINION: This receives high marks by women golfers, for good reason. The course does not penalize you with awkward landing areas when playing the forward tees. – Loralei

DIRECTIONS: From downtown Los Angeles (about 130 miles east to the course): Take I-10 east, exit at Cook Street and head south. Turn left on Country Club Drive and left again on Desert Falls Parkway.

DESERT WILLOW GOLF RESORT (resort, 36 holes, fry, hurdzan & cook 1997) . . . .

38995 Desert Willow Drive
Palm Desert, CA 92260
(760) 346-7060
desertwillow.com

	YARDAGE	PAR	RATING	SLOPE
FRONT	5079	72	69.0	120
MIDDLE	6173	72	69.7	125
BACK	7057	72	74.1	138

$65 - $165

WHAT TO EXPECT: Huge bunkers, together with the natural desert, dominate the landscape and make up the challenge of this new, popular desert course.

OUR OPINION: With its Arroyo Desert look, it's a little bit of Phoenix in Palm Springs. Course conditioning is excellent; I don't think we saw another divot or ball mark all day. This is tough course, but fair. The women we played with (all 36 handicappers) thought it was a fun course. The five sets of tees work. – Frank

NOTES: The yardage listed is for the Firecliff Course.

DIRECTIONS: From downtown Los Angeles (about 120 miles east to the course): Take I-10 east, exit at Cook Street and head south. Turn right on Country Club Drive and make another right into the course.

EMERALD DESERT GOLF & RV RESORT (public, 9 holes) . . . .

76-000 Frank Sinatra Drive
Palm Desert, CA 92211
(760) 345-4770
emeralddesert.com

	YARDAGE	PAR	RATING	SLOPE
FRONT	-	-	-	-
MIDDLE	-	-	-	-
BACK	1330	28	-	-

$15 - $22

WHAT TO EXPECT: This is a short nine-hole course with one par 4. The challenge of the course is provided by water, which comes into play on six of nine holes.

DIRECTIONS: From downtown Los Angeles (about 130 miles east to the course): Take I-10 east, exit on Cook Street, and head south. Turn left on Frank Sinatra Drive. Emerald Desert is on the left.

INDIAN RIDGE COUNTRY CLUB (members only, 36 holes, arnold palmer) . . . .

76-375 Country Club Drive
Palm Desert, CA 92211
(760) 772-7222
indianridgecc.com

	YARDAGE	PAR	RATING	SLOPE
FRONT	4923	72	68.6	121
MIDDLE	6735	72	72.5	132
BACK	7081	72	74.3	137

$75 - $100

WHAT TO EXPECT: Indian Ridge has the Grove Course and the Arroyo Course. The Grove course is more of a traditional desert course with plenty of water and palm trees. The Arroyo Course has a high-desert feel, with some forced carries and large natural waste bunkers. Both layouts have large, undulating green sites.

NOTES: The yardage listed is for the Grove Course.

DIRECTIONS: From downtown Los Angeles (about 130 miles east to the course): Take I-10 east, exit at Cook Street and head south. Turn left on Country Club Drive. The club is on the right, just past El Dorado.

IRONWOOD COUNTRY CLUB (members only, 36 holes, ted robinson) . . . .

73-735 Irontree Drive
Palm Desert, CA 92260
(760) 346-0551
ironwoodcc.com

	YARDAGE	PAR	RATING	SLOPE	
FRONT	5940	72	74.6	132	**$70 - $70**
MIDDLE	6810	72	72.6	125	
BACK	7268	72	74.8	132	

WHAT TO EXPECT: There are two scenic courses, the North and South. The North Course plays among the homes and measures a little more than 5,700 yards. The South is long (7,200 yards) and driver friendly with lots of water, sand, rolling terrain, and flat greens.
NOTES: The yardage listed is for the South Course.
DIRECTIONS: From downtown Los Angeles (about 120 miles east to the course): Take I-10 east, exit at Monterey and turn right. Cross Highway 111 and the road turns into Highway 74. Turn left on Haystack and right on Portola. The entrance is on the left.

LAKES COUNTRY CLUB, THE (members only, 27 holes, ted robinson) . . . .

161 Old Ranch Road
Palm Desert, CA 92211
(760) 568-4321
thelakescc.com

	YARDAGE	PAR	RATING	SLOPE	
FRONT	5378	72	71.0	127	**$65 - $125**
MIDDLE	6287	72	69.6	116	
BACK	6704	72	71.9	121	

WHAT TO EXPECT: There are plenty of lakes on all three Lakes Courses. The North and East Courses are lined with condominiums, and the water comes into play mostly on the front of the greens. The South Course is the longest course, and features abundant landing areas. All the courses have fairly big undulating greens.
NOTES: The yardage listed is for the South/North combination.
DIRECTIONS: From downtown Los Angeles (about 130 miles east to the course): Take the I-10 east, exit Cook Street and turn right. Turn left on Country Club Drive and then a quick right on Lakes. The entrance is on the right.

MARRAKESH COUNTRY CLUB (members only, 18 holes, ted robinson 1968) . . . .

47-000 Marrakesh Drive
Palm Desert, CA 92260
(760) 568-2660

	YARDAGE	PAR	RATING	SLOPE	
FRONT	3220	60	57.9	92	**$50 - $90**
MIDDLE	-	-	-	-	
BACK	3614	60	56.8	86	

WHAT TO EXPECT: The course is located in a housing development. This is a hilly, narrow executive layout with well-guarded, average-size greens, four lakes and plenty of trees. The longest hole on the course is a little more than 300 yards.
NOTES: Reciprocal play with other members only clubs is allowed. The course is closed in October.
DIRECTIONS: From downtown Los Angeles (about 120 miles east to the course): Take I-10 east, exit at Monterey Avenue, and head south. Turn left on Country Club Drive. Turn right on Portola Avenue, to the club entrance.

MARRIOTT DESERT SPRINGS RESORT AND SPA (resort, 36 holes, ted robinson 1987) . .

74-855 Country Club Drive
Palm Desert, CA 92260
(760) 341-1756
desertspringsgolfclub.com

	YARDAGE	PAR	RATING	SLOPE
FRONT	6143	72	69.2	123
MIDDLE	6381	72	70.3	126
BACK	6762	72	72.1	130

$55 - $160

WHAT TO EXPECT: The Marriott contains two feel-good resort courses. There are plenty of traps, palm trees, and water along the way to keep you entertained. For the most part, the Desert Springs is forgiving, with open fairways and large greens that reward good shots. For the average golfer who is having a good day, a career score is possible.

OUR OPINION: This is a nice resort with fun layouts, but if you are just going to play the courses, check the rates before you play. Don't get me wrong; we like these golf courses; but for $160, you should not only have fun, but be inspired, and that won't happen here. – Shaw

NOTES: The yardage listed is for the Palms Course.

DIRECTIONS: From downtown Los Angeles (about 120 miles east to the course): Take I-10 east, exit at Cook Street and head south. Turn right on Country Club Drive to the resort.

MARRIOTT'S SHADOW RIDGE RESORT (resort, 18 holes, nick faldo 2000) . . . .

9002 Shadow Ridge Road
Palm Desert, CA 92211
(760) 674-2700
golfshadowridge.com

	YARDAGE	PAR	RATING	SLOPE
FRONT	5158	71	69.6	119
MIDDLE	6552	71	71.4	128
BACK	6924	71	73.2	132

$50 - $140

WHAT TO EXPECT: Set against the Santa Rosa Mountains, this is Nick Faldo's first championship design in the states. The course offers ample fairways, with bold bunkering and greens, along with subtle undulations that reward and encourage a variety of shots. Miss the putting surfaces here and your ball will invariably roll into a tightly mowed collection area or into a green-side bunker. A deft touch will be required to make par.

OUR OPINION: This is an excellent layout that will test all of your golfing skills. The bunkers are beautiful to look at, as long as you are not in one of them. We recommend this course highly, unless you have money to burn we don't recommend paying $140 for green fees. Play it during the week, twilight, or in the off-season. – The Mole

DIRECTIONS: From downtown Los Angeles (about 130 miles east to the course): Take I-10 east, exit at Monterey Avenue and head south. The entrance is on the east side, about two miles down.

MONTEREY COUNTRY CLUB (members only, 27 holes, ted robinson) . . . .

41-500 Monterey Avenue
Palm Desert, CA 92260
(760) 346-1115
americangolf.com

	YARDAGE	PAR	RATING	SLOPE	
FRONT	5814	72	74.0	131	**$80 - $105**
MIDDLE	5898	72	67.9	117	
BACK	6185	72	69.4	119	

WHAT TO EXPECT: The South and West Courses are narrow with trees and condominiums lining the fairways. Hit your ball ten yards off the fairway and you will be adding two strokes to your scorecard. There is plenty of water on these two courses, but most can be avoided by the smart player. The East Course is flatter. The water on this course is more intimidating and harder to avoid, especially for the women, who have a few long, forced carries. T he greens are fairly large with tricky, subtle breaks.

NOTES: The yardage listed is for the South and West nines. Reciprocal play with other members only clubs is allowed.

DIRECTIONS: From downtown Los Angeles (about 120 miles east to the course): Take I-10 east, exit onto Monterey Avenue, and drive south to the club.

MOUNTAIN VISTA GOLF COURSE AT SUN CITY (semi-private, 36 holes, greg nash

38-180 Del Webb Boulevard
Palm Desert, CA 92211
(760) 200-2200
mountainvistagolf.com

	YARDAGE	PAR	RATING	SLOPE	
FRONT		72			**$33 - $89**
MIDDLE		72			
BACK		72			

WHAT TO EXPECT: There are two 18-hole courses, the Santa Rosa and the San Gorgonio. The Santa Rosa has wider fairways that slope on either side. Take advantage of the first six holes; they are the easiest. Starting with the seventh hole, you will encounter water and long par 3s and one of the most demanding finishing holes in the desert. For the average golfer, expect to lose four golf balls. The San Gorgonio course has smaller, undulating greens with narrow fairways outlined by water and bunkers.

DIRECTIONS: From downtown Los Angeles (about 130 miles east to the course): Take I-10 east, exit at Washington, and turn left to the course.

OASIS COUNTRY CLUB, THE (semi-private, 18 holes, david rainville) . . . .

42-330 Casbah Way
Palm Desert, CA 92211
(760) 345-2715

	YARDAGE	PAR	RATING	SLOPE	
FRONT	3100	60	56.9	85	**$60 - $60**
MIDDLE	3100	60	54.3	89	
BACK	3489	60	56.2	92	

WHAT TO EXPECT: This is a short, executive course with water everywhere. The golfer prone to errant shots will find out quickly that this course is only an oasis for abused golf balls tired of being topped, sliced, hooked, and looking for a good place to hide.

DIRECTIONS: From downtown Los Angeles (about 130 miles east to the course): Take I-10 east, exit at Washington Street and turn right. Turn right on Hovley Lane. The course is on the left.

PALM DESERT COUNTRY CLUB (semi-private, 27 holes, william p. bell) . . . .

77-200 California Drive
Palm Desert, CA 92211
(760) 345-2525

	YARDAGE	PAR	RATING	SLOPE
FRONT	5843	72	72.5	121
MIDDLE	6360	72	69.3	111
BACK	6643	72	70.9	116

$20 - $75

WHAT TO EXPECT: The Championship Course, as well as the nine-hole executive course, is traditional in style. Both feature fairly level terrain and are surrounded by homes that will come into play for the severe hooker or slicer.
NOTES: The yardage listed is for the Championship Course.
DIRECTIONS: From downtown Los Angeles (about 130 miles east to the course): Take I-10 east, exit Washington, and turn right. Turn right on Avenue of the States and go about 3 miles to the course.

PALM DESERT GREENS COUNTRY CLUB (members only, 18 holes, ted robinson 1970) .

73-750 Country Club Drive
Palm Desert, CA 92260
(760) 346-2941

	YARDAGE	PAR	RATING	SLOPE
FRONT	3680	63	59.6	95
MIDDLE	3680	63	57.0	88
BACK	4088	63	58.9	93

$15 - $30

WHAT TO EXPECT: This is an older, traditional-style executive course. User friendly, the course has plenty of mature trees, wide-tarmac fairways, an abundance of water, and greens that are well protected by sand.
DIRECTIONS: From downtown Los Angeles (about 120 miles east to the course): Take the I-10 east, exit onto Monterey Avenue and head south. Turn left on Country Club Drive. If you reach Portola, you have gone too far.

PALM DESERT RESORT COUNTRY CLUB (semi-private, 18 holes, ted robinson) . . . . . .

77-333 Country Club Drive
Palm Desert, CA 92211
(760) 345-2781
pdrcc.com

	YARDAGE	PAR	RATING	SLOPE
FRONT	5462	72	71.5	121
MIDDLE	6343	72	69.4	112
BACK	6616	72	70.9	117

$30 - $90

WHAT TO EXPECT: This is a fairly forgiving course for anyone who can hit it moderately straight. To keep you entertained, you will find six lakes, rolling terrain, 65 sand traps, and a variety of trees. Homes are found throughout the course.
DIRECTIONS: From downtown Los Angeles (about 130 miles east to the course): Take I-10 east, exit at Cook Street, and head south. Turn left at Country Club Drive. The course is about three lights down.

PALM VALLEY COUNTRY CLUB (members only, 36 holes, ted robinson) . . . .

39-205 Palm Valley Drive
Palm Desert, CA 92211
(760) 345-2737

	YARDAGE	PAR	RATING	SLOPE
FRONT	5294	72	71.8	129
MIDDLE	6324	72	69.8	118
BACK	6545	72	70.9	120

$95 - $110

WHAT TO EXPECT: Palm Valley has two courses, The Championship Course and the Challenge Course. The Championship Course has the yardage while the Challenge Course has the bite. Lined with palm trees, the Championship Course features tranquil waterfalls and member-friendly fairways. With 19 lakes, the Challenge Course lives up to its name. Placement is everything. Either bring good iron play or an abundance of golf balls.
NOTES: The yardage listed is for the Championship Course. Reciprocal play with other members only clubs is allowed.
DIRECTIONS: From downtown Los Angeles (about 130 miles east to the course): Take I-10 east, exit on Cook Street, and turn right. Turn left on Country Club Drive and then left again on Palm Valley Drive.

PORTOLA COUNTRY CLUB (members only, 18 holes) . . . .

42-500 Portola Avenue
Palm Desert, CA 92260
(760) 568-1592

	YARDAGE	PAR	RATING	SLOPE
FRONT	-	-	-	-
MIDDLE	-	-	-	-
BACK	2124	54	-	-

$10 - $15

WHAT TO EXPECT: This is a par-3 course located in a mobile home park.
DIRECTIONS: From downtown Los Angeles (about 120 miles east to the course): Take I-10 east, exit at Monterey Avenue, and go south. Turn left on Country Club Drive and then right on Portola Avenue.

SANTA ROSA COUNTRY CLUB (members only, 18 holes, len gerkin) . . . .

38-105 Portola Avenue
Palm Desert, CA 92260
(760) 568-5717

	YARDAGE	PAR	RATING	SLOPE
FRONT	5231	70	70.1	113
MIDDLE	5443	70	71.0	115
BACK	6443	67	65.1	112

$40 - $40

WHAT TO EXPECT: The course is currently under renovation and will be open in late 2001.
NOTES: Reciprocal play with other members only clubs is allowed.
DIRECTIONS: From downtown Los Angeles (about 120 miles east to the course): Take I-10 east, exit at Cook Street, and turn right. Turn right on Frank Sinatra Drive and then left on Portola Avenue. The course is on the right.

SHADOW MOUNTAIN GOLF CLUB (members only, 18 holes, gene sarazen) . . . .

73-800 Ironwood
Palm Desert, CA 92260
(760) 346-8242

	YARDAGE	PAR	RATING	SLOPE
FRONT	5200	71	69.7	117
MIDDLE	5393	71	70.8	120
BACK	5393	70	66.3	114

$30 - $60

WHAT TO EXPECT: The shadow of Shadow Mountain comes from the forest of palm trees that line the fairways. Although the fairways are narrow, the real challenge comes around the greens. An accurate short game is needed to navigate the small greens, which are well protected by bunkers.
NOTES: Reciprocal play with other members only clubs is allowed.
DIRECTIONS: From downtown Los Angeles (about 120 miles east to the course): Take I-10 east, exit at Monterey, and turn right. Turn left on to Highway 111. Turn right on San Luis Rey. Go until it ends and turn left in to the club.

SUNCREST COUNTRY CLUB (public, 9 holes, richard watson) . . . .

73-450 Country Club Drive
Palm Desert, CA 92260
(760) 340-2467

	YARDAGE	PAR	RATING	SLOPE
FRONT	1948	33	60.6	96
MIDDLE	2361	33	61.3	98
BACK	2473	33	62.3	101

$20 - $30

WHAT TO EXPECT: This is a level, open executive course with some water holes and one par 5.
DIRECTIONS: From downtown Los Angeles (about 120 miles east to the course): Take I-10 east, exit at Monterey Avenue, and turn right. Turn left on Country Club Drive. Make a left at the first light into the entrance.

WOODHAVEN COUNTRY CLUB (members only, 18 holes, harold heers) . . . .

41-555 Woodhaven Drive East
Palm Desert, CA 92211
(760) 345-7513
woodhavencc.com

	YARDAGE	PAR	RATING	SLOPE
FRONT	5254	70	70.0	117
MIDDLE	5794	70	72.4	122
BACK	5794	70	67.1	118

$50 - $90

WHAT TO EXPECT: Set on 100 acres with 500 homes lining the fairways, accuracy is a must off the tee. The greens are small and level. The attraction of this golf course is the distance, or lack of it. At 5,800 yards the older, younger, or weaker golfer can compete with the bigger hitters.
NOTES: Reciprocal play with other members only clubs is allowed.
DIRECTIONS: From downtown Los Angeles (about 130 miles east to the course): Take I-10 east, exit at Washington Street, and turn right to head south. The Course is about one-half mile down on the right, just before Hovely.

CANYON COUNTRY CLUB (members only, 18 holes, william f. bell 1961) . . . .

1100 Murray Canyon Drive
Palm Springs, CA 92264
(760) 327-1321
canyoncountryclub.com

	YARDAGE	PAR	RATING	SLOPE
FRONT	5862	72	73.7	127
MIDDLE	6488	72	70.6	121
BACK	6880	72	72.3	125

$65 - $80

WHAT TO EXPECT: This is a level course with two large lakes. The fairways are surrounded by homes, which can cause severe frustration for the golfer who sprays the ball off the tee and plays by the rules.
DIRECTIONS: From downtown Los Angeles (about 115 miles east to the course): Take I-10 east to Highway 111 into Palm Springs. Turn left on Vista Chino and then right on Sunrise. When the road bends, turn left on Toledo. Toledo turns right and becomes Murray Canyon Drive.

CANYON SOUTH GOLF COURSE (public, 18 holes, william p. bell) . . . .

1097 Murray Canyon Drive
Palm Springs, CA 92264
(760) 327-2019

	YARDAGE	PAR	RATING	SLOPE
FRONT	5645	71	72.0	116
MIDDLE	6205	71	68.6	109
BACK	6536	71	70.8	119

$15 - $70

WHAT TO EXPECT: This is a straightforward, no-frills course with wide fairways. The course is unique from many of the area's layouts because it is sheltered from the wind.
DIRECTIONS: From downtown Los Angeles (about 115 miles east to the course): Take I-10 east to Highway 111 into Palm Springs. Turn left on Vista Chino and then right on Sunrise. When the road bends, turn left on Toledo. Toledo becomes Murry Canyon Drive.

MESQUITE GOLF CLUB (public, 18 holes, bert stamps) . . . .

2700 East Mesquite Avenue
Palm Springs, CA 92264
(760) 323-9377
americangolf.com

	YARDAGE	PAR	RATING	SLOPE
FRONT	5248	72	70.7	120
MIDDLE	5888	72	68.0	118
BACK	6210	72	69.5	122

$45 - $85

WHAT TO EXPECT: Mesquite is unusual in that it has six relatively short par 5s and six relatively long par 3s. There are plenty of water and 65 bunkers. The course is challenging enough for the good golfer and resort friendly for the less skilled.
DIRECTIONS: From downtown Los Angeles (about 115 miles east to the course): Take I-10 east, exit at Gene Autry, and head south. Take a right on Vista Chino and then a left on Farrell for about three miles to Mesquite.

O'DONNELL GOLF CLUB (members only, 9 holes, tom o'donnell 1928) . . . .

301 North Belardo Road
Palm Springs, CA 92262
(760) 325-2259

	YARDAGE	PAR	RATING	SLOPE
FRONT	2601	35	69.9	116
MIDDLE	-	-	-	-
BACK	2601	35	65.2	108

$44 - $44

WHAT TO EXPECT: This is an open course with small greens and water that comes into play on one hole.

NOTES: This was the first course built in Palm Springs.

DIRECTIONS: From downtown Los Angeles (about 110 miles east to the course): Take I-10 east take the Vista Chino/Date Palm exit. Turn right on Date Palm and then left on Palm Canyon. Turn right on Amado and enter the desert museum parking lot to get to the club.

PALM SPRINGS COUNTRY CLUB (public, 18 holes) . . . .

2500 Whitewater Club Road
Palm Springs, CA 92262
(760) 323-2626

	YARDAGE	PAR	RATING	SLOPE
FRONT	5228	72	72.4	118
MIDDLE	5869	72	66.6	110
BACK	6201	72	68.9	115

$40 - $60

WHAT TO EXPECT: This is a typical, older, parkland-style course set in the desert with wide, level fairways and mature trees.

NOTES: The course often closes in late spring until fall.

DIRECTIONS: From downtown Los Angeles (about 110 miles east to the course): Take I-10 east, exit Palm Drive and turn right. This turns into Gene Autry Trail. Make a right on Vista Chino and then another right on Whitewater Club Road.

TAHQUITZ CREEK, A GOLF RESORT (public, 36 holes, william p. bell) . . . .

1885 Golf Club Drive
Palm Springs, CA 92264
(760) 328-1005
palmergolf.com

	YARDAGE	PAR	RATING	SLOPE
FRONT	5206	72	70.0	119
MIDDLE	6249	72	69.9	123
BACK	6649	72	71.8	125

$50 - $90

WHAT TO EXPECT: The Legend Course is the older of the two courses. The average golfer will find this is a fun, playable course. The Resort Course is an enjoyable but tougher venue with cactus, palms, sand, and water. This is one of the better, more difficult public access layouts in the area. When the wind blows, the degree of difficulty increases significantly.

OUR OPINION: Tahquitz Creek has two enjoyable courses. Play both if you get the chance. – Brad

NOTES: The yardage listed is for the Resort Course.

DIRECTIONS: From downtown Los Angeles (about 115 miles east to the course): Take I-10 east, exit Palm Drive/Gene Autry Trail and turn right on Gene Autre. Turn left on Ramon Road and then right on Crossley. The driving range on the right.

TOMMY JACOBS' BEL AIR GREENS (public, 9 holes, len girken 1967) . . . .

1001 South El Cielo Road
Palm Springs, CA 92264
(760) 322-6062
superpages.com

	YARDAGE	PAR	RATING	SLOPE	
FRONT	-	-	-	-	
MIDDLE	-	-	-	-	**$9 - $19**
BACK	1800	32	57.0	92	

WHAT TO EXPECT: This is a mature course with medium-sized greens and trees guarding the fairways. You will find water on about half the holes.

DIRECTIONS: From downtown Los Angeles (about 115 miles east to the course): Take I-10 east, exit at Gene Autry Trail and turn right. Take another right on Ramon Road and then a left on El Cielo Road. The course is on the right.

ANTELOPE VALLEY COUNTRY CLUB (members only, 18 holes, william bell, sr. 1953) . .

39800 Country Club Drive
Palmdale, CA 93551
(661) 947-3400

	YARDAGE	PAR	RATING	SLOPE	
FRONT	6157	74	76.5	129	
MIDDLE	6408	72	70.2	122	**$35 - $55**
BACK	6740	72	71.9	121	

WHAT TO EXPECT: Sand, water, trees, and wind will keep you on your toes at Antelope. The fairways are lined with trees, and the greens are well guarded by bunkers, but beware of the rough. Missing the fairways can be a painful experience, literally. Originally cut out of a forest of Joshua trees (part of the cactus family), the course still has many of trees.

NOTES: Guests are restricted on weekends and holidays until noon.

DIRECTIONS: From within Palmdale: Off Highway 14 take the Rancho Vista Boulevard/Avenue P exit. Head east only about a quarter mile to Country Club Drive. Turn left to the club.

DESERT AIRE GOLF COURSE (public, 9 holes) . . . .

3620 East Avenue P
Palmdale, CA 93550
(661) 538-0370

	YARDAGE	PAR	RATING	SLOPE	
FRONT	2775	35	71.5	116	
MIDDLE	3031	36	-	-	**$6 - $14**
BACK	3178	36	68.3	106	

WHAT TO EXPECT: The trees lining the fairways of this level course won't cause much trouble for golfers off the tee. In fact, they are helpful in blocking the wind and providing shade during the summer months. The greens are medium-sized, and one lake comes into play.

DIRECTIONS: From within Palmdale: Off Highway 14, take the Avenue P/Rancho Vista exit. Drive east about four miles to get to the course.

RANCHO VISTA GOLF COURSE (public, 18 holes, ted robinson) . . . .

3905 Club Rancho Drive
Palmdale, CA 93351
(661) 272-9903
ranchovista.com

	YARDAGE	PAR	RATING	SLOPE
FRONT	5262	-	-	-
MIDDLE	-	-	-	-
BACK	6632	-	-	-

$38 - $45

WHAT TO EXPECT: This residential development features water; there are ten lakes in all. With plenty of wind and immature trees, an accurate punch shot comes in handy.
DIRECTIONS: From within Palmdale: Off Highway 14, take the Avenue P/Rancho Vista exit. Head west on Rancho Vista Boulevard. Turn right on Town Center Drive and then left on Bolz Ranch Road. Turn right on Club Rancho Drive.

PRIMM VALLEY GOLF CLUB (resort, 36 holes, tom fazio 1997) . . . .

31900 South Las Vegas Boulevard
Primm, NV 89019
(702) 679-5510
primmvalleyresorts.com

	YARDAGE	PAR	RATING	SLOPE
FRONT	5397	72	72.1	124
MIDDLE	6540	72	71.7	130
BACK	7132	72	74.6	138

$55 - $195

WHAT TO EXPECT: A fortune was spent crafting the flat desert and importing trees to build these two courses. While the stylized Tom Fazio bunkering is similar on each course, as is the wind, the Lakes Course incorporates a traditional layout, lots of trees, and you guessed it, man-made lakes. The Desert Course features cacti, waste areas and plenty of bunkers.
OUR OPINION: These are two solid courses. One course is not significantly better than the other, (neither is worth $195) so don't worry about which one you play. The higher handicapper may prefer the desert course because there are fewer places to lose golf balls. – The Mole
NOTES: The yardage listed is for the Desert Course.
DIRECTIONS: From the Las Vegas Airport (about 42 miles southwest to the course): Take I-15 south. This course at the California/Nevada border. Exit at Yates Well Road and head north.

MEADOWLARK GOLF CENTER (public, 9 holes) . . . .

43625 60th Street West
Quartz Hill, CA 93536
(661) 943-2022

	YARDAGE	PAR	RATING	SLOPE
FRONT	929	27	-	-
MIDDLE	-	-	-	-
BACK	1112	27	-	-

$8 - $8

WHAT TO EXPECT: Meadowlark is a par-3 course and teaching center.
DIRECTIONS: From Palmdale (about 10 miles northwest to the course): Take Highway 14 toward Lancaster. Exit at Avenue K and go west. Turn right on 60th Street West, and the golf center is on the left.

CLUB AT MORNINGSIDE, THE (members only, 18 holes, jack nicklaus 1982) . . . .

39-033 Morningside Drive
Rancho Mirage, CA 92270
(760) 321-1555

	YARDAGE	PAR	RATING	SLOPE
FRONT	5448	72	71.8	124
MIDDLE	6404	72	70.6	122
BACK	6773	72	72.7	127

$85 - $85

WHAT TO EXPECT: This refined, manicured links-style is one of the most engaging layouts in the Coachella Valley. Even though it occupies an essentially flat site, this playable Jack Nicklaus design provides many entertaining options.
DIRECTIONS: From downtown Los Angeles (about 120 miles east to the course): Take I-10 east, exit at Ramon Road and turn right. Turn left on Bob Hope Drive and then right on Country Club Drive. Turn right on Morningside Drive, and the club entrance is on the left.

DESERT ISLAND GOLF & COUNTRY CLUB (members only, 18 holes, d. muirhead) . . . .

71-777 Frank Sinatra Drive
Rancho Mirage, CA 92270
(760) 328-0841

	YARDAGE	PAR	RATING	SLOPE
FRONT	5604	72	72.2	120
MIDDLE	6310	72	69.8	118
BACK	6684	72	71.7	123

$65 - $130

WHAT TO EXPECT: Instead of a course with an island green, this is a residential community set on an island, with a golf course bordering the lake. Not a long course, Desert Island stresses accuracy off the tee and precise iron play onto small greens. Although water comes into play on one-third of the holes, it is your putter that will make or break your round. The greens are not only small, but some are severely undulating.
DIRECTIONS: From downtown Los Angeles (about 120 miles east to the course): Take I-10 east, exit at Ramon Road/Bob Hope Drive, and go right. Turn left on Bob Hope Drive. Turn right on Frank Sinatra Drive.

MISSION HILLS COUNTRY CLUB (members only, 54 holes, muirhead, palmer, dye) . .

34-600 Mission Hills Drive
Rancho Mirage, CA 92270
(760) 324-9400
missionhills.com

	YARDAGE	PAR	RATING	SLOPE
FRONT	5684	72	73.6	132
MIDDLE	6906	72	73.1	127
BACK	7221	72	74.8	133

$50 - $225

WHAT TO EXPECT: There are three courses are Mission Hills Country Club: the Dinah Shore, the Pete Dye, and the Arnold Palmer Courses. The all have different personalities. The Dinah Shore Course meanders around mildly undulating terrain and boasts some strong green-side bunkering and strategic water hazards. It has become a demanding driving course. The Pete Dye Course is a stadium venue with moguls, lakes, and enormous bunkers. The Arnold Palmer has the most water but also is the most tame of the three layouts.
NOTES: The yardage listed is for the Dinah Shore Tournament Course. Reciprocal play with other member only clubs is allowed.
DIRECTIONS: From downtown Los Angeles (about 120 miles east to the course): Take I-10 east, exit at Bob Hope Drive/Ramon Road. Turn left on Bob Hope and right on Dinah Shore Drive. The entrance is about a mile past the Westin.

RANCHO LAS PALMAS COUNTRY CLUB (resort/private, 27 holes, ted robinson) . . . . .

42-000 Bob Hope Drive
Rancho Mirage, CA 92270
(760) 862-4551

	YARDAGE	PAR	RATING	SLOPE
FRONT	5256	70	70.2	124
MIDDLE	5725	70	66.3	112
BACK	6128	70	67.8	115

$125 - $135

WHAT TO EXPECT: The three courses are the North, South and West. None of the courses is particularly long. They can be narrow in spots, with condos coming into play for the golfer who has trouble hitting fairways. On windy days you will find these courses less windy than many of the neighboring facilities.
NOTES: The yardage listed is for the South/West nines. Reciprocal play with other members only clubs is allowed.
DIRECTIONS: From downtown Los Angeles (about 120 miles east to the course): Take I-10 east, exit at Bob Hope Drive/Ramon Road and head south on Bob Hope Drive. Take the second entrance on the left. The first entrance is for the Marriott.

RANCHO MIRAGE COUNTRY CLUB (semi-private, 18 holes, harold heers 1985) . . . . . .

38-500 Bob Hope Drive
Rancho Mirage, CA 92270
(760) 324-4711
ranchomiragegolf.com

	YARDAGE	PAR	RATING	SLOPE
FRONT	5309	70	70.5	117
MIDDLE	5823	70	68.0	119
BACK	6211	70	69.4	122

$25 - $95

WHAT TO EXPECT: Big hitters had better keep control of their driver on this rather short course. Accuracy is paramount as water hazards are the dominant feature.
DIRECTIONS: From downtown Los Angeles (about 120 miles east to the course): Take I-10 east, exit at Bob Hope Drive/Ramon Road and head south on Bob Hope Drive.

SPRINGS CLUB, THE (members only, 18 holes, desmond muirhead) . . . .

One Duke Drive
Rancho Mirage, CA 92270
(760) 328-0590
springsclub.com

	YARDAGE	PAR	RATING	SLOPE
FRONT	5614	72	72.6	127
MIDDLE	6279	72	70.1	124
BACK	6637	72	71.9	128

$70 - $70

WHAT TO EXPECT: This is a straightforward, playable desert course with wide fairways. The course features an island green.
DIRECTIONS: From downtown Los Angeles (about 120 miles east to the course): Take I-10 east, exit at Bob Hope Drive, and turn right. Turn left on Bob Hope Drive. The club is on the right.

SUNRISE COUNTRY CLUB (members only, 18 holes, ted robinson) . . . .

71-601 Country Club Drive
Rancho Mirage, CA 92270
(760) 328-6549

	YARDAGE	PAR	RATING	SLOPE
FRONT	3837	64	61.3	101
MIDDLE	-	-	-	-
BACK	3837	64	56.9	85

$40 - $40

WHAT TO EXPECT: Sunrise is an executive course with wide fairways, some water and medium-sized flat greens.
NOTES: Reciprocal play with other members only clubs is allowed.
DIRECTIONS: From downtown Los Angeles (about 120 miles east to the course): Take the I-10 east, exit at Bob Hope, and turn right on Country Club Drive, which is past the Eisenhower Medical Center. Sunrise is on the left.

TAMARISK COUNTRY CLUB (members only, 18 holes, william p. bell) . . . .

70-240 Frank Sinatra Drive
Rancho Mirage, CA 92270
(760) 328-2141

	YARDAGE	PAR	RATING	SLOPE
FRONT	6219	72	69.5	115
MIDDLE	6555	72	70.9	119
BACK	6881	72	72.6	123

$72 - $72

WHAT TO EXPECT: Flat, well-bunkered, and with many rows of trees, Tamarisk is a good test of golf. This course is one of the oldest in the desert. Ben Hogan was once the pro here.
DIRECTIONS: From downtown Los Angeles (about 120 miles east to the course): Take I-10 east, exit at Date Palm, and turn right. Turn left on Gerald Ford and then a right on Duval. Turn left on Frank Sinatra Drive and the club is on the left.

THUNDERBIRD COUNTRY CLUB (members only, 18 holes, dawson & hughes 1951) . . .

70-612 Highway 111
Rancho Mirage, CA 92270
(760) 328-2161

	YARDAGE	PAR	RATING	SLOPE
FRONT	5854	72	74.2	133
MIDDLE	6179	71	69.4	126
BACK	6460	71	70.7	129

$90 - $90

WHAT TO EXPECT: This is a flat course with water coming into play on five holes and homes lining half the fairways.
DIRECTIONS: From downtown Los Angeles (about 120 miles east to the course): Take I-10 east and exit at Bob Hope. Take Bob Hope south, and turn right on Country Club Drive. The club is on the left, on the corner of Highway 111 and Country Club Drive.

WESTIN MISSION HILLS RESORT - DYE COURSE (public, 18 holes, pete dye 1987) . . .

71-501 Dinah Shore Drive
Rancho Mirage, CA 92270
(760) 328-3198
troongolf.com

	YARDAGE	PAR	RATING	SLOPE
FRONT	4841	70	67.4	107
MIDDLE	6161	70	69.6	126
BACK	6677	70	72.2	131

$56 - $150

WHAT TO EXPECT: This is a classic Dye design with pot bunkers, large greens, and some, but not an overabundance of railroad ties. Large, undulating, and firm greens make this course a challenge. Golfers need to be 90 yards or closer to hold these greens. The player who is hitting from 150 yards out is going to be in for a long day. Water comes into play on more than half the holes.

OUR OPINION: If you love Pete Dye designs, you will love this course. If you hate Pete Dye designs, you will hate this course. If you're on a budget, play here during the offseason, when rates are reasonable. – Frank

DIRECTIONS: From downtown Los Angeles (about 120 miles east to the course): Take I-10 east, exit onto Ramon Street and turn right. Turn left on Bob Hope and then right on Dinah Shore Drive.

WESTIN MISSION HILLS RESORT - PLAYER COURSE (public, 18 holes, gary player) . . .

70-705 Ramon Road
Rancho Mirage, CA 92270
(760) 770-2908
troongolf.com

	YARDAGE	PAR	RATING	SLOPE
FRONT	6023	72	68.5	115
MIDDLE	6605	72	71.3	124
BACK	7021	72	73.4	131

$150 - $175

WHAT TO EXPECT: This is a very playable resort course. The Player Course has plenty of water, but it can easily be avoided by most golfers. It has more than enough length to be challenging, and is exposed to the desert wind.

OUR OPINION: Gary Player believes that a shot well struck to a green should give you a birdie putt, so there are no mountainous undulations on the greens. They are well kept and run true. Landscaping has grown in over the years to make the course more natural. The only downside is that every time we play, there seems to be a lot of construction, which distracts from some natural beauty. The course is playable for all handicaps. – Frank

DIRECTIONS: From downtown Los Angeles (about 120 miles east to the course): Take I-10 east, exit at Ramon Road and turn right.

CHINA LAKE GOLF COURSE (military, 18 holes, george bell 1957) . . . .

411 Midway Drive
Ridgecrest, CA 93555
(760) 939-2990

	YARDAGE	PAR	RATING	SLOPE
FRONT	5506	72	71.2	120
MIDDLE	6541	72	70.7	114
BACK	6850	72	72.5	119

$10 - $18

WHAT TO EXPECT: This is an easy walking course with some slope and small greens. Water comes into play on three holes. Keeping the ball on the right side of the fairways will allow you a better angle to the greens.

NOTES: This military course allows public play.

DIRECTIONS: From Mojave (about 55 miles northeast to the course): Go north on Highway 14 for about 40 miles to Highway 178. Then turn right and drive east for 13 miles to the entrance of China Lake Naval Weapons Station. The course is on Midway Drive.

IVEY RANCH COUNTRY CLUB (semi-private, 9 holes, william f. bell) . . . .

74-580 Varner Road
Thousand Palms, CA 92276
(760) 343-2013

	YARDAGE	PAR	RATING	SLOPE
FRONT	2322	35	66.4	107
MIDDLE	2473	35	63.3	98
BACK	2633	35	64.9	102

$35 - $35

WHAT TO EXPECT: Just keep it in the fairway and you will be ok. It's one of the few courses nowadays where you don't need a degree in geometry to figure it out. The only trouble you will find on this layout is if you are wild off the tee.

DIRECTIONS: From downtown Los Angeles (about 115 miles east to the course): Take I-10 east, exit on Monterey, and go over the freeway. Turn right on Varner Road.

DESERT WINDS COMBAT CENTER GOLF COURSE (military, 18 holes) . . . .

MCCS MCAGCC Combat Golf Assoc.
Twentynine Palms, CA 92278
(760) 830-6132

	YARDAGE	PAR	RATING	SLOPE
FRONT	5998	72	70.0	113
MIDDLE	6370	72	70.2	116
BACK	6905	72	72.7	121

$5 - $12

WHAT TO EXPECT: This is a challenging desert course that sits along a hillside. You can literally see every hole from the clubhouse. The fairways are runway wide; the greens are larger on the front nine and smaller on the back. Out-of-bounds, wind, and heat can all be factors.

DIRECTIONS: From San Bernardino (about 90 miles northeast to the course): Take I-10 east to the Highway 62 turnoff to Twentynine Palms. Upon entering Twentynine Palms, turn left at Adobe Road. There is signs for the base. Ask at the gate for further directions.

ROAD RUNNER DUNES GOLF RESORT (resort, 9 holes, lawrence hughes) . . . .

4733 Desert Knoll Road
Twentynine Palms, CA 92277
(760) 367-5770

	YARDAGE	PAR	RATING	SLOPE
FRONT	2584	36	70.8	117
MIDDLE	-	-	-	-
BACK	3027	36	70.1	115

$11 - $21

WHAT TO EXPECT: This is a flat course with ample greens and plenty of trees. The course has eight traps and water that comes into play on two holes.
NOTES: The course has R.V. hookup, as well as condos.
DIRECTIONS: From San Bernardino (about 90 miles northeast to the course): Take I-10 east to the Highway 62 turnoff to Twentynine Palms. Go through town and turn left on Utah Trail. Turn left on Amboy, and the course is on the right.

BLUE SKIES COUNTRY CLUB (semi-private, 18 holes, j.w. hale) . . . .

55-100 Martinez Trail
Yucca Valley, CA 92284
(760) 365-0111

	YARDAGE	PAR	RATING	SLOPE
FRONT	5757	73	71.6	119
MIDDLE	6115	71	68.7	108
BACK	6400	71	69.8	115

$15 - $30

WHAT TO EXPECT: Although trees are prominent throughout the course, you will find Blue Skies to be a friendly driving course with little rough. There are some strategically placed bunkers and two lakes that come into play on only two holes.
DIRECTIONS: From San Bernardino (about 72 miles northeast to the course): Take I-10 east to Highway 62 toward Twentynine Palms. Go about 18 miles and turn left on Camino del Cielo. Turn right on Martinez Trail, to the club.

Green Pages

Green Pages

ARCHITECTS

Here is a list of talented California architects, as well as some designers from out of state. All have left their mark on California. You never know when you are going to have the urge to build a golf course.

● ALGIE M. PULLEY, JR.

1190 Glen Rd.
Lafayette, CA 94549
(925) 284-9214

● AMERICAN SOCIETY OF GOLF COURSE ARCHITECTS

221 N. LaSalle St., Ste. 3500
Chicago, IL 60601
(312) 372-7090
asgca.org

Call the American Society of Golf Course Architects for a complete list of members.

● ANDREW RAUGUST

4170 Yacht Harbor Dr.
Stockton , CA 95204
(209) 942-1200

Andrew Raugust's credits include the Reserve at Spanos Park Golf Club in Stockton.

● BLISS GOLF DESIGN

1689 Willowside Rd.
Santa Rosa, CA 95401
(707) 578-4273

Credits include: Rooster Run in Petaluma and Windsor Golf Club in Windsor.

● BRADFORD BENZ

5965 Almaden Expwy., Ste. 210
San Jose, CA 95120
(408) 323-8010

● CAL OLSON GOLF ARCHITECTURE

30448 Rancho Viejo Rd., Ste. 100
San Juan Capistrano, CA 92675
(714) 641-6654
calolson.com

Credits include: Coyote Hills Golf Club in Fullerton and Sierra Star in Mammoth.

● CARY BICKLER

1110 Rosecrans St., Ste. 207
San Diego, CA 92106
(619) 223-3240
bickler.com

Credits include: Borrego Springs Golf Resort & Country Club in Borrego Springs and Encinitas Ranch in Encinitas.

● CASEY O'CALLAGHAN GOLF COURSE DESIGN

3151 Airway Avenue, Ste. R-1
Costa Mesa, CA 92626
(714) 433-2359

● DAVID GINKEL DESIGN

9810 Wilford Way
Gilroy, CA 95020
(408) 848-1724
ginkeldesign.com

Credits include: redesign of Sharon Heights Country Club in Menlo Park.

● DON BOOS DESIGN

1437 Wingdam Dr.
Murphys, CA 95247
(209) 728-8526

Credits include: Greenhorn Creek Golf Club in Angels Camp.

● GOLF PROPERTIES DESIGN

3369 Dehesa Rd.
El Cajon, CA 92019
(619) 442-8100

Golf Properties Design is currently doing preliminary work on projects in California, Mexico, and Washington.

● GOLFPLAN
  PO Box 1823
  Santa Rosa, CA 95402
  (707) 526-7190
  golfplan.com
Ron Fream's credits include:
RedHawk Golf Club in Temecula,
Desert Falls Country Club in Palm
Desert, and Carmel Mountain Ranch
Golf Course in San Diego.

● GRAVES AND PASCUZZO
  4990 Hillsdale Circle, Ste. B
  El Dorado Hills, CA 95762
  (916) 941-8692
The team of Robert Muir Graves and
Damian Pascuzzo credits include:
Sterling Hills Golf Club in Camarillo
and Westridge Golf Club in La
Habra.

● HALSEY DARAY GOLF
  9001 Grossmont Blvd.
  La Mesa, CA 91941
  (619) 463-9285
Credits include: River Course at
Alisal in Solvang.

● JMP DESIGN
  14651 Big Basin Way
  Saratoga, CA 95070
  (408) 867-5600
  jmpgolf.com
Credits include: Wildhawk Golf Club
in Sacramento.

● JOHNNY MILLER DESIGN, LTD.
  1875 Century Park East, #1150
  Los Angeles, CA 90067
  (310) 553-0330
  johnnymillerdesign.com
Credits include: Whitney Oaks Golf
Club in Rocklin and Brighton Crest
Country Club in Friant.

● KNOTT - BROOKS - LINN GOLF
DESIGN GROUP
  236 Castro St., Ste. 3
  Mountain View, CA 94041
  (650) 968-9036
  knottbrookslinn.com
Both Donald Knott and Gary Linn
were part of Robert Trent Jones II's
team for over 20 years.

● LANDMARK GOLF COMPANY
  74-947 Highway 111, Ste. 200
  Indian Wells, CA 92210
  (760) 776-6688
  landmarkgolf.com

● MICHAEL S. JOHNSTONE, AIA
  6114 Lasalle Ave., Ste. 329
  Oakland, CA 94611
  (510) 531-2296
  michaelsjohnstone.com

● NELSON & HAWORTH
  3030 Bridgeway
  Sausalito, CA 94965
  (415) 332-2889
  nelsonhaworth.com

● NICKELS GOLF GROUP, LTD.
  100 Galli Dr., Ste. 5
  Novato, CA 94949
  (415) 884-0626
  nickelsgolf.com
Redesigning credits include: Santa
Rosa Country Club in Santa Rosa,
Burlingame Golf Course in
Burlingame, and the Meadowood
Resort in St. Helena.

● PIRKL ASSOCIATION
  33752 Bridgehampton Dr.
  Dana Point, CA 92629
  (949) 248-7098
Credits include: Rio Hondo Golf and
Country Club in Downey.

● RAINVILLE-BYE

100 W. Main St., Ste. 11
Tustin, CA 92780
(714) 838-7200
Credits include: Yucaipa Valley
Golf Club in Yucaipa and Mission
Hills of Hayward.

● ROBERT TRENT JONES II

705 Forest Ave.
Palo Alto, CA 94301
(650) 326-3833
rtj2.com
Credits include: Bodega Harbour in
Bodega Bay, Poppy Hills in Pebble
Beach, Resort at Squaw Creek in
Lake Tahoe, Rancho San Marcos in
Santa Barbara, and CordeValle in
San Martin.

● ROBINSON GOLF

30131 Town Center Dr., Ste. 268
Laguna Niguel, CA 92677
(949) 363-5870
golfdesign.com
Ted Robinson is credited with
designing over 60 courses in
California.

● SCHMIDT-CURLEY

8180 N. Hayden Dr., Ste. D-200
Scottsdale, AZ 85258
(602) 483-1994
Credits include: Landmark at Oak
Quarry in Riverside and Talega in
San Clemente.

● STRATEGIC GOLF DESIGN

2027 Grahn Dr.
Santa Rosa, CA 95404
(707) 545-7431
Sandy-Lyle.com
John Millhouse, Rick Elliot, and Tim
Kent, formerly of Golfplan, have
formed Strategic Golf Design and an
association with Sandy Lyle Golf
Design. Strategic Golf Design
currently has projects in Alabama,
Nicaragua, and Northern California.

● THOMPSON GOLF PLANNING

1510 Grant Ave., Ste. 305
San Francisco, CA 94945
(415) 878-2020
thompsongolf.com

● TOM JOHNSON GOLF DESIGN

PO Box 1540
Pleasanton, CA 94566-1540
(925) 462-6213
tsjgolf.com
Tom Johnson has designed courses
in Japan, the Pacific Rim countries,
Europe, and the United States.

ART

● CYPRESS CLASSICS
PO Box 5999
Oxnard, CA 93031
(800) 473-8504
cypress-classics.com
Cypress Classics is the exclusive publisher of artist Noble Powell III. Noble has painted 20 portraits of the world's greatest golf landscapes. Cypress Classics artwork is sold worldwide. You can call for a catalog or visit the showroom on-line.

● GOLF COLLECTORS SOCIETY
PO Box 241042
Cleveland, OH 44124
(440) 460-3979
golfcollectors.com

● GOLF LINKS TO THE PAST
636 West Diversey Pkwy., #110
Chicago, IL 60614
(800) 449-4097
golflinkstothepast.com
They specialize in golf art, memorabilia, and rare books. Golf Links to the Past has the exclusive licensing rights to sell Bobby Jones art, memorabilia, and photographs.

● GOLF SCENES & PORTRAITS
23248 Coso Drive
Mission Viejo, CA 92692
(949) 458-9151
Steve Winke paints commissioned fine art using your favorite golf photo.

● JB PUBLISHERS
4208 Douglas Blvd., Ste. 200
Granite Bay, CA 95746
(916) 677-2442
You may not recognize the name, but chances are if you live in California, you have seen some of JB Publishers work. In the last 15 years, JB Publishers' have done over 200 limited-edition prints and paintings. Ninety-percent of all their work is commissioned, but they do sometimes have overruns. They currently have thirty prints in publication.

● JOANN DOST GOLF EDITIONS, LLC
PO Box 827
Pebble Beach, CA 93953
(831) 375-3678
joanndost.com
Joann Dost Golf Editions produces commissioned fine art photography, editorial material, and advertising. Joann Dost is one of the world's most renowned photographers of golf landscapes. She shot many of the photos for PEBBLE BEACH: THE OFFICIAL HISTORY.

● KARL FARRIS GOLF SCULPTURES
72540 Betty Lane
Rancho Mirage, CA 92270
(760) 568-1746
golfsculptures.com
Karl Farris was commissioned to do limited edition sculptures of four famous golfers. Karl's 19-inch high sculptures of Arnold Palmer, Greg Norman, Walter Hagen, and Bobby Jones were recently purchased and are now be displayed by the British Golf Museum at St. Andrews. All four golfers depicted have won the British Open. For details on how to purchase one of these limited edition pieces visit his website.

ASSOCIATIONS

● AMERICAN JUNIOR GOLF
ASSOCIATION
1980 Sports Club Dr.
Brazelton, GA 30517
(770) 868-4200
ajga.com

● AMERICAN SINGLES GOLF
ASSOCIATION
PO Box 470493
Charlotte, NC 28247
(888) 465-3628

● ASSOCIATION OF DISABLED
AMERICAN GOLFERS
PO Box 2647
Littleton, CO 80161
(303) 738-1675
adag.org

● AT&T PEBBLE BEACH JUNIOR
GOLF ASSOCIATION
PO Box 4548
Carmel, CA 93921
(831) 625-1555
The AT&T Pebble Beach Junior Golf
Association is a local non-profit
organization created in 1988. They
introduce the game of golf to young
people between the ages 7-17 who
live and attend school on the
Monterey Peninsula. Membership is
free. The association has 1,750
junior golfers who have benefited.
They provide instructional clinics,
teaches children etiquette, and
hosts several tournaments.

● BAY AREA GOLF ASSOCIATION
2407 Pinehurst
Discovery Bay, CA 94514
(925) 516-9690

● CALIFORNIA GOLF WRITERS
ASSOCIATION
PO Box 1049
Pebble Beach, CA 93953
(831) 375-1747
To join the California Golf Writers
Association, you must submit three
published samples of your writing.
The membership is $30 per year.

● CALIFORNIA SENIORS' GOLF
ASSOCIATION
PO Box 1157
Pebble Beach, CA 93953
(831) 625-4653

● CENTRAL CALIFORNIA GOLF
ASSOCIATION
3374 E. Simpson
Fresno, CA 93703
(209) 227-8937

● CLUB MANAGERS ASSOCIATION OF
AMERICA
1733 King St.
Alexandria, VA 22314
(703) 739-9500

● DESERT JUNIOR GOLF
ASSOCIATION
41-945 Boardwalk, Ste. G
Palm Desert, CA 92211
(760) 341-4323
scpga.org
The Desert Junior Golf Association
is now a part of the Southern
California Junior Golf Association
run by the Southern California PGA.

● EXECUTIVE WOMEN'S GOLF
ASSOCIATION
300 Ave. of Champions, Ste. 140
Palm Beach Gardens, FL 33418
(800) 407-1477
This association has local chapters
throughout the country. Their goal
is to bring executive women
together to share the golfing
experience.

● FAMILY GOLF ASSOCIATION
2 E. Broad St.
Hopewell, NJ 08525
(609) 466-8191
familygolf.org
They promote family fun and values
through golf.

● FELLOWSHIP OF CHRISTIAN
ATHLETES
8701 Leeds Rd.
Kansas City, MO 64129
(800) 289-0909
fca.org

● GOLF COURSE SUPERINTENDENTS
ASSOCIATION OF AMERICA
1421 Research Park Dr.
Lawrence, KS 66049
(800) 472-7878
gcsaa.org

● GOLF COURSE SUPERINTENDENTS
ASSOCIATION OF CENT. CALIFORNIA
PO Box 27093
Fresno, CA 93729
(209) 298-4853

● GOLF COURSE SUPERINTENDENTS
ASSOCIATION OF NO. CALIFORNIA
PO Box 3360
Diamond Springs, CA 95619
(530) 626-0931

● GOLF COURSE SUPERINTENDENTS
ASSOCIATION OF SO. CALIFORNIA
5198 Arlington Ave., Ste. 700
Riverside, CA 92504
(909) 784-1623

● IMPERIAL VALLEY JUNIOR GOLF
ASSOCIATION
238 S. 8th St.
El Centro, CA 92243
(760) 353-3900

● JUNIOR AMATEUR GOLF
SCHOLARS
4981 Lemon Ave.
Cypress, CA 90630
(714) 952-3316
jagstour.com

● JUNIOR GOLF ASSOCIATION OF
NORTHERN CALIFORNIA
114 Arroyo Ct.
Santa Cruz, CA 95060
(831) 425-0367
jganc.com

● KERN COUNTY JUNIOR GOLF
ASSOCIATION
PO Box 281
Bakersfield, CA 93302
(661) 834-2994

● LINK TO LIFE
1706 Chester Ave.
Bakersfield, CA 93301
(661) 322-5601
Link to Life promotes breast cancer
awareness through golf.

● LONG BEACH JUNIOR GOLF
ASSOCIATION
6700 East Carson St.
Long Beach, CA 90808
(562) 431-1886

● NATIONAL ASSOCIATION OF GOLF
TOURNAMENT DIRECTORS
212 South Henry St., Ste. 200
Alexandria , VA 22314
(888) 899-2483
nagtd.com

● NATIONAL CLUB ASSOCIATION
1120 20th St. NW, Ste. 725
Washington, DC 20036
(202) 822-9822
natlclub.org

● NATIONAL COLLEGIATE ATHLETIC
ASSOCIATION
PO Box 6222
Indianapolis, IN 46206
(317) 917-6222
ncaa.org

● NATIONAL GOLF FOUNDATION
1150 South US Hwy. 1, Ste. 401
Jupiter, FL 33477
(561) 744-6006
ngf.org

● NATIONAL MINORITY GOLF
FOUNDATION
7226 N. 16th St.
Phoenix, AZ 85020
(602) 943-8399
nmgf.org

● NCGA
PO Box NCGA
Pebble Beach, CA 93953
(831) 625-4653
ncga.org
Northern California Golf Association

● NCPGA
411 Davis St., Ste. 103
Vacaville, CA 95688
(707) 449-4742
ncpga.com
Northern California Section of the
PGA of America

● NORTHERN CALIFORNIA MINORITY
JUNIOR GOLF SCHOLARSHIP
PO Box 246152
Sacramento, CA 95824
(916) 455-3076

● NORTHERN CALIFORNIA NINER'S
ASSOCIATION
3891 Bayview Circle
Concord, CA 94520
(925) 825-5239

● NORTHERN NEVADA GOLF
ASSOCIATION
PO Box 5630
Sparks, NV 89432
(775) 673-4653
nnga.org

● PACIFIC WOMEN'S GOLF
ASSOCIATION
8396 Riesling Way
San Jose, CA 95135
(408) 238-8092
golfpwga.org

● PGA OF AMERICA
PO Box 109601
Palm Beach Gardens, FL 33410
(561) 624-8400
pgahq.com

● PUBLIC LINKS GOLF ASSOCIATION
OF SOUTHERN CALIFORNIA
7035 Orangethorpe Ave., Ste. E
Buena Park, CA 90621
(800) 272-7542
plga.org

● RETIRED MILITARY GOLFERS
ASSOCIATION
28441 Chat Dr.
Laguna Niguel, CA 92677
(949) 831-3703
exwebservices.com/RMGA

● ROYAL AND ANCIENT GOLF CLUB
St. Andrews, Fife KY16 9JD
Scotland, UK
(011) 44-133-447-2112
randa.org
Royal and Ancient Golf Club of St.
Andrews

● SAN DIEGO JUNIOR GOLF
ASSOCIATION
3333 Camino del Rey South, #100
San Diego, CA 92108-3836
(619) 280-8505
They host the San Diego Junior
World Golf Tournament. The
four-day tournament attracts over
1,000 junior golfers from the United
States and as many as 30 other
countries.

● SAN DIEGO WOMEN'S GOLF
ASSOCIATION
13956 Capewood Lane
San Diego, CA 92128
(858) 673-1127

● SANTA BARBARA JUNIOR GOLF
ASSOCIATION
5410 Hales Lane
Carpinteria, CA 93013
(805) 684-4380

● SANTA CRUZ COUNTY JUNIOR
GOLF ASSOCIATION
PO Box 3360
Santa Cruz, CA 95063
(831) 457-7993
sccjga.com

● SCGA
PO Box 7186
North Hollywood, CA 91615
(818) 980-3630
scga.org
Southern California Golf Association

● SCPGA
601 South Valencia Ave., Ste. 200
Brea, CA 92823
(714) 776-4653
scpga.org
Southern California Section of the
PGA of America

● SHIVAS IRONS SOCIETY
PO Box 222339
Carmel, CA 93922
(831) 626-4566

● THE SENIORS GOLF ASSOCIATION
PO Box 5110
Santa Maria, CA 93456
(877) 928-6691

● USGA
PO Box 708
Far Hills, NJ 07931
(908) 234-2300
usga.com
United States Golf Association

● USGA GREEN SECTION
SOUTHWEST REGION
505 N. Tustin Ave., Ste. 121
Santa Ana, CA 92705
(714) 542-5766

● VALLEY JUNIOR GOLF
ASSOCIATION
PO Box 891777
Temecula, CA 92589
(909) 506-4766

● VENTURA COUNTY JUNIOR GOLF
ASSOCIATION
PO Box 7569
Ventura, CA 93006
(805) 535-1232
vcjga.com

● WESTERN AMERICAN GOLF
ASSOCIATION
402 W. Arrow Hwy., Ste. 10
San Dimas, CA 91773
(909) 592-1281

● WESTERN STATES GOLF
ASSOCIATION
7845 Medinah Ct.
Pleasanton, CA 94588
wsgagolf.org

● WOMEN'S GOLF ASSOCIATION OF
NORTHERN CALIFORNIA
5776 Stoneridge Mall Rd. #160
Pleasanton, CA 94588
(925) 737-0963
wganc.com

● WOMEN'S NINE HOLE GOLF
ASSOCIATION
90 Bear Gulch Rd.
Portola Valley, CA 94028
(650) 851-0814

● WOMEN'S PUBLIC LINKS GOLF
ASSOCIATION OF SO. CALIFORNIA
7035 Orangethorpe Ave., Ste. F
Buena Park, CA 90621
(714) 994-4799
justgolf.org

● WOMEN'S SOUTHERN CALIFORNIA
GOLF ASSOCIATION
402 W. Arrow Hwy., Ste. 10
San Dimas, CA 91773
(909) 592-1281
womensgolf.org

CELEBRITY/PRO-AM TOURNAMENTS

Ever wondered what it would be like to play on tour? Have you ever imagined the feeling of stepping through the ropes and having the starter call your name? Do you want to experience the adrenaline rush on the first tee when you ask your caddy to pull out your driver?

If you answered yes to any of the above, but carry a handicap that is hovering somewhere around your age, don't give up the dream.

With several PGA, Senior PGA, LPGA, and Mini-Tour events held in California, there is bound to be a pro-am to suit your fantasy. The only downside? The cost. The average PGA pro-am runs around $2,500.

For those who want to spend a little less, there are several celebrity - amateur tournaments where players can mingle with stars of sport and screen.

● AT&T PEBBLE BEACH NATIONAL
PRO-AM
PO Box 869
Monterey, CA 93942
(831) 649-1533
attpbgolf.com
Originally named the Crosby Pro-Am, this PGA event is regarded as the premier celebrity golf tournament. The tournament is played on Pebble Beach, Spyglass, and Poppy Hills. The AT&T has featured participants such as Bill Murray, Tommy Smothers, Clint Eastwood, Ken Griffey, Jr., Jerry Rice, and Ray Romano. The tournament takes place in February. For amateurs who want to play in the event – good luck, there's usually a healthy waiting list.

● BUICK INVITATIONAL
   3333 Camino del Rio S., Ste. 100
   San Diego, CA 92108-3836
   (800) 888-2842
   buickinvitational.com

● CELEBRITY QUARTERBACK GOLF
   SHOOT-OUT
   Buckingham Golf & Country Club
   Kelseyville, CA
   (707) 279-4863
   konoctiharbor.com
Here's your chance to play with 20
former NFL quarterbacks. Past
signal callers who have played in
the event include Joe Montana, Billy
Kilmer, Tom Flores, Daryl
Lamonica, and Johnny Unitas. A
few years ago, they were begging
for participants, but now very few
playing spots are available.

● FRANK SINATRA CELEBRITY
   INVITATIONAL
   69730 Highway 111, Ste. 215
   Rancho Mirage, CA 92270
   (800) 377-8277
   sinatracenter.org
Players get a chance to play with
celebrities such as Don Johnson,
Robert DeNiro, Robert Wagner and
many others. The cost is $3,750 per
playing spot. Larger sponsorships
are available. A playing spot
includes two days of golf with a
celebrity, pairing party, luncheon,
concert, awards party, and more.
This event benefits the Barbara
Sinatra Children's Center. The
event usually takes place in
February and golf is played at
Desert Willow Resort, with the
events off-site. The Frank Sinatra
Celebrity Invitational has a
reputation for being spectator
friendly. Most celebrities are
gracious enough to allow pictures
and autographs.

● NABISCO CHAMPIONSHIP
   34-600 Mission Hills Dr.
   Rancho Mirage, CA 92270
   (760) 324-4546
   nabiscochampionship.com
The Nabisco Championship
Tournament is held at the Mission
Hills Country Club.

● NISSAN OPEN
   350 South Bixel St., Ste. 100
   Los Angeles, CA 90017
   (800) 752-6736
   nissanopen.com
The Nissan Open runs a Celebrity,
Pro-Am, and Corporate
Tournaments.

● PALM SPRINGS CELEBRITY GOLF
   CLASSIC
   333 N. Palm Canyon Dr., Ste. 217
   Palm Springs, CA 92262
   (800) 914-4533

● WORLD PRO-AMS
   PO Box 200
   Shawnee, PA 18356
   (800) 797-9464
   golftournamenttours.com
World Pro-Ams have grown from
one tournament at Pebble Beach to
over a dozen events, such as
pro-ams, amateur two-man team
events and fathers/son venues, held
annually worldwide. During that
time, more than 2,000 golf
professionals and over 7,000
amateur golfers have participated in
World Pro-Am events. The Wilson
Pro-Am, Father/Son Team
Championship, World Pro-Am, and
World Two-Man are held in Pebble
Beach.

CHARITIES

● AT&T PEBBLE BEACH JUNIOR
GOLF ASSOCIATION
PO Box 4548
Carmel, CA 93921
(831) 625-1555
This local non-profit organization
was created in 1988. They
introduce the game of golf to young
people between the ages 7-17 who
live and attend school on the
Monterey Peninsula. Membership is
free. The association has benefited
over 1,750 junior golfers. Through
the Kenny Stout Memorial Golf
Foundation, they provide clubs free
to children who wouldn't otherwise
be able to afford them.

● CHARITY GOLF ONLINE
4951 Reforma Rd.
Woodland Hills, CA 91364
(818) 225-8255
CharityGolfOnline.com
The ultimate site for finding charity
events in Southern California.

● GOLFNET LONG DISTANCE AND
MORE
39511 Gallaudet Dr., Ste. 270
Fremont, CA 94538
(800) 717-4653
golfnetphone.com
GolfNet Long Distance and More
provides efficient long-distance
phone service designed especially
for the golf industry. GolfNet uses
the proceeds to provide free golf
clinics for underprivileged children.

● LINK TO LIFE
1706 Chester Ave.
Bakersfield, CA 93301
(661) 322-5601
Link to Life promotes breast cancer
awareness through golf. They host
an LPGA tournament and their funds
help provide free mammograms.

● SAN DIEGO INNER CITY GOLF
FOUNDATION
5276 Church Ward St.
San Diego, CA 92114
(619) 264-4319
The San Diego Inner City Golf
Foundation provides lessons and
tournaments for inner city kids.

● SAY GOLF
4427 Freeport Blvd.
Sacramento, CA 95822
(916) 455-7888
Sacramento Area Youth provides
much needed services for junior
golfers in the area.

● SCPGA FOUNDATION
601 South Valencia Ave., Ste. 200
Brea, CA 92823
(714) 776-4653
scpga.org
The SCPGA Foundation has assumed
administrative oversight of those
programs associated with junior
golf, high school golf programming,
scholarships, and at-risk youth
programming. They are a nonprofit
organization that, among other
things, hosts more than 90
tournaments a year for junior
golfers.

● THE PRO KIDS GOLF ACADEMY
4085 52nd St.
San Diego, CA 92105
(619) 582-4704
The Pro Kids Golf Academy &
Learning Center is a program that
gives inner city children a chance to
learn and play golf. Since its
inception, the Pro Kids Golf
Academy and Learning Center at
Colina Park has enrolled over 3000
children and teens. The teaching
pros conduct over 250 classes per
year and their monthly tournaments
attract about 70 players. Their
students played about 10,000 rounds
on the course last year.

DISCOUNTS

Restrictions or no restrictions, you could be paying too much for your next round of golf. Here are several options for saving money on your next trip to the links.

● AMERICAN GOLF PLAYERS
  ASSOCIATION
  3443 N. Central Ave., Ste. 819
  Phoenix, AZ 85012
  (888) 790-2472
  agpa.com
The American Golf Players Association offers discounts at over 45 American Golf Corporation courses in California. The two most popular memberships range in price from $29.95 to $49.95. Several other types of memberships are available. Memberships can include discounts on green fees, merchandise, club rentals, and the John Jacobs School of Golf.

● CLUB 19 GOLF AND TRAVEL
  SAVINGS
  PO Box 222594
  Carmel, CA 93922-2594
  (800) 347-6119
  club19golf.com
Club 19 provides discounts to over 550 golf courses in California, Oregon, Washington, British Columbia, Nevada, and Arizona. In California there are discounts at over 200 courses. Club 19 is also a travel club. It offers five or six hosted trips a year all over the world. Each vacation is seven nights and eight days. With membership, you also receive a vacation pass, which includes discounts of up to 50 percent off hotel rooms.

● GOLF EXTRA
  PO Box 25868
  Santa Ana, CA 92799
  (800) 598-4653
  golfxtra.com
Golf Extra offers Southern California golfers several different types of memberships. A full membership runs around $99 and includes a free sleeve of golf balls every month, preferred tee time privileges, green fee discounts, and monthly tournaments.

● NEXT DAY GOLF
  41905 Boardwalk, Ste. A2
  Palm Desert, CA 92211
  (760) 345-8463
  parteegolf.com
If you can wait until the day before you play in Palm Springs, you can receive discounted green fees at over 33 courses in the Palm Springs area.

● PASSPORT TO PALM SPRINGS
  2012 Southridge Dr.
  Palm Springs, CA 92264
  (760) 321-4588
Passport to Palm Springs offers discount green fees at over 30 courses in Palm Springs. There are also discounts on attractions, lodging, services, and dining.

● PASSPORT TO PHOENIX
  2012 Southridge Dr.
  Palm Springs, CA 92264
  (760) 321-4588
Passport to Phoenix offers discount green fees in and around Phoenix. There are also discounts on attractions, lodging, services, and dining.

● STAND-BY-GOLF

1555 S. Palm Canyon Dr.
Palm Springs, CA 92264
(866) 224-2665
stand-bygolf.com

Stand-by-Golf covers courses in Palm Springs, Las Vegas, Hawaii, and Florida. They purchase tee times from courses the night before and sell them to golfers at discounts ranging from 25 to 50 percent.

● THE GOLF DIGEST PASSBOOK

2530 E. Broadway, Ste. B
Tucson , AZ 85716
(800) 950-4653
golfpassbook.com

The Golf Digest Passbook offers discounts at over 450 courses in the Western United States. It offers savings at over 50 driving ranges and 15 PGA, Senior PGA, and LPGA tournaments. There are also savings on over 25 stay-and-play packages at resorts in the west.

● WEST COAST GOLF VALUE BOOK

15650 Vineyard Blvd., Ste. 152
Morgan Hill, CA 95037
(800) 949-1415
2for1golf.com

The West Coast Value Book offers savings at more than 200 golf courses and practice facilities throughout California and Hawaii.

EXHIBITIONS

● GREAT NORTHERN CALIFORNIA GOLF EXPO

851 81st Ave., Ste. 230
Oakland, CA 94621
(888) 746-7522
golfexpo.net

They run two shows in California. The Sacramento Show is held February 22-24, 2002 at the Cal Expo. The San Mateo Show is held March 8-10, 2002. The shows feature over 200 booths, including equipment manufacturers, apparel companies, resorts, and other related businesses.

● SOUTHERN CALIFORNIA GOLF EXPO

1360 South Coast Hwy.
Laguna Beach, CA 92651
(949) 376-6942
socalgolfexpo.com

This is held at the Long Beach Convention Center. Visit their website or call for more information.

● SPORTSLINK PRODUCTIONS

12290 Torrey Pines Dr.
Auburn, CA 95602
(530) 268-0144
golfshowtime.com

Sportslink Productions has three California shows. Sacramento is scheduled for February 6-8, 2002, Sonoma County is scheduled for February 16-17, 2002, and the East Bay is scheduled for February 23-24, 2002. For more information call Sportslink. The shows feature equipment, apparel, resorts, and free lessons from local PGA professionals.

● THE GOLF EXPO

601 S. Valencia Ave., Ste. 200
Brea, CA 92823
(714) 776-4653
scpga.org

The Southern California PGA Golf Expo is held in early March, in Pomona. It is put on by the Southern California PGA section and the SCGA. The event draws over 20,000 participants and more than 200 exhibitors. Exhibitors include leading manufacturers of equipment and apparel, the latest training aids, travel discounts, and free instruction by Southern California PGA members. Call for current dates.

FUNDRAISING

Golf fundraising is becoming increasingly popular for adding extra cash to your charity event. Here is a list of companies that are in the business of making money from other people's money.

● BETTERGOLF.NET

625 Broadway, Ste. 1000
San Diego, CA 92101
(888) 768-3463
bettergolf.net

Bettergolf.net brings you ClubFinder. This enables golfers to label their clubs so that they can easily be identified and returned. ClubFinder protects the golfer's privacy by not displaying information such as the golfer's name, home address, and telephone number. The ClubFinder program can be used by golf organizations as a method to raise money.

● GOLF MARKETING WORLD WIDE

3030 Keane Dr.
Carmichael, CA 95608
(916) 484-7749
hole-in-won.com

Golf Marketing World Wide can help raise money by organizing hole-in-one, putting, and other contests.

● INTERACTIVE FUNDRAISING

1364 Country Club Dr.
Los Altos, CA 94024
(800) 572-4331
interactivegolf.com

Interactive Fundraising can provide your charity or corporate event with contests such as the Predict-Your-Distance Challenge, $500,000 World Putting Contest, and the Arnold Palmer Scratch-off Scorecards.

● JOANN DOST GOLF EDITIONS, LLC

PO Box 827
Pebble Beach, CA 93953
(831) 375-3678
joanndost.com
Golf Editions produces
commissioned fine art photography,
and advertising. They have
produced several high-end golf
calendars used for fundraising.
Joann Dost is one of the world's
best photographers of golf
landscapes.

● NITELITE GOLF

PO Box 1200
Wolfeboro, NH 03896
(800) 282-1533
Nitelite Golf can help run a night
tournament on your favorite golf
course. It bills itself as, "the
second most fun you can have in the
dark."

● SPORTS STUFF

4061 E. Castro Valley Blvd. #115
Castro Valley, CA 94552
(510) 881-0487
SportsStuffAuctions.com
Are looking to do a a sports auction
at your next event? Sports Stuff
provides charity fundraisers with
high-end, quality memorabilia for
silent or live auctions. They come
and set up the display themselves,
and talk to your patrons about the
pieces. It is a no-risk situation for
your group. If it doesn't sell, they
take it back without a charge to you.
In the past 18 months, they have
helped charities raise over
$300,000.

● THE GOLF CHALLENGE

4951 Reforma Rd.
Woodland Hills, CA 91364
(818) 225-8255
CharityGolfOnline.com
The Golf Challenge presents a
unique way to receive donations
from those participants who can't
play in your event.

● THE GOLF DIGEST PASSBOOK

2530 E. Broadway, Ste. B
Tucson , AZ 85716
(800) 950-4653
golfpassbook.com
The Golf Passbook offers discounts
at over 450 courses in the Western
United States. It offers savings at
over 50 driving ranges and 15 PGA,
Senior PGA, and LPGA tournaments.
There are savings on over 25
stay-and-play packages at resorts in
the West. For more information on
how to use The Golf Passbook for
fundraising, call toll free.

● WEST COAST GOLF VALUE BOOK

15650 Vineyard Blvd., Ste. 152
Morgan Hill, CA 95037
(800) 949-1415
2for1golf.com
The West Coast Value Book offers
savings at over 200 golf courses
and practice facilities throughout
California. For more information on
how to raise money by selling the
West Coast Value Book, log on to
the website.

GOLF COURSE INSURANCE

- **ACCORDIA UNDERWRITERS**
  11017 Cobble Rock Dr.
  Rancho Cordova, CA 95670
  (916) 231-1741

- **FAIRWAY UNDERWRITERS**
  191 Pawtucket Blvd.
  Lowell, MA 01854
  (800) 662-2141
  Fairway Underwriters insures over 850 courses nationwide and 45 in California.

HISTORY

Although golf has a rich history, finding more information about it can be challenging, especially in California. We have found several sources you might find interesting while researching the game.

- **GOLF COLLECTORS SOCIETY**
  PO Box 241042
  Cleveland, OH 44124
  (440) 460-3979
  golfcollectors.com

- **GOLF LINKS TO THE PAST**
  636 W. Diversey Pkwy., Ste. 110
  Chicago, IL 60614
  (800) 449-4097
  golflinkstothepast.com
  They specialize in golf art, memorabilia, and rare books. Experts on the legends of golf, they have the exclusive licensing rights to sell Bobby Jones art, memorabilia, and photographs.

- *Pebble Beach: The Official History*
  PO Box 827
  Pebble Beach, CA 93953
  sleepingbearpress.com
  PEBBLE BEACH: THE OFFICIAL HISTORY is the most recent historical account of the Pebble Beach Golf Links. This 224-page book gives a spectacular account of one of the world's most famous golf courses and includes over 380 photos. You can find the book at nearly every major book store and on the web.

● THE RALPH W. MILLER GOLF
   LIBRARY/MUSEUM
   City of Industry, CA
   (626) 968-3737

The core of the library's holdings is the private golf collection of the late Ralph W. Miller. Mr. Miller was a prominent attorney who gathered the information for forty years, prior to 1974. For the history of golf in Southern California, this is a must-see. The library contains museum items and a collection of books, art, videos, and journals. It also can help you with research.

Unfortunately, at time of press, the library is homeless. It is currently in storage, until a permanent home is found. The number listed is for the City of Industry Chamber of Commerce. Call them for the latest update.

● THE UNITED STATES GOLF
   ASSOCIATION
   PO Box 708
   Far Hills, NJ 07931
   (908) 234-2300
   usga.com

The website offers many options, including website tours of the USGA Museum and the Library.

HOLE-IN-ONE INSURANCE

Hole-in-one-insurance allows you to run contests at selected par 3s. If a player hits a hole-in-one, he or she can win a new car, a cruise, or even cash. All you pay is a small insurance fee. Before you run out and buy insurance, remember just carrying insurance may not be enough. Read the rules and regulations carefully. Placing the tee markers a few yards the wrong direction, or not having a witness, can be a costly mistake.

● AMERICAN HOLE 'N ONE
   55 Slitt St.
   Buford, GA 30573
   (800) 822-2257

● FLAGSTICK GUARANTEE
   PO Box 62851
   Colorado Springs, CO 80962
   (800) 521-2727

● GOLF MARKETING, INC.
   3937 Springleaf Dr.
   Stone Mountain, GA 30083
   (404) 294-9708

● GOLF MARKETING WORLD WIDE
   1 Timberline
   Norwalk, CT 06854
   (800) 959-5322
   hole-in-won.com

Golf Marketing World Wide provides hole-in-one insurance, putting contests, skill challenges, and speciality items.

● HOLE IN ONE, INC.
   1911 SE 32nd Terrace
   Cape Coral, FL 33904
   (800) 572-8798

● HOLE IN ONE INTERNATIONAL
6170 Ridgeview Ct., Ste. A
Reno, NV 89509
(800) 827-2249
h101.com

● INTERACTIVE GOLF
1364 Country Club Dr.
Los Altos, CA 94024
(800) 572-4331
interactivegolf.com

● NATIONAL HOLE-IN-ONE
ASSOCIATION
11910 Greenville Ave.
Dallas, TX 75243
(800) 527-6944

● SCA PROMOTIONS, INC.
8300 Douglas Ave., Ste. 625
Dallas, TX 75225
(888) 860-3700
scapromotions.com

● SPORTWORX
5404 McEver Rd.
Oakwood, GA 30566
(888) 967-2323
sportworx.com.

● TEE (TOURNAMENT EVENT
ENTERPRISES)
1575 Adrian Rd., Ste. B
Burlingame, CA 94010
(650) 697-5946

● TSI SPORTS INCORPORATED
PO Box 1320
Flowery Branch, GA 30542
(800) 356-7868

JUNIORS ONLY

This section is dedicated to anything
related to the junior golfer.

● AMERICAN JUNIOR GOLF
ASSOCIATION
1980 Sports Club Dr.
Brazelton, GA 30517
(770) 868-4200
ajga.com

● AT&T PEBBLE BEACH JUNIOR
GOLF ASSOCIATION
PO Box 4548
Carmel, CA 93921
(831) 625-1555
The AT&T Pebble Beach Junior Golf
Association is a local non-profit
organization created in 1988. They
introduce the game of golf to young
people between the ages 7-17 who
live and attend school on the
Monterey Peninsula. Membership is
free. The association has 1,750
junior golfers who have benefited.
The association provides
instructional clinics, teaches
children etiquette, and hosts several
tournaments.

● CYPRESS GOLF CLUB JUNIOR
PROGRAM
4921 Katella Ave.
Los Alamitos, CA 90720
(714) 527-1800

● DESERT JUNIOR GOLF
ASSOCIATION
41-945 Boardwalk, Ste. G
Palm Desert, CA 92211
(760) 341-4323
scpga.org
The Desert Junior Golf Association
is now a part of the Southern
California Junior Golf Association
run by the Southern California PGA.

● FELLOWSHIP OF CHRISTIAN
ATHLETES
8701 Leeds Rd.
Kansas City, MO 64129
(800) 289-0909
fca.org
Fellowship for Christian Athletes
run several golf camps. Call for
California locations. These camps
combine golf with spiritual
enrichment. The instructors are
college coaches, PGA club pros,
and PGA, LPGA, and Nike touring
professionals. Scholarships are
available.

● HAGGIN OAKS JUNIOR GOLF
CAMPS
3645 Fulton Ave.
Sacramento, CA 95821
(916) 575-2525
hagginoaks.com
Haggin Oaks has been running
junior camps for nearly 25 years.
The emphasis is on learning the
fundamentals and having fun on the
course. Five-day courses are run
throughout the summer by PGA and
LPGA professionals. Fees range
from around $100 to $200 and
include two meals per day, hats,
shirt, instruction and playing time.
Call for hotel information.

● IMPERIAL VALLEY JUNIOR GOLF
ASSOCIATION
238 S. 8th St.
El Centro, CA 92243
(760) 353-3900

● JUNIOR AMATEUR GOLF
SCHOLARS
4981 Lemon Ave.
Cypress, CA 90630
(714) 952-3316
jagstour.com

● JUNIOR GOLF ASSOCIATION OF
NORTHERN CALIFORNIA
114 Arroyo Ct.
Santa Cruz, CA 95060
(831) 425-0367

● JUNIOR GOLF SCOREBOARD
4470 Cox Rd., Ste. 136
Glen Allen, VA 23060
(888) 549-GOLF
juniorgolfscoreboard.com
Juniorgolfscoreboard.com is the
ultimate site for finding a place to
play. You will find more than 1,300
events to choose from throughout
the United States, Canada, and even
a few in Europe.

● KERN COUNTY JUNIOR GOLF
ASSOCIATION
PO Box 281
Bakersfield, CA 93302
(661) 834-2994

● LA JOLLA CLUB GOLF COMPANY
2445 Cades Way
Vista, CA 92083
(800) 468-7700
lajollaclub.com
La Jolla Club Golf Company designs
a line of clubs specifically made for
kids.

● LONG BEACH JUNIOR GOLF
ASSOCIATION
6700 East Carson St.
Long Beach, CA 90808
(562) 431-1886

● NIKE JUNIOR GOLF CAMPS -
RESIDENT
919 Sir Francis Drake Blvd.
Kentfield, CA 94904
(800) 645-3226
ussportscamps.com
There are many locations throughout
California and Nevada.

● NIKE JUNIOR GOLF CAMPS -
WEEK-LONG
919 Sir Francis Drake Blvd.
Kentfield, CA 94904
(800) 645-3226
ussportscamps.com
There are many locations throughout
California and Nevada.

● NIKE PARENT-CHILD GOLF SCHOOL
919 Sir Francis Drake Blvd.
Kentfield, CA 94904
(800) 645-3226
ussportscamps.com
The Parent-Child schools includes a
4-to-1 student to teacher ratio. All
instructors are LPGA or PGA
certified. The camps include
on-course lessons, video, lunch,
workbook, and gift pack. Locations
include Carmel, San Diego, Palm
Springs, Santa Barbara, Stanford
and Las Vegas.

● NOR CAL FAMILY GOLF
CHAMPIONSHIP
1575 Adrian Rd., Ste. B
Burlingame, CA 94010-2107
(650) 692-6261
hookedongolf.com
See "San Francisco Junior Golf
Championship."

● NORTHERN CALIFORNIA MINORITY
JUNIOR GOLF SCHOLARSHIP
PO Box 246152
Sacramento, CA 95824
(916) 455-3076

● OAK CREEK GOLF SCHOOL -
JUNIOR GOLF CAMPS
One Golf Club Drive
Irvine, CA 92620
(949) 653-5384

● RIDGELINE COUNTRY CLUB -
JUNIOR GOLF CAMPS
1051 N. Meads
Orange, CA 92869
(714) 538-5030

● ROOSTER RUN
2301 E. Washington St.
Petaluma, CA 94954
(707) 778-1211
roosterrun.com
Rooster Run Golf Club puts on
several junior golf camps from
spring break through fall. The
camps run Monday through Thursday
and are staffed by PGA
professionals. Junior camps include
a 5-to-1 student to teacher ratio, use
of clubs, lunch, T-shirt, and prizes
for each camper.

● SAN DIEGO INNER CITY GOLF
FOUNDATION
5276 Church Ward St.
San Diego, CA 92114
(619) 264-4319
The San Diego Inner City Golf
Foundation provides lessons and
tournaments for inner city kids in
San Diego.

● SAN DIEGO JUNIOR GOLF
ASSOCIATION
3333 Camino del Rey South, #100
San Diego, CA 92108-3836
(619) 280-8505
The San Diego Junior Golf
Association puts on the San Diego
Junior World Golf Tournament. The
four day tournament attracts over
1,000 junior golfers from the United
States and as many as 30 other
countries.

● SAN FRANCISCO JUNIOR GOLF
CHAMPIONSHIP
1575 Adrian Rd., Ste. B
Burlingame, CA 94010-2107
(650) 692-6261
hookedongolf.com
Entering its 10th year in business, San Francisco Golf Services is the parent company of Hooked On Golf. Formed as a broad-based service company, it focuses on golf in the San Francisco Bay Area. Founded by former PGA-Tour player John Abendroth, the company has run the San Francisco Junior Golf Championship for ten years. It also manages the Northern California Family Golf Championship.

● SANTA BARBARA JUNIOR GOLF
ASSOCIATION
5410 Hales Lane
Carpinteria, CA 93013
(805) 684-4380

● SANTA CRUZ COUNTY JUNIOR
GOLF ASSOCIATION
PO Box 3360
Santa Cruz, CA 95063
(831) 457-7993
sccjga.com

● SCPGA JUNIOR GOLF
FOUNDATION
601 South Valencia Ave., Ste. 200
Brea, CA 92823
(714) 776-4653
scpga.org
The SCPGA Foundation hosts more than 90 tournaments a year for junior golfers. Boys and girls ages 7-17 compete in these events against other juniors their own age regardless of skill level. In the first months of the operations, the foundation brought the game to more than 3,500 inner city, at-risk children.

In 1999, SCPGA began the the Junior Tour Cup. The series will be offered to a maximum of 200 of Southern California's best junior golfers who demonstrate superior play in the Foundation's Junior Golf Program.

● STANFORD JUNIOR GOLF CAMP
641 E. Campus Drive
Stanford, CA 94305-6150
(877) 611-0236
stanford.edu
Stanford Golf Camps for boys and girls are for juniors 11 to 18 years of age. The co-ed camps have morning and afternoon instruction in putting, course management, long and short game, etiquette and rules. Campers will also have a chance to play on the course as well as enjoy other activities, such as swimming and basketball. For young golfers with a strong game, a players' camp is available with on-course instruction and course management instruction. Enrollment is limited to 40 campers with handicaps of 10 or better.

● THE PRO KIDS GOLF ACADEMY
   4085 52nd St.
   San Diego, CA 92105
   (619) 582-4704
Since its inception, the Pro Kids
Golf Academy and Learning Center
at Colina Park has enrolled over
3,000 children and teens. The
teaching pros conduct over 250
classes per year and their monthly
tournaments attract about 70
players. Their students played
about 10,000 rounds on the course
last year.

● TUSTIN RANCH GOLF CLUB -
  JUNIOR CAMP
   12442 Tustin Ranch Rd.
   Tustin, CA 92782
   (714) 573-7029

● US KIDS GOLF
   3040 Northwoods Pkwy.
   Norcross, GA 30071
   (888) 3-USKIDS
   uskidsgolf.com
US Kids Golf, designers of custom
golf clubs for kids 3-12, know the
importance of well fitted clubs.
With clubs that are properly fitted,
youngsters can develop a swing that
will last. They also offer an
extensive line of kid size
accessories. Check their website
for a listing of where their clubs can
be found in California.

● VALLEY JUNIOR GOLF
  ASSOCIATION
   PO Box 891777
   Temecula, CA 92589
   (909) 506-4766

● VENTURA COUNTY JUNIOR GOLF
  ASSOCIATION
   PO Box 7569
   Ventura, CA 93006
   (805) 535-1232
   vcjga.com

NOVELTY

● CARLSBAD BAGS, INC.
   3320 Piragua St.
   Carlsbad, CA 92009
   (888) 878-7375

● PRO TOUR MEMORABILIA
   16556 Arminta St.
   Van Nuys, CA 91406
   (800) 465-3511
   protourmem.com
Pro Tour Memorabilia specializes in
tee prizes, corporate gifts, and
individual gifts that are hand signed
by the professional. It has a wide
selection of items including clubs,
photos, and other golf items. If you
are looking for a unique golf gift,
call for a free catalog.

● STUART KERN AMERICA
   1165 West Walnut St.
   Compton, CA 90220
   (800) 735-1361
Stuart Kern America produces
leather goods and desk accessories.

OWNER/MANAGEMENT GROUPS

Owner/management groups are the wave of the future. Don't be surprised in the next few years if a club near you is run by a management firm. As more and more courses open throughout the state, the competition is going to be fierce. In California, many high-end daily-fee courses are already fighting over the same golfers. Not everyone is going to survive. In the past, management groups have been looked down upon because of their profit-first mentality. Although management groups will always be interested in the bottom line, a new breed of management group has arrived in the state. They are marketing-savvy and understand that the best way to increase play is by providing better customer service and a better product. With so much competition in the state, California golfers will be the ultimate winners.

● AMERICAN GOLF CORPORATION
2951 28th Street
Santa Monica, CA 90405
(310) 664-4000
americangolf.com
American Golf is the largest golf management company in the United States. It manages 65 courses in California. Its properties in California include Oakhurst in Clayton, Tilden Park in Berkeley, and RiverWalk in the San Diego area.

● ARNOLD PALMER GOLF MANAGEMENT
6751 Forum Drive, Ste. 200
Orlando, FL 32821
(407) 926-2500
palmergolf.com
Arnold Palmer Golf Management properties include Tahquitz Creek in Palm Springs and the Presidio Golf Course in San Francisco.

● CLUB CORPORATION OF AMERICA
650 Town Center, Ste. 570
Costa Mesa, CA 92626
(714) 662-1381
clubcorp.com
Club Corporation has more than 230 owned and managed properties on five continents, ranging from premier country clubs and world-class resort destinations to business and sports clubs and semi-private golf courses. For information on courses in California visit the website.

● COURSECO, INC.
PO Box 1619
Petaluma, CA 94954
(707) 763-0335
courseco.com
CourseCo, Inc., is involved with several courses, including Riverside Golf Course in Fresno, Mather Golf Course, Deep Cliff Golf Course in Cupertino, and Crystal Springs Golf Course in Burlingame.

● EMPIRE GOLF
14670 Cantova Way
Rancho Murieta, CA 95683
(916) 354-3040
empiregolf.com
Empire Golf manages Cherry Island, Santa Rosa Fairgrounds, La Contenta Golf Club, and Ancil Hoffman.

● ENVIROMENTAL GOLF, INC.
24121 Ventura Boulevard
Calabasas, CA 91302
(818) 223-8500
envgolf.com
Environmental Golf manages
several clubs in California including
Glenn Annie Golf Club, Sandpiper,
Sterling Hills, the Links at
RiverLakes Ranch, and Westridge
Golf Club.

● JC GOLF
1441 N. Twin Oaks Valley Blvd.
San Diego, CA 92128
(760) 591-4653
jcresortsgolf.com
Rancho Bernardo Inn in San Diego,
and Encinitas Ranch are among JC
Golf Resorts properties.

● LANDMARK GOLF COMPANY
74-947 Highway 111, Ste. 108
Indian Wells, CA 92210
(760) 776-6688
landmarkgolf.com
The Landmark Golf Company owns
and operates the new Landmark Golf
Club.

● TROON GOLF
15044 N. Scottsdale Rd., Ste. 300
Scottsdale, AZ 85254
(888) TROON-US
troongolf.com
Troon Golf manages golf courses
nationwide, eleven in California
alone. Some of their California
sites include Carmel Valley Ranch,
Robinson Ranch, and Monarch
Beach.

● WALTERS GOLF
5500 E. Flamingo Road
Las Vegas, NV 89122
(888) 397-2999
Walters Golf operates Stallion
Mountain, Desert Pines and Royal
Links in Nevada.

PHOTOGRAPHY

Beautiful photos of your course are
a must for advertising and
promotion. Although there aren't
many photographers in California
who specialize in shooting golf
courses, the few that call the
Golden State home produce some of
the world's finest photos.

● AIDAN BRADLEY
721 E. Gutierrez St.
Santa Barbara, CA 93103
(805) 962-8466
Aidan Bradley Photography credits
include: Sandpiper, Rancho San
Marcos, The Badlands, and many
others across the United States and
throughout the world.

● ELAN PHOTOGRAPHY
Newport Beach, CA
(714) 219-0505
Elan provides same day golf photos
for your tournament or corporate
outing.

● JB PUBLISHERS
4208 Douglas Blvd., Ste. 200
Granite Bay, CA 95746
(916) 677-2442
In the last 15 years, JB Publishers
have done over 200 limited edition
prints and paintings. Ninety-percent
of their work is commissioned, but
they do sometimes have overruns.
They currently have thirty prints in
publication.

● JOANN DOST GOLF EDITIONS, LLC
PO Box 827
Pebble Beach, CA 93953
(831) 375-3678
joanndost.com
You may not have heard of Joann Dost, but chances are you have seen her work. One of the few photographers commissioned to shoot Pebble Beach, Joann Dost travels all over the world photographing the world's best courses.

● KAUFMAN GOLF PHOTOGRAPHY
1446 Francisco St.
San Francisco, CA 94123
(415) 409-2238
Robert Kaufman, an award-winning photographer has 20 years experience in shooting and working in the golf industry.

● MICHAEL PALMER PHOTOGRAPHY
16332 Balassi Rd.
Hacienda Heights, CA 91745
(626) 336-3707
Michael Palmer Photography does both tournament and golf course photography.

● PANOFOTOS
Website
panofotos.com
PanoFotos are 360 degree seamless photographs for use on the internet. On the internet site, you can stand on the tee box, and with your mouse, turn yourself around to see what's in front of you, behind you and to either side.

PUBLICATIONS

● CHURM PUBLISHING
1451 Quail St., Ste. 110
Newport Beach, CA 92660
(949) 833-9895
orangecountygolf.net
Churm Publishing produces Orange County Golf, Los Angeles Golf and San Diego Golf. These are informative, well written magazines in full color.

● Crittenden Golf News
PO Box 189010
Coronado, CA 92178
(619) 437-6250
Crittenden Golf News is primarily dedicates itself to the business of golf.

● Executive Golfer Magazine
2171 Campus Dr., Ste. 330
Irvine, CA 92612
(949) 752-6474

● Fairways & Greens Magazine
PO Box 50701
Reno, NV 89513-0701
(775) 772-9370
fairwaysgreens.com
Fairways and Greens is a well-written, bimonthly magazine that serves golfers in northern Nevada, northern and central California, and Oregon. This magazine provides in-depth golf coverage to golfers of every level who love to play the game and want to improve their skills. It clues you in on some of the finest courses throughout the west.

● *Focus on Golf*

Los Angeles Times Square
Los Angeles, CA 90053
(213) 237-6124

Six to seven times a year, the Los Angeles Times produces an expanded golf section that wraps around the sports page. The edition comes out the Thursday prior to a major or special tournament, such as the Ryder Cup.

● *Fore*

PO Box 7186
North Hollywood, CA 91615
(818) 980-3630
scga.org

Produced for the members of the Southern California Golf Association, this magazine is published six times a year.

● *Golf Index*

444 Burchett St.
Glendale, CA 91209
(800) 374-6339
golf-index.com

● *Golf Tips Magazine*

12121 Wilshire Blvd., Ste. 1200
Los Angeles, CA 90025
(310) 820-1500
golftipsmag.com

Golf Tips Magazine is the in-depth instruction and equipment magazine.

● *Golf Today*

204 Industrial Rd.
San Carlos, CA 94070
(800) 465-3788
golftodaymagazine.com

Golf Today produces a monthly tabloid magazine that features golf course reviews, new products, golf news, discount coupons, tournament schedules and articles. The magazine is distributed free of charge through golf shops and courses throughout California, Nevada, Utah, and Arizona.

● *Golfer's Guide*

2604-B El Camino Real, Ste. 274
Carlsbad, CA 92008
(760) 599-5894

● *Junior Golf Magazine*

PO Box 2210
Palm Springs, CA 92263-2210
(760) 323-0204
juniorgolf.com

● *NCGA News*

PO Box NCGA
Pebble Beach, CA 93953
(831) 625-4653
ncga.org

NCGA News magazine is published quarterly by the Northern California Golf Association for its members.

● *North Valley Golf Times*

PO Box 4827
Chico, CA 95927
(530) 879-1877
justdogolf.tv

This tabloid-style magazine covers golf from Oregon to Northern California.

● *Northern California Golf Guide*

4471 D St.
Sacramento, CA 95819
(916) 452-6200
norcalgolfguide.com

The Northern California Golf Guide is published yearly by Sacramento Magazine. The magazine provides several golf related articles, golf maps, and over 230 golf listings for courses in the Bay Area, Lake Tahoe, Reno/Carson Valley, and southern and central Oregon. Details on the latest edition can be found on the website.

● *Palm Springs Life*

303 N. Indian Canyon Dr.
Palm Springs, CA 92262
(760) 325-2333
desertgolfguide.com

Each summer Palm Springs Life magazine comes out with a guide to Palm Springs golf. Check the website for year-round information.

● *San Diego Golfer*

100 S. Sunrise Way, Ste. 257
Palm Springs, CA 92262
(760) 323-3630

San Diego Golfer covers San Diego County. Produced by Sports Media, this tabloid magazine covers tournament news, course news, views and opinions, real estate, golf business, and much more.

● *Schwing!*

PO Box 884570
San Francisco, CA 94188-4570
(415) 671-2428
gotballs.com

Schwing! is geared to younger golfers and is a breath of fresh air in the stuffy world of golf. The writing and graphics are cutting edge in this quarterly publication. The magazine is distributed worldwide and can be found in California at Barnes & Noble, Borders, and Tower Book stores. For a subscription you can call 888-520-9099.

● *Sierra Nevada Golf Country*

916 Angus St.
Carson City, NV 89703
(775) 885-8096
sierragolfcountry.com

Sierra Nevada Golf Country is published six times a year by Sierra Nevada Publishing.

● *Southern California Golf*

100 S. Sunrise Way, Ste. 257
Palm Springs, CA 92262
(760) 323-3630

Desert Golf covers Palm Springs and the surrounding Coachella Valley. Produced by Sports Media, this tabloid magazine covers tournament news, course news, views and opinions, real estate, golf business, and much more.

● *Tee Shots*

411 Davis St., Ste 103
Vacaville, CA 95688
(707) 449-4742
ncpga.com

Northern California Section of the PGA of America produces this magazine for its members. Advertising is accepted.

● *Vegas Golfer*

2290 Corporate Circle Dr. # 280
Henderson, NV 89014
(702) 990-2585

Vegas Golfer is produced six times a year and is distributed primarily in the Las Vegas area.

● *Wine Country Golf Guide*

884 Second St.
Santa Rosa, CA 95404
(707) 578-3300
golfguide.org

This free guide to wine country courses is distributed at local courses, stores, and businesses throughout Sonoma, Napa, Marin, San Francisco, Solano, Lake, and Mendocino counties. There are several discount coupons for green fees in the guide.

PUTTING GREENS

Here are four advantages to having a putting green in your backyard:

1) less maintenance - most putting greens use synthetic turf

2) environmentally friendly - putting greens never need fertilizer

3) adds value to your home - provided the prospective buyer plays golf

4) saves money - how many bets have you lost because you never find time to practice putting?

● ALL-PRO PUTTING GREENS
16315 Piuma
Cerritos, CA 90703
(714) 374-9271
All-Pro Putting Greens of California offers state-of-the-art synthetic turf that duplicates the look, feel, and roll of a bent-grass green. Call for a free estimate.

● BACK NINE GREENS
Website
(800) 583-6619
backninegreens.com

● FIVE STAR PUTTING GREENS
1002 River Rock Dr.
Folsom, CA 95630
(800) 990-8030

● GREEN DREAMS
(714) 734-9212
Constructed of a specially designed synthetic turf which is top-dressed with sand, the finished product rolls like a country club green without the maintenance. Green Dreams is an authorized Putting Green International dealer.

● ONE PUTT GREENS
22541 Aspen St., Ste. D
Lake Forest, CA 92630
(760) 930-1005
One Putt specializes in the design and installation of synthetic putting greens that consist of both synthetic fibers and natural aggregates that look and play like natural bent grass. They also install sand traps and chipping areas.

● PROFESSIONAL PUTTING GREENS
28562 Oso Pkwy., Ste. 528
Rancho Sta. Margarita, CA 92688
(949) 709-5889

● PUTTMASTERS
1360 Los Conejos
Fallbrook, CA 92028
(619) 339-3537
puttmasters.com
Puttmasters covers all of Southern California

● SOUTHWEST PUTTING GREENS
5148 Heddell Ct., Ste. D
Las Vegas, NV 89118
(702) 253-0094

● TAP-IN TURF PRODUCTS
PO Box 2109
Cupertino , CA 95014-1017
(888) 880-4TAP
Tap-In Turf Products specializes in high-quality, synthetic putting greens for home and business.

● TOUR TRUE TECHNOLOGY
384 Oyster Point Blvd., Ste. 14
South San Francisco, CA 94080
(650) 244-0690
tourtrue.com
They specialize in indoor/outdoor putting greens and practice facilities for both commercial and home use.

SCHOOLS

California has golf schools for adults, juniors, and even ones for both parent and child. Prices range from $99 a week for group lessons at the local muni, to $3,000 a week to be pampered at a high-end resort. Whatever your price range, call and ask questions to find the school that best suits your needs.

● AMERICAS FAVORITE GOLF SCHOOLS

1295 SE Port St. Lucie Blvd.
Port St. Lucie, FL 34952
(800) 365-6640
afgs.com

Americas Favorite Golf Schools has several locations and include two, three or five night's accommodations, five hours of instruction, plus on course play with your professional, green fees and carts. During and after class, a daily video is available to review your swing. All students have unlimited use of the range. Americas Favorite Golf School uses a 5-to-1 player to-professional ratio. Call for current locations.

● AVIARA GOLF ACADEMY

7447 Batiquitos Drive
Carlsbad, CA 92009
(800) 433-7468
kipputt.com

The Aviara Golf Academy runs year round at the Four Seasons Resort Aviara. Two and three-day sessions are available with a 4-to-1 student-teacher ratio. Costs range from $800 to $1,200.

● AVILA BEACH GOLF ACADEMY

Avila Beach Road
Avila Beach, CA 93424
(805) 595-4000
avilabeachresort.com

● CALIFORNIA AND LAS VEGAS GOLF SCHOOLS

40015 Sierra Hwy., Ste. B-290
Palmdale, CA 93550
(800) 894-9593
weteachgolf.com

Bruce Baird's California and Las VegasGolf Schools offer customized classes to fit each student's needs. One to five day courses are available, but students have been known to book up to six weeks of training. Locations include the Monterey Peninsula, San Diego, and Las Vegas.

● CARMEL VALLEY RANCH GOLF SCHOOL

1 Old Ranch Rd.
Carmel Valley, CA 93923
(831) 626-2510

Located at the world famous Carmel Valley Ranch resort, the golf school includes three days of instruction and on-course playing time. Other activities available are tennis, horseback riding, bicycling, fishing, windsurfing, and sailing. Shared lodging and breakfast are included in the costs, which can range from around $800 to $2,000.

● COMPUSPORT ACADEMY OF GOLF AT PRIMM VALLEY GOLF CLUB

31900 S. Las Vegas Blvd.
Primm, NV 89019
(800) 266-7877
compusport.com

The CompuSport Academy is only one of four places in the world that offer you a biomechincal view of your swing. The process allows you to build a model of your swing using your own specifications. The CompuSport Academy will then superimpose your model swing against your current swing, showing your strengths and weaknesses. During the week you will work to match that model swing. Schools range from one to three days and include lodging, instruction, golf, and your own take-home video. Prices range from $545 for the one-day school to $1,995 for the three-day school.

● DAVE PELZ GOLF SCHOOLS

1310 R.R. 620 South, B-1
Austin, TX 78734
(800) 824-8899
pelzgolf.com

The emphasis at the Dave Pelz Scoring Game School is putting, bunker play, and wedge shots. Dave Pelz, a former NASA researcher, uses various hi-tech training aids, along with exercises, to help students shave unwanted strokes from their game. Locations include PGA West and the Napa Valley.

● FELLOWSHIP OF CHRISTIAN ATHLETES JUNIOR GOLF CAMPS

8701 Leeds Rd.
Kansas City, MO 64129
(800) 289-0909
fca.org

Call for California locations. These camps combine golf with spiritual enrichment. The instructors are college coaches, PGA club pros, and PGA, LPGA, and Nike touring professionals. Scholarships are available.

● GOLF UNIVERSITY

17550 Bernardo Oaks Dr.
San Diego, CA 92128
(800) 426-0966
golfuniversity.com

Golf University is held at the Rancho Bernardo Inn. They have a 4-to-1 student to teacher ratio.

● JIM MCLEAN GOLF SCHOOL

56-150 PGA Blvd.
La Quinta, CA 92253
(760) 564-7144
jimmclean.com

The Jim McLean Golf School in California is located at PGA West. Schools range from one to six days. The six-day school includes 43 hours of instruction, a 3-to-1 student to teacher ratio, five rounds of golf with cart, and a Jim McLean Golf School gift package. Schools run year round. Classes in June, July, August, and September have reduced rates.

● JOHN JACOBS GOLF SCHOOL

7825 East Redfield Rd.
Scottsdale, AZ 85260
(800) 472-5007
jacobsgolf.com

The John Jacobs School of Golf features teachers who are either PGA or LPGA certified. Golf school packages include accommodations, meals, rounds of golf, and group functions. Call to find locations throughout California.

457

● LA COSTA GOLF SCHOOL
2100 Costa del Mar Rd.
Carlsbad, CA 92009
(760) 438-9111
lacosta.com

● NIKE GOLF SCHOOLS - ADULT
919 Sir Francis Drake Blvd.
Kentfield, CA 94904
(800) 645-3226
ussportscamps.com
The school includes a 4-to-1 student to teacher ratio. All instructors are LPGA or PGA certified. The camps include on-course lessons, video, lunch, workbook, and gift pack.

● NIKE JUNIOR GOLF CAMPS - RESIDENT
919 Sir Francis Drake Blvd.
Kentfield, CA 94904
(800) 645-3226
ussportscamps.com
Check for locations and ages.

● NIKE JUNIOR GOLF CAMPS - WEEK-LONG
919 Sir Francis Drake Blvd.
Kentfield, CA 94904
(800) 645-3226
ussportscamps.com
There are many locations throughout California and Nevada.

● NIKE PARENT-CHILD GOLF SCHOOL
919 Sir Francis Drake Blvd.
Kentfield, CA 94904
(800) 645-3226
ussportscamps.com
The Parent-Child schools includes a 4-to-1 student to teacher ratio. All instructors are LPGA or PGA certified. The camps include on-course lessons, video, lunch, workbook, and gift pack. Locations include Carmel, San Diego, Palm Springs, Santa Barbara, Stanford and Las Vegas.

● OJAI VALLEY INN ACADEMY OF GOLF
905 Country Club Drive
Ojai, CA 93023
(805) 646-2420
ojairesort.com

● PEBBLE BEACH GOLF ACADEMY
17 Mile Drive
Pebble Beach, CA 93953
(800) 654-9300
pebblebeach.com
The Pebble Beach Academy has sessions running from July through December. The program includes accommodations at the Inn at Spanish Bay, continental breakfasts, and two days of instruction, Guests will also receive rounds of golf on the famed Pebble Beach Golf Links and the Links at Spanish Bay.

● PROFESSIONAL GOLFERS CAREER COLLEGE
PO Box 892319
Temecula, CA 92589-2319
(800) 877-4380
progolfed.com
Are you looking for a career in the golf business? Professional Golfer Career College might be your answer. They offer a 16-month, four semester program where golfers can improve their skills as well as learn about the business of golf.

● SCHOOL OF GOLF FOR WOMEN AT SINGING HILLS RESORT

3007 Dehasa Rd.
El Cajon, CA 92019
(619) 442-3425
Singinghills.com

Singing Hills Golf Club & Resort offers a golf school for women. The facility includes use of a private practice range, 36 holes of championship golf, 18-hole par-3 course, four chipping and pitching greens, six practice bunkers, and four practice greens. Three-and five-day classes are available.

● SEA PINES GOLF RESORT

1945 Solano St.
Los Osos, CA 93402
(888) SEA-PINE
SeaPinesGolfResort.com

● SHAW GUIDES

Website
shawguides.com

For detailed information on golf camps all over the country, check out .shawguides.com.

● SONOMA MISSION INN GOLF ACADEMY

17700 Arnold Drive
Sonoma, CA 95476
(888) 713-4653
smigolfacademy.com

The Sonoma Golf Club offers one to three-day golf school packages. Golf packages include instruction, a room at the world-famous Sonoma Mission Inn, and rounds of golf.

● STANFORD JUNIOR GOLF CAMP

641 E. Campus Drive
Stanford, CA 94305-6150
stanford.edu

Stanford Golf Camps are for juniors 11 to 18 years of age. The co-ed camps have morning and afternoon instruction in putting, course management, long and short game, etiquette and rules. Campers will also have a chance to play on the course as well as enjoy other activities, such as swimming and basketball. For young golfers with a strong game, a players' camp is available with on-course instruction and course management instruction. Enrollment is limited to 40 campers with handicaps of 10 or better.

● TROON GOLF INSTITUTE

71-501 Dinah Shore Drive
Rancho Mirage, CA 92270
(760) 328-4303

● UNITED STATES SCHOOLS OF GOLF

718 1/2 East Main
Richmond, IN 47374
(800) 354-7415
ussog.com

Four United States Schools of Golf are located in California. Each school includes five hours of daily instruction, green fees, range privileges, cart fees, a 4-to-1 student to teacher ratio, a take-home video of your swing, bag storage, and hotel accommodations.

● VIP GOLF ACADEMY

7356 Pine Creek Way
Port St. Lucie, FL 34986
(800) 679-2916
vipgolfacademy.com

The VIP Golf Academy has a 1-to-1 teacher to student ratio, lasting from one to five days. Call for California locations.

SPEAKERS/ENTERTAINMENT

Looking for something unique for your charity or corporate event? This section includes several different ideas that can separate your event from the pack.

● CORPORATE GOLF

PO Box 1332
Pebble Beach, CA 93953
(831) 655-5916

Corporate Golf manages approximately 140 professional tour players, while also conducting clinics and tournament outings for large corporations. It is able to provide comedians, trick shot artists, and long-drive champions.

● DIVOT THE CLOWN

5883 S.E. Riverboat Drive
Stuart , GA 34997
(561) 283-1240
mindspring.com/~divottheclown/

Divot the Clown and Kevin Compare are Class A PGA professionals. They perform one of the most entertaining trick-shot shows you will ever see. Together they have a rare combination of showmanship and athletic ability. They also can demonstrate sound golf swing fundamentals.

● HOOKED ON GOLF

1620 Burlingame Avenue
Burlingame, CA 94010
(650) 692-6261
hookedongolf.com

Hooked On Golf hosts John Abendroth and Mitch Juricich are available for personal appearances. They perform seminars and clinics for charity and corporate events.

● LONG DRIVERS OF AMERICA

840 W. 9th St., Ste. E
Upland, CA 91786
(888) 233-4654
longdrives.com

If you are planning a tournament or an event and want to include a long-drive demonstration, contact Long Drivers of America for further information on how to arrange an appearance. Visit the website for tournament schedules and information.

● PIN-UP GOLF

15030 Ventura Blvd., Ste. 308
Sherman Oaks, CA, CA 91403
(888) 849-3004
pinupgolf.com

Pin-Up Golf provides beautiful hostesses to meet, greet, and socialize with players. They can help you raise money by selling, and signing posters and calendars, monitoring hole-in-one or closest-to-the-hole contests, selling raffle tickets, selling premium cigars, operating putting contests, and much more. Even if you are not interested, its worth checking out the website.

● SOUTHERN CALIFORNIA GOLF

Website
(909) 699-1886
southerncaliforniagolf.com

Don't have time to set up entertainment for your clients? Southern California Golf is a full-service organization that can take care of all your clients golfing needs.

● THE ALLEN AGENCY INC.

23852 Pacific Coast Hwy. #401
Malibu, CA 90265
(800) 516-9090
celeberityspeakig.com

They specialize in sports celebrity speakers.

● THE MULLIGAN MAN
   4951 Reforma Rd.
   Woodland Hills, CA 91364
   (818) 225-8255
   themulliganman.com
If you are need of a Master of
Ceremonies for your next event, the
Mulligan Man is your guy. He also
is a donation resource, and can
provide on-course entertainment.

TEE PRIZES

Finding the correct tee prize has
always been difficult, whether your
budget is $5 per player or $150 per
player. Here are some places we
thought you might try.

● A.S.A.P MARKETING
   PMB 8469, P.O. Box 2428
   Pensicola, FL 32513-2482
   (800) 665-5222
   asapmarketing.com
A.S.A.P. provides awards, golf
clothing, accessories, and
tournament prizes.

● ASSOCIATED BUSINESS PRODUCTS
   2329 Circadian Way
   Santa Rosa, CA 95407
   (707) 527-6022
ABP provides prizes and tee gifts
and corporate logo items including
shirts, jackets, hats, awards, golf
balls, tees, shoes, bags, and
umbrellas. Call for a catalog.

● CORPORATE GOLF
   701 Pennsylvania Ave., Loft 109
   San Francisco, CA 94107
   (415) 648-1070
   corporate-golf.com
Corporate Golf, the Fortune 500's
Pro Shop is a provider of pro-line
golf merchandise and services for
corporate events. It provides a
comprehensive selection of
top-quality, name-brand golf
apparel, headgear, accessories, and
equipment.

● FICI.COM

2967 Nationwide Pkwy.
Brunswick, OH 44212
(800) 886-3367
fici.com

Golf Promotional Products offers
everything from logo imprinted golf
balls, logo imprinted clubs, tees,
hats, head covers, and apparel.
They also offers awards, tee packs,
and accessories.

● GEIGER BROTHERS WEST

295 N. Crane Road
Oakdale, CA 95361
(209) 847-9529

Place your tournament logo or
company logo on brand names such
as Bobby Jones, Antigua and
Munsingwear.

● GINO'S AWARDS, INC.

28749 Chagrin Blvd.
Woodmere, OH 44122
(216) 831-6565
ginosonline.com

Gino's offers awards, plaques,
clocks, crystal, hole-in-one-awards,
money clips, cigar holders and
much more.

● IN THE LOOP GOLF

1206 Fourth Street
Santa Rosa, CA 95404
(707) 569-8481
InTheLoopGolf.com

Wouldn't you have loved to have
received the Golf California
Survival Guide as a tee prize?
Discount pricing available starting
at 24 players. Call us for more
information.

● INTERACTIVE GOLF

1364 Country Club Drive
Los Altos, CA 94024
(800) 572-4331
interactivegolf.com

● KAUFMAN TOURNAMENT
PHOTOGRAPHY

1446 Francisco Street
San Francisco, CA 94123
(415) 409-2238

Robert Kaufman Photography
provides tournament photography
for both small and large outings.

● PRO TOUR MEMORABILIA

16556 Arminta St.
Van Nuys, CA 91406
(800) 465-3511
protourmem.com

Pro Tour Memorabilia specializes in
tee prizes, corporate gifts, and
individual gifts that are hand signed
by the professional. It has a wide
selection of items including clubs,
photos, and and other golf items. If
you are looking for a unique golf
gift, call for a free catalog.

● ROB'S TEE HOUSE

PO Box 8120
San Luis Obispo, CA 93403
(805) 544-3880
robsteehouse.com

Everyone needs tees. Rob's offers
several different styles and logo
options. They also offer other golf
accessories.

● SCENIC GOLF INTERNATIONAL

121 Bernoulli Circle
Oxnard, CA 93030
(800) 544-6536
scenicgolf.com

Scenic Golf International provides a
video for golfers on a par 3 hole.
They can also provide your
tournament with tee signs and
award plaques.

● STORM DUDS RAIN GEAR

100 Frank Mossburg Drive
Attleboro, MA 02703
(800) 637-7246

● THE GOLF COLLECTION GOLF SHOP

Website
(888) DOGLEG-8
golfcollection.com

The Golf Collection on-line catalog is part of the the Golf Collection retail store in Long Island, New York. The retail store is a four-time winner of "Americas 100 Best Golf Shops." They have also been named "Best of the Web" for gifts by the The Best in Golf, a Golf Magazine publication. The Golf Collection Golf Shop carries clubs, bags, shoes, balls, and accessories. It holds one of the largest selections of golf gifts, furniture, and novelties in the nation. If you don't find what you are looking for on-line, give them a call.

● THE GOLF DIGEST PASSBOOK

2530 E. Broadway, Ste. B
Tucson , AZ 85716
(800) 950-4653
golfpassbook.com

The Golf Passbook offers discounts at over 450 courses in the Western United States. It offers savings at over 50 driving ranges and 15 PGA, Senior PGA, and LPGA tournaments. There are also savings on over 25 stay-and-play packages at resorts in the west. Great tee prize

● THE GOLF PEOPLE

16203 Westwoods Business Park
Ellisville, MO 63021-4506
(800) 334-7757
thegolfpeople.com

The Golf People offers a 48-page catalog with golf awards, tee prizes, and favors. Over 100 items are available for you to imprint your company name or logo.

● THE LINKSKEEPER

39 Varda Landing Rd.
Sausalito, CA 94965
(415) 332-8155
linkskeeper.com

Linkskeeper makes logo divot repair tools and other accessories such as money clips and key chains for tournament tee prizes, corporate premiums, and golf companies.

● WATCHIT

442 Wekiva Cove Road
Longwood , FL 32779
(407) 788-1216

WATCHIT is leader in promotional watches with corporate or tournament logos.

● WEST COAST GOLF VALUE BOOK

15650 Vineyard Blvd., Ste. 152
Morgan Hill, CA 95037
(800) 949-1415
2for1golf.com

The West Coast Value Book offers savings at over 200 golf courses and practice facilities throughout California. This makes a good tee prize.

TEE PRIZES/NOVELTY

● CYPRESS CLASSICS

PO Box 5999
Oxnard, CA 93031
(800) 473-8504
cypress-classics.com
Cypress Classics sells upscale gifts
and prizes for tournaments and
corporate events. It also sells golf
art. Call for a catalog or visit the
showroom on-line.

● GOLF EDITIONS

Website
golfeditions.com
Unique invitations and reply cards
designed specifically for corporate
executives, their clients, as well as
for pro shops, tournaments, gifts
and special occasions.

● PACIFIC ETCHED GLASS AND CRYSTAL

2046 Sunset Drive
Pacific Grove, CA 93950
(831) 373-0683
pacificglass.com
They specialize in gifts, trophies,
and awards for tournaments, as well
as corporate and charity events.
Check the website, or if you are
visiting the Monterey Peninsula, call
for directions and visit the
showroom in Pacific Grove.

● SPORTS SPECTRUM GREETING CARDS

324 S. Pacific Coast Hwy., #201
Redondo Beach, CA 90277
(800) 752-9426
sportsgreetingcards.com
As the name suggests, they have an
entire spectrum of different greeting
cards, including golf. Check out
their website.

TEE TIMES

Tired of waking up at 4 a.m. to make
your next tee time? Tee time
services are coming in vogue. Most
can save you the hassle of trying to
book a time, while a few can even
save you some money.

● ADVANCE GOLF

79211 Bermuda Dunes
Bermuda Dunes, CA 92201
(760) 324-3560
Advance Golf provides individual
and group tee times for the Palm
Springs area.

● BOOK4GOLF.COM

Website
book4golf.com

● DESERT GOLF RESERVATIONS

73766 US Highway 111
Palm Desert, CA 92260
(760) 341-2662
Desert Golf is a reservation system
for all the PGA West courses.

● GOLF A LA CARTE

3261 Cambridge Court
Palm Springs, CA 92264
(877) 887-6900
palmspringsgolf.com
Golf a la Carte was established in
1988 and rated, the "best of the tee
time services" by Sunset Magazine.
It guarantees tee times up to 90
days in advance, one year in
advance for large groups. There is
no surcharge. You have your choice
of over 30 clubs in the Palm Springs
area, and Golf a la Carte will be
happy to make recommendations.

● LAS VEGAS PREFERRED TEE TIMES

5500 East Flamingo Road
Las Vegas, NV 89122
(888) 368-7833

● M & M TEE TIMES

7445 Girand Avenue
La Jolla, CA 92037
(858) 456-8366

M & M Tee Times provides reservations for all the finer courses in and around San Diego, including Torrey Pines.

● NEXT DAY GOLF

41905 Boardwalk, Ste. A2
Palm Desert, CA 92211
(760) 345-8463
parteegolf.com

Courses call Next Day Golf with their open tee times for - you guessed it - the next day. If you can wait until the day before you play, you can receive discounted green fees at over 33 courses in the Palm Springs area.

● PALM SPRINGS TEE TIMES

303 Indian Canyon Dr.
Palms Springs, CA 92262
(760) 324-5012
palmspringsteetimes.com

Palm Springs Tee Times specializes in tee times for the Palm Springs area with a human touch. They provide a very fast response and are very knowledgeable about the area. They work with over 30 courses.

● STAND-BY-GOLF

1555 South Palm Canyon Drive
Palm Springs, CA 92264
(866) 224-2665
stand-bygolf.com

Stand-by-Golf covers courses in the Palm Springs area, Las Vegas, Hawaii and Florida. They purchase tee times from courses the night before and sell them to golfers at discounts ranging from 25 to 50 percent.

TOURNAMENT AND EVENT PLANNING

Running a charity or corporate event is hard work, especially if you plan on trying to enjoy the event yourself. California has an abundance of qualified tournament and event planners who can make the event a stress-free and memorable experience for all.

● ADVANTAGE GOLF

2551 San Ramon Valley Blvd.
San Ramon, CA 94583
(800) 753-9538

Advantage Golf takes care of everything from the planning of, to execution of an event. They can provide signs, contests, tee prizes, celebrity speakers, promotional products, and much more.

● CORPORATE GOLF

PO Box 1332
Pebble Beach, CA 93953
(831) 655-5916

Corporate Golf manages approximately 140 professional tour players, also while conducting clinics and tournament outings for large corporations. They are able to provide comedians, trick shot artists, and long-drive champions.

● CORPORATE GOLF MANAGEMENT

44489 Town Centre Way, #260
Palm Desert, CA 92260
(760) 341-7542
corporategolfmanagement.com

Corporate Golf Management specializes in golf management for corporate, group, and incentive travel.

● CREATIVE EVENTS

26080 Carmel Ranch Boulevard
Carmel, CA 93923
(831) 624-7200

● GREAT GOLF EVENTS

5250 West 94th Terrace
Prairie Village, KS 66207
(888) 324-9515
greatgolfevents.com

Great Golf Events is a nationwide, single-source, golf events company. They do everything from finding a site to producing the event. They have associations with Nike, American Golf, Adams, and American Hole-in-One.

● HOOKED ON GOLF

1620 Burlingame Avenue
Burlingame, CA 94010
(650) 692-6261
hookedongolf.com

Entering its 10th year in business, San Francisco Golf Services is the parent company of Hooked On Golf. Formed as a broad-based service company, it focuses on golf in the San Francisco Bay Area. Founded by former PGA TOUR player John Abendroth, the company has been involved with many corporate and charity golf events as either a consultant, event manager, or instructional golf clinic. For information on consulting for either golf events or golf products, e-mail him at igolfswing@aol.com or telephone.

● HUNTER PUBLIC RELATIONS

PO Box 1049
Pebble Beach, CA 93953
(831) 375-1747
hunter-pr.com

Hunter Public Relations (HPR) specializes in the development and execution of public relations strategies and special events, primarily for the hospitality and golf industries.

With offices on both coasts, HPR has wide access to major media at national, regional, and local levels. Its worldwide network of contacts, proprietary media lists, and relationships, developed over the past 15 years, gives HPR a competitive edge in the marketplace.

● INTERACTIVE GOLF

1364 Country Club Drive
Los Altos, CA 94024
(800) 572-4331
interactivegolf.com

Interactive Golf can provide charity or corporate events with complete event management, hole-in-one insurance, logo tee prizes, and awards.

● M & M TEE TIMES

7445 Girand Avenue
La Jolla, CA 92037
(858) 456-8366

M & M Tee Times provides tee times for the San Diego area, as well as organizing and running corporate events.

● NITELITE GOLF

PO Box 1200
Wolfeboro, NH 03896
(800) 282-1533

Nitelite Golf can help you run a night tournament at your favorite golf course. It bills itself as, "the second most fun you can have in the dark."

● PALM SPRINGS GOLF VACATIONS

74945 Sheryl Avenue
Palm Desert, CA 92260
(800) 774-6531
golfdestinations.com

Palm Springs Golf Vacations specializes in individual and corporate outings in the Palm Springs area.

● PAR-TEE GOLF

Website
Palm Desert, CA
(800) PAR-TEE-1
parteegolf.com

Par-Tee Golf specializes in reservations for golf, hotel, and cars in the Palm Springs area. Tournament services are also available.

● SPECTRUM GOLF

6390 E. Thomas Road, Ste. 300
Scottsdale, AZ 85251
(800) 577-3787
spectrum-golf.com

Spectrum Golf is owned and operated by PGA TOUR professionals. Spectrum specializes in creating customized events of all sizes.

● TEE (TOURNAMENT EVENT ENTERPRISES)

1575 Adrian Road, Ste. B
Burlingame, CA 94010
(650) 697-5946

Tournament Event Enterprises provides customized golf tournament services for businesses and organizations. The company is run by Mitch Juricich, creator and co-host of television's Hooked on Golf.

● THE BERKELEY GROUP, LLC

2461 Santa Monica Blvd. #506
Santa Monica, CA 90404
(310) 543-5346

The Berkeley Group produces corporate, charity, and celebrity golf tournaments. They also plan golf outings, retreats, specialty, and VIP golf events.

● THE RICHLIN GROUP

13428 Maxella Avenue, Ste. 278
Marina del Rey, CA 90292
(800) 254-4653
trgolf.com

The Richlin Group exclusively arranges and promotes tournaments.

● TOURNAMENT CREATIONS

514 North Coast Highway, Ste. F
Oceanside, CA 92054
(760) 966-0782
tournamentcreations.com

Tournament Creations specializes in organizing charity, corporate, and celebrity events in California, Arizona, and Nevada.

● WOLF COMMUNICATIONS

2245 Sunlit Ann Drive
Santa Rosa , CA 95403
(707) 575-4415

Wolf Communications is a public relations and advertising firm that specializes in outdoor recreation. Clients include golf courses and golf industry cooperative marketing organizations (golf courses and lodging properties). The Santa Rosa-based agency develops comprehensive PR campaigns, advertising programs, promotions, and special events.

TOURS, INDEXED

Index Tours are set up so amateurs with handicaps and professionals can compete in the same event. Participants can win cash or prizes, with winners receiving up to $1,000. For golfers wanting to keep their amateur status, be sure to check the rules carefully before accepting any cash or prizes.

● SDG TOUR
PO Box 3488
Quartz Hill, CA 93536-0488
(800) 433-7342
sdgtour.com

Single Digit Tour events take place all over the state. Entrants must have a 9.9 handicap or less. So players don't lose their amateur status, good-anywhere gift certificates are given as prizes. The tour follows all USGA guidelines and events are held once a month. The top ten point finishers from Northern California face-off against the top ten point finishers of Southern California for the Founders Cup.

● THE PEPSI TOUR
14272 Wick Boulevard
San Leandro, CA 94577
(800) 614-GOLF
pepsitour.com

The Pepsi Tour is owned and operated by All Golfers Tour Association, a California corporation founded in 1994. They organize, promote, and conduct golf tournaments at some of the best country clubs and public courses on the west coast. The tour has two separate divisions. The Open Division is for the professional and the best amateur golfers who play in low gross competitions. The Indexed Division is for non-amateur and amateur players of all skill levels that play in handicapped or flighted low-gross competitions. Events are held in Northern California, Southern California, Arizona, and Nevada. For more information call 800-614-GOLF or log on to the website at pepsitour.com.

TOURS, PROFESSIONAL

What separates the PGA TOUR player from the mini-tour player? Nerve, a little luck, knowing how to win, and the ability to grind out one tour stop after another without going crazy. Hitting the road is the only way to push your game to the limit.

● BUY.COM TOUR

112 PGA Tour Boulevard
Ponte Vedra Beach, FL 32082
(904) 285-3700
pgatour.com

Once the Ben Hogan Tour, formally the Nike Tour, and soon to be the ex-BUY.COM Tour, these events, run by the PGA TOUR, usually have open qualifiers on Monday. As many as 200 golfers play for seven or eight tournament spots. To gain an exemption on the BUY.COM Tour, players must make it through the final stage of PGA TOUR qualifying school. The top fifty golfers who don't make the PGA TOUR gain a one-year exemption. Many of today's biggest names on the PGA TOUR got their starts here.

● CASCADE GOLF TOUR

418 Fredrick Street SE
Olympia, WA 98501
(360) 786-8486
cascadegolftour.com

Located in Washington, the Cascade Tour has 20 events with an average purse of $11,000. The tour is open to all professionals and amateurs with handicaps of nine or less.

● DAKOTAS PROFESSIONAL GOLF TOUR

600 James Place
Yankton, SD 57078
(605) 665-2383

The Dakotas Tour runs eight three-to-four day events, four two-day events and six one-day events. The tournament season begins in July and ends in late September.

● GOLDEN STATE TOUR

PO Box 710
Pauma Valley, CA 92061
(760) 742-1461
gstour.com

The Golden State Tour has been around for 17 years. Graduates include Jim Furyk, Tom Lehman, and Brent Geiberger. Over 100 events are held each year, with a total purse of $1,000,000. The tour runs year-round and is open to both professionals and amateurs. For more information on playing the Golden State Tour, contact Doug Ives at the the tournament office.

● LPGA TOUR

100 International Golf Drive
Daytona, FL 32124
(904) 274-6200
lpga.com

● PGA TOUR

112 PGA Tour Boulevard
Ponte Vedra Beach, FL 32082
(904) 285-3700
pgatour.com

The quickest way to the PGA TOUR is Q (qualifying) school, better known as "hell" by its participants. Several stages of Q-school are held in California. Even though the entry fee is well over $3,000, so many hackers have attempted to qualify that golfers must now have a letter of recommendation to apply.

● PLAYERS WEST

4900 Hopyard, Ste. 100
Pleasanton, CA 94588
(925) 463-4841
playerswest.com

The Players West tour is a professional tour for women golfers. The top ten finishers on the money list each year earn a $2,500 scholarship to cover expenses for the LPGA qualifying school. In the past nine years, over 54 former Players West golfers have made it to the LPGA. This is considered the Hogan/Nike/Buy.com Tour for women.

● SENIOR PGA TOUR

112 PGA Tour Boulevard
Ponte Vedra Beach, FL 32082
(904) 285-3700
pgatour.com

TRAVEL

Whether planning a golf trip in the Golden State or halfway around the world, you may want to consider using a travel agent that specializes in golf tours. A golf travel agent can save you money, time, and hassles. Now all you have to worry about is keeping your head down, knees bent, rotating your shoulder, and releasing your hands...

● AGS GOLF TOURS

Website
(888) 529-2448
A-G-S-golf.com

AGS Golf Tours specializes in golf vacations in England, Scotland, and Ireland.

● BALBOA TRANSPORTATION

11552 Alborada Drive
San Diego, CA 92127
(800) 350-3053
balboatransportation.com

Balboa will transport a golf outing to courses in-and-around the San Diego/Baja California area. It can accommodate groups ranging from 8 to 36 players.

● CLASSIC GOLF & LEISURE

75706 McLachlin Court
Palm Desert, CA 92216
(760) 772-2560

● CLUB 19 GOLF AND TRAVEL
SAVINGS
PO Box 222594
Carmel, CA 93922-2594
(800) 347-6119
club19golf.com

Club 19 provides discounts to over 550 golf courses in California, Oregon, Washington, British Columbia, Nevada, and Arizona. In California, there are discounts at over 200 courses. Club 19 is also a travel club. It offers five or six hosted trips a year, all over the world. Each vacation is seven nights and eight days. With membership, you also receive a vacation pass, which includes discounts of up to 50 percent off hotel rooms. Call and mention the California Services Directory and receive $10 off the $49 membership fee. Shipping and handling is $3.

● DESERT GOLF CONCIERGE
42240 Green Way, Ste. E
Palm Desert, CA 92211
(760) 346-4850

Desert Golf Events manages, plans, and produces corporate and individual golf travel packages. Call for a free consultation.

● GOLF DESTINATIONS
11230 Sorrento Valley Road #215
San Diego, CA 92121
(800) 335-3534
golfdestinationsonline.com

Golf Destinations covers Europe, nearly every golf destination in the US, Australia, South Africa, Asia, the Caribbean and much more. In addition to packages to Europe and the Southeast, they also books packages to special events, such as the PGA Championship. Check the website for details.

● GOLF DESTINATIONS
INTERNATIONAL
74945 Sheryl Avenue
Palm Desert, CA 92260
(760) 346-3331

● GOLF HOLIDAYS INTERNATIONAL
50-855 Washington Street
La Quinta, CA 92253
(888) 465-3499

● GOLF & LEISURE INTERNATIONAL
22312 Philiprim Street
Woodland Hills, CA 91367
(818) 340-3600
golfleisure.com

Golf and Leisure International arranges trips to the Masters, the US Open, and the PGA Championship.

● GOLF SAN DIEGO
PO Box 6215
San Diego, CA 92166
(619) 226-1749

● GOLF TOURS OF SCOTLAND
Scotland
(800) 847-8064

● GOLF TRAVEL CENTER
668 Las Gallinas Avenue
San Rafael, CA 94903
(888) 383-3633
golftravelcenter.com

Golf Travel Center books trips to Hawaii, Canada, California, Arizona, and Europe. They can arrange every aspect of your golf vacation.

● INTERNATIONAL FAIRWAYS, LTD.

1446 Francisco Street
San Francisco, CA 94123
(415) 409-2238

International Fairways provides golf hospitality from Augusta to St. Andrews. They can get you into the US Open, British Open, the Masters, and PGA Championship. Packages include accommodations, tickets, food, and entertainment.
International Fairways also offers custom excursions to Scotland and Ireland.

● PALM SPRINGS GOLF VACATIONS

74945 Sheryl Avenue
Palm Desert, CA 92260
(800) 774-6531
golfdestinations.com

Palm Springs Golf Vacations specializes in individual and corporate outings in the Palm Springs area.

● PAR-TEE GOLF

Website
Palm Desert, CA
(800) PAR-TEE-1
parteegolf.com

Par-Tee Golf offers reservations for golf, hotel, and cars in the Palm Springs area. Tournament services and packages are also available.

● PASSPORT TO PALM SPRINGS

2012 Southridge Drive
Palm Springs, CA 92264
(760) 321-4588

Passport to Palm Springs offers discount green fees at over 30 courses in the Palm Springs area. There are also discounts on attractions, lodging, services, and dining.

● PASSPORT TO PHOENIX

2012 Southridge Drive
Palm Springs, CA 92264
(760) 321-4588

Passport to Phoenix offers discount green fees in Phoenix and its surrounding area. There are also discounts on attractions, lodging, services, and dining.

● PLAYERS CHOICE GOLF TOURS

5711-1 Independence Circle
Fort Meyers, FL 33912
(800) 477-8687
pchoice.com

Players Choice has PGA Section professionals on staff to arrange custom golf tours of Florida, California, Arizona, Las Vegas, Hawaii, and Europe.

● RESORT GOLF VACATIONS

2441 Bellevue Avenue
Daytona Beach, FL 32114
(800) 351-9575
resort-golf.com

Resort Golf Vacations books resort vacations in the US, Mexico, and the Caribbean. Included in all packages are resort accommodations, tee times, green fees, taxes, and service charges.

● SPECTRUM GOLF VACATIONS

6390 E. Thomas Road, Ste. 300
Scottsdale, AZ 85251
(800) 577-3787
spectrum-golf.com

Spectrum Golf Vacations is owned and operated by PGA TOUR professionals. Spectrum specializes in creating customized, once-in-a-lifetime golf vacations and events. Spectrum guarantees tee times and exceptional resort selections in premiere golf destinations such as Phoenix/Scottsdale, Palm Springs, Las Vegas, and Los Cabos, Mexico.

● SPORTS EMPIRE
   PO Box 6169
   Lakewood, CA 90714-6169
   (800) 255-5258
   sportsempire.org
Sports Empire runs golf tours all over the world. They specialize in packages to California, Arizona, and Hawaii.

● THE GOLF DIGEST PASSBOOK
   2530 East Broadway, Ste. B
   Tucson , AZ 85716
   (800) 950-4653
   golfpassbook.com
The Golf Passbook offers discounts at over 450 courses in the Western United States. It offers savings at over 50 driving ranges and 15 PGA, Senior PGA, and LPGA tournaments. There are also savings on over 25 stay-and-play packages at resorts in the west.

● TRAVEL EXPERTS
   2607 Denver Street
   San Diego, CA 92110
   (619) 276-0200
Travel Experts specializes in golf and ski vacations.

● WINE N MORE.COM
   13375 Frati Lane
   Sebastopol, CA 95472
   (877) 994-9463
   winenmore.com
Wine N More.com specializes in all inclusive golf packages to Golf Resorts in the California Wine Country, Las Vegas, and Reno. Destinations include Silverado Country Club, Sonoma Mission Inn, Pebble Beach, and several others.

WOMEN ONLY

This chapter is dedicated to everything that is related to women's golf.

● BLOOMINGBAGS
   722 Genevieve Avenue, Ste. A
   Solana Beach, CA 92075
   (800) 443-2247
   bloomingbags.com
Bloomingbags manufacture's designer women's golf bags and accessories. Products can be ordered from the company on-line.

● DANA LEE SPORTSWEAR
   PO Box 3953
   Thousand Oaks, CA 91359-0953
   (888) 393-2548
Dana Lee produces excellent quality women's sportswear and beautiful outerwear in the low-to-moderate price range. Dana Lee Sportswear can be found at golf facilities, resorts, and some retail stores. The garments are sized and made in the USA.

● EXECUTIVE WOMEN'S GOLF ASSOCIATION
   300 Avenue of Champions #140
   Palm Beach Gardens, FL 33418
   (800) 407-1477
The Executive Women's Golf Association has local chapters throughout the country. The goal of the Executive Women's Golf Association is to bring executive women together to share the golfing experience.

● KAREN KANE GOLF
   2275 East 37th Street
   Los Angeles, CA 90058-1435
   (323) 588-0000
   karenkane.com
Karen Kane Golf provides fashionable, stylish, and tasteful, women's golf wear.

● LPGA Tour

100 International Golf Drive
Daytona, FL 32124
(904) 274-6200
lpga.com

● Ojai Valley Inn Academy of Golf

905 Country Club Drive
Ojai, CA 93023
(805) 646-2420
ojairesort.com

The Academy of Golf offers women's only sessions.

● Players West

4900 Hopyard, Ste. 100
Pleasanton, CA 94588
(925) 463-4841
playerswest.com

The Players West tour is a professional tour for women golfers. The top ten finishers on the money list each year earn a $2,500 scholarship to cover expenses for the LPGA qualifying school. In the past nine years, over 54 former Players West golfers have made it to the LPGA. This is considered the Hogan/Nike/Buy.com Tour for women.

● San Diego Women's Golf Association

13956 Capewood Lane
San Diego, CA 92128
(858) 673-1127

● School of Golf for Women at Singing Hills Resort

3007 Dehasa Road
El Cajon, CA 92019
(619) 442-3425
Singinghills.com

Singing Hills Golf Club & Resort offers a golf school for women. The facility includes use of a private practice range, 36 holes of championship golf, 18-hole par-3 course, four chipping and pitching greens, six practice bunkers, and four practice greens. Three-and five-day classes are available.

● Take Two Sportswear

1300 Bristol Street N., Ste. 100
Newport Beach, CA 92660
(800) 600-5010

Take Two pioneered the velcro closure. The visor adjusts to the individual's head size. Each visor weighs less than two ounces and is machine washable. Most visors are logo friendly. Call for ordering guidelines or where to find a local retailer.

● Women's Golf Association of Northern California

5776 Stoneridge Mall Road #160
Pleasanton, CA 94588
(925) 737-0963
wganc.com

● Women's Nine Hole Golf Association

90 Bear Gulch Road
Portola Valley, CA 94028
(650) 851-0814

● Women's Southern California Golf Association

402 W. Arrow Highway, Ste. 10
San Dimas, CA 91773
(909) 592-1281
womensgolf.org

Directory Index

City Index

495

Index and Scoring Log

How do you rank among the California Golfers?
Let us know how many you've played: intheloopgolf.com

Sample Golden State Golf Club	Public	(707) 569-8481	Santa Rosa	p. 1
Notes	*Great layout but greens are wacky. Well worth playing again.*		Date **2-9-02**	Par (24) **65**

3-Par at Four Points Sheraton	Resort	(858) 715-1763	San Diego	p. 356
Notes			Date	Par (24)

Adams Springs Golf Course	Public	(707) 928-9992	Loch Lomond	p. 127
Notes			Date	Par (34)

Admiral Baker Golf Course	Military	(619) 556-5520	San Diego	p. 356
Notes			Date	Par (72)

Adobe Creek Golf Club	Public	(707) 765-3000	Petaluma	p. 131
Notes			Date	Par (72)

Aetna Springs Golf Course	Public	(707) 965-2115	Pope Valley	p. 133
Notes			Date	Par (35)

Airways Golf Course	Public	(559) 291-6254	Fresno	p. 226
Notes			Date	Par (68)

Alhambra Golf Course	Municipal	(626) 570-5059	Alhambra	p. 252
Notes			Date	Par (70)

How do you rank among the California Golfers? Let us know how many you've played: intheloopgolf.com

Aliso Creek Golf Course	Public	(949) 499-1919	Laguna Beach	p. 327
Notes			Date	Par (32)

Aliso Viejo Golf Club	Public	(949) 598-9200	Aliso Viejo	p. 318
Notes			Date	Par (71)

Allen's Golf Course	Public	(530) 241-5055	Redding	p. 61
Notes			Date	Par (31)

Almaden Golf & Country Club	Members only	(408) 268-3959	San Jose	p. 169
Notes			Date	Par (72)

Alondra Park Golf Course	Municipal	(310) 217-9919	Lawndale	p. 263
Notes			Date	Par (72)

Alta Sierra Golf & Country Club	Semi-Private	(530) 273-2010	Grass Valley	p. 102
Notes			Date	Par (72)

Alta Vista Country Club	Members only	(714) 528-1103	Placentia	p. 330
Notes			Date	Par (72)

Altadena Golf Course	Public	(626) 797-3821	Altadena	p. 252
Notes			Date	Par (36)

Anaheim "Dad Miller" Golf Course	Public	(714) 765-3481	Anaheim	p. 318
Notes			Date	Par (71)

Anaheim Hills Golf Club	Public	(714) 998-3041	Anaheim	p. 318
Notes			Date	Par (71)

How do you rank among the California Golfers? Let us know how many you've played: intheloopgolf.com

Ancil Hoffman Golf Course	Public	(916) 482-3284	Carmichael	p. 97
Notes			Date	Par (72)

Angel Park Golf Club	Resort	(888) 446-5358	Las Vegas	p. 390
Notes			Date	Par (71)

Annandale Golf Course	Members only	(626) 795-8253	Pasadena	p. 273
Notes			Date	Par (70)

Antelope Greens Golf Course	Public	(916) 334-5764	Antelope	p. 92
Notes			Date	Par (58)

Antelope Valley Country Club	Members only	(661) 947-3400	Palmdale	p. 416
Notes			Date	Par (72)

Anthem Country Club	Members only	(702) 914-7888	Las Vegas	p. 390
Notes			Date	Par (72)

Anthem, The Revere at	Public	(702) 259-4653	Henderson	p. 378
Notes			Date	Par (72)

Apple Mountain Golf Resort	Resort	(530) 647-7400	Camino	p. 96
Notes			Date	Par (71)

Apple Valley Country Club	Members only	(760) 242-3125	Apple Valley	p. 292
Notes			Date	Par (71)

Arbuckle Golf Club	Semi-Private	(530) 476-2470	Arbuckle	p. 92
Notes			Date	Par (36)

Arcadia Golf Course	Public	(626) 443-9367	Arcadia	p. 253

Notes

Date	Par (54)

ArrowCreek Golf Club	Public	(775) 850-4653	Reno	p. 78

Notes

Date	Par (72)

Arrowhead Country Club	Members only	(909) 882-1638	San Bernardino	p. 309

Notes

Date	Par (72)

Arrowhead Golf Course	Public	(530) 233-3404	Alturas	p. 54

Notes

Date	Par (36)

Arroyo Fairways Mobile Home Club &	Members only	(909) 927-1610	Hemet	p. 298

Notes

Date	Par (27)

Arroyo Seco Golf Course	Public	(323) 255-1506	South Pasadena	p. 278

Notes

Date	Par (54)

Auburn Lake Trails Golf Course	Members only	(530) 885-6526	Cool	p. 98

Notes

Date	Par (29)

Auburn Valley Country Club	Members only	(530) 269-1837	Auburn	p. 93

Notes

Date	Par (72)

Auld Course, The	Public	(619) 482-4666	Chula Vista	p. 342

Notes

Date	Par (72)

Avila Beach Resort	Public	(805) 595-4000	Avila Beach	p. 187

Notes

Date	Par (71)

How do you rank among the California Golfers? Let us know how many you've played: intheloopgolf.com

Avondale Golf Club	Members only	(760)	345-3712	Palm Desert	p. 405
Notes				Date	Par (72)

Azusa Greens Country Club	Public	(626)	969-1727	Azusa	p. 253
Notes				Date	Par (70)

Badlands Golf Club	Semi-Private	(702)	363-0754	Las Vegas	p. 391
Notes				Date	Par (72)

Bailey Creek Golf Course	Public	(530)	259-4653	Lake Almanor	p. 57
Notes				Date	Par (72)

Bakersfield Country Club	Members only	(661)	871-4121	Bakersfield	p. 221
Notes				Date	Par (72)

Balboa Park Golf Course	Public	(619)	239-1632	San Diego	p. 357
Notes				Date	Par (72)

Bali Hai Golf Club	Public	(888)	397-2499	Las Vegas	p. 391
Notes				Date	Par (71)

Barbara Worth Golf Resort	Semi-Private	(760)	356-5842	Holtville	p. 381
Notes				Date	Par (71)

Barona Creek Golf Club	Public	(619)	387-7018	Lakeside	p. 350
Notes				Date	Par (72)

Bartley Cavanaugh Golf Course	Public	(916)	665-2020	Sacramento	p. 112
Notes				Date	Par (71)

Bayonet/Blackhorse Golf Course	Public	(831)	899-7271	Seaside	p. 210
Notes				Date	Par (72)

Baywood Golf & Country Club	Members only	(707)	822-3688	Arcata	p. 122
Notes				Date	Par (72)

Bear Creek Golf Club	Members only	(909)	677-8631	Murrieta	p. 303
Notes				Date	Par (72)

Bear Mountain Golf Course	Public	(909)	585-8002	Big Bear Lake	p. 293
Notes				Date	Par (35)

Bear's Best	Public	(702)	804-8500	Las Vegas	p. 392
Notes				Date	Par (72)

Beau Pre Golf Club	Semi-Private	(707)	839-2342	McKinleyville	p. 127
Notes				Date	Par (71)

Bel Air Country Club	Members only	(310)	440-2423	Los Angeles	p. 266
Notes				Date	Par (70)

Belmont Country Club	Members only	(559)	251-5076	Fresno	p. 227
Notes				Date	Par (72)

Benbow Valley RV Resort & Golf Course	Public	(707)	923-2777	Garberville	p. 125
Notes				Date	Par (35)

Bennett Valley Golf Course	Municipal	(707)	528-3673	Santa Rosa	p. 134
Notes				Date	Par (72)

Bermuda Dunes Country Club	Members only	(760)	345-2771	Bermuda Dunes	p. 370
Notes				Date	Par (72)

Bernardo Heights Country Club	Members only	(858)	487-3440	San Diego	p. 357
Notes				Date	Par (72)

Bethel Island Golf Course	Public	(925)	684-2654	Bethel Island	p. 223
Notes				Date	Par (72)

Bidwell Park Golf Course	Public	(530)	891-8417	Chico	p. 54
Notes				Date	Par (72)

Big Canyon Country Club	Members only	(949)	644-5404	Newport Beach	p. 329
Notes				Date	Par (72)

Bigfoot Golf & Country Club	Semi-Private	(530)	629-2977	Willow Creek	p. 65
Notes				Date	Par (35)

Bighorn Golf Club	Members only	(760)	341-4653	Palm Desert	p. 406
Notes				Date	Par (72)

Bijou Municipal Golf Course	Public	(530)	542-6097	South Lake Tahoe	p. 81
Notes				Date	Par (32)

Bing Maloney Golf Course	Public	(916)	433-2283	Sacramento	p. 112
Notes				Date	Par (72)

Birch Hills Golf Course	Public	(714)	990-0201	Brea	p. 319
Notes				Date	Par (59)

How do you rank among the California Golfers? Let us know how many you've played: intheloopgolf.com

Birnam Wood Golf Club	Members only	(805)	969-0919	Santa Barbara	p. 207
Notes				Date	Par (71)

Bishop Country Club	Semi-Private	(760)	873-5828	Bishop	p. 70
Notes				Date	Par (71)

Bixby Village Golf Course	Public	(562)	498-7003	Long Beach	p. 264
Notes				Date	Par (29)

Black Gold Golf Club	Public	(714)	961-0060	Yorba Linda	p. 335
Notes				Date	Par (72)

Black Mountain Country Club	Semi-Private	(702)	565-7933	Henderson	p. 378
Notes				Date	Par (72)

Black Oak Golf Course	Public	(530)	878-1900	Auburn	p. 94
Notes				Date	Par (36)

Blackberry Farm Golf Course	Municipal	(408)	253-9200	Cupertino	p. 152
Notes				Date	Par (29)

Blackhawk Country Club	Members only	(925)	736-6550	Danville	p. 154
Notes				Date	Par (72)

Blacklake Golf Course	Public	(805)	343-1214	Nipomo	p. 198
Notes				Date	Par (72)

Blue Rock Springs Golf Course	Municipal	(707)	643-8476	Vallejo	p. 141
Notes				Date	Par (71)

How do you rank among the California Golfers? Let us know how many you've played: intheloopgolf.com

Blue Skies Country Club	Semi-Private	(760) 365-0111	Yucca Valley	p. 423
Notes		Date	Par (71)	

Blythe Golf Course	Public	(760) 922-7272	Blythe	p. 370
Notes		Date	Par (73)	

Bodega Harbour Golf Links	Semi-Private	(707) 875-3538	Bodega Bay	p. 122
Notes		Date	Par (70)	

Bolado Park Golf Course	Public	(831) 628-9995	Tres Pinos	p. 243
Notes		Date	Par (35)	

Bonita Golf Club	Public	(619) 267-1103	Bonita	p. 340
Notes		Date	Par (71)	

Borrego Springs Golf Resort & Country	Resort	(760) 767-3330	Borrego Springs	p. 370
Notes		Date	Par (72)	

Boulder City Golf Course	Public	(702) 293-9236	Boulder City	p. 372
Notes		Date	Par (72)	

Boulder Creek Golf & Country Club	Resort	(831) 338-2121	Boulder Creek	p. 150
Notes		Date	Par (65)	

Boulder Ridge, The Golf Club at	Members only	(408) 323-9900	San Jose	p. 170
Notes		Date	Par (72)	

Boundary Oak Golf Course	Public	(925) 934-4775	Walnut Creek	p. 180
Notes		Date	Par (72)	

Bradshaw Ranch Golf Course	Public	(916)	363-6549	Sacramento	p. 112
Notes				Date	Par (27)

Braemar Country Club	Members only	(818)	345-6520	Tarzana	p. 280
Notes				Date	Par (70)

Brea Golf Course	Public	(714)	529-3003	Brea	p. 319
Notes				Date	Par (58)

Brentwood Country Club	Members only	(310)	451-8011	Los Angeles	p. 266
Notes				Date	Par (72)

Brentwood Golf Club	Public	(925)	516-3400	Brentwood	p. 224
Notes				Date	Par (72)

Bridges at Rancho Santa Fe, The	Members only	(858)	759-7200	Rancho Santa Fe	p. 354
Notes				Date	Par (71)

Bridges Golf Club, The	Public	(925)	735-4253	San Ramon	p. 175
Notes				Date	Par (73)

Brighton Crest Golf & Country Club	Semi-Private	(559)	299-8586	Friant	p. 229
Notes				Date	Par (72)

Broken Spoke Golf Course	Public	(760)	353-4653	El Centro	p. 377
Notes				Date	Par (30)

Brookside Country Club	Members only	(209)	956-7888	Stockton	p. 239
Notes				Date	Par (72)

Brookside Golf Club	Public	(626) 796-8151	Pasadena	p. 273
Notes			Date	Par (72)

Brookside Golf Course	Municipal	(775) 856-6009	Reno	p. 78
Notes			Date	Par (35)

Brooktrails Golf Course	Public	(707) 459-6761	Willits	p. 142
Notes			Date	Par (56)

Buchanan Fields Golf Course	Public	(925) 682-1846	Concord	p. 152
Notes			Date	Par (31)

Buckingham Golf & Country Club	Semi-Private	(707) 279-4863	Kelseyville	p. 126
Notes			Date	Par (36)

Buena Park Golf Center	Public	(714) 562-0840	Buena Park	p. 319
Notes			Date	Par (27)

Buena Vista Golf Course	Public	(661) 398-9720	Taft	p. 242
Notes			Date	Par (72)

Buenaventura Golf Course	Public	(805) 642-2231	Ventura	p. 214
Notes			Date	Par (72)

Burlingame Country Club	Members only	(650) 342-0750	Hillsborough	p. 157
Notes			Date	Par (70)

Butte Creek Country Club	Members only	(530) 343-8292	Chico	p. 55
Notes			Date	Par (72)

How do you rank among the California Golfers? Let us know how many you've played: intheloopgolf.com

Calabasas Golf & Country Club	Members only	(818)	222-3222	Calabasas Park	p. 255

Notes

Date	Par (72)

California Country Club	Members only	(626)	968-4222	Whittier	p. 285

Notes

Date	Par (72)

California Golf Club	Members only	(650)	589-0144	South San	p. 178

Notes

Date	Par (72)

Calimesa Country Club	Public	(909)	795-2488	Calimesa	p. 293

Notes

Date	Par (70)

Callaway Golf Center	Public	(702)	897-9500	Las Vegas	p. 392

Notes

Date	Par (27)

Camarillo Springs Golf Course	Public	(805)	484-1075	Camarillo Springs	p. 189

Notes

Date	Par (72)

Camelot Golf Course	Public	(661)	824-4107	Mojave	p. 403

Notes

Date	Par (36)

Cameron Park Country Club	Members only	(530)	672-7900	Cameron Park	p. 96

Notes

Date	Par (72)

Camino Heights Golf Club	Semi-Private	(530)	644-0190	Camino	p. 96

Notes

Date	Par (31)

Campers Inn RV & Golf Course	Public	(530)	724-3350	Dunnigan	p. 99

Notes

Date	Par (27)

How do you rank among the California Golfers? Let us know how many you've played: intheloopgolf.com

Campus Commons Golf Course	Public	(916) 922-5861	Sacramento	p. 112
Notes			Date	Par (29)

Candlewood Country Club	Members only	(562) 941-5310	Whittier	p. 285
Notes			Date	Par (70)

Canyon Country Club	Members only	(760) 327-1321	Palm Springs	p. 414
Notes			Date	Par (72)

Canyon Crest Country Club	Members only	(909) 274-7906	Riverside	p. 306
Notes			Date	Par (72)

Canyon Gate Country Club	Members only	(702) 363-0303	Las Vegas	p. 392
Notes			Date	Par (72)

Canyon Lake Golf Club	Members only	(909) 246-1782	Canyon Lake	p. 294
Notes			Date	Par (71)

Canyon Lakes Country Club	Public	(925) 735-6511	San Ramon	p. 175
Notes			Date	Par (71)

Canyon Oaks Country Club	Members only	(530) 343-1116	Chico	p. 55
Notes			Date	Par (72)

Canyon South Golf Course	Public	(760) 327-2019	Palm Springs	p. 414
Notes			Date	Par (71)

Carlton Oaks Country Club	Resort	(619) 448-8500	Santee	p. 362
Notes			Date	Par (72)

How do you rank among the California Golfers? Let us know how many you've played: intheloopgolf.com

Carmel Mountain Ranch	Public	(858) 487-9224	San Diego	p. 357
Notes			Date	Par (71)

Carmel Valley Ranch	Semi-Private	(831) 626-2510	Carmel	p. 189
Notes			Date	Par (70)

Carson Valley Golf Course	Public	(775) 265-3181	Gardnerville	p. 73
Notes			Date	Par (71)

CasaBlanca Golf Club	Resort	(888) 711-4653	Mesquite	p. 402
Notes			Date	Par (72)

Cascades Golf Club, The	Public	(818) 833-8900	Sylmar	p. 279
Notes			Date	Par (71)

Casserly Golf Course	Public	(831) 724-1654	Watsonville	p. 215
Notes			Date	Par (27)

Casta del Sol Golf Course	Public	(949) 581-0940	Mission Viejo	p. 328
Notes			Date	Par (60)

Castle Creek Golf Course	Semi-Private	(760) 749-2422	Escondido	p. 345
Notes			Date	Par (72)

Castle Oaks Golf Club	Public	(209) 274-0167	Ione	p. 103
Notes			Date	Par (71)

Castlewood Country Club	Members only	(925) 485-2250	Pleasanton	p. 165
Notes			Date	Par (72)

How do you rank among the California Golfers? Let us know how many you've played: intheloopgolf.com

Course	Type	Phone	City	Page
Catalina Island Golf Course	Resort	(310) 510-0530	Avalon	p. 253
Notes			Date	Par (32)
Cathedral Canyon Country Club	Semi-Private	(760) 328-6571	Cathedral City	p. 373
Notes			Date	Par (72)
Chalk Mountain Golf Club	Public	(805) 466-8848	Atascadero	p. 186
Notes			Date	Par (72)
Champions Golf Links	Public	(916) 688-9120	Sacramento	p. 113
Notes			Date	Par (30)
Chaparral Country Club	Members only	(760) 340-1501	Palm Desert	p. 406
Notes			Date	Par (60)
Chardonnay Golf Club	Public/Privat	(707) 257-1900	Napa	p. 128
Notes			Date	Par (72)
Cherry Hills Golf Club	Semi-Private	(909) 679-1182	Sun City	p. 310
Notes			Date	Par (72)
Cherry Island Golf Course	Municipal	(916) 991-6875	Elverta	p. 101
Notes			Date	Par (72)
Chester Washington Golf Course	Public	(323) 756-6975	Los Angeles	p. 266
Notes			Date	Par (73)
Chevy Chase Country Club	Members only	(818) 244-8461	Glendale	p. 259
Notes			Date	Par (33)

China Lake Golf Course	Military	(760) 939-2990	Ridgecrest	p. 422
Notes			Date	Par (72)

Chuck Corica Golf Complex	Public	(510) 522-4321	Alameda	p. 148
Notes			Date	Par (70)

Chula Vista Municipal Golf Course	Public	(619) 479-4141	Bonita	p. 340
Notes			Date	Par (73)

Churn Creek Golf Course	Public	(530) 222-6353	Redding	p. 61
Notes			Date	Par (36)

Cimarron Golf Resort	Public	(760) 770-6060	Cathedral City	p. 373
Notes			Date	Par (71)

Cinnabar Hills Golf Club	Public	(408) 323-7815	San Jose	p. 170
Notes			Date	Par (72)

Claremont Country Club	Members only	(510) 655-2431	Oakland	p. 162
Notes			Date	Par (68)

Claremont Golf Course	Public	(909) 624-2748	Claremont	p. 256
Notes			Date	Par (32)

Clear Lake Riviera Golf Club	Public	(707) 277-7129	Kelseyville	p. 126
Notes			Date	Par (35)

Club at Morningside, The	Members only	(760) 321-1555	Rancho Mirage	p. 418
Notes			Date	Par (72)

How do you rank among the California Golfers? Let us know how many you've played: intheloopgolf.com

Course	Type	Phone	City	Page
Cobb Meadows Golf Course	Public	(707) 928-5276	Cobb	p. 123
		Date		Par (33)
Cold Springs Golf & Country Club	Members only	(530) 622-4567	Placerville	p. 108
		Date		Par (72)
Colina Park Golf Course	Public	(619) 582-4704	San Diego	p. 358
		Date		Par (54)
Colonial Country Club	Members only	(909) 925-2664	Hemet	p. 298
		Date		Par (54)
Colony Country Club, The	Public	(909) 677-2221	Murrieta	p. 303
		Date		Par (65)
Colton Golf Club	Public	(909) 877-1712	Colton	p. 296
		Date		Par (57)
Colusa Golf & Country Club	Semi-Private	(530) 458-5577	Colusa	p. 98
		Date		Par (36)
Compton Golf Course	Public	(562) 633-6721	Compton	p. 257
		Date		Par (27)
Contra Costa Country Club	Members only	(925) 685-8288	Pleasant Hill	p. 165
		Date		Par (72)
Copper River Country Club	Members only	(559) 434-5200	Fresno	p. 227
		Date		Par (72)

CordeValle Golf Club	Members only	(408)	695-4590	San Martin	p. 173
Notes				Date	Par (72)

Cordova Golf Course	Public	(916)	362-1196	Sacramento	p. 113
Notes				Date	Par (63)

Coronado Municipal Golf Course	Public	(619)	435-3121	Coronado	p. 343
Notes				Date	Par (72)

Corral de Tierra Country Club	Members only	(831)	484-1325	Corral de Tierra	p. 191
Notes				Date	Par (72)

Costa Mesa Country Club	Public	(714)	540-7500	Costa Mesa	p. 320
Notes				Date	Par (72)

Coto de Caza Golf & Racquet Club	Members only	(949)	858-2770	Coto de Caza	p. 321
Notes				Date	Par (72)

Cottonwood at Rancho San Diego	Public	(800)	455-1902	El Cajon	p. 344
Notes				Date	Par (72)

Country Club of Rancho Bernardo	Members only	(858)	487-1212	San Diego	p. 358
Notes				Date	Par (72)

Country Village Golf Course, The	Members only	(909)	685-7466	Mira Loma	p. 301
Notes				Date	Par (27)

Coyote Creek Golf Club	Public	(408)	463-1400	Morgan Hill	p. 161
Notes				Date	Par (72)

How do you rank among the California Golfers? Let us know how many you've played: intheloopgolf.com

Coyote Hills Golf Course	Semi-Private	(714) 672-6800	Fullerton	p. 323
Notes			Date	Par (70)

Coyote Moon Golf Course	Public	(530) 587-0886	Truckee	p. 84
Notes			Date	Par (72)

Craig Ranch Golf Course	Public	(702) 642-9700	North Las Vegas	p. 404
Notes			Date	Par (70)

Creekside Golf Course	Public	(209) 571-5123	Modesto	p. 234
Notes			Date	Par (72)

Cresta Verde Golf Club	Public	(909) 737-2255	Corona	p. 296
Notes			Date	Par (71)

Crosby National Golf Club, The	Members only	(858) 756-6300	Rancho Santa Fe	p. 354
Notes			Date	Par (-)

Cross Creek Golf Club	Semi-Private	(909) 506-3402	Temecula	p. 311
Notes			Date	Par (71)

Crow Canyon Country Club	Members only	(925) 735-8300	Danville	p. 154
Notes			Date	Par (69)

Crystal Springs Golf Course	Public	(650) 342-0603	Burlingame	p. 150
Notes			Date	Par (72)

Crystalaire Country Club	Members only	(661) 944-2111	Llano	p. 402
Notes			Date	Par (72)

Cypress Golf Club	Public	(714) 527-1800	Los Alamitos	p. 328

Notes		Date	Par (71)

Cypress Golf Course	Public	(650) 992-5155	Colma	p. 151

Notes		Date	Par (29)

Cypress Lakes Golf Course	Military	(707) 448-7186	Vacaville	p. 140

Notes		Date	Par (72)

Cypress Point Club	Members only	(831) 624-2223	Pebble Beach	p. 201

Notes		Date	Par (72)

Cypress Ridge Golf Course	Public	(805) 474-7979	Arroyo Grande	p. 186

Notes		Date	Par (72)

D'Andrea Golf & Country Club	Semi-Private	(775) 331-6363	Sparks	p. 82

Notes		Date	Par (71)

Dairy Creek Golf Course	Public	(805) 782-8060	San Luis Obispo	p. 206

Notes		Date	Par (71)

Darkhorse Golf Club	Public	(530) 269-7900	Auburn	p. 94

Notes		Date	Par (72)

Date Palm Country Club	Semi-Private	(760) 328-1315	Cathedral City	p. 373

Notes		Date	Par (58)

David L. Baker Memorial Golf Center	Public	(714) 418-2152	Fountain Valley	p. 322

Notes		Date	Par (62)

Davis Golf Course	Municipal	(530) 756-4010	Davis	p. 99
Notes			Date	Par (67)

Dayton Valley Golf Club	Semi-Private	(775) 246-7888	Dayton	p. 72
Notes			Date	Par (72)

De Anza Country Club	Members only	(760) 767-5577	Borrego Springs	p. 371
Notes			Date	Par (72)

De Bell Golf Course	Public	(818) 845-5052	Burbank	p. 254
Notes			Date	Par (71)

De Laveaga Golf Course	Public	(831) 423-7212	Santa Cruz	p. 176
Notes			Date	Par (72)

Deep Cliff Golf Course	Public	(408) 253-5357	Cupertino	p. 153
Notes			Date	Par (60)

Del Mar Country Club	Members only	(858) 759-5520	Rancho Santa Fe	p. 354
Notes			Date	Par (72)

Del Monte Golf Course	Public	(831) 373-2700	Monterey	p. 196
Notes			Date	Par (72)

Del Norte Golf Course	Public	(707) 458-3214	Crescent City	p. 123
Notes			Date	Par (35)

Del Paso Country Club	Members only	(916) 483-0401	Sacramento	p. 113
Notes			Date	Par (72)

Club	Type	Phone	City	Page
Del Rio Country Club	Members only	(209) 545-0013	Modesto	p. 234
Notes		Date	Par (72)	
Del Rio Country Club	Semi-Private	(760) 344-0085	Brawley	p. 372
Notes		Date	Par (70)	
Delano Golf Course	Public	(661) 725-7527	Delano	p. 225
Notes		Date	Par (32)	
Desert Aire Golf Course	Public	(661) 538-0370	Palmdale	p. 416
Notes		Date	Par (36)	
Desert Crest Country Club	Semi-Private	(760) 329-8711	Desert Hot	p. 375
Notes		Date	Par (27)	
Desert Dunes Golf Club	Semi-Private	(760) 251-5366	Desert Hot	p. 375
Notes		Date	Par (72)	
Desert Falls Country Club	Semi-Private	(760) 340-4653	Palm Desert	p. 406
Notes		Date	Par (72)	
Desert Horizons Country Club	Members only	(760) 340-4651	Indian Wells	p. 381
Notes		Date	Par (72)	
Desert Inn Golf Club	Resort	(702) 733-4290	Las Vegas	p. 393
Notes		Date	Par (72)	
Desert Island Golf & Country Club	Members only	(760) 328-0841	Rancho Mirage	p. 418
Notes		Date	Par (72)	

How do you rank among the California Golfers? Let us know how many you've played: intheloopgolf.com

Desert Pines Golf Club	Public	(702) 388-4400	Las Vegas	p. 393
Notes			Date	Par (71)

Desert Princess Country Club	Resort	(760) 322-2280	Cathedral City	p. 374
Notes			Date	Par (72)

Desert Rose Golf Course	Public	(702) 431-4653	Las Vegas	p. 393
Notes			Date	Par (71)

Desert Willow Golf Club	Public	(702) 263-4653	Henderson	p. 378
Notes			Date	Par (60)

Desert Willow Golf Resort	Resort	(760) 346-7060	Palm Desert	p. 407
Notes			Date	Par (72)

Desert Winds Combat Center Golf Course	Military	(760) 830-6132	Twentynine Palms	p. 422
Notes			Date	Par (72)

Diablo Country Club	Members only	(925) 837-9233	Diablo	p. 154
Notes			Date	Par (71)

Diablo Creek Golf Course	Municipal	(925) 686-6262	Concord	p. 152
Notes			Date	Par (71)

Diablo Grande Golf Club	Resort/Priva	(209) 892-4653	Patterson	p. 236
Notes			Date	Par (72)

Diablo Hills Golf Course	Public	(925) 939-7372	Walnut Creek	p. 180
Notes			Date	Par (34)

Diamond Bar Golf Course	Public	(909) 861-8282	Diamond Bar	p. 257
Notes			Date	Par (72)

Diamond Oaks Golf Course	Public	(916) 783-4947	Roseville	p. 110
Notes			Date	Par (73)

Diamond Valley Golf Club	Public	(909) 767-0828	Hemet	p. 298
Notes			Date	Par (72)

Discovery Bay Country Club	Members only	(925) 634-0704	Byron	p. 224
Notes			Date	Par (71)

Dominguez Golf Course & Practice Center	Public	(310) 719-1942	Carson	p. 255
Notes			Date	Par (54)

Doubletree Carmel Golf Resort	Resort	(858) 485-4145	San Diego	p. 358
Notes			Date	Par (72)

Dove Canyon Country Club	Members only	(949) 858-2888	Dove Canyon	p. 322
Notes			Date	Par (71)

Dragon at Gold Mountain, The	Resort	(800) 368-7786	Graeagle	p. 74
Notes			Date	Par (72)

DragonRidge Golf Club	Semi-Private	(702) 614-4444	Henderson	p. 379
Notes			Date	Par (72)

Dry Creek Ranch Golf Club	Public	(209) 745-2330	Galt	p. 230
Notes			Date	Par (72)

	Dryden Park Golf Course	Public	(209) 577-5359	Modesto	p. 234
Notes				Date	Par (72)

	Eagle Creek Golf & Learning Center	Public	(805) 461-7500	Atascadero	p. 187
Notes				Date	Par (27)

	Eagle Crest Golf Club	Public	(760) 737-9762	Escondido	p. 345
Notes				Date	Par (72)

	Eagle Crest Golf Club	Semi-Private	(702) 240-1320	Las Vegas	p. 394
Notes				Date	Par (60)

	Eagle Glen Golf Club	Public	(909) 272-4653	Corona	p. 296
Notes				Date	Par (72)

	Eagle Ridge Golf Club	Public	(408) 846-4531	Gilroy	p. 191
Notes				Date	Par (72)

	Eagle Valley Golf Course	Public	(775) 887-2380	Carson City	p. 71
Notes				Date	Par (72)

	Eagle's Nest Golf Course	Public	(530) 465-2424	Klamath River	p. 56
Notes				Date	Par (32)

	EastLake Country Club	Public	(619) 482-5757	Chula Vista	p. 343
Notes				Date	Par (72)

	Eaton Canyon Golf Course	Public	(626) 794-6773	Pasadena	p. 274
Notes				Date	Par (35)

How do you rank among the California Golfers? Let us know how many you've played: intheloopgolf.com

Echo Hills Golf Club	Public	(909)	652-2203	Hemet	p. 299
Notes				Date	Par (35)

Edgewood Tahoe Golf Course	Public	(775)	588-3566	Stateline	p. 83
Notes				Date	Par (72)

El Caballero Country Club	Members only	(818)	345-2221	Tarzana	p. 280
Notes				Date	Par (71)

El Camino Country Club	Members only	(760)	757-0321	Oceanside	p. 351
Notes				Date	Par (72)

El Cariso Golf Course	Public	(818)	367-6157	Sylmar	p. 279
Notes				Date	Par (62)

El Dorado Hills Golf Club	Public	(916)	933-6552	El Dorado Hills	p. 99
Notes				Date	Par (61)

El Dorado Park Golf Course	Public	(562)	430-5411	Long Beach	p. 264
Notes				Date	Par (72)

El Macero Country Club	Members only	(530)	753-5621	El Macero	p. 100
Notes				Date	Par (72)

El Niguel Country Club	Members only	(949)	496-5767	Laguna Niguel	p. 327
Notes				Date	Par (72)

El Prado Golf Courses	Public	(909)	597-1753	Chino	p. 295
Notes				Date	Par (72)

How do you rank among the California Golfers? Let us know how many you've played: intheloopgolf.com

El Rancho Verde Royal Vista Golf Club	Semi-Private	(909) 875-5346	Rialto	p. 305
Notes			Date	Par (72)

El Rivino Country Club	Public	(909) 684-8905	Riverside	p. 306
Notes			Date	Par (73)

El Segundo, The Lakes at	Public	(310) 322-0202	El Segundo	p. 258
Notes			Date	Par (29)

El Toro Golf Course	Public	(949) 726-2577	Irvine	p. 324
Notes			Date	Par (72)

Eldorado Country Club	Members only	(760) 346-8081	Indian Wells	p. 381
Notes			Date	Par (72)

Elkhorn Country Club	Members only	(209) 477-0252	Stockton	p. 239
Notes			Date	Par (71)

Elkins Ranch Golf Course	Public	(805) 524-1440	Fillmore	p. 191
Notes			Date	Par (71)

Emerald Desert Golf & RV Resort	Public	(760) 345-4770	Palm Desert	p. 407
Notes			Date	Par (28)

Emerald Hills Golf Club	Public	(650) 368-7820	Redwood City	p. 166
Notes			Date	Par (27)

Emerald Isle Golf Course	Public	(760) 721-4700	Oceanside	p. 351
Notes			Date	Par (56)

Emerald Lakes Golf Center	Public	(916) 685-4653	Elk Grove	p. 100
Notes			Date	Par (33)

Emerald River Golf Course	Public	(702) 298-4653	Laughlin	p. 401
Notes			Date	Par (72)

Emerson Lake Golf Course	Public	(530) 257-6303	Susanville	p. 63
Notes			Date	Par (36)

Empire Lakes Golf Course	Public	(909) 481-6663	Rancho	p. 304
Notes			Date	Par (72)

Empire Ranch Golf Course	Public	(775) 885-2100	Carson City	p. 71
Notes			Date	Par (72)

Encinitas Ranch Golf Course	Public	(760) 944-1936	Encinitas	p. 345
Notes			Date	Par (72)

Escalon Golf Course	Public	(209) 838-1277	Escalon	p. 226
Notes			Date	Par (28)

Escondido Country Club	Members only	(760) 746-4212	Escondido	p. 346
Notes			Date	Par (70)

Eureka Golf LLC	Municipal	(707) 443-4808	Eureka	p. 124
Notes			Date	Par (70)

Exeter Golf Course	Public	(559) 592-4783	Exeter	p. 226
Notes			Date	Par (30)

Fairbanks Ranch Country Club	Members only	(858)	259-8819	Rancho Santa Fe	p. 355

Notes		Date	Par (72)

Fairgrounds Golf Center	Public	(707)	577-0755	Santa Rosa	p. 134

Notes		Date	Par (30)

Fairmount Golf Course	Public	(909)	682-2202	Riverside	p. 306

Notes		Date	Par (36)

Fall River Valley Golf & Country Club	Resort	(530)	336-5555	Fall River Mills	p. 56

Notes		Date	Par (72)

Fallbrook Golf Club	Public	(760)	728-8334	Fallbrook	p. 347

Notes		Date	Par (72)

Farms Golf Club, The	Members only	(858)	756-5585	Rancho Santa Fe	p. 355

Notes		Date	Par (72)

Feather River Inn Golf Course	Public	(530)	836-2722	Blairsden	p. 70

Notes		Date	Par (35)

Feather River Park Resort	Public	(530)	836-2328	Blairsden	p. 70

Notes		Date	Par (35)

Fig Garden Golf Course	Semi-Private	(559)	439-2928	Fresno	p. 227

Notes		Date	Par (72)

Ford Park Golf Course	Public	(562)	927-8811	Bell Gardens	p. 254

Notes		Date	Par (54)

Forebay Golf Course	Public	(209)	826-3637	Santa Nella	p. 238
Notes				Date	Par (36)

Forest Lake Golf Club	Public	(209)	369-5451	Acampo	p. 220
Notes				Date	Par (66)

Forest Meadows Golf Course	Resort	(209)	728-3439	Murphys	p. 106
Notes				Date	Par (60)

Fountaingrove Club, The	Semi-Private	(707)	579-4653	Santa Rosa	p. 135
Notes				Date	Par (72)

Four Seasons Resort Aviara	Public/Resort	(760)	603-6900	Carlsbad	p. 341
Notes				Date	Par (72)

Franklin Canyon Golf Course	Public	(510)	799-6191	Hercules	p. 156
Notes				Date	Par (72)

French Camp Golf Course & RV Park	Public	(209)	234-3030	Manteca	p. 233
Notes				Date	Par (70)

Friendly Hills Country Club	Members only	(562)	698-0331	Whittier	p. 285
Notes				Date	Par (70)

Friendly Valley Golf Launch	Members only	(661)	252-9859	Newhall	p. 271
Notes				Date	Par (28)

Ft. Washington Golf & Country Club	Members only	(559)	434-9120	Fresno	p. 227
Notes				Date	Par (72)

Fullerton Golf Course	Public	(714) 871-5141	Fullerton		p. 323
Notes				Date	Par (67)

Furnace Creek Golf Course	Resort	(760) 786-2301	Death Valley		p. 374
Notes				Date	Par (70)

Gavilan Golf Course	Public	(408) 846-4920	Gilroy		p. 192
Notes				Date	Par (30)

General Old Golf Course	Public	(909) 697-6690	Riverside		p. 306
Notes				Date	Par (72)

Genoa Lakes, The Golf Club at	Resort	(775) 782-4653	Genoa		p. 73
Notes				Date	Par (72)

Gilroy Golf Course	Public	(408) 848-0490	Gilroy		p. 192
Notes				Date	Par (35)

Glen Annie Golf Club	Public	(805) 968-6400	Goleta		p. 192
Notes				Date	Par (71)

Glenbrook Golf Course	Members only	(775) 749-5201	Glenbrook		p. 74
Notes				Date	Par (35)

Glendora Country Club	Members only	(626) 335-3713	Glendora		p. 260
Notes				Date	Par (72)

Gleneagles International Golf Course	Public	(415) 587-2425	San Francisco		p. 167
Notes				Date	Par (36)

Glenn Golf & Country Club	Public	(530)	934-9918	Willows	p. 65
Notes				Date	Par (36)

Glenoaks Golf Club	Public	(626)	335-7565	Glendora	p. 260
Notes				Date	Par (27)

Gold Hills Country Club	Semi-Private	(530)	246-7867	Redding	p. 61
Notes				Date	Par (72)

Golden Era Golf Course	Public	(909)	654-0130	Gilman Hot	p. 298
Notes				Date	Par (36)

Golden Gate Park Golf Course	Public	(415)	751-8987	San Francisco	p. 167
Notes				Date	Par (27)

Golf Club at Quail Lodge, The	Resort	(831)	620-8808	Carmel	p. 189
Notes				Date	Par (71)

Golf Club at Tahoe Donner, The	Semi-Private	(530)	587-9440	Truckee	p. 84
Notes				Date	Par (72)

Golf Resort at Indian Wells, The	Resort	(760)	346-4653	Indian Wells	p. 382
Notes				Date	Par (72)

Goose Creek Golf Club	Public	(909)	735-3982	Mira Loma	p. 301
Notes				Date	Par (70)

Graeagle Meadows Golf Course	Semi-Private	(530)	836-2323	Graeagle	p. 74
Notes				Date	Par (72)

How do you rank among the California Golfers? Let us know how many you've played: intheloopgolf.com

Granite Bay Golf Club	Members only	(916) 791-5379	Granite Bay	p. 102
Notes			Date	Par (71)

Green Hills Country Club	Members only	(650) 583-0882	Millbrae	p. 160
Notes			Date	Par (71)

Green River Golf Club	Public	(714) 970-8411	Corona	p. 297
Notes			Date	Par (72)

Green Tree Golf Club	Public	(707) 448-1420	Vacaville	p. 141
Notes			Date	Par (71)

Green Tree Golf Course	Public	(760) 245-4860	Victorville	p. 313
Notes			Date	Par (72)

Green Valley Country Club	Members only	(707) 864-0473	Suisun	p. 140
Notes			Date	Par (72)

Green Valley Oaks	Public	(530) 677-4653	Rescue	p. 109
Notes			Date	Par (72)

Greenhorn Creek	Semi-Private	(209) 736-8111	Angels Camp	p. 92
Notes			Date	Par (72)

Griffith Park Golf Club	Public	(323) 664-2255	Los Angeles	p. 267
Notes			Date	Par (72)

Hacienda Golf Club	Members only	(562) 697-3610	La Habra Heights	p. 262
Notes			Date	Par (71)

Haggin Oaks Golf Complex	Municipal	(916)	481-4653	Sacramento	p. 114

Notes

Date	Par (72)

Half Moon Bay Golf Links	Public	(650)	726-4438	Half Moon Bay	p. 155

Notes

Date	Par (72)

Hank's Swank Par 3	Public	(559)	252-7077	Fresno	p. 228

Notes

Date	Par (27)

Hansen Dam Golf Course	Municipal	(818)	896-0050	Pacoima	p. 272

Notes

Date	Par (72)

Harbor Park Golf Course	Public	(310)	549-4953	Wilmington	p. 286

Notes

Date	Par (36)

Harding Park Golf Course	Public	(415)	661-1865	San Francisco	p. 168

Notes

Date	Par (72)

Healdsburg Tayman Park Golf Course	Public	(707)	433-4275	Healdsburg	p. 125

Notes

Date	Par (34)

Heartwell Golf Course	Public	(562)	421-8855	Long Beach	p. 264

Notes

Date	Par (54)

Heritage Palms Golf Club	Semi-Private	(760)	772-7334	Indio	p. 383

Notes

Date	Par (72)

Hesperia Golf & Country Club	Semi-Private	(760)	244-9301	Hesperia	p. 299

Notes

Date	Par (72)

Hidden Hills Golf Club & Resort	Resort	(209)	852-2242	La Grange	p. 103

Notes		Date	Par (72)

Hidden Oaks Golf Course	Public	(805)	967-3493	Santa Barbara	p. 207

Notes		Date	Par (27)

Hidden Springs Country Club	Public	(760)	329-8816	Desert Hot	p. 376

Notes		Date	Par (29)

Hidden Valley Country Club	Members only	(775)	857-4742	Reno	p. 78

Notes		Date	Par (72)

Hidden Valley Golf Club	Public	(909)	737-1010	Norco	p. 304

Notes		Date	Par (72)

Hidden Valley Lake Country Club	Semi-Private	(707)	987-3035	Middletown	p. 127

Notes		Date	Par (72)

Hiddenbrooke Golf Club	Public	(707)	558-1140	Vallejo	p. 141

Notes		Date	Par (72)

Highland Falls Golf Club	Resort	(702)	254-7010	Las Vegas	p. 394

Notes		Date	Par (72)

Highland Springs Village Golf Course	Members only	(909)	845-3060	Cherry Valley	p. 294

Notes		Date	Par (28)

Hillcrest Country Club	Members only	(310)	553-8911	Los Angeles	p. 267

Notes		Date	Par (71)

Horse Thief Country Club	Resort	(661) 823-8571	Tehachapi	p. 242
Notes			Date	Par (72)

Hunter Ranch Golf Course	Public	(805) 237-7444	Paso Robles	p. 200
Notes			Date	Par (72)

Hyatt Newporter	Public	(949) 729-6193	Newport Beach	p. 329
Notes			Date	Par (27)

Incline Village, The Golf Courses at	Resort	(775) 832-1146	Incline Village	p. 75
Notes			Date	Par (72)

Indian Camp Golf Course	Public	(530) 667-2922	Tulelake	p. 63
Notes			Date	Par (28)

Indian Creek Country Club	Public	(916) 652-5546	Loomis	p. 105
Notes			Date	Par (32)

Indian Hills Golf Club	Public	(909) 360-2090	Riverside	p. 307
Notes			Date	Par (70)

Indian Palms Country Club	Semi-Private	(760) 347-2326	Indio	p. 383
Notes			Date	Par (72)

Indian Ridge Country Club	Members only	(760) 772-7222	Palm Desert	p. 407
Notes			Date	Par (72)

Indian Springs Country Club	Semi-Private	(760) 775-3360	La Quinta	p. 385
Notes			Date	Par (72)

Indian Valley Golf Club	Public	(415)	897-1118	Novato	p. 130

Notes		Date	Par (72)

Indian Wells Country Club	Members only	(760)	360-0861	Indian Wells	p. 382

Notes		Date	Par (72)

Indio Golf Course	Public	(760)	347-9156	Indio	p. 384

Notes		Date	Par (54)

Industry Hills Golf Club	Public	(626)	810-4653	City of Industry	p. 256

Notes		Date	Par (72)

Iron-Wood Nine Golf Course	Public	(562)	916-8400	Cerritos	p. 256

Notes		Date	Par (29)

Ironwood Country Club	Members only	(760)	346-0551	Palm Desert	p. 408

Notes		Date	Par (72)

Ivey Ranch Country Club	Semi-Private	(760)	343-2013	Thousand Palms	p. 422

Notes		Date	Par (35)

J.B. Golf Course	Public	(209)	886-5670	Farmington	p. 226

Notes		Date	Par (27)

Jack Tone Golf	Public	(209)	599-2973	Ripon	p. 237

Notes		Date	Par (62)

Javier's Fresno West Golf Course	Public	(559)	846-8655	Kerman	p. 230

Notes		Date	Par (72)

Jess Ranch Golf Club	Public	(760) 240-1800	Apple Valley	p. 292
Notes			Date	Par (65)

Joe Mortara Golf Course	Public	(707) 642-5146	Vallejo	p. 142
Notes			Date	Par (28)

Jurupa Hills Country Club	Public	(909) 685-7214	Riverside	p. 307
Notes			Date	Par (70)

Kelly Ridge Golf Course	Semi-Private	(530) 589-0777	Oroville	p. 59
Notes			Date	Par (33)

Kern River Golf Course	Public	(661) 872-5128	Bakersfield	p. 221
Notes			Date	Par (70)

Kern Valley Country Club	Public	(760) 376-2828	Kernville	p. 76
Notes			Date	Par (36)

King City Golf Course	Public	(831) 385-4546	King City	p. 231
Notes			Date	Par (35)

Kings Country Club	Members only	(559) 582-0740	Hanford	p. 230
Notes			Date	Par (72)

Kings River Golf & Country Club	Members only	(559) 897-2077	Kingsburg	p. 231
Notes			Date	Par (72)

Kings Valley Golf Course	Public	(707) 464-2886	Crescent City	p. 123
Notes			Date	Par (28)

How do you rank among the California Golfers? Let us know how many you've played: intheloopgolf.com

Knollwood Country Club	Public	(818) 363-8161	Granada Hills	p. 261
			Date	Par (72)

Notes

La Cañada–Flintridge Country Club	Members only	(818) 790-0155	La Cañada	p. 261
			Date	Par (70)

Notes

La Contenta Golf Club	Semi-Private	(209) 772-1081	Valley Springs	p. 116
			Date	Par (71)

Notes

La Costa Resort and Spa	Resort/Priva	(760) 438-9111	Carlsbad	p. 342
			Date	Par (72)

Notes

La Cumbre Country Club	Members only	(805) 682-3131	Santa Barbara	p. 207
			Date	Par (71)

Notes

La Jolla Country Club	Members only	(858) 454-2505	La Jolla	p. 348
			Date	Par (72)

Notes

La Mirada Golf Course	Public	(562) 943-7123	La Mirada	p. 262
			Date	Par (70)

Notes

La Purisima Golf Course	Public	(805) 735-8395	Lompoc	p. 195
			Date	Par (72)

Notes

La Quinta Country Club	Members only	(760) 564-4151	La Quinta	p. 385
			Date	Par (72)

Notes

La Quinta Resort & Club: Citrus Course	Members only	(760) 564-7620	La Quinta	p. 385
			Date	Par (72)

Notes

La Quinta Resort & Club: Dunes &	Resort	(760) 564-7686	La Quinta	p. 386
Notes			Date	Par (72)

La Rinconada Country Club	Members only	(408) 395-4220	Los Gatos	p. 159
Notes			Date	Par (70)

Laguna Seca Golf Club	Public	(831) 373-3701	Monterey	p. 196
Notes			Date	Par (71)

Laguna Woods Golf Club	Members only	(949) 597-4336	Laguna Woods	p. 327
Notes			Date	Par (71)

Lahontan Golf Club	Members only	(530) 550-2424	Truckee	p. 85
Notes			Date	Par (72)

Lake Almanor Country Club	Semi-Private	(530) 259-2868	Lake Almanor	p. 57
Notes			Date	Par (35)

Lake Almanor West Golf Course	Public	(530) 259-4555	Chester	p. 54
Notes			Date	Par (36)

Lake Arrowhead Country Club	Members only	(909) 337-3515	Lake Arrowhead	p. 300
Notes			Date	Par (71)

Lake Chabot Golf Course	Public	(510) 351-5812	Oakland	p. 162
Notes			Date	Par (70)

Lake Elizabeth Golf & Ranch Club	Public	(661) 724-1221	Lake Elizabeth	p. 389
Notes			Date	Par (70)

Lake Forest Golf & Practice Center	Public	(949) 859-1455	Lake Forest	p. 328
Notes			Date	Par (29)

Lake Merced Golf & Country Club	Members only	(650) 755-2239	Daly City	p. 153
Notes			Date	Par (72)

Lake of the Pines Country Club	Members only	(530) 269-1544	Auburn	p. 94
Notes			Date	Par (71)

Lake Redding Golf Course	Public	(530) 243-5531	Redding	p. 61
Notes			Date	Par (31)

Lake Ridge Golf Course	Public	(775) 825-2200	Reno	p. 79
Notes			Date	Par (71)

Lake San Marcos Country Club	Resort/Priva	(760) 744-1310	Lake San Marcos	p. 349
Notes			Date	Par (72)

Lake Shastina Golf Resort	Resort	(530) 938-3205	Weed	p. 64
Notes			Date	Par (72)

Lake Tahoe Golf Course	Resort	(530) 577-0788	South Lake Tahoe	p. 81
Notes			Date	Par (71)

Lake Tamarisk Golf Club	Public	(760) 227-3203	Desert Center	p. 375
Notes			Date	Par (35)

Lake View Executive Course	Public	(775) 727-6388	Pahrump	p. 405
Notes			Date	Par (59)

Lake Wildwood Country Club	Members only	(530)	432-1163	Penn Valley	p. 107
Notes				Date	Par (72)

Lakes Country Club, The	Members only	(760)	568-4321	Palm Desert	p. 408
Notes				Date	Par (72)

Lakeside Golf Club	Members only	(818)	985-3335	Burbank	p. 254
Notes				Date	Par (70)

Lakeview Golf Club	Public	(760)	352-6638	El Centro	p. 377
Notes				Date	Par (33)

Lakewood Country Club	Public	(562)	429-9711	Lakewood	p. 263
Notes				Date	Par (72)

Lancaster Golf Center	Public	(661)	726-3131	Lancaster	p. 389
Notes				Date	Par (27)

Landmark Golf Club	Public	(760)	347-2326	Indio	p. 384
Notes				Date	Par (72)

Landmark Golf Club at Oak Quarry	Public	(909)	685-1440	Riverside	p. 307
Notes				Date	Par (72)

Las Posas Country Club	Members only	(805)	482-4518	Camarillo	p. 187
Notes				Date	Par (71)

Las Positas Golf Course	Municipal	(925)	455-7820	Livermore	p. 157
Notes				Date	Par (72)

Las Vegas Country Club	Members only	(702) 734-1122	Las Vegas	p. 394
Notes			Date	Par (72)

Las Vegas Golf Club	Public	(702) 646-3003	Las Vegas	p. 395
Notes			Date	Par (72)

Las Vegas National Golf Club	Public	(702) 734-1796	Las Vegas	p. 395
Notes			Date	Par (71)

Las Vegas Paiute Golf Resort	Resort	(800) 711-2833	Las Vegas	p. 396
Notes			Date	Par (72)

Lawrence Links Golf Course	Public	(916) 332-7800	Antelope	p. 92
Notes			Date	Par (36)

Legacy Golf Club, The	Public	(702) 897-2187	Henderson	p. 379
Notes			Date	Par (72)

Legends Golf Club at Rancho Lucerne	Public	(760) 955-5976	Lucerne Valley	p. 300
Notes			Date	Par (-)

Lemoore Golf Course	Public	(559) 924-9658	Lemoore	p. 231
Notes			Date	Par (72)

Lighthouse Golf Course	Public	(916) 372-4949	West Sacramento	p. 117
Notes			Date	Par (70)

Likely Place R.V. & Golf	Public	(530) 233-6676	Likely	p. 57
Notes			Date	Par (36)

How do you rank among the California Golfers? Let us know how many you've played: intheloopgolf.com

Course	Type	Phone	City	Page
Lincoln Hills Golf Club	Public	(916) 434-7450	Lincoln	p. 104
Notes			Date	Par (72)
Lincoln Park Golf Course	Municipal	(415) 221-9911	San Francisco	p. 168
Notes			Date	Par (68)
Lindero Country Club	Semi-Private	(818) 889-1158	Agoura Hills	p. 252
Notes			Date	Par (29)
Lindsay Municipal Golf Course	Municipal	(559) 562-1144	Lindsay	p. 231
Notes			Date	Par (27)
Links Course at Paso Robles, The	Public	(805) 227-4567	Paso Robles	p. 200
Notes			Date	Par (72)
Little River Inn Golf Club	Resort	(707) 937-5667	Little River	p. 126
Notes			Date	Par (70)
LJS Golf Club	Public	(909) 413-3290	Moreno Valley	p. 301
Notes			Date	Par (28)
Lockeford Springs Golf Course	Public	(209) 333-6275	Lodi	p. 232
Notes			Date	Par (72)
Lomas Santa Fe Country Club	Members only	(858) 755-1547	Solana Beach	p. 363
Notes			Date	Par (72)
Lomas Santa Fe Executive Golf Course	Public	(858) 755-0195	Solana Beach	p. 363
Notes			Date	Par (28)

How do you rank among the California Golfers? Let us know how many you've played: intheloopgolf.com

Lone Tree Golf Course	Public	(925)	706-4220	Antioch	p. 149

Notes		Date	Par (72)

Los Altos Golf & Country Club	Members only	(650)	947-3110	Los Altos	p. 158

Notes		Date	Par (71)

Los Amigos Country Club	Public	(562)	862-1717	Downey	p. 257

Notes		Date	Par (70)

Los Angeles Country Club, The	Members only	(310)	276-6104	Los Angeles	p. 267

Notes		Date	Par (71)

Los Angeles Royal Vista Golf Course	Semi-Private	(909)	595-7441	Walnut	p. 283

Notes		Date	Par (71)

Los Arroyos Golf Club	Public	(707)	938-8835	Sonoma	p. 138

Notes		Date	Par (29)

Los Coyotes Country Club	Members only	(714)	994-7777	Buena Park	p. 320

Notes		Date	Par (72)

Los Feliz Municipal Golf Course	Public	(323)	663-7758	Los Angeles	p. 268

Notes		Date	Par (27)

Los Prados Golf Course	Semi-Private	(702)	645-5696	Las Vegas	p. 396

Notes		Date	Par (70)

Los Robles Golf Course	Public	(805)	495-6421	Thousand Oaks	p. 213

Notes		Date	Par (69)

How do you rank among the California Golfers? Let us know how many you've played: intheloopgolf.com

Los Serranos Country Club	Public	(909)	597-1711	Chino Hills		p. 295

Notes		Date	Par (74)

Los Verdes Golf Course	Public	(310)	377-7888	Rancho Palos		p. 275

Notes		Date	Par (71)

Lost Canyons Golf Club	Public	(805)	522-4653	Simi Valley		p. 211

Notes		Date	Par (72)

Lyons Golf Course	Public	(209)	937-7905	Stockton		p. 240

Notes		Date	Par (32)

Mace Meadow Golf & Country Club	Semi-Private	(209)	295-7020	Pioneer		p. 108

Notes		Date	Par (72)

Madera Golf & Country Club	Members only	(559)	674-2682	Madera		p. 232

Notes		Date	Par (72)

Madera Municipal Golf Course	Municipal	(559)	675-3504	Madera		p. 232

Notes		Date	Par (121)

Maderas Golf Club	Semi-Private	(858)	726-4653	Poway		p. 352

Notes		Date	Par (72)

Maggie Hathaway Golf Course	Public	(323)	755-6285	Los Angeles		p. 268

Notes		Date	Par (27)

Malibu Country Club	Public	(818)	889-6680	Malibu		p. 270

Notes		Date	Par (72)

Mallard Lake Golf Course	Public	(530) 674-0475	Yuba City	p. 117
Notes			Date	Par (34)

Manteca Park Golf Course	Public	(209) 825-2500	Manteca	p. 233
Notes			Date	Par (72)

Marbella Golf & Country Club	Members only	(949) 248-8590	San Juan	p. 333
Notes			Date	Par (70)

Mare Island Golf Club	Public	(707) 562-4653	Vallejo	p. 142
Notes			Date	Par (70)

Marin Country Club	Members only	(415) 382-6707	Novato	p. 130
Notes			Date	Par (72)

Marine Memorial Golf Course	Military	(760) 725-4704	Camp Pendleton	p. 341
Notes			Date	Par (72)

Marrakesh Country Club	Members only	(760) 568-2660	Palm Desert	p. 408
Notes			Date	Par (60)

Marriott Desert Springs Resort and Spa	Resort	(760) 341-1756	Palm Desert	p. 409
Notes			Date	Par (72)

Marriott Hotel Golf Course - Manhattan	Public	(310) 546-4551	Manhattan Beach	p. 270
Notes			Date	Par (27)

Marriott's Shadow Ridge Resort	Resort	(760) 674-2700	Palm Desert	p. 409
Notes			Date	Par (71)

Marshall Canyon Golf Club	Public	(909)	593-8211	La Verne	p. 262
Notes				Date	Par (71)

Marshallia Ranch Golf Course	Military	(805)	734-1333	Vandenberg AFB	p. 214
Notes				Date	Par (72)

Mather Golf Course	Public	(916)	364-4353	Mather	p. 106
Notes				Date	Par (72)

Mayacama Golf Club	Members only	(707)	543-8040	Santa Rosa	p. 135
Notes				Date	Par (72)

McCloud Golf Course	Public	(530)	964-2535	McCloud	p. 58
Notes				Date	Par (37)

McInnis Park Golf Center	Public	(415)	492-1800	San Rafael	p. 174
Notes				Date	Par (31)

Meadow Club	Members only	(415)	456-9393	Fairfax	p. 155
Notes				Date	Par (71)

Meadow Lake Golf Club	Semi-Private	(760)	749-1620	Escondido	p. 346
Notes				Date	Par (71)

Meadow Land	Public	(209)	669-6777	Hilmar	p. 230
Notes				Date	Par (29)

Meadowlark Golf Center	Public	(661)	943-2022	Quartz Hill	p. 417
Notes				Date	Par (27)

Meadowlark Golf Course	Public	(714) 846-1364	Huntington Beach p. 323
Notes		Date	Par (70)

Meadowmont Golf Course	Public	(209) 795-1313	Arnold	p. 93
Notes			Date	Par (36)

Meadowood Resort Hotel Golf Course	Members only	(707) 963-3646	St. Helena	p. 139
Notes			Date	Par (31)

Meadows Del Mar Golf Club, The	Resort	(877) 530-0636	San Diego	p. 359
Notes			Date	Par (71)

Menifee Lakes Country Club	Semi-Private	(909) 672-3090	Menifee	p. 300
Notes			Date	Par (72)

Menlo Country Club	Members only	(650) 366-9910	Redwood City	p. 166
Notes			Date	Par (70)

Merced Golf & Country Club	Members only	(209) 722-3357	Merced	p. 233
Notes			Date	Par (72)

Merced Hills Golf Club	Public	(209) 383-4943	Merced	p. 234
Notes			Date	Par (72)

Mesa Verde Country Club	Members only	(714) 549-0522	Costa Mesa	p. 320
Notes			Date	Par (71)

Mesquite Golf Club	Public	(760) 323-9377	Palm Springs	p. 414
Notes			Date	Par (72)

	Micke Grove Golf Links	Public	(209) 369-4410	Lodi	p. 232
Notes				Date	Par (72)

	Mile Square Golf Club	Public	(714) 968-4556	Fountain Valley	p. 322
Notes				Date	Par (72)

	Mill Valley Golf Course	Municipal	(415) 388-9982	Mill Valley	p. 159
Notes				Date	Par (33)

	Mira Vista Country Club	Members only	(510) 237-7045	El Cerrito	p. 155
Notes				Date	Par (71)

	Miramar Memorial Golf Club	Military	(858) 577-4155	San Diego	p. 359
Notes				Date	Par (72)

	Mission Bay Golf Course	Public	(858) 490-3370	San Diego	p. 359
Notes				Date	Par (58)

	Mission Hills Country Club	Members only	(760) 324-9400	Rancho Mirage	p. 418
Notes				Date	Par (72)

	Mission Hills Golf Course	Public	(510) 888-0200	Hayward	p. 156
Notes				Date	Par (30)

	Mission Hills Little League Golf Course	Public	(818) 892-3019	Mission Hills	p. 270
Notes				Date	Par (27)

	Mission Lakes Country Club	Semi-Private	(760) 329-8061	Desert Hot	p. 376
Notes				Date	Par (71)

How do you rank among the California Golfers? Let us know how many you've played: intheloopgolf.com

Mission Trails Golf Course	Public	(619)	460-5400	San Diego	p. 360
Notes				Date	Par (71)

Mission Viejo Country Club	Members only	(949)	582-1020	Mission Viejo	p. 328
Notes				Date	Par (72)

Modesto Municipal Golf Course	Municipal	(209)	577-5360	Modesto	p. 235
Notes				Date	Par (35)

Moffett Field Golf Course	Military	(650)	603-8026	Sunnyvale	p. 178
Notes				Date	Par (72)

Mojave Resort Golf Course	Resort	(702)	535-4653	Laughlin	p. 401
Notes				Date	Par (72)

Monarch Bay Golf Club	Public	(510)	895-2162	San Leandro	p. 172
Notes				Date	Par (71)

Monarch Beach Golf Links	Resort	(949)	240-8247	Dana Point	p. 321
Notes				Date	Par (70)

Montanera Golf Club	Members only	(925)	258-1020	Orinda	p. 163
Notes				Date	Par ()

Montclair Golf Course	Public	(510)	482-0422	Oakland	p. 163
Notes				Date	Par (27)

Montebello Country Club, The	public	(323)	725-0892	Montebello	p. 270
Notes				Date	Par (71)

How do you rank among the California Golfers? Let us know how many you've played: intheloopgolf.com

Montecito Country Club	Members only	(805)	969-0800	Santa Barbara	p. 208

Notes		Date	Par (71)

Monterey Country Club	Members only	(760)	346-1115	Palm Desert	p. 410

Notes		Date	Par (72)

Monterey Park Golf Course	Public	(323)	266-2241	Monterey Park	p. 271

Notes		Date	Par (29)

Monterey Peninsula Country Club	Members only	(831)	372-8141	Pebble Beach	p. 201

Notes		Date	Par (72)

Monterey Pines Golf Course	Public	(831)	656-2167	NPS Monterey	p. 198

Notes		Date	Par (69)

Montreux Golf & Country Club	Members only	(775)	849-9496	Reno	p. 79

Notes		Date	Par (72)

Moraga Country Club	Members only	(925)	376-2253	Moraga	p. 161

Notes		Date	Par (71)

Moreno Valley Ranch Golf Course	Public	(909)	924-4444	Moreno Valley	p. 302

Notes		Date	Par (72)

Morgan Run Resort and Club	Members only	(858)	756-3255	Rancho Santa Fe	p. 355

Notes		Date	Par (71)

Morro Bay Golf Course	Public	(805)	782-8060	Morro Bay	p. 197

Notes		Date	Par (71)

How do you rank among the California Golfers? Let us know how many you've played: intheloopgolf.com

Mount Huff Golf Course	Public	(530) 284-6204	Crescent Mills	p. 56
Notes			Date	Par (32)

Mount Shasta Resort Golf Course	Resort	(530) 926-3052	Mount Shasta	p. 59
Notes			Date	Par (70)

Mount St. Helena Golf Course	Public	(707) 942-9966	Calistoga	p. 123
Notes			Date	Par (34)

Mount Whitney Golf Club	Public	(760) 876-5795	Lone Pine	p. 76
Notes			Date	Par (36)

Mount Woodson Golf Club	Semi-Private	(760) 788-3555	Ramona	p. 353
Notes			Date	Par (70)

Mountain Meadows Golf Course	Public	(909) 623-3704	Pomona	p. 274
Notes			Date	Par (72)

Mountain Shadows Golf Resort	Public	(707) 584-7766	Rohnert Park	p. 133
Notes			Date	Par (71)

Mountain Springs Golf Club	Public	(209) 532-1000	Sonora	p. 115
Notes			Date	Par (72)

Mountain View Country Club	Public	(909) 737-9798	Corona	p. 297
Notes			Date	Par (72)

Mountain View Golf Club	Public	(805) 525-1571	Santa Paula	p. 210
Notes			Date	Par (69)

How do you rank among the California Golfers? Let us know how many you've played: intheloopgolf.com

Mountain Vista Golf Course at Sun City	Semi-Private	(760)	200-2200	Palm Desert	p. 410
Notes				Date	Par (72)

MountainGate Country Club	Members only	(310)	476-2800	Los Angeles	p. 268
Notes				Date	Par (72)

Muroc Lake Golf Course	Military	(661)	277-3469	Edwards	p. 377
Notes				Date	Par (72)

Napa Golf Course	Municipal	(707)	255-4333	Napa	p. 129
Notes				Date	Par (72)

Napa Valley Country Club	Members only	(707)	252-1114	Napa	p. 129
Notes				Date	Par (72)

National City Golf Course	Public	(619)	474-1400	National City	p. 350
Notes				Date	Par (34)

Navy Golf Course - Seal Beach	Military	(714)	527-4401	Cypress	p. 321
Notes				Date	Par (72)

Needles Municipal Golf Course	Public	(760)	326-3931	Needles	p. 404
Notes				Date	Par (70)

Nevada County Country Club	Semi-Private	(530)	273-6436	Grass Valley	p. 102
Notes				Date	Par (35)

New Horizons Golf Course	Members only	(310)	325-3080	Torrance	p. 280
Notes				Date	Par (27)

Newport Beach Country Club, The	Members only	(949)	644-9680	Newport Beach	p. 329

Notes

Date	Par (71)

Newport Beach Golf Course	Public	(949)	852-8681	Newport Beach	p. 329

Notes

Date	Par (59)

North Golf Course	Semi-Private	(909)	679-9668	Sun City	p. 310

Notes

Date	Par (61)

North Kern Golf Course	Public	(661)	399-0347	Bakersfield	p. 221

Notes

Date	Par (72)

North Las Vegas Par-3	Public	(702)	633-1833	North Las Vegas	p. 404

Notes

Date	Par (27)

North Ranch Country Club	Members only	(818)	889-9421	Westlake Village	p. 284

Notes

Date	Par (72)

North Ridge Country Club	Members only	(916)	967-5716	Fair Oaks	p. 101

Notes

Date	Par (71)

Northgate Golf Club	Public	(775)	747-7577	Reno	p. 79

Notes

Date	Par (72)

Northstar at Tahoe Golf Course	Resort	(530)	562-2490	Truckee	p. 85

Notes

Date	Par (72)

Northwood Golf Club	Public	(707)	865-1116	Monte Rio	p. 128

Notes

Date	Par (36)

How do you rank among the California Golfers? Let us know how many you've played: intheloopgolf.com

Norwalk Golf Center		Public	(562) 921-6500	Norwalk	p. 272

Notes		Date	Par (27)

O'Donnell Golf Club		Members only	(760) 325-2259	Palm Springs	p. 415

Notes		Date	Par (35)

Oak Creek Golf Club		Public	(949) 653-7300	Irvine	p. 324

Notes		Date	Par (71)

Oak Creek Golf Course		Public	(530) 529-0674	Red Bluff	p. 60

Notes		Date	Par (35)

Oak Patch Golf Course		Public	(559) 733-5000	Visalia	p. 244

Notes		Date	Par (29)

Oak Tree Country Club		Members only	(661) 821-5144	Tehachapi	p. 242

Notes		Date	Par (36)

Oak Valley Golf Club		Public	(909) 769-7200	Beaumont	p. 293

Notes		Date	Par (72)

Oakdale Golf & Country Club		Members only	(209) 847-2924	Oakdale	p. 107

Notes		Date	Par (72)

Oakhurst Country Club		Semi-Private	(925) 672-9737	Clayton	p. 151

Notes		Date	Par (72)

Oakmont Country Club		Members only	(818) 542-4292	Glendale	p. 259

Notes		Date	Par (72)

Oakmont Golf Club	Semi-Private	(707)	539-0415	Santa Rosa	p. 136
Notes				Date	Par (71)

Oakmoore Golf Course	Tournaments	(209)	462-6712	Stockton	p. 240
Notes				Date	Par (36)

Oaks North Executive Course	Public	(858)	487-3021	San Diego	p. 360
Notes				Date	Par (60)

Oasis Country Club, The	Semi-Private	(760)	345-2715	Palm Desert	p. 410
Notes				Date	Par (60)

Oasis Golf Club, The	Resort/Semi-	(702)	346-7820	Mesquite	p. 402
Notes				Date	Par (71)

Ocean Meadows Golf Course	Public	(805)	968-6814	Goleta	p. 193
Notes				Date	Par (36)

Ocean Trails Golf Club	Public	(877)	799-GOLF	Rancho Palos	p. 275
Notes				Date	Par (72)

Oceanside Center City Golf Course	Public	(760)	433-8590	Oceanside	p. 351
Notes				Date	Par (66)

Oceanside Golf Course	Public	(760)	433-1360	Oceanside	p. 352
Notes				Date	Par (72)

Ojai Valley Inn & Spa	Resort	(805)	646-2420	Ojai	p. 199
Notes				Date	Par (70)

Old Brockway Golf Course	Public	(530) 546-9909	Kings Beach	p. 76
Notes			Date	Par (36)

Old Ranch Country Club	Members only	(562) 596-4611	Seal Beach	p. 334
Notes			Date	Par (72)

Old River Golf Course	Public	(209) 830-8585	Tracy	p. 243
Notes			Date	Par (36)

Olivas Park Golf Course	Public	(805) 677-6771	Ventura	p. 214
Notes			Date	Par (72)

Olympic Club, The	Members only	(415) 587-8338	Daly City	p. 153
Notes			Date	Par (71)

Orinda Country Club	Members only	(925) 254-0811	Orinda	p. 163
Notes			Date	Par (72)

Outdoor Resort & Country Club	Members only	(760) 328-3834	Cathedral City	p. 374
Notes			Date	Par (54)

Pacific Golf & Country Club	Members only	(949) 498-3771	San Clemente	p. 331
Notes			Date	Par (72)

Pacific Grove Golf Course	Public	(831) 648-5777	Pacific Grove	p. 200
Notes			Date	Par (70)

Painted Desert Golf Course	Public	(702) 645-2880	Las Vegas	p. 396
Notes			Date	Par (72)

Pajaro Valley Golf Club	Public	(831) 724-3851	Royal Oaks	p. 204
Notes			Date	Par (72)

Pala Mesa Resort	Resort	(800) 722-4700	Fallbrook	p. 348
Notes			Date	Par (72)

Palm Desert Country Club	Semi-Private	(760) 345-2525	Palm Desert	p. 411
Notes			Date	Par (72)

Palm Desert Greens Country Club	Members only	(760) 346-2941	Palm Desert	p. 411
Notes			Date	Par (63)

Palm Desert Resort Country Club	Semi-Private	(760) 345-2781	Palm Desert	p. 411
Notes			Date	Par (72)

Palm Lake Golf Course	Public	(909) 629-2852	Pomona	p. 274
Notes			Date	Par (27)

Palm Lakes Golf Course	Public	(559) 291-4050	Fresno	p. 228
Notes			Date	Par (62)

Palm Meadows Golf Course	Public	(909) 382-2002	San Bernardino	p. 309
Notes			Date	Par (72)

Palm Royale Golf Course	Public	(760) 345-9701	La Quinta	p. 386
Notes			Date	Par (54)

Palm Springs Country Club	Public	(760) 323-2626	Palm Springs	p. 415
Notes			Date	Par (72)

Palm Valley Country Club	Members only	(760)	345-2737	Palm Desert	p. 412
Notes				Date	Par (72)

Palm Valley Golf Club	Semi-Private	(702)	363-4373	Las Vegas	p. 397
Notes				Date	Par (72)

Palms Golf Club, The	Members only	(760)	771-2606	La Quinta	p. 386
Notes				Date	Par (70)

Palms Golf Club, The	Resort	(800)	621-0187	Mesquite	p. 403
Notes				Date	Par (72)

Palo Alto Golf Course	Public	(650)	856-0881	Palo Alto	p. 164
Notes				Date	Par (72)

Palo Alto Hills Golf & Country Club	Members only	(650)	948-2320	Palo Alto	p. 164
Notes				Date	Par (71)

Palo Cedro Golf Club	Semi-Private	(530)	547-3012	Palo Cedro	p. 60
Notes				Date	Par (36)

Palos Verdes Golf Club	Semi-Private	(310)	375-2759	Palos Verdes	p. 273
Notes				Date	Par (71)

Paradise Knolls Golf Course	Public	(909)	685-7034	Riverside	p. 308
Notes				Date	Par (72)

Paradise Pines Golf Course	Public	(530)	873-1111	Magalia	p. 58
Notes				Date	Par (34)

Paradise Valley Golf Course	Public	(707)	426-1600	Fairfield	p. 124
Notes				Date	Par (72)

Park Place, The Greens at	Public	(949)	250-7888	Irvine	p. 325
Notes				Date	Par (56)

Pasadera Country Club	Members only	(831)	647-2421	Monterey	p. 196
Notes				Date	Par (71)

Pasatiempo Golf Course	Semi-Private	(831)	459-9155	Santa Cruz	p. 177
Notes				Date	Par (70)

Paso Robles Golf Club	Public	(805)	238-4722	Paso Robles	p. 201
Notes				Date	Par (71)

Pauma Valley Country Club	Members only	(760)	742-1230	Pauma Valley	p. 352
Notes				Date	Par (71)

Peach Tree Golf & Country Club	Members only	(530)	743-2039	Marysville	p. 105
Notes				Date	Par (72)

Peacock Gap Golf & Country Club	Semi-Private	(415)	453-4940	San Rafael	p. 174
Notes				Date	Par (71)

Pebble Beach Golf Links	Resort	(831)	624-3811	Pebble Beach	p. 202
Notes				Date	Par (72)

Pelican Hill Golf Club	Public	(949)	760-0707	Newport Coast	p. 330
Notes				Date	Par (71)

Peninsula Golf & Country Club, The	Members only	(650)	638-2239	San Mateo	p. 173
Notes				Date	Par (71)

Penmar Golf Course	Public	(310)	396-6228	Venice	p. 283
Notes				Date	Par (33)

Petaluma Golf & Country Club	Members only	(707)	762-7041	Petaluma	p. 132
Notes				Date	Par (35)

Peter Hay Golf Course	Public	(831)	625-8518	Pebble Beach	p. 202
Notes				Date	Par (27)

PGA of Southern California at Oak Valley	Public	(877)	PGA-2500	Calimesa	p. 294
Notes				Date	Par (72)

PGA West: Greg Norman Course	Semi-Private	(760)	564-3900	La Quinta	p. 387
Notes				Date	Par (72)

PGA West: Private Courses	Members only	(760)	564-7100	La Quinta	p. 387
Notes				Date	Par (72)

PGA West: TPC Stadium & Nicklaus	Semi-Private	(760)	564-7170	La Quinta	p. 388
Notes				Date	Par (72)

Pheasant Run Golf Club	Public	(559)	665-3411	Chowchilla	p. 225
Notes				Date	Par (72)

Phoenix Lake Golf Course	Public	(209)	532-0111	Sonora	p. 115
Notes				Date	Par (35)

How do you rank among the California Golfers? Let us know how many you've played: intheloopgolf.com

	Pin High Family Golf Center	Public	(408)	934-1111	Alviso	p. 148
Notes					Date	Par (30)

	Pine Meadows Golf Course	Public	(925)	228-2881	Martinez	p. 159
Notes					Date	Par (28)

	Pine Mountain Club	Members only	(805)	242-3734	Pine Mountain	p. 236
Notes					Date	Par (30)

	Pine Mountain Lake Country Club	Semi-Private	(209)	962-8620	Groveland	p. 103
Notes					Date	Par (70)

	Pismo State Beach Golf Course	Public	(805)	481-5215	Grover Beach	p. 194
Notes					Date	Par (27)

	Pittsburg's Delta View Golf Course	Municipal	(925)	439-4040	Pittsburg	p. 165
Notes					Date	Par (70)

	Plantation Golf Club, The	Members only	(760)	775-3688	Indio	p. 384
Notes					Date	Par (72)

	Pleasant Hills Golf Course	Public	(408)	238-3485	San Jose	p. 170
Notes					Date	Par (72)

	Pleasanton Fairways Golf Course	Public	(925)	462-4653	Pleasanton	p. 166
Notes					Date	Par (30)

	Plumas Lake Golf & Country Club	Semi-Private	(530)	742-3201	Marysville	p. 105
Notes					Date	Par·(71)

Plumas Pines Golf Resort	Resort	(530)	836-1420	Graeagle	p. 75
Notes				Date	Par (72)

Point Mugu Golf Club	Military	(805)	989-7109	Point Mugu	p. 204
Notes				Date	Par (35)

Polvadero Golf Course	Public	(559)	935-3578	Coalinga	p. 225
Notes				Date	Par (36)

Ponderosa Golf Course	Public	(530)	587-3501	Truckee	p. 85
Notes				Date	Par (35)

Poplar Creek Golf Course	Public	(650)	522-4653	San Mateo	p. 173
Notes				Date	Par (70)

Poppy Hills Golf Course	Public	(831)	622-8239	Pebble Beach	p. 202
Notes				Date	Par (72)

Poppy Ridge Golf Course	Public	(925)	456-8202	Livermore	p. 157
Notes				Date	Par (72)

Porter Valley Country Club	Members only	(818)	368-2919	Northridge	p. 271
Notes				Date	Par (70)

Porterville Golf Course	Municipal	(559)	784-9468	Porterville	p. 236
Notes				Date	Par (34)

Portola Country Club	Members only	(760)	568-1592	Palm Desert	p. 412
Notes				Date	Par (54)

Preserve Golf Club, The	Members only	(831)	626-6584	Carmel	p. 190
Notes				Date	Par (72)

Presidio Golf Course	Public	(415)	561-4661	San Francisco	p. 168
Notes				Date	Par (72)

Presidio Hills Golf Course	Public	(619)	295-9476	San Diego	p. 360
Notes				Date	Par (54)

Primm Valley Golf Club	Resort	(702)	679-5510	Primm	p. 417
Notes				Date	Par (72)

Pruneridge Golf Club	Public	(408)	248-4424	Santa Clara	p. 176
Notes				Date	Par (31)

Quail Ranch Golf Club	Public	(909)	654-2727	Moreno Valley	p. 302
Notes				Date	Par (72)

Quarry at La Quinta, The	Members only	(760)	777-1100	La Quinta	p. 388
Notes				Date	Par (72)

Rams Hill Country Club	Semi-Private	(760)	767-5124	Borrego Springs	p. 371
Notes				Date	Par (72)

Ranch Course at the Alisal	Resort	(805)	688-4215	Solvang	p. 212
Notes				Date	Par (72)

Rancho Bernardo Inn	Resort	(858)	675-8500	San Diego	p. 361
Notes				Date	Par (72)

Rancho Cañada Golf Club	Public	(800) 536-9459	Carmel	p. 190
Notes			Date	Par (71)

Rancho Carlsbad Golf Course	Public	(760) 438-1772	Carlsbad	p. 342
Notes			Date	Par (56)

Rancho del Pueblo	Public	(408) 347-0990	San Jose	p. 171
Notes			Date	Par (28)

Rancho del Rey Golf Club	Public	(209) 358-7131	Atwater	p. 221
Notes			Date	Par (72)

Rancho Duarte Golf Club	Public	(626) 357-9981	Duarte	p. 258
Notes			Date	Par (31)

Rancho La Quinta Country Club	Members only	(760) 777-7799	La Quinta	p. 388
Notes			Date	Par (72)

Rancho Las Palmas Country Club	Resort/Priva	(760) 862-4551	Rancho Mirage	p. 419
Notes			Date	Par (70)

Rancho Maria Golf Club	Public	(805) 937-2019	Santa Maria	p. 209
Notes			Date	Par (72)

Rancho Mirage Country Club	Semi-Private	(760) 324-4711	Rancho Mirage	p. 419
Notes			Date	Par (70)

Rancho Murieta Country Club	Members only	(916) 354-2400	Rancho Murieta	p. 109
Notes			Date	Par (72)

How do you rank among the California Golfers? Let us know how many you've played: intheloopgolf.com

Course	Type	Phone	City	Page
Rancho Park Golf Course	Public	(310) 839-4374	Los Angeles	p. 269
Notes			Date	Par (71)
Rancho San Joaquin Golf Course	Public	(949) 786-5522	Irvine	p. 325
Notes			Date	Par (72)
Rancho San Marcos Golf Course	Public	(805) 683-6334	Santa Barbara	p. 208
Notes			Date	Par (71)
Rancho Santa Fe Golf Club	Members only	(858) 756-3094	Rancho Santa Fe	p. 356
Notes			Date	Par (72)
Rancho Sierra Golf Club	Public	(661) 946-1080	Lancaster	p. 389
Notes			Date	Par (35)
Rancho Solano Golf Course	Public	(707) 429-4653	Fairfield	p. 124
Notes			Date	Par (72)
Rancho Vista Golf Course	Public	(661) 272-9903	Palmdale	p. 417
Notes			Date	Par (-)
Raspberry Hill, Golf Course at	Public	(530) 878-7818	Auburn	p. 95
Notes			Date	Par (29)
Recreation Park Golf Course	Public	(562) 494-5000	Long Beach	p. 265
Notes			Date	Par (72)
Red Hawk Golf Club	Semi-Private	(775) 626-6000	Sparks	p. 82
Notes			Date	Par (72)

Red Hill Country Club	Members only	(909)	982-4559	Rancho	p. 305
Notes				Date	Par (72)

Red Rock Country Club	Members only	(702)	304-5600	Las Vegas	p. 397
Notes				Date	Par (72)

Redhawk Golf Club	Public	(909)	302-3850	Temecula	p. 311
Notes				Date	Par (72)

Redlands Country Club	Members only	(909)	793-1295	Redlands	p. 305
Notes				Date	Par (70)

Redwood Empire Golf & Country Club	Members only	(707)	725-5194	Fortuna	p. 125
Notes				Date	Par (72)

Reece Point Golf Course	Military	(530)	788-0192	Beale AFB	p. 95
Notes				Date	Par (72)

Reflection Bay Golf Club	Public	(702)	740-4653	Henderson	p. 379
Notes				Date	Par (72)

Reserve, The	Members only	(760)	674-2240	Indian Wells	p. 382
Notes				Date	Par (72)

Resort at Squaw Creek	Resort	(530)	581-6637	Olympic Valley	p. 77
Notes				Date	Par (71)

Rhodes Ranch Golf Club	Public	(888)	311-8337	Las Vegas	p. 397
Notes				Date	Par (72)

Richmond Country Club	Members only	(510)	232-7815	Richmond	p. 167
Notes				Date	Par (72)

Ridge Golf Course, The	Public	(530)	888-7888	Auburn	p. 95
Notes				Date	Par (71)

Ridgeline Executive Golf Course	Public	(714)	538-5030	Orange	p. 330
Notes				Date	Par (32)

Ridgemark Country Club Resort	Semi-Private	(831)	634-2222	Hollister	p. 194
Notes				Date	Par (72)

Rio Bravo Country Club	Members only	(661)	871-4653	Bakersfield	p. 222
Notes				Date	Par (72)

Rio Hondo Golf & Country Club	Public	(562)	927-2329	Downey	p. 258
Notes				Date	Par (71)

Rio la Paz Golf Club	Semi-Private	(530)	656-2182	Nicolaus	p. 107
Notes				Date	Par (71)

Rio Secco Golf Club	Resort	(888)	867-3226	Henderson	p. 380
Notes				Date	Par (72)

Rio Vista Golf Club	Public	(707)	374-2900	Rio Vista	p. 237
Notes				Date	Par (72)

River Bend Golf & Country Club	Members only	(530)	246-9077	Redding	p. 62
Notes				Date	Par (32)

How do you rank among the California Golfers? Let us know how many you've played: intheloopgolf.com

River Course at the Alisal	Public	(805)	688-6042	Solvang	p. 212
Notes				Date	Par (72)

River Island Country Club	Semi-Private	(559)	784-9425	Porterville	p. 237
Notes				Date	Par (72)

River Oaks Golf Course	Public	(209)	537-4653	Ceres	p. 225
Notes				Date	Par (58)

River Ridge Golf Club	Public	(805)	983-4653	Oxnard	p. 199
Notes				Date	Par (72)

River Ridge Golf Course	Public	(562)	692-9933	Pico Rivera	p. 274
Notes				Date	Par (29)

River View Golf Club	Public	(714)	543-1115	Santa Ana	p. 333
Notes				Date	Par (70)

Riverbend Golf Club	Public	(559)	432-3020	Madera	p. 233
Notes				Date	Par (72)

RiverLakes Ranch, The Links at	Public	(661)	587-5465	Bakersfield	p. 222
Notes				Date	Par (72)

Riverside Golf Course	Public	(909)	682-3748	Riverside	p. 308
Notes				Date	Par (72)

Riverside Golf Course	Public	(559)	275-5900	Fresno	p. 228
Notes				Date	Par (72)

Riverview Golf & Country Club	Members only	(530)	224-2250	Redding	p. 62
Notes				Date	Par (72)

Riverwalk Golf Club	Public	(619)	296-4653	San Diego	p. 361
Notes				Date	Par (72)

Riviera Country Club	Members only	(310)	459-5395	Pacific Palisades	p. 272
Notes				Date	Par (71)

Road Runner Club	Public	(760)	767-5373	Borrego Springs	p. 371
Notes				Date	Par (54)

Road Runner Dunes Golf Resort	Resort	(760)	367-5770	Twentynine Palms	p. 423
Notes				Date	Par (36)

Robinson Ranch	Public	(661)	252-7666	Santa Clarita	p. 278
Notes				Date	Par (72)

Roddy Ranch, The Club at	Public	(925)	978-4653	Antioch	p. 149
Notes				Date	Par (72)

Rolling Hills Country Club	Members only	(310)	326-7731	Rolling Hills	p. 275
Notes				Date	Par (70)

Roosevelt Executive Golf Course	Public	(323)	665-2011	Los Angeles	p. 269
Notes				Date	Par (33)

Rooster Run Golf Club	Public	(707)	778-1211	Petaluma	p. 132
Notes				Date	Par (72)

Roseville Rolling Greens Golf Club	Public	(916) 797-9986	Roseville	p. 110
Notes			Date	Par (27)

Rosewood Lakes Golf Course	Municipal	(775) 857-2892	Reno	p. 80
Notes			Date	Par (72)

Rossmoor Golf Course	Members only	(925) 933-2607	Walnut Creek	p. 180
Notes			Date	Par (72)

Round Hill Country Club	Members only	(925) 837-7424	Alamo	p. 148
Notes			Date	Par (71)

Royal Links Golf Club	Public	(702) 450-8000	Las Vegas	p. 398
Notes			Date	Par (72)

Ruby Hill Golf Club	Members only	(925) 417-5850	Pleasanton	p. 166
Notes			Date	Par (72)

Saddle Creek Golf Club	Semi-Private	(209) 785-3700	Copperopolis	p. 98
Notes			Date	Par (72)

Sail Ho Golf Course	Public	(619) 523-5003	San Diego	p. 361
Notes			Date	Par (29)

Salinas Fairways Golf Course	Municipal	(831) 758-7300	Salinas	p. 205
Notes			Date	Par (71)

Salinas Golf & Country Club	Members only	(831) 449-1526	Salinas	p. 205
Notes			Date	Par (72)

How do you rank among the California Golfers? Let us know how many you've played: intheloopgolf.com

San Bernardino Golf Course	Public	(909) 885-2414	San Bernardino	p. 309

Notes	Date	Par (70)

San Clemente Golf Course	Public	(949) 361-8380	San Clemente	p. 331

Notes	Date	Par (72)

San Diego Country Club	Members only	(619) 422-0108	Chula Vista	p. 343

Notes	Date	Par (72)

San Dimas Canyon Golf Course	Public	(909) 599-2313	San Dimas	p. 276

Notes	Date	Par (72)

San Francisco Golf Club	Members only	(415) 469-4122	San Francisco	p. 169

Notes	Date	Par (71)

San Gabriel Country Club	Members only	(626) 287-6052	San Gabriel	p. 277

Notes	Date	Par (71)

San Geronimo Golf Course	Public	(415) 488-4030	San Geronimo	p. 169

Notes	Date	Par (72)

San Joaquin Country Club	Members only	(559) 439-3359	Fresno	p. 228

Notes	Date	Par (72)

San Jose Country Club	Members only	(408) 258-3636	San Jose	p. 171

Notes	Date	Par (70)

San Jose Municipal Golf Course	Municipal	(408) 441-4653	San Jose	p. 171

Notes	Date	Par (72)

San Juan Hills Country Club	Public	(949) 493-1167	San Juan	p. 333

Notes

Date	Par (71)

San Juan Oaks Golf Club	Public	(831) 636-6115	San Juan Bautista	p. 206

Notes

Date	Par (72)

San Luis Obispo Country Club	Members only	(805) 543-4035	San Luis Obispo	p. 206

Notes

Date	Par (72)

San Luis Rey Downs	Public/Resort	(800) 783-6967	Bonsall	p. 340

Notes

Date	Par (72)

San Ramon Royal Vista Golf Club	Public	(925) 828-6100	San Ramon	p. 175

Notes

Date	Par (72)

San Vicente Inn & Golf Club	Semi-Private	(760) 789-3477	Ramona	p. 353

Notes

Date	Par (72)

Sandpiper Golf Course	Public	(805) 968-1541	Goleta	p. 193

Notes

Date	Par (72)

Sands R.V. Resort	Public	(760) 251-1173	Desert Hot	p. 376

Notes

Date	Par (32)

Santa Ana Country Club	Members only	(714) 545-7260	Santa Ana	p. 334

Notes

Date	Par (72)

Santa Anita Golf Course	Public	(626) 447-7156	Arcadia	p. 253

Notes

Date	Par (71)

Santa Barbara Golf Club	Public	(805)	687-7087	Santa Barbara	p. 208

Notes | Date | Par (70) |

Santa Clara Golf & Tennis Club	Public	(408)	980-9515	Santa Clara	p. 176

Notes | Date | Par (72) |

Santa Maria Country Club	Members only	(805)	937-2027	Santa Maria	p. 209

Notes | Date | Par (72) |

Santa Rosa Country Club	Members only	(760)	568-5717	Palm Desert	p. 412

Notes | Date | Par (67) |

Santa Rosa Golf & Country Club	Members only	(707)	546-6617	Santa Rosa	p. 136

Notes | Date | Par (72) |

Santa Teresa Golf Club	Public	(408)	225-2650	San Jose	p. 171

Notes | Date | Par (71) |

Saratoga Country Club	Members only	(408)	253-5494	Saratoga	p. 177

Notes | Date | Par (34) |

Saticoy Country Club	Members only	(805)	485-5216	Camarillo	p. 188

Notes | Date | Par (72) |

Saticoy Golf Course	Public	(805)	647-6678	Ventura	p. 215

Notes | Date | Par (34) |

Sawtooth on the St. Johns	Public	(559)	564-1503	Woodlake	p. 246

Notes | Date | Par (71) |

How do you rank among the California Golfers? Let us know how many you've played: intheloopgolf.com

SCGA Members' Club	Public	(909) 677-7446	Murrieta		p. 303
Notes				Date	Par (72)

Scholl Canyon Golf & Tennis Club	Public	(818) 243-4100	Glendale		p. 260
Notes				Date	Par (60)

Sea Aire Golf Course	Public	(310) 316-9779	Torrance		p. 280
Notes				Date	Par (27)

Sea 'N' Air Golf Course	Military	(619) 545-9659	Coronado		p. 344
Notes				Date	Par (72)

Sea Pines Golf Resort	Resort	(805) 528-1788	Los Osos		p. 195
Notes				Date	Par (31)

Sea Ranch Golf Links, The	Public	(707) 785-2468	Sea Ranch		p. 137
Notes				Date	Par (72)

Seabee Golf Course of Port Hueneme,	Military	(805) 982-2620	Port Hueneme		p. 204
Notes				Date	Par (71)

Seacliff Country Club	Members only	(714) 536-7575	Huntington Beach		p. 324
Notes				Date	Par (72)

Seascape Golf Club	Resort	(831) 688-3213	Aptos		p. 186
Notes				Date	Par (71)

Sebastopol Golf Course	Public	(707) 823-9852	Sebastopol		p. 137
Notes				Date	Par (31)

	Selma Valley Golf Course	Public	(559) 896-2424	Selma	p. 238
Notes				Date	Par (69)

	Sepulveda Golf Complex	Public	(818) 986-4560	Encino	p. 259
Notes				Date	Par (72)

	Sequoia Woods Country Club	Members only	(209) 795-2141	Arnold	p. 93
Notes				Date	Par (70)

	Sequoyah Country Club	Members only	(510) 632-4069	Oakland	p. 163
Notes				Date	Par (70)

	Serrano Country Club	Members only	(916) 933-5716	El Dorado Hills	p. 100
Notes				Date	Par (72)

	Seven Hills Golf Club	Public	(909) 925-4815	Hemet	p. 299
Notes				Date	Par (72)

	Seven Oaks Country Club	Members only	(661) 664-6474	Bakersfield	p. 222
Notes				Date	Par (72)

	Shadow Creek Golf Club	Resort	(866) 260-0069	North Las Vegas	p. 404
Notes				Date	Par (72)

	Shadow Lakes Golf Club	Public	(888) 876-6687	Brentwood	p. 224
Notes				Date	Par (72)

	Shadow Mountain Golf Club	Members only	(760) 346-8242	Palm Desert	p. 413
Notes				Date	Par (70)

Shadowridge Country Club	Members only	(760)	727-7706	Vista	p. 363

Notes

	Date	Par (72)

Shady Canyon Golf Club	Members only			Irvine	p. 325

Notes

	Date	Par (71)

Shandin Hills Golf Club	Public	(909)	886-0669	San Bernardino	p. 310

Notes

	Date	Par (72)

Sharon Heights Golf & Country Club	Members only	(650)	854-6429	Menlo Park	p. 159

Notes

	Date	Par (72)

Sharp Park Golf Course	Public	(650)	359-3380	Pacifica	p. 164

Notes

	Date	Par (72)

Shasta Valley Golf Course	Public	(530)	842-2302	Montague	p. 58

Notes

	Date	Par (36)

Shelter Cove Golf Course	Public	(707)	986-1464	Shelter Cove	p. 138

Notes

	Date	Par (32)

Sherwood Country Club	Members only	(805)	496-3036	Thousand Oaks	p. 213

Notes

	Date	Par (72)

Sherwood Forest Golf Course	Public	(559)	787-2611	Sanger	p. 238

Notes

	Date	Par (71)

Shorecliffs Golf Course	Public	(949)	492-1177	San Clemente	p. 332

Notes

	Date	Par (72)

Shoreline Golf Links	Municipal	(650) 969-2041	Mountain View	p. 162
Notes			Date	Par (72)

Siena Golf Club	Public	(888) 689-6469	Las Vegas	p. 398
Notes			Date	Par (72)

Sierra Golf Course	Public	(530) 622-0760	Placerville	p. 108
Notes			Date	Par (31)

Sierra La Verne Country Club	Members only	(909) 596-2100	La Verne	p. 263
Notes			Date	Par (71)

Sierra Lakes Golf Club	Public	(909) 350-2500	Fontana	p. 297
Notes			Date	Par (72)

Sierra Meadows - Ranch Course	Semi-Private	(559) 642-1343	Oakhurst	p. 235
Notes			Date	Par (70)

Sierra Meadows - River Creek Course	Public	(559) 683-3388	Ahwahnee	p. 220
Notes			Date	Par (36)

Sierra Nevada Golf Ranch	Public	(775) 782-7700	Genoa	p. 73
Notes			Date	Par (72)

Sierra Sage Golf Course	Public	(775) 972-1564	Reno	p. 80
Notes			Date	Par (71)

Sierra Star Golf Club	Resort	(760) 924-4653	Mammoth Lakes	p. 77
Notes			Date	Par (70)

Sierra View Country Club	Members only	(916) 783-4600	Roseville	p. 111
Notes			Date	Par (72)

Sierra View Golf Course of Visalia	Public	(559) 732-2078	Visalia	p. 244
Notes			Date	Par (72)

Silver Creek Valley Country Club	Members only	(408) 239-5775	San Jose	p. 172
Notes			Date	Par (72)

Silver Lakes Country Club	Members only	(760) 245-7435	Helendale	p. 377
Notes			Date	Par (72)

Silver Oak Golf Club	Public	(775) 841-7000	Carson City	p. 71
Notes			Date	Par (71)

Silverado Country Club & Resort	Resort	(707) 257-5460	Napa	p. 129
Notes			Date	Par (72)

SilverStone Golf Club	Resort	(877) 888-2127	Las Vegas	p. 398
Notes			Date	Par (72)

Simi Hills Golf Course	Public	(805) 522-0803	Simi Valley	p. 211
Notes			Date	Par (71)

Sinaloa Golf Course	Public	(805) 581-2662	Simi Valley	p. 211
Notes			Date	Par (27)

Singing Hills Resort	Resort	(619) 442-3425	El Cajon	p. 344
Notes			Date	Par (72)

How do you rank among the California Golfers? Let us know how many you've played: intheloopgolf.com

Skyline Country Club Ranch	Members only	(760)	749-3233	Valley Center	p. 363
Notes				Date	Par (29)

Skylinks Golf Course	Public	(562)	429-0030	Long Beach	p. 265
Notes				Date	Par (72)

Skywest Golf Course	Public	(510)	317-2300	Hayward	p. 156
Notes				Date	Par (72)

Snowcreek Golf Course	Resort	(760)	934-6633	Mammoth Lakes	p. 77
Notes				Date	Par (35)

Soboba Springs Royal Vista Golf Course	Public	(909)	654-9354	San Jacinto	p. 310
Notes				Date	Par (73)

Sonoma Mission Inn Golf and Country	Resort	(707)	996-0300	Sonoma	p. 139
Notes				Date	Par (72)

Soule Park Golf Course	Public	(805)	646-5633	Ojai	p. 199
Notes				Date	Par (72)

South Gate Golf Course	Public	(323)	357-9613	South Gate	p. 278
Notes				Date	Par (27)

South Hills Country Club	Members only	(626)	332-3222	West Covina	p. 283
Notes				Date	Par (71)

Southern Highlands Golf Club	Members only	(702)	263-1000	Las Vegas	p. 399
Notes				Date	Par (72)

Southridge Golf Course	Public	(530) 755-4653	Sutter	p. 116
Notes			Date	Par (72)

SouthShore Golf Club	Members only	(702) 558-0022	Henderson	p. 380
Notes			Date	Par (71)

Spanish Bay, The Links at	Resort	(831) 647-7495	Pebble Beach	p. 203
Notes			Date	Par (72)

Spanish Hills Golf & Country Club	Members only	(805) 389-1644	Camarillo	p. 188
Notes			Date	Par (71)

Spanish Trail Golf & Country Club	Members only	(702) 364-0357	Las Vegas	p. 399
Notes			Date	Par (-)

Spanos Park, The Reserve at	Semi-Private	(209) 477-4653	Stockton	p. 240
Notes			Date	Par (72)

Spring Creek Golf & Country Club	Members only	(209) 599-3630	Ripon	p. 238
Notes			Date	Par (72)

Spring Hills Golf Course	Public	(831) 724-1404	Watsonville	p. 215
Notes			Date	Par (71)

Spring Valley Golf Course	Public	(408) 262-1722	Milpitas	p. 160
Notes			Date	Par (70)

Spring Valley Lake Country Club	Members only	(760) 245-7921	Victorville	p. 313
Notes			Date	Par (72)

Springs Club, The	Members only	(760) 328-0590	Rancho Mirage	p. 419

Notes

Date	Par (72)

Springtown Golf Course	Public	(925) 455-5695	Livermore	p. 158

Notes

Date	Par (35)

Spyglass Hill Golf Course	Semi-Private	(831) 625-8563	Pebble Beach	p. 203

Notes

Date	Par (72)

St. Stanislaus Golf Club	Public	(209) 538-2828	Modesto	p. 235

Notes

Date	Par (28)

Stallion Mountain Country Club	Members only	(702) 450-8044	Las Vegas	p. 399

Notes

Date	Par (72)

Stanford University Golf Course	Members only	(650) 323-0944	Stanford	p. 178

Notes

Date	Par (71)

Steele Canyon Golf Club	Semi-Private	(619) 441-6900	Jamul	p. 348

Notes

Date	Par (71)

Sterling Hills Golf Club	Public	(805) 987-3446	Camarillo	p. 188

Notes

Date	Par (71)

Stevinson Ranch	Public	(209) 668-8200	Stevinson	p. 239

Notes

Date	Par (72)

Stockdale Country Club	Members only	(661) 832-0587	Bakersfield	p. 223

Notes

Date	Par (71)

Stockton Golf & Country Club	Members only	(209)	466-6221	Stockton	p. 241

Notes

	Date	Par (71)

Stoneridge Country Club	Members only	(858)	487-2117	Poway	p. 353

Notes

	Date	Par (72)

StoneTree Golf Club	Public	(415)	209-6090	Novato	p. 131

Notes

	Date	Par (72)

Strawberry Farms Golf Club	Public	(949)	551-1811	Irvine	p. 326

Notes

	Date	Par (72)

Studio City Golf Course	Public	(818)	761-3250	Studio City	p. 279

Notes

	Date	Par (27)

Summitpointe Golf Club	Public	(408)	262-8813	Milpitas	p. 160

Notes

	Date	Par (72)

Sun City Golf Club	Semi-Private	(916)	774-3850	Roseville	p. 111

Notes

	Date	Par (72)

Sun Lakes Country Club	Members only	(909)	845-2135	Banning	p. 292

Notes

	Date	Par (72)

Sun Valley Golf Course	Public	(619)	466-6102	La Mesa	p. 349

Notes

	Date	Par (27)

Suncrest Country Club	Public	(760)	340-2467	Palm Desert	p. 413

Notes

	Date	Par (33)

Sundale Country Club	Semi-Private	(661)	831-5224	Bakersfield	p. 223

Notes		Date	Par (72)

Sunken Gardens Golf Course	Public	(408)	739-6588	Sunnyvale	p. 179

Notes		Date	Par (29)

Sunnyside Country Club	Members only	(559)	255-6871	Fresno	p. 229

Notes		Date	Par (72)

Sunnyvale Golf Course	Municipal	(408)	738-3666	Sunnyvale	p. 179

Notes		Date	Par (70)

Sunol Valley Golf Club	Public	(925)	862-0414	Sunol	p. 179

Notes		Date	Par (72)

Sunridge Golf Club	Public	(775)	267-4448	Carson City	p. 72

Notes		Date	Par (72)

Sunrise Country Club	Members only	(760)	328-6549	Rancho Mirage	p. 420

Notes		Date	Par (64)

Sunrise Golf Course	Members only	(916)	723-0481	Citrus Heights	p. 97

Notes		Date	Par (31)

Sunrise Vista Golf Club	Military	(702)	652-2602	Las Vegas	p. 400

Notes		Date	Par (72)

Sunset Hills Country Club	Members only	(805)	495-5407	Thousand Oaks	p. 213

Notes		Date	Par (71)

Sunset Ridge Golf Course	Public	(805) 347-1070	Santa Maria	p. 210
Notes			Date	Par (28)

Sunset Whitney Country Club	Members only	(916) 624-2610	Rocklin	p. 109
Notes			Date	Par (72)

Swallows Nest Golf Course	Members only	(916) 927-6481	Sacramento	p. 114
Notes			Date	Par (30)

Swenson Park Golf Course	Municipal	(209) 937-7360	Stockton	p. 241
Notes			Date	Par (72)

Sycamore Canyon Golf Club	Public	(661) 854-3163	Arvin	p. 220
Notes			Date	Par (72)

Table Mountain Golf Club	Public	(530) 533-3922	Oroville	p. 59
Notes			Date	Par (72)

Tahoe City Golf Course	Public	(530) 583-1516	Tahoe City	p. 83
Notes			Date	Par (33)

Tahoe Paradise Golf Course	Public	(530) 577-2121	Tahoe Paradise	p. 84
Notes			Date	Par (64)

Tahquitz Creek, A Golf Resort	Public	(760) 328-1005	Palm Springs	p. 415
Notes			Date	Par (72)

Talega Golf Club	Public	(949) 369-6226	San Clemente	p. 332
Notes			Date	Par (72)

Tamarisk Country Club	Members only	(760)	328-2141	Rancho Mirage	p. 420
				Date	Par (72)

Notes

Teal Bend Golf Club	Public	(916)	922-5209	Sacramento	p. 114
				Date	Par (72)

Notes

Tecolote Canyon Golf Club	Public	(858)	279-1600	San Diego	p. 362
				Date	Par (58)

Notes

Tehama Golf Club	Members only	(831)	624-5549	Carmel Valley	p. 190
				Date	Par (72)

Notes

Temecula Creek Inn Golf Resort	Resort	(800)	642-4653	Temecula	p. 312
				Date	Par (72)

Notes

Temeku Hills Golf & Country Club	Public	(909)	694-9998	Temecula	p. 312
				Date	Par (72)

Notes

Three Rivers Golf Course	Public	(559)	561-3133	Three Rivers	p. 242
				Date	Par (35)

Notes

Thunder Canyon Country Club	Members only	(775)	884-4597	Washoe Valley	p. 85
				Date	Par (72)

Notes

Thunderbird Country Club	Members only	(760)	328-2161	Rancho Mirage	p. 420
				Date	Par (71)

Notes

Tierra del Sol Golf Club	Public	(760)	373-2384	California City	p. 372
				Date	Par (72)

Notes

How do you rank among the California Golfers? Let us know how many you've played: intheloopgolf.com

Tierra Oaks, The Golf Club at	Members only (530) 275-0887	Redding	p. 62
Notes		Date	Par (72)

Tierra Rejada Golf Club	Public (805) 531-9300	Moorpark	p. 197
Notes		Date	Par (72)

Tijeras Creek Golf Club	Public (949) 589-9793	Rancho Santa	p. 331
Notes		Date	Par (72)

Tilden Park Golf Course	Public (510) 848-7373	Berkeley	p. 150
Notes		Date	Par (70)

Tommy Jacobs' Bel Air Greens	Public (760) 322-6062	Palm Springs	p. 416
Notes		Date	Par (32)

Torrey Pines Golf Course	Public (858) 452-3226	La Jolla	p. 349
Notes		Date	Par (72)

TPC at Summerlin	Members only (702) 256-0222	Las Vegas	p. 400
Notes		Date	Par (72)

TPC at the Canyons	Public (702) 256-2000	Las Vegas	p. 401
Notes		Date	Par (71)

Tracy Golf & Country Club	Members only (209) 835-9463	Tracy	p. 243
Notes		Date	Par (72)

Tradition Golf Club	Members only (760) 564-1067	La Quinta	p. 389
Notes		Date	Par (72)

Trinity Alps Golf & Country Club	Semi-Private	(530)	623-5411	Weaverville	p. 64

Notes

Date	Par (31)

Tucker Oaks Golf Course	Public	(530)	365-3350	Redding	p. 63

Notes

Date	Par (36)

Tulare Golf Course	Public	(559)	686-5300	Tulare	p. 244

Notes

Date	Par (72)

Turkey Creek Golf Club	Public	(916)	434-9100	Lincoln	p. 104

Notes

Date	Par (72)

Turlock Golf & Country Club	Members only	(209)	634-4976	Turlock	p. 244

Notes

Date	Par (72)

Tuscan Ridge Golf Club	Semi-Private	(530)	343-3862	Chico	p. 55

Notes

Date	Par (-)

Tustin Ranch Golf Club	Public	(714)	730-1611	Tustin	p. 335

Notes

Date	Par (72)

Twain Harte Golf Club	Public	(209)	586-3131	Twain Harte	p. 116

Notes

Date	Par (29)

Twelve Bridges Golf Club	Public	(916)	645-7200	Lincoln	p. 104

Notes

Date	Par (72)

Twin Creeks Golf Course	Public	(831)	758-7333	Salinas	p. 205

Notes

Date	Par (31)

Twin Lakes Golf Course	Public	(805) 964-1414	Goleta	p. 193
Notes			Date	Par (29)

Twin Oaks Golf Course	Public	(760) 591-4653	San Marcos	p. 362
Notes			Date	Par (72)

Ukiah Municipal Golf Course	Municipal	(707) 467-2832	Ukiah	p. 140
Notes			Date	Par (69)

Upland Hills Country Club	Semi-Private	(909) 946-4711	Upland	p. 312
Notes			Date	Par (70)

Valencia Country Club	Members only	(661) 287-1880	Valencia	p. 281
Notes			Date	Par (72)

Valencia, The Greens at	Public	(661) 222-2900	Valencia	p. 281
Notes			Date	Par ()

Valle Grande Golf Course	Public	(661) 832-2259	Bakersfield	p. 223
Notes			Date	Par (72)

Valley Club of Montecito, The	Members only	(805) 969-4681	Santa Barbara	p. 209
Notes			Date	Par (72)

Valley Gardens Golf Course	Public	(831) 438-3058	Scotts Valley	p. 177
Notes			Date	Par (31)

Valley Hi Country Club	Members only	(916) 423-2170	Elk Grove	p. 101
Notes			Date	Par (72)

Valley Oaks Golf Course	Public	(559)	651-1441	Visalia	p. 245

Notes		Date	Par (72)

Van Buren Golf Center	Public	(909)	688-2563	Riverside	p. 308

Notes		Date	Par (57)

Van Buskirk Golf Course	Public	(209)	937-7357	Stockton	p. 241

Notes		Date	Par (72)

Van Nuys Golf Course	Public	(818)	785-3685	Van Nuys	p. 282

Notes		Date	Par (30)

Verdugo Hills Golf Course	Public	(818)	352-3282	Tujunga	p. 281

Notes		Date	Par (54)

Via Verde Country Club	Members only	(909)	599-8486	San Dimas	p. 277

Notes		Date	Par (72)

Victoria Club	Members only	(909)	684-5035	Riverside	p. 308

Notes		Date	Par (72)

Victoria, The Links of	Public	(310)	323-6981	Carson	p. 255

Notes		Date	Par (72)

Village Country Club	Members only	(805)	733-3537	Lompoc	p. 195

Notes		Date	Par (72)

Village Green Golf Course	Public	(559)	456-4653	Fresno	p. 229

Notes		Date	Par (30)

How do you rank among the California Golfers? Let us know how many you've played: intheloopgolf.com

Villages Golf & Country Club, The	Members only	(408)	274-3220	San Jose	p. 172

Notes		Date	Par (72)

Vineyard Golf Club, The	Public	(760)	735-9545	Escondido	p. 346

Notes		Date	Par (70)

Vintage Club, The	Members only	(760)	862-2076	Indian Wells	p. 383

Notes		Date	Par (72)

Vintner's Golf Club	Public	(707)	944-1992	Yountville	p. 143

Notes		Date	Par (34)

Virginia Country Club	Members only	(562)	424-5211	Long Beach	p. 265

Notes		Date	Par (71)

Visalia Country Club	Members only	(559)	734-1458	Visalia	p. 245

Notes		Date	Par (72)

Vista Valencia Golf Course	Public	(661)	253-1870	Valencia	p. 282

Notes		Date	Par (61)

Vista Valley Country Club	Members only	(760)	758-5275	Vista	p. 364

Notes		Date	Par (71)

Warner Springs Ranch Golf Course	Semi-Private	(760)	782-4270	Warner Springs	p. 364

Notes		Date	Par (72)

Wasco Valley Rose Golf Course	Public	(661)	758-8301	Wasco	p. 245

Notes		Date	Par (72)

Washoe County Golf Course	Public	(775) 828-6640	Reno	p. 80
Notes			Date	Par (72)

Wawona Golf Course	Public	(209) 375-6572	Wawona	p. 86
Notes			Date	Par (35)

Weed Golf Course	Public	(530) 938-9971	Weed	p. 64
Notes			Date	Par (35)

Welk Resort	Resort	(760) 749-3225	Escondido	p. 347
Notes			Date	Par (62)

Wente Vineyards, The Course at	Public	(925) 456-2475	Livermore	p. 158
Notes			Date	Par (72)

Westchester Golf Course	Public	(310) 649-9166	Westchester	p. 284
Notes			Date	Par (53)

Western Hills Golf & Country Club	Members only	(714) 528-6400	Chino Hills	p. 295
Notes			Date	Par (72)

Westin Mission Hills Resort - Dye Course	Public	(760) 328-3198	Rancho Mirage	p. 421
Notes			Date	Par (70)

Westin Mission Hills Resort - Player	Public	(760) 770-2908	Rancho Mirage	p. 421
Notes			Date	Par (72)

Westlake Golf Course	Public	(818) 889-0770	Westlake Village	p. 284
Notes			Date	Par (67)

Westridge Golf Club	Public	(562)	690-4200	La Habra		p. 326
Notes				Date	Par (72)	

Whispering Lakes Golf Course	Public	(909)	923-3673	Ontario		p. 304
Notes				Date	Par (72)	

Whitehawk Ranch, The Golf Club at	Resort	(800)	332-4295	Clio		p. 72
Notes				Date	Par (71)	

Whitney Oaks Golf Club	Public	(916)	632-8333	Rocklin		p. 110
Notes				Date	Par (71)	

Whittier Narrows Golf Course	Public	(626)	288-1044	Rosemead		p. 276
Notes				Date	Par (72)	

Wikiup Golf Course	Public	(707)	546-8787	Santa Rosa		p. 137
Notes				Date	Par (29)	

Wilcox Oaks Golf Club	Members only	(530)	527-7087	Red Bluff		p. 60
Notes				Date	Par (69)	

Wildcreek Golf Course	Resort	(775)	673-3100	Sparks		p. 83
Notes				Date	Par (72)	

Wildhawk Golf Club	Public	(916)	688-4653	Sacramento		p. 115
Notes				Date	Par (72)	

WildHorse Golf Club	Public	(702)	434-9000	Henderson		p. 380
Notes				Date	Par (72)	

Wildhorse Golf Course	Public	(530) 753-4900	Davis	p. 99
Notes			Date	Par (72)

Wildwood Mobile Country Club	Members only	(626) 968-2338	Hacienda Heights	p. 261
Notes			Date	Par (27)

William Land Park Golf Course	Public	(916) 277-1207	Sacramento	p. 115
Notes			Date	Par (34)

Willow Creek Golf Course	Public	(877) 779-4653	Pahrump	p. 405
Notes			Date	Par (71)

Willow Park Golf Course	Public	(510) 537-8989	Castro Valley	p. 151
Notes			Date	Par (71)

Willowbrook Golf Course	Public	(619) 561-1061	Lakeside	p. 350
Notes			Date	Par (36)

Willowick Golf Club	Public	(714) 554-0672	Santa Ana	p. 334
Notes			Date	Par (71)

Wilshire Country Club, The	Members only	(323) 934-1121	Los Angeles	p. 269
Notes			Date	Par (71)

Winchester Country Club	Members only	(530) 878-9585	Meadow Vista	p. 106
Notes			Date	Par (72)

Windsor Golf Club	Public	(707) 838-7888	Windsor	p. 143
Notes			Date	Par (72)

How do you rank among the California Golfers? Let us know how many you've played: intheloopgolf.com

Wolf Creek at Paradise Canyon	Public	(866) 252-GOLF	Mesquite	p. 403
Notes			Date	Par (72)

Wolf Run Golf Club	Semi-Private	(775) 851-3301	Reno	p. 81
Notes			Date	Par (71)

Wood Ranch Golf Club	Members only	(805) 522-7262	Simi Valley	p. 212
Notes			Date	Par (72)

Woodbridge Golf & Country Club	Members only	(209) 369-2371	Woodbridge	p. 246
Notes			Date	Par (73)

Woodcreek Golf Club	Municipal	(916) 771-4653	Roseville	p. 111
Notes			Date	Par (72)

Woodhaven Country Club	Members only	(760) 345-7513	Palm Desert	p. 413
Notes			Date	Par (70)

Woodland Hills Country Club	Members only	(818) 347-1476	Woodland Hills	p. 286
Notes			Date	Par (70)

Woodley Lakes Golf Course	Public	(818) 787-8163	Van Nuys	p. 282
Notes			Date	Par (72)

Yolo Fliers Country Club	Members only	(530) 662-8050	Woodland	p. 117
Notes			Date	Par (72)

Yorba Linda Country Club	Members only	(714) 779-2461	Yorba Linda	p. 335
Notes			Date	Par (71)

Yosemite Lakes Park Golf Course	Members only	(559)	642-2562	Coarsegold	p. 97
Notes				Date	Par (31)

Yucaipa Valley Golf Club	Public	(909)	790-6522	Yucaipa	p. 313
Notes				Date	Par (72)

Zaca Creek Golf Course	Public	(805)	688-2575	Buellton	p. 187
Notes				Date	Par (29)

The acknowledgment — why?

It seems the only people who read the acknowledgments are the ones you forget to mention, so why write one? Is it an unwritten law? Will I be considered anti-establishment if I don't do one? At home one night, I asked my wife (the one who has patiently stood by me throughout this project) "Do I really need to write an acknowledgment?" Her reply was simple: "You will do anything to avoid writing." She knows me too well.

Still, the question intrigued me, so I went to my publishers, Greg Redmond and Chris Bronis, who shared in my vision and were the guiding checkbook behind this project. Do I need to write an acknowledgment? Before they answered, Greg wanted to study my question for "legal reasons" and Chris wanted to do a per-word breakdown of the cost of an acknowledgment page.

Frustrated, I went to my co-author, Bob Fagan, and to my contributors and friends, Andy Lipschultz, Frank McClung, Shannon Millhouse, Mark Anderson, Mike Jackson, Kyle Morgan, Robert Walker, Phyllis Redmond, James Pisenti, Dave Morgan, Val Verhunce, Brad Sevier, Dave McClung, Debbie Bronis, The Mole, Carolyn Perkins, Mike Mazzaffari, Loralei Abels, Ted Horton, Emmy Mooreminister, Karen Stumbaugh, Scott Humphry, Sandy Loughran, Byron Cone, Joann Dost, Bob Reade, Vince Mastracco, Morgan Abbott, Dino Minatta, Gregg Stumbaugh, Robert Kaufman, Eric Firpo, Dean Loughran, Nancy Bernstein, Sterling Anderson, and George Tucker. One by one, I asked them the simple question. Do I need to write an acknowledgment? Not one of them could give me a straight answer. For some reason though, they kept repeating the spelling of their names.

It became apparent that this question was too big for individuals, so I began emailing the organizations that assisted me for the last year. Impressive organizations like the NCGA, NCPGA, SCPGA, SCGA, CGCOA, Studio M, Fairways and Greens, Churm Publications, Hunter Public Relations, Creative Spiral, Wolf Communications, Banta Books, and Sunbelt Publications. I waited and waited, but no one responded to my question. They probably didn't check their email.

In desperation, I turned to my parents, who gave me life and my kids new sneakers. But, they weren't speaking to me. Apparently, I forgot to acknowledge them in my last book.

To make a long story shorter, I never did get an answer to the question, but I did come to the conclusion that it takes a hell of a lot of good people to make a book.

Thank you all -

Shaw Kobre

Authors

Shaw Kobre -
Shaw is the author of three editions of *California Golf*, and has been writing about golf since 1995. Before becoming a writer, he was the director of a Nike Tour event in Sonoma County for five seasons. Shaw lives in Santa Rosa with his wife, Kim and two sons, Alec and Rylan. Shaw, once a 9.2 index, has driven himself insane by switching from right-handed to left-handed golf and back again, several times. At this time, he can play poorly from either side.

Bob Fagan -
A former golf professional, Bob was the Executive Director of the Northern California PGA from 1991-1998. Today, he is a management consultant specializing in startups and troubled operations both in and outside the golf industry. He also consults on golf facility operations and serves as an expert golf witness. Bob is one of the most extensively traveled golfers in America. During his 38 years of golf, he has played nearly 1,450 courses, more than 400 in California alone. A fine player, Fagan owns more 75 course records. He grew up in Pennsylvania and was schooled in Florida where he won at the state, collegiate, and professional levels. More recently, he was the California Golf Writers Association 2001 Champion. Also a member of the Golf Writers Association of America, Bob resides in Pleasanton, and has a daughter, Kelly, and a son, Matthew.

Contributors

AKA the "Our" behind "Our Opinions"
Along with Shaw Kobre and Bob Fagan look for the first names from the following people to see their opinions of various courses. Do you agree? Disagree? Have a favorite contributor? Let us know at intheloopgolf@aol.com.

Andy Lipschultz -
Andy works in the entertainment industry and has no ties to the golf industry. Because of this, he would like to be thought of as the Jed Leland of golf writing (in case that's confusing, here's a hint: Joseph Cotton). He is a journalism graduate of Cal State University, Northridge, and has written about golf for Los Angeles Magazine. He is also the author of the Random House Book *How The Grinch Stole Hollywood*. If you get so angry reading his reviews that you want to take him out to a golf course and kick his a**, you probably could—he plays to a 12.

The Mole -
The Mole's identity is unknown, even to us. We do know that he is an industry insider, who cannot speak his mind openly for fear that he would lose his job. The Mole has access to some of the state's best clubs, both public and private.

Loralei Abels -
Having played golf since childhood, Loralei embarked in the golf industry with the goal to introduce more people to the game. She is currently Director of Marketing of Access Golf. She is a staff player with Cleveland Golf and spokeswomen for its line of ladies clubs. She still finds time to operate the Loralei Abels Golf School, teaching women's clinics throughout Europe four times a year. Finally, Loralei is a member of the Sunriver Women's Golf Forum, developed to promote the growth of women's golf.

Val Verhunce -
Val is the Director of Instruction at Rooster Run Golf Club in Petaluma, and is co-founder of The Putting Edge School. He is also president of the Junior Golf Association of Sonoma County. Val played golf at the University of South Florida and Texas Wesleyan College. He spent three years playing professionally on the mini-tour circuit before becoming a PGA Professional in 1986. He resides in Santa Rosa with his wife, Terri and two daughters, Bailey and Madelynn.

Brad Sevier -
Brad has been enjoying the game of golf for 20 years. He currently plays to 11.7 index. Mr. Sevier is in the commercial real estate finance business in Los Angeles. He currently resides in Manhattan Beach with his wife Nicole and two sons, Jack and Adam.

Frank McClung -
Frank is the Sales Director for Toshiba America. He learned to play golf from his grandfather at the age of seven and currently plays to a 10 index. He has played golf extensively all over the world. He currently resides in Fremont with his wife, Cheryl and two boys Mac and Taylor.

Nancy Bernstein - Research/Editing
Nancy didn't pick up a club until 10 years ago, but golf runs in her family. Before working on the Golf California Survival Guide, she worked on the Nike Tour event in Sonoma County, and for the past couple of years, has volunteered as a media liaison for the AT&T Pebble Beach Pro-Am. Her degree from USC was in creative writing, and her father is very happy to see her actually doing something with it.

Our Cover Course — Genoa Lakes

How ironic, that the cover course for the first edition of the *Golf California Survival Guide* is not located in California. From a borders stand point, very ironic. From a golfing standpoint, it is not that ironic, because Genoa and the surrounding Reno-Lake Tahoe area golf courses are supported by California golfers.

The Golf Club at Genoa Lakes is located in historic Genoa, Nevada. The facility opened on July 4, 1993 and is set just east of Lake Tahoe, at the foot of the Sierra Nevada.

The course is a collaboration between PGA Tour Pro, Peter Jacobsen and golf course architect, John Harbottle III. The Golf Club at Genoa Lakes is a semi-private course with a links-style, championship layout. The course plays to a par 72 and stretches from 5,008 to 7,263 yards, with four sets of tees. The layout winds along the Carson River and natural wetlands, creating water hazards on 14 holes.

The Golf Club at Genoa Lakes has played host to the Nevada State Amateur, Sierra Nevada PGA Chapter, American Junior Golf Association, and the 2001 U.S. Open qualifying.

A $10 million renovation has just been completed, which includes the clubhouse, pro shop, 19th hole lounge, locker rooms, interactive training centers, snack bar, patio and two new tennis courts. The banquet pavilion can accommodate group functions as well as weddings.

For more information about the course go to page 73 or visit their website, at www.genoalakes.com.